CONVEYANCING
LAW AND PRACTICE IN SCOTLAND

CONVEYANCING LAW AND PRACTICE IN SCOTLAND

by

JOHN M. HALLIDAY

M.A., LL.B. (Glasgow), LL.D. (Edin.).

Emeritus Professor of Conveyancing in the
University of Glasgow

Volume I

I General Principles
II Moveable Conveyancing

Published under the auspices of

THE SCOTTISH UNIVERSITIES LAW INSTITUTE

EDINBURGH
W. GREEN & SON LTD.
1985

First published in 1985

© 1985. THE SCOTTISH UNIVERSITIES LAW INSTITUTE

ISBN   0   414   00760   3

Printed in Great Britain
by
Thomson Litho Ltd., East Kilbride, Scotland

PREFACE

THE object of this work is to provide practitioners in Scotland with an up-to-date statement of conveyancing law and practice. Substantive law is touched upon only in so far as directly related to the adjective law of conveyancing, and even within that field the increase in specialism introduced by modern statutes and developed in practice in particular types of transaction renders it impossible to treat many topics adequately within the compass of a general textbook. The reader will find that in many areas this book does little more than direct him to the relevant law, and the styles offered are restricted to the transactions most frequently encountered in practice, but the constraints of space have rendered this *apologia pro omissis* inevitable.

This volume deals with certain principles applicable to conveyancing generally and also to moveable conveyancing. Heritable conveyancing, trusts and succession and deeds having taxation objectives will be dealt with in subsequent volumes. At the time of writing comprehensive legislation affecting companies, bankruptcy and insolvency is in course of enactment and will be noticed also in subsequent volumes.

I am indebted to the supervising committee of the Scottish Universities Law Institute and in particular to Professor J.A.M. Inglis and Emeritus Professor A.J. McDonald who have made many valuable suggestions regarding the text. On specialist topics I have received invaluable assistance from professional colleagues, notably Mr. Thomas Gardiner, Mr. James H. Campbell, Mr. John A. Campbell, Mr. J. Cameron Henderson and Professor R.B. Jack, which I gratefully acknowledge, and from Mr. I.J.S. Talman who has read the final text. I have also to acknowledge the co-operation of Clydesdale Bank plc in furnishing certain styles. Miss Candice Blackwood has given me unstinting help in the background research and is responsible for the preparation of the table of statutes. I have also to acknowledge the secretarial assistance of Miss Shelagh Barclay and Mrs. Thérèse Still in converting the manuscript into typescript and the patient labours of my wife in the preparation of the index and table of cases. Finally I must pay tribute to the skill and care of the publishers, W. Green & Son Ltd., in printing and producing the book. I am, however, solely responsible for the book in its final form.

The law is stated as at December 31, 1984, although some subsequent changes have been incorporated.

J.M. HALLIDAY

v

NOTE

In several styles included in this volume, stamp duty of 50p is indicated as appropriate. Since the volume went to press, the fixed stamp duty of 50p has been abolished in many cases by s. 85 and Sched. 24 of the Finance Act 1985.

CONTENTS

LIST OF ABBREVIATIONS

Anton	Professor A. E. Anton, *Private International Law*, 1967.
Bell, *Arbitration*	J. M. Bell, *Law of Arbitration in Scotland*, 2nd ed., 1877.
Bell, *Comm.*	Professor G. J. Bell, *Commentaries on the Law of Scotland and the Principles of Mercantile Jurisprudence*, 7th ed., 1870.
Bell, *Prin.*	Professor G. J. Bell, *Principles of the Law of Scotland*, 10th ed., 1899.
Bell, (Montgomerie)	Professor A. M. Bell, *Lectures on Conveyancing*, 3rd ed., 1882.
Burns	John Burns, *Conveyancing Practice according to the Law of Scotland*, 4th ed., 1957.
Clive	Eric M. Clive, *The Law of Husband and Wife in Scotland*, 2nd ed., 1982.
Craigie, (*Heritable Rights*)	John Craigie, *Scottish Law of Conveyancing, Heritable Rights*, 3rd ed., 1899.
Craigie, (*Moveable Rights*)	John Craigie, *Scottish Law of Conveyancing, Moveable Rights*, 2nd ed., 1894.
Currie	James G. Currie, *Confirmation of Executors in Scotland*, 7th ed., by A. E. McRae, 1973.
Dickson	W. G. Dickson, *Law of Evidence in Scotland*, 3rd ed., 1887.
Ersk.	Professor John Erskine of Carnock, *An Institute of the Law of Scotland*, 8th ed., 1871.
Gloag, *Contract*	Professor W. M. Gloag, *Law of Contract*, 2nd ed., 1929.
Gloag & Henderson	Professor W. M. Gloag and Professor R. C. Henderson, *Introduction to the Law of Scotland*, 8th ed., by A. B. Wilkinson and W. A. Wilson, 1980.
Gloag & Irvine	Professor W. M. Gloag and J. M. Irvine, *Law of Rights in Security, Heritable and Moveable and Cautionary Obligations*, 1897.
Goudy	Henry Goudy, *Law of Bankruptcy in Scotland*, 4th ed., 1914.
Halliday	Professor J. M. Halliday, *Conveyancing and Feudal Reform (Scotland) Act 1970*, 2nd ed., 1977.
Halsbury	*Halsbury's Laws of England*, 4th ed.
Lindley	*Partnership*, 14 ed., 1979.
McLaren	John, Lord McLaren, *Law of Wills and Succession*, 3rd ed., 1894.
Marshall	Enid A. Marshall, *Scots Mercantile Law*, 1983.

Menzies, *Lectures*	Professor Allan Menzies, *Lectures on Conveyancing according to the Law of Scotland*, revised ed., 1900.
Menzies, *Trustees*	A. J. P. Menzies, *Law of Scotland affecting Trustees*, 2nd ed., 1913.
Miller, J. B.	Professor J. B. Miller, *The Law of Partnership in Scotland*, 1973.
Palmer	*Company Law* 23rd ed., 1982.
Paton & Cameron	G. C. H. Paton and J. G. S. Cameron, *Law of Landlord and Tenant*, 1967.
Rankine, *Leases*	Professor Sir John Rankine, *Law of Leases in Scotland*, 3rd ed., 1916.
R.T.P.B.	Registration of Title Practice Book, 1981.
Stair	Sir James Dalrymple, Viscount Stair, *Institutions of the Law of Scotland*, Tercentenary ed., 1981.
Stewart, Graham	J. Graham Stewart, *Treatise on the Law of Diligence*, 1898.
Walker, *Contract*	Professor D. M. Walker, *Law of Contracts and Related Obligations in Scotland*, 2nd ed., 1985.
Walker, *Prin.*	Professor D. M. Walker, *Principles of Scottish Private Law*, 3rd. ed., 1982.
Walker, *Judicial Factors*	N. M. L. Walker, *Judicial Factors*, 1974.
Walker & Walker	A. G. Walker and N. M. L. Walker, *The Law of Evidence in Scotland*, 1964.
Wilson	Professor W. A. Wilson, *The Law of Scotland relating to Debt*, 1982.
Wilson and Duncan	Professor W. A. Wilson and A. G. M. Duncan, *Trusts, Trustees and Executors*, 1975.
Wood, *Lectures*	Professor J. P. Wood, *Lectures on Conveyancing* 1903.

TABLE OF CASES

xi

TABLE OF STATUTES

PART I

GENERAL PRINCIPLES

INTRODUCTION

Conveyancing

1–01   Conveyancing is that branch of law which deals with the preparation of deeds. It is the body of law and procedure which relates to the constitution, transfer and discharge by written documents of rights and obligations in connection with property of all kinds, both moveable and heritable. Although the ambit of conveyancing can be thus broadly defined it forms part of an integrated system of law and cannot be confined to a neatly sealed-off compartment. The capacity of parties to grant deeds involves the law of persons and of trusts, the preparation of documents creating rights or obligations requires consideration of the principles of obligations and contract, the validity of deeds creating securities is subject to the ultimate test of insolvency or bankruptcy of the granter, the execution of deeds and the effect thereon of subsequent actings of parties involve the law of evidence and the enforcement or vindication of rights to property demands knowledge of the appropriate civil remedies and court procedures. In this work the various branches of substantive law which relate to the preparation of deeds are touched upon, but necessarily briefly, and in many situations it will be necessary for the conveyancer to consult standard works of reference on the particular topics. For example, in this chapter the treatment of rights in property is arranged in relation to the characteristics of property which are of importance in the preparation of deeds relating to it; for an account of the substantive law of property and its classification as moveable or heritable reference should be made to Walker, *Principles*, Volume III, or Gloag and Henderson, Chapters xxxvi to xl.

Classification of deeds

1–02   Deeds may be classified:

(a) *In relation to function*, as (i) deeds of constitution which create rights or obligations; (ii) deeds of transfer whereby an existing right is transferred to another person; or (iii) deeds of discharge whereby an existing right or obligation is extinguished.

(b) *In relation to the time when they take effect*, as (i) *inter vivos* deeds which become operative either immediately or at some specified date or time which is not dependent upon the life of any person, or (ii) *mortis causa* deeds which take effect only upon the death of a person, usually the granter.

(c) *In relation to their form*, as (i) unilateral deeds granted by one person or by several persons having the same or related interests, or (ii) bilateral or multilateral deeds granted by two or more persons having different interests.

Structure of deeds

1–03   The essential elements of a deed, however complex, are identifiable. Briefly they comprise:

(i) *the inductive or narrative clause*, which specifies the names and designations of the granters or parties and the consideration or cause of granting,

(ii) *the operative or dispositive clause*, which contains the words which create, transfer or discharge, as the case may be, the rights or obligations with which the deed is concerned,

(iii) *ancillary or executory clauses*, which deal with subordinate or detailed matters designed to make the deed fully effective, and

(iv) *the attestation clause or testing clause* in probative deeds, which contains the particulars of execution, the written evidence of observance of the solemnities which give the deed obligatory force in law.[1]

Material of deeds

1–04   In early times deeds were written on parchment or vellum but now always on paper. Formerly where more than one sheet was required they were battered together, each sheet being pasted firmly at the foot of the preceding one, and all the sheets were kept in the form of a roll. The more convenient method of preparing deeds bookwise was authorised by the Deeds Act 1696[2] which provided that each page should be numbered and the number of pages should be mentioned at the end of the last page.[3] The requirement of numbering each page was repealed by the Act 19 & 20 Victoria c. 89 and the need to specify the total number of pages at the end was abolished by section 38 of the Conveyancing (Scotland) Act 1874.

Medium with which deeds written

1–05   Deeds may be written in ink, but a deed written in pencil will not be denied effect on that account.[4] It is obviously desirable, however, that deeds should be written in a comparatively permanent medium, less easily susceptible of alteration than pencil. If a deed is written in ink but

---

[1] For a fuller analysis of the structure of deeds see Chap. 4 *infra*.

[2] Act 1696 c. 15.

[3] The provisions of the 1696 Act as to signature of pages have now been superseded by s. 44 of the Conveyancing and Feudal Reform (Scotland) Act 1970—see Chap. 3.

[4] *Williamson* v. *Kennedy* (1857) 19 D. 443; *Muir's Trs.* (1869) 8 M. 53; *Simsons* v. *Simsons* (1883) 10 R. 1247.

has alterations made in pencil there is a presumption, not conclusive but rebuttable, that the alterations were merely deliberative in character.[5] Most professionally prepared deeds are now typewritten[6] or produced on word processors or other modern equipment.

Language of deeds

1–06   Deeds were formerly written in Latin but the use of English has long been normal practice. The Crown Charters Act 1847[7] permitted charters from the Crown to be written in English and the last normal use of Latin in formal deeds, the notary's docquet at the end of an instrument of sasine, vanished with the disappearance of such instruments in 1858.[8]

Delivery of deeds

1–07   Normally in *inter vivos* transactions a deed, in order to be effective, must not only be executed but also delivered to the grantee in order to put it outwith the control of the granter to alter or destroy it, although certain actings of parties may be equivalent to delivery or may raise a presumption that delivery has taken place. In the case of testamentary deeds, however, delivery is not required; the deed is revocable during the granter's lifetime but on his death it is deemed to be the expression of his testamentary intentions and is effective without delivery. Nor do bilateral or multilateral deeds require delivery; when fully executed by all parties they create rights or obligations in favour of or binding upon persons having different interests and no special significance can be attached to the possession of the completed deed by any one of them.[9]

Completion of title

1–08   The execution and delivery of a deed confers or transfers rights upon or to the grantee in a question with the granter but in the case of deeds affecting many kinds of property it is necessary to complete the title of the grantee by registration or other appropriate procedure in order to make the right effective against third parties, *i.e.* to create a *jus in re* in the property which is the subject of the deed. Familiar examples are the registration of a transfer of shares in the books of the company or of a deed relating to heritable property in the Register of Sasines or procuring registration of the title in the Land Register of Scotland or the

---

[5] *Munro's Exrs.* v. *Munro* (1890) 18 R. 122; *Currie's Trs.* v. *Currie* (1904) 7 F. 364. *Cf. Lamont* v. *Magistrates of Glasgow* (1887) 14 R. 603.
[6] See *Simpson's Trs.* v. *Macharg & Son* (1902) 9 S.L.T. 398.
[7] s. 25.
[8] Titles to Land (Scotland) Act 1858, s. 1.
[9] For a more detailed examination of the principles of delivery see Chap. 9 *infra*.

intimation to the debtor of the assignation of a right to an obligation of payment of money.

RIGHTS IN PROPERTY

Rights and interests in property

1–09 In transactions relating to property a deed, in order to be fully effective, must be granted and concurred in by all persons having rights or interests in the property adverse to the right conferred on the grantee by the deed. Alternatively persons having such adverse rights or interests may by a separate deed executed contemporaneously discharge or restrict them so that they cannot compete with or adversely affect the grantee's right under the principal deed. The legal effect of the deed and the form in which it is framed, however, depend upon the character of the various rights of those who grant or consent to it.

Personal and real rights

1–10 In relation to property the broad distinction between a personal right (*jus in personam*) and a real right (*jus in re*) has been recognised from the earliest times by the institutional writers.[10] As it has been expressed by Bell[11]:

> "Of the rights relative to property, another division has been made by lawyers into those which depend upon the engagement or obligation of the person to give the thing, or to make it available to another, in perpetual or temporary use; and those in which, by immediate connection with the thing itself, without the intervention of another, it is said to belong to the person. Rights of the former kind are sometimes termed Personal Rights relative to things, being only available by demand against a particular person. Rights of the latter kind are called Real Rights, and are available against the thing itself, in whose hands soever it may be found. The former the Roman lawyers called Jura ad Rem, the latter Jura in Re."

For the purposes of conveyancing this broad distinction requires further analysis.

Rights dependent upon obligation before transfer or conveyance

1–11 Where a right depends upon a contract or other obligation which has not yet been implemented by an appropriate document of transfer it may be described as a right which is purely personal, enforceable, if need be, by an action directed against the obligant. Such a right has been referred to as *jus crediti* or *jus actionis*. It is a right which, before becoming real, requires "the intervention of another," *i.e.* the granting

---

[10] Stair, I, i, 22; Ersk., III, i, 2.
[11] *Prin.*, Intro., 3.

of an appropriate document of transfer by the obligant.[11a] A familiar example is the right of a purchaser who has concluded a valid agreement for the sale and purchase of heritable property. In such a situation the conversion of the purely personal right into a *jus in re* or right of property is dependent upon the ability of the obligant to grant an appropriate document of conveyance as a first step and the occurrence of any event which precludes him from doing so will prevent the acquisition of a right of property by the obligee. Should the seller become bankrupt before granting a disposition, the property will vest in his trustee,[12] who may disclaim the contract leaving the purchaser to claim damages against the sequestrated estate, a claim which may be of little value. If the seller is a limited company which becomes insolvent before granting a disposition the effect is similar.[13] The property is still part of the company's assets; on a winding up the liquidator may claim ownership of the property and disclaim the contract of sale; if a receiver is appointed under an "all assets" floating charge the property as part of the company's assets becomes subject to a fixed security which is preferable to the purely personal right of the purchaser.[14] The limitations of the purely personal right of a purchaser under a contract of sale of heritable property are important if the purchaser resells or grants a security over the property. He is not a person who has a right to land under section 3 of the Conveyancing (Scotland) Act 1924 or a right to an interest in land under section 12(1) of the Conveyancing and Feudal Reform (Scotland) Act 1970; he has only a right to require the original seller to grant a conveyance or a security and the consent of that person is necessary to a valid disposition or standard security in favour of the subsequent purchaser or lender. The original purchaser may dispose of rights under the contract of sale by an assignation intimated to the original seller, but on the principle of *assignatus utitur jure auctoris* the right of the assignee is vulnerable to the occurrence of any event which precludes the original seller from implementing his obligation.

1–12   Another illustration of a purely personal right is that of a legatee under a trust disposition and settlement whereby the whole estate of the testator has been conveyed to trustees for purposes which include a bequest of property to the legatee. Until the trustees have transferred or conveyed the property in implement of the bequest the legatee's right may be affected by any circumstances which preclude the trustees from

---

[11a] The term *jus ad rem* has been used either interchangeably with a *jus crediti* or *jus actionis* where the claim is to the transfer of specific property which still requires the intervention of another or as denoting the higher right where a transfer or conveyance of the property has been granted but the right has not yet been made real but can be made so without such intervention (as described in para. 1–13 *infra*). In *Edmond* v. *Magistrates of Aberdeen* (1858) 3 Macq. App. 116, Lord Cranworth (at 122) suggested a practical distinction that a *jus ad rem* indicated a right of the latter category. Probably the situation is that a *jus ad rem* may comprehend a right of either category, being a right to a specific property which is not yet a real right.

[12] Bankruptcy (Scotland) Act 1913, s. 97(2).

[13] Companies Act 1985, s. 623.

[14] Companies Act 1985, s. 469(7).

so implementing it, *e.g.* if the testator's estate is insufficient to satisfy all the bequests made, each of the legacies bequeathed will, in appropriate order, be subject to abatement or, if the estate of the testator is insolvent, will be wholly lost on the rule that a testator cannot confer benefit upon legatees unless the claims of his creditors have first been satisfied. Accordingly the legatee may dispose of his right by assignation intimated to the trustees but the right taken by the assignee is vulnerable to abatement or loss similarly. If the legacy is of heritable property the legatee cannot grant a valid disposition; a conveyance by the trustees in implement of the legacy is required in order to provide an acceptable link in title.

Rights after transfer or conveyance but before completion of title

1–13   Once a document of transfer or conveyance has been executed and delivered in implement of a purely personal right the legal position is significantly altered. In Scots law there is a clear distinction between a contract or obligation on the one hand and a conveyance or *traditio* on the other hand.[15] The basic rule of *traditionibus non nudis pactis dominia rerum transferuntur* applies to the effect that in a question between the parties the document of transfer or conveyance, when duly delivered, transfers a right of ownership to the grantee. As between the granter or his executors and the grantee or his representatives delivery of the document of transfer or conveyance excludes the property from the ownership of the granter.[16] The grantee may dispose of the property to a third party by an appropriate document of transfer or conveyance, or may create a security over it, deducing his title in appropriate form.[17] It may be observed that a transaction of sale of goods forms an exception to the distinction between contract and conveyance above outlined since in terms of section 17 of the Sale of Goods Act 1979 the property in specific goods sold under a contract of sale is transferred to the purchaser when the parties to the contract intend it to be transferred, *i.e.* the property in the goods passes by virtue of the contract itself on the intended date of transfer.[18]

1–14   In the case of many kinds of property, however, the right conferred by a delivered deed of transfer or conveyance requires some further procedure in order to make it a real right of property or *jus in re* valid against third parties, *e.g.* intimation to the debtor of an assignation, registration of a transfer of shares in the books of the company,

---

[15] See T. B. Smith, *Short Commentary*, 280.

[16] *Thomas* v. *Lord Advocate*, 1953 S.C. 151.

[17] A deduction of title is required in a disposition or heritable security to be recorded in the Register of Sasines (Conveyancing (Scotland) Act 1924, s. 3; Conveyancing and Feudal Reform (Scotland) Act 1970, s. 12), but not in a deed relating to an interest registered in the Land Register of Scotland if evidence of the necessary links is produced to the Keeper (Land Registration (Scotland) Act 1979, s. 15(3)).

[18] The exception is not usually of significance for conveyancing purposes since a contract of sale of goods is not normally followed by any further deed of transfer.

registration of the deed or title to heritable property or securities in the Register of Sasines or the Land Register of Scotland or possession under a lease with the alternative of registration where the lease is registrable. In general, it is the date when title to the transferred right is completed that is the criterion of preference in questions with third parties proponing a competing right or effecting diligence. Some of the situations in which a competition of rights may occur are considered in the following paragraphs.

1-15 **(a) Competition with other deeds.** Where the granter of the deed has mistakenly or fraudulently granted a competing deed to another party, both grantees having acted in good faith, the criterion of preference is the date when the appropriate procedure for completion of title[19] is effected, irrespective of the dates of granting of the competing deeds.

1-16 **(b) Competition with arresters.** Where the subject-matter of the deed is a moveable debt or obligation which is arrested by a creditor of the granter before intimation of the assignation, whether absolute or in security, the arrester is preferred to the assignee.[20] If the intimation and the arrestment are made on the same day and the hour at which each was effected is not clear they will rank *pari passu*.[21]

1-17 **(c) Competition with adjudgers.** Where the deed is a conveyance of land priority as between the grantee and an adjudger, irrespective of the dates of the deed or the decree of adjudication, is determined in favour of whichever party first obtains a real right by registration.[22] If, when the issue arises, neither party is infeft, priority is regulated by the respective dates of the conveyance and the decree.[23] If the deed is a lease or an assignation of a lease possession must have followed before the decree of adjudication was pronounced.[24]

1-18 **(d) Competition with trustee in bankruptcy of granter.** If the deed is an assignation of a debt or moveable right which has not been intimated to the debtor or obligant before the date of sequestration, the trustee in bankruptcy has a preferable right since the incorporeal moveable estate of the bankrupt vests in the trustee as if intimation had been made at that date.[25] If the subject-matter of the deed is moveable property but some form of registration is required to complete the grantee's title, such as shares of a company, shares in a ship or a mortgage thereon, or a

---

[19] *e.g. Rainford* v. *Keith* [1905] 2 Ch. 147 (shares of company); Policies of Assurance Act 1867, s. 3 (assurance policies); Merchant Shipping Act 1894, s. 33; Mortgaging of Aircraft Order 1972 (S.I. 1972 No. 1268), art. 14(2); Patents Act 1977, s. 33; Real Rights Act 1693 (titles to land registered in the Register of Sasines); Land Registration (Scotland) Act 1979, s. 3(4) (real rights registered in the Land Register of Scotland); *Rodger* v. *Crawford* (1867) 6 M. 24 (registrable leases).
[20] Ersk., III, vi, 19; *Lord Advocate* v. *Royal Bank of Scotland Ltd.*, 1978 S.L.T. 38, 41.
[21] *Inglis* v. *Edward* (1630) Mor. 2773.
[22] Graham Stewart, *Diligence*, 635, and authorities there cited.
[23] *Gordon* v. *Rae* (1822) 2 S. 78.
[24] *Inglis & Co.* v. *Paul* (1829) 7 S. 469.
[25] Bankruptcy (Scotland) Act 1913, s. 97(1).

patent, priority depends upon the respective dates when registration is completed by the grantee or the trustee.[26] If the deed is a conveyance of land the trustee in bankruptcy acquires only a personal right by virtue of his act and warrant since the statutory vesting is not equivalent to infeftment; the reference to recording of the deemed adjudication in section 97(2) of the Bankruptcy (Scotland) Act 1913 is to registration in the Register of Inhibitions and Adjudications, not the Register of Sasines.[27] Accordingly there is a race for registration between the grantee of the conveyance and the trustee, priority being accorded to whichever of them first completes his title.[28] If the deed is a non-registrable lease or an assignation thereof which has not been followed by possession before the date of sequestration, the trustee's right is preferable since he is deemed to have a decree of adjudication on that date and the rule already stated in paragraph 1–17 applies.

1–19 **(e) Competition with liquidator of company granter.** Although winding up a company does not have the effect of vesting its assets in the liquidator and they remain the property of the company, the effect of winding up is stated in section 538 of the Companies Act 1985 in terms which echo the corresponding provisions of section 97 of the Bankruptcy (Scotland) Act 1913. The liquidator must then administer the assets of the company as so affected and distribute them in accordance with the rights and preferences of creditors and contributories. The result of competition between the grantee of a deed executed and delivered by the company before winding up and its liquidator would appear to be effectively the same as in the case of the bankruptcy of an individual granter as already outlined in paragraph 1–18 *supra*.[29,30]

1–20 **(f) Competition with receiver of assets of company granter.** Where the subject-matter of the deed is such that completion of the grantee's title would be effected by intimation to the debtor in the debt or obligation transferred, the receiver's right would be preferred if intimation had not been made when the floating charge crystallised on the appointment of the receiver.[31] The position with regard to rights transferred by a deed which requires some form of registration in order to complete the grantee's title is not entirely clear. Section 13(7) of the Companies (Floating Charges and Receivers) (Scotland) Act 1972 (now section 469(7) of the Companies Act 1985) provides that on the appointment of a receiver the

---

[26] *Morrison* v. *Harrison* (1876) 3 R. 406: statutory provisions cited in para. 1–15 *supra*.
[27] For an explanation of this construction see Goudy, *Bankruptcy*, 256.
[28] In the case of heritable property or a heritable security the trustee may complete title by notarial instrument duly recorded—Titles to Land Consolidation (Scotland) Act 1868, s. 25.
[29] See *Gibson* v. *Hunter Home Designs Ltd.* (in liquidation), 1976 S.C. 23. (In that case the deed (a feu disposition) had not been delivered but there was opinion *obiter* that even after delivery the grantee would only have a personal right and his acquisition of a real right would be dependent upon recording in the Register of Sasines).
[30] The procedure for completion of title to heritable property or a heritable security in s. 25 of the 1868 Act is also available to a liquidator.
[31] *Forth & Clyde Construction Co. Ltd.* v. *Trinity Timber & Plywood Co. Ltd.*, 1984 S.L.T. 94.

floating charge by virtue of which he was appointed shall attach to the property then subject to the charge and such attachment shall have effect as if the charge were a fixed security over the property to which it has attached. "Fixed security" is defined in relation to any property of a company by section 31(1) of the 1972 Act (now section 486 of the 1985 Act) as any security which on the winding up of a company in Scotland would be treated as an effective security over that property and (without prejudice to that generality) includes a security over that property, being a heritable security within the meaning of section 9(8) of the Conveyancing and Feudal Reform (Scotland) Act 1970. In the *Forth & Clyde Construction Co. Ltd.*[32] case the Lord President (Emslie) said, "By the language of s. 13(7) one is, in my opinion, driven to ask, in attempting to define the effect of attachment of particular property, what kind of security over that property, other than by way of diligence, would be treated by the law of Scotland on the winding-up of the company in this jurisdiction as an effective security." The application of that dictum to the situation where there is competition between the grantee of a delivered deed which requires registration for completion of title and a receiver, however, is unclear. It may be argued that to constitute an effective security on the winding up of a company the deed must have been registered so that the receiver is deemed to have a title completed by registration whenever the charge attaches, *i.e.* a title preferable to that of the grantee of the deed, so that there is no race for registration as in a competition with a liquidator,[33] but *quaere* until the point is clarified by judicial decision.

Practice

1–21   In order to minimise the risks of possible challenge to a personal right to property outlined in paragraphs 1–08 to 1–17 *supra* the duty of the conveyancer is to ensure that (a) where the right depends solely upon contract or obligation a document of transfer or conveyance of it is prepared, executed and delivered as expeditiously as is practicable and (b) when such a document has been delivered any further steps necessary to create a real right in the property are carried out without delay.

Real rights

1–22   When a valid deed transferring or burdening a right of property has been delivered and any appropriate procedure for completing a real right has been carried out, the grantee's real right in the property or security which is the subject of the deed is effective against challenge by

---

[32] 1984 S.L.T. 94, 96.
[33] The receiver would on this view be in a stronger position than a liquidator. That is not altogether illogical. The unsecured creditors and the liquidator had not, prior to winding up, any kind of security, whereas the holder of the floating charge had an inchoate security capable of being transformed into a fixed security by appointment of a receiver.

any person. He may grant any further deed transferring, modifying, burdening or discharging the right. In general it is unnecessary in any such deed to deduce the title of the granter. In assignations of moveable rights it is competent to specify any title connecting that of the granter to that of the original obligee, but the statutory provision is permissive, not mandatory.[34] A deduction of title is not required in the assignation of a policy of assurance by a successor of the person originally entitled to the policy[35] nor in a transfer of or security over shares of a company, a ship or a share thereof, an aircraft mortgage or a patent granted by a person who is the registered proprietor of it. In deeds relating to heritable property or heritable securities it is unnecessary for a person having a recorded or registered title to deduce title in any feu grant, disposition, heritable security or ground annual or assignation, discharge or deed of restriction thereof.[36] An assignation or conveyance of any obligation or right of relief or other right connected with lands, the title to which obligation or right does not pass under a general assignation, or deemed assignation,[37] of writs in a disposition or feu grant, may be in the form of Schedule M to the Conveyancing (Scotland) Act 1874[38] which contains a clause of deduction of title: that is not truly an exception to the general rule because the general assignation of writs does not assign the writs to any effect beyond what is appropriate to them as feudal titles, so that the granter of the assignation or conveyance does not have a recorded title to the obligation, right of relief or other right. If such obligation or right has been entered in the title sheet of an interest in land registered in the Land Register of Scotland no assignation of the obligation or right is now necessary.[39]

QUALIFICATIONS AND RESTRICTIONS OF RIGHT OR TITLE TO PROPERTY

Intrinsic and extrinsic qualifications

1–23   The right of a person to grant deeds affecting property may be qualified by provisions either (a) contained at length or referred to in the deed which constitutes his right or title to the property, or (b) contained in a separate deed not referred to in the deed which constitutes that right or title. In the former case the qualification of the right is intrinsic to the title; in the latter case the title is *ex facie* absolute and unqualified but the qualifications of it appear from a separate deed and are extrinsic

---

[34] Transmission of Moveable Property (Scotland) Act 1862, ss. 1, 4 and Scheds. A and B.

[35] Policies of Assurance Act 1867, s. 5 and Sched.

[36] The former requirement of deduction of title in an assignation of a registered lease or assignations, deeds of restriction or discharges of heritable securities or ground annuals where the granter was not the original creditor was abolished in circumstances where he has a recorded title—Conveyancing and Feudal Reform (Scotland) Act 1970, s. 47 and Sched. 10.

[37] By the Land Registration (Scotland) Act 1979, s. 16(1) or (2).

[38] s. 50.

[39] Land Registration (Scotland) Act 1979, s. 15(4).

to the title. The distinction between intrinsic and extrinsic qualifications may have significant effects which may be illustrated in the cases of trusts and securities.

1–24 **(a) Trusts.** Where property is held in trust and the fiduciary character of the right or title of the trustees is intrinsic, as in an *inter vivos* or a testamentary conveyance of the property in trust, the rules of the common law were that any dealing with the property by the trustees which was outwith the powers conferred in or necessarily implied by the trust deed or was at variance with the terms or purposes of the trust had the results that (i) any right to or over the property acquired by the other party to the dealing was reducible and so was unmarketable,[40] and (ii) the trustees incurred personal liability to the beneficiaries for breach of trust.[41] These rules were not altered by section 4 of the Trusts (Scotland) Act 1921, which conferred certain general powers on trustees, since the statutory powers were exercisable only where the acts of the trustees were not at variance with the terms or purposes of the trust. The first of these rules, however, was significantly altered by section 2 of the Trusts (Scotland) Act 1961 in the case of certain kinds of transactions. Subsection (1) of that section provides that where, after August 27, 1961, trustees enter into a transaction whereby they purport to do any act of the description specified in paragraphs (*a*) to (*ee*) of section 4 of the 1921 Act (sales, the granting of feus or leases, borrowing on the security of the trust estate, excambions and acquiring residential property as a residence for occupation by a beneficiary) the validity of the transaction and of any title acquired by the second party under the transaction shall not be challengeable by the second party or any other person on the ground that the act in question is at variance with the terms or purposes of the trust.[42] The second of the rules above mentioned, the personal liability of the trustees to beneficiaries for breach of trust, remains unchanged.[43] Another limited protection is given to executors (who are also trustees within the definition in the Trusts (Scotland) Act 1921[44]) by section 17 of the Succession (Scotland) Act 1964. Where any person has in good faith and for value acquired title to or any interest in or security over heritable property which has vested in an executor directly or indirectly from (a) the executor or (b) a person deriving title directly from the executor, the title so acquired is not challengeable on the ground that the confirmation was reducible or has in fact been reduced or, in a case

---

[40] *Bruce* v. *Stewart* (1900) 2 F. 948.

[41] Bell, *Prin.*, s. 2000; *Hood* v. *Macdonald's Tr.*, 1949 S.C. 24.

[42] The underlying reason for the change was that it was thought to be inequitable that the title of a person transacting for value with trustees should be perilled upon his construction of a trust deed which, especially when it was not professionally prepared, was ambiguous as to the powers of the trustees. The protection given by the subsection, however, is not restricted to transactions for value nor need the second party be *in bona fide*; it is available even when the transaction is obviously *ultra vires* of the trustees.

[43] 1961 Act, s. 2(2).

[44] s. 2 as extended to include an executor dative by Succession (Scotland) Act 1964, s. 20.

falling within (b), that the title should not have been transferred to the person mentioned.[45]

Apart from the statutory protection given by section 2 of the 1961 Act and section 17 of the 1964 Act in the circumstances in which they apply, the rules of the common law remain.[46]

1–25   Where the title of trustees to property is *ex facie* absolute and the qualification which establishes its fiduciary character is contained in a separate deed not referred to in the title of the trustees, *i.e.* is extrinsic, the validity of the right or title of a second party who transacts with the trustees depends upon good faith. If the second party acquires property or an interest in property for value in *bona fide* ignorance of the latent trust, his title is not reducible on challenge by a beneficiary of the trust.[47] On the other hand if the second party had knowledge of the existence of the fiduciary character of the right or title of the trustees, he is in the same position as if the qualification was intrinsic to the title of the trustees, *i.e.* the title which he acquires as a result of the transaction has the protection given by section 2 of the 1961 Act in cases to which it applies but in other cases he must be satisfied that the trustees have power to enter into the transaction and that it is not at variance with the terms or purposes of their trust. In a question between the trustees and beneficiaries the trustees incur liability for breach of trust if the transaction was *ultra vires* or at variance with the terms or purposes of the trust, irrespective of whether the title acquired by the second party to the transaction is challengeable or not.

1–26   The character of the fiduciary qualification of the title of a trustee as intrinsic or extrinsic does not in general affect the situation where diligence is directed against the trust property or the trustee is sequestrated. Diligence creditors can only attach property as their debtor has it subject to any qualification of trust whether patent on the face of his title or latent.[48] On the sequestration of an individual trustee the property which passes to his trustee in bankruptcy does not include property held by the bankrupt in trust even although the trust qualification was extrinsic to his title.[49]

1–27   **(b) Securities.** Whether a title to property is merely in security may be established intrinsically, where the deed which constitutes it creates expressly a security only, or extrinsically, where the title is *ex facie* absolute but is qualified by a separate agreement or back letter whereby the true character of the deed as creating merely a security is

---

[45] It may be noted that the protection given by s. 17 is only available where the second party to the transaction has acted in good faith.

[46] *e.g.* the title derived from a transaction with a tutor who is also a trustee under the 1921 Act is not protected from reduction on the ground of minority and enorm lesion.

[47] *Redfearn* v. *Somervails* (1813) 1 Dow's App. 50.

[48] *Brugh* v. *Forbes* (1715) Mor. 10213.

[49] *Heritable Reversionary Co. Ltd.* v. *Millar* (1892) 19 R. (H.L.) 43.

acknowledged. A title to a heritable security for a debt[50] created on or after November 27, 1970, will be in the former category since it can only be in the form of a standard security,[51] but the title to heritable securities created before that date may be in either category. The title to securities over moveable property may also be in either category.

1-28 *Deeds which are intrinsically securities.* Where the nature of the title as being merely a right in security is evident from the deed which creates it or any deed referred to therein which establishes that fact, the creditor in the security may only deal with it as such, observing any conditions contained in the security deed or imposed by law upon the powers of a creditor to deal with property of the kind involved, and a third party transacting with the creditor must ensure that these conditions have been complied with if the validity of the transaction is to be unchallengeable.

1-29 *Deeds involving ex facie absolute transfer.* Where the title to the property is *ex facie* absolute and the fact that it is truly held in security is disclosed in a separate deed the position of persons dealing with the creditor is less clear. If the qualifying deed simply acknowledges that the property, notwithstanding the *ex facie* absolute transfer or conveyance, was truly in security of a loan, so that the debtor could require a retrocession or reconveyance upon its repayment, the qualifying deed creates a personal or contractual obligation or a *pactum de retrovendendo.*[52] (It may be that the language of the qualifying deed creates a trust, as by the use of the words "in trust,"[53] in which case the rules as to property held on a latent trust apply).[54] In circumstances where the qualifying deed creates a contractual obligation a number of important questions in conveyancing practice may arise; these are considered in the following paragraphs.

1-30 (i) *The rights of the creditor to deal with the security property and the validity of the title acquired by the other party.* If the creditor sells or grants a security over the property to a third party who is unaware of the fact that the creditor is not absolute proprietor and transacts for value the validity of the title which he acquires cannot be challenged successfully by the debtor even if the transaction was not authorised by the qualifying deed. If, however, the debtor learns of a proposed sale or grant of security which is in breach of the terms of the qualifying deed, he may interdict the proposed transaction.[55] Where in the case of an absolute disposition of heritable property the qualifying

---

[50] For definition of "debt" see Conveyancing and Feudal Reform (Scotland) Act 1970, s. 9(8)(c).
[51] *Ibid.*, s. 9(3).
[52] *Campbell* v. *Bertram* (1865) 4 M. 23, 28; *National Bank of Scotland Ltd.* v. *Union Bank of Scotland Ltd.* (1885) 13 R. 380 *per* Lord President Inglis at 413; on appeal (1886) 14 R. (H.L.) 1.
[53] *Heritable Reversionary Co. Ltd.* v. *Millar, supra.*
[54] For a full discussion of the circumstances in which the qualifying deed creates either a contractual obligation or a trust see Wilson and Duncan, *Trusts,* 8–12.
[55] *Lucas* v. *Gardner* (1876) 4 R. 194.

back letter or agreement was recorded in the Register of Sasines, the writers of leading text books took the view that the effect of that recording was to make the obligation to denude a real limitation of the disponee's right.[56] The effect upon the validity of the title acquired by a third party transacting with the creditor is not altogether clear. If the back letter or qualifying agreement does no more than record that the debtor is entitled to a reconveyance upon repayment, there may be an argument that the creditor before repayment may exercise the power of sale that his original absolute infeftment confers and that his only obligation is to account to the debtor for the proceeds after repayment of the loan.[57] For a solicitor acting for the other party to the transaction with the creditor the safe rule of practice is to ensure that the transaction is authorised by the qualifying deed and, if that is unclear, to obtain the consent of the debtor. In cases where the absolute title is to moveable or heritable property and the existence of the qualifying agreement is known to the third party the practice rule is similar, since otherwise the third party may not be transacting in good faith, which can never safely be recommended.[57a] If the creditor does sell or burden the property in breach of the terms of the qualifying agreement or, in the case of a sale, upon terms which do not obtain the best price, he will be liable in damages to the debtor.[58]

1–31 (ii) *The residual rights of the debtor.* When a debtor has granted an *ex facie* absolute conveyance of heritable property qualified by an unrecorded back letter or agreement to the effect that the conveyance was truly in security, the residual right which remains in the debtor varies if (a) he was originally infeft in the property, or (b) he was not so infeft. In the words of Lord Kinnear[59]:

> "the difference between the position of a debtor infeft who dispones his estate to his creditors by an absolute disposition but really in security and that of the defender, who had never at any time a right of property in the subjects, is very material indeed. The doctrine is that a security in the form of an absolute disposition but qualified by a back-bond declaring the title to be limited to a definite security is neither more nor less than a heritable security, and therefore that the granter's title of property remains entire subject to the security. It follows that the granter of the disposition remaining in possession has a perfectly valid and sufficient title to dispose of the property in any way provided he does not trench on the security. Nothing hinders him to sell, subject of course to the security,—or to grant other postponed securities, either in the same form

---

[56] Bell, *Prin.*, s. 912; Menzies, *Lectures*, 892, 893; Montgomerie Bell, *Lectures*, 1174. See also *Dundee Calendering Co.* v. *Duff* (1869) 8 M. 289 *per* L.P. Inglis at 294.

[57] *Scottish Heritable Security Co.* v. *Allan, Campbell & Co.* (1876) 3 R. 333 *per* L.P. Inglis at 340; *Duncan* v. *Mitchell* (1893) 21 R. 37.

[57a] *Rodger (Builders) Ltd.* v. *Fawdry*, 1950 S.C. 483.

[58] *Park* v. *Alliance Heritable Security Co.* (1880) 7 R. 546; *Baillie* v. *Drew* (1884) 12 R. 199 (in both cases the claim of damages was unsuccessful); *Rimmer* v. *Thomas Usher & Son Ltd.*, 1967 S.L.T. 7.

[59] In *Ritchie* v. *Scott* (1899) 1 F. 728 at 736: followed in *Edinburgh Entertainments Ltd.* v. *Stevenson*, 1926 S.C. 363 and cited with approval in *Scobie* v. *William Lind & Co. Ltd.*, 1967 S.L.T. 9.

> or any other, but the principle is that a security in this form, being merely a security after all in substance, although in the form of a disposition absolute, does not divest the granter even feudally, and he is therefore in a position to deal with his estate by virtue of his own original title, and requires no other right or authority, so long as he leaves his creditor's security unimpaired."

His Lordship contrasted that position with that of a person who had not been infeft but had granted an absolute conveyance to a creditor: "But then the right to deal with the estate in this way depends entirely on the original title, on which the trust or security is merely a burden, and therefore the doctrine is altogether unavailing to support a lease flowing from a person in the position of the defender, who had no original title but only a *jus crediti*." The doctrine that a remanent infeftment remains in the infeft granter of an *ex facie* absolute disposition seems inconsistent with earlier decisions and judicial *dicta*[60] and has been criticised,[61] but it has been directly affirmed in the two latest decisions of the Inner House, in *Ritchie* and *Edinburgh Entertainments Ltd.*, and is in conformity with the realities of the situation.

1–32   The granter of an *ex facie* absolute assignation of incorporeal moveable rights qualified by an agreement that the assignation was truly in security retains a reversionary right which can be assigned absolutely or in security, intimation of the subsequent assignation being made to the grantee of the original *ex facie* absolute assignation.[62]

1–33   *Assignation.* Where the nature of a grant as a security is established intrinsically in the deed which creates it, the security may be assigned by assignation or conveyance, the title of the assignee being completed by appropriate mode. If the nature of the grant as a security is established extrinsically by a separate document assignation normally requires more complex documentation. It is competent to obtain from the creditor an absolute retrocession, transfer or reconveyance of the security subjects, the title of the debtor being completed in appropriate form, and the personal obligation of debt, usually contained in the separate deed, can be discharged by a receipt or discharge separate or endorsed thereon; the security subjects will then be available for the creation of a security to the assignee or new creditor. In the case of certain kinds of security, *e.g.* a pre-1970 security over heritable property, it was possible to combine the reconveyance by the original creditor and the conveyance to the new creditor in a single document on a narrative that the first conveyance was truly in security of a loan which had been repaid and that the debtor had requested and consented to a conveyance by the original creditor to

---

[60] *e.g. Gardyne* v. *Royal Bank of Scotland* (1851) 13 D. 912 (opinion of consulted judges at 939, 940); *National Bank of Scotland Ltd.* v. *Union Bank of Scotland Ltd.* (1885) 13 R. 380, *per* Lord Kinnear at 405; on appeal (1886) 14 R. (H.L.) 1, *per* Lord Watson at 3, 4.
[61] J. M. Halliday, *Conveyancing Review*, I, 5.
[62] See *Nelson* v. *National Bank of Scotland Ltd.*, 1936 S.C. 570.

the new creditor followed by an absolute conveyance to the new creditor with the debtor's consent, duly recorded, the obligation for repayment of the new loan and the nature of the conveyance as being truly in security of the loan being contained in a separate agreement between the debtor and the new creditor or assignee. Where the title to moveable property is completed by a form of registration which is not adapted to complex deeds, *e.g.* registration of shares in companies, the assignation may be effected by an absolute transfer of the shares by the original creditor in favour of the assignee, duly registered, together with an agreement amongst the original creditor, the debtor and the assignee narrating the arrangement for assignation of the debt and confirming that the transfer is truly in security of the debt now owed to the assignee. If the security has been created intrinsically by a deed which on the face of it creates a security, a partial assignation may be granted containing a ranking clause regulating the respective priorities of the portions of the debt due to the original creditor and the assignee. If the security has been constituted by absolute transfer or conveyance it is difficult to effect a partial assignation because of the problems of having two persons who are *ex facie* proprietors of the security subjects and to make provisions for ranking which will be effective on the security subjects (as distinct from a personal bargain between the two creditors). In such circumstances it is usually more convenient to have the security subjects retrocessed or reconveyed to the debtor and new securities created in favour of the two creditors which are *ex facie* security deeds, although it is necessary to ensure that the priority of the original security is not thereby lost by any diligence used after it was created.

1–34 *Discharge.* Where the fact that the grant was in security appears intrinsically in the deed which creates it, a simple receipt for the sum lent granted by the creditor effectively extinguishes the security, since the grant of security was ancillary to the obligation to repay and falls upon its discharge.[63] As a matter of proper practice, however, it will usually be desirable, where the original security deed has been intimated, recorded or registered, to clear the record by intimating, recording or registering a formal discharge of the security. Where the nature of the grant as being a security is established extrinsically by separate deed it is almost always proper conveyancing procedure to have the property which has been assigned or conveyed *ex facie* absolutely retrocessed or reconveyed to the debtor and his title completed appropriately. A narrative of the fact that the absolute assignation or conveyance was truly in security of a debt which has now been repaid may be contained in the retrocession or reconveyance or, if not, evidenced by a receipt or discharge, separate or endorsed, of the obligation of debt created by the separate deed. In the case of *ex facie* absolute dispositions of heritable

---

[63] *Cameron* v. *Williamson* (1895) 22 R. 293.

property a relatively simple form of discharge may now be used instead of reconveyance.[64]

Restrictions upon rights in property

1–35   The freedom of a person to grant deeds affecting a right or interest in property may be subject to restrictions imposed by law or inherent in a limited title or stipulated in the conditions of his title.

1–36   **(a) Corporeal moveable property.** The only proprietary title to corporeal moveable property is that of ownership: there cannot be, as in the case of heritable subjects, co-existing rights of ownership of superior and vassal.[65] Nevertheless the owner of corporeal moveable property may be subject to restraints upon dealing with it imposed by law upon particular kinds of such property, *e.g.* a registered British ship, if it is to continue to be registered as such, may be transferred only to a qualified person[66] and the transfer must be in the form of a bill of sale,[67] or an aircraft registered in the United Kingdom cannot continue to be so registered if an unqualified person becomes entitled to a legal or beneficial interest therein.[68] If an interest in the property is less than that of ownership, such as a liferent, the liferenter has a mere usufruct and his power to deal with the property is limited to the extent of his interest, or if he possesses the property on hire he may only deal with it subject to the contractual conditions of the hiring.

1–37   **(b) Incorporeal moveable property.** Such property consists in essence of legal rights or claims but even an absolute owner may only exercise or transfer them subject to restraints imposed by law from the nature of the subject, *e.g.* a person entitled to legal rights in the estate of a deceased spouse or parent who has died testate may only enforce the rights on condition of forfeiting testamentary provisions in his favour under the principle of election and if the right involves *delectus personae* it may not be transferable. Moreover a right of this kind may be subordinate, such as a mere liferent or a right of security over the property or use of it under licence from the owner, when it will be subject to the limitations of a liferent interest or the conditions imposed conventionally in the security deed or licence, as the case may be.

1–38   **(c) Heritable property.** Several estates in land, each of which are rights of ownership, may co-exist in a single heritable property, such as ownership of a superiority or a feu or a sub-feu. There may also be subordinate rights such as those enjoyed only in liferent or created by leases or

---

[64] Conveyancing and Feudal Reform (Scotland) Act 1970, s. 40 and Sched. 9. As to circumstances in which a reconveyance containing an appropriate narrative may still be preferable, see Halliday, *C. & F.R.A. 1970*, para. 5–25.
[65] See Walker, *Principles*, III, 367.
[66] Merchant Shipping Act 1894, ss. 1, 25.
[67] *Ibid.*, s. 24.
[68] Air Navigation Order 1980 (S.I. 1980 No. 1965), art. 4.

servitudes. All of these rights, whether of ownership or less, are subject to restraints in use or disposal of the land in which they exist imposed by law or in conditions of title.

–39 *(i) Rights of ownership.* The owner of any estate in land may be restricted in its use by the common law, as by principles of the law of neighbourhood or the existence of a servitude of necessity in favour of an adjacent proprietor, or by statute, as by the requirement of planning permission for certain kinds of development. The right of an owner freely to use or dispose of his heritable property may also be, and commonly is, restricted conventionally by conditions of title. Not all conditions may lawfully be created as real burdens on land[69] but there remains a wide variety of conditions which may be imposed and substantially restrict use. The right of an owner freely to dispose of his land or an interest in it, subject always to conditions which are real and binding upon singular successors, cannot be fettered,[70] save that he can no longer create an entail,[71] or a liferent beyond a certain period,[72] and clauses of pre-emption or redemption may, subject to certain statutory conditions,[73] restrict his right to sell.[74] Sub-feuing cannot lawfully be prohibited.[75]

–40 *(ii) Subordinate rights.* Subordinate rights or interests in heritable property are also subject to restrictions imposed by the common law either from the nature of the right or of the property, *e.g.* a liferenter may only let for the duration of the liferent or the dominant owner of a servitude may not increase the burden of it, or by statute, *e.g.* leases of agricultural holdings or of dwelling-houses are subject to statutory provisions.[76] Restrictions upon use or disposal may also be imposed conventionally in a document which created the subordinate right, *e.g.* a lease may contain not only detailed restrictions as to use but may prohibit, absolutely or subject to the consent of the landlord, assignation or subletting, and additionally real conditions which affect the right of the owner from whom or whose authors the subordinate title was derived continue to burden the subordinate right.

–41 *(iii) Real and personal conditions.* Conditions in titles to heritable property may be real, in the sense that they continue to burden the land irrespective of the person who may acquire rights or interests in it, or personal, in the sense that they create rights and obligations relating to

---

[69] As to the kinds of conditions that cannot be constituted as real burdens see *Tailors of Aberdeen* v. *Coutts* (1834) 13 S. 266; (1840) 1 Rob. App. 296; 3 R.L.C. 269.
[70] Act 20 Geo. II, c. 50, s. 10.
[71] Entail Act 1914, s. 2.
[72] Law Reform (Miscellaneous Provisions) (Scotland) Act 1968, s. 18.
[73] Conveyancing Amendment (Scotland) Act 1938, s. 9; Land Tenure Reform (Scotland) Act 1974, ss. 12, 13.
[74] *Preston* v. *Earl of Dundonald's Creditors* (1805) 3 R.L.C. 289; *McElroy* v. *Duke of Argyll* (1902) 4 F. 885.
[75] Conveyancing (Scotland) Act 1874, s. 22.
[76] *e.g.* Agricultural Holdings (Scotland) Act 1949, as amended; Rent (Scotland) Act 1984.

land upon the parties to the deed which contains them and their executors but do not affect singular successors.[77] The duty of a solicitor acting for a person acquiring the property or an interest in it is to explain the import of any real conditions which will affect his client and ensure that they are acceptable: he need not be concerned with regard to personal conditions which will not be binding upon his client. A solicitor acting for the person conveying the property or interest should be concerned with the observance of conditions whether real or personal in order to ensure that the former are imported into the bargain and that a breach of the latter does not involve his client in liability for damages.

---

[77] The distinction is discussed fully in a later chapter.

CHAPTER 2

CAPACITY AND POWER TO GRANT DEEDS

23

ALIENS

2–01 IN time of peace aliens[1] have the same rights as British subjects in relation to heritable or moveable property,[2] save that they cannot be the owners of, or of a share in, a British ship[3] and that in general they are not qualified to hold a legal or beneficial interest by way of ownership in an aircraft registered in the United Kingdom.[4] They may inherit property upon intestacy and may dispose of it testamentarily.[5]

2–02 In wartime, however, contracts made after war has commenced with enemy aliens not resident within the United Kingdom, unless under a licence from the Crown, are illegal and void, and cannot be enforced even after peace has been concluded.[6] If an enemy alien is domiciled

---

[1] *i.e.* persons other than British subjects as defined in the British Nationality Acts 1948 to 1981.
[2] Status of Aliens Act 1914, s. 17.
[3] Merchant Shipping Act 1894, s. 1; Status of Aliens Act 1914, s. 17 as amended by British Nationality Act 1948, s. 34(3) and Sched. 4, Pt. II.
[4] Air Navigation Order 1980, (S.I. 1980 No. 1965), art. 4.
[5] Status of Aliens Act 1914, s. 17.
[6] *Willison* v. *Patteson* (1817) 7 Taunt. 439.

and is within the United Kingdom and has complied with any statutory requirements as to registration he may act in a representative capacity, *e.g.* as an executor-dative,[7] and he may enter into and enforce contracts.[8] The rights of an enemy alien to property remain,[9] and will be restored to him when peace returns.[10] A company, although registered in the United Kingdom and conducting its business there, may be an enemy alien if effectively controlled by persons who are such.[11]

PUPILS

Status of Pupils

2–03 Pupils, *i.e.* boys under the age of 14 and girls under the age of 12, are not recognised in law as having an independent legal personality. A pupil himself has no capacity to grant deeds, and any deed which he purports to grant is void.[12] He may be required to pay a reasonable price for necessaries sold and delivered to him,[13] and money lent to him and used for his benefit may be recovered from him,[14] but these are obligations imposed or implied by law and are not contractual.

Tutors

2–04 Since a pupil has no legal capacity, his property is administered by his tutor. The tutor of a pupil child may be (1) his father and mother who have equal rights of administration exercisable by either alone,[15] (2) a tutor nominate appointed testamentarily by either parent to act jointly with the surviving parent or alone if the other parent is dead,[16] (3) a tutor nominate appointed to administer a particular provision by the person who makes the provision,[17] (4) a tutor-at-law or tutor-dative appointed by the court under common law where both parents are dead,[18] or (5) a factor *loco tutoris* appointed by the court either where no parent survives or where there may be a conflict of interest between a parent and the child.[19]

---

[7] *Schulze*, 1917 S.C. 400; *Crolla*, 1942 S.C. 21.

[8] *Schulze, Gow & Co.* v. *Bank of Scotland*, 1914 2 S.L.T. 455.

[9] *Ertel Beiber & Co.* v. *Rio Tinto Co.* [1918] A.C. 260.

[10] *Penney* v. *Clyde Shipbuilding and Engineering Co. Ltd.*, 1920 S.C. (H.L.) 68.

[11] *Daimler Co.* v. *Continental Tyre and Rubber Co. (Great Britain) Ltd.* [1916] 2 A.C. 307.

[12] Erskine, *Inst.*, I, vii, 14; *Sinclair* v. *Stark* (1828) 6 S. 336, 340; *Hill* v. *City of Glasgow Bank* (1879) 7 R. 68, 74.

[13] Sale of Goods Act 1979, s. 3(2).

[14] *Scott's Tr.* v. *Scott* (1887) 14 R. 1043.

[15] Guardianship Act 1973, s. 10.

[16] Guardianship of Infants Act 1925, s. 5.

[17] Bell, *Prin.*, ss. 2071, 2094. A clause is commonly inserted in wills appointing the trustees as tutors or curators to any beneficiaries who are in nonage.

[18] *Dick* v. *Douglas*, 1924 S.C. 787. This procedure is now seldom used; the appointment of a factor *loco tutoris* is usually sought.

[19] *Balfour Melville* (1903) 5 F. 347; *Speirs*, 1946 S.L.T. 203.

Powers of Tutors

2–05 Any parent acting as tutor to his or her pupil child, whether at common law or by virtue of the Guardianship of Children (Scotland) Acts 1886 to 1973, is deemed to be a trustee within the meaning of the Trusts (Scotland) Acts 1921 and 1961.[20] A tutor nominate, tutor-at-law, tutor-dative or factor *loco tutoris* is in the same position.[21]

2–06 As a deemed trustee the tutor has power to enter into any of the transactions specified in section 4 of the 1921 Act, so long as these are not at variance with the terms or purposes of the trust. Since normally there is no document which defines the terms or purposes of the tutor's office,[22] his power to enter into any particular transaction depends upon whether it is consistent with the purposes of his appointment.[23] *Prima facie* the duty of a tutor or curator is to preserve the estate of the ward rather than to alienate or alter it,[24] but where property is held simply as an investment then it would be within the tutor's powers to sell and reinvest in accordance with the normal practice of proper management of investments; where the property is of the nature of a family residence or has some special family connection the tutor would have no power to dispose of it.[25] Where doubt exists as to the power of the tutor to enter into any particular transaction his proper course is to apply to the court[26] for special power under section 5 of the 1921 Act, and the court may grant authority for the proposed act, even although it is at variance with the terms or purposes of the tutor's office, on being satisfied that it is in all the circumstances expedient for the execution of the deemed trust.

2–07 (a) **Sale and purchase of heritable property**. On the foregoing principles a tutor has power to sell the ward's heritable property if it is of the nature of an investment, but not if it is the family dwelling-house.[27]

2–08 A trustee has no general statutory power to purchase heritable property but may acquire any interest in residential accommodation reasonably required to provide a suitable residence for any of the beneficiaries.[28] That provision would probably enable a tutor to purchase residential accommodation for his ward. Otherwise he would require to seek special authority from the court.

---

[20] Guardianship of Infants Act 1925, s. 10.

[21] Trusts (Scotland) Act 1921, s. 2 as amended by Trusts (Scotland) Act 1961, s. 3.

[22] An appointment of a factor *loco tutoris*, in the absence of any crave for special powers, is customarily made simply with the usual powers.

[23] *Cunningham's Tutrix*, 1949 S.C. 275, 276.

[24] *Macqueen* v. *Tod* (1899) 2 F. 1069; *Linton* v. *Inland Revenue*, 1928 S.C. 209, *per* Lord President (Clyde) at 213, 214.

[25] *Cunningham's Tutrix, supra* at 277.

[26] The Court of Session: 1921 Act, s. 2.

[27] *Cunningham's Tutrix, supra*, explaining decisions in *Dempster*, 1926 S.L.T. 157 and *Brunton*, 1928 S.N. 112, and discussing dictum of Lord President (Clyde) in *Linton* v. *Inland Revenue, supra*; *Leslie's J.F.*, 1925 S.C. 464, 473.

[28] Trusts (Scotland) Act 1961, s. 4.

2–09   (b) Feus. The feuing of individual plots of a large estate, particularly where there has been a practice of granting such feus and that practice was consistent with proper management of the estate, would not be at variance with the purposes of the tutor's office and would be within his powers.[29] On the other hand the conversion of a whole landed estate into a superiority might be.[30] Elements in favour of the existence of the power would be a history of granting feus of the estate prior to the tutor taking office[31] or the location of the land being such that feuing was a natural development for which the land was suitable and loss would result if that course was not adopted.[32]

2–10   (c) Leases. A tutor has power to grant leases, including mineral leases, to abate rents, lordships or royalties in leases and to accept renunciations of leases, but all subject to the statutory provision that any such act is not at variance with the purposes of his office.[33] Whether the granting of a lease would be at variance with those purposes is a question of circumstances. Where property is held as an investment the granting of leases on terms appropriate to the nature of the property would be an ordinary act of management and would probably justify the granting even of long registrable leases of commercial property in accordance with modern practice. If property had already been let when the tutor entered upon his office, a renewal of the lease or the grant of a new lease would be within his powers.[34]

2–11   The powers of trustees under the 1921 Act to grant mineral leases are discussed in para. 2–57 *infra*. The duties of a tutor in that matter, however, may be significantly different. The working of certain minerals, particularly by extraction from the surface, can affect adversely the amenity of an estate. Where such workings already existed when the tutor's office commenced, a renewal of the leases or even the grant of new leases would probably be within his powers, but if a lease of minerals is to be granted in an area hitherto unaffected by mineral workings, the proper course may be to postpone the decision between commercial advantage and loss of amenity until the pupil comes of age, since the primary duty of the tutor is to preserve the estate rather than to alter its character. If a tutor wishes to grant a new mineral lease in such circumstances it would be advisable to seek the authority of the court.

2–12   Where the pupil is the tenant under a lease, the tutor requires the authority of the court to renounce it.[35] The tutor may renew an existing

---

[29] *Marquess of Lothian's C.B.*, 1927 S.C. 579 (relating to a *curator bonis* but the *ratio* is applicable to a tutor).
[30] *Ibid.*, at 585.
[31] *Pettigrew's Exrs.* (1890) 28 S.L.R. 14.
[32] *Campbell* (1880) 7 R. 1032.
[33] Trusts (Scotland) Act 1921, s. 4.
[34] *Dick's Trs.* v. *Robertson* (1901) 3 F. 1021.
[35] *Warden* (1829) 7 S. 848.

tenancy or undertake a new let for the purpose of providing residential accommodation reasonably required for occupation by the pupil,[36] but otherwise he requires the authority of the court to take property on let.

2–13 **(d) Securities.** A tutor has power to borrow money on the security of the trust estate or any part thereof, both heritable and moveable, if that is not at variance with the purposes of his office.[37] Where the ward's estate was already burdened with securities when the tutor took office variation of the terms of the securities or their discharge and replacement by new securities of similar amount would be ordinary acts of administration and within his powers.[38] If, however, the tutor proposed to grant a new security, as where capital was required to supplement the ward's income or for some particular purpose, there could be a question as to the necessity or advisability of burdening the estate in that way, and it would probably be wise to seek the authority of the court. It has been suggested that borrowing to pay off another debt might be a proper course.[39]

2–14 The powers of trustees to invest the funds of the trust estate in securities over heritable or moveable property are considered in paras. 2–63 to 2–72 *infra*. Where the estate of the ward when it comes under the administration of a tutor initially includes securities over property it would not be inconsistent with the purposes of his office to retain any security so long as the personal obligation and the subject of the security remain satisfactory, or even to vary the terms of the security for the benefit of the ward, *e.g.* by negotiating an increase in the rate of interest. That course would be justifiable as being the preservation and administration of the estate as it came into the hands of the tutor. Where, however, a new security over property is being contemplated it would seem doubtful whether such an investment, involving in periods of inflation devaluation of the invested capital, is appropriate to the purposes of the tutor's office, and special power should be sought from the court. If the security was over heritable property the tutor would for his own protection observe the provisions as to independent valuation and limitation of the amount lent contained in section 30 of the Trusts (Scotland) Act 1921.

2–15 **(e) Excambions.** Section 4 of the 1921 Act authorises a tutor to excamb any part of the ward's heritable estate, again subject to the qualification that such an act is not at variance with the purposes of his office. Excambions of small pieces of ground would be competent, but the exchange of any major item of the ward's heritage for other land might well be inconsistent with the tutor's primary duty of preserving the estate.

---

[36] Trusts (Scotland) Act 1961, s. 4.
[37] Trusts (Scotland) Act 1921, s. 4.
[38] *Henderson's Trs.* (1901) 8 S.L.T. 431.
[39] N. M. L. Walker, *Judicial Factors*, 105; *Grant* (1889) 16 R. 365.

2–16   (f) Arbitration. Section 4 of the 1921 Act also authorises a tutor to compromise or submit and refer all claims connected with the estate of the pupil where to do so would not be at variance with the purposes of his office. That provision would normally authorise a tutor to enter into submissions to arbitration in relation to any claims on behalf of or against the ward's estate.

MINORS

Status of Minors

2–17   Minors, *i.e.* boys who have attained the age of 14 and girls who have attained the age of 12 but who in neither case have attained the age of 18, have legal personality and can grant deeds, but the law gives certain protection against the results of transactions which have been entered into rashly or involve serious loss, notably that they may be reduced within the period of the *quadriennium utile.* A minor has capacity to grant or consent to deeds, but it is limited by reason of the special protection which the law affords to him on account of his inferior judgment or discretion.[40]

2–18   The father and mother, or either of them if only one survives, are automatically curators or curator to their minor children, each parent while both survive being entitled to exercise the right of curator without the other.[41] A curator may also be appointed (1) by nomination by the minor's parent,[42] (2) by the court on petition by the minor,[43] or (3) by a factor *loco tutoris* automatically becoming *curator bonis* when the child attains puberty.[44] If both parents are dead, the minor may have no curator.

Minors having Curators

2–19   The legal position of a curator is fundamentally different from that of a tutor. When a deed is granted by a minor, it is the act of the minor himself; the curator's function as adviser to the minor in the management of his affairs is to consent to the particular deed. It is settled that a deed granted by a minor who has a curator without the consent of the curator is null,[45] save where (1) the minor has engaged in trade, business or a profession when he may be liable for his business engagements,[46] (2) he has held himself out as of full age and was reasonably believed to be

[40] Bell, *Prin.*, s. 2088.
[41] Guardianship Act 1973, s. 10.
[42] Tutors and Curators Act 1696; Guardianship Act 1973, s. 10.
[43] Administration of Justice (Scotland) Act 1933, s. 12.
[44] Judicial Factors (Scotland) Act 1889, s. 11.
[45] *O'Donnell* v. *Brownieside Coal Co. Ltd.*, 1934 S.C. 534; *Faulds* v. *British Steel Corporation*, 1977 S.L.T. (Notes) 18.
[46] *McFeetridge* v. *Stewarts & Lloyds Ltd.*, 1913 S.C. 773.

so,[47] or (3) the consideration received by the minor has been profitably expended for his benefit. A deed granted by a curator alone is null.[48]

2–20 The curator of a minor is a trustee for the purposes of the Trusts (Scotland) Acts 1921 to 1961,[49] and has power to enter into any of the transactions specified in section 4 of the 1921 Act, as amended by the 1961 Act, where his action is not at variance with the purposes of his office. There is a significant distinction, however, between the position of a curator and that of a tutor. Since a pupil has no contractual capacity the validity of any transaction entered into by his tutor depends solely upon the powers of his tutor and a contract made by his tutor which is at variance with the purposes of his office is challengeable for want of power. A minor has full power to contract with the consent of his curator and if that consent is given, even although the curator's action in doing so is at variance with the purposes of his office, it would seem that the transaction cannot be challenged on the ground of want of power. (It may of course be open to reduction later on the grounds of minority and enorm lesion). Certainly it would not appear that an application to the court for special powers would be required.[50]

Minors having no Curator

2–21 A minor who has no curator, or who is forisfamiliated, has full powers to grant deeds alone, subject always to his right to reduce them subsequently on the ground of minority and enorm lesion.[51]

Powers of Minors with Consent of Curators and Minors having no Curator

2–22 In general a minor, with consent of his curator if he has one, or a minor who has no curator acting alone, has full powers to grant deeds of all kinds, subject always to the risk of reduction on the ground of minority and enorm lesion.

(a) Heritable property—feu, sale and purchase

2–23 He may grant feus and sell[52] or purchase heritable property. He may also dispose of it testamentarily.[53]

---

[47] *Wilkie* v. *Dunlop & Co.* (1834) 12 S. 506.

[48] Bell, *Prin.*, s. 2096.

[49] Trusts (Scotland) Act 1921, s. 2.

[50] *Wallace* v. *Wallace*, Mar. 8, 1817, F.C.; *Gillam's Curator* (1908) 15 S.L.T. 1043: contrast *Gilligan's Curator* (1908) 15 S.L.T. 1042.

[51] *Hill* v. *City of Glasgow Bank* (1879) 7 R. 68, *per* Lord President Inglis at 74, 75; *McFeetridge* v. *Stewarts & Lloyds Ltd.*, 1913 S.C. 773.

[52] *Wallace* v. *Wallace, supra.*

[53] Succession (Scotland) Act 1964, s. 28.

(b) Leases

2-24   He may grant leases, even of a duration longer than the period of minority,[54] or undertake tenancies.

(c) Securities

2-25   He may also borrow money and grant securities over his heritable or moveable property which are valid if the money is applied for his benefit[55] and in principle he has power to invest funds in securities.

Reduction before Expiry of Quadriennium Utile

2-26   A transaction with a tutor on behalf of a pupil or with a minor with consent of his curator or by a minor alone who has no curator are reducible at any time within the period of four years after the pupil or minor has attained majority on the ground of minority and enorm lesion.[56] Where the transaction has been entered into by a tutor and involves an act which trustees have power to do under section 4(1)(*a*) to (*ee*) of the Trusts (Scotland) Act 1921, as amended, although it is incompetent to challenge the validity of the title given on the ground that the actings of the tutor were at variance with the terms or purposes of his deemed trust by reason of the protection afforded by section 2 of the Trusts (Scotland) Act 1961,[57] as amended by section 8 of the Law Reform (Miscellaneous Provisions) (Scotland) Act 1980,[58] there would appear to be no bar to a challenge of the transaction on the ground of minority and enorm lesion. The statutory protection clearly has no application to transactions by a minor who has no curator, nor would it avail against a challenge of transactions by a minor with consent of his curator, since (1) the power to enter into the transaction is that of the minor and his curator merely consents, and (2) the protection does not extend against challenge on the ground of minority and lesion.

2-27   For the purposes of conveyancing practice the effect of these provisions may be summarised thus:

     (1) Where a transaction is entered into by a minor alone who has no curator, the statutory protection afforded to the other party to the transaction or any other person has no application and the transaction may be reducible within the *quadriennium utile*. It follows that any such transactions are inadvisable. In particular, a person who purchases heritable property should receive a title which is free from the possibility of challenge. In circumstances where both parties wish to proceed with a sale and purchase of heritable property practical safeguards against the

---

[54] *Alexander* v. *Thomson* (1813) Hume 411.
[55] *Harkness* v. *Graham* (1836) 14 S. 1015.
[56] For a discussion of the circumstances in which such transactions may be challenged on this ground, see Walker, *Principles*, I, 205, 206 and Walker, *Contracts* (2nd ed.), 5–28 to 5–35.
[57] 9 & 10 Eliz. 2, c. 57.
[58] 1980 c. 55.

risk of subsequent challenge by the minor should be taken, *e.g.* the sale should be made after adequate advertisement at the best price that can reasonably be obtained, possibly supported by a valuation made by an independent surveyor, so that it would be difficult to establish enorm lesion, and the purchaser's solicitor should have advised his client in writing of the risk involved.

(2) Where the transaction is entered into by a tutor or by a minor with consent of his curator (neither the tutor nor curator being subject to the supervision of the Accountant of Court) and the act is one which trustees are empowered to do by section 4 of the 1921 Act, its validity and any title acquired by the other party or any other person will normally be immune from subsequent challenge on the ground that it was at variance with the purposes of the office of the tutor or curator but remains vulnerable to challenge on the ground of minority and enorm lesion and the practical safeguards suggested above in transactions with a minor alone should be adopted. Moreover, if the transaction should be at variance with the purposes of the office of the tutor or curator, he may become liable in damages in a question with his ward, and, should there be any doubt on the matter, it may be advisable to apply to the court for power to enter into the transaction: whether the application is granted or refused as unnecessary, the tutor or curator is protected,[59] and the approval of the court will render subsequent reduction on the ground of minority and lesion unlikely.

(3) Where the transaction is entered into by a judicial factor, such as a factor *loco tutoris* or *curator bonis*, and the act is one which a trustee is empowered to do under section 4(1)(*a*) to (*ee*) of the 1921 Act, then, if the consent of the Accountant of Court has been obtained in compliance with the procedure outlined in paragraph 2–83 *infra*, the transaction will be treated as not being at variance with the terms or purposes of the factor's trust and the statutory protection will be available, but technically only against challenge on the ground that the act was at variance with the purposes of the factor's office.[60]

2–28 Certain precautions may be taken to reduce the risk of subsequent reduction by a minor in transactions of sale and purchase of heritable property, loan and security and discharge of rights.

(a) Sales and purchases of heritable property

2–29 The safeguards which are advisable in sales of heritable property by a minor have already been considered.[61] In the case of a purchase by a minor he may refuse to complete on the ground that the price is excessive or the conditions unduly onerous.[62] If the minor has a curator who is

---

[59] See *Bristow*, 1965 S.L.T. 225.
[60] Trusts (Scotland) Act 1961, s. 2(2)–(6) as added by the Law Reform (Miscellaneous Provisions) (Scotland) Act 1980, s. 8.
[61] Para. 2–27, *supra*.
[62] Burns, *Conveyancing Practice* (4th ed.), 310.

a party to the contract, however, there may be personal liability on his part. It is suggested that the curator's personal liability should be made express in the contract by inserting a guarantee by the curator in his individual capacity that the purchase will be implemented. If the minor has no curator, a guarantee from a responsible person should be sought.

(b) Loans and securities

2–30   Lesion is presumed where a loan is made to a minor on the security of his property and the transaction may be reduced unless the lender can demonstrate that the money has been applied for the benefit of the minor,[63] and the creditor is entitled to require evidence that it has been so applied or to have the loan repaid.[64] It is obvious that in practice such transactions should be avoided.

(c) Discharges

2–31   Lesion is presumed in the case of a gratuitous discharge[65] and a discharge for consideration granted by a minor is also reducible on proof of lesion.[66] The problem of discharges by tutors or minors and curators arises frequently in the administration of executry or trust estates when a beneficiary is in nonage. Where a legacy or vested share of residue becomes payable to a pupil his tutor is entitled to require payment to him as guardian of the beneficiary although, if the tutor is in embarrassed circumstances, the executor or trustees may require caution.[67] Since a receipt or discharge granted by a tutor on behalf of a pupil or by a minor, even with the consent of his curator, is open to reduction by the pupil or minor within the *quadriennium utile*[68] it is usual in practice for executors or trustees to seek to withhold payment until the beneficiary attains majority. Unless there is urgent need of the money the claim to payment before majority is seldom pressed, and if there is such need the executors or trustees should be satisfied that the money is being applied for the beneficiary's benefit. In many wills a clause is inserted which authorises the executors or trustees, if a legacy or share of residue falls to a beneficiary who is in nonage, either to retain the bequest until the beneficiary attains majority or to pay it to the legal guardian or the person for the time being having the custody of the beneficiary whose discharge shall be sufficient exoneration. The value of such a clause is that (1) it enables the executors or trustees to withhold payment until the beneficiary attains majority, thus negativing the right of a tutor or minor

---

[63] *Harkness* v. *Graham* (1833) 11 S. 760, 761.
[64] *Ferguson* v. *Yuill* (1835) 13 S. 886.
[65] *McFeetridge* v. *Stewarts & Lloyds Ltd.*, 1913 S.C. 773, 791.
[66] *Robertson* v. *S. Henderson & Sons Ltd.* (1904) 6 F. 770: *McFeetridge* v. *Stewarts & Lloyds Ltd.*, *supra.*
[67] McLaren, *Wills and Succession* (3rd ed.), 1173; *Dumbreck* v. *Stevenson* (1861) 4 Macq. 86; *Murray's Trs.* v. *Bloxsom's Trs.* (1887) 15 R. 233.
[68] The validity of a discharge is not protected by s. 2 of the 1961 Act.

to require payment before that event, and (2) if payment is made to the guardian and the money is dissipated the beneficiary cannot claim repetition from the executors or trustees since the payment has been made with the authority of the testator so that it is a condition of the bequest.

(d) Gratuitous deeds

2–32 There is a conclusive presumption of lesion in the case of deeds granted by a tutor or minor gratuitously, *e.g.* donations of significant value or cautionary obligations.[69]

SPOUSES

Married Women

2–33 A married woman now has the same powers of disposal of her heritable or moveable property as if she were unmarried, and any deed or writing executed by her with reference to heritable estate in Scotland or moveable estate is valid and effectual without the consent of her husband.[70] No married person, either wife or husband, is, by reason only of minority, subject to the curatory of his or her parent or any person appointed by the parent[71] nor is a wife, by reason only of minority, subject to the curatory of her husband.[72]

2–34 A married woman may enter into contracts and incur obligations as if she were not married, and her husband is not liable in respect of any contract which she may enter into or obligation she may incur on her own behalf.[73] If however she acts as agent for her husband or within the scope of authority given by him expressly or impliedly, then her husband is liable for performance of obligations so undertaken by her: the former *praepositura* or presumed authority to purchase household necessities has now been abolished.[73a]

Donations between Spouses

2–35 Donations *inter virum et uxorem* are irrevocable by the donors, but any such donation completed within a year and a day before the sequestration of the estates of the donor is revocable at the instance of the creditors of the donor.[74]

---

[69] *McFeetridge* v. *Stewarts & Lloyds Ltd.*, *supra* at 791.
[70] Married Women's Property (Scotland) Act 1920, s. 1.
[71] Law Reform (Husband and Wife) (Scotland) Act 1984, s. 3(1).
[72] *Ibid.*, s. 3(2).
[73] 1920 Act, s. 3.
[73a] Law Reform (Husband and Wife) (Scotland) Act 1984, s. 7.
[74] 1920 Act, s. 5.

Statutory Provisions—Particular Kinds of Property

2-36 As to the powers of spouses to effect policies of life assurance under the Married Women's Policies of Assurance (Scotland) Act 1880 as amended by the Married Women's Policies of Assurance (Amendment) (Scotland) Act 1980, see the undernoted text.[75] The statutory restraints upon the powers of an entitled spouse to deal with the matrimonial home imposed by the Matrimonial Homes (Family Protection) (Scotland) Act 1981[76] are considered in a later chapter in relation to sales of dwelling-houses.

PERSONS OF UNSOUND MIND

Incapax with no Curator

2-37 A person of unsound mind cannot effectively grant a deed since he lacks the mental capacity to understand what he is doing, and any deed which he purports to grant is null.[77] Nor can the purported transaction be enforced even if the other party to it was unaware of the fact that he was dealing with a person of unsound mind.[78]

Incapax with Curator

2-38 When a *curator bonis* is appointed by the court the *incapax* has no further control of his property[79] and the curator manages it on his behalf. A curator appointed by the court is normally a judicial factor; as such he is a trustee within the definitions of the Trusts (Scotland) Act 1921 and has the general powers conferred on a trustee thereby.[80,81]

INTOXICATED PERSONS

2-39 A person who is so intoxicated as to be unaware of what he is doing is incapable of giving a true consent and accordingly lacks the capacity to enter into obligations.[82] It would appear, however, that an obligation undertaken in that condition can only be avoided if the party repudiates it as soon as he recovers his senses and becomes aware of what he has done.[83]

---

[75] Walker, *Principles*, I, 242, 243.
[76] c. 59.
[77] *Gall* v. *Bird* (1855) 17 D. 1027.
[78] *John Loudon & Co.* v. *Elder's Curator Bonis*, 1923 S.L.T. 226.
[79] *Lang* (1847) 10 D. 148; *Macgregor* (1848) 11 D. 285.
[80] Trusts (Scotland) Act 1921, ss. 2, 4: Trusts (Scotland) Act 1961, s. 3.
[81] As to powers of judicial factors generally, see para. 2–81 *infra*.
[82] Stair, I, x, 13; Ersk., III, i, 16; *Taylor* v. *Provan* (1864) 2 M. 1226.
[83] *Pollok* v. *Burns* (1875) 2 R. 497.

TRUSTEES

Powers under Trust Deed

-40   The powers of trustees to perform acts of administration and to grant or accept any relevant deeds depend primarily upon the terms of the trust deed under which they act, on the principle that the truster could have dealt as he pleased with the property which he has placed in trust and so may direct or empower the trustees to deal with it either expressly in terms of the trust deed[84] or impliedly in fulfilment of the directions or powers which it contains.[85]

Statutory Powers

-41   In addition certain powers are conferred on trustees by the Trusts (Scotland) Act 1921[86] as amended by the Trusts (Scotland) Act 1961[87] and the Trustee Investments Act 1961.[88] These statutes, other than the Trustee Investments Act 1961, apply only to Scottish trusts and include any trust constituted by any deed or other writing, or by private or local Act of Parliament, or by Royal Charter, or by resolution of any corporation or public or ecclesiastical body and the appointment of any tutor, curator or judicial factor by deed, decree or otherwise,[89] and for this purpose a judicial factor means any person holding a judicial appointment as a factor or curator on another person's estate.[90] "Trustee" includes any trustee under any trust whether nominated, appointed, judicially or otherwise, or assumed, whether sole or joint, and whether or not entitled to receive any benefit under the trust or any remuneration as trustee for his services, and any trustee *ex officio*, executor nominate, tutor, curator and judicial factor[91] and an executor dative.[92]

-42   Section 4 of the 1921 Act, as amended, empowers trustees to do certain acts in relation to the property of the trust including sale, feuing, leasing and borrowing on security, excambion and purchase of residential accommodation for a beneficiary, subject always to the qualification that any such act is not at variance with the terms or purposes of the trust, and by implication to grant or consent to any deeds necessary or incidental to the performance of such acts. Whether an act is at variance with the terms or purposes of the trust must be determined upon a construction of the trust deed. Although an act is not expressly forbidden by the deed it may be at variance with its purposes.[93] On the other hand

---

[84] *Goodsir* v. *Carruthers* (1858) 20 D. 1141, 1145.
[85] *Moss's Trs.* v. *King*, 1952 S.C. 523.
[86] 11 & 12 Geo. 5, c. 58, ss. 4, 5.
[87] 9 & 10 Eliz. 2, c. 57, s. 4.
[88] 9 & 10 Eliz. 2, c. 62, s. 10.
[89] 1921 Act, s. 2.
[90] 1961 Act, s. 3.
[91] 1921 Act, s. 2.
[92] Succession (Scotland) Act 1964, s. 20.
[93] *Tennent's J.F.* v. *Tennent*, 1954 S.C. 215, 225.

even although an act is not necessary for the purposes of the trust it may not be at variance with them.[94] It is clear that the statutory powers are not exercisable if the act proposed is at variance with *either* the terms *or* the purposes of the trust deed,[95] *e.g.* a general power of sale might not authorise the sale of a particular property which was the subject of a bequest in liferent or fee; for that an express power of sale would be necessary.[96]

2–43   Section 5 of the 1921 Act enables the Court of Session, on the petition of trustees under a trust to which the Act applies but excluding any trust constituted by private or local Act of Parliament,[97] to authorise the trustees to do any of the acts mentioned in section 4 as amended, notwithstanding that such an act is at variance with the terms or purposes of the trust, on being satisfied that such act is in all the circumstances expedient for the execution of the trust. The court may dismiss the petition as unnecessary[98] or may grant it,[99] but even if it is dismissed as unnecessary the court may in a proper case allow the expenses of the petition to be met from the trust estate.[1]

Protection of Persons transacting with Trustees

2–44   In transactions entered into on or after August 27, 1961, in which trustees purport to do in relation to the trust estate any of the acts described in paragraphs (*a*) to (*ee*) of section 4(1) of the 1921 Act, as amended, the validity of the transaction and of any title acquired by the second party under the transaction or any other person is not challengeable on the ground that the act in question was at variance with the terms or purposes of the trust.[2]

Nobile Officium

2–45   Where neither the trust deed nor the Trusts Acts confer a power which the trustees wish to exercise, the trustees may apply to the Court of Session to authorise the proposed act in the exercise of the *nobile officium*. This equitable jurisdiction has been exercised sparingly by the court. Where the trust deed has defined the powers of the trustees the court will seldom confer a higher power[3] and in practice the *nobile officium* is exercised only "where something administrative or executive is wanting in the constituting document to enable the trust purposes to be

---

[94] *Marquess of Lothian's C.B.*, 1927 S.C. 579, 586.
[95] *Marquess of Lothian's C.B.*, *supra* at 584.
[96] *Christie's Trs.*, 1946 S.L.T. 309, 310.
[97] For trusts in which a petition under s. 5 was not competent see *Church of Scotland General Trustees*, 1931 S.C. 704, and *Edinburgh Royal Infirmary Board of Management*, 1959 S.C. 393.
[98] *Christie's Trs.*, 1946 S.L.T. 309; *Cunningham's Tutrix*, 1949 S.C. 275.
[99] *Chalmers Hospital (Banff) Trs.*, 1923 S.C. 220; *Darwin's Trs.*, 1924 S.L.T. 778.
[1] *Cunningham's Tutrix*, *supra*.
[2] Trusts (Scotland) Act 1961, s. 2.
[3] *Hall's Trs.* v. *McArthur*, 1918 S.C. 646, 652.

effectually carried out."[4] In the field of conveyancing practice the court has used the *nobile officium* to exercise an auxiliary jurisdiction in authorising the sale of Scottish heritage by trustees acting under an English trust who had obtained an order by the courts in England that such a sale was expedient,[5] and in special circumstances to purchase heritable property.[6]

Retrospective Sanction by the Court of ultra vires Acts

2-46 The court will normally refuse to sanction retrospectively *ultra vires* acts of trustees either on a petition under section 5 of the 1921 Act[7] or on an application for exercise of the *nobile officium*,[8] but may do so in exceptional circumstances.[9]

(a) Sale of trust property

2-47 The principles which determine the power of trustees to sell trust property apply to sales of both heritable and moveable property,[10] but most of the reported decisions relate to the sale of heritable property. A power of sale may be conferred by the trust deed either specially in relation to particular property or generally in the form of an unqualified power to sell the trust estate heritable and moveable, or it may be implied from the terms of the trust deed as necessarily incidental to the carrying out of its directions or purposes, or it may be conferred statutorily by section 4 of the 1921 Act, as amended, if sale, although neither expressly nor impliedly authorised by the trust deed, is not at variance with its terms or purposes.

2-48 A power of sale of heritable property was implied under the trust deed (a) where the deed directed division of an estate comprising heritable and moveable property,[11] (b) where the deed directed the division of estate heritable and moveable or the proceeds thereof,[12] and (c) where the deed contained a direction to pay the truster's debts and the moveable estate was insufficient for that purpose.[13] A power conferred under an English will to sell real estate was held impliedly to authorise the sale of Scottish heritable property acquired by the testator after

---

[4] *Hall's Trs., supra* at 650; *Scott's Hospital Trs.*, 1913 S.C. 289; *Anderson's Trs.*, 1921 S.C. 315.
[5] *Pender's Trs.* 1907 S.C. 207 *Harris's Trs.*, 1919 S.C. 432; *Campbell-Wyndham-Long's Trs.*, 1951 S.C. 685.
[6] *Fletcher's Trs.*, 1949 S.C. 330.
[7] Retrospective validation was refused under the corresponding s. 3 of the Trusts (Scotland) Act 1867 in *Clyne* (1894) 21 R. 849.
[8] *Dow's Trs.*, 1947 S.C. 524; *East Kilbride District Nursing Ass.*, 1951 S.C. 64; *Horne's Trs.*, 1952 S.C. 70.
[9] *Christie's Trs.*, 1932 S.C. 189; *Campbell-Wyndham-Long's Trs.*, 1962 S.C. 132.
[10] *Marquess of Lothian's C.B.*, 1927 S.C. 579, 587.
[11] *Boag* v. *Walkinshaw* (1872) 10 M. 872.
[12] *Thomson's Trs.* v. *Thomson* (1897) 25 R. 19.
[13] *Mackinnon Campbell's Trs.* v. *Campbell* (1838) 1 D. 153; *Graham* v. *Graham's Trs.* (1850) 13 D. 420.

execution of the will.[14] On the principle that the owner of a *pro indiviso* share of common property may always pursue an action of division and sale, a trustee who had no power of sale was held entitled to enforce that right.[15] Where the trust estate included securities which might involve liability, *e.g.* shares with unlimited liability, then, even if the trustees were directed to hold the trust estate and there was no express power of sale, it was held that the trustees had a duty to sell.[16] It is suggested, however, that the *ratio* of this decision cannot be safely extended to the situation where trustees are directed to hold heritable property which is subject to significant contingent liabilities, *e.g.* for major reconstruction or repair or the costs of demolition; if in such circumstances the trustees have no express or implied power of sale the proper course is to present a petition to the court under section 5 of the 1921 Act on the ground that a sale is expedient.[17]

2–49   The statutory power of sale of trustees and the power of the court to authorise sales were both significantly amplified by sections 4 and 5 of the 1921 Act. Under sections 2 and 3 of the Trusts (Scotland) Act 1867[18] a power of sale, if not conferred expressly or by implication under the trust deed, could be obtained only with the authority of the court upon a petition under section 3; under section 4 of the 1921 Act the necessity for judicial authority is dispensed with if the sale is not at variance with the terms or purposes of the trust. Moreover, the power of the court to authorise sale under section 3 of the 1867 Act was exercisable only if it was "expedient for the execution of the trust and not inconsistent with the intention thereof"; the latter requirement was not included in the corresponding section 5 of the 1921 Act and the court may authorise a sale if it is expedient for the execution of the trust.[19] The decisions under the earlier statute must therefore be read with due regard to the ampler powers conferred by the later statute.

2–50   For the exercise of the statutory power of sale it is essential that the sale must not be at variance with *either* the terms *or* the purposes of the trust deed.[20] Where the trust deed contains a general power of sale but its purposes provide that a particular property be held in fee or liferent for a particular beneficiary, a sale may be permissible with the consent of the beneficiary concerned, since the general power is applicable *prima facie* to all items of the trust estate and the right of objection is available only to the beneficiary and that right is negatived by his consent.[21] If, however, the trust deed does not contain a general power of

---

[14] *Phipps* v. *Phipps' Trs.*, 1914 1 S.L.T. 239.
[15] *Craig* v. *Fleming* (1863) 1 M. 612.
[16] *Brownlie* v. *Brownlie's Trs.* (1879) 6 R. 1233.
[17] See *Fiddes' Trs.* (1899) 7 S.L.T. 67; *Taylor's Trs.* v. *Tailyour*, 1927 S.C. 288.
[18] 30 & 31 Vict., c. 97.
[19] See *Leslie's J.F.*, 1925 S.C. 464, 472 *per* Lord Sands.
[20] See para. 2–42 *supra*.
[21] *Charlton's Trs.* (1901) 9 S.L.T. 130.

sale and there is a specific provision in favour of a beneficiary in liferent so that *prima facie* a sale would be at variance with the purposes of the trust, the trustees, while the liferent subsists, have no power of sale under the trust deed or the statute and the consent of the beneficiary does not assist since, as a mere usufructuary, he has no power of sale either. It is clear that an express prohibition of sale of heritage excludes the statutory power,[22] a power of sale subject to particular exceptions negatives the statutory power as regards the excepted properties,[23] but a direction to sell the truster's whole heritable estate with two exceptions did not prevent the trustees being authorised to sell the excepted properties.[24] A prohibition against selling before a specified date excludes the statutory power *quoad* a sale prior to that date.[25] If a power of sale is not negatived expressly or by necessary implication from the terms of the trust deed and a sale would in the relevant circumstances be instrumental in achieving the principal design and objects of the trust, the statutory power may be available,[26] although for the avoidance of doubt in such cases, a petition under section 5 of the 1921 Act may be advisable. The expression of a wish that certain property be made over to beneficiaries does not amount to a prohibition of sale where a general power of sale is conferred.[27]

2–51   Where trustees have no power to sell either under the provisions of the trust deed or under section 4 of the 1921 Act they may obtain such power from the court on a petition under section 5 of the 1921 Act if the court is satisfied that a sale is expedient for the execution of the trust. Petitions by trustees for power to sell heritable property under section 5 have been granted in circumstances where the intention of the truster was to apply the income from heritage for specified purposes but the income had become insufficient for those purposes.[28] Petitions under section 5 should be brought in the first instance before the Lord Ordinary, but, if the petition involves a scheme of administration of a charitable or other permanent endowment, the scheme must be finally adjusted and settled by the Inner House.[29]

2–52   Trustees having powers of sale, whether conferred by the trust deed or by the 1921 Act, may sell by public roup or private bargain unless otherwise directed by the trust deed or on authority given by the court, and minerals may be reserved.[30] Trustees have a duty to secure the best

---

[22] *Hay's Trs.* v. *Hay Miln* (1873) 11 M. 694.

[23] *Whyte's Factor* v. *Whyte* (1891) 18 R. 376.

[24] *Sutherland's Trs.* (1892) 29 S.L.R. 903.

[25] *Marshall's Trs.* (1897) 24 R. 478.

[26] For examples see *Weir's Trs.* (1877) 4 R. 876; *Downie* (1879) 6 R. 1013; *Deacons of the Incorporated Trades of Perth* v. *Hunt* (1881) 18 S.L.R. 585; *Richardson* (1898) 6 S.L.T. 241; *Christie's Trs.* (1904) 11 S.L.T. 786; *Jamieson's Trs.*, 1909 1 S.L.T. 36.

[27] *Jamieson* v. *Allardice* (1872) 10 M. 755.

[28] *e.g. Chalmers Hospital (Banff) Trs.*, 1923 S.C. 220; *Darwin's Trs.*, 1924 S.L.T. 778.

[29] Trusts (Scotland) Act 1921, s. 26; *Viscountess Ossington's Trs.*, 1965 S.C. 410.

[30] Trusts (Scotland) Act 1921, s. 6.

price reasonably obtainable, and should not impose conditions which militate against that unless they are designed to protect the amenity or value of other property forming part of the trust estate. It is a matter of commercial judgment whether trustees should accept a lower offer which is unconditional in preference to a higher offer contingent upon the obtaining of planning permission for a proposed development. Trustees have less freedom than a seller who is an individual to accept a lower offer, or to release an offerer from a completed contract; if practicable such actions should have the consent of beneficiaries having among them a vested interest in the trust estate. It is doubtful whether trustees can properly sell at a price fixed by arbitration[31]; the safer course is to test the market by advertisement. In certain circumstances, e.g. where it is doubtful whether a property may be sold more advantageously in separate lots, it may be desirable to obtain the advice of surveyors or estate agents, but in the normal case of sale of a single property where there are no obvious difficulties of choice of method it is thought that trustees may sell after advertisement without such advice.

(b) Purchase of heritable property

2–53 Trustees have no power at common law to purchase heritable property, nor do they have any general statutory power to do so[32]; such a power must be conferred expressly or by necessary implication from the terms of the trust deed or by a decision of the Court of Session in exercise of the nobile officium.

2–54 A limited power to purchase heritable property is conferred upon trustees to whom the Trusts (Scotland) Act 1921 applies by section 4(1)(ee)[33] which authorises them to acquire with the funds of the trust estate any interest in residential accommodation (whether in Scotland or elsewhere) reasonably required to enable them to provide a suitable residence for occupation by any of the beneficiaries, subject to the qualification that such an act is not at variance with the terms or purposes of the trust. The word "purposes" is not confined to the trust purposes set forth in the trust deed but includes the general purposes underlying the creation of the trust.[34] Where there is doubt on the matter a petition by the trustees for authority to make the acquisition may be presented under section 5 of the 1921 Act.

2–55 Power to purchase heritable property may be granted by the Court of Session under the nobile officium in exceptional circumstances where it is clearly expedient in the interests of the trust.[35] It may also be

---

[31] Menzies on Trustees, 215.
[32] Buchan v. Muirhead's Trs. (1901) 9 S.L.T. 24.
[33] Added to the 1921 Act by the Trusts (Scotland) Act 1961, s. 4.
[34] Bristow, 1965 S.L.T. 225, 226.
[35] For examples, see Wardlaw's Trs. (1902) 10 S.L.T. 349; Anderson's Trs., 1921 S.C. 315; Fletcher's Trs., 1949 S.C. 330.

competent for the power to be conferred by way of an enlargement of the powers of trustees upon approval by the court of an arrangement for variation of trust purposes under section 1 of the Trusts (Scotland) Act 1961.[36]

(c) Feus

2–56   Trustees within the meaning of the Trusts (Scotland) Act 1921 may grant feus if not at variance with the terms or purposes of the trust[37] and may petition for power to feu under section 5 of that Act, and the Court of Session may grant the power even where feuing is at variance with these terms or purposes if satisfied that it is expedient for the execution of the trust.

(d) Leases

2–57   Trustees of trusts as defined in the Trusts (Scotland) Act 1921 have power under section 4(1)(c) to grant leases of any duration (including mineral leases) of the heritable estate or any part thereof, subject to the qualification that such an act is not at variance with the terms or purposes of their trust.

2–58   (i) *Leases not exceeding 20 years.* Leases of property held for investment may be granted by trustees in the exercise of their powers of administration of the trust estate.[38] Where property was already let by the truster, trustees have an implied power to enter into a new lease on the expiry of the existing period of tenancy.[39] A lease of property not formerly let by the truster, such as a family dwelling-house, may involve different considerations,[40] but if the house is not required as a residence by any of the members of the truster's family and it is inexpedient to sell it, letting for a short period or periods may be a sensible act of administration. If the property let is a dwelling-house it is suggested that trustees should normally seek to grant short tenancies as defined in section 34 of the Tenants' Rights, Etc. (Scotland) Act 1980[41] rather than protected tenancies which are not within that definition.

2–59   (ii) *Long leases exceeding 20 years.* The granting of long leases will seldom be consonant with the terms or purposes of a family trust, save when the prospective duration of the trust is very long and in such cases the trust deed will frequently confer express power on the trustees. In a case where the trust estate was directed to be held until the death of the last survivor of the truster's children the court granted authority to the

---

[36] 9 & 10 Eliz. 2, c. 57; *Henderson*, 1981 S.L.T. (Notes) 40.
[37] Trusts (Scotland) Act 1921, s. 4(1)(b).
[38] *Campbell* v. *Wardlaw* (1883) 10 R. (H.L.) 65, 69; *Noble's Trs.*, 1912 S.C. 1230.
[39] *Dick's Trs.* v. *Robertson* (1901) 3 F. 1021.
[40] *Noble's Trs., supra per* Lord Johnston at 1234.
[41] 1980 c. 52.

trustees to enter into a lease for 999 years.[42] A direction not to sell or dispose of heritage impliedly negatived the power of trustees to grant a lease of 99 years since that amounted to an alienation of the property.[43] The development of valuable commercial or industrial property by the use of long leases is now normal practice, but where trustees are involved as granters of such leases the trust is usually a convenient vehicle in the documentation of the project and the beneficiaries are companies involved in the operation; in such circumstances the granting of long leases is not at variance with the purposes of the trust.

2–60   (iii) *Mineral leases.* Mineral leases of any duration may now be granted by trustees,[44] and a power of sale contained in the trust deed will authorise the granting of mineral leases since that is virtually a sale of part of the subjects.[45] Clearly trustees have power to grant mineral leases where the mineral field has formerly been leased by the truster, but it has been doubted whether they would have power to open up new mineral fields.[46]

2–61   (iv) *Administration of leases.* Under the 1921 Act[47] trustees have powers to remove tenants, to abate or reduce rent temporarily or permanently and to accept renunciations of leases. Clearly they would have power also to increase rents under rent review clauses or where permitted by law under the Rent Acts.

2–62   (v) *Trustees as lessees.* There is no general power to take subjects on lease under the Trusts Acts but trustees may do so if accommodation is reasonably required for the provision of a suitable residence for occupation by any of the beneficiaries.[48] In any other case trustees require power under the trust deed.

(e) Securities

2–63   **Trustees as lenders.** The powers of trustees to invest the trust funds in securities depend primarily on the trust deed but may be modified or enlarged by statute, notably the Trustee Investments Act 1961.[49] Certain principles of common law applicable to trustees, such as the prohibition of transactions in which a trustee may be *auctor in rem suam*, must also be kept in view. It is convenient to consider also the procedures which should be adopted by trustees to minimise the risk of liability to beneficiaries in respect of improper or unfortunate investments with security.

---

[42] *Birkmyre* (1881) 8 R. 477.
[43] *Petrie's Trs.* v. *Ramsay* (1868) 7 M. 64.
[44] Trusts (Scotland) Act 1921, s. 4(1)(c).
[45] *Naismith's Trs.* v. *Naismith*, 1909 S.C. 1380.
[46] *Campbell* v. *Wardlaw* (1883) 10 R. (H.L.) 65, 67, 70.
[47] s. 4(1)(c) and (m).
[48] Trusts (Scotland) Act 1921, s. 4(1)(ee) added by Trusts (Scotland) Act 1961, s. 4.
[49] 9 & 10 Eliz. 2, c. 62.

2–64　Powers under trust deed. Many trust deeds confer ample powers of investment upon the trustees, but such provisions are strictly construed.[50] In particular, power to retain securities does not imply a power to purchase securities of a similar kind,[51] nor does it absolve trustees from the duty of preserving the trust estate by continuing to consider the advisability of retaining them.[52] In the absence of special powers in the trust deed, the trustees are restricted to making investments in securities authorised by statute or common law.

2–65　Statutory powers. The statutory powers of investment in securities are now regulated principally by the Trustee Investments Act 1961. The powers of investment authorised by the Act are not limited by provisions contained in any instrument, *e.g.* any trust deed, made before August 3, 1961 (other than an enactment or an instrument made under an enactment) but are exercisable only in so far as a contrary intention is not expressed in any Act or instrument made under an enactment, whenever passed or made, or in any instrument made after August 3, 1961.[53] The Act thus operates to enlarge the powers of investment conferred by a trust deed made before that date, but may be limited by provisions expressing a contrary intention made after that date. In this connection any rule of Scots law whereby a testamentary writing may be deemed to be made on a date other than that on which it was actually executed is to be disregarded,[54] *i.e.* the date of a will for this purpose is the date of signature, not the date of the death of the testator.

2–66　　The Act authorises investments of various categories specified in the First Schedule, to which additions may be made by Order in Council.[55] Briefly these are (1) narrower-range investments not requiring advice from a person reasonably believed by the trustees to be qualified by his ability in and practical experience of financial matters,[56] (2) narrower-range investments requiring such advice,[57] which include loans on heritable security in Scotland,[58] and (3) wider-range investments,[59] which also require such advice.[60] The "advice" must have been given or subsequently confirmed in writing.[61] The powers of investment conferred by the Act are additional to and do not derogate from any special powers of investment exercisable by the trustees,[62] but any such special

---

[50] For examples of judicial interpretation of powers conferred in trust deeds, see Wilson and Duncan, 339–342.
[51] Menzies, 353.
[52] *Thomson's Trs.* v. *Davidson*, 1947 S.C. 654.
[53] s. 1(3).
[54] s. 1(3).
[55] s. 12.
[56] First Sched., Pt. I.
[57] First Sched., Pt. II.
[58] *Ibid.*, Pt. II, 13.
[59] *Ibid.*, Pt. III.
[60] s. 6(2).
[61] s. 6(5).
[62] s. 3(1).

power conferred on trustees before August 3, 1961, has effect as a power of investment in the like manner and under the like provisions as provided by the Act.[63] In the exercise of his powers of investment a trustee must have regard to the need for diversification of the trust's investments and the suitability to the trust of investments of the kind proposed and of the particular investment contemplated.[64] Where trustees in the exercise of powers conferred by the Act invest in wider-range securities the trust fund requires to be divided into two parts, equal at the time of division, consisting respectively of narrower-range and wider-range investments and the Act contains further provisions as to the treatment of increases in value of the property in either part, the allocation of new items of property accruing to the trust fund and the treatment of "special-range property" being investments which trustees are specifically authorised to make in terms of the trust deed.[65] These provisions relate more to trust management than conveyancing; for a more detailed consideration of them see the text referred to.[66]

2–67   Certain powers of investment are conferred on trustees by the Trusts (Scotland) Act 1921, although these are used comparatively seldom in practice. Trustees having power to invest in real securities may, unless expressly forbidden by the trust deed, invest on any charge, or any mortgage on such charge, made under the Improvement of Lands Acts 1864 and 1899 or on any charge created for payment of estate or other Government duty under the Finance Act 1894 or the Finance (1909–10) Act 1910.[67] Trustees having power to invest in mortgages or bonds of any company may, unless the contrary is expressed in the trust deed, invest in debenture stock of the company.[68] Trustees having power to invest in the purchase of land or on heritable security may do so notwithstanding that the same is charged by an absolute order under the Improvement of Land Act 1864 unless the terms of the trust expressly provide otherwise.[69] Trustees, unless authorised by the terms of the trust, may not apply for, purchase, acquire or hold beyond a reasonable time for realisation or conversion into registered or inscribed stock any certificate to bearer or other bond or document payable to bearer.[70]

2–68   **Heritable securities.** Trustees have power to invest in loans on heritable security in Scotland and in mortgages of freehold property in England and Wales and Northern Ireland and of leasehold property in those latter countries where the unexpired term at the time of investment is not less than 60 years,[71] and do not require to take advice on the suitability

---

[63] s. 3(2).
[64] s. 6(1).
[65] ss. 2, 3(3).
[66] Wilson and Duncan, 350–354.
[67] 1921 Act, s. 12(1).
[68] 1921 Act, s. 12(2).
[69] 1921 Act, s. 13 as amended by Statute Law (Repeals) Act 1977.
[70] 1921 Act, s. 15(1).
[71] Trustee Investments Act 1961, First Sched., Pt. II, 13.

of the particular loan.[72] In making loans on heritable security trustees should have regard to the provisions of section 30 of the Trusts (Scotland) Act 1921 which are:

> "(1) Any trustee lending money on the security of any property shall not be chargeable with breach of trust by reason only of the proportion borne by the amount of the loan to the value of such property at the time when the loan was made, provided that it shall appear to the court that in making such loan the trustee was acting upon a report as to the value of the property made by a person whom the trustee reasonably believed to be an able practical valuator instructed and employed independently of any owner of the property, whether such valuator carried on business in the locality where the property is situated or elsewhere, and that the amount of the loan by itself or in combination with any other loan or loans upon the property ranking prior to or *pari passu* with the loan in question does not exceed two equal third parts of the value of the property as stated in such report, and this section shall apply to a loan upon any property on which the trustees can lawfully lend.
> (2) This section shall apply to transfers of existing securities as well as to new securities, and in its application to a partial transfer of an existing security the expression "the amount of the loan" shall include the amount of any other loan or loans upon the property ranking prior to or *pari passu* with the loan in question."

The section relieves trustees of liability for a loan that may subsequently prove to be insufficiently secured: strictly, it does not impose a duty upon trustees to require a valuation,[73] nor is the fact that a valuation has not been obtained conclusive against the trustees where there is a deficiency in the security,[74] but in practice trustees should always have the protection of an independent valuation. It is essential that the valuator is employed by the trustees and is in no way instructed or influenced by the borrower,[75] and his fee should not be dependent upon the loan transaction being carried through.[76] The employment of a valuator does not relieve the trustees of the responsibility of making up their own minds as to the sufficiency of the security or the amount of the loan[77]; they should consider the whole circumstances of the proposed loan transaction and should not treat the valuation as justification for advancing two-thirds of the value contained in the report.[78] The report of the valuator should deal with both the capital value of the property and, in the case of let property, the current rental and the provisions for rent reviews. If the property is occupied by the borrower, the trustees should inquire as to his financial resources and his ability to pay interest on the

---

[72] *Ibid.*, s. 6(7).
[73] *Palmer* v. *Emerson* [1911] 1 Ch. 758.
[74] *Boyd* v. *Greig*, 1913 1 S.L.T. 398.
[75] *Boyd* v. *Greig, supra; Shaw* v. *Cates* [1909] 1 Ch. 389; *Re Solomon, Nore* v. *Meyer* [1912] 1 Ch. 261.
[76] *Marquis of Salisbury* v. *Keymer* (1909) 25 T.L.R. 278.
[77] *Boyd* v. *Greig, supra.*
[78] *Shaw* v. *Cates, supra.*

loan from income.[79] The valuator should be informed that the valuation is required in relation to a proposed loan by trustees, with some indication of its suggested amount and duration. The report should deal with matters relevant to the particular property including, according to the nature of the property, such matters as (i) leases and the terms thereof, (ii) restrictions on use or any significant servitudes, (iii) the use class of the property if any development is proposed, (iv) the price paid when the property was acquired and the date of acquisition, (v) the structural condition and state of repair of the buildings and, if the buildings or any extensions are of recent construction, that planning permission and building warrants were obtained, (vi) the risk of subsidence or settlement, (vii) drainage and access rights and the availability of public services such as electricity, gas and water, (viii) in the case of property used for a trade or business the existence of all requisite licences, (ix) in the case of property which includes machinery or valuable fittings whether these are heritable or moveable, (x) in the case of landed estates the rights of tenants of agricultural holdings, and (xi) repairs or improvements which should be carried out as a condition of the loan. The report should conclude with a valuation of the property and a statement of the maximum amount of the loan which might safely be made. Upon some of those matters the valuator may be unable to obtain reliable information, in which event inquiries should be made by the solicitor for the trustees before the loan transaction is completed.

2–69   The Trusts (Scotland) Act 1921 provides that where a trustee has improperly advanced trust money on a heritable security which would, at the time of investment, have been a proper investment for a less sum than was actually advanced, the security will be deemed an authorised investment for such less sum, and the trustee shall only be liable to make good the sum advanced in excess thereof with interest.[80]

2–70   Further provisions for relieving trustees against liability for breach of trust where they acted honestly and reasonably and ought fairly to be excused and for relief against a beneficiary at whose request or instigation the breach was committed are contained in sections 32(1) and 31 respectively of the 1921 Act. Trustees may also claim relief from liability by reason of an immunity clause in the trust deed; the extent of the immunity conferred is considered in a later chapter relating to the framing of trust deeds.

2–71   A person borrowing money from trustees and granting heritable security should be satisfied that the lending is not at variance with the terms or purposes of the trust since the validity of such a transaction, not being an act which trustees are empowered to do under section 4(1)(a)

---

[79] See *Maclean* v. *Soady's Tr.* (1888) 15 R. 966 as to the acceptance of a postponed heritable security where the borrower was plainly in continuing need of finance.
[80] s. 29.

to (*ee*) of the 1921 Act, does not have the benefit of the protection given to persons transacting with trustees under section 2 of the Trusts (Scotland) Act 1961.

(f) Excambions

2–72   Trustees had no power to excamb heritable property of the trust at common law but may do so in the exercise of the statutory power conferred by section 4(1)(*e*) of the Trusts (Scotland) Act 1921 subject to the condition that the act is not at variance with the terms or purposes of the trust.

(g) Arbitration

2–73   Trustees have power under section 4(1)(*i*) of the 1921 Act to compromise or to submit and refer all claims connected with the trust estate provided that to do so is not at variance with the terms or purposes of the trust. This power may properly be exercised to resolve questions between trustees and third parties but not to determine questions as to the rights or claims of beneficiaries since the decision of the arbiter in such circumstances may well amount to a variation of the purposes of the trust.[81]

Auctor in Rem Suam

2–74   Any transaction entered into by a trustee in which there is or may be a conflict between his personal interest as an individual and the interests of the trust is reducible by a beneficiary or other person having an interest to challenge, since it involves a breach of the established principle that a trustee may not be *auctor in rem suam*.[82] Indirect transactions such as a sale of trust property to a firm of which the trustee is a partner[83] or a company of which he is a director[84] are voidable. Nor can the principle be avoided by the trustee resigning office after he has derived some advantage from knowledge acquired or a business relationship established from his position as a trustee[85]; if a trustee is likely to be involved in a transaction where his interest as an individual may conflict with his interest as a trustee his proper course is to resign office and transact on an equal footing with any other third party. Transactions vulnerable to challenge include the purchase by a trustee of property forming part of the trust estate[86] or of the interest of a liferenter,[87] loans by the

---

[81] *Tennent's J.F.* v. *Tennent*, 1954 S.C. 215, 225, 226.
[82] *York Buildings Co.* v. *Mackenzie* (1795) 3 Pat.App. 378; *Hamilton* v. *Wright* (1842) 1 Bell's App. 574; *Aberdeen Ry.* v. *Blaikie Bros.* (1853) 1 Macq. 461; *Perston* v. *Perston's Trs.* (1863) 1 M. 245; *Mags. of Aberdeen* v. *University of Aberdeen* (1877) 4 R. (H.L.) 48; *Hall's Trs.* v. *McArthur*, 1918 S.C. 646; *Inglis* v. *Inglis*, 1983 S.L.T. 437.
[83] *Ex p. Moore* (1881) 51 L.J. Ch. 72.
[84] *Dunn* v. *Chambers* (1897) 25 R. 247.
[85] *Halley's Trs.* v. *Halley*, 1920 2 S.L.T. 343.
[86] *Hamilton* v. *Wright*, *supra*.
[87] *Davis* v. *Davis* (1908) 16 S.L.T. 380.

trustee to the trust[88] or by the trust to the trustee,[89] or the renewal in his own name of a lease previously held by the trust.[90] A trustee may, however, transact with a beneficiary, as by purchasing the beneficiary's interest in the trust estate, but it must be demonstrated that the trustee acted fairly and gave full information to the beneficiary and paid a full price.[91] A conflict of interests may arise in relation to partnerships, as where a partner of a deceased testator has been appointed as one of his testamentary trustees who are empowered to participate in carrying on the business; in such circumstances any new partnership arrangements should not result in the partner-trustee receiving an increased share of profits.[92] Where a business carried on by the trustees is converted into a limited company the trustees cannot as individuals take shares.[93]

Foreign Trustees

2–75 The powers of trustees of an English or foreign trust to grant deeds are regulated primarily by the provisions of the trust deed. Transactions relating to moveable property, if authorised by the trust deed, may be carried out in Scotland so long as they are not illegal nor inconsistent with Scots law.[94] In transactions relating to heritable property in Scotland it is necessary to consider the respective spheres of the law of the domicile of the trust and of Scots law as the *lex situs*. The proper law of the trust regulates the interpretation of the trust deed and the powers of the trustees; the Scottish Trusts Acts do not apply to foreign trusts.[95] So far as relating to heritable property in Scotland, however, the provisions of the deed and the powers conferred on the trustees must not conflict with the law of Scotland.[96] The question arises frequently in relation to the powers of trustees under foreign trusts to sell heritable property situated in Scotland. If the trustees have express power to do so under the trust deed or by statute, then the sale may be effected and no power need be sought from the Scottish court.[97] If there is any doubt as to the power of the trustees to sell, the opinion of a barrister or counsel expert in the law of the domicile of the trust should be obtained. If the trustees do not have the necessary power an application should be made to the court having jurisdiction over the trust for an order that the proposed sale is competent and expedient, and thereafter an application should be made to the Court of Session to authorise the sale in the exercise of the

---

[88] *Croskery* v. *Gilmour's Trs.* (1890) 17 R. 697, 700; *Wilson* v. *Smith's Trs.*, 1939 S.L.T. 120.
[89] *Perston* v. *Perston's Trs.*, *supra*; *Ritchies* v. *Ritchie's Trs.* (1888) 15 R. 1086; *Templeton* v. *Burgh of Ayr*, 1912 1 S.L.T. 421.
[90] *McNiven* v. *Peffers* (1868) 7 M. 181; *Halley's Trs.* v. *Halley*, *supra*.
[91] *Buckner* v. *Jopp's Trs.* (1887) 14 R. 1006, 1023; *Dougan* v. *Macpherson* (1902) 4 F. (H.L.) 7.
[92] *Lawrie* v. *Lawrie's Trs.* (1892) 19 R. 675.
[93] *Taylor* v. *Hillhouse's Trs.* (1901) 9 S.L.T. 31.
[94] Anton, *Private International Law*, 478.
[95] *Carruthers' Trs. and Allan's Trs.* (1896) 24 R. 238.
[96] *Philipson-Stow* v. *Inland Revenue* [1961] A.C. 727, 761.
[97] *Phipps* v. *Phipps' Tr.*, 1914 1 S.L.T. 239.

nobile officium.[98] The authorisation may extend to a continuing series of transactions, such as feuing or leasing, and further applications for each feu or lease are not required.[99] Save in exceptional circumstances,[1] retrospective sanction to *ultra vires* acts by foreign trustees will not be given.[2] It should be kept in view that the provisions as to the validity of a title granted by trustees by a transaction which is at variance with the terms or purposes of the trust contained in section 2 of the Trusts (Scotland) Act 1961 have no application to foreign trustees.

EXECUTORS

2–76 An executor-nominate is a trustee within the meaning of the Trusts (Scotland) Acts 1921 and 1961.[3] He has all the powers conferred upon him under the will by which he was appointed or by statute. An executor-dative in the administration of the estate of a deceased person has the whole powers and is subject to the same obligations, limitations and restrictions which gratuitous trustees have, or are subject to, under any enactment or under common law, and is a trustee within the definition of that term in the Trusts (Scotland) Acts above mentioned, save only that he has no power to resign or assume new trustees.[4] An executor remains subject to challenge under common law in respect of actions which infringe the rule against being *auctor in rem suam.*[5]

2–77 Although the powers of an executor have been assimilated by statute to those of a trustee there remains a clear distinction between the position of an executor and that of a trustee. A trustee is a fiduciary depositary of the trust estate for the purposes prescribed in the trust deed, which may involve holding of property and management of investments. An executor represents the deceased and, subject to any directions in the deceased's will, his functions are to settle debts and to administer, realise and distribute the estate.[6] This distinction may be important when it has to be determined whether an act is at variance with the purposes of the executor's deemed trust; his powers of investment may be less ample than those of a trustee.

2–78 Two important statutory protections are available in respect of transactions by an executor. (1) The validity of any transaction of the

---

[98] *Carruthers' Trs. and Allan's Trs.* (1896) 24 R. 238; *Allan's Trs.* (1897) 24 R. 718; *Pender's Trs.*, 1907 S.C. 207; *Harris's Trs.*, 1919 S.C. 432; *Campbell-Wyndham-Long's Trs.*, 1951 S.C. 685; *Campbell, Pet.*, 1958 S.C. 275.
[99] *Pender's Trs.*, *supra*; *Campbell, Pet.*, *supra*.
[1] *e.g. Campbell-Wyndham-Long's Trs.*, 1962 S.C. 132.
[2] *Horne's Trs.*, 1952 S.C. 70; *Prudential Assurance Co. Ltd.*, 1952 S.L.T. 121.
[3] 1921 Act, s. 2.
[4] Succession (Scotland) Act 1964, s. 20.
[5] *Inglis* v. *Inglis*, 1983 S.L.T. 437.
[6] *Globe Insurance Co.* v. *McKenzie* (1850) 7 Bell's App. 296, 319; *Lawson's Tr.* v. *Lawson*, 1938 S.C. 632.

descriptions specified in paragraphs (*a*) to (*ee*) of subsection (1) of s. 4 of the 1921 Act and of any title acquired by the second party under the transaction or any other person is not challengeable on the ground that the executor's act was at variance with the terms or purposes of his deemed trust.[7] (2) Where any person has in good faith and for value acquired title to any interest in or security over heritable property which has vested in an executor for the purposes of administration directly or indirectly from the executor or a person deriving title directly from the executor the title is not challengeable on the ground that the confirmation was reducible or has in fact been reduced or, in the case of a person deriving title directly from the executor, on the ground that the title should not have been transferred to that person.[8] This latter protection applies not only to titles given in transactions with an executor or a person deriving title directly from him but also in the situation where the executor has intervened to give a title for the purpose of implementing the provisions of an entail or a destination in the title to the property.[9]

2–79   Section 2 of the 1961 Act does not contain an express requirement that the other person transacting with trustees must act in good faith. In 1961 the devolution of the right of the deceased to heritable property was regulated by the deceased's will or testamentary writing which required to be examined as part of a prescriptive progress of titles and the object of section 2 was to absolve the person transacting with his trustees from the need to peril his title upon a construction of the will or testamentary writing, which might indicate that the transaction was at variance with its terms or purposes. Accordingly the fact that *prima facie* the transaction was so at variance did not affect its validity on the ground that the other person was not transacting in good faith. After the passing of the 1964 Act the right of an executor-nominate to deal with heritable property was based, not on the deceased's will or testamentary writing, but, by virtue of section 14 of the Act, upon the confirmation of the executor. A third party transacting for value with a person who has derived title from an executor need not examine the will or testamentary writing and in practice should not do so lest it disclose that the executor may have transferred the property to the wrong person and raise questions as to good faith.

JUDICIAL FACTORS

2–80   The powers of a judicial factor to grant deeds depend upon (1) the power conferred by the court on his appointment or special powers granted by the court in an application by the factor, and (2) the powers

---

[7] Trusts (Scotland) Act 1961, s. 2.
[8] Succession (Scotland) Act 1964, s. 17.
[9] *Ibid.*, s. 18(4).

conferred by the Trusts (Scotland) Act 1921 upon a judicial factor as a trustee.[10,11]

–81 Normally a judicial factor is appointed with the "usual powers." Judicial factors may be appointed in a wide variety of circumstances[12] and the scope of "usual powers" depends upon the nature of his duties. The duty of a factor *loco tutoris* or a *curator bonis* to a minor or *incapax* is primarily to conserve the estate of the ward[13] whereas a factor appointed to wind up the affairs of a partnership has the duty and the power to realise its assets[14] and the like power may be implied when a factor is appointed on a trust estate and realisation of assets of the trust may be necessary for payment of its debts,[15] to effect a distribution of the estate in accordance with the purposes in the trust deed[16] or when a sale is necessary to implement the truster's directions.[17]

–82 Judicial factors may exercise the powers conferred on trustees by section 4 of the Trusts (Scotland) Act 1921 where such acts are not at variance with the terms or purposes of his trust. Where a factor is appointed on a trust estate the terms and purposes of his trust will be contained in the relevant trust deed,[18] but in other cases where there is no trust deed the purposes must be ascertained by reference to the purposes for which the estate has been put under the management of the factor.[19] For example, factors on intestate estates or partnership estates plainly have power to realise assets of the estates for the purpose of winding them up. It is more difficult to determine whether realisation is at variance with the purpose of the deemed trust of a factor *loco tutoris* or a *curator bonis* whose primary duty is the preservation of the estate, but the sale of heritable property held as an investment[20] or the continuance of a previous policy of granting feus[19] or even a development of land appropriate to the nature of the subjects and in the commercial interests of the ward's estate may be within the factor's powers.

–83 If doubt exists as to the power of a factor to enter into any transaction which is outwith the ordinary course of factorial management or to do any act which is within the general powers contained in section 4 of the 1921 Act but may be at variance with the purposes of the factor's office

[10] 1921 Act, s. 2; Trusts (Scotland) Act 1961, s. 3; 1921 Act, s. 4.
[11] For a fuller discussion of the powers of judicial factors see N. M. L. Walker, *Judicial Factors*, 75–82.
[12] See *Leslie's J.F.*, 1925 S.C. 464 at 469.
[13] *Macqueen* v. *Tod* (1899) 1 F. 1069; *McAdam's Exr.* v. *Souters* (1904) 7 F. 179, 181.
[14] *Cooper & Son's J.F.*, 1931 S.L.T. 26.
[15] *Brown's Factor* (1902) 9 S.L.T. 490.
[16] *Wharrie's J.F.*, 1916 1 S.L.T. 345.
[17] *Stirling's J.F.*, 1917 1 S.L.T. 165; *McLeay*, 1921 1 S.L.T. 340.
[18] But a judicial factor appointed with "usual powers" has only the powers of a trustee at common law or by statute and does not have any special powers given to the trustees in the original trust deed: *Carmichael's J.F.*, 1971 S.L.T. 336.
[19] *Marquess of Lothian's C.B.*, 1927 S.C. 579 at 584.
[20] *Cunningham's Tutrix*, 1949 S.C. 275.

it may be authorised by the court on the application of the factor.[21] The occasions for such applications in respect of acts which the factor is empowered to do under section 4(1)(*a*) to (*ee*) of the 1921 Act may be diminished so far as the interests of the other party to the transaction are concerned by reason of the protection given by section 2 of the Trusts (Scotland) Act 1961. In the case of transactions by a judicial factor that protection is conditional upon the consent of the Accountant of Court having been obtained.[22]

Where an application is made to the Accountant of Court for consent the Accountant may grant the application if (a) he considers that the doing of the act is in the best interests of the ward or any person to whom the ward owes a duty of support, (b) the Accountant is satisfied that the judicial factor is not expressly prohibited by the terms of his appointment from doing the act, and (c) notification has been made to the persons specified in the Rules of Court of the proposed application, the act to which it relates and their right to object thereto within 28 days of the posting of the notice.[23] It is understood that where any objections are stated the practice of the Accountant is to withhold his consent, leaving the matter to be resolved by application to the court. Notwithstanding the provisions of section 2 of the 1961 Act a factor may in his own interests seek the authority of the court to a transaction which may be at variance with the purposes of his office, since persons interested in the estate under the factor's charge may seek to hold him liable for any loss to the estate which may result.[24]

TRUSTEES IN SEQUESTRATION

2–84 The general duties of a trustee in bankruptcy are to manage, realise and recover the bankrupt's estate, wherever situated, and convert the same into money with a view to distribution thereof amongst his creditors.[25] The powers of the trustee with which conveyancers are concerned relate mainly to sale of the moveable and heritable property of the estate and the closely related matter of the procedures which must be observed in exercising those powers.

Sale of Moveable Property

2–85 The Bankruptcy (Scotland) Act 1913 contains no specific requirements and few special provisions as to the method of sale of the moveable property of the bankrupt. The private sale of book debts is incompetent on the view that the trustee's duty is to recover them from the debtors.[26]

---

[21] Judicial Factors Act 1849, s. 7; Trusts (Scotland) Act 1921, s. 5.
[22] 1961 Act, s. 2(1).
[23] R. 200A, added by S.I. 1980 No. 1803.
[24] *Barclay*, 1962 S.C. 594.
[25] Bankruptcy (Scotland) Act 1913, s. 78.
[26] *Stewart* v. *Crookston* and *Galbraith* v. *Stewart*, 1910 S.C. 609. Book debts may be sold by auction but only after 12 months from the date of sequestration, 1913 Act, s. 133.

To facilitate the realisation of non-vested or contingent rights of the bankrupt the trustee may effect insurances on the life of the bankrupt.[27] Where the estate of the bankrupt includes the copyright in any work or any interest in such copyright sales of the work or of the bankrupt's right or interest may be made by the trustee only on terms which will secure to the author of the work payment of the royalties which he would have been entitled to receive from the bankrupt.[28]

Sale of Heritable Property

(a) Sale by the trustee

–86   The creditors may determine whether the property is to be realised by public sale or by private sale.[29] Such a decision may be made by the creditors at the meeting held after the examination of the bankrupt or at any other meeting called for the purpose and if that decision has been made before a heritable creditor having a power of sale has commenced proceedings for sale or if such proceedings, after being commenced before the decision of the creditors, have thereafter been unduly delayed, the creditor is not entitled to interfere with the sale by the trustee.[30]

–87   Where the sale is made by public auction the upset price and the manner of sale are fixed by the trustee with the consent of the commissioners, but the upset price must be sufficient to pay the debt, principal, interest and expenses, of any heritable creditor having security over the property.[30] The sale should be made after advertisement under articles of roup in accordance with normal practice. If a sale is not effected on the first exposure, the property may be re-exposed at a reduced upset price, again fixed by the trustee with the consent of the commissioners.

–88   The property may be sold by private bargain with the concurrence of (1) a majority of creditors in number and value, (2) the heritable creditors, if any, and (3) the Accountant of Court on such terms and conditions as to price and otherwise as the trustee with the concurrence of those parties may fix.[31] The concurrence of the Accountant is conclusive evidence that the concurrence of the requisite majority of creditors has been obtained.[31] The practice of the Accountant of Court is to require the trustee (i) to exhibit missives showing the proposed terms and conditions of sale, (ii) to exhibit a valuation or other satisfactory evidence

---

[27] 1913 Act, s. 78.
[28] 1913 Act, s. 102.
[29] *Ibid.*, s. 92.
[30] *Ibid.*, s. 110.
[31] *Ibid.*, s. 111.

of the value of the property, (iii) to exhibit minutes of creditors and commissioners or other satisfactory evidence that those parties approve of the sale, and (iv) to lodge a list of creditors with the amount of their claims, showing those who have concurred, and a certificate in prescribed terms that the list of creditors is full and correct, and that the whole heritable creditors holding heritable securities affecting the property and a majority in number and value of the ordinary creditors have concurred in the proposed sale and in its terms and conditions.[32] If those requirements are met the Accountant will pronounce an order granting his concurrence, but he does not sign the disposition.[32] It has been observed[33] that the consent of the commissioners is not required by section 111 but presumably they would sign the disposition in favour of the purchaser if the Accountant has issued an order concurring in the sale. An inhibitor, although he holds what may be regarded as a security over heritage,[34] is not a heritable creditor for the purposes of section 111 since the trustee can convey the property notwithstanding the existence of an inhibition.[35] Creditors who must be included in the list of ordinary creditors and in the computation of the majority in number and value are, with the exception of heritable creditors having security over the property which is being sold, restricted to those who have lodged claims in the sequestration. Preferential creditors,[36] creditors holding securities over other parts of the bankrupt's estate, and probably also deferred creditors, if they have lodged claims, are included, but creditors whose claims are under £20 are excluded.[37] Heritable creditors having security over the property which is being sold who have lodged claims must be included for the full amount of their debt without deduction of the value of their security.[38]

2–89 **Provisional sales.** It would appear competent, if a favourable offer is received before the procedure for obtaining the requisite consents has been carried through, for the trustee to enter into a contract for sale of the heritable property subject to the condition that the necessary consents are obtained and that, if these are not obtained, the contract will be cancelled without liability for damages upon either party.[39]

2–90 **Combined sales.** It may be advantageous to sell two or more properties together or to sell a property with goodwill, machinery and stock for an inclusive price. There would seem no impediment to adopting such a course provided that, if there are different heritable creditors having

---

[32] Notes by Accountant of Court for Guidance of Trustees in Sequestrations, para. XVI, published in *The Parliament House Book.*
[33] Burns, 317.
[34] *Mitchell* v. *Motherwell* (1888) 16 R. 122.
[35] 1913 Act, ss. 97, 100.
[36] *Ibid.*, s. 118.
[37] *Ibid.*, s. 96.
[38] *Ibid.*, s. 55.
[39] Burns, 316.

security over the several parts, agreement can be reached between the trustee and the heritable creditors as to apportionment of the *cumulo* price.[40]

2–91 **Compromises.** In certain circumstances, *e.g.* where a heritable creditor is willing to discharge his claim in exchange for a conveyance of the burdened property, the trustee may accept such a compromise instead of bringing the property to sale by virtue of his power to compromise claims under section 172 of the 1913 Act.[41]

(b) Sale by heritable creditors or by trustee with concurrence of heritable creditors

2–92 A creditor having security over heritable property of the bankrupt which is preferable to the right of the trustee may sell the security subjects if entitled to do so in terms of the security notwithstanding the sequestration and it is competent for the trustee to concur in the sale to fortify the title. The heritable creditor can be required by the court to account for any surplus of the price.[42]

2–93 A creditor having a heritable security over property of the bankrupt, with power to sell, may concur with the trustee in bringing the property to sale. The trustee sells the property in his own name and executes the articles of roup and the conveyance to the purchaser with the consent of the heritable creditor and the commissioners. The price is paid by the purchaser to the parties legally entitled thereto and, so far as not paid at the time of the delivery of the conveyance, is consigned in bank. Such payment or consignation frees and discharges the property sold and the purchaser from the security of the consenting creditor, whether the debt in his security is satisfied or not, and from all securities postponed to that of the consenting creditor.[43]

2–94 Sections 108 and 109 of the 1913 Act were enacted at a time when a creditor under a bond and disposition in security could sell only by public auction. A heritable creditor under a bond and disposition in security or a standard security may now sell by private bargain,[44] and a question arises as to the concurrence of or sale by the trustee under the sections when the sale is made by private bargain. In the case of a sale by a heritable creditor under section 108 (in which there is no specific reference to sale by public auction) it is thought that the trustee, if satisfied with the terms of the sale, may concur in the sale although it would be advisable to obtain the consent of the commissioners. As a general rule,

---

[40] *Op. cit.*, 317.
[41] *Dalzell* v. *Denniston* (1876) 4 R. 222; *Douglas* v. *Maclachlan* (1881) 8 R. 470.
[42] 1913 Act, s. 108.
[43] *Ibid.*, s. 109.
[44] Conveyancing and Feudal Reform (Scotland) Act 1970, ss. 25, 35.

however, the trustee should not concur; the heritable creditor should be left to effect a sale under the powers in his security, thus preserving the right of the trustee to challenge the validity of the sale, if so advised, on the ground that the price was not the best that could be reasonably obtained or that the exercise of the power of sale by the heritable creditor has not been *ex facie* regular.[45] It is thought that the procedure under section 109 would be incompetent if the sale is by private bargain, since in terms the section relates to sale by public auction.

Foreign Elements

(a) Power of Scottish trustee with regard to estate of bankrupt situated abroad

2–95   The act and warrant of the trustee transfers to and vests in him the moveable estate and effects of the bankrupt, wherever situated, as at the date of the sequestration,[46] and will be enforced in England or Northern Ireland.[47] As regards foreign countries, while in theory it is for the courts of the country where the moveables are situated to decide to what extent it will recognise a Scottish sequestration, in practice they will normally do so and the Scottish courts will interdict creditors from pursuing proceedings abroad to recover assets of the bankrupt situated there.[48] In general, therefore, it may be assumed that the trustee has power to deal with the moveable estate of the bankrupt wherever situated.[49]

2–96   The act and warrant also transfers to and vests in the trustee the whole property of the bankrupt[50] and "property" is defined as including every kind of property heritable and moveable and "heritable" includes "real."[51] In the case of real property in England and Northern Ireland the act and warrant requires to be registered in the Chief Court of Bankruptcy.[52] In the case of other foreign countries it is for the courts of the relevant foreign country to determine the effect of a Scottish sequestration on immoveable property in conformity with the *lex situs*, and it is necessary for the trustee to apply to the Court of Session to make an order requesting the appropriate foreign court to act as auxiliary to the Court of Session and have the act and warrant registered.[53] Subject to these procedures being carried out the trustee has power to deal with immoveable property abroad.

---

[45] *Ibid.*, s. 38 applied to standard securities by s. 32.
[46] 1913 Act, s. 97.
[47] (English) Bankruptcy Act 1914, s. 121.
[48] *Lindsay* v. *Paterson* (1840) 2 D. 1373.
[49] For a fuller discussion see Anton, 436, 437.
[50] 1913 Act, s. 97.
[51] *Ibid.*, s. 2.
[52] *Ibid.*, s. 97.
[53] *Murphy's Tr.*, 1933 S.L.T. 632.

(b) Power of foreign trustee with regard to estate of bankrupt situated in Scotland

2–97   In general foreign sequestrations are recognised in Scotland as conferring a title on the trustee to recover moveable property of the bankrupt situated in Scotland and indeed an application for authority to do so has been dismissed as unnecessary.[54]

2–98   The certificate of appointment of an English trustee in bankruptcy, for all purposes of any law in force in Scotland requiring registration or recording of conveyances of heritable property, is deemed to be a conveyance of such property and may be registered or recorded accordingly,[55] and on request by an English or Northern Irish court having jurisdiction in bankruptcy the Court of Session will exercise an auxiliary jurisdiction to enforce any order by such a court.[56] The procedure is (1) to produce and register in the petition department the order of adjudication in bankruptcy and the order appointing the trustee, (2) to have those orders, with the certificates of the petition department thereon, recorded in the Register of Inhibitions and Adjudications, and (3) either to record a notice of title in the appropriate Register of Sasines or have an entry made on the relevant title sheet of the Land Register of Scotland. The powers of sale of an English or Northern Irish trustee are those conferred upon a trustee in bankruptcy by English or Northern Irish law[57]; he does not have the powers of a Scottish trustee such as to sell without the consent of inhibitors[58] or to sell by public auction with the consent of a heritable creditor to the effect of clearing the title of postponed securities.[59] Other foreign trustees in bankruptcy require the authority of the Court of Session to sell heritable property of the bankrupt which is situated in Scotland but that authority will normally be given on appropriate conditions.[60]

TRUSTEES UNDER TRUST DEEDS FOR CREDITORS

2–99   A trustee under a trust deed for creditors has the powers conferred by the trust deed and has the statutory powers of a trustee under the Trusts (Scotland) Acts 1921 and 1961, notwithstanding that the trustee is remunerated for his services.[61] The hazard of the trust deed being superseded by sequestration and precautions in procedure on sale by the trustee

---

[54] *Araya* v. *Coghill*, 1921 S.C. 462.
[55] (English) Bankruptcy Act 1914, s. 53(4).
[56] *Ibid.*, ss. 121, 122.
[57] *e.g.* an English trustee may sell by public auction or private bargain without consents—(English) Bankruptcy Act 1914, s. 55.
[58] *Murphy's Tr.* v. *Aitken*, 1983 S.L.T. 78.
[59] Bankruptcy (Scotland) Act 1913, s. 109.
[60] *Araya* v. *Coghill, supra.*
[61] Trusts (Scotland) Act 1921, s. 2; *Royal Bank of Scotland* (1893) 20 R. 741; *Clark's Tr.* v. *McRostie*, 1908 S.C. 196.

under a trust deed to provide against that event are considered later in relation to trust deeds for creditors.

COMPANIES

2–100 The powers of companies incorporated under the Companies Acts to enter into transactions and grant deeds are now determined by (1) the law as it existed before the European Communities Act 1972, and (2) the provisions of section 9(1) of that Act. The effect of the Act is that the former *ultra vires* principles are not superseded for all purposes but do not operate adversely against persons dealing with the company in good faith.

The Law before the European Communities Act 1972

2–101 The objects of a company are specified in its memorandum of association and the powers of its directors in its articles of association. These are public documents and persons dealing with a company were deemed to have notice of their contents, and so had the duty of examining those documents to ascertain the powers of the company and of its directors to enter into contracts. As a result of that doctrine of constructive notice *ultra vires* acts by a company could be classified broadly in three categories: (1) acts which were *ultra vires* of the company, (2) acts which were *intra vires* of the company but *ultra vires* of its directors, and (3) acts which were *intra vires* of the company or its directors, as the case might be, only if certain procedures or formalities were observed. Acts falling within the first category were void and could not be ratified by the shareholders,[62] nor could the company be barred from pleading the nullity.[63] Acts within the second category could be ratified by decision of a general meeting called for the purpose,[64] and so validated retrospectively. In cases within the third category the company might be barred from pleading that a contract was invalid on the rule of the *Royal British Bank* v. *Turquand*[65] on the basis that the person transacting with the company was entitled to assume that its "indoor management" was in order.[66]

The Law after Section 9(1) of the European Communities Act 1972

2–102 Section 9(1) of the Act (effective as from January 1, 1973) provides that in favour of a person dealing with a company in good faith, any transaction decided on by the directors shall be deemed to be one which is

---

[62] *Ashbury Railway Carriage and Iron Co.* v. *Riche* (1875) L.R. 7 H.L. 653.
[63] *General Property Investment Co.* v. *Matheson's Trs.* (1888) 16 R. 282, 291.
[64] *Irvine* v. *Union Bank of Australia* (1877) 2 App. Cas. 366; *Grant* v. *United Kingdom Switchback Rlys. Co.* (1888) 40 Ch.D. 135.
[65] (1856) 6 E. & B. 327.
[66] As to the limits of the rule see Gloag, *Contract*, 116, 117.

within the capacity of the company to enter into, and the power of the directors to bind the company shall be deemed to be free of any limitation under the memorandum or articles of association; and a party to such a transaction so decided on shall not be bound to inquire as to the capacity of the company to enter into it or as to any such limitation on the powers of the directors, and shall be presumed to have acted in good faith unless the contrary is proved. The effect of the subsection, briefly stated, is that invalidity of transactions within any of the three categories listed in paragraph 2–101 *supra* cannot be pleaded by the company against a person transacting with it provided that (a) that person acted in good faith and (b) the transaction was decided upon by the directors. The former rules of the common law still apply internally, *e.g.* in questions between the company and the directors or between the directors and shareholders, and probably the person contracting with the company may still plead as against the company that it has acted *ultra vires* since the object of the subsection is to protect him and not to diminish his rights under the existing law.[67]

LIQUIDATORS OF COMPANIES

2–103 In view of the nature of the duties of the liquidator of a company the powers with which conveyancers are usually concerned are those involving sale of the company's property in relation to the rights of secured creditors and creditors who have used diligence.

Winding-up by Court

2–104 A liquidator in a winding-up by the court (i) has power with the sanction of the court or the committee of inspection to perform certain acts,[68] including (a) bringing or defending actions on behalf of the company, (b) carrying on the business of the company, and (c) other specified powers including compromising claims; and (ii) has power without any sanction to perform certain other acts,[69] including the sale of the heritable and moveable property of the company and raising money on the security of the company's assets. The exercise by the liquidator of the statutory powers is subject to the control of the court and any creditor or contributory may apply to the court with regard to the exercise or proposed exercise of any of those powers.[70] In the winding-up of a Scottish company the court may provide by order that the liquidator may, where there is no committee of inspection, exercise any of the powers (a) or (b) in (i) above without the sanction or intervention of the court and,

---

[67] Palmer, 127.
[68] Companies Act 1985, s. 539(1).
[69] *Ibid.*, s. 539(2).
[70] *Ibid.*, s. 539(3).

subject to general rules, the liquidator has the same powers as a trustee on a bankrupt estate.[71]

Voluntary Winding-up

2–105   The liquidator may, in the case of a members' voluntary winding-up with the sanction of an extraordinary resolution of the company, and in the case of a creditors' voluntary winding-up with the sanction of the court or the committee of inspection or (if there is no such committee) a meeting of creditors, exercise any of the powers given by paragraphs (*d*), (*e*) and (*f*) of subsection (1) of section 539 of the 1985 Act (payment of classes of creditors in full and compromises with creditors or contributories).[72] He may, without sanction, exercise any of the other powers given to a liquidator in a winding-up by the court, including power to sell the heritable or moveable property and to borrow on the security of its assets.[73] In a voluntary winding-up of a Scottish company the liquidator, subject to general rules, has the same powers as a trustee on a bankrupt estate.[74]

Winding-up subject to Supervision of Court

2–106   The liquidator has the same powers as a liquidator in a voluntary winding-up subject to any restrictions imposed by the court, provided that he may not exercise the powers given by paragraphs (*d*), (*e*) and (*f*) of subsection (1) of section 539 of the 1985 Act except with the sanction of the court or, where the court order for supervision was made after a creditors' voluntary winding-up, with the sanction of the court or the committee of inspection, or (if there is no such committee) a meeting of the creditors.[75]

Effect of Winding-up on Diligence—Inhibitions

2–107   Section 623(2) and (3) of the 1985 Act provides that a winding-up of a company registered in Scotland shall be equivalent, in the case of the moveable property of the company, to an arrestment in execution and decree of furthcoming and to an executed or completed poinding, and, in the case of heritable property, to a decree of adjudication for payment of the whole debts of the company subject to such preferable heritable rights and securities as existed at the date of commencement of the winding-up and are valid and unchallengeable and a right to poind the ground of limited effect in competition with the liquidator.[76] The provisions of subsections (2) and (3) echo the language of section 97 of the

---

[71] *Ibid.*, s. 539(4), (5).
[72] *Ibid.*, s. 598(1).
[73] *Ibid.*, s. 598(2).
[74] *Ibid.*, s. 598 applying s. 539(5) to voluntary winding-up.
[75] *Ibid.*, ss. 609, 610.
[76] *Ibid.*, s. 623.

Bankruptcy (Scotland) Act 1913 with appropriate modifications since the property of a bankrupt vests in his trustee on sequestration whereas in the winding-up of a company it remains the property of the company but is administered by the liquidator. Section 623 of the 1985 Act does not contain in the case of a liquidator, as section 97 of the 1913 Act does in the case of a trustee in sequestration, an express statement that the right of the liquidator is not challengeable on the ground of a prior inhibition. The view has been expressed[77] that a purchaser from a trustee in sequestration is not affected by inhibitions against the bankrupt but that the position is otherwise in the liquidation of a company. It is thought that this view is not well-founded, for the following reasons: (1) An inhibition is a prohibitory diligence which does not vest a real right in the inhibitor[78] and cannot prevail against the deemed adjudication constiP-tuted by subsection (3) of section 623. (2) An inhibition strikes at future *voluntary* acts and winding-up, at least a winding-up at the instance of creditors, is not a voluntary act of the company. (3) In subsection (2) of the section relating to moveable property, it is the decree of furthcoming or executed poinding that creates a real right of property in the subject; the comparable process required to render an inhibition real is adjudication.[79] It is submitted that the effect of an inhibition, which has not been followed by adjudication, in a question with a liquidator of the inhibited company, at least when the winding-up is at the instance of creditors, is that the liquidator may sell the property without the consent of the inhibitor but must accord the inhibitor a preference over posterior creditors in ranking.[80,81] Where a prior inhibition exists the liquidator when selling should not undertake an obligation to deliver or exhibit a clear search.[82]

Sale by Liquidator of Heritable Property burdened by Securities

2–108 Section 623(4) of the 1985 Act applies the provisions of sections 108 to 113 and 116 of the Bankruptcy (Scotland) Act 1913 to the realisation of the heritable property of a company in liquidation where that property is affected by heritable rights and securities.[83] Section 111 of the 1913 Act does not derogate from the liquidator's powers of sale under section 539(2)(a) of the 1985 Act; a liquidator may sell heritable property of the company by private bargain with the consent of the heritable creditors without requiring the concurrence of the general creditors and the Accountant of Court.[84]

---

[77] Burns, 300, 301.
[78] Graham Stewart, 551.
[79] *Op. cit.*, 561.
[80] As in sequestrations—*Baird & Brown* v. *Stirrat's Tr.* (1872) 10 M. 414.
[81] See Palmer, 1282.
[82] *Dryburgh* v. *Gordon* (1896) 24 R. 1.
[83] See paras. 2–92 to 2–94 *supra*.
[84] *Liquidator of Style & Mantle Ltd.* v. *Prices Tailors Ltd.*, 1934 S.C. 548 (decided on corresponding section of Companies Act 1929).

Applications by Liquidator to Court

2–109   Section 539(3) (in a winding-up by the court) and section 602 (in a voluntary winding-up) of the 1985 Act permit the liquidator or a creditor or contributory to apply to the court with respect to the exercise of the powers of the liquidator. The procedure in the Court of Session is by motion or note in the petition process made to the liquidation judge (winding-up by the court or subject to supervision by the court) or by petition (voluntary winding-up)[85]: in the sheriff court the procedure is by written note in the petition process (winding-up by the court or subject to the supervision of the court) or by petition (voluntary winding-up).[86] These provisions may be of use where a liquidator proposes to enter into a transaction which is outwith the powers specified in sections 539 or 598 of the Act and it is doubtful whether it is authorised by paragraph (h) of subsection (2) of the former section as being necessary for winding-up and distribution. In a case where liquidators proposed to sell property of the company to the Board of Trade and the Board were represented on the committee of inspection the court authorised the sale on an application under section 307 of the Companies Act 1948 (now section 602 of the 1985 Act).[87] A liquidator has no power to purchase heritable property; for that the authority of the court would be required.

Powers of Liquidators—England and Northern Ireland

2–110   Since the 1985 Act is a United Kingdom statute the powers of the liquidator of a Scottish company in relation to property of the company situated in England or Northern Ireland and of the liquidator of an English or Northern Irish company in relation to property of the company situated in Scotland are those conferred by sections 539 and 598 of the Act, subject to the qualification that in the case of real or heritable property the *lex situs* regulates the rights of parties as regards securities or diligences. The 1985 Act contains provision for the reciprocal enforcement of orders of the English or Northern Irish courts and interlocutors or decrees of the Scottish courts in proceedings for winding-up.[88]

RECEIVERS

General Powers

2–111   A receiver of the property of a company appointed by the holder of a floating charge or by the court may exercise over that part of the property and undertaking of the company attached by the charge the powers

---

[85] Rules of Court, r. 215(a) and (b).
[86] S.R. & 0. 1930 No. 234 as amended by S.I. 1948 No. 2293, paras. 47, 48.
[87] *Liquidators of North British Locomotive Co. Ltd.* v. *Lord Advocate*, 1963 S.C. 272.
[88] s. 570.

given to him by the instrument creating the charge and also, so far as not inconsistent with any provision in that instrument, has the powers specified in section 471 of the Companies Act 1985.[89] The statutory powers include sale, feuing or other method of disposal of the property by public roup or private bargain with or without advertisement, the borrowing of money and granting securities therefor over the property, granting leases of the property and taking on lease any property required or convenient for the business of the company. He may use the company's seal and execute in the name and on behalf of the company any deed or other document. After the appointment of a receiver the directors of the company are not entitled to deal in any way with the property of the company attached by the charge.[90]

Limitations of Receiver's Powers—Diligence and Securities

112 The powers of a receiver are subject to the rights of any person who has effectually executed diligence on all or any part of the property before the receiver was appointed, and the rights of creditors who hold over all or any part of the property of the company a fixed security or a floating charge having priority over, or ranking *pari passu* with the floating charge by virtue of which the receiver was appointed.[91] If a receiver sells or disposes, or desires to sell or dispose, of property which is subject to a security or interest of, or burden or encumbrance in favour of, a creditor whose right ranks prior to, or *pari passu* with, or postponed to the floating charge by virtue of which the receiver was appointed, or if the property or an interest in it has been affected or attached by effectual diligence, and the receiver is unable to obtain the consent of the creditor or the person who has executed the diligence to the sale or disposal, he may apply to the court for authority to sell or dispose of the property free of the security, burden, encumbrance or diligence.[92] The court may grant authority on such terms or conditions as it thinks fit, but a fixed security over the property which ranks prior to the floating charge by virtue of which the receiver was appointed must be met or provided for in full.[93] When the transfer or conveyance so authorised has been granted by the receiver, completion of the grantee's title by intimation, registration or recording as may be appropriate disencumbers the property of the security, burden or encumbrance affecting it and frees it from the executed diligence.[94] Two observations may be made as to the construction of those provisions, *viz.*: (1) The wording "sells or disposes, or is desirous of selling or disposing" indicates that the receiver may apply

---

[89] For powers in the instrument creating the charge see floating charges, Vol. 3, *infra*.
[90] *Imperial Hotel (Aberdeen) Ltd.* v. *Vaux Breweries Ltd.*, 1978 S.L.T. 113.
[91] 1985 Act, s. 471(2).
[92] *Ibid.*, s. 477(1).
[93] *Ibid.*, s. 477(2).
[94] *Ibid.*, s. 477(3).

to the court either after or before entering into the contract of sale. It is suggested, however, that in practice the authority of the court should be sought prior to the conclusion of a contract for sale, unless there are compelling reasons for urgency, and if there are such reasons the contract should contain a provision that if the conditions imposed by the court are unacceptable to the receiver he should be free of the bargain without liability for damages. (2) Although it is expressly provided that the claims of a creditor holding a prior fixed security must be met or provided for in full there is no such provision in the case of a creditor who has effectually executed diligence. It seems improbable, however, that the court when granting authority would restrict or derogate from the rights obtained by a creditor who had effectually executed diligence, but it may possibly enlarge them.[95]

(a) Diligence creditors

2–113   An arrestment which has not been followed by a furthcoming is not effectively executed diligence to which a receiver's right is subject,[96] nor apparently is an inhibition effected after the granting of the floating charge but before the appointment of a receiver if the inhibitor has not adjudicated.[97] It is unclear, however, whether a receiver can sell heritable property subject to such an inhibition without either obtaining the consent of the inhibitor or applying to the court under section 477 of the 1985 Act because the wording of subsection (1) of that section refers to property "affected or attached by effectual diligence." An inhibition is not effectual to attach the property—that requires an adjudication—but it is effectual in the sense that it affects the property since a trustee in sequestration or a liquidator who has a preferable right to sell the property must give effect to the inhibition as creating a preference in ranking over posterior creditors.[98] It is thought that the safe course in practice is for a receiver, if he cannot obtain the consent of the inhibitor, to make application under section 477 and to qualify the contract of sale appropriately with regard to producing clear searches. It is submitted that the decision in *Armour and Mycroft, supra,* does not establish the right of an inhibitor to receive the free proceeds of sale of the property after the claims of the holder of the floating charge have been satisfied. An inhibition secures simply a preference for the inhibitor over posterior creditors; the decision referred to was made by the court in the exercise of its

---

[95] See comment on *Armour and Mycroft, Petrs.*, 1983 S.L.T. 453, in para. 2–113 *infra.*

[96] *Lord Advocate* v. *Royal Bank of Scotland Ltd.*, 1976 S.L.T. 130; affd. 1977 S.C. 155; 1978 S.L.T. 38.

[97] This contention was accepted in *Armour and Mycroft, supra,* at 455. It seems that this was a logical concession: an inhibition strikes at future voluntary acts of the person inhibited, whereas sale by the receivers was not an act of the company but of the holders of floating charges making effective a right which antedated the inhibition.

[98] See *Lord Advocate* v. *Royal Bank of Scotland Ltd., supra* 1977 S.C. at 173, 174; *Armour and Mycroft, supra* at 455.

equitable power under the corresponding provisions of subsection (2) of section 21 of the Companies (Floating Charges and Receivers) (Scotland) Act 1972 in the special circumstances of the case.

(b) Secured creditors

2–114   Where property of a company is subject to both a floating charge and a fixed security arising by operation of law, the latter has priority over the charge[99] and over the receiver's rights which derive from it. Fixed securities arising by operation of law include lien and landlord's hypothec.[1] Subject to any ranking agreement contained in the floating charge or any instrument altering it, a fixed security in which the creditor's right has been made real before the floating charge has attached ranks prior to the right of the receiver.[2] The receiver may sell the property either with the consent of the prior creditor or with the authority of the court on an application under section 477 of the 1985 Act which may be granted only on condition that the prior security has been met or provided for in full.[3]

Receivers Appointed in the United Kingdom

2–115   A receiver appointed under the law of any part of the United Kingdom in consequence of a charge which, as created, was a floating charge may exercise his powers in any other part of the United Kingdom so far as such exercise is not inconsistent with the law applicable there.[4] So a receiver appointed by an English company by virtue of a floating charge created by a Scottish company may exercise over property situated in Scotland which is attached by the charge the powers conferred in the instrument which created the charge or conferred by English law so far as not inconsistent with the law of Scotland. Where a receiver had been appointed by an English company over property of a Scottish company it was held that the right of the receiver to moneys due to the Scottish company was preferable to that of a creditor of that company who had arrested the moneys subsequent to the appointment of the receiver.[5]

[99] 1985 Act, s. 464(2).
[1] In *Cumbernauld Development Corp.* v. *Mustone Ltd.*, 1983 S.L.T. (Sh.Ct.) 55 it was conceded in an action of sequestration for rent that the right of a receiver ranked prior to the landlords' hypothec. The correctness of this concession is doubtful. The hypothec of a landlord created by a lease entered into before the appointment of a receiver is a security arising by operation of law which can be made effective by sequestration (*Dundee Corporation* v. *Marr*, 1971 S.C. 96, 100) and it would be illogical in that situation for a receiver to be in a better position than a trustee in bankruptcy (Bankruptcy (Scotland) Act 1913, s. 115) or a liquidator (Companies Act 1985, s. 623; *Anderson's Trs.* v. *Donaldson*, 1908 S.C. 38).
[2] 1985 Act, s. 464(4).
[3] *Ibid.*, s. 477(2).
[4] Administration of Justice Act 1977, s. 7.
[5] *Gordon Anderson (Plant) Ltd.* v. *Campsie Construction Ltd. and Anglo Scottish Plant Ltd.*, 1977 S.L.T. 7 (decided under the former s. 15(4) of the 1972 Act now repealed but effectively replaced by s. 7 of the 1977 Act, *supra*).

CHARTERED INCORPORATIONS

2–116 Bodies incorporated by royal charter have, subject to any restrictions contained in the charter, full power to contract and grant deeds and in particular may enter into any transaction in furtherance of the objects for which they were established.[6] Interdict is competent against any act which is *ultra vires*,[7] but the court will allow a reasonably wide discretion to the body in the determination of whether or not an act is in the reasonable furtherance of its objects.[8]

PUBLIC OR STATUTORY CORPORATIONS

2–117 Public corporations established by statute or corporations constituted by or under the provisions of a statute may enter into contracts and grant deeds which are within powers expressly conferred by the statute or are in furtherance of or incidental to the purposes for which the corporation was established, but any act which is outwith these powers is *ultra vires* and void.[9] A corporation cannot enter into an agreement to abstain from the future exercise of its full statutory powers[10] or to use land for a purpose which is incompatible with the statutory purposes for which it was acquired.[11]

LOCAL AUTHORITIES

2–118 Local authorities may do anything which is calculated to facilitate, or is conducive or incidental to, the discharge of any of their functions[12] and have other express statutory powers, *e.g.* to acquire land by agreement or compulsorily and to erect buildings.[13] Local authorities may make standing orders with regard to the making of contracts by them and must make standing orders with regard to the making of contracts for the supply of goods or materials or the execution of works, but a person contracting with a local authority is not bound to inquire whether the standing orders have been complied with, and non-compliance with such orders does not invalidate a contract.[14] Further provisions as to the powers of planning authorities in relation to the acquisition, appropriation for particular purposes and disposal of land and the development of land are contained in Part VI of the Town and Country Planning (Scotland) Act 1972, as amended.

---

[6] *Conn* v. *Corporation of Renfrew* (1906) 8 F. 905.
[7] *Sanderson* v. *Lees* (1842) 22 D. 24.
[8] *Kilmarnock Mags.* v. *Aitken* (1849) 11 D. 1089; *Conn* v. *Corporation of Renfrew, supra.*
[9] *D. & J. Nicol* v. *Dundee Harbour Trs.*, 1915 S.C. (H.L.) 7; *Grieve* v. *Edinburgh & District Water Trs.*, 1918 S.C. 700. *Cf. Roberts* v. *British Railways Board* [1964] 3 All E.R. 651.
[10] *Ayr Harbour Trs.* v. *Oswald* (1883) 10 R. (H.L.) 85.
[11] *British Transport Commission* v. *Westmorland County Council* [1958] A.C. 126.
[12] Local Government (Scotland) Act 1973, s. 69.
[13] *Ibid.*, ss. 70–92.
[14] *Ibid.*, s. 81.

UNINCORPORATED ASSOCIATIONS

119 Unincorporated associations such as clubs or societies normally have a constitution and/or rules which regulate the rights and liabilities of members and the powers of a committee of management. The title to heritable property belonging to or leased by the association is usually taken in the names of trustees for the association and their powers to deal with the property, and the consents required and procedure to be adopted, are defined in the constitution or rules. Trustees for the association will usually be within the definition of that term in the Trusts (Scotland) Act 1921 since the constitution or the conveyance by which the property was acquired is a deed or writing creating the trust and so persons dealing with the trustees in a transaction within the scope of subsection (1)(*a*) to (*ee*) of section 4 of that Act may have the protection given by section 2 of the Trusts (Scotland) Act 1961 against challenge of the validity of the transaction on the ground that the transaction is at variance with the terms or purposes of the trust. It is still the practice, however, for a person contracting with the trustees in relation to the property of an association to examine the relevant constituting documents. He will normally require to do so in order to verify the personnel of the trustees and that they have been properly appointed, and it is in the interests of the trustees (who are not protected by section 2 of the 1961 Act) and the other party to the transaction to avoid all question by ensuring to the satisfaction of the solicitors for both parties that the proposed transaction is within the powers of the trustees or has been duly authorised by the committee or members and is being carried out in conformity with any procedures required.

FRIENDLY SOCIETIES

120 Friendly societies are usually registered under the Friendly Societies Acts, now consolidated in the Friendly Societies Act 1974. A registered society must have rules which are registered under the Act[15] and trustees[16] in whom the property of the society is vested.[17] A society may, if its rules so provide, hold land or purchase it or take it on lease, in all cases in the names of the trustees, and may sell, excamb, grant securities over or lease such land, and no purchaser, assignee, lender on security or tenant is bound to enquire as to the authority of the trustees for such transactions.[18] Persons transacting with the trustees of Scottish societies also will have the protection given by section 2 of the Trusts (Scotland) Act 1961 in relation to acts of the trustees which are within the ambit of section 4(1)(*a*) to (*ee*) of the Trusts (Scotland) Act 1921. The powers of

---

[15] Friendly Societies Act 1974, ss. 8, 17.
[16] *Ibid.*, s. 24.
[17] *Ibid.*, s. 54.
[18] *Ibid.*, s. 53.

the trustees in a question with members of the society are regulated by its rules.

TRADE UNIONS

2–121   A trade union which is not a special register body[19] is not an incorporated body and all property belonging to it is vested in trustees in trust for the union.[20] It is capable of making contracts[19] and granting appropriate deeds. The rules of the trade union must make provision with regard to the purposes for which and the manner in which any property or funds of the union are authorised to be applied or invested.[21]

BUILDING SOCIETIES

2–122   Building societies are incorporated bodies registered under the Building Societies Acts, the statute currently in force being the Building Societies Act 1962. A society must have rules which prescribe *inter alia* the purposes to which its funds may be applied.[22] In relation to land a society may (i) so far as is necessary for the purpose for which it is established hold land with the right of foreclosure, (ii) purchase, build, hire or take on lease a building for conducting its business, (iii) purchase or hold on lease land for the purpose only of erecting on it a building for conducting its business, and (iv) sell, exchange or let the whole or any part of property mentioned in (ii) or (iii) above.[23] It may unite with, and transfer its engagements to, another society.[24] A society is prohibited from advancing money on the security of feudal or leasehold property which is subject to a prior mortgage unless the prior mortgage is in favour of the society, but it may advance on the security of land which is subject to a charge imposed by a local authority under statutory powers.[25] When selling heritable property under powers contained in a mortgage the society must take reasonable care to ensure that the price is the best that can reasonably be obtained.[26]

INDUSTRIAL AND PROVIDENT SOCIETIES

2–123   A society for carrying on any industry, business or trade (including dealings of any description with land) may be registered under the Industrial and Provident Societies Acts 1965 to 1978.[27] The society must have rules which are submitted in Scotland with the application for registration to

---

[19] Under the Industrial Relations Act 1971.
[20] Trade Union and Labour Relations Act 1974, s. 2.
[21] *Ibid.*, s. 6(3).
[22] Building Societies Act 1962, s. 4.
[23] *Ibid.*, s. 7.
[24] *Ibid.*, ss. 18–20.
[25] *Ibid.*, s. 32.
[26] *Ibid.*, s. 36(1).
[27] 1965 Act, s. 1.

the assistant registrar of friendly societies for Scotland.[28] The powers of the society are determined by its rules and the statutes, and it may hold or purchase land or take land on lease, and may sell, exchange, grant a heritable security over or lease such land and erect, alter or pull down buildings upon it.[29] No purchaser, assignee, creditor in a heritable security or tenant is bound to inquire as to the authority for any dealing with land by the society.[29] A society may amalgamate with or transfer its engagements to another society, or may be converted into or amalgamate with or transfer its engagements to a company incorporated under the Companies Acts.[30]

PARTNERSHIPS

Partnership as a legal person

124 A partnership in Scots law is a legal person distinct from the individual partners, but it is not a full legal person which has contractual capacity: it acts through the agency of its partners and "the acts of every partner who does any act for carrying on in the usual way business of the kind carried on by the firm of which he is a member bind the firm and his partners, unless the partner so acting has in fact no authority to act for the firm in the particular matter, and the person with whom he is dealing either knows that he has no authority, or does not know or believe him to be a partner."[31]

Acts in the business of the firm

125 A partner has authority to bind the firm in transactions which are in the ordinary course of the firm's business. For examples of such transactions see the undernoted texts.[32] A distinction may be drawn between acts which are usual in the ordinary course of conduct of the trade, business or profession in which the firm is engaged and acts which, although related to the business of the firm in the sense that they are necessary for its operations, are not a normal recurring incident of its business. So a partner in a theatrical business, which normally entered into short-term leases of premises for the performance of entertainment, could bind the firm to a lease of such premises for a winter season,[33] but a lease of premises for a longer period as offices from which the business of a trading or professional firm would be carried on should be entered into by all the partners. Again a partner of a professional firm may bind the firm in acts normally done on behalf of its clients, or in the purchase for the

---

[28] *Ibid.*, s. 2.
[29] *Ibid.*, s. 30.
[30] *Ibid.*, ss. 50–52.
[31] Partnership Act 1890, s. 5.
[32] Gloag, *Contract*, 150; Walker, *Contracts* (2nd ed.), 5–52.
[33] *Cooke's Circus Buildings Co. Ltd.* v. *Welding* (1894) 21 R. 339.

firm's own use of consumable supplies or minor equipment which will require replacement, but *quaere* as regards the acquisition of major items of equipment which will be used for a much longer period?

Knowledge of partner's authority

2–126   The ostensible authority of a partner to bind the firm is limited by the statutory qualification that it does not extend to acts which the partner had no authority to do *and* the person with whom he is dealing either knows that he has no such authority or does not know or believe him to be a partner.[34] It has been judicially stated that a partner cannot give a guarantee so as to bind the firm since that is not one of the powers which a partner has,[35] but much depends upon the nature of the business: a partner in a firm of solicitors acting for a seller of heritable property normally grants an obligation to clear the records of incumbrances or diligences disclosed by a search and it has not been doubted that such an obligation binds the firm.[36] Where, however, the letter of obligation was granted by a partner on behalf of his firm in respect of a loan transaction for his private interest, and that fact was known to the lender, the obligation was held not to be binding on the firm unless the partner had special authority.[37]

Partners as trustees of firm's property

2–127   Since a partnership cannot sustain the feudal relationship the title to heritable property belonging to a firm is usually taken in the names of partners as trustees for the firm and the titles to leases and valuable property or investments of the firm are often also so taken. Prior to the enactment of the Trusts (Scotland) Act 1961 the practice when such property was being sold was to require the signatures of all partners to the disposition or other relevant document of transfer. The underlying reason was that, in the absence of any special powers contained in the document of title, a sale might be at variance with the purposes of the trust and so not authorised by section 4 of the Trusts (Scotland) Act 1921 and, since the transaction was not part of the usual business of the firm, the trustee partners or partner, if they did not comprise the whole of the current partners of the firm, did not have authority to bind the firm to the sale. Where the personnel of the partners had changed since the title was taken there could also be a question whether the firm as now existing was the same firm as that for which the property was held in trust.[38] Section 2 of the 1961 Act has now simplified such problems, at least as regards dealings with heritable property owned or leased by a

---

[34] Partnership Act 1890, s. 5.
[35] *Shiell's Trs.* v. *Scottish Property Investment Building Society* (1884) 12 R. (H.L.) 14, *per* Lord Blackburn at 23.
[36] *e.g. Dryburgh* v. *Gordon* (1896) 24 R. 1.
[37] *Walker* v. *Smith* (1906) 8 F. 619.
[38] See Burns, 311.

partnership. The title to such property devolves according to the nature and tenure thereof,[39] *i.e.* it is regulated in accordance with the law of trusts, and so the title of a person transacting with the trustees for the firm has the protection afforded by section 2 of the 1961 Act. If the transaction was unauthorised, however, the trustee partners remain liable to the other partners and possibly, depending upon the terms of the trust contained in the title deed by which it was constituted and any subsequent agreement regulating the devolution of the beneficial interest, the former partners or their representatives.

---

[39] Partnership Act 1890, s. 20(2).

CHAPTER 3

EXECUTION OF DEEDS

*Probative deeds, privileged writings and writings admissible in modum
    probationis*

3–01   In relation to their mode of execution deeds or writings may be classified as (1) probative deeds which comply with the statutory solemnities
for the execution of formal deeds and are of themselves, without further
evidence, sufficient proof of the obligations or rights which they impose
or confer, (2) privileged writings which, although not probative, are in
point of form as valid for their purposes as deeds executed in conformity
with the statutory solemnities, *e.g.* holograph writings or documents *in re
mercatoria*, and (3) deeds which do not fall within either of those categories but are admissible to establish the existence of certain obligations for
the constitution of which probative or privileged writing is not required
by law. In *Paterson* v. *Paterson*[1] a distinction was made between *obligationes literis*, obligations which require writing for their constitution and
for which probative or privileged writings are necessary, and other obligations which require writing, not for their constitution, but only for
their proof (*in modum probationis*). Documents of the kind last mentioned and the nature of the obligations for the proof of which they may
be used are matters within the field of the law of evidence[2]; the present
chapter relates only to probative deeds and privileged writings.

PROBATIVE DEEDS

Definition and application

3–02   In this chapter the term probative deed denotes a deed which is
executed in accordance with the solemnities prescribed by the authenti-

---

[1] (1897) 25 R. 144.
[2] See Walker and Walker, *Evidence*, Chap. IX.

cation statutes.[3] Solemn execution is required for the constitution of any of the *obligationes literis* such as contracts relating to heritage, including securities over heritable property but excepting leases for not more than a year, and contracts of service for more than a year,[4] subject always to (i) the privileges accorded by law to holograph writings,[5] (ii) the principles whereby informal writings may be validated subsequently by *rei interventus* or homologation,[6] and (iii) the exception of bonds or obligations relating to moveables involving an amount not exceeding £8·33.[7]

The authentication statutes

3–03   Solemnities to be observed in the execution of probative deeds were prescribed by a series of statutes, generally known as the authentication statutes, enacted in the sixteenth and seventeenth centuries, and these, with certain amendments made in more recent legislation, regulate the requirements for formal execution of such deeds.[8] For an account of the evolution of the requirements of execution of formal deeds through these statutes and their interpretation by the courts see the texts cited.[9]

Requirements for execution of probative deeds

3–04   The requirements for formal execution of a probative deed in modern practice may be summarised thus:

(1) The deed must be subscribed and (where appropriate) sealed by the granter or granters and any consenting parties, personally or vicariously by other persons duly authorised, on the last page, and any inventory, appendix, schedule, plan or other document annexed must also be subscribed and (where appropriate) sealed on the last page.[10] A will or testamentary writing, however, must be subscribed by the granter, personally or vicariously, on every page and at the end, or, if it consists of a single sheet, at the end.

(2) The granter or granters and any consenting parties must sign in the presence of, or acknowledge his or their signature to, at least two competent witnesses who must subscribe on the last page.[10a]

---

[3] For a list of these see para. 3–03.

[4] For a full discussion of obligations which are, or are doubtfully within, the category of *obligationes literis* see Gloag, *Contract*, Chap. X; Walker and Walker, *Evidence*, Chap. IX; Walker, *Contracts*, 2nd ed., 13–23.

[5] See para. 3–46 *et seq*.

[6] See paras. 15–17 to 15–21 (Vol. 2).

[7] The Subscription of Deeds Act 1579 (1579 c. 80) required solemn execution of "bandes and obligations of great importance," interpreted as relating to obligations involving more than £100 Scots.

[8] The principal statutes are the Subscription of Deeds Act 1540 (1540 c. 117); Subscription of Deeds Act 1579 (1579 c. 80); Writs Act 1672 (1672 c. 7); The Lyon King of Arms Act 1672 (1672 c. 21); Subscription of Deeds Act 1681 (1681 c. 5); Deeds Act 1696 (1696 c. 15); Conveyancing (Scotland) Act 1874, ss. 38, 39; Conveyancing and Feudal Reform (Scotland) Act 1970, s. 44.

[9] Menzies, *Lectures*, Chaps. IV–IX; Montgomerie Bell, *Lectures*, Chaps. I–III; Wood, *Lectures*, Pt.II, Chaps. II, III.

[10] Conveyancing and Feudal Reform (Scotland) Act 1970, s. 44.

[10a] The acknowledgement need not be in words: *Cumming* v. *Skeoch's Trs.* (1879) 6 R. 963.

(3) The witnesses must be designed in the deed (normally in the test-ing clause) or by the addition of their designations after their signatures.

Subscription by Granter of or Party to the Deed

(a) Style of signature

3–05   A man or an unmarried woman signs his or her surname in full, pre-faced by (i) the christian names in full, or (ii) any recognised contraction of any of the christian names, or (iii) the initials of the christian names, or (iv) any combination of (i), (ii) and (iii). All christian names appear-ing in the deed should be represented in the signature and, if not, the omission should be referred to in the testing clause. In the converse case, where a christian name or initial appears in the signature but is not included or represented in the name of the person in the deed, it is thought that the deed is not thereby invalidated so long as the discre-pancy is noticed appropriately in the testing clause; so long as the name and designation of the party as appearing in the deed is sufficiently iden-tifying, the fact that a christian name has been omitted should not be fatal. A married woman signs her husband's surname prefaced by her own christian names, or recognised contractions or initials thereof. She may sign her maiden surname instead of her husband's surname,[11] but as these are alternatives it is strictly incorrect to sign both or to insert before the signature of her married name the initial of her maiden name although it has been decided that to do so is not a material error.[12] The surname preceded by "Mr." or "Mrs." but without christian names or initials is not a valid signature[13] but if there is a proper signature the fact that it is prefaced by "Mr." or "Mrs." will not invalidate it.[14]

3–06   A deed is not probative if the signature consists merely of the granter's initials.[15] There are decisions in older cases where deeds, although only signed by initials of the granters, were sustained, but those deeds were not probative since their validity was dependent upon other evidence such as that the granter was accustomed to subscribe in that way[16] or that he was unable to write his full surname.[17] The making of a mark[18] or a partial signature and mark[19] is not a valid subscription. It is not essential that a signature be legible.[20]

---

[11] Dunlop v. Greenlees' Trs. (1863) 2 M.1.
[12] Grieve's Trs. v. Japp's Trs., 1917 1 S.L.T. 70.
[13] Allan and Crichton, Petrs., 1933 S.L.T. (Sh.Ct.) 2, doubting the decision in the old case of Gordon v. Murray (1765) Mor. 16818.
[14] Ferguson, 1959 S.C. 56, where the sufficiency of the signature of a witness "Mme. Pion Roux" was not challenged.
[15] Gardner v. Lucas (1878) 5 R. (H.L.) 105.
[16] Ker v. Gibson (1693) Mor. 16805; Crosbie and Pickens v. Pickens (1749) Mor. 16814.
[17] Weir v. Ralston, June 22, 1813, F.C.
[18] Crosbie v. Wilson (1865) 3 M. 870; Morton v. French, 1908 S.C. 171.
[19] Donald v. McGregor, 1926 S.L.T. 103.
[20] Stirling Stuart v. Stirling Crawfurd's Trs. (1885) 12 R. 610.

(b) Method of signature

3–07 The signature must be wholly the act of the granter. It is not a valid signature if the hand of the writer is guided by another person[21] (although it is permissible to have the hand supported by the wrist[22]) or is made by a person unable to write who simply copied his name over lines made with a pin by another.[23] Retouching of a poorly-made signature by the signatory himself does not affect its validity.[24] The use of an embossed stamp[24] or a cyclostyle[25] does not constitute signature. The fact that a signature is written on erasure does not invalidate it.[26]

(c) Position of signature

3–08 A probative document must be subscribed, except when granted by the Sovereign who superscribes. The signature should be adhibited on the last page of the deed and at the end of any inventory, appendix, schedule, plan or other annexed document, and also, in the case of wills or testamentary writings, at the foot of each page.[27] Even in holograph writings, where the rigid statutory rules regarding authentication of documents are somewhat relaxed,[28] subscription is essential to the validity of a document.[29]

3–09 The requirement of subscription of every page of a deed remains applicable to wills or testamentary writings. If the deed is written on a single sheet, folded to form several pages, subscription on the last page only is sufficient, since the Deeds Act 1696 applies to deeds written bookwise on more than one sheet.[30] If the deed consists of only one sheet and the signature appears on the last page only, it is essential that the pages are connected by the wording running on or by a catchword as in *Russell's Exr. v. Duke*.[31] In *Ferguson*[32] a will in English form on one sheet of paper, folded so as to form four pages, contained the entire testamentary matter on the first page and beneath it the signature of the testator and part of a docquet of attestation, and the third page contained the remainder of the docquet and the signatures of two witnesses. It was held that there was a sufficient connecting link between the first and third pages so that the witnesses' signatures could be deemed to be

---

[21] *Moncrieff* v. *Monypenny* (1710) Mor. 15936. See also *Clark's Exr.* v. *Cameron*, 1982 S.L.T. 68.

[22] *Noble* v. *Noble* (1875) 3 R. 74.

[23] *Crosbie and Pickens* v. *Pickens, supra*.

[24] *Stirling Stuart* v. *Stirling Crawfurd's Trs., supra*.

[25] *Whyte* v. *Watt* (1893) 21 R. 165.

[26] *Brown* v. *Duncan* (1888) 15 R. 511.

[27] Conveyancing and Feudal Reform (Scotland) Act 1970, s. 44.

[28] *Lorimer's Exrs.* v. *Hird*, 1959 S.L.T. (Notes) 8, *per* Lord President (Clyde) at 8. See para. 3–49.

[29] *Foley* v. *Costello* (1904) 6 F. 365; *Taylor's Exrs.* v. *Thom*, 1914 S.C. 79; *McLay* v. *Farrell*, 1950 S.C. 149; *Robbie* v. *Carr*, 1959 S.L.T. (Notes) 16; *Boyd* v. *Buchanan*, 1964 S.L.T. (Notes) 108.

[30] *Smith* v. *Bank of Scotland* (1824) 2 Shaw's App. 265. Contrast *McCrummen's Trs.* v. *Edinburgh and Glasgow Bank* (1859) 21 D. (H.L.) 3.

[31] 1946 S.L.T. 242.

[32] 1959 S.C. 56.

subscriptions, along with the testator's, of the body of the deed contained on the first page. Where the deed was a bank order form which contained a testamentary instruction on one side and only the signature of the testatrix on the other side it was decided that there was no proper subscription; there was no connecting link between the testamentary provisions on one side of the form and the signature on the other.[33]

Signature or Execution—Particular Persons or Bodies

3–10 **Peers** subscribe their title alone, using their highest title if more than one, unless the deed has some relation to an inferior title when it may be added to their subscription.

Wives of peers subscribe their husband's title prefixed by their own christian names.

Eldest sons of peers may subscribe their courtesy title.

Partnerships normally execute formal deeds by the firm name adhibited by one of the partners together with the signatures of all the individual partners, all the signatures being attested.

Bodies incorporated by Royal Charter or Act of Parliament normally have the mode of executing deeds prescribed in the constituting Charter or Act, usually involving the use of a seal under regulations or rules specified.

Companies incorporated under the Companies Acts must have a seal and it is affixed to formal deeds. Section 36(3) of the Companies Act 1985 provides that a deed to which a company is a party shall be held to be validly executed according to the law of Scotland on behalf of the company if it is executed in accordance with the provisions of the Act or is sealed with the common seal of the company and subscribed on behalf of the company by two of the directors or by a director and secretary of the company, and such subscription on behalf of the company shall be binding whether attested by witnesses or not. The subsection permits two methods of execution of deeds by a company, namely (a) execution in accordance with the provisions of the Act, *i.e.* in accordance with the regulations in the company's articles of association adopted under section 7 of the Act, or (b) sealing and subscription by two directors or by a director and the secretary. The two methods are alternative; execution which complies with the requirements of either is valid.[34] Although as a matter of strict construction the concluding provision of the subsection dispensing with the need for witnessing applies to the second method, it is thought that if the articles of association of the company regulating the use of the seal do not specify that witnesses are required then witnesses are unnecessary if the first method is adopted. In practice the use of the second method is preferable; it avoids the need of examining the

---

[33] *Baird's Trs.* v. *Baird*, 1955 S.C. 286.
[34] *Clydesdale Bank (Moore Place Nominees) Ltd.* v. *Snodgrass*, 1939 S.C. 805.

articles of association since it is a proper alternative method directly authorised by statute. Burns[35] points out that, although Table A of the Companies Acts of 1908 and 1929 provided that the seal be affixed in the presence of the signing officers of the company, Table A of the 1948 Act omitted this direction and concludes that if the seal and the requisite signatures *de facto* appear on the document it is not necessary that the sealing and subscribing be done together.

The liquidator of a company executes deeds granted by the company in liquidation by affixing the seal of the company and subscribing his own name as liquidator. Witnesses are required. Particulars of the liquidator's appointment will appear in the deed or its testing clause.

The receiver of property of a company in receivership executes deeds by the company and the receiver by affixing the seal of the company and subscribing his own name as receiver. Again witnesses are required. Particulars of the receiver's appointment will be narrated in the deed.

Industrial and provident societies execute deeds by sealing with the common seal of the society and subscription by two members of the committee and the secretary; and witnesses are not required.[36]

Friendly societies. The property of a friendly society is vested in trustees for the society[37] who execute deeds relating to property by the signatures of the trustees or a majority and quorum of them attested by witnesses, subject to any special provisions in the rules of the society.

Trade unions. The property of a trade union is normally vested in trustees who execute deeds relating to it as above indicated in relation to friendly societies.

Local authorities execute deeds by sealing with the common seal of the council and subscription by two members of the council and the proper officer of the council and witnesses are not required, but execution in any other manner provided in a local Act is a competent alternative. A person transacting with the council is not bound to inquire whether the authority to affix the seal has been duly given.[38]

Building societies must have a common seal and rules governing its use.[39] Reference may be made to the rules of the particular society and any relevant resolutions made in accordance with the rules regulating the execution of deeds by the society.

Specially authorised persons—attorneys or factors. Frequently companies, building societies or other bodies who have to execute many deeds authorise specified officers under powers contained in the constituting documents to execute deeds on behalf of the particular body. In such cases the resolution made in accordance with such powers should be specified in the testing clause, *e.g.* "these presents consisting of this

---

[35] at 8.
[36] Industrial and Provident Societies Act 1965, s. 36.
[37] Friendly Societies Act 1974, s. 54.
[38] Local Government (Scotland) Act 1973, s. 194.
[39] Building Societies Act 1962, ss. 1–4.

and the two preceding pages are executed on behalf of us the X Building Society at [*place*] on [*date*] by being sealed with our common seal and subscribed by [*names, designations and offices of the authorised signatories*] as authorised by resolution of the board [*directors*] made in accordance with the Rules of the said Society before these witnesses [*named and designed*]." Also individual persons or trustees may authorise a factor and commissioner to execute deeds on their behalf. The document appointing such authorised signatories should in like manner be specified in the testing clause.

3–11   **Foreign persons or bodies**. *Inter vivos* deeds by foreign persons or bodies relating to moveables, if executed abroad, may be executed by any method valid in accordance with the law of the place of execution.[40] If the deeds relate to heritable property in Scotland, however, the *lex loci situs* applies and they must be executed in accordance with the requirements of Scots law. In the case of testamentary deeds, if (i) words are used which would by common law[41] or by statute[42] carry moveable estate in Scotland and (ii) there is an intention to carry Scottish heritable property, then the deed may be executed in the manner required or permitted by the law of Scotland in the case of any testamentary writing.[43] It follows that if a will of an Englishman is executed in accordance with the law of England and purports to deal with Scottish heritage then, since such a will would enable an executor to deal with moveables in Scotland, it also confers on the executor a right to administer the Scottish heritage.[44]

Witnesses

(a) Competent witnesses

3–12   The following persons are not competent witnesses: (1) persons (male or female) who are under 14 years of age; (2) blind persons (who cannot see the granter subscribe and, although they may hear him acknowledge his subscription, cannot accurately connect the acknowledgment with the deed); (3) persons of unsound mind; (4) persons who sign the deed as principals; and (5) persons who cannot write. It is necessary that the witness should know the granter,[45] but introduction at the time of execution is sufficient.[46] A witness is not disqualified from attesting a signature because he or she is related to the granter or has an interest in

---

[40] *Purvis' Trs.* v. *Purvis' Exrs.* (1861) 23 D. 812, 831.
[41] *Purvis' Trs.* v. *Purvis' Exrs.*, *supra*.
[42] Wills Act 1963. See paras. 3–77 *et seq*.
[43] Titles to Land Consolidation (Scotland) Act 1868, s. 20; *Connel's Trs.* v. *Connel* (1872) 10 M. 627; *Studd* v. *Studd's Trs.* (1880) 8 R. 249; (1883) 10 R. (H.L.) 53; *Browne* (1882) 20 S.L.R. 76.
[44] *Connel's Trs.* v. *Connel*, *supra*.
[45] Subscription of Deeds Act 1681 (1681 c. 5).
[46] *Brock* v. *Brock*, 1908 S.C. 964.

the subject-matter of the deed[47] and a will was sustained as validly attested where one of the witnesses was a trustee nominated therein.[48] Nevertheless it is suggested that in practice it is preferable that witnesses should be independent persons, since attestation by persons interested in the deed may be an element in circumstances where reduction of a deed is sought on extrinsic grounds such as undue influence. It is not necessary that a witness should have any knowledge of the contents of the deed; he or she is merely witnessing the act of signature by the granter.[49]

(b) Style of signature

3–13 The signature of a witness should correspond with the name of the witness as appearing in the testing clause of the deed, each christian name being represented in the signature in full or by a recognised contraction or initial. Where there is no such correspondence the fact may be noted in the testing clause, e.g. Thomas Robert Jones (subscribing his usual signature "Tom Jones").

(c) Position and method of signature

3–14 The witnesses should subscribe on the last page of the deed, normally opposite the signature of the granter which they attest, adding the word "Witness" after their signatures, although it is in order for that word to be written by someone else.[50] Where the same witnesses attest the signatures of several parties who all subscribe on a single occasion, it is unnecessary for the witnesses to sign more than once. In an old case[51] it was decided that, even although the granters subscribed at different times, a single signature by a witness who had seen all the granters sign was sufficient, but this decision must now be regarded as impliedly disapproved by the decisions and dicta in later cases which emphasise that execution is a single act and should be performed unico contextu.[52] The witnesses may add their designations after their signatures, or someone else may do so,[53] or alternatively the witnesses may be fully named and designed in the testing clause of the deed. It was decided in Hogg v. Campbell[54] that a granter may acknowledge his subscription to two witnesses separately at different times but, although this decision has not been overruled, the best practice is that both witnesses should be present together at the time of signature or when the signature is acknowledged.

---

[47] Simsons v. Simsons (1883) 10 R. 1247.
[48] Mitchell v. Miller (1742) Mor. 16900.
[49] Ormistoun v. Hamilton (1708) Mor. 16890.
[50] Gibson v. Walker, June 16, 1809, F. C., at 324.
[51] Edmonstone v. Edmonstone (1749) Mor. 16901.
[52] Walker v. Whitwell, 1916 S.C. (H.L.) 75; Hynd's Tr. v. Hynd's Trs., 1955 S.C. (H.L.) 1.
[53] Conveyancing (Scotland) Act 1874, s. 38.
[54] (1864) 2 M. 848.

84 EXECUTION OF DEEDS

(d) Time of signature

3–15   The witnesses should sign immediately after subscription by the party
whose signature they attest, but there may be a question as to how long
afterwards it is permissible for the witnesses to sign without endangering
the validity of the execution. In several cases considerable latitude was
allowed, *e.g.* deeds have been sustained by the courts where (i) the witnesses signed in another room within a quarter of an hour later, the
deed having been out of their sight in the interval,[55] (ii) the witnesses
took the deed back to an office and signed three-quarters of an hour
after hearing the granter acknowledge his signature,[56] and (iii) missives
of sale were signed four months later by persons who had been present
when the missives were signed by the parties but had not been asked at
the time to act as witnesses.[57] The *ratio* of these decisions, however,
must be regarded as questionable in the light of the later decision in
Walker v. *Whitwell.*[58] In that case a will written by the granter's son was
signed by the granter in presence of another person, who signed as a witness, and the son, who did not. After the death of the granter her son,
acting on legal advice, also signed as a witness. In the Court of Session a
court of seven judges decided by a majority that the will was validly
executed but on appeal to the House of Lords that decision was unani-
mously reversed. The ground of decision was that attestation by subscribing witnesses is not merely evidence of the fact of execution, but is
an indispensable part of the statutorily prescribed solemnities; a witness
is only entitled to attest a signature at the request, actual or implied, of
the granter and the continuing request, like any mandate, falls upon the
death of the person who has made it. It follows that (i) signature of a
deed by a witness after the death of the party whose signature he seeks
to attest is incompetent, (ii) so also is attestation by a person who has
seen the party sign by stealth or without the knowledge and assent of the
signatory, and (iii) the signatures of the witnesses form part of a single
act of execution of the deed and should, as part of the essential solemnities, be adhibited, in a reasonable sense, *unico contextu* without undue
lapse of time.[59]

(e)   Reduction of deeds on grounds of defects in attestation

3–16   The onus which rests upon a person challenging the validity of a deed
ex facie probative is heavy, particularly where the granter's signature is
admitted and the ground of challenge is defective attestation.[60] The evidence of the instrumentary witnesses alone, when they admit their signatures, but testify that they do not remember having signed, or even

[55] *Frank* v. *Frank* (1795) Mor. 16824.
[56] *Thomson* v. *Clarkson's Trs.* (1892) 20 R. 59.
[57] *Stewart* v. *Burns* (1877) 4 R. 427.
[58] 1914 S.C. 560; revd. 1916 (H.L.) 75; overruling *Tener's Trs.* v. *Tener's Trs.* (1879) 6 R. 1111.
[59] See also *Hynd's Tr.* v. *Hynd's Trs.*, 1955 S.C. (H.L.) 1 at 19.
[60] *Smith* v. *Bank of Scotland* (1824) 2 Shaw's App. 265, 286, 287.

deny having seen the granter sign or heard him acknowledge his subscription, is regarded with suspicion and is not usually preferred to the evidence afforded by their signatures on the deed.[61] Evidence by one of the witnesses alone, without any other evidence, would clearly be insufficient to reduce the deed.[62] Other evidence, *e.g.* that neither the granter nor the witnesses were present at the place and time at which the deed bore to have been executed, may suffice.[63]

-17 Where a granter seeks to reduce his own deed on the ground of a latent defect in attestation he may be met with the defence of personal bar or *rei interventus* since other parties have been induced to transact with the granter in reliance on a deed which is *ex facie* probative.[64]

Testing Clause

(a) Function

-18 The function of the testing clause is to record the particulars of execution which give the deed its probative character. It also serves (i) to mention any discrepancies between the full names of the parties or witnesses and their signatures as appended to the deed, and (ii) to notice any alterations, interlineations or erasures.[65]

(b) Form

-19 The testing clause may be either in the full form, short form or docquet form. The full form as normally used contains a statement of the number of pages (any plan, inventory or other appendix being mentioned), a statement that the deed has been subscribed by the granter or granters (mentioning any discrepancy between the names of the granter or granters and their signatures), the place or places and the date or dates of subscription and the full christian names and surnames and designations of the witnesses (mentioning any disconformity between the names as stated in the testing clause and as represented in their signatures[66]). Neither the number of pages[67] nor the place or date of execution is a necessary ingredient of the clause but it is good practice to include them. The number of pages may be of evidential value in

---

[61] *Sibbald* v. *Sibbald* (1776) Mor. 16906; *Frank* v. *Frank* (1795) Mor. 16824; *Condie* v. *Buchan* (1823) 2 S. 385; *Cleland* v. *Cleland* (1838) 1 D.254; *Donaldson* v. *Stewart* (1842) 4 D. 1215, 1217; *Morrison* v. *Maclean's Trs.* (1862) 24 D. 625, 629; (1863) 1 M. 304; *Baird's Tr.* v. *Murray* (1883) 11 R. 153, 156; *Stirling Stuart* v. *Stirling Crawfurd's Trs.* (1885) 12 R. 610, 626; *McArthur* v. *McArthur's Trs.*, 1931 S.L.T. 463.

[62] *Forrest* v. *Low's Trs.*, 1907 S.C. 1240.

[63] *Young* v. *Paton*, 1910 S.C. 63 (although the deed was not necessarily reduced since it had been delivered for onerous causes—see para. 3–17).

[64] *Baird's Tr.* v. *Murray, supra; National Bank of Scotland* v. *Campbell* (1892) 19 R. 885; *Young* v. *Paton, supra; MacLeish* v. *British Linen Bank*, 1911 2 S.L.T. 168; *Boyd* v. *Shaw*, 1927 S.C. 414.

[65] See paras. 3–24 to 3–26.

[66] Although a minor discrepancy may not invalidate *Richardson's Trs.* (1891) 18 R. 1131, 1133; *Speirs* v. *Speirs' Trs.* (1878) 5 R. 923.

[67] Conveyancing (Scotland) Act 1874, s. 38.

non-testamentary deeds where each page is not identified by subscription, the place and date of signature may assist in establishing the genuineness or otherwise of the deed in the event of subsequent challenge[68] and the date is of importance in testamentary deeds to determine whether it was the latest expression of the testator's intentions. If inadequate space has been left for the testing clause it is thought that it would be incompetent to complete it below the signatures of the granters; the Subscription of Deeds Act 1681 requires that the witnesses be designed "in the bodie of the writ," although such a defect might be regarded as an informality of execution remediable by a decree on an application under section 39 of the Conveyancing (Scotland) Act 1874. The proper practice is to insert the whole of the testing clause in the last page which contains part of the substance of the deed. If part or the whole of the testing clause is upon a new page above the subscription of the granters which has been adhibited only on that page, and particularly if that page is upon a separate sheet, the granters will have signed only a blank page or sheet. If the testing clause is connected by a catchword and there are no suspicious circumstances the deed may be sustainable as valid,[69] but the safe course is to have the deed re-engrossed so that the testing clause is accommodated wholly on the final page of the deed itself or, if time does not permit, to have the deed signed by the granters on every page.

3–20   The short form of testing clause usually states the number of pages (mentioning any appendix), the fact that it has been subscribed by the granter or granters, the place or places and date or dates of signature and that it has been so subscribed before the witnesses whose subscriptions and designations are appended. The docquet form merely states that the deed has been signed by the granter or granters at a place or places on a date or dates in presence of (the names and designations of the witnesses being specified below the docquet). The short and the docquet forms are widely used in practice. They obviate the risk of typing errors in the full form of testing clause but on the other hand they are less suitable if alterations in the deed or discrepancies between the names and the signatures of the granters have to be noticed. The designations of the witnesses need not be written by the witnesses themselves.[70]

(c) Errors in testing clauses

3–21   In practice there should be no material error in the testing clause, and no erasure, interlineation or alteration in the record of any essential particular of execution. Whether such an error will deprive the deed of its probative character is a question of circumstances depending on the nature and importance of the mistake. Where the surname of a witness

---

[68] See *Young* v. *Paton, supra*.
[69] *McLaren* v. *Menzies* (1876) 3 R. 1151: *Russell's Exr.* v. *Duke*, 1946 S.L.T. 242.
[70] Conveyancing (Scotland) Act 1874, s. 38.

was written on erasure in the clause it was decided that the deed was nevertheless valid since the witness's own signature supplied the omission of his surname in the testing clause (it was necessary to regard the surname in the testing clause as *pro non scripto* on account of the unauthenticated erasure).[71]

Where an error occurs in the typing or writing of the testing clause the proper course is to recommence the clause from the point where the error has been made, introducing the correct version by words such as "that is to say." Since the function of the clause is to record the necessary particulars of execution and the corrected version does that sufficiently it should not matter that an evident error has been made in the record as originally rendered which has been openly corrected. The new version, however, should not appear wholly in the margin of the deed: that might raise a question whether the designations of the witnesses were recorded, as the 1681 Act requires, in the body of the deed.

(d) Time of completion

22 The testing clause may be completed after subscription at any time before the deed is registered for preservation or founded on in court.[72,73] Where a deed had been sent for registration in the Books of Council and Session and thereafter it was desired to amend an error in the testing clause, it was necessary to petition the Court of Session to authorise the Keeper to give access to the deed for the purpose of making the amendment at the sight of the Keeper.[74] Mere production of a deed in court is distinct from founding upon it; only the latter prevents completion of the testing clause.[75] Apart from these limits a lapse of time, even a very long time, does not constitute an objection to completion of a testing clause; in one case a delay of 32 years was held not to be a ground of objection to the deed.[76]

(e) Testing clause cannot alter provisions of deed

23 A testing clause cannot be used to alter or affect the provisions of the deed itself, and any purported alteration of or addition to the terms of the deed which is inserted in the testing clause will be disregarded. The reason is evident: the deed which the granter signed contained no testing clause and any modification of its terms contained in that clause may well have been inserted without his authority or consent.[77]

---

[71] *McDougall* v. *McDougall* (1875) 2 R. 814.

[72] Conveyancing (Scotland) Act 1874, s. 38.

[73] Registration in the Register of Sasines for publication does not prevent an error in the testing clause being amended and the deed may be recorded of new (Titles to Land Consolidation (Scotland) Act 1868, s. 143). See also Land Registration (Scotland) Act 1979, s. 8(2).

[74] *Caldwell* (1871) 10 M. 99.

[75] *Millar* v. *Birrell* (1876) 4 R. 87: *cf. Hill* v. *Arthur* (1870) 9 M. 223.

[76] *Blair* v. *Earl of Galloway* (1827) 6 S. 51.

[77] *Smiths* v. *Chambers' Trs.* (1877) 5 R. 97, affd. 5 R. (H.L.) 151; *Blair* v. *Assets Co. Ltd.* (1896) 23 R. (H.L.) 36.

Alterations in Probative Deeds

(a) Principles of construction

3–24   The presumption of law is that alterations in or additions to formal attested deeds are deemed to have been made after the deed has been executed and delivered and, save for the statutory provisions contained in section 39 of the Conveyancing (Scotland) Act 1874, the presumption is irrebuttable.[78] Accordingly, if an alteration or addition has not been authenticated, it is regarded as *pro non scripto*. In the case of an erasure where the words erased are not legible, it will be presumed that they were of importance, but an objector is not entitled to substitute anything he pleases with a view to destroying the deed.[79] The rules of construction may be broadly stated thus: (1) If an unauthenticated alteration or addition has been made in words which are not of material importance, the fact that they are disregarded does not destroy the effectiveness of the deed. (2) If it occurs in words which are of material importance to a part of the deed which is separable, the result is to invalidate only that part of the deed; the remainder of the deed will receive effect in accordance with its terms.[80] (3) If it occurs in words which are essential to the validity of the whole deed, then it is destructive of the whole deed.

(b) Material alterations

3–25   What is a material alteration or addition depends upon the nature of the deed.[81] Plainly essential matters in all deeds are the names and designations of the parties, the operative words of the dispositive clause and the particulars of execution required by the statutory solemnities such as the designations of the witnesses either in the body of the deed or after their subscriptions. Examples of material elements in particular deeds are in a disposition the description of the property conveyed, in a bond the sum of money or in a cautionary obligation the obligation which is guaranteed. For illustrations of alterations which were fatal to the validity of the deed see the cases cited,[82] and for examples of cases where alterations had the effect of vitiating only part of the deed see the undernoted decisions.[83] In certain circumstances, as where the alterations were made in the granter's own hand in testamentary deeds and there was no suspicion of fraud, the deeds were upheld.[84] In *Cattanach's*

---

[78] *Kedder* v. *Reid* (1840) 1 Rob. App. 183; *Boswell* v. *Boswell* (1852) 14 D. 378; *Munro* v. *Butler Johnstone* (1868) 7 M. 250, 256.

[79] *McDougall* v. *McDougall, supra.*

[80] *Abernethie* v. *Forbes* (1835) 13 S. 263, 268, 269 (a case relating to a blank portion of a deed, but the principle applies to any other nullity).

[81] Stair, IV, xlii, 19.

[82] *Pitillo* v. *Forrester* (1671) Mor. 11536; *Lawrie* v. *Reid* (1712) Mor. 12284; *Merry* v. *Howie* (1801) Mor. App. v. Writ No. 3; *Gibson* v. *Walker*, June 16, 1809, F.C.; *Shepherd* v. *Grant's Trs.* (1844) 6 D. 164, affd. (1847) 6 Bell's App. 153; *Munro* v. *Butler Johnstone, supra.*

[83] *Kemps* v. *Ferguson* (1802) Mor. 16949; *Adam* v. *Drummond*, June 12, 1810, F.C.

[84] *Earl of Traquair* v. *Henderson* (1822) 1 S. 527; *Robertson* v. *Ogilvie's Trs.* (1844) 7 D. 236.

Tr. v. *Jamieson*[85] the testing clause contained a declaration regarding erasures in the deed which was obviously false, but the deed was sustained since the erased parts, which occurred in the description of the lands in a bond and disposition in security, were not essential to a sufficient description of the security subjects.

(c) Practice

3–26 If an alteration or addition of material importance requires to be made in a formal deed the proper course is to insert it in the margin of the deed with a caret in the body of the deed indicating where the insertion is to be interpolated and to have the marginal addition sidescribed by the granter or granters by signing his or their christian names or initials on one side and his or their surnames on the other, and in addition the alteration or addition should be declared in the testing clause with a statement that it was made prior to subscription, *e.g.* "under declaration that the words 'five hundred' were inserted to read between the words 'thousand' and 'pounds' occurring on the fifth line of page first hereof all prior to subscription." If an alteration or addition, whether made by way of marginal addition, deletion, interlineation or erasure, is not material in the sense that, even if disregarded, it would not affect the deed or the part of the deed in which it occurs, it is not strictly necessary to have it authenticated by the granter or granters, but the normal practice is to mention it in the testing clause as having been made prior to subscription.

(d) Alterations in testamentary deeds

3–27 The decisions of the courts in relation to alterations of probative testamentary deeds may involve two distinct principles, namely (1) whether or not an alteration made at or prior to the execution of the original deed is effective, when the rules are the same as for other attested writs,[86] or (2) whether or not an alteration made subsequently by the testator should receive effect, when the relevant rules are those which permit revocation or variation by the testator of a solemnly executed testamentary deed and the test is whether the alteration was made *animo revocandi* so that the deed as altered represents the final testamentary intention of the testator. Frequently such subsequent alterations are holograph of the testator and in effect constitute a holograph codicil made by amendment of the formal deed rather than by a separate writing, so that the less rigorous requirements for authentication of holograph writings, although not entirely applicable, may to

---

[85] (1884) 11 R. 972.
[86] *Macdonald* v. *Cuthbertson* (1890) 18 R. 101, 104–105, 108; *Walker* v. *Whitwell*, 1916 S.C. (H.L.) 75, 79, 84.

some extent influence the decisions.[87] It is necessary to read the judgments in such cases with this distinction clearly in mind, since opinions delivered in the context of a case where subsequent amendments to testamentary deeds were being considered may not be wholly relevant in relation to the law of authentication of deeds.

3-28   The *locus classicus* of the principles which regulate subsequent alterations in testamentary writings made with a view to revocation or alteration of the provisions of an earlier formally attested principal deed is the judgment of Lord McLaren in *Pattison's Trs.* v. *University of Edinburgh*,[88] which may be summarised thus:

(1) If a will is found with the signature cancelled, or with lines drawn through the dispositive or other essential clause, then, on proof that the cancellation was done by the testator or by his order with the intention of revoking the will, it will be held to have been revoked: otherwise it is treated as still subsisting.

(2) If a will is found with one or more legacies or particular provisions scored out, that raises no question as to the revocation of the whole will but only of the provisions concerned, and these will not be held to be revoked unless upon evidence that the scoring out was done by the testator himself or on his direction with the intention of revoking the clause. Of such intention initialling of the deletion by the testator is normally sufficient evidence. Deletions not initialled or authenticated by the testator will be regarded as ineffective.

(3) If a will is found with marginal or interlineal additions, even in the testator's handwriting, these are not effective unless authenticated by the signature or initials of the testator.[89]

(4) If a will contains words scored out and others substituted, the cancellation is conditional on the substituted words taking effect, *i.e.* if the substituted words are rejected on the ground of lack of authentication, the deletion is also disregarded and the will takes effect in its original form.

3-29   The effect of deletions or alterations made by a testator on a copy of a will depends upon the circumstances and they will be effective only if the court is satisfied that they were made with the intention of altering the principal will and are authenticated by the testator.[90] The validity of a revocation is not affected by the fact that the testator acted under a misapprehension.[91]

---

[87] See Walker and Walker, *Evidence*, 191.
[88] (1888) 16 R. 73 at 76, 77.
[89] For examples of such authenticated alterations which were effective, see *Royal Infirmary of Edinburgh* v. *Lord Advocate* (1861) 23 D. 1213; *Caledonian Banking Co.* v. *Fraser* (1874) 44 S.L.R. 345; *Hogg's Exrs.* v. *Butcher*, 1947 S.N. 141, 190. For unauthenticated alterations held ineffective, see *Brown* v. *Maxwell's Exrs.* (1884) 11 R. 821; *Petticrew's Trs.* v. *Pettigrew* (1884) 12 R. 249. For a very special case, see *Gray's Trs.* v. *Dow* (1900) 3 F. 79.
[90] *Thomson's Trs.* v. *Bowhill Baptist Church*, 1956 S.C. 217.
[91] *Speirs* v. *Graham* (1829) 8 S. 268; *Thomson's Trs.* v. *Bowhill Baptist Church, supra.*

(e) Statutory provisions regarding erasures

–30 Notarial instruments and notices of title. Since these documents do not effect conveyances or transfers of ownership but merely feudalise existing rights the rules with regard to erasures therein have been relaxed by statute. The Erasures in Deeds (Scotland) Act 1836 was made applicable to all instruments,[92] to the effect that all such instruments are not challengeable on the ground that any part thereof is written on erasure unless it is proved that the erasure was made for the purpose of fraud or that the record thereof in the Register of Sasines is not conformable to the deed as presented for registration.

–31 Record of deed in Register of Sasines. As regards the record of any deed in the Register of Sasines the Conveyancing (Scotland) Act 1874 provides in section 54 that no challenge of any deed recorded in the Register on the ground that any part of the record of such deed is written on erasure shall receive effect unless it is proved that the erasure was made for the purpose of fraud or that the record is not conformable to the deed as presented for registration.

(f) Blanks in deeds

–32 If a blank occurs in a probative deed when it is founded upon, the deed is not probative as regards the part of it which contains the blank space. If the blank is in a material part of the deed, then the deed is ineffectual[93]; if the blank, although material, occurs in a separable part of the deed only the part containing the blank is invalidated and the remainder of the deed will receive effect.[94] If a blank space in a deed has been filled up after execution but before it is founded upon and the words so inserted have not been authenticated by the granter, then the onus rests upon the party founding upon the deed of showing that the words were inserted in the blank space with the knowledge and consent of the granter.[95]

–33 Blanks in deeds partly printed. Printed forms of deeds are frequently used for wills or commercial contracts of a standard type, blank spaces being left for completion by the persons who use them. A strict application of the foregoing principles would deny probative quality to such deeds since the party founding on them would require to establish that the blanks had been filled up before execution or subsequently with the granter's consent. Special statutory provision has been made for such deeds by section 149 of the Titles to Land Consolidation (Scotland) Act 1868 (as modified by section 38 of the Conveyancing (Scotland) Act

---

[92] Titles to Land Consolidation (Scotland) Act 1868, s. 144—now applicable to notices of title: Conveyancing (Scotland) Act 1924, s. 6.
[93] *Graham* v. *Mags. of Montrose* (1830) 4 W. & S. 346.
[94] *Abernethie* v. *Forbes* (1835) 13 S. 263.
[95] *Earl of Buchan* v. *Scottish Widows' Fund Society* (1857) 19 D. 551.

1874) to the effect that deeds having a testing clause may be partly written and partly engraved or lithographed and, provided that in the testing clause the date is expressed, such deeds shall be as valid and effectual as if they had been wholly in writing. The result apparently is that, if the date is stated in the testing clause, the rules above explained regarding blanks in deeds do not apply to partly-printed deeds and if duly attested they are accorded the status of probative writs.[96]

3–34 **The Blank Bonds and Trusts Act 1696 (c. 25).** Deeds containing blanks in the names of the grantees may be null by statute under the Act, which was passed to prohibit the former practice of leaving the name of the grantee of a bond blank so that it was transferable by delivery. The Act provided that no bonds, assignations, dispositions or other deeds be subscribed blank in the names of the grantees and that the names of the grantees be inserted before or at the time of subscription or at least in the presence of the subscribing witnesses before delivery of the deed, on pain of nullity. The Act does not apply to bills of exchange, orders *in re mercatoria*, bills of lading or bearer shares of companies. If a deed was blank as regards the name of the grantee at the time of execution but the name was supplied before delivery, it will be presumed to have been completed properly before delivery unless the contrary is proved.[97] The nullity does not apply to the whole deed although the Act, literally construed, would have that effect; in *Abernethie* v. *Forbes*[98] a deed of entail was granted in which the name of the last substitute was left blank, and the deed was held valid as regards all the heirs whose names had been inserted before subscription, the nullity affecting only the last substitute. An example of a deed which was found null under the 1696 Act and also under the rules regulating the execution of probative deeds is *Pentland* v. *Hare*[98a] where a trust deed was subscribed in India with the names of the trustees left blank and these were later inserted in Scotland.

Additional Solemnities Prescribed by Granter

3–35 It is competent for the granter of a deed to impose additional solemnities of execution, at least in the case of a testamentary deed, and failure to observe these may be fatal to the validity of the deed, even although its execution complies with the solemnities prescribed by law. A holograph will which concluded with a clause, "In testimony of this being my last will and testament I hereby set my hand and seal," had been signed and sealed originally but when found the seal had been torn off. The

---

[96] See *Nisbet* (1897) 24 R. 411, where a proof under s. 39 of the 1874 Act was allowed, not because the will concerned had blanks filled up, but because the witnesses were not designed.
[97] *Ruddiman* v. *Merchant Maiden Hospital* (1746) Mor. 11562.
[98] (1835) 13 S. 263.
[98a] (1829) 7 S. 640.

House of Lords, reversing the decision of the Court of Session, held that the removal of the seal revoked the will.[99]

Notarial Execution

–36   A deed may be executed notarially on behalf of a person who is blind or unable to write. Provision for notarial execution was made in a number of older statutes[1] and the current procedure is contained in section 18(1) of the Conveyancing (Scotland) Act 1924. That section provides that any deed, instrument or writing granted after the commencement of the Act (August 1, 1924), whether relating to land or not, may, after having been read over to the granter, be validly executed on his behalf, if he from any cause, temporary or permanent, is blind or unable to write, by a law agent or notary public, or a justice of the peace, or, as regards wills or other testamentary writings, by a parish minister acting in his own parish or his assistant and successor so acting, subscribing the same in the presence of the granter and by his authority, all before two witnesses who have heard the deed, instrument or writing read over to the granter and have heard or seen such authority given, and a holograph docquet in the form of Schedule I to the Act, or in any words to the like effect, precedes the signature of the law agent, notary public, justice of the peace, or parish minister or his assistant or successor, as the case may be.

(a) Application

‌–37   The provisions of the subsection apply to any deed which is to be solemnly executed on behalf of any person who for any cause, temporary or permanent, is blind or unable to write, and the granter must declare that he is in that condition.[2] It is not applicable to stock transfers which do not require to be attested.[3] A blind person may, if he so desires, sign a deed himself,[4] but it is undesirable that he should do so because of the possibility of fraud.

(b) Who may execute deeds notarially

‌–38   The deed may be executed on behalf of the granter by a solicitor[5] or a notary public or a justice of the peace or, in the case of wills or other testamentary writings only, a parish minister acting in his own parish or his assistant or successor so acting. A solicitor need not have taken out his annual practising certificate,[6] and a qualified solicitor employed as a

---

[99] *Nasmyth* v. *Hare* (1821) 1 Shaw's App. 65. See also *Campbell's Trs.* v. *Campbell* (1903) 5 F. 366.
[1] Act 1540 c. 117; Act 1579 c. 80; Subscription of Deeds Act 1681 (c. 5); Conveyancing (Scotland) Act 1874, s. 41.
[2] 1924 Act, Sched. I.
[3] Stock Transfer Act 1963, s. 1(2).
[4] *Duff* v. *Earl of Fife* (1823) 1 Shaw's App. 498; *Ker* v. *Hotchkis* (1837) 15 S. 983.
[5] Now the normal designation of a law agent: Solicitors (Scotland) Act 1933, s. 49.
[6] *Stephen* v. *Scott*, 1927 S.C. 85.

clerk by a firm of solicitors may execute a deed notarially.[7] The Church of Scotland (Property and Endowments) Amendment Act 1933 provides[8] that the power conferred by section 18 of the 1924 Act is vested in the holder of any charge in the Church of Scotland as minister, or colleague and successor, or assistant and successor, and whether appointed without time limit or for a period of years. The power may be exercised throughout the whole parish in which the charge or any part of it is situated. A certificate by the Principal Clerk to the General Assembly is conclusive evidence of the parish in which the charge is situated.

(c) Disqualifying interest

3–39   It has always been necessary that a notary public should in the exercise of his functions be disinterested and independent. So, when he executes a deed notarially on behalf of an incapacitated granter, it is essential to the validity of the deed that he should have no interest in its subject-matter. Interests which disqualify a person from executing a deed notarially include (i) that one of two notaries who executed a trust disposition and settlement on behalf of the granter was appointed as a trustee, the trustees being empowered to appoint a factor with a salary,[9] (ii) that a partner of the notary was appointed one of three trustees in the will with the usual power to appoint one of their number to act as solicitor for the trust and receive remuneration,[10] even when in such a case the notary had acted, due to the illness of the granter, in circumstances of special urgency,[11] or (iii) that the notary was appointed by the will to be law agent on the estate.[12] The rigour with which the rule is applied is demonstrated by the decision in *Crawford's Trs.* v. *Glasgow Royal Infirmary*[13] where a will had been personally executed by the testatrix in which she appointed a partner in a firm of solicitors as one of her trustees with the usual power to appoint one of their number as solicitor in the estate and where subsequently a codicil (which conferred no benefit on the notary or his firm) was executed notarially by another partner of the firm. The codicil was held to be invalid since it fell to be treated as *unum quid* with the will under which the notary had a disqualifying interest. In *Irving* v. *Snow*[14] a domiciled Scotsman made a will in England which was notarially executed on his behalf by a Scottish solicitor who was appointed sole executor and declared that he was entitled to charge fees. It was admitted that the will was validly executed for the purpose of probate in England and so was valid for the purpose

---

[7] *Hynd's Tr.* v. *Hynd's Trs.*, 1955 S.C. 1, 14, 21.
[8] s. 13.
[9] *Ferrie* v. *Ferrie's Trs.* (1863) 1 M. 291.
[10] *Finlay* v. *Finlay's Trs.*, 1948 S.C. 16; *Paterson's Exrs.*, 1956 S.L.T. (Sh.Ct.) 44. But *contra* where the will contained no power to the trustees to employ a solicitor: *McIldowie* v. *Muller*, 1982 S.L.T. 154.
[11] *Gorrie's Tr.* v. *Stiven's Exrx.*, 1952 S.C. 1.
[12] *Newstead* v. *Dansken*, 1918 1 S.L.T. 136.
[13] 1955 S.C. 367.
[14] 1956 S.C. 257.

of admission to confirmation in Scotland under section 2 of the Wills Act 1861, but opinions were reserved as to the effect of the will and in particular the enforceability of the clause providing for the remuneration of the executor. It is probably unobjectionable for a solicitor employed by a firm of solicitors but not a partner to execute a deed notarially if he personally has no beneficial interest in its subject-matter even although his employers have,[15] and it was decided that a will was valid under which a county clerk was appointed trustee and executor although it was executed notarially by the depute county clerk.[16] It was decided in the old case of *Craig* v. *Richartson*[17] that the same notary cannot subscribe on behalf of both parties to a contract and, although it was held that such procedure was competent in the execution of a mutual settlement revocable by either party,[18] opinions on the matter in *Lang* v. *Lang's Trs.*[19] where the deed was a marriage contract, suggest that in circumstances where a deed is executed notarially on behalf of more than one party, and certainly where the parties may have different and possibly conflicting interests, different notaries should execute on behalf of each party.[20]

(d) Procedure

3–40   The granter, the notary and the two witnesses being assembled together the deed is read over verbatim (usually by the notary) to the granter, the granter declares that he is blind or unable to write, as the case may be, and gives authority, audible or visible, so that the witnesses may hear or see it, to the notary to sign the deed on his behalf. The notary then writes on the last page of the deed in his own handwriting a docquet in the form of Schedule I to the 1924 Act or words to the like effect and signs his name below the docquet on the last page and also, but only if the deed is a testamentary writing, at the foot of each of the preceding pages, and the witnesses immediately thereafter sign as witnesses on the last page. The notary should also sign any plans, schedules or appendices annexed to the deed. It is essential that the docquet, as well as the signature, is holograph of the notary: the equivalent of the granter's signature is not merely the signature of the notary but also his docquet which must, equally with his signature, be in his own hand.[21] The signature of the notary, both at the end of the docquet and, in

---

[15] *Hynd's Tr.* v. *Hynd's Trs.*, *supra* at 14, 21: *Fraser's Exr.*, 1955 S.L.T. (Sh.Ct.) 35.

[16] *Aitken*, 1965 S.L.T. (Sh.Ct.) 15.

[17] (1610) Mor. 16829.

[18] *Graeme* v. *Graeme's Trs.* (1868) 7 M. 14.

[19] (1889) 16 R. 590.

[20] The strict rules as to disqualifying interest of the notary, while unimpeachable in principle, can have inequitable results in the case of testamentary deeds. Although the notary or his partners may lose fees, the major sufferers are the intended beneficiaries who have normally had no part in the improper actings. Should the result not be that the notary or his partners are excluded from all benefit but that, if there are no suspicious circumstances, the will should be effective in other respects?

[21] *Henry* v. *Reid* (1871) 9 M. 503; *Irvine* v. *McHardy* (1892) 19 R. 458; *Kissack* v. *Webster's Trs.* (1894) 2 S.L.T. 172; *Campbell* v. *Purdie* (1895) 22 R. 443.

testamentary deeds, on each preceding page is simply his normal signature of his own name. It is unnecessary for the notary to sign also at the end of the deed above the docquet.[22] The witnesses should sign opposite the signature of the notary at the end of the docquet on the last page of the deed. In *Hynd's Tr.* v. *Hynd's Trs.*, *supra*, Lord Morton of Henryton thought it a valid objection that the witnesses did not sign in that position,[23] but Lord Reid and Lord Keith considered that the deed would not thereby have been invalidated.[24] It is essential that the whole procedure is carried out *unico contextu*; the reading over, the giving of authority by the granter, the writing of the docquet and signature by the notary and the signing by the witnesses all form part of a single act of execution to be completed in the presence of the granter, the notary and the witnesses.[25] Thereafter the testing clause is inserted in the deed in the usual form as if the granter had signed personally. It is competent to apply to the court under section 39 of the Conveyancing (Scotland) Act 1874[26] in order to put right an informality of execution in a notarially executed deed,[27] but the procedures prescribed in section 18(1) of the 1924 Act are thought to be essential solemnities, not mere formalities, and it would appear that, for example, a defect such as the notary's docquet not being holograph could not be cured by an application under section 39 of the 1874 Act.

Informalities of Execution

3-41   Under the older authentication statutes the failure to observe any of the prescribed solemnities of execution resulted in nullification of the deed, even although the disconformity was comparatively slight. For example, mistakes in the christian name[28] or surname[29] or designation[30] of witnesses were fatal to the validity of the deed. On the other hand where the name of a witness was "Davys" but it was rendered in the testing clause as "Davis" the deed was sustained since the discrepancy consisted of a single letter and the witness was sufficiently identified by his designation.[31] In short, either an irregularity in execution was so trivial that it did not invalidate or, if the error was more serious, the deed was null—there was no intermediate category of defect, with the result that a deed which was undeniably genuine could be invalidated by a comparatively minor mistake in or deviation from the statutory solemnities of execution. Section 39 of the Conveyancing (Scotland) Act 1874,

---

[22] *Mathieson* v. *Hawthorns & Co.* (1899) 1 F. 468: 1924 Act, Sched. I, note.
[23] at 11.
[24] at 20, 27; *Hardie* v. *Hardie*, Dec. 6, 1810, F.C.
[25] *Hynd's Tr.* v. *Hynd's Trs.*, *supra*.
[26] See para. 3–41.
[27] Conveyancing (Scotland) Act 1924, s. 18(2), amending the previous law (*Campbell* v. *Purdie*, *supra*).
[28] *Abercromby* v. *Innes* (1707) Mor. 17022.
[29] *Archibalds* v. *Marshall* (1787) Mor. 16907.
[30] *Graham's Creditors* v. *Grierson* (1752) Mor. 16902.
[31] *Dickson's Trs.* v. *Goodall* (1820) Hume 925.

however, provides that no deed, instrument or writing subscribed by the granter or maker thereof, and bearing to be attested by two witnesses subscribing, and whether relating to land or not, shall be deemed invalid or denied effect according to its legal import because of any informality of execution, but the burden of proving that such deed, instrument or writing so attested was subscribed by the granter or maker and by the witnesses shall lie on the party using or upholding the same. The proof may be led in any action or proceeding in which the deed, instrument or writing is founded on or objected to, or in a special application to the Court of Session or to the sheriff within whose jurisdiction the defender in any such application resides, to have it declared that the deed, instrument or writing was subscribed by the granter or maker and the witnesses. Defects in execution may now be classified in three categories, namely (1) one so minor that it can be disregarded or the deficiency can be supplied without applying to the court under section 39, (2) one so serious that it is more than an informality of execution and cannot be declared valid under the section, or (3) one which is sufficiently material that it cannot be disregarded but not so serious that it irremediably invalidates the deed, *i.e.* an informality of execution that can be cured by a finding of the court under the section.

–42 *Minor defects which may be disregarded as not affecting the probative character of the deed.* Examples are: (1) Failure to complete the testing clause of a will until after the death of the granter—the omission could be supplied by insertion of the clause even after the death of the granter.[32] The case cited was decided before the 1874 Act was in operation: now an application under section 39 is competent when the later decisions cited in paragraph 3–44 *infra* are available as precedents. (2) An error of a single letter in the surname of a witness.[33] (3) The designation of a witness as "their" servant instead of "our" servant.[34] (4) A will where the signature of the testator, admittedly genuine, had been superimposed upon erasure.[35] (5) A deed in which two granters who were married women included in their signatures the initial of their maiden names.[36]

–43 *Defects so serious as to invalidate the deed beyond the possibility of cure under section 39.* Examples are: (1) A deed signed by the granter and "witnesses" who neither saw the signature nor heard it acknowledged, so that there was really no witnessing at all.[37] (2) A will signed by one of the witnesses after the death of the granter.[38] (3) A minute of enactment

[32] *Veasey* v. *Malcolm's Trs.* (1875) 2 R. 748.
[33] *Dickson's Trs.* v. *Goodall, supra.*
[34] *Speirs* v. *Speirs' Trs.* (1878) 5 R. 923.
[35] *Brown* v. *Duncan* (1888) 15 R. 511.
[36] *Grieve's Trs.* v. *Japp's Trs.*, 1917 1 S.L.T. 70.
[37] *Smyth* v. *Smyth* (1876) 3 R. 573; *Forrest* v. *Low's Trs.*, 1907 S.C. 1240.
[38] *Walker* v. *Whitwell*, 1916 S.C. (H.L.) 75.

following on a sale by public roup which was attested by only one witness and had been founded upon so that subsequent signature by the witness would have been incompetent under section 38 of the 1874 Act.[39] (4) A testamentary writing which was not properly subscribed by the granter.[40] (5) A notarially executed will in which the solemnities required by section 18 of the Conveyancing (Scotland) Act 1924 had not been observed, *e.g.* where the signatures of the notary and the witnesses were not made *unico contextu*.[41]

3-44 *Defects which are informalities of execution.* Applications under section 39 of the 1874 Act which have been entertained as competent include the following: (1) A testamentary writing which was not signed by the granter on every page.[42] (2) A will, duly signed and witnessed, but of which the testing clause had not been completed at the time of the testator's death.[43] (3) Testamentary writings, signed and witnessed, where the designations of the witnesses were not contained in the deeds nor appended to their signatures,[44] even when the writing had been founded on in court so that the easier remedy available under section 38 of the 1874 Act of adding the designations of the witnesses could no longer be adopted.[45] (4) A disposition containing a discrepancy between the surname of a witness in the testing clause and in his signature.[46] (5) A will containing unauthenticated deletions and interlineations with no designations of the witnesses.[47]

3-45 *Practice.* The principal provenance of section 39 of the 1874 Act is in relation to testamentary deeds or writings, where questions as to the validity of execution of the documents frequently arise after the death of the testator. Solicitors acting in the administration of the estate should examine the execution of the testamentary document *before* applying for confirmation so that any defects, such as omissions of the testing clause or failure to design the witnesses, can be corrected or supplied under section 38 of the Act. If the nature of the defect is such that it cannot be thus rectified then an application to the sheriff court may be made under section 39 of the Act which will be refused (when the defect is more than an informality of execution) or dismissed as unnecessary (when the defect is trivial) or granted (where there is an informality of execution within the meaning of the section). It is thus practicable to

---

[39] *Moncrieff* v. *Lawrie* (1896) 23 R. 577.
[40] *Baird's Trs.* v. *Baird*, 1955 S.C. 286.
[41] *Hynd's Tr.* v. *Hynd's Trs., supra.*
[42] *McLaren* v. *Menzies* (1876) 3 R. 1151; *Brown* (1883) 11 R. 400; *Shiell*, 1936 S.L.T. 317; *Bogie's Exrs.* v. *Bogie*, 1953 S.L.T. (Sh.Ct.) 32; *Ferguson*, 1959 S.C. 56; *Bisset*, 1961 S.L.T. (Sh.Ct.) 19; *McNeill* v. *McNeill*, 1973 S.L.T. (Sh.Ct.) 16.
[43] *Addison* (1875) 2 R. 457; *Inglis' Trs.* v. *Inglis* (1901) 4 F. 365.
[44] *Nisbet* (1897) 24 R. 411; *Garrett* (1883) 20 S.L.R. 756.
[45] *Thomson's Trs.* v. *Easson* (1878) 6 R. 141.
[46] *Richardson's Trs.* (1891) 18 R. 1131. Lord McLaren at 1133 doubted whether the discrepancy (a single letter) would have invalidated the deed at common law. *Cf. Dickson's Trs.* v. *Goodall, supra.*
[47] *Elliot's Exrs.*, 1939 S.L.T. 69.

obtain a judicial decision as to the validity of the document by a comparatively inexpensive process.

PRIVILEGED WRITINGS

3–46 There are certain deeds or writings to which the law gives effect although some of the statutory solemnities required for probative deeds are lacking. These are referred to herein as privileged writings. Examples are writings which are holograph of the granter or are adopted by him as holograph, deeds or writings which, although not formally executed, are adopted by another probative or holograph document, *inter vivos* deeds executed abroad in relation to moveables and testamentary deeds executed abroad in relation to both moveable and heritable estate, documents *in re mercatoria*, particular deeds or writings for which less formal methods of execution are authorised by statute and deeds which are not of great importance.

Holograph Writings

3–47 If a document is wholly in the handwriting of the granter and subscribed by him, it will receive effect although not attested by witnesses. The basis of this privilege is that "the handwriting of any party, through a whole deed, is more difficult to be imitated or counterfeited, and therefore less exposed to forgery, than the bare subscription by a party of his name; and both writing and subscribing a deed is a more trustworthy and deliberate expression of intention than merely subscribing a deed written by another."[48]

3–48 Subject to the rules relating to documents adopted as holograph[49] and documents partly printed and partly holograph,[50] a deed or writing must be shown by the person founding upon it, to be wholly, or in its essential parts, in the handwriting of the granter and subscribed by him if it is to be effective in law without attestation.[51]

3–49 The writing may be in pencil,[52] or partly in ink and partly in pencil,[53] and it is effective as a holograph document even if it purported to be attested but was not in fact witnessed at all since the witnesses neither saw the granter sign nor heard him acknowledge his subscription,[54] or if the granter had apparently contemplated that it should be witnessed but

---

[48] Montgomerie Bell, *Lectures*, 78. See also Stair, IV, xlii, 6; Ersk., III, ii, 22; W. A. Wilson, "In Modum Probationis," 1968 J.R. 193; *Callander* v. *Callander's Trs.* (1863) 2 M. 291, 301.

[49] See para. 3–62.

[50] See paras. 3–56 to 3–59.

[51] Bell, *Prin.*, s. 20; *Macdonald* v. *Cuthbertson* (1890) 18 R. 101, 106; *Bridgeford's Exr.* v. *Bridgeford*, 1948 S.C. 416, 419, 420; *Tucker* v. *Canch's Tr.*, 1953 S.C. 270, 274, 276, 277; Walker and Walker, *Evidence*, 209.

[52] *Muir's Trs.* (1869) 8 M. 53; *Tait's Trs.* v. *Chiene*, 1911 S.C. 743.

[53] *Manson* v. *Edinburgh Royal Institution*, 1948 S.L.T. 196.

[54] *Yeats* v. *Yeats' Trs.* (1833) 11 S. 915; *Harley* v. *Harley's Exr.* 1957 S.L.T. (Sh.Ct.) 17.

that was not done,[55] or if an intended testing clause followed the granter's signature but was not completed and the writing was not witnessed.[56] In the last-mentioned case[56] the Lord President (Clyde) observed: "The rigid statutory rules applicable in cases of attestation of deeds, designed to protect parties against fraud, have no place in regard to a holograph document where the writing and signature are admittedly those of the granter."

3–50   A holograph writing is not exempt from the requirement of subscription by the granter. If it is unsigned it will normally be regarded as incomplete and not a concluded deed which the granter intended to be legally effective. It is essential that the document is *subscribed*; superscription is not enough,[57] nor is a signature in the margin of the deed,[58] and where a holograph will was signed and further provisions followed which were unsigned the unsigned part was held to be ineffectual.[59]

3–51   The privileges accorded to holograph writings, however, extend to the admissibility of a less formal style of subscription than is required in formally attested documents. Signature by initials may be sufficient,[60] or signature of an accustomed contraction of the granter's christian name alone[61] or even simply "Mum" in a letter to the granter's daughter expressing testamentary intentions.[62] Moreover it is not necessary that all pages of a holograph testamentary writing be signed so long as there is a signature on the last page and parole evidence may be admitted to establish in the case of doubt to which pages the subscription applies.[63]

Holograph writings are not probative

3–52   It should be emphasised that holograph documents are not probative deeds. The latter constitute, by themselves and without other evidence, proof of the rights and obligations which they confer or impose, whereas a holograph writing, in order to be effectual, must be proved by the party who upholds it to be in the handwriting of the granter and subscribed by him.[64] Nor does a statement contained in the body of the writing that it is in the granter's handwriting alter the onus of proof in that matter. If the genuineness of the document as a writing holograph of the granter is challenged a statement *in gremio* that it is so is of no value as evidence and gives rise to no presumption unless the signature is admitted or proved to be that of the granter.[65]

---

[55] *Gunnell's Trs.* v. *Jones* (1915) 1 S.L.T. 166.

[56] *Lorimer's Exrs.* v. *Hird*, 1959 S.L.T. (Notes) 8.

[57] *Foley* v. *Costello* (1904) 6 F. 365; *Taylor's Exrs.* v. *Thom*, 1914 S.C. 79; *Dickerson* (1959) 75 Sh.Ct.Rep. 126.

[58] *Robbie* v. *Carr*, 1959 S.L.T. (Notes) 16.

[59] *McLay* v. *Farrell*, 1950 S.C. 149. Cf. *Fraser's Exrx.* v. *Fraser's C.B.*, 1931 S.C. 536.

[60] *Spiers* v. *Home Spiers* (1879) 6 R. 1359; *Lowrie's J.F.* v. *McMillan's Exrx.*, 1972 S.C. 105.

[61] *Draper* v. *Thomason*, 1954 S.C. 136.

[62] *Rhodes* v. *Peterson*, 1972 S.L.T. 98.

[63] *Spiers* v. *Home Spiers, supra*; *Cranston* (1890) 17 R. 410, 411.

[64] *Anderson* v. *Gill* (1858) 20 D. 1326; 3 Macq. 180.

[65] *Harper* v. *Green*, 1938 S.C. 198.

Proof of testamentary holograph writings—statutory provision

3–53   In circumstances where the authenticity of a holograph testamentary writing is challenged the rule of law as stated in *Anderson* v. *Gill* and *Harper* v. *Green*, *supra*, applies and the person seeking to uphold the document must establish to the satisfaction of the court that the handwriting and signature are those of the granter, but there are many cases where there is no such challenge but it is necessary to establish the effectiveness of a testamentary holograph document as a link in title to property. As regards moveable estate it was the practice in commissary proceedings, based upon the decision in *Cranston*,[66] to accept without further evidence a will which bore *in gremio* to be holograph. If no such statement was contained in it the practice of the commissary courts was to require the affidavits of two satisfactory witnesses who knew the testator's handwriting and deponed that the will and signature were in the handwriting of the testator. As regards heritable estate the practice was for some time similar but the decision in *Frederick* v. *Craig*[67] raised doubts as to the soundness of that practice. In that case it was decided, in relation to a will which did not bear *in gremio* to be holograph, that a purchaser of heritable property was entitled to require a decision of the court, on evidence, that the will was holograph of the deceased, and it was observed *obiter* that a declaration *in gremio* of a holograph will that it had been written by the subscriber afforded only *prima facie* evidence of its authenticity and the practice of recognising that such a declaration shifted the normal onus of proof was not easy to explain upon principle. The decision recalled the qualifications expressed by Lord Shand in *Cranston, supra*,[68] that, "before such a document [a holograph will] can be held to be entitled to effect in any question of title, or of transfer of property, it is clear that some evidence is necessary to instruct that it was truly the deed of the alleged granter,—that is, that it is in his handwriting" and that "according to sound principle proof that the writing is that of the deceased should be required in such cases before confirmation is granted." An Act of Sederunt of July 19, 1935 authorised a simple mode of proof by way of a petition to the sheriff which was served upon the heir-at-law and such other persons as the sheriff might decide. The sheriff could accept as evidence two or more affidavits by persons familiar with the testator's handwriting and such persons were not disqualified from deponing by reason of having a patrimonial interest in the estate. Later, section 11 of the Conveyancing Amendment (Scotland) Act 1938 gave retrospective validation to holograph wills which had been accepted under the former practice by providing that any writing of a testamentary character on which confirmation of executors-nominate had been issued before the commencement of the Act (July 1, 1938) should be deemed to be probative.

---

[66] (1890) 17 R. 410.
[67] 1932 S.L.T. 315.
[68] At 413, 414.

3–54   Section 5 of the Wills Act 1963 (applicable where the death of the testator occurred after January 1, 1964) provided that any testamentary instrument should be treated as probative for the purpose of the conveyance of heritable property in Scotland if (a) confirmation of executors to property disposed of in the instrument had been issued in Scotland, or (b) probate, letters of administration or other grant of representation issued outwith Scotland in respect of property disposed of in the instrument had been certified in Scotland under section 14 of the Confirmation of Executors Act 1858 or sealed in Scotland under section 2 of the Colonial Probates Act 1892. The Succession (Scotland) Act 1964[69] (applicable where the death of the testator occurred on or after September 10, 1964) repealed section 5 of the 1963 Act but substantially re-enacted its provisions[70] save that they apply to any property, whether heritable or moveable.[71] Section 21 of the 1964 Act provides that confirmation of an executor to property disposed of in a holograph testamentary disposition shall not be granted unless the court is satisfied by evidence consisting at least of an affidavit by each of two persons that the writing and signature of the disposition are in the handwriting of the testator. Accordingly, whether or not the will contains a declaration that it is holograph of the testator, it is now necessary, both for moveable and heritable property affected by it, that evidence of the identity of the handwriting and signature be furnished. Neither the 1963 Act nor the 1964 Act are retrospective in effect.[72]

Date of holograph writings

3–55   Save in the case of testamentary writings[73] and acknowledgments of intimation of assignations,[74] holograph writings, even though admitted or proved to be genuine, do not of themselves establish the accuracy of the date they bear.[75] The date in the document may be of value as evidence, but it is not conclusive, and the onus of proving the date, when it is material, rests on the party who seeks to uphold the deed.

Writings partly holograph

3–56   In a series of cases regarding printed will forms where blank spaces had been filled up in the testator's own hand and subscribed by him or her the courts have had to consider whether the document was entitled to the privileges of a holograph document so that it was effective

---

[69] s. 34 and Sched. 3.
[70] s. 32.
[71] The requirement of certification in Scotland of English or Northern Irish probates, letters of administration or grants of representation is now superseded provided that the grant notes the domicile of the deceased as being in England, Wales or Northern Ireland (Administration of Estates Act 1971, Sched. 1, para. 5).
[72] 1963 Act, s. 7; 1964 Act, s. 37(1)(d).
[73] Conveyancing (Scotland) Act 1874, s. 40.
[74] *Gray* v. *Duke of Hamilton* (1708) Rob. App. 1.
[75] *Waddel* v. *Waddel's Trs.* (1845) 7 D. 605; *Dyce* v. *Paterson* (1847) 9 D. 1141.

without being attested. Although the decisions related to printed will forms, it is thought that the principles enunciated by the court apply also to unattested documents where the non-holograph parts are typewritten or written by another hand and to deeds which are not testamentary.[76]

3–57 In the earlier decisions the principle was that, if the document was to be valid as a holograph writing, all the essential parts required to be in the handwriting of the testator, the printed words being formal or superfluous in the sense that, if struck out or disregarded, there would still be a completed expression of the granter's testamentary intention.[77] Lord President Inglis[78] indicated that the essential parts included, *quoad* the appointment of executors, the words appointing them, and the words of gift or bequest and a description of the gift or bequest. That stringent test was not satisfied in *Macdonald* v. *Cuthbertson*,[78a] where the holograph parts were only the name of the testator, the names of the executor and of the universal legatees, the actual words of bequest and the description of the subject-matter of the bequest being printed in the will form. In *Carmichael's Exrs.* v. *Carmichael*[79] the holograph parts comprised the name and designation of the testator, the appointment of and the names and designations of the executors, the name of the testator's wife and the subjects bequeathed to her in liferent and the words of bequest, the names of the legatees and the subject-matter of the residuary bequest. It was decided that the will was valid, since the holograph portions sufficiently expressed the testamentary intentions of the writer. Although the rules laid down in the case of *Macdonald* v. *Cuthbertson*, *supra*, were expressly applied it may be noted that in the case of the liferent bequest the actual words of the bequest were printed but the absence of such words (on the principle that they were disregarded) was not considered essential even although there was no verb which governed the substantive items of the bequest.[80]

3–58 In more recent decisions it would appear that some relaxation of the earlier strict rules has been admitted. In *Bridgeford's Exr.* v. *Bridgeford*[81] the test adopted was to determine whether the sense of the document as a whole could be gathered from the holograph portion; if so, the document including the printed parts should be read as a whole provided always that there was no antinomy between the document as a whole and the holograph portion.[82] In that case a will, in which the name and address of the testatrix, the name and address of the

---

[76] Walker and Walker, *Evidence*, 211.
[77] *Macdonald* v. *Cuthbertson* (1890) 18 R. 101, 108; *Paterson's Trs.* v. *Joy*, 1910 S.C. 1029, 1035, 1036.
[78] In *Macdonald* v. *Cuthbertson, supra* at 105.
[78a] *Supra.*
[79] 1909 S.C. 1387.
[80] *Carmichael's Exrs.* v. *Carmichael, supra* at 1389.
[81] 1948 S.C. 416.
[82] at 421.

executrix, the name and address of the universal legatee and the subject-matter of the bequest to her were holograph, but the actual words of appointment of the executrix and of the bequest to the legatee were printed, was held to be valid since the printed portions were non-essential or superfluous. In *Tucker* v. *Canch's Tr.*[83] it was emphasised that the decision in *Bridgeford's Exr.* v. *Bridgeford* did not involve any departure from the principle laid down in *Macdonald* v. *Cuthbertson* in the sense that the primary test was whether the essentials of a will were contained in the holograph parts but, if that test was satisfied, the document was to be construed as a whole. In *Tucker* v. *Canch's Tr.* the printed parts were clearly essential and not superfluous and the will was determined to be invalid. In *Gillies* v. *Glasgow Royal Infirmary*[84] the holograph parts were the name and address of the testator, the word "To" followed by the names and addresses of legatees and the amounts of their legacies, the words "Residue, divided into 4 equal parts, to" followed by the names of four charities and the name and designation of the executor. The actual words of bequest of the pecuniary legacies and of the residue and of appointment of the executor were printed. The will was sustained as a valid testamentary writing.

3–59   To sum up, the principles now applicable appear to be: (1) If the holograph portions of a testamentary writing contain the essentials of a will and the non-holograph parts are non-essential or superfluous effect will be given to the whole document, including the non-holograph parts, so long as these are not inconsistent with the holograph portions. (2) The actual words of appointment of executors and the actual words making bequests are formal and not essential and may be non-holograph provided the executors and the legatees and the subject-matter of the bequests to them are identified or described in holograph writing in the appropriate places in the document so that the intention of the granter to make the appointment or bequests is sufficiently clear.[85]

Alterations to holograph writings

3–60   (a) **Inter vivos deeds**. Alterations in holograph *inter vivos* deeds which have been delivered are in the same position as alterations in delivered attested deeds, and require authentication as in formal deeds to rebut the presumption that they were made after delivery and without the authority of the granter. If alterations are not so authenticated they will be disregarded: if they occur in essential matters they will invalidate the deed or will render the portion of the deed, if separable, ineffective.[86]

3–61   (b) **Testamentary deeds.** In the case of holograph testamentary deeds the relevant question is not whether the alterations were made in an

---

[83] 1953 S.C. 270, *per* Lord Patrick at 275 and Lord Mackintosh at 277.
[84] 1960 S.C. 438.
[85] *Quaere* as to the appointment of executors in proceedings for confirmation: *Campbell*, 1963 S.L.T. (Sh.Ct.) 10.
[86] Montgomerie Bell, *Lectures*, 73.

effective form before execution but whether, although made after execution, they are codicillary in effect and represent the final testamentary intentions of the testator. The rules as to authentication of alterations to probative testamentary deeds[87] are not applicable to alterations upon holograph testamentary writings.[88] Alterations to holograph wills are clearly effective if they are authenticated by the signature or initials of the testator, but it is not necessary that they be so authenticated. Unauthenticated alterations to such deeds, if made in the testator's own handwriting, are in the same situation as alterations in a probative deed which are expressly mentioned in the testing clause as having been made by the granter.[89] Words written on erasure in a holograph will, even although important, were given effect without having been authenticated,[90] as also were unauthenticated deletions.[91] The general presumption is that when holograph testamentary writings containing alterations are found apparently undisturbed there is a presumption of fact that the alterations were made by the testator.[92] That presumption may be rebutted if it appears that a deletion was accidental and not intentional[93] or that the amendments were deliberative notes rather than the expression of a concluded intention, e.g. where the original will was written in ink and the holograph amendments were in pencil, when there is a rebuttable presumption that the amendments were merely deliberative.[94] It has been judicially observed that a deleted word which is still legible may be referred to in order to ascertain the original intention of the testator with a view to determining the meaning of the parts which had been left standing.[95] The foregoing rules and presumptions apply to alterations which are holograph of the granter of a holograph deed; alterations to a holograph deed which are not in the handwriting of the granter would require to be authenticated by him in the same way as alterations to a formally attested deed.

Writings expressly Adopted as Holograph in the Writings themselves

3–62 A deed or writing which is printed, typewritten or written by a person other than the granter may be accorded the privileges of a holograph writing if the granter adds in his own handwriting at the end of the deed the words, "Adopted as holograph," normally immediately before his signature but it is not a ground of objection that the words be written

---

[87] See para. 3–28.
[88] *Magistrates of Dundee* v. *Morris* (1858) 3 Macq. 134, 152.
[89] *Robertson* v. *Ogilvie's Trs.* (1844) 7 D. 236, 242; *Hogg's Exrs.* v. *Butcher*, 1947 S.N. 141; affd. 1947 S.N. 190.
[90] *Robertson* v. *Ogilvie's Trs.*, *supra*.
[91] *Milne's Exr.* v. *Waugh*, 1913 S.C. 203.
[92] *Ibid.*, 208; *Allan's Exrx.* v. *Allan*, 1920 S.C. 732.
[93] *Magistrates of Dundee* v. *Morris*, *supra* at 152, 153.
[94] *Munro's Exrs.* v. *Munro* (1890) 18 R. 122; *Currie's Trs.* v. *Currie* (1904) 7 F. 364; *Lamont* v. *Magistrates of Glasgow* (1887) 14 R. 603.
[95] *Magistrates of Dundee* v. *Morris*, *supra* at 164; *Chapman* v. *Macbean* (1860) 22 D. 745, 747.

below the signature.[96] Other words may have the same effect, *e.g.* "accepted as holograph" or any words which expressly or by clear implication adopt the writing as being holograph of the granter.[97] Where the deed or writing comprises more than one page either each page should be so adopted or the signature on the last page should clearly identify the writing adopted, *e.g.* "This and the four preceding pages adopted as holograph." In theory it is the docquet that is the operative part of the document, the non-holograph part being in a similar position to a paper apart imported into it.[98]

3–63   The purpose, and the effect, of the docquet of adoption as holograph is to render binding upon the granter a document or writing which, without the docquet, would not be so.[99] Accordingly, in *Harvey* v. *Smith*[1] it was decided that an offer to purchase heritable property which was adopted as holograph by an illiterate man, not separately advised, who the court was satisfied on evidence did not understand the effect of the phrase as making the offer irrevocably binding, did not have that effect. The *ratio decidendi* of this decision has been criticised,[2] but it remains the law.

3–64   The docquet of adoption may be used in bilateral or multilateral contracts but all parties who did not write the contract must, if it is to be binding, separately adopt it by a docquet in their own handwriting. A document by co-obligants written by one of the parties and merely signed by the others, without any docquet adopting it as holograph, was found not to be binding upon one of the parties who simply signed it,[3] and the party who has actually written the document is not bound if his liability was conditional upon all the parties being bound.[4] Docquets of adoption as holograph are in common use in missive letters between solicitors on behalf of purchasers and sellers of heritable property, and all the letters on both sides should be so adopted or, if not, the concluding letters on behalf of each party should adopt all the preceding correspondence on his behalf. If the missive letters are not holograph or adopted as holograph by both parties either may resile even if the letters on his side of the correspondence were in obligatory form.[5]

3–65   The docquet adopting the document as holograph must itself be in the handwriting of the granter. In one very special case[6] a typewritten will and codicil with the words "accepted as holograph" also typewritten

---

[96] *Gavine's Tr.* v. *Lee* (1883) 10 R. 448.
[97] *Maitland's Trs.* v. *Maitland* (1871) 10 M. 79, 84.
[98] *McBeath's Trs.* v. *McBeath*, 1935 S.C. 471, 477.
[99] *Campbell's Trs.* v. *Campbell* (1903) 5 F. 366, 372.
[1] (1904) 6 F. 511. Followed in *Maclaine* v. *Murphy*, 1958 S.L.T. (Sh.Ct.) 49.
[2] Gloag, *Contract*, 95–96; Walker and Walker, *Evidence*, 212.
[3] *Miller* v. *Farquharson* (1835) 13 S. 838. An opinion to the contrary in *Dickson* v. *Blair* (1871) 10 M. 41 at 46 seems plainly wrong in principle.
[4] Gloag, *Contract*, 201; Bell, *Prin.*, s. 250.
[5] *Malcolm* v. *Campbell* (1891) 19 R. 278.
[6] *McBeath's Trs.* v. *McBeath*, 1935 S.C. 471.

followed by a pen signature were sustained by a narrow majority of a court of seven judges, but both the will and the codicil contained a statement *in gremio* that they had been typed by the granter, and it was admitted that owing to a physical disability the granter for some time prior to his death had invariably used a typewriter for his written communications and that the whole of the documents in question had been typed by him. A subsequent attempt to extend the ambit of this decision to a typed will signed by the testator but not containing *in gremio* a statement that it had been typewritten by the granter and not having any statement, either written or typewritten, that it was adopted or accepted as holograph, was unsuccessful.[7]

Writings Adopted by another Deed or Writing

General principle

3–66 A deed or writing which of itself is ineffectual by reason of lack of any of the statutory solemnities of execution required for a probative deed or as not being entitled to the privileges accorded by common law to holograph writings may nevertheless be rendered effective if it is homologated or adopted by another effectively executed deed or writing which expressly or by necessary implication validates the defective deed. The adoption may be made by a subsequent deed or writing which renders an earlier inoperative deed effective or may be made antecedently by an effective deed which directs that effect be given to subsequent informally executed writings. The principle applies to both *inter vivos*[8] and *mortis causa*[9] deeds or writings. Strictly the defective deeds are not privileged since their effectiveness derives, not from any privilege accorded by law to them, but from the fact that they are homologated or adopted by another effective deed or writing.

Adoption by subsequent deed or writing

3–67 The subsequent validating deed or writing may be formally executed or holograph. An example of the former is *Callander* v. *Callander's Trs.*,[10] where a bond of provision, improperly executed since the writer of the deed was not designed, was sustained as effective by being adopted in later related probative writings which referred to the bond and assumed its validity. More commonly the subsequent writing is holograph in the form of a codicil or note which treats the original defective testamentary document as effective.[11] A document of

---

[7] *Chisholm* v. *Chisholm*, 1949 S.C. 434.

[8] *e.g. McGinn* v. *Shearer*, 1947 S.C. 334.

[9] *e.g. McIntyre* v. *McFarlane's Trs.*, March 1, 1821, F.C.; *Callander* v. *Callander's Trs.* (1863) 2 M. 291.

[10] (1863) 2 M. 291.

[11] For example see *McIntyre* v. *McFarlane's Trs.*, *supra*; *Liddle* v. *Liddle* (1898) 6 S.L.T. 218; *Cross' Trs.* v. *Cross* 1921 1 S.L.T. 244; *Craik's Exrx.* v. *Samson*, 1929 S.L.T. 592.

acknowledgment of a loan, not holograph of the debtor, was validated by the addition of the words, "Received the sum of £50 stg.," in the handwriting of the debtor and signed by him.[12]

3–68 Even an unsubscribed document may be rendered effective by another effectively executed writing which plainly identifies it and adopts it.[13] The unsubscribed document, however, is validated only in so far as its terms are not inconsistent with those of the document which adopts it.[14] A signed description of the unsigned document in the envelope which contains it does not amount to an effective document which adopts the unsigned enclosure.[15]

Adoption by antecedent deed

3–69 It is competent for a testator in an effectively executed testamentary deed to provide that effect shall be given to other testamentary writings made by him even although the latter are not executed in a manner which would otherwise be required by law. The principles to be applied in determining whether the other less formal document is to be effective have been stated in the decision of Lord Justice-Clerk Cooper (who delivered the opinion of a court of seven judges) in *Waterson's Trs.* v. *St. Giles Boys Club*,[16] and may be summarised as follows: (1) The first question to be answered in such cases is a pure question of construction, *viz.* whether the particular writing satisfies the description and fulfils the requisites sought to be prescribed by the principal settlement.[17] (2) A direction to implement the provisions of "any writing under my hand," without more, does not dispense with the requirement that the writing be subscribed by the granter.[18] (3) If the direction is to give effect to "any writing under my hand or subscribed (or signed) by me" it will be effective to adopt unsigned writings since it is clear that "under my hand" is used in a special sense and does not mean "subscribed by me."[19] In a recent case[20] where the principal settlement directed the trustees "to implement all legacies and others which may be contained in any future writings subscribed by me however otherwise informal the same may be," it was held that the direction did not validate a subsequent unsigned codicil but did validate a further signed codicil *quoad*

---

[12] *Christie's Trs.* v. *Muirhead* (1870) 8 M. 461.
[13] *Stenhouse* v. *Stenhouse*, 1922 S.C. 370, *per* Lord President (Clyde) at 372, 373; *Fraser's Exrx.* v. *Fraser's C.B.*, 1931 S.C. 536; *Campbell's Exrs.* v. *Maudslay*, 1934 S.L.T. 420; *Muir* v. *Muir*, 1950 S.L.T. (Notes) 40.
[14] *Macphail's Trs.* v. *Macphail*, 1940 S.C. 560.
[15] *Taylor's Exrs.* v. *Thom*, 1914 S.C. 79; *Macphail's Trs.* v. *Macphail*, *supra*.
[16] 1943 S.C. 369.
[17] *Ibid.*, at 374.
[18] *Ibid.*, at 374, 375; *Inglis* v. *Harper* (1831) 5 W. & S. 785; *Wilsone's Trs.* v. *Stirling* (1861) 24 D. 163; *Young's Trs.* v. *Ross* (1864) 3 M. 10; *Fraser* v. *Forbes' Trs.* (1899) 1 F. 513; *Hamilton's Trs.* v. *Hamilton* (1901) 4 F. 266; *Morton* v. *French*, 1908 S.C. 171. The earlier decision to the contrary in *Ronalds' Trs.* v. *Lyle*, 1929 S.C. 104, was overruled in *Waterson's Trs.*
[19] *Crosbie* v. *Wilson* (1865) 3 M. 870; *Lamont* v. *Magistrates of Glasgow* (1887) 14 R. 603.
[20] *Macrorie's Exrs.* v. *McLaren*, 1982 S.L.T. 295.

the legacies contained therein but did not otherwise make it an effective testamentary settlement which revoked earlier testamentary deeds.

3–70 The incorporation of directions of this kind in formal wills is commonly used in practice since it enables the granter to provide for the distribution of jewellery or effects, and to alter his or her directions from time to time as the items bequeathed or the selected legatees are changed without the need to execute formal codicils or a new will. The normal form of clause runs:

> "And I direct my trustees [executor] to pay or deliver such legacies and to fulfil such instructions as I may leave by any writing under my hand, however informal if indicative of my intentions."

A clause in those terms will not validate unsigned writings and it is desirable that it should not do so since it may impose on the trustees or executor a difficult decision whether unsigned notes or jottings were merely an aide-memoire or deliberative rather than expressive of a concluded testamentary intention; a signature remains the best evidence of the latter.

3–71 Provisions in a formal deed for the adoption of less formal writings are also useful in a discharge and ratification of trustees by the residuary legatees. Where the administration of the trust is complete save for one or two items which cannot immediately be realised and are not in a condition to be conveniently distributed amongst a number of legatees, a formal discharge and ratification may be signed reserving the rights of the legatees in respect of these items and, to avoid the necessity of a subsequent formal deed when distribution of the items or of the proceeds of their realisation becomes practicable, a provision may be inserted in the principal deed of discharge that a simple receipt for such items by the legatees will be a sufficient discharge in respect of them. It may be observed that this method is inappropriate where the share of a legatee who is in nonage is retained until he attains majority, since the legatee has not signed the full discharge and ratification and so has not authorised the acceptance of an informal document of receipt in respect of his share. In such circumstances a formal discharge will still be required when the retained interest is later distributed, but it may be considerably shortened by incorporating therein a reference to the narrative, accounts and scheme of division in the earlier discharge and ratification in terms whereby these are approved and adopted by the signatory legatee.

Writings in re mercatoria

3–72 In order to facilitate the conduct of business the common law has long permitted some relaxation of the statutory solemnities of execution in the case of documents *in re mercatoria*. Such documents are effectual, though not written by the obligant, provided they are subscribed by him and the authenticity of the subscription is not challenged.[21]

"This exemption of mercantile writings is a privilege conceded to the necessary rapidity of the operations of trade, and to the confidential methods of transacting business, which, amidst numerous dealings between traders, are necessary and unavoidable; fortified by the additional circumstance, that they often regulate transactions between subjects of different states, among whom the peculiarities of municipal law cannot be admitted."[22]

Privileges accorded to mercantile writings

3–73   The privileges of such writings are: (1) They are effective though neither holograph nor attested provided they are subscribed by the parties,[22] and parole evidence of the genuineness of the signature, if challenged, is admissible.[23] (2) Subscription by initials, or by mark, is sufficient if proved or admitted to be genuine and the accustomed mode of the person transacting business.[24] (3) The date of the writing does not, as in the case of holograph writs, require to be independently proved, at least for its ordinary mercantile purpose.[25]

Writings within the category of res mercatoria

3–74   Writings *in re mercatoria* have been generally defined as, "all the variety of engagements, or mandates, or acknowledgments, which the infinite occasions of trade may require,"[26] and "obligations *in re mercatoria*" is a phrase which is widely interpreted.[27] The following are clearly included within the category of documents *in re mercatoria*: (1) bills of exchange[28]; (2) promissory notes[29]; (3) bank cheques[30]; (4) orders for goods[31]; (5) guarantees in or in connection with a mercantile transaction,[32] but not personal guarantees by a third party in respect of cash advances to a customer,[33] the test being whether the guarantee was

---

[21] *Ramsay & Hay* v. *Pyronon* (1632) Mor. 16963; *Thomson* v. *Gilkison* (1830) 9 S. 520; *Nicholson* v. *Stuart's Exr.* (1896) 3 S.L.T. 233.

[22] Bell, *Comm.*, I. 342.

[23] Walker and Walker, *Evidence*, 102.

[24] Bell, *Comm.*, I, 343. In the case of signature by mark it may be necessary that the document was read over to and adopted by the party (*Rose* v. *Johnston* (1878) 5 R. 600 at 603, 604). See also *Craig* v. *Scobie* (1832) 10 S. 510 and *Forbes' Exrs.* v. *Western Bank* (1856) 16 D. 242, 807.

[25] Bell, *Comm.*, I, 343; Walker and Walker, *Evidence*, 102. But where the date is material, as in bankruptcy, the trustee may require additional evidence of the date (*Purvis* v. *Dowie* (1869) 7 M. 764).

[26] Bell, *Comm.*, I, 342.

[27] *Beardmore & Co.* v. *Barry*, 1928 S.C. 101, 110; affd. 1928 S.C. (H.L.) 47.

[28] These were recognised at common law as documents *in re mercatoria* and require only signature (Bills of Exchange Act 1882, s. 3(1)). As to signature by parties or with their authority see Walker and Walker, *Evidence*, 104–106.

[29] Bills of Exchange Act 1882, s. 83(1).

[30] *Ibid.*, s. 73; Bell, *Comm.*, I, 342.

[31] Bell, *Comm.*, I, 342.

[32] *Paterson* v. *Wright*, Jan. 31, 1810, F.C., affd. 6 Pat. App. 38; *Dykes* v. *Roy* (1869) 7 M. 357; *B.O.C.M. Silcock Ltd.* v. *Hunter*, 1976 S.L.T. 217.

[33] *Johnston* v. *Grant* (1844) 6 D. 875.

granted in a course of dealing between merchants[34]; (6) offers and acceptances to sell or buy goods or merchandise or to transport them from place to place.[35]

3–75   Writings of a special character which have been decided to be *in re mercatoria* include (1) an obligation by a director of a company to take shares undertaken as part of a compromise of an earlier transaction to subscribe on request for shares,[36] (2) an agreement to take advertising space,[37] (3) an obligation to purchase an engine and fittings in heritable premises and to relieve the seller of his obligations under a lease of the premises,[38] (4) a submission and decree-arbitral in a question as to seed supplied being conform to sample,[39] (5) a letter from a bank acknowledging that bonds, originally held for another party, were held on account of others,[40] (6) a warrant by ironfounders undertaking to deliver iron to the order of a specified person,[41] and (7) docquets approving, acknowledging or discharging entries in business books or accounts.[42]

Writings not admitted as writings in re mercatoria

3–76   These include (1) a lease of business premises,[43] (2) the engagement of a salesman for more than one year,[44] and (3) the acknowledgment of a loan.[45]

Foreign Deeds

3–77   **Inter vivos deeds relating to moveables.** The mode of execution of deeds by foreign persons or bodies has already been touched upon briefly.[46] The original concept was that deeds regarding moveables executed abroad were effectively executed by any method valid in accordance with the law of the place of execution. The rule was *locus regit actum.* The law was encapsulated in the dictum of Lord President Inglis in *Purvis' Trs.* v. *Purvis' Exrs.*[47] "All instruments (without distinction, except in the case of conveyance of land) executed abroad according to the solemnities of the place of execution, must receive effect in Scotland, exactly in the same way as if they were executed in Scotland, according

---

[34] *B.O.C.M. Silcock Ltd.* v. *Hunter, supra* at 224.
[35] Bell, *Comm.*, I, 342.
[36] *Beardmore & Co.* v. *Barry, supra.*
[37] *United Kingdom Advertising Co.* v. *Glasgow Bag-Wash Laundry*, 1926 S.C. 303.
[38] *Kinninmont* v. *Paxton* (1892) 20 R. 128.
[39] *Dykes* v. *Roy* (1869) 7 M. 357.
[40] *Stuart* v. *Potter, Choate & Prentice*, 1911 1 S.L.T. 377.
[41] *Commercial Bank* v. *Kennard* (1859) 21 D. 864.
[42] For a fuller discussion of the kind of docquets which have the privilege of writings *in re mercatoria*, see Walker and Walker, *Evidence*, 102–104.
[43] *Danish Dairy Co.* v. *Gillespie*, 1922 S.C. 656.
[44] *Stewart & McDonald* v. *McCall* (1869) 7 M. 544.
[45] It is not now material that such a document is not *in re mercatoria* since it need not be holograph or tested (*Paterson* v. *Paterson* (1897) 25 R. 144).
[46] at para. 3–11.
[47] (1861) 23 D. 812, 831.

to the solemnities of the Act of 1681.''[48] But where the document is a contract it may be effectively executed if the execution conforms to the law of the place of performance of the contract.[49]

3–78   Where a document is executed in Scotland for use abroad, as when a power of attorney is granted in favour of a representative of a company authorising him to conclude a contract on behalf of the company in a foreign country, evidence that the power of attorney has been validly executed in accordance with the law of Scotland is usually provided by having the document notarised by a docquet placed upon it by a notary public certifying that it has been executed by the granting company in accordance with the law of Scotland and by having a further docquet placed upon it by the provost or other public officer of the place of execution in Scotland certifying the status and signature of the notary. In the case of a document executed abroad which is tendered in Scotland comparable evidence of the authenticity of the deed and its compliance with the law of the country of execution may be required.

3–79   Inter vivos deeds relating to Scottish heritable property. Such deeds in order to be valid must be executed in accordance with the law of Scotland, wherever executed. The *lex loci situs* applies.

Testamentary deeds

3–80   (1) Deaths prior to January 1, 1964
    (a) Moveable estate. The common law of Scotland extended to testamentary deeds relating to moveable property which were executed abroad the same privilege as that accorded to *inter vivos* deeds regarding moveables similarly executed, namely, that the law of Scotland recognised them as valid if executed in accordance with the law of the place of execution.[50] The privilege was further extended by the Wills Act 1861 (applicable only to British subjects and moveable estate). The Act provided that, in addition to the recognition of wills relating to moveables made in accordance with the law of the place of execution, a principle already established by common law in Scotland by the decision in *Purvis' Trs.*, wills of personal estate made out of the United Kingdom by a British subject were valid if executed in accordance with (1) the law of the testator's domicile at the time of the making of the will, and (2) the law of that part of the British Empire where he had his domicile of origin, and also provided that no change of domicile made after the execution of the will revoked it or affected its construction.

---

[48] So a security over moveables (a life insurance policy) was held to be effectively constituted by mere delivery in England and intimation to the insurance company, since English law recognises a security so created, and so the security was valid in a question with the Scottish insurance company (*Scottish Provident Institution* v. *Cohen* (1888) 16 R. 112).
[49] *Valery* v. *Scott* (1876) 3 R. 965. For a fuller discussion see Anton, *Private International Law*, 202–205.
[50] *Purvis' Trs.* v. *Purvis' Exrs., supra.*

3–81 *(b) Heritable estate.* The original rule of the common law was that testamentary deeds disposing of heritable property required to be in the form of *de praesenti* conveyances, and that rule applied also to Scottish wills executed abroad. Section 20 of the Titles to Land Consolidation (Scotland) Act 1868 provided that the word "dispone" or other words importing a conveyance *de praesenti* were no longer necessary and that, where any testamentary deed or writing purporting to convey or bequeath lands contains with reference to such lands any word or words which would, if used in a will or testament with reference to moveables, be sufficient to confer upon the executor or upon the grantee or legatee of such moveables a right to claim or receive the same, such deed or writing, if duly executed in the manner required or permitted by the law of Scotland, would be deemed to be valid as a settlement on the grantee or legatee of the lands to which it applied.[51] The requirements now are (i) that the will discloses an intention to carry heritable estate,[52] and (ii) that it is executed in the manner required or permitted by the law of Scotland in the case of a will relating to moveable estate. The 1868 Act was construed as applying to a foreign will dealing with Scottish heritage,[53] and so a will which indicated an intention to deal with Scottish heritage and was executed abroad in a manner which was recognised at common law or under the Wills Act 1861 in the case of a will relating to moveable estate was also effective to carry the Scottish heritage.

3–82 **(2) Deaths on or after January 1, 1964—both moveable and heritable estate**

The common law as regards wills executed abroad relating to moveable and heritable property remains, but the statutory provisions of the Wills Act 1861 have been extended. The Wills Act 1963 (applicable where the testator dies on or after January 1, 1964) repealed the 1861 Act and substituted wider provisions which apply to wills executed in any foreign state (not merely wills by British subjects) and to both moveable and immoveable estate. A will is treated as properly executed if its execution conforms to the internal law in force in (i) the territory where it was executed, or (ii) the territory where, at the time of its execution or of the testator's death, he was domiciled or had his habitual residence, or (iii) a state of which, at either of those times, he was a national.[54] Moreover, a will is treated as properly executed, so far as it disposes of immoveable property, if its execution conforms to the law in force in the territory where the property is situated.[55] A will executed on board a vessel or aircraft is treated as properly executed if its execution

---

[51] As amended by the Succession (Scotland) Act 1964, s. 34(1) and Sched. 2, but effecting no significant alteration on the matter of validity of the will.

[52] *Hardy's Trs.* (1871) 9 M. 736; *McLeod's Trs.* v. *McLeod* (1875) 2 R. 481; *Clarke's Trs.* v. *Clarke's Exrs.*, 1925 S.C. 431.

[53] *Connel's Trs.* v. *Connel* (1872) 10 M. 627; *Browne* (1882) 20 S.L.R. 76; *Studd* v. *Cook* (1883) 10 R. (H.L.) 53.

[54] s. 1.

[55] s. 2(1)(*b*).

conforms to the internal law in force in the territory with which, having regard to its registration and other relevant circumstances, the vessel or aircraft is most closely connected.[56] A will which revokes a will, or a provision contained in a will, which would be treated as properly executed will be regarded as properly executed if its execution conforms to any law by reference to which the revoked will or provision would be treated as properly executed.[57] As regards the exercise of powers of appointment, the will which does so is treated as properly executed if the execution of the will conforms to the law governing the essential validity of the power[58] and is not to be treated as informally executed by reason only that its execution was not in accordance with any formal requirements contained in the instrument creating the power.[59] If a law in force outside the United Kingdom requires special formalities to be observed by testators, or witnesses to a will to have certain qualifications, these requirements are to be treated as formal requirements only, notwithstanding any rule of law to the contrary.[60] The construction of a will is not altered by any change in the testator's domicile after it has been executed.[61]

Formal validity and essential validity

3–83   It should be kept in view that the rules relating to the execution of foreign wills at common law or under the Wills Act 1963 regulate only the formal validity of a will. Its essential validity remains a matter to be determined by the law of the testator's last domicile. For example, a will executed abroad by a testator who died domiciled in Scotland, although recognised for the purposes of admission to confirmation, would not defeat rights of *jus relictae* and legitim,[62] and a provision in a foreign will directing feuing of lands in Scotland for annual feuduties would be ineffective.[63]

Deeds and Writings Executed in Accordance with Special Statutory Provisions

3–84   Various statutes prescribe special modes of execution of documents to which they relate. Some of the more important are:

Companies Act 1985. The memorandum and articles of association of a company may be attested by one witness.[64] As already noted,[65] contracts on behalf of a company may be executed by being sealed and

---

[56] s. 2(1)(*a*).
[57] s. 2(1)(*c*).
[58] s. 2(1)(*d*).
[59] s. 2(2).
[60] s. 3, *i.e.* they are informalities of execution not necessarily fatal to the effectiveness of the will.
[61] s. 4.
[62] *Purvis' Trs.* v. *Purvis' Exrs.*, *supra*, at 823.
[63] Land Tenure Reform (Scotland) Act 1974, s. 1.
[64] ss. 2(6), (7) 3.
[65] para. 3–10.

subscribed by two directors or by one director and the secretary without the need of being attested by witnesses.[66]

Stock Transfer Act 1963. Transfers of certain securities, including government securities (but not those registered in the Post Office Register), securities issued by companies (other than companies limited by guarantee or unlimited companies), local authority securities and units of a trust scheme, may be executed by the transferor and need not be attested.[67]

Merchant Shipping Act 1894. Bills of sale or mortgages of ships and transfers of such mortgages need be attested by only one witness.[68]

Consumer Credit Act 1974. Provision is made by regulations under the Act which prescribe the manner in which a regulated agreement is to be executed by the debtor or hirer and the creditor or owner.[69]

Trustee Savings Bank Act 1969. Provision is made by regulations prescribing the manner in which and the persons by whom any document used in connection with a trustee savings bank is to be signed or executed.[70]

National Savings Bank Act 1971. Provision is made by regulations for execution of documents relating to transactions in the National Savings Bank.[71]

Crown Writs

3–85   The statutes applicable to the testing of deeds are not applicable to crown writs, which are written under the seal of Chancery without a testing clause, any alterations being authenticated by the initials of the Director of Chancery.[72]

Quasi-Judicial Writs—Arbitrations

3–86   In arbitrations relating to heritable property the contract of submission and the award of the arbiter must be attested or holograph,[73] but less formally executed submissions or awards may become binding if followed by *rei interventus*, homologation or adoption.[74] Arbitrations regarding agricultural leases form an exception to this general rule under common law which required only that submissions and awards be signed but not attested nor holograph,[75] but it appears that in statutory arbitrations under the Agricultural Holdings (Scotland) Act 1949 submissions and awards should be witnessed or holograph.[76]

---

[66] s. 36(3).
[67] s. 1.
[68] ss. 24(2), 31(1) and 37.
[69] s. 61; S.I. 1983 No. 1553.
[70] s. 86; Trustee Savings Bank Regulations 1972 (S.I. 1972 No. 583).
[71] ss. 2, 8; National Savings Bank Regulations 1972 (S.I. 1972 No. 764).
[72] *Catton* v. *MacKenzie* (1874) 1 R. 488.
[73] *McLaren* v. *Aikman*, 1939 S.C. 222.
[74] *Otto* v. *Weir* (1871) 9 M. 660, 661.
[75] *McLaren* v. *Aikman, supra*, at 227; for earlier decisions see Walker and Walker, *Evidence*, 95.
[76] Agricultural Holdings (Specification of Forms) (Scotland) Instrument 1960 (S.I. 1960 No. 1337).

3–87   In other arbitrations the general rule is that, if the submission be formally executed, so also should be the award,[77] subject always to the principles of subsequent validation by *rei interventus*, homologation or adoption. Submissions and awards *in re mercatoria* need not be formally executed,[78] nor where the arbitration relates to matters of small importance.[79] Apart from these exceptions it would seem that submissions and awards should be attested or holograph but the authorities are by no means uniform.[80] A remit for valuation to a man of skill and his decision must be as formal as in other arbitration proceedings,[81] but this rule is frequently elided in practice by a stipulation in a contract providing for reference to a man of skill that he will act as an expert and not as an arbiter.

3–88   A judicial reference by parties or their solicitors may be signed without being attested[82] and is binding when the court interpones its authority to it.[83] The report of the referee may also be signed without witnesses and is a sufficient basis for a decree giving effect to it.[84]

3–89   A joint memorial for the opinion of counsel and counsel's opinion may be signed without attestation in accordance with normal practice.[85]

Deeds not of Great Importance

3–90   The Subscription of Deeds Act 1579 (c. 80) required observance of the statutory solemnities of execution in all deeds relating to heritage and bonds and obligations "of great importance." That provision has been construed in practice as exempting from those requirements documents relating to moveable property of a value not exceeding £100 Scots (now £8·33).[86]

---

[77] *McLaren* v. *Aikman, supra*, at 227, 229.

[78] *Dykes* v. *Roy* (1869) 7 M. 357, 360; *Hope* v. *Crookston Bros.* (1890) 17 R. 868; *McLaren* v. *Aikman, supra*, at pp. 227–228.

[79] See para. 3–90.

[80] See Walker and Walker, *Evidence*, 98.

[81] *Stewart* v. *Williamson*, 1909 S.C. 1254, 1258; 1910 S.C. (H.L.) 47; *McLaren* v. *Aikman, supra*, at 228, 229.

[82] Bell, *Arbitration*, s. 513.

[83] *Ibid.*, s. 519; Dickson, *Evidence*, s. 563.

[84] Bell, *Arbitration*, ss. 533, 534.

[85] *Dykes* v. *Roy, supra*, at p. 360; *Fraser* v. *Lord Lovat* (1850) 7 Bell's App. 171.

[86] Menzies, *Lectures*, 155; *Ferguson* v. *Macpherson* (1758) Mor. 16848.

CHAPTER 4

GENERAL STRUCTURE OF DEEDS AND COMMON CLAUSES

General structure of deeds

1–01   However complex formal deeds may be the arrangement of clauses
normally follows a logical order which is similar in most deeds. Briefly
the order is: (1) The inductive clause which contains (a) the names and
designations of parties and (b) the narrative. In unilateral deeds this
clause contains the name(s) and designation(s) of the granter or granters
or in bilateral or multilateral deeds the names and designations of all the
parties. The names and designations of consenting parties may appear in
the inductive clause but in unilateral deeds are more usually contained
in the operative clause. The narrative part of the clause states the consideration or cause of granting. (2) The operative or dispositive clause
containing the act or acts of the granter or granters—the "doing" clause
which effects the purpose of the deed and makes the grant or defines the
obligations undertaken in favour of the grantees or parties. In unilateral
deeds this clause normally specifies the names and designations of any
consenters and of the grantee or grantees. (3) Executory clauses, varying according to the nature of the deed, which are necessary or desirable
in order to make the deed fully effective, *e.g.* warrandice, penalty or
irritancy clauses. (4) The attestation or testing clause which contains the
particulars of execution that give the deed its probative character. In
bilateral or multilateral contracts operative and executory provisions are
frequently immixed either in the deed itself or in related schedules as a
matter of convenience of drafting.

I. Inductive Clause

(a) Parties

1–02   The full christian names, surnames and addresses of the parties and consenters should be stated,[1] but it is sufficient if they are identified in the
deed since the maxim *falsa demonstratio non nocet dummodo constet de
persona* applies.[2] Where the deed is one in a continuing progress of writs
the designation of the granter should be linked with his designation in
the immediately preceding writ if it has altered in the interval. If a
granter acts in a particular character by virtue of which he is legally
entitled to the subject-matter of the deed, as in the case of a trustee, the
deed runs in his own name, specifying the capacity in which he acts and
the deed, decree or other document by which he was appointed. If the
granter has no legal entitlement to the subject-matter of the deed but
acts as an agent for a principal who is so entitled, as in the case of an
attorney or factor and commissioner, the deed should run in the name of
the principal and the signature by the agent should be explained in the

---

[1] Although the names and designations of grantees or consenters may be contained in the operative
clause it is convenient to deal with matters relating to parties and consenters together.
[2] *Scottish Union Insurance Co.* v. *Calderwood* (1836) 14 S. 667.

testing clause specifying the instrument whereby he is authorised to execute the deed.[3] However it is thought that in the latter case it is not a ground of objection to the validity of the deed if it runs in the name of the agent, specifying his authority, and deeds by an attorney or a factor and commissioner framed in that manner are acceptable in practice. Similar principles apply in relation to grantees. If the deed confers rights or benefits upon persons acting in a particular capacity, such as trustees, the deed should be granted in their favour in that capacity, stating the deed, decree or instrument by which they were appointed. If the deed effects a transaction negotiated by a representative of an incapacitated person or by an agent on behalf of his principal the grant is made in favour of the principal, not the agent.[4]

4–03   In practice there are certain exceptions to these general principles. Transfers of stocks, shares or debentures of English companies, or Scottish companies which do not recognise trusts, are normally taken (a) in the case of trustees in the names of the trustees as individuals without mention of their fiduciary capacity, or (b) in the individual name of the tutor of a pupil child or the *curator bonis* of a person of unsound mind without mention of their capacity, not in the name of the ward, since that course facilitates disposal of the security if that becomes desirable in the interests of proper management of the ward's investments. The fact that the investments form part of the trust funds or the estate of the ward, as the case may be, should be noted informally on the certificate for the security.

Special parties

4–04   **Companies.** It is peculiarly important that deeds granted by or in favour of an incorporated company should state the name of the company precisely as rendered in its certificate of incorporation. Minor errors in the names of individual persons may not invalidate the deed if they are sufficiently identified, on the principle of *falsa demonstratio*, but the separate legal *persona* created by incorporation of a company exists only in the company whose name is registered and so a deed intended to be granted by or in favour of that company but which renders its name inaccurately is granted by or to a body which has no legal entity. In practice a supplementary corroborative deed is necessary. If the discrepancy occurred in the name of the company which granted the deed and that company is in liquidation when the error is observed, the corrective deed should be granted by the company and its liquidator, but if the liquidator has been discharged on conclusion of the winding-up recourse

---

[3] The distinction is that persons having a fiduciary right or title to the subject-matter of the deed are the only persons who can properly grant it. An agent acts as representing his principal with authority to execute the deed and technically the correct place to explain that authority is in the clause relating to its execution.

[4] The main reason is that the right or title conferred by the deed should be conceived in favour of the person to whom in law it belongs. It also simplifies conveyancing practice since no further procedure is necessary upon termination of the authority of the representative or agent.

may be had to the Queen's and Lord Treasurer's Remembrancer since the right or property purported to be conveyed by the deed would have remained technically *in bonis* of the company and would have accrued to the Crown as *bona vacantia*.[5] The Remembrancer normally is prepared to grant a corroborative deed on being satisfied as to the circumstances and on payment of his legal expenses. If the discrepancy occurred in the name of the grantee company the corroborative deed may be obtained from the granter or from his executor or, if a company, from the company itself or the company and its liquidator or the Queen's and Lord Treasurer's Remembrancer, as the case may be. The principle is that a deed in favour of a non-existent body does not divest the granter of the right of property which it purported to transfer so that the granter or his or its representatives remain *in titulo* to grant a corroborative deed.

4–05 Companies in liquidation. Upon its liquidation a company remains vested in its own assets, but the liquidator is entitled to administer them.[6] So deeds by a company in liquidation are granted by the company and its liquidator specifying the decree or the relevant resolution or resolutions by which he was appointed. In a members' voluntary winding-up the resolution will be that of the company.[7] In the case of a creditors' voluntary winding-up the resolution will be (i) that of the company confirmed by that of the creditors, (ii) that of the company where the creditors have made no other nomination, or (iii) that of the creditors where they have nominated a liquidator other than the liquidator nominated by the company.[8]

4–06 Receivers. The assets of the company remain vested in it but, in so far as they fall within the assets included in the floating charge by virtue of which the receiver was appointed, the receiver is entitled to administer them to the exclusion of the directors of the company.[9] So deeds affecting such assets are granted by the company and the receiver, narrating the floating charge or debenture by virtue of which the appointment of the receiver was made and the instrument of appointment or decree of court by which he was appointed.

4–07 Trustees on trust estate. The assets comprised in a trust estate are vested fiducially in the trustees. Deeds by or to trustees run in the names of the individual trustees, with their designations, specifying the trust deed under which they act by reference to the name and designation of the truster and its date and, if registered, the date of its registration.[10]

---

[5] Companies Act 1985, s. 654.
[6] *Bank of Scotland* v. *Liquidators of Hutchison, Main & Co. Ltd.*, 1913 S.C. 255, 262–263.
[7] Companies Act 1985, s. 580.
[8] *Ibid.*, s. 589.
[9] *Imperial Hotel (Aberdeen) Ltd.* v. *Vaux Breweries Ltd.*, 1978 S.C. 86.
[10] The facility of describing deeds by reference to the names, without designations, of the granter permitted by s. 8 and Sched. D to the Conveyancing (Scotland) Act 1924 is applicable to deeds affecting lands which are referred to in another deed; it does not apply to granters or grantees of a deed itself.

Where assumed trustees are involved it is unnecessary to refer to the deeds of assumption in the inductive or operative clauses: it is sufficient to describe them as "the trustees now acting under" the original trust deed.[11]

4-08 Trustee under trust deed for creditors. The practice is the same as for trustees on a trust estate.

4-09 Trustee in bankruptcy. The assets of the bankrupt vest in the trustee by virtue of his act and warrant.[12] Deeds are granted by the trustee (designed) of the bankrupt (designed) specifying the act and warrant.

4-10 Partnerships. *(i) Deeds constituting obligations undertaken by or in favour of a firm.* Any instrument relating to the business of a firm may create an obligation binding on the firm if undertaken in the name of the firm and signed by any partner or authorised person.[13] Formal deeds which are not, or possibly are not, within the scope of the ordinary business of the firm should be granted by the firm and all the partners thereof, making it clear, if that be the situation, that the obligation is undertaken by the firm and not by the partners as individuals. (The partners will, of course, be liable as guarantors of the firm's obligations but will not be primarily responsible).[14] Frequently, however, in relation to banking facilities the obligation is undertaken by the firm and all the partners as such partners and as individuals jointly and severally. In the case of a formal deed creating an unsecured obligation in favour of a partnership the document should be granted in favour of the firm *socio nomine*, although the names of the partners may be added for the purpose of identifying the firm, *e.g.* "The Glasgow Tinfoil Company, metal merchants, 16 Albert Square, Glasgow, (of which firm the partners are [*names and designations*])." If the original firm is dissolved and its assets are taken over by a new firm the right to the obligation should be assigned to the new firm in order to give it a title to sue on the obligation.[15] Such an assignation should be granted by the original firm and its partners: if the original firm has been dissolved by the death of a partner or by agreement before that has been done the assignation may be granted by the surviving partner or partners (who can sue for a debt due to the firm[16]).

**4-11 *(ii) Partnership property.* The title to feudal property owned by a firm is

---

[11] In deeds relating to land or heritable securities it may be necessary to deduce the title of trustees who grant the deed—Conveyancing (Scotland) Act 1924, s. 3; Conveyancing and Feudal Reform (Scotland) Act 1970, s. 12. In moveable conveyancing the title of trustees who grant the deed, if different from the trustees in whose favour the title to the asset concerned originally stood, should be linked by specifying the deeds by which the present trustees acquired right: that may be done in the inductive clause or later in the deed—see Conveyancing (Scotland) Act 1874, s. 50 and Sched. M.
[12] Bankruptcy (Scotland) Act 1913, s. 97.
[13] Partnership Act 1890, s. 6. See Miller, *Partnership*, 220–229.
[14] 1890 Act, s. 9; Miller, *ibid.*, 159–160.
[15] *A. & A. Campbell* v. *Campbell's Exrs.*, 1910 2 S.L.T. 240.
[16] *Nicoll* v. *Reid* (1877) 5 R. 137.

taken in the names of the partners as trustees for the firm since the firm itself cannot sustain the feudal relationship. The conveyance will be granted in favour of the partners and the survivors and survivor of them as trustees for the partnership. Securities in favour of the partnership should be taken in the name of the firm *quoad* the personal obligation and *quoad* the grant of security in favour of the partners and the survivors and survivor of them as trustees for the firm. Leases may be granted in favour of the firm *socio nomine*[17] although there may be some doubt whether that is competent if the name of the firm is merely a descriptive one.[18] In practice such leases should be taken in favour of the partners and the survivors and survivor of them as trustees for the firm who should be bound jointly and severally with the firm for the performance of the obligations of the tenants.[19] Dispositions of the heritable property of the firm are granted by the trustees or the survivors or survivor, as also are assignations of heritable securities held by the firm, usually with the consent of the individual partners. Since the title to and interest in any heritable estate which belongs to a partnership devolves according to the nature and tenure thereof,[20] the title to property held in trust for a firm devolves in accordance with the law of trusts. So the original trustees or the survivors of them remain *in titulo* to deal with the property or security taken in their names as trustees, notwithstanding that the original partnership has terminated and its assets are now held for a new firm; the position usually is that the new firm is beneficially entitled to the assets and the trustees hold them for the new firm. From the point of view of the grantee the consent of all the partners (whether of the original firm if it still exists or the new firm for whom they are now held) may not be strictly necessary since the title obtained from the trustees may be protected under section 2 of the Trusts (Scotland) Act 1961, but such consent is desirable in the interests of the trustees since the disposal may well be at variance with the terms or purposes for which the assets were originally acquired. Assignations of leases taken in the names of trustees for a firm may be granted by the trustees, also with the consent of all partners, provided that, where there has been a change in the *persona* of the firm, the lease has not thereby terminated.

4–12 Pupils and tutors. Deeds on behalf of a pupil are granted by the tutors or tutor, stating their or his office as guardian of the pupil and, if a tutor has been judicially appointed, specifying the decree of appointment. Deeds in favour of a pupil are granted to the pupil, not the tutors or tutor.

4–13 Minors and curators. The power to grant deeds is in the minor and so they run in his name with consent of his curators or curator (if any).

---

[17] *Denniston Macnayr & Co.* v. *Macfarlane* (1808) Mor. App., *voce* Tack 15; Bell, *Prin.*, s. 357.
[18] Rankine, *Leases*, 86.
[19] Paton and Cameron, 63.
[20] Partnership Act 1890, s. 20(2).

Deeds in favour of the minor are granted to him, the consent of the curator to the transaction being included in the narrative clause.

4–14 Persons of unsound mind. Deeds granted on behalf of an *incapax* run in the name of his curator specifying the decree appointing him. Deeds in favour of the *incapax* are granted to the *incapax*, not his curator.

4–15 Judicial factors. Where the factory is on the estate of a living ward, such as factories *loco tutoris* or as *curator bonis*, deeds are granted in favour of the ward as the actual owner and it is unnecessary for the factor to connect himself with the title to the ward's property.[21] On a sale or disposal of the property of a ward who has no legal capacity, such as a pupil or *incapax*, the factor grants the deed, not as *dominus* but as a guardian who supplies that deficiency in the ward in the exercise of his functions. Where the ward is a minor the *dominium* of his property is in the minor himself and he has capacity to grant deeds affecting it but the consent of the factor is required to supplement the minor's judgment.

4–16   The position is otherwise where there is no identifiable person who is *dominus* of the property, as in the case of a judicial factor on a trust estate or on the sequestrated estates of a deceased person. In such cases the right or title to the property of the estate is vested fiducially in the factor and deeds are granted by or to the factor.[22]

4–17 Consenters. Consent to a deed is required by persons who have an interest in the subject-matter of the deed which is not that of a principal but might adversely affect the right of the granter to grant the deed or the right taken by the grantee under it. Common examples of consent are (i) that of the holder of a security over property conveyed by the deed to the effect of disburdening it of the security, (ii) that of an agent who has purchased the property conveyed by the deed to the effect of authorising the conveyance to his principal, (iii) that of a beneficiary having a vested right in trust property to a conveyance of it by the trustees which may be at variance with the powers of the trustees, or (iv) that of a party who may have a possible right to any part of property conveyed by the deed either by reason of some ambiguity in the title of the granter or because of a right in the property which may conflict with the right given to the grantee, *e.g.* the right of a non-entitled spouse in a matrimonial home.[22a]

4–18 Effect of consent. Where consent is given in respect of a particular interest specified in the deed and the consenter grants warrandice from fact and deed only, the effect of the consent is merely *non repugnantia, i.e.* the consenter relinquishes any rights which he may at the time have in a question with the grantee, but not his rights against the granter or any

---

[21] *Scott* (1856) 18 D. 624, 626; *Maconochie* (1857) 19 D. 366, 372.
[22] *Scott, supra,* at 626; Walker, *Judicial Factors,* 83.
[22a] Matrimonial Homes (Family Protection) (Scotland) Act 1981, s. 6(1).

other person, and the consent does not import a discharge or conveyance of the right in respect of which it is given. So the consent of a creditor in a heritable security to a disposition of the security subjects is normally expressed as disburdening the subjects of the security so that the disponee may have full enjoyment of them, but it does not imply a discharge of the consenting creditor's right to require repayment of the secured loan from the disponer nor an assignation of it to the disponee.[23] Moreover, the consent is referable to the interest of the consenter as it exists at the time when the consent is given, and if the consenter subsequently acquires another interest in the subject-matter of the deed he will not be held as having consented in respect of that new interest.[24] If, however, the consenter grants absolute warrandice any right in the subject-matter of the deed which subsequently accrues to him accresces to the benefit of the grantee of the deed.[25] Where a person who is the true owner of subjects conveyed *a non domino* consents for all right, title and interest competent to him in the premises, he effectually conveys the subjects to the grantee; and the effect of his consent is not simply *non repugnantia*.[26]

4–19   **Practice.** The implications of these principles in practice are important. It is difficult to figure all the circumstances in which consents to a deed may be required but the following rules in the more usual situations are suggested: (1) Where a secured creditor consents to a conveyance of the security subjects the deed should specify the interest in respect of which consent is given, *e.g.* "with the consent of A.B. to the effect of disburdening as by his signature hereto he hereby disburdens the subjects hereby conveyed of [*specify the security deed*]," and the warrandice of the consenter should be from fact and deed only. (2) Where a person has concluded a contract of purchase on behalf of another the deed of conveyance in favour of the principal should narrate that the purchase was made by the agent on behalf of the principal, the agent's consent should be for all right, title and interest competent to him in the premises but his warrandice should be from fact and deed only. Where, however, there has been a subsale, as when A sells to B and B without taking a title resells to C, B's warrandice should be absolute—he is a principal in fact although a consenter in form. (3) Where there is some ambiguity in the title of the granter of a deed of conveyance to the property conveyed and consent is given by the person who may be entitled to challenge the granter's title in any respect, the consent should be for all right, title and interest, present and future, in the premises, but if the consenter is receiving no significant consideration his warrandice should be restricted to fact and deed. (4) Where residuary legatees consent to a

---

[23] Menzies, *Lectures*, 500; Craigie, *Heritable Rights*, 84.
[24] *Forbes* v. *Innes* (1668) Mor. 7759; *Stuart* v. *Hutchison* (1681) Mor. 7762; Erskine, II, vii, 4; *Buchan* v. *Cockburn* (1739) 1 R.L.C. 33.
[25] Craigie, *op. cit.*, 83, 84.
[26] *Mounsey* v. *Maxwell* (1808) Hume 237; *Sorley's Trs.* v. *Grahame* (1832) 10 S. 319.

deed of conveyance on sale by trustees the consent should be for all right, title and interest, present and future, and, since the consenters will in effect receive the benefit of the consideration, their warrandice should be absolute. (The warrandice granted by the trustees in its normal form, *i.e.* from their own facts and deeds and binding the trust estate and the beneficiaries therein in absolute warrandice, would probably have that effect but if the consent of the residuary legatees has been specifically incorporated in the deed the safe course for the grantee is to include expressly the absolute warrandice of the consenters also.)

(b) Narrative

4–20   Function of clause. The function of the narrative part of the inductive clause is to explain the purpose or reason for granting. In many deeds the object of granting is self-evident but in others a brief narrative assists in rendering the deed fully intelligible. The narrative may have important legal implications, as establishing the character of the deed as gratuitous or onerous, to determine liability to and the amount of any stamp duty payable upon it or to make the deed fully effective.

4–21   Gratuitous or onerous deeds. If a deed is gratuitous the older form of narrative in grants by individuals, still in common use, is "for love, favour and affection." Where such words are inappropriate, as in grants by corporate or unincorporated bodies, the usual phraseology is "for certain good causes," sometimes with the addition of the words "but without any consideration" if it is desired to indicate clearly that the deed is by way of gift. If a deed is granted in exchange for payment of a price the amount thereof will be stated, but if for any reason it is not desired to disclose the price on the face of the deed the narrative may run "for certain good and onerous causes and considerations."[27] In bilateral or multilateral deeds, *e.g.* a lease, where there are obligations imposed on each of the parties, it is impracticable to summarise the considerations in the initial narrative, and a brief statement of the agreement of parties to enter into the transaction in the terms after contained is sufficient.

4–22   Stamp Act 1891. Section 5 of the Stamp Act 1891 requires that all the facts and circumstances affecting the liability of any instrument to stamp duty, or the amount of the duty with which it is chargeable, are to be fully and truly set forth in the instrument. Since the object of the section is to prevent fraud, however, there is no objection in practice, if for any reason it is not desired to disclose the consideration on the face of the deed, to express in the narrative that the deed is granted for certain good and onerous causes, or not to refer to any consideration, provided that the whole circumstances relative to liability for and the amount of

---

[27] As to stamp duty on such deeds, see para. 4–22.

stamp duty are disclosed to the Stamp Office when the deed is submitted for adjudication of duty.

–23 Discharge. It is peculiarly important in documents of discharge that the narrative is accurate. A false narrative, particularly in circumstances where the granter was not separately advised and might have been misled, may be fatal to the validity of the discharge.[28] Moreover, it is desirable that the narrative in a deed of discharge is full and comprehends all claims which were in the contemplation of the parties when the deed was granted. General words of discharge will not cover claims which were not so contemplated.[29] It follows that in a discharge and ratification granted by beneficiaries in favour of trustees at the conclusion of the administration of a trust all actings of the trustees which may have been outwith their powers or at variance with the terms or purposes of the trust should be fully disclosed in the narrative of the deed, since otherwise the beneficiaries may subsequently challenge the effectiveness of the discharge on the ground that they were unaware of those matters.[30]

–24 Illegal consideration—pacta illicita. Deeds involving contracts may be illegal if the object of the contract or the mode of its performance is illegal either at common law or by statute. For an account of the various grounds on which a deed effecting a contract may be void by reason of illegality, see Walker, *Contracts*, 11–17 to 11–33.

II. OPERATIVE OR DISPOSITIVE CLAUSE

–25 Function and contents. This clause contains the act of the granter and is the principal clause of the deed. Its content varies with the nature of the deed, as undertaking obligations, assigning, conveying or transferring property or discharging obligations or extinguishing rights. It also contains, especially in unilateral deeds, the name and designation of the grantee and any destination to other persons in succession.

–26 Construction of deed. In the construction of deeds constituting or giving effect to a contract the whole deed may be looked at in order to ascertain the terms of the bargain.[31] There is, however, an important exception to that rule in the construction of conveyances of land. In deeds of that kind the dispositive clause, if unambiguous, is decisive of any question relating to the matters with which it deals, *i.e.* the extent of the land conveyed and any real burdens imposed thereon or other qualifications of the grant, the identity of the grantee and the meaning of any

---

[28] *Graham* v. *Magistrates of Montrose* (1830) 4 W. & S. 346; *Glass* v. *McIntosh* (1825) 4 S. 1; *Thomson* v. *Thomson* (1829) 8 S. 156.

[29] *Dickson* v. *Halbert* (1854) 16 D. 586, 597; *Burns' Trs.* v. *Burns' Trs.*, 1911 2 S.L.T. 392, 394; *Dickson's Trs.* v. *Dickson's Trs.*, 1930 S.L.T. 226; *Armour* v. *Glasgow Royal Infirmary*, 1909 S.C. 916.

[30] See *Johnstone* v. *Mackenzie's Trs.*, 1911 S.C. 321, revd. 1912 S.C. (H.L.) 106 on other grounds.

[31] Gloag, *Contract*, 399; *North British Oil and Candle Co.* v. *Swann* (1868) 6 M. 835.

destination. The conclusive quality of the dispositive clause in conveyances of land is not affected by the provisions of other clauses, even although these may indicate that the intention of the granter has not been accurately effected in the dispositive clause.[32] As it has been put by Baron Hume[33]:

> "The dispositive is certainly the ruling clause, the main text for construction of the charter; and it is not ordinarily to be controuled, refuted, or done away, by any of the after clauses, where they happen to be repugnant to or derogatory from it . . . if in itself clear, and express, and full, it vests an immediate estate in the disponee in its own terms; and this cannot be taken back, or be withheld from him, in virtue of any mention that is made of different or less beneficial terms, or of higher and more advantageous terms, in the other members of the instrument, of which it is not the proper business or destination to settle these matters."

It is only if the terms of the dispositive clause are ambiguous that it is permissible to refer to other clauses of the deed to resolve the ambiguity, e.g. where the dispositive clause of a deed could be read as being a conveyance of the lands or of the superiority the narrative clause was considered to determine that only the superiority was conveyed.[34]

III. EXECUTORY CLAUSES

4–27   Executory clauses are of various kinds appropriate to the type of deed but two of them, the clause of warrandice and the clause of consent to registration for preservation or execution, are of common occurrence in many different kinds of deed and may be considered generally.

(1) Warrandice

Nature of warrandice

4–28   Warrandice in its absolute form is a personal obligation by the granter of a deed that the deed and the right thereby granted shall be effectual to the grantee and that if the grantee suffers loss or damage by reason of reduction of the deed, or eviction, total or partial, from any property conveyed by the deed, or any act or deed of the granter or his predecessors in title, or any defect in the title of the granter to the property conveyed by the deed, the granter will make good that loss or damage. The extent of warrandice as above stated may be qualified in the clause of warrandice itself by restricting the obligation to simple warrandice or to warrandice from fact and deed only. The obligation of warrandice is applicable principally in deeds creating personal obligations, selling or conveying heritable or moveable property or constituting securities over

---

[32] *Cooper Scott* v. *Gill Scott*, 1924 S.C. 309.
[33] *Lectures*, IV, 134.
[34] *Orr* v. *Mitchell* (1893) 20 R.(H.L.) 27.

such property. It may be express or implied by law from the nature of the transaction. In sales of moveable property its effect is prescribed and the right to contract out of that effect is limited by statute[35] and in conveyances of and securities over heritable property its effect is defined by statute.[36]

4–29 **Express and implied warrandice.** Warrandice may be expressly stated in a clause of warrandice contained in the deed. If not expressly stated it may be implied by law from the nature of the transaction. Warrandice, when expressed, supersedes the warrandice which would have been implied by law,[37] subject to any statutory provisions which prohibit or affect the construction of provisions purporting to contract out of or modify implied terms of certain contracts.[38]

Degrees of warrandice

4–30 **(a) Simple warrandice.** This is the least onerous degree of warrandice, and is implied by law in gratuitous deeds. The granter undertakes that he will not in future voluntarily do anything to prejudice the right given to the grantee by the deed.[39] It does not protect the grantee against future deeds which the granter was under a prior obligation to grant nor against any existing burdens or defects in property conveyed by the deed or the granter's title to it. The granter who is making a donation simply transfers the right to the property conveyed as it stands subject to any burdens and restrictions upon it or qualifications in his right to it but undertakes that he will not voluntarily do anything in future that will derogate from the grant. If expressed the clause runs either, "And I grant simple warrandice," or, "I warrant these presents to the said A [and his foresaids] against all future voluntary deeds to be granted by me."

4–31 **(b) Warrandice from fact and deed.** This warrandice is more onerous: it protects the grantee not only against future deeds of the granter but against his own former deeds or actings. It gives a right of recourse only against acts or deeds of the granter himself; it does not indemnify against acts of third parties such as a successful challenge by another person of the granter's title to property conveyed by the deed. It is implied in assignations of debts, in which case there is also implied warrandice *debitum subesse, i.e.* that the debt assigned is a valid and subsisting obligation. The warranty of the validity of the debt applies also to the obligations of cautioners, and if the obligation of any cautioner has been discharged the cedent will be liable for any loss thereby sustained

---

[35] See para. 4–43.
[36] See paras. 4–33, 4–37.
[37] *Coventry* v. *Coventry* (1834) 12 S. 895; *Strong* v. *Strong* (1851) 13 D. 548; *Macalister* v. *Macalister's Exrs.* (1866) 4 M. 495.
[38] *e.g.* Unfair Contract Terms Act 1977, s. 20 in relation to contracts of sale or hire-purchase of goods.
[39] *Alexander* v. *Lundies* (1675) Mor. 940.

by the assignees.[40] Warrandice *debitum subesse* does not guarantee the ability of the debtor to pay, even if the warrandice in the assignation is expressed as absolute; that would require an express guarantee of solvency.[41] The usual form of the clause is, "I grant warrandice from fact and deed only," or, in the older form, "I grant warrandice from my own proper[42] facts and deeds only." It is appropriate to deeds granted by persons acting in a fiduciary capacity, *e.g.* trustees normally grant warrandice from fact and deed only and, if the warrandice appropriate to the transaction is absolute, bind the trust estate under their charge and the beneficiaries therein in absolute warrandice. A trustee who personally grants any higher degree of warrandice may be liable for burdens created by a third party.[43] It is suggested by Erskine[44] that, in a conveyance where the title is doubtful or the consideration is inadequate, warrandice is implied only from fact and deed, but this proposition is doubtful[45]; the proper course in any such transaction is to express the warrandice which is to be granted.

4–32   (c) **Absolute warrandice.** This is the most onerous degree of warrandice. It not only protects the grantee against the past or future acts or deeds of the granter but gives recourse against any defect in the title of the granter to property conveyed and against eviction, total or partial, therefrom on any ground existing prior to the granting of the deed. It is implied in transactions of sale or security and in onerous transactions generally. It is implied also in leases[46] although the landlord's obligations under warrandice may be affected by the tenant's knowledge of limitations in the landlord's title when the lease was granted or failure by the tenant to prevent encroachment by third parties.[47]

Warrandice—heritable rights

4–33   (a) **Conveyances.** In dispositions of land the statutory form of the clause "And I grant warrandice," is defined as implying, unless specially qualified, absolute warrandice as regards the lands and writs and evidents and warrandice from fact and deed as regards the rents.[48] Since the definition applies to any disposition it is necessary to modify the clause in deeds where absolute warrandice with those implications is inappropriate, *e.g.* in a gratuitous disposition an express clause of simple warrandice should be inserted.[49] Absolute warrandice in conveyances of land

---

[40] *Reid* v. *Barclay* (1879) 6 R. 1007.
[41] *Barclay* v. *Liddel* (1671) Mor. 16591.
[42] "My own proper" is tautologous emphatic; it does not imply any reference to the quality of the fact or deed.
[43] *Horsbrugh's Trs.* v. *Welch* (1886) 14 R. 67, although in the circumstances warrandice from fact and deed only would have been enough to impose liability.
[44] II, iii, 25.
[45] Montgomerie Bell, *Lectures*, 216.
[46] *Middletons* v. *Yorstoun* (1826) 5 S. 162; *Middletons* v. *Megget* (1828) 7 S. 76.
[47] See Paton and Cameron, 128–129 and authorities there cited.
[48] Titles to Land Consolidation (Scotland) Act 1868, s. 8.
[49] See *Macalister* v. *Macalister's Exrs.* (1866) 4 M. 495 (relating to a lease but the principle would apply to a disposition).

guarantees that there shall be no eviction from the lands conveyed and that the writs assigned will be available and effectual for maintaining the grantee in possession of those lands.[50]

4-34 *Loss or damage covered by warrandice.* Several situations may be figured in which a claim against a seller under a grant of absolute warrandice would emerge.

(1) Where a third party successfully propones a prior and preferable title to the whole or part of the lands conveyed.

(2) Where a third party has a valid feu right to the *dominium utile* of the whole or part of lands conveyed without exception of feu rights from warrandice.

(3) Where minerals have been effectively reserved to a superior or other person and no reference to the reservation has been made in the conveyance of the property, since on the principle of ownership *a coelo usque ad centrum* the grantee will have been extruded from ownership of part of the subjects conveyed.

(4) Where the property conveyed or part thereof, not being of a character which is normally subject to leasing, is found to be subject to a lease, whether or not registered, and leases have not been excepted from warrandice. The existence of a lease may not in all circumstances be a breach of warrandice—see paragraph 4-38(6) *infra*—but it will be if entry with vacant possession has been specified in the conveyance.

(5) Where the land conveyed is subject to a servitude which in the circumstances is of an onerous character and has not been disclosed in the title deeds or incorporated in the conveyance.[50a]

(6) Where the land conveyed is subject to a real burden which was not contained or incorporated by reference in the conveyance and which involves the purchaser in loss.[50a]

(7) The existence of a heritable security over the land to which the purchase had not been made subject.[51]

(8) In the case of a conveyance of flatted property where, either expressly or by virtue of the common law of the tenement, (a) a right of exclusive property in, *e.g.* the *solum* or roof has purported to have been conveyed and it is discovered that a third party has a prior title to a right of common property in that part of the property, or (b) a right of common property in the *solum*, roof or walls has purported to be conveyed and it is discovered that a third party has a prior title to exclusive ownership of any of those parts.

4-35 *Warrandice in registered titles.* If a conveyance of property is to be registered in the Land Register for Scotland a clause of warrandice is still appropriate, but the legal effects may differ in some respects. Various typical situations are considered in the *Registration of Title Handbook*,

---

[50] *Brownlie* v. *Miller* (1880) 7 R. (H.L.) 66, 83.
[50a] See para. 4-45.
[51] *Dewar* v. *Aitken* (1780) Mor. 16637.

paragraph H.3.06, which gives detailed guidance as to the rights of parties in relation to warrandice and the statutory indemnity under section 12 of the Land Registration (Scotland) Act 1979. The principles which regulate the rights of parties where a conveyance has been granted by A in favour of B with absolute warrandice and B's title has been registered may be stated broadly thus:

(1) If the statutory indemnity is excluded either by reason of the loss arising from a defect or burden of a kind in respect of which there is no entitlement to indemnity under section 12(3) of the Act or by reason of an express exclusion from indemnity upon registration, then B must rely for relief upon A's warrandice.

(2) If the loss is insured under the statutory indemnity and is also a breach of warrandice then (a) if B suffers loss by rectification of his title at the instance of the holder of a preferable competing title he may elect either to claim under the statutory indemnity or under warrandice but, if he chooses the former, the Keeper will be subrogated to his rights against the seller under the obligation of warrandice (section 13 of the Act) or (b) if for any reason, *e.g.* that the holder of the competing title was not in possession of the disputed area when registration of B's title was effected so that B's registered title is invulnerable, then the holder of the competing title may claim to be indemnified under the Act or, if A was also the author of the competing title, he may claim against A under the warrandice in the conveyance of the land to him by A or subrogate the Keeper to his rights thereunder.

It should be emphasised that the rights of parties as above outlined may be affected by wrongful or negligent acts of the parties.

4–36   **(b) Leases.** In leases the clause normally runs, "And I grant absolute warrandice."[52] In assignations of registered leases the statutory clause, "And I grant warrandice," implies absolute warrandice as in a disposition of lands,[53] but in assignations of unregistered leases warrandice may be from fact and deed as regards the landlord's power to grant the lease, which the cedent does not warrant, and absolute warrandice as regards the cedent's own title, but the higher degree of absolute warrandice may be given. Absolute warrandice indemnifies the tenant against eviction, partial[54] or total,[55] from the subjects let. If the tenant's interest under a long (registrable) lease has been registered in the Land Register, the general principles as to the statutory indemnity and warrandice explained in paragraph 4–35 apply *mutatis mutandis* but it should be noted that, where the competing title is that of the landlord, the claim of the landlord to statutory indemnity is excluded under section 12(3)(*m*)

---

[52] The statutory clause, "And I grant warrandice," does not have the effect of absolute warrandice when contained in the lease itself, so that absolute warrandice, though normally implied, should be expressed.

[53] Registration of Leases (Scotland) Act 1857, s. 20.

[54] *Dougall* v. *Magistrates of Dunfermline*, 1908 S.C. 151, 160.

[55] *Menzies* v. *Duke of Queensberry's Exrs.* (1832) 11 S. 18.

of the 1979 Act if it arises from any information omitted from the title sheet of the interest of the landlord (except so far as relating to the constitution or amount of rent and adequate information regarding that has been made available to the Keeper).

4–37 **(c) Securities.** In heritable securities the statutory clause, "And I grant warrandice," imports, unless specially qualified, absolute warrandice as regards the lands and the title-deeds thereof and warrandice from fact and deed as regards the rents.[56] The statutory forms of assignation of heritable securities do not include a clause of warrandice, but, if granted for consideration, warrandice would be implied of the validity and continued existence of the obligation of the debtor and the sufficiency of the cedent's title to the security. It should be kept in view that the cedent may incur liability under warrandice in which he would not have been involved if the security had been discharged instead of being assigned. For example, if the personal obligation has been altered,[57] or payments to account of the sum due have been received, or the rate of interest reduced, or deeds postponing or restricting the security have been granted, the cedent would incur liability to the assignee unless appropriate qualifications are made in the assignation. In circumstances where an assignation rather than a discharge is being granted at the instance of the debtor, as when the creditor has sought repayment and the debtor has arranged for a new lender, the original creditor should not incur any greater liability than if a discharge had been granted and should modify the terms of an assignation appropriately.[58]

Loss or damage not covered by warrandice

4–38 Absolute warrandice does not indemnify against every eventuality which may affect the value of heritable property or peaceful possession of it by the grantee. In particular it does not indemnify against:

(1) Defects, whether evident or latent, in the physical condition of the property.[59]

(2) Losses or burdens natural to the right[60] or arising from the legal effects of ownership.[61]

(3) Servitudes, unless of a very burdensome description[62] such as was the case in *Urquhart* v. *Halden*.[63] In *Welsh* v. *Russell*,[64] although the

---

[56] Titles to Land Consolidation (Scotland) Act 1868, s. 119; Conveyancing and Feudal Reform (Scotland) Act 1970, s. 10(2).

[57] As by discharge of cautioners: *Jackson* v. *Nicoll* (1870) 8 M. 408.

[58] See Burns, 556, 557; *Russell's Trs.* v. *Mudie* (1857) 20 D. 125.

[59] *Aberdeen Development Co.* v. *Mackie, Ramsay & Taylor*, 1977 S.L.T. 177, 181. (See articles: R. Black, 1982 J.R. 31; *contra* D. J. Cusine, 1983 J.L.S. 228; J. M. Halliday, 1983 J.R. 1.)

[60] Bell, *Prin.*, s. 895; *MacRitchie's Trs.* v. *Hope* (1836) 14 S. 578; *Brownlie* v. *Miller* (1880) 7 R. (H.L.) 66.

[61] *Lumsden* v. *Gordon* (1682) Mor. 16606; *Plenderleath* v. *Earl of Tweeddale* (1800) Mor. 16639; *Brownlie* v. *Miller, supra.*

[62] Erskine, II, iii, 31; Bell, *Prin.*, s. 895.

[63] (1835) 13 S. 844.

[64] (1894) 21 R. 769.

decision was against the pursuer in respect that the remedy sought was inappropriate, the opinions delivered indicated that a servitude of way in favour of a neighbour through the pursuer's garden might found a claim under warrandice. Clearly a servitude of passage which prevents the development of land purchased expressly for that purpose would found a claim on warrandice.[65]

(4) Destruction of the property by some natural cause, such as disappearance of an island in a river, or by *damnum fatale* such as fire. If the subjects so affected are let, the remedy of the tenant is not a claim under warrandice but abandonment of the lease on the principle of *rei interitus*.[66]

(5) Loss arising from supervenient legislation, where again in leasehold cases the remedy of the tenant is to abandon the lease.[67]

(6) It has been decided[68] that a lease of the property is not a burden which founds a claim under warrandice in a disposition of the subjects but, while this decision is in accordance with certain older authorities, the safe course in practice is to except existing leases from warrandice without prejudice to the right of the grantee to make any proper challenge of their validity which would not give the tenant a right of recourse against the granter, *e.g.* "And I grant warrandice but excepting from all warrandice the current lets and leases and all statutory rights of tenancy, occupancy or possession affecting the said subjects or any part thereof but without prejudice to the right of the said disponee and his foresaids to challenge or impugn the same on any ground in law not inferring warrandice against me." In *Wight* v. *Earl of Hopeton*[69] a disposition was granted with a clause of warrandice in effectively those terms and the purchaser was held to be personally barred from challenging a lease which by reason of having no definite ish was not valid against a singular successor of the landlord since the tenant could have recovered damages against the disponer/landlord under the warrandice contained in the lease. Such a provision will not protect a person having a personal right of possession which is not a lease against challenge of that right by a singular successor of the owner of the subjects.[70]

Qualifications of express warrandice—particular cases

4–39   In certain transactions it may be appropriate to qualify absolute warrandice by excepting from it existing burdens upon the land conveyed which the grantee is accepting, *e.g.* a disposition of a landed estate of which the whole or parts have been feued, when the clause normally

---

[65] *e.g.* as in *Armia Ltd.* v. *Daejan Developments Ltd.*, 1979 S.C. (H.L.) 56, although the issue was the right to resile from missives of purchase, not warrandice.
[66] *Duff* v. *Fleming* (1870) 8 M. 769.
[67] *Tay Salmon Fisheries Co. Ltd.* v. *Speedie*, 1929 S.C. 593; *Mackeson* v. *Boyd*, 1942 S.C. 56.
[68] *Lothian and Borders Farmers Ltd.* v. *McCutchion*, 1952 S.L.T. 450.
[69] (1763) Mor. 10461.
[70] *Mann* v. *Houston*, 1957 S.L.T. 89.

runs, "And I grant warrandice but excepting therefrom the existing feu rights but without prejudice to the right of the grantee to challenge or impugn the same on any ground in law not inferring warrandice against me [or my foresaids]." An exception in these terms will not protect existing feu rights which have not been made real by infeftment.[71] A similar qualification has already been mentioned as regards existing leases, although technically these may not be burdens.[72] Servitudes, at least if they are onerous, should similarly be excepted from warrandice. Likewise in a conveyance of land subject to heritable securities for which liability is being accepted by the purchaser, the securities should be excepted from the grant of absolute warrandice. In a grant of a standard security any prior or *pari passu* securities should be excepted or referred to.[73] Where a person agreed to sell "all his right and interest" in certain lands and stipulated that the warrandice should be from fact and deed only, it was decided that he was bound to grant a disposition of the lands, and not merely of his interest in them, with a clause of warrandice limited to fact and deed.[74] In leases of minerals it is usual to qualify warrandice to the effect that the existence or quality of the minerals, or the success of the trials, is not guaranteed but simply that, if the minerals are there, they are let in terms of the lease.[75]

Warrandice—moveable rights

4-40   In deeds creating obligations or assigning moveable property it is not usual to include a clause of express warrandice, the degree of warrandice implied being left to implication of law.

The styles of clause for simple[76] or fact and deed[77] warrandice, if expressed, have already been mentioned. If absolute warrandice is granted the clause may run "I bind myself to warrant these presents at all hands [and against all mortals as law will]."

Assignations

4-41   The warrandice granted in an assignation of a moveable debt requires care. The risk of the cedent becoming liable to the assignee in the event of any alteration having been made in the terms of the obligation assigned on the implied warrandice *debitum subesse* has already been noticed.[78] If a debt is assigned upon which the cedent has already done diligence a declaration should be inserted prohibiting the assignee from using the name and instance of the cedent in any further steps in

---

[71] *Ceres School Board* v. *McFarlane* (1895) 23 R. 279.
[72] See para. 4–38.
[73] Halliday, 1970 C. & F.R.A. 126, 127.
[74] *Hay* v. *Corporation of Aberdeen*, 1909 S.C. 554.
[75] Montgomerie Bell, *Lectures*, 1206.
[76] para. 4–30.
[77] para. 4–31.
[78] paras. 4–31, 4–37.

diligence, since otherwise the cedent might incur liability for any expenses awarded to the debtor.[79]

Discharges

4–42   In a discharge of a particular debt the warrandice, if expressed, is usually absolute. Where the discharge is combined with an assignation or retrocession of security the warrandice is absolute as regards the discharge and from fact and deed only as regards the assignation or retrocession.[80] In the case of a discharge and ratification by beneficiaries in favour of trustees at the close of administration of a trust the obligation to free and relieve the trustees of claims, with absolute warrandice, should be limited to the amount received by each granting beneficiary.

Contracts of sale, credit sale, conditional sale and hire-purchase

4–43   The warranties by a seller of goods or other corporeal moveables depend partly upon the express warranties in the contract of sale or hire-purchase and also upon the terms, including warranties, implied by statute.[81] The warranties implied by statute in such contracts differ in certain respects from warrandice in other deeds which are the subject of this chapter. The remedy under warrandice at common law consists in making good the loss, whereas in contracts of sale of goods or hire-purchase the remedy for material breach may lie in rejection of the goods and certain warranties cannot be excluded or the liability of the seller restricted in terms of statutory provisions. Warranties in contracts of sale and hire-purchase are considered when dealing with the terms of such contracts.[82]

Effect of warrandice

4–44   Warrandice is a contingent obligation which arises only upon eviction, partial or total, of the grantee from the right or property guaranteed. If, however, the ground of eviction is unquestionable and stems from the act of the granter of the warrandice himself, a claim under warrandice is prestable without waiting for eviction.[83] Moreover, if the granter disputes his liability under the obligation of warrandice the grantee is entitled to have that question determined immediately.[84] Where an action for reduction of the title warranted had been raised and the granter of the warrandice became bankrupt, it was held that the claimant under warrandice was entitled to be ranked as a contingent creditor

---

[79] Wood, *Lectures*, 582.
[80] Wood, *Lectures*, 601.
[81] Consumer Credit Act 1974; Unfair Contract Terms Act 1977; Sale of Goods Act 1979.
[82] See para. 8–07.
[83] Bell, *Prin.*, s. 895; *Smith* v. *Ross* (1672) Mor. 16596.
[84] *Lord Melville* v. *Erskine's Trs.* (1842) 4 D. 385; *Leith Heritages Co.* v. *Edinburgh and Leith Glass Co.* (1876) 3 R. 789.

on the bankrupt's estate and to have a dividend set aside to meet the contingent claim until the action of reduction had been finally decided.[85]

4–45 The claim available to the grantee under warrandice is to be relieved of the loss incurred by reason of the eviction; it does not entitle him to rescind the contract.[86] So where the price of teinds purchased from the Crown was unpaid and remained a burden on lands sold and payment was claimed from the purchaser by the Crown the seller was liable under warrandice to relieve the purchaser thereof.[87] Where a bond and disposition in security had been granted and, before it had been recorded, the subjects were sold to a purchaser who was unaware of the existence of the bond, and the purchaser without taking infeftment resold the subjects with absolute warrandice, the intermediate purchaser was found liable to relieve the ultimate purchaser of the burden of the security when it was recorded prior to the latter's title.[88] When a farm was let by a burgh with absolute warrandice reserving to the landlords the privilege of fishing by themselves or others having written authority from them and it was found that other parties had right to fish as members of the community and ratepayers of the burgh, damages were awarded to the tenant for partial eviction by way of a reduction in rent.[89] On the other hand warrandice warrants peaceful possession of the property and the sufficiency of the title to it, but does not guarantee any particular result in law, as in a case where subjects believed to have been held of the Crown were later ascertained to be held of a subject superior who exacted a casualty.[90]

4–46 It was decided in *Leith Heritages Co.* v. *Edinburgh and Leith Glass Co.*[91] that, in circumstances where a disposition had been granted with absolute warrandice and it was later discovered that the seller had no title to one parcel of the lands conveyed and the purchaser's agent admitted that he was aware of that fact when the disposition was prepared, the court was entitled, in considering a claim for breach of warrandice, to look beyond the technicalities of conveyancing language and to refuse the claim. This decision must be regarded as of doubtful authority, however, since it is inconsistent with the principle emphasised in later decisions of the House of Lords[92] that the disposition when accepted becomes the sole measure of the rights of the contracting parties and supersedes all previous communings. That principle has recently been reaffirmed in *Winston* v. *Patrick*,[92a] distinguishing earlier decisions where there were special circumstances where the principle

---

[85] *Fraser* v. *McIver* (1860) 22 D. 1190.
[86] *Welsh* v. *Russell* (1894) 21 R. 769.
[87] *Briggs' Trs.* v. *Dalyell* (1851) 14 D. 173.
[88] *Dewar* v. *Aitken* (1780) Mor. 16637.
[89] *Dougall* v. *Magistrates of Dunfermline*, 1908 S.C. 151.
[90] *Brownlie* v. *Miller*, 1880 7 R. (H.L.) 6.
[91] (1876) 3 R. 789.
[92] *Lee* v. *Alexander* (1883) 10 R. (H.L.) 91; *Orr* v. *Mitchell* (1893) 20 R. (H.L.) 27.
[92a] 1981 S.L.T. 41.

was modified by agreement—these are considered more fully in a later chapter dealing with the relationship between the contract of sale and the disposition.

Measure of damages

4–47   In *Cairns* v. *Howden*[93] the question was raised, but not decided, whether the measure of the claim under absolute warrandice in a case of total eviction was the price paid or the value of the subjects at the date of eviction. It would appear that the latter view is preferable,[94] but it may substantially increase the potential liability, particularly where land is sold for development when the value of the developed property may be many times the value of the undeveloped site conveyed. It also points to the advisability, in covering a defective title by an insurance indemnity, of providing an appropriate increase over the sale price to allow for the effect of inflation or the value of any development contemplated.

Transmissibility of obligation and claim

4–48   The obligation of the granter of warrandice is personal and, if a claim arises after the death of the granter, is prestable against his executors.[95] In special circumstances, where an obligation of absolute warrandice of a lease of fishings was granted by an heir of entail and expressed as binding the granter and his successors in the entailed lands, it was held that he had no legal right to bind succeeding heirs of entail and that the granter's executors were not liable since they derived no benefit under the lease.[96]

4–49   A successor of the purchaser is entitled to found on an obligation of warrandice granted to his predecessor in title by virtue of the clause of assignation of writs in the disposition in favour of the successor, and the original purchaser of the lands, even although he has ceased to own them, also has a title to sue.[97]

Course of action on threat of eviction

4–50   If eviction is threatened the grantee of the obligation of warrandice should notify the granter of it. The granter may elect to undertake the defence or he may leave the grantee to do so. In the latter event the grantee may decline to defend, at least where it is clear that there is no effective defence.[98] If the grantee defends the action it is prudent to keep the granter informed of the line of defence, lest he may

---

[93] (1870) 9 M. 284.
[94] Erskine, II, iii, 30; Bell, *Prin.*, s. 895; *Welsh* v. *Russell, supra, per* Lord McLaren at pp. 773, 774. See R. A. A. McCall-Smith, "An Aspect of Warrandice," 1972 S.L.T. (News) 41.
[95] *Duchess of Montrose* v. *Stuart* (1887) 15 R. (H.L.) 19.
[96] *Duke of Bedford* v. *Earl of Galloway's Tr.* (1904) 6 F. 971.
[97] *Christie* v. *Cameron* (1898) 25 R. 824.
[98] See *Welsh* v. *Russell, supra, per* Lord Kinnear at 775.

subsequently seek to avoid liability under warrandice on the ground that the defence was misconducted, although the success of such an argument would seem doubtful when he had declined to undertake the defence himself. If the defence succeeds the grantee is not entitled to recover the expenses of the defence; warrandice protects against eviction, but does not guarantee that no person will unsuccessfully challenge the grantee's right.[99] On the other hand if the defence fails the grantee is entitled to claim the loss suffered on eviction together with the expenses of the unsuccessful defence.[1]

Duration of obligation of warrandice—registered title

–51   If warrandice is granted in relation to a heritable right it is extinguished by the long negative prescription 20 years after the date when eviction occurs since that is the date when the obligation becomes enforceable.[2] For practical purposes, however, the limit of the granter's obligation as regards eviction is the expiry of the period of positive prescription upon a title recorded in the Register of Sasines, since the title of the grantee, when followed by peaceful possession without judicial interruption for that period, becomes unchallengeable. If the title is registered in the Land Register of Scotland subject to an exclusion of indemnity the position is similar; the exclusion of indemnity does not amount to eviction, and possession peaceably and without judicial interruption for the period of positive prescription effectively precludes challenge.[3] If the title is registered without exclusion of indemnity, however, the claim under warrandice of the registered proprietor or the holder of the competing title, as the case may be,[4] prescribes in 20 years from the date when the loss is incurred and the Keeper may enforce the claim within the same period by virtue of his right of subrogation.

Real warrandice

–52   Real warrandice consisted in the conveyance of other subjects as security against eviction from the subjects to which the warrandice applied: on eviction from the latter, the grantee of the warrandice acquired a right of entry to the security subjects. It was implied in contracts of excambion. This form of warrandice is now obsolete. The Conveyancing (Scotland) Act 1924[5] made it incompetent to dispone lands in real warrandice of a conveyance of other lands on or after January 1, 1925, and provided that real warrandice would not arise *ex lege* from any contract or agreement entered into after that date.

---

[99] Montgomerie Bell, *Lectures*, 219; *Inglis* v. *Anstruther* (1771) Mor. 16633.
[1] *Dougall* v. *Magistrates of Dunfermline*, 1908 S.C. 151. *Cf. Stephen* v. *Lord Advocate* (1878) 6 R. 282.
[2] Prescription and Limitation (Scotland) Act 1973, s. 7.
[3] *Ibid.*, s. 1 as amended by Land Registration (Scotland) Act 1979, s. 10.
[4] See para. 4–35.
[5] s. 14(1).

(2) Registration for Preservation and Execution

(a) Introduction

4-53   Registration of deeds or writs may be effected for three distinct purposes, for preservation, for execution or for publication. The object of registration for preservation is to ensure that important deeds are preserved safely in a public register from which extracts (official copies) may be issued which are of equivalent legal effect to the principals. Registration for execution is designed to facilitate and expedite the enforcement of obligations constituted in a probative deed by way of a consent of the obligant inserted in the deed to registration of it for execution which dispenses with the need for court action and authorises a summary form of diligence. Registration for publication relates to deeds affecting land and serves the double purpose of making rights to and burdens or securities upon land real and providing public information regarding them.

4-54   The origins and development of registration for preservation and registration for execution are closely linked and may be conveniently treated together. Registration for publication has a quite separate history and is now in course of being superseded by registration of title—it is considered separately in relation to heritable conveyancing.

(b) Registration for execution

4-55   **History.** Registration for execution originated earlier than registration for preservation, the latter being a development which arose out of the former. The original objective of a clause of consent to registration for execution was to enable the creditor in a specific obligation contained in a formal deed to enforce that obligation, without the expense and possible delay of pursuing an action for implement in court, simply by presenting the deed constituting the obligation and containing the consent to the appropriate court of law which would then, in respect of the formal undertaking which the debtor could not evade, pronounce a decree of implement. In the early developments of the concept the clause obliged the debtor to appear in court and consent to decree, later it took the form of a mandate by the debtor to a named procurator to appear in court and consent to decree on behalf of the debtor, then the practice became to leave the name of the mandatory blank and ultimately the procuratory disappeared leaving only a simple consent to registration for execution.[6]

4-56   **Recording ad longum.** In accordance with the custom of recording a decree of court *ad longum* in the court books, it was and remains the

---

[6] For a fuller account of the history of registration for execution, see Menzies, *Lectures*, 183–188; *Encyclopaedia of the Laws of Scotland*, Vol. 12, pp. 363–367.

practice, when a deed containing a consent to registration for execution is presented for registration, that the deed upon which the court relies is engrossed at length in the court books as a preamble to the decree which implements the obligation contained in the deed. So registration for execution involves registration of the whole deed in the court books and an extract is issued which contains the text of the whole deed and the decree of the court authorising implement is appended to it. As to the form of the extract and the appended decree which authorises diligence in modern practice, see paragraph 4–67 *infra*.

4–57 **Registration after death of creditor or debtor.** The theoretical concept of consent to registration for execution required that both the creditor[7] and the debtor[8] should be living, but that requirement was statutorily removed *quoad* both the creditor[9] and the debtor,[10] and registration for execution is competent even when either of the original parties is deceased. These statutes only authorised registration after the death of either party: further procedure is necessary as regards diligence in such circumstances—see paragraphs 4–68, 4–72 and 4–73 *infra*.

(c) Registration for preservation

4–58 **History.** Shortly after the process of registration of deeds for execution became established it was appreciated that it was in the interests of the parties to any deed of importance to have the principal registered and preserved in a public register from which official extracts could be obtained when required. If a deed was registered for execution the fact that it was automatically so preserved was an incidental benefit, and so, even when execution was not contemplated, the practice arose of recording deeds in the registers of the courts simply for preservation.

4–59 Originally a procuratory or clause of consent to registration for preservation required to be inserted in the deed, probably from an imperfect analogy with that requirement in the case of registration for execution, but it was soon evident that there was no need for such consent since no additional powers, such as that of doing summary diligence, resulted from the safe preservation of a deed recording obligations and rights to which all the parties concerned had formally agreed. The Registration Act 1698 (c. 4) provided that it would be lawful to register probative writs for conservation in any public register competent, without a clause of registration contained in the writs. The Act provided for the principal writ to be returned to the ingiver and that an extract would make entire faith in the same manner as if the writs had been registered by virtue of a clause of registration, except in the case of improbation. The Registration of Writs (Scotland) Act 1868 altered the

---

[7] *Channel* v. *Seton* (1693) Mor. 839.
[8] *Brown* v. *Binnie* (1635) Mor. 14994.
[9] Registration Act 1693 (c. 15).
[10] Registration Act 1696 (c. 39).

practice of returning the principal writ to the ingiver and prohibited the giving up of a writ given in for registration in the Books of Council and Session, whether before or after it had been booked, except with the express authority of the Lords of Council and Session under such conditions and limitations as were expressed in that authority, and the giving out of writs given in to be registered in any register was also prohibited. The circumstances in which and the conditions upon which writs given in for registration may be given out by authority of the court are treated in paragraph 4–70 *infra*.

(d) Registration for preservation and execution

4–60   **Form and effect of clause.** Short forms of clauses of consent to registration for preservation, or for preservation and execution, were prescribed by various statutes now consolidated in the Titles to Land Consolidation (Scotland) Act 1868,[11] the statutory form being, "And I consent to registration hereof for preservation" or "for preservation and execution." In any deed, whether relating to land or not, the statutory clause, unless specially qualified, imports "a consent to registration and a procuratory of resignation in the Books of Council and Session, or other judges' books competent, therein to remain for preservation; and also, if for execution, that letters of horning, and all necessary execution shall pass thereon, upon six days' charge, on a decree to be interponed thereto in common form."[12] The consent to registration for preservation is unnecessary and in standard securities the form of clause prescribed reads simply, "And I consent to registration for execution,"[13] and is defined as importing, unless specially qualified, a consent to registration in the Books of Council and Session, or, as the case may be, in the books of the appropriate sheriff court, for execution.[14]

4–61   **Registers competent.** Registration for preservation or execution is competent in either the Books of Council and Session or the books of the appropriate sheriff court,[15] save that feu charters by subject superiors[16] and minutes of resignation by trustees[17] may be registered only in the Books of Council and Session. The consent to registration may specify a particular register, in which case registration can be effected only in that register, but such a restriction is seldom imposed in practice.

4–62   **Jurisdiction.** A consent to registration for execution in its general form authorises registration in either of the registers above mentioned. Registration in the Books of Council and Session may be effected when the granter of the obligation resides in Scotland or is otherwise subject to

---

[11] Scheds. B and FF (No. 1).
[12] 1868 Act, s. 138.
[13] Conveyancing and Feudal Reform (Scotland) Act 1970, Sched. 2, Form A.
[14] s. 10(3).
[15] Act 49 Geo. III, c. 42 (1809).
[16] Act 1693 c. 35.
[17] Trusts (Scotland) Act 1921, s. 19.

the jurisdiction of the Court of Session, and diligence may proceed upon the decree of registration by messenger-at-arms, not by sheriff officer, anywhere in Scotland. Registration in the sheriff court books, however, is competent only if the granter of the obligation is designed in the deed as residing within the jurisdiction of the court from which the extract decree is to be issued and he still resides within that jurisdiction when the registration decree is enforced. If the granter has changed his residence to another jurisdiction then diligence may be done by sheriff officer only after presenting the extract decree of registration with a minute endorsed thereon to the Petition Department of the Court of Session or to the sheriff within whose jurisdiction the granter now resides and obtaining a *fiat ut petitur* or a warrant of concurrence.[18]

–63 Judgments extension—recognition. Until recently an extract of a writ registered in the Books of Council and Session with a warrant for diligence appended, being equivalent to a decree of the Court of Session, could be enforced in England and Northern Ireland in accordance with the provisions of the Judgments Extension Act 1868, whereas an extract of a writ registered in the sheriff court books could not be so enforced since the Inferior Courts Judgments Extension Act 1882 contained no corresponding provision. Section 4 of the Civil Jurisdiction and Judgments Act 1982 (which repeals the Acts of 1868 and 1882) now provides for the enforcement of judgments of the Court of Session or the sheriff court in such matters in any other of the contracting states of the European Economic Community.

–64 Writs which may competently be registered for execution. Subject to the exception of certain documents undermentioned,[19] it is competent to register for execution only probative writs[20] which contain a consent to registration for execution.[21] Moreover, an obligation for payment of money constituted by the writ must be sufficiently definite as to amount and time of payment and identification of the creditor and debtor that it could properly be incorporated in a court decree. If the obligation expressed in the writ is for payment of an indefinite sum, as in the case of a bond of cash credit or a personal bond for all moneys due on accounts with a bank, the obligation may be made specific if the writ contains provision for the conclusive ascertainment of the amount due at any particular time, as by a certificate of the creditor or an officer of the creditor bank. In such cases the writ may be presented for registration along with the certificate (the latter does not require to be registered) when a warrant authorising summary diligence in respect of the amount stated in the certificate will be issued.[22] A provision in a writ

---

[18] Debtors (Scotland) Act 1838, s. 13.
[19] See para. 4–66.
[20] *Carnoway* v. *Ewing* (1611) Mor. 14988.
[21] *Erskine* (1710) Mor. 14997; Titles to Land Consolidation (Scotland) Act 1868, s. 138.
[22] *Fisher* v. *Syme & Stewart* (1828) 7 S. 97; *Paisley Union Bank* v. *Hamilton* (1831) 9 S. 488.

that a stated account certified by the specified officer would constitute the amount due does not preclude the debtor from showing that the amount so certified is erroneous.[23] An obligation to pay on a future indeterminate date cannot be enforced by summary diligence but if the obligation is to pay on a future fixed date a warrant for summary diligence may be obtained qualified by the words "the terms of payment being always first come and bygone."[24] Summary diligence is competent in the sheriff court against a partnership under a firm or trading or descriptive name[25] and against the individual partners[26] but not against a person who is not a partner although he may have incurred liability on the principle of holding out.[27]

4–65   An obligation *ad factum praestandum* may be enforced by registration for execution of a probative writ which constitutes it, provided that the obligation is sufficiently precise that it could be made the subject of a decree requiring performance of a specified act; a charge against the tenant upon an extract registered lease of a farm to implement the whole obligations of the lease was held incompetent.[28]

4–66   Writs registrable for execution without clause of consent. Bonds or obligations in favour of the Crown may be registered for execution as if they contain a clause of consent to registration for execution, and diligence is competent thereon as upon a probative bond containing such a clause.[29] Summary diligence is also competent upon bills of exchange and promissory notes,[30] but not upon cheques.[31] For the requirements as to the validity of a bill of exchange upon the protest of which summary diligence may follow see the undernoted text.[31a]

4–67   Warrants for execution of summary diligence. When an extract of a deed or writ containing a consent to registration for execution has been registered in the Books of Council and Session or in the books of the appropriate sheriff court the keeper or assistant keeper of the register or the sheriff clerk, as the case may be, inserts at the end of the extract a warrant in the form: "And the said Lords grant [*or* the Sheriff grants] warrant for all lawful execution hereon." Warrants for execution inserted in extracts of protests of bills of exchange or promissory notes are as nearly as may be in the same form.[32] Such warrants upon extracts of deeds or protests authorise diligence against the debtor's moveable estate[33]; if it

---

[23] *Smith* v. *Drummond* (1829) 7 S. 792.
[24] Debtors (Scotland) Act 1838, Sched. 1.
[25] Sheriff Courts (Scotland) Act 1907, r. 14(1).
[26] *Drew* v. *Lumsden* (1865) 3 M. 384.
[27] *Brember* v. *Rutherford* (1901) 4 F. 62.
[28] *Hendry* v. *Marshall* (1878) 5 R. 687.
[29] Exchequer Court (Scotland) Act 1856, s. 38.
[30] Bills of Exchange Act 1681; Inland Bills Act 1696; Bills of Exchange (Scotland) Act 1772; Bills of Exchange Act 1882, s. 98.
[31] *Glickman* v. *Linda*, 1950 S.C. 18.
[31a] Wilson, *Law of Scotland relating to Debt*, 240.
[32] Writs Execution (Scotland) Act 1877, ss. 1, 2 and Sched.
[33] *Ibid.*, s. 3.

is proposed to do diligence against the debtor's heritable property application for letters of diligence must be made.

-68 Changes in creditor or debtor. The procedure outlined above for registration of a deed or writ for execution is competent, save for the exception aftermentioned, only if the creditor and debtor are those named in the deed. If the original creditor has died or assigned the deed before it has been registered for execution, his executor or the assignee, as the case may be, must register the deed and obtain an extract and then apply to the Petition Department of the Court of Session for letters of horning.[34] If the creditor dies or assigns the deed after it has been registered for execution, the confirmation should contain or the assignation should assign the extract decree and the executor or assignee may then present the extract together with the confirmation or the assignation to the Petition Department or the sheriff clerk and obtain a *fiat ut petitur* or warrant of concurrence.[35] If a charge has been given the execution of the charge should also be produced. If the original debtor has died summary diligence is incompetent and the debt must be constituted against his executors by ordinary action.[36] There is an exception to this rule in the case of a heritable security where either (i) a person has taken the security subjects by a conveyance containing *in gremio* an agreement that the personal obligation in the security shall transmit against him and the conveyance has been signed by him, or (ii) a person has taken the security subjects by succession, gift or bequest and an agreement has been executed by that person to the transmission of the personal obligation against him.[37]

-69 Diligence against heritable property. An extract decree of registration for execution authorises summary diligence only against the debtor's moveable property. If it is proposed to do diligence against the debtor's heritable property it is necessary to raise the appropriate form of action, *e.g.* adjudication or maills and duties.

-70 Withdrawal of writ presented for registration. The Registration of Writs (Scotland) Act 1868[38] prohibited the giving up of a writ which had been presented for registration in the Books of Council and Session, whether before or after it had been booked, except with the express authority of the Lords of Council and Session. In one case a testamentary deed was given in to be recorded after the death of the granter, but, before booking, a clerical error was discovered in the testing clause and the principal beneficiary and the solicitor by whom it had been prepared petitioned the court to allow access to the deed for adding certain words to the

---

[34] *Mitchell* v. *St. Mungo Lodge of Ancient Shepherds*, 1916 S.C. 689.
[35] Debtors (Scotland) Act 1838, ss. 7, 12 and Scheds. 5, 9.
[36] *Kippen* v. *Hill* (1822) 2 S. 105.
[37] Conveyancing (Scotland) Act 1874, s. 47; Conveyancing (Scotland) Act 1924, s. 15, applied to standard securities by the Conveyancing and Feudal Reform (Scotland) Act 1970, s. 32.
[38] s. 1—see para. 4–59.

testing clause. The court, without pronouncing any judgment as to the effect of the proposed amendment, authorised it to be made at the sight of the keeper of the register, but it was questioned whether an amendment could competently be allowed upon any part of the deed other than the testing clause.[39] In a subsequent case the court permitted an unbooked deed to be withdrawn in order that it might be signed by the instrumentary witnesses in the presence of the Keeper of the Register of Deeds.[40] Withdrawal of the principal writ after it has been booked may be permitted, but only if the court is satisfied that it is necessary in the interests of justice and that the production of an extract is insufficient.[41] Withdrawal may be allowed where the validity of the document is challenged on the ground of forgery or other matters which depend upon the examination of the original document.[42]

4–71 **Summary of practice in registration for execution.** *(i) Original debtor and original creditor.* The deed containing the consent to registration for execution is presented to the Keeper of the Books of Council and Session or the sheriff clerk. The deed is registered and an extract containing a full copy of the deed is issued with a warrant authorising all lawful execution thereon.[43]

4–72 *(ii) Change in creditor.* As to the procedure where there has been a change in the creditor, see paragraph 4–68 *supra.* In practice, if the deed is being assigned after it has been registered, the extract of the deed *and* the decree should both be assigned. If the deed has not been registered the original creditor should be asked to register it and then assign the extract and the decree. A minute may then be endorsed on the extract and presented to the Court of Session or the appropriate sheriff clerk[44] producing the assignation and any prior writs constituting the assignee's title, when the clerk will subjoin *fiat ut petitur* with the date and his signature and will date and initial each production. If the original creditor is deceased and the deed has been registered, the confirmation should include both the deed and the decree of registration, when the executor may adopt the procedure by minute as outlined above. If the confirmation does not include the decree an eik should be obtained which does so. If the deed has not been registered before the death of the original creditor his executor may register it but must then apply to the Petition Department for letters of horning and poinding; summary diligence is incompetent. Where there has been a change in personnel of the original trustees who were the creditors, as by deed of assumption or a statutory provision substituting successors, summary diligence is not competent and the new trustees must proceed by way of letters of

---

[39] *Caldwell* (1871) 10 M. 99.
[40] *Murray* (1904) 6 F. 840.
[41] *Western Bank & Liquidators* (1868) 6 M. 656.
[42] *Chenevix-Trench*, 1917 S.C. 168 and other cases there cited.
[43] The form of warrant is prescribed in the Schedule to the Writs Execution (Scotland) Act 1877.
[44] The form of minute is prescribed in No. 5 of the Schedule to the Debtors (Scotland) Act 1838.

horning,[45] but *quaere* whether that is necessary where the creditors are survivors of the original trustees whose succession is automatic in terms of the original deed.

4–73 *(iii) Change in debtor.* The foregoing procedures are applicable only where there has been no change in the original debtor. If the original debtor is deceased summary diligence is incompetent and the debt must be constituted against his representative by ordinary action.[46]

4–74 *(iv) Heritable securities.* In heritable securities where a new debtor has undertaken the personal obligation upon purchase of, or succession to, the security subjects summary diligence is competent if the new debtor has signed a bond of corroboration containing a consent to registration for execution or has consented to the personal obligation transmitting against him by a provision in the conveyance of the subjects to him on the lines of Form No. 2 of Schedule A to the Conveyancing (Scotland) Act 1924 and has signed the conveyance or, where the new debtor has taken the security subjects by succession, gift or bequest, he has executed an agreement to the transmission of the obligation against him.[47] When the obligation has transmitted against the new proprietor under the 1874 Act as amended by the 1924 Act the creditor may present a minute to the Petition Department of the Court of Session or the appropriate sheriff clerk in the form prescribed in Schedule K to the 1874 Act, when the clerk to the court or the sheriff clerk will append *fiat ut petitur* with the date and his signature, upon which summary diligence may proceed. In relation to the statutory transmission of the personal obligation in a heritable security the following points should be noted. (1) It is not necessary that the original bond or standard security has been registered for execution but it must have contained a consent to registration for that purpose. (2) The procedure is available only against a person who has acquired the security subjects from the original debtor and is, at the time when the minute is presented, the proprietor of those subjects.[48] (3) It follows that it is not available for diligence against the representatives of an original debtor who is deceased (unless they have signed an agreement to transmission of the obligation against them) or by a derivative creditor against the original debtor.[49] (4) Since the warrant craved in the minute is only to charge, it is doubtful whether it would authorise arrestment or poinding.[49] (5) The procedure is available to an assignee of the original creditor[50] who must refer in the minute to the assignation by which he acquired right to the security. Burns[51] expresses the view that it is unnecessary to refer to the writs,

---

[45] *Mitchell* v. *St. Mungo Lodge of Ancient Shepherds*, 1916 S.C. 689.
[46] *Kippen* v. *Hill* (1822) 2 S. 105.
[47] 1924 Act, s. 15 amending Conveyancing (Scotland) Act 1874, s. 47.
[48] See form in Sched. K to 1874 Act.
[49] Burns, 45.
[50] Sched. K to 1874 Act.
[51] at 47.

other than the last one, whereby the assignee acquired title to the security, but this seems doubtful in view of the terms of Schedule K which requires specification of the assignation "or other writ or writs forming the title in the creditor's person," and it is thought that the safer course is to mention the whole series of writs whereby the title of the new creditor was acquired. (6) When the procedure is used by the executor of the original creditor it is suggested that the executor should have completed title by infeftment and that the minute should narrate the confirmation and notice of title.[52] (7) The original deed constituting the security or an extract of it from the Books of Council and Session or the Register of Sasines and the other writs (if any) forming the creditor's title to the security must be produced along with the minute.[53]

4–75   **Registration for publication combined with registration for preservation and/or execution.** Where a deed may be recorded in the Register of Sasines for publication it may also be registered in the Books of Council and Session for preservation and, if it contains the necessary consent, for execution. The warrant of registration placed on the deed should state the extent of registration required, thus: "Register on behalf of the within named A.B. for preservation [*or* for preservation and execution] as well as for publication in the Register of the County of X."[54] The principal deed is retained in the register and an extract or extracts are issued: the deed is recorded at length in the Register of Sasines and is indexed in the Books of Council and Session. If a deed has originally been registered for preservation and publication only, an extract of it may subsequently, if the deed contained a consent to registration for execution, be registered for that purpose. The extract is presented bearing a warrant of registration for preservation and execution and an extract will be issued with the required warrant for execution thereon.[55]

4–76   **Registration for execution in relation to registration of title.** If a deed which contains a consent to registration for execution is submitted to the Keeper in the process of registration of a title in the Land Register and it is desired also to register the deed for execution, the applicant should so instruct the Keeper in a covering letter which should state also the number of extracts required. An extract or extracts having the necessary warrant for execution will then be issued. If a title has been registered but registration for execution has not been requested at that time, the deed containing the consent to registration will be returned by the Keeper along with other documents submitted in support of the application for registration in the Land Register. The deed should be retained with the land certificate and if subsequently it is desired to do

---

[52] See Sched. K.
[53] As to practice where the title to the security has been registered in the Land Register, see para. 4–76.
[54] Land Registers (Scotland) Act 1868, s. 12 and Sched. A (No. 3), as amended by Conveyancing (Scotland) Act 1924, Note 2 to Sched. F.
[55] Writs Execution (Scotland) Act 1877, s. 6.

summary diligence the principal deed[56] may be presented with a warrant of registration for preservation and execution endorsed thereon when an extract with a warrant authorising summary diligence will be issued.[57] If the deed is a standard security in respect of which a charge certificate has been issued, the charge certificate to which the original standard security has been attached should be returned to the Keeper who will remove the standard security, register it in the Books of Council and Session and thereafter re-issue the charge certificate with the extract from the Books of Council and Session authorising summary diligence attached.[58]

---

[56] An office copy provided under s. 6(5) of the Land Registration (Scotland) Act 1979 is not acceptable for this purpose.

[57] The provisions of s. 6 of the Writs Execution (Scotland) Act 1877 are not affected by registration of title: Land Registration (Scotland) Act 1979, Sched. 3.

[58] R.T.P.B. s. D. 1.25.

PART II

MOVEABLE CONVEYANCING

Introduction

5–01   The document traditionally used for the creation of a relatively long-term obligation of debt, with intermediate interest, was the personal bond. It is still used in its original or an abbreviated form for that purpose and is of conveyancing importance since it is the basic style employed for the creation of obligations, both pecuniary and for performance, in many deeds relating both to moveable and heritable property. A simpler type of document creating an obligation for payment or repayment of money, normally used when implement is contemplated within a shorter period, is the IOU. Documents which constitute a primary obligation for payment of money, such as a personal bond, a bond of annuity, a bond of cash credit or an IOU are considered in this chapter. Documents which create secondary or contingent obligations of debt are treated in Chapter 6.

I. Personal Bond

History

5–02   Until the Reformation the laws against usury prohibited the taking of interest upon money and various devices such as the sale of annual rents from land were employed to circumvent the prohibition. The normal form of document creating an obligation of debt, without interest, was the ticket, which contained a brief statement that the granter was justly addebted to the grantee in a stated sum with an obligation upon the granter and his heirs, successors and executors to make payment to the grantee, his heirs or assignees on a specified date under penalty in case of failure. The Act 1587 c. 52 recognised the commercial sense of lending money at interest and permitted such transactions with interest at 10 per cent. Thereafter the personal bond was evolved containing the form of acknowledgment of indebtedness in the ticket, specification of the date of payment under penalty and payment of interest until that date.[1]

Style

5–03   The full traditional form of personal bond for money lent is:

I, A (*designed*) grant me to have instantly borrowed and received from B (*designed*) the sum of £   Sterling, which sum I bind and oblige myself, my executors and representatives whomsoever all jointly and severally without the necessity of discussing them in their order to repay to the said B, his executors or assignees whomsoever, at the term of Whitsunday next within (*place of payment*), with a fifth part more of liquidate penalty in case of failure, and the interest of the said principal sum at the rate of   per centum per annum from the date hereof to the said term of payment and half-yearly, termly and proportionally thereafter during the non-payment thereof, and that at two terms in the year, Whitsunday and Martinmas, by equal portions, beginning the first payment of the said interest at the term of Whitsunday next for the interest due preceding that date, and the next term's payment thereof at Martinmas following and so forth half-yearly, termly and proportionally thereafter during the non-payment of the principal sum, with a fifth part more of the interest due at each term of liquidate penalty in case of failure in the punctual payment thereof: And I consent to registration for preservation and execution. (*To be attested*)

Parties—variations

5–04   (a) **Several obligants.** A bond by several granters bound jointly and severally may run:

We, A, B and C (*all designed*) grant us to have instantly borrowed and received from D (*designed*) the sum of £   , which sum we bind ourselves jointly and severally and our respective executors and assignees whomsoever all jointly and severally without the necessity of discussing them in their order to repay *etc.*

---

[1] For a fuller account see Menzies, *Lectures*, 216–222.

The word "severally" creates liability *in solidum*,[2] but other expressions have the same result, *e.g.* the phrase normally used "jointly and severally,"[3] or "conjunctly and severally,"[4] or "as co-principals and full debtors,"[5] or "as full debtors."[6] *Pro rata* liability is implied if the obligants are bound simply or in terms *pro rata*, but "jointly"[7] or "conjunctly,"[8] used alone, or "each for his own part"[9] also infer that the liability is *pro rata*.

If the obligants are to be bound only *pro rata* (which is less advantageous to the creditor but may occasionally be acceptable) the operative provision may be:

> bind and oblige ourselves, each *pro rata* [and for equal proportions of the said sum] *or* [to the extent of £   ] and interest thereon only" and our respective executors and representatives whomsoever without the necessity of discussing them in their order to repay *etc.*

5–05   If the obligants are bound jointly and severally, the fact that one of them does not sign, or that some defect in the bond so far as relating to the obligation of any of the granters renders it unenforceable against him, releases the other granters from liability under the bond.[10] The same result does not follow when the obligants undertake liability *pro rata* each for a specified sum, but may do so if their liability is for equal shares of a total sum since the loss of one co-obligant increases the liability of the others. Co-obligants in a joint and several obligation may be released if the creditor discharges one of them without the consent of the others,[11] but it may not necessarily have that result: when the bond was granted and delivered the right of relief amongst the granters *inter se* was effectively created and may not be lost by a unilateral discharge of one of them by the creditor.[12] The sequestration of one of the co-granters of a bond does not release the others from liability,[13] but accession by the creditor to a trust deed for creditors by one of the co-granters, if not assented to by the others, may do so. Other acts by the creditor without the consent of the co-obligants may affect the enforceability of the bond, *e.g.* giving time or releasing a security. For provisions that may be inserted in the bond with a view to preventing the

---

[2] Montgomerie Bell, *Lectures*, 262.

[3] Bell, *Prin.*, s. 56; *Fleming* v. *Gemmill*, 1908 S.C. 340.

[4] *Police Commissioners of Dundee* v. *Straton* (1884) 11 R. 586; *Burns* v. *Martin* (1887) 14 R. (H.L.) 20.

[5] *Cleghorn* v. *Yorston* (1707) Mor. 14624.

[6] *Cloberhill* v. *Ladyland* (1631) Mor. 14623.

[7] *Coats* v. *Union Bank of Scotland*, 1928 S.C. 711; 1929 S.C. (H.L.) 114.

[8] *Campbell* v. *Farquhar* (1724) Mor. 14626.

[9] Bell, *Comm.*, I, 362.

[10] *Paterson* v. *Bonar* (1844) 6 D. 987; *Scottish Provincial Assurance Co.* v. *Pringle* (1858) 20 D. 465. These decisions related to cautioners but the principle seems applicable to joint and several obligations generally: each granter was entitled to contribution from the others and his liability may be significantly enlarged if he does not have that right against one of them.

[11] *Morgan* v. *Smart* (1872) 10 M. 610, but involving a special provision in relation to cautioners in the Mercantile Law Amendment Act 1856, s. 9.

[12] See Wilson, *Law of Scotland Relating to Debt*, 149.

[13] Bankruptcy (Scotland) Act 1913, s. 52.

release of the granters in various circumstances see the *Encyclopaedia of Scottish Legal Styles*, Volume 2, page 4.

5–06 **(b) Partnerships.** A bond by a firm may be granted simply in the firm name, which has the effect of binding the firm and the partners jointly and severally,[14] but the better practice is to make the liability expressly joint and several by the firm and its partners so that summary diligence may be competent against each or all of them, thus:

> We, the firm of A B & Co. (*designed*), and we, A, B and C (*all designed*), the individual partners of the said firm as such partners and as trustees[15] for the said firm and as individuals grant us to have instantly borrowed and received from D (*designed*) the sum of £ , which sum we the said firm of A B & Co., bind and oblige ourselves and our successors and we the said A, B and C bind and oblige ourselves as such partners and trustees and as individuals and our respective executors and representatives whomsoever, all without the necessity of discussing them in their order, and all the obligations hereby undertaken being joint and several, to repay *etc.*

5–07 A bond in favour of a firm may be granted in favour of the firm *socio nomine*, without mention of the partners, but it must be kept in view that if the firm alters by reason of changes in the personnel of the partners an assignation may be necessary as a preliminary to court action to enforce the obligation. As to summary diligence in such circumstances see paragraph 4–68 *supra*. Alternatively the bond may be written in favour of partners as trustees for the firm, in which case it is thought that the named partners as trustees may sue and do diligence notwithstanding a change in the firm since the fact that the beneficiaries in a trust have altered does not affect the title of the trustees to recover an asset of the trust.

5–08 When a business is carried on by a sole partner there is no separate legal *persona*. Bonds by or in favour of the partner may run in the name of the individual designed as "carrying on the business of under the name of X Y & Co. at (*address*)," but where the bond is for all moneys due on a running account it may be preferable to design the granter without reference to his business in order to avoid any implication that the obligation relates only to sums advanced for the purposes of the business.

5–09 **(c) Companies.** A bond granted by an incorporated company runs in the registered name of the company (*designed*) and binds the company, itself and its successors jointly and severally and its capital, stock and assets. If directors are required to join personally in the obligation the style may be modelled on that in paragraph 5–06 *supra*. Bonds in favour of a company are granted in favour of the company (*designed*) and its successors and assignees.

---

[14] Partnership Act 1890, s. 9.
[15] There may be assets such as heritable property which are held by partners as trustees for the firm.

5–10   **(d) Trustees**. Trustees who grant personal bonds for money borrowed for the purposes of the trust should not bind themselves personally; the obligation should be created against the trustees and their successors in office in their fiduciary capacity and the trust estate under their charge, thus:

> We, A, B and C (*all designed*), the trustees acting under (*specify deed of trust*), grant us to have instantly borrowed and received for the purposes of the said (*deed of trust*) from D (*designed*) the sum of £   , which sum we bind ourselves and our successors as trustees foresaid, but not personally or individually, and the trust estate under our charge, jointly and severally without the necessity of discussing them in their order to repay *etc.*

Bonds in favour of trustees should be granted in favour of the trustees as such, specifying the deed of trust under which they act, and their successors in office as trustees.

Narrative

5–11   The word "instantly" is appropriate where the money passes against delivery of the bond. If the money has been advanced previously the wording is adjusted appropriately, *e.g.* "I, A (*designed*) acknowledge that I owe to B (*designed*) the sum of £   ," perhaps with an indication of the account or transaction whereby the indebtedness arose, *e.g.* "being the balance due to him on a trading account for goods supplied."[16] If the money has been advanced partly before and partly against delivery, "instantly" should be replaced by "now and formerly." If the transaction is not one of loan the acknowledgment of borrowing and receiving will be omitted; the obligation will simply be to make payment.

Operative clause

5–12   This clause gives the deed its distinctive character, as compared with a mere acknowledgment of debt, and constitutes an undertaking to repay with interest subsisting until discharged or otherwise extinguished. The amount and the interest should be specific or ascertainable in terms of the deed so that registration for execution may be competent on default.

Debtor's succession

5–13   If the granter of the bond is deceased when the obligation thereunder is enforced the creditor may sue the debtor's executor or his representatives, *i.e.* the persons who benefit from the debtor's estate, who are bound jointly and severally without the benefit of discussion. Normally

---

[16] As to the consequences of misstating an existing indebtedness to be an instant advance in affecting onus of proof and precluding summary diligence, see *Keith* v. *Cairney*, 1916 1 S.L.T. 245; 1917 1 S.L.T. 202.

the creditor will elect to proceed against the executor of the debtor who will have the whole free assets of the estate available to meet the claim. After the expiry of six months from the date of the debtor's death his executor is bound to pay any debt properly due *primo venienti*[17] and if he makes payment to beneficiaries without providing for all debts actually due and known to him he incurs personal liability to the creditors.[18] The creditor in the bond may elect to pursue the beneficiaries, who as representatives of the deceased debtor are bound severally by the obligation, but can only recover from them to the extent that they have respectively benefited from the debtor's estate.[19] The renunciation of the benefit of discussion was formerly of importance in respect that in its absence the creditor was bound to observe a particular order in proceeding against the heirs to the heritable property of the debtor.[20] It is now of less importance since the whole estate of the debtor, both heritable and moveable, vests in his executor and the creditor will usually pursue the executor for payment. The renunciation may still be of value, however, if for any reason the creditor wishes to proceed first against a representative of the deceased debtor who has taken heritable property by virtue of a special destination in circumstances where a debt created by the deceased may be enforced against the person succeeding under the destination.[21] When the benefit of discussion is renounced the creditor may proceed against the representatives of the deceased debtor, whether they have succeeded to moveable or heritable estate, in any order and, although that result would probably follow from the obligation binding the debtor and his representatives jointly and severally,[22] it is advisable that the benefit of discussion be expressly renounced.

Creditor's succession

5–14   Originally rights of a long-term character were regarded as heritable and so a personal bond, after the first term when payment could have been required was past, was heritable in the succession of the creditor. Up to that date it was moveable since the creditor might have contemplated enforcing repayment at that time and it was not yet clear that a long-term investment was intended,[23] and a bond which contained no

---

[17] *Taylor & Ferguson Ltd.* v. *Glass's Trs.*, 1912 S.C. 165.

[18] *Lamond's Trs.* v. *Croom* (1871) 9 M. 662; *Heritable Securities Investment Association* v. *Miller's Trs.* (1893) 20 R. 675.

[19] *Welch's Exrs.* v. *Edinburgh Life Assurance Co.* (1896) 23 R. 772. The decision turned on the construction of s. 12 of the Conveyancing (Scotland) Act 1874 relating to the liability of heirs in heritage but the principle applies: beneficiaries are representatives of the debtor only to the extent that they benefit from his estate and he had no power to obligate them further.

[20] See Burns, 19.

[21] *e.g.* where the destination was contained in a title to feudal property (*Renouf's Trs.* v. *Haining*, 1919 S.C. 497, 507; *Steele* v. *Caldwell*, 1979 S.L.T. 228) but not in a title to leasehold property (*Robertson's Tr.* v. *Roberts*, 1982 S.L.T. 22).

[22] *Burns* v. *Martin* (1887) 14 R. (H.L.) 20, 25.

[23] *Gray* v. *Walker* (1859) 21 D. 709.

provision for payment of interest was moveable.[24] The common law was altered by the Act 1641 c. 57, re-enacted by the Bonds Act 1661 c. 32, which provided that bonds containing an obligation for payment of interest, excepting bonds expressly excluding executors, would be moveable in succession.[25] The Succession (Scotland) Act 1964 did not repeal the Act of 1661 with the result that, although executors cannot effectively be excluded since the whole estate of a deceased person vests for the purposes of administration in his executor, personal bonds expressed as excluding executors, after the first term for payment is past, are heritable in the succession of the creditor. Such bonds are thus excluded in the computation of legal rights and, if by testamentary disposition heritable estate in general terms is bequeathed to particular beneficiaries, such bonds will fall within the bequest. If a bond which excludes the creditor's executors is assigned it becomes moveable in the succession of the assignee unless the assignation also has excluded executors. A personal bond is moveable in the succession of the creditor but can be made heritable if the creditor wishes to do so by expressly excluding his executors; when it is assigned the intention of the original creditor is no longer relevant and it is the intention of the assignee which matters, so that if he wishes to alter the succession to the bond from that which the law would otherwise imply he must exclude executors in the assignation.[26]

Date of payment

5–15   The date of payment stated should be the first term at which interest will become payable after the date of the bond, so that repayment may be demanded at that term or at any time thereafter. Whenever that term is past the obligation of the debtor is a liquid debt upon which summary diligence is competent. If there has been a bargain that repayment will not be required for a longer period it is suggested that the date of repayment inserted in the bond should nevertheless be the first term upon which interest will become payable after the date of the bond, the arrangement that payment will not be required before the later date being incorporated in a separate back letter and made conditional upon punctual payment of interest in the meantime.

Place of payment

5–16   The obligation of the debtor is to make payment on the date and at the place specified in the bond. The most convenient place is the creditor's place of business or that of his bankers. The debtor is not bound to make payment at any other place. The general rule as regards the place of payment of debts is that payment should be tendered at the residence

---

[24] Ersk., II, ii, 29.
[25] Other exceptions specified in the Act are now obsolete or have been superseded by subsequent legislation.
[26] See Burns, 19.

or place of business of the creditor,[27] and if no place of payment is specified in a bond it is thought that the address of the creditor stated in the bond would be implied.

Penalty clause

5–17   The origin of the one-fifth part more was the Adjudications Act 1672 c. 19, which provided that a creditor in an adjudication for debt was entitled to have adjudged to him as much of the debtor's lands as was equivalent in value to the amount of the debt with a fifth part more since he was not receiving payment in cash. The phrase was adopted by conveyancers as an appropriate penalty on default and became an established clause of style. Since it is a penalty unrelated to the potential loss it is not enforceable in accordance with its terms, but it does cover the actual expenses and loss incurred by the creditor through the debtor's default. Moreover, if the bond is secured, the actual expenses and loss are, by virtue of the penalty clause, covered by the security and in competition have the same ranking as the principal and interest.[28]

5–18   The expenses covered by the penalty clause include (1) the expenses awarded by the court in an action (whether defended or not) by the creditor against the debtor to recover the loan and interest; (2) the expenses of diligence enforcing the decree[29] or of a charge following upon registration for execution[30]; (3) the expenses incurred by the creditor in defending his right under the bond against challenge by a third party, even although no expenses had been found due in the litigation with the third party[31]; (4) where a cautioner has been required to pay the amount due under the bond and has obtained an assignation from the creditor, the expenses of the assignation and interest on both the principal and interest which the cautioner has paid to the creditor[32]; and (5) in the case of a bond with heritable security, the expenses of the creditor in successfully defending his conduct when intromitting with the rents of the security subjects while in possession of them.[33]

5–19   If the creditor desires to impose an obligation on the debtor to pay expenses of a kind which may not be included within the ambit of the penalty clause, that may be done by inserting a clause either in the bond or in a separate back letter which stipulates for such expenses expressly.

5–20   The penalty clause is enforceable "in the case of failure." "Failure" occurs whenever the debtor fails to make payment after it has been demanded by the creditor. Where the debtor's obligation was

---

[27] *Haughhead Coal Co.* v. *Gallocher* (1903) 11 S.L.T. 156.
[28] *Jameson* v. *Beilby* (1835) 13 S. 865; *Orr* v. *Mackenzie* (1839) 1 D. 1046; *Bruce* v. *Scottish Amicable Life Assurance Society*, 1907 S.C. 637.
[29] *Gordon* v. *Maitland* (1761) Mor. 10050.
[30] Menzies, *Lectures*, 228.
[31] *Ramsay* v. *Goldie* (1826) 4 S. 737.
[32] *Inglis* v. *Renny* (1825) 4 S. 113.
[33] *Bruce* v. *Scottish Amicable Life Assurance Society*, *supra*.

constituted in a bond and disposition in security and the creditor had served a schedule of intimation, requisition and protest in the statutory form requiring repayment with notice that, if repayment had not been made on the expiry of three months, the security subjects might be sold, it was decided that the debtor was in default if he did not make payment forthwith.[34] The notice calling-up a standard security[35] has a similar format (although the period is two months) and default will occur if payment is not tendered by the debtor upon receipt of the notice.

Interest

5–21   The obligation of the debtor is to make payment of interest at the rate and on the dates stated in the bond. If, however, the debtor is an individual or a partnership or other unincorporated body not consisting entirely of bodies corporate and the court finds the credit bargain of which the bond forms part to be extortionate it may reopen the credit agreement so as to do justice between the parties,[36] and the modification which the court is empowered to make may involve a reduction in the stipulated rate of interest.[37] If there is an omission to specify the liability for or rate of interest in the bond, interest is nevertheless payable *ex lege* on money lent,[38] unless there are special circumstances which indicate that payment of interest was not intended by the lender.[39] The rate of interest implied in such cases formerly was "legal interest" of 5 per cent, but now it will vary according to the circumstances,[40] *e.g.* the rate of interest current on unsecured loans, secured loans or consigned money. Interest, although payable at the stipulated terms, accrues *de die in diem*.

5–22   The provision in the bond for a fifth part more of interest unpaid is a penalty which is not in terms enforceable. If penal interest is to be imposed effectively the method is to stipulate for a higher rate in the bond qualified by a back letter restricting the rate of interest to the intended rate conditional upon punctual payment. "Punctual payment" is strictly construed.[41]

Compound interest

5–23   Compound interest, *i.e.* when interest on the principal sum due and unpaid at each term is added to the principal and interest thereafter is payable on the aggregate sum, is not payable unless expressly stipulated for in the bond. Payments made to account, in the absence of an express

---

[34] *McAra* v. *Anderson*, 1913 S.C. 931.
[35] Conveyancing and Feudal Reform (Scotland) Act 1970, Sched. 6, Form A.
[36] Consumer Credit Act 1974, ss. 137, 189.
[37] As to the matters which may be taken into account by the court in determining whether a credit bargain is extortionate, see Wilson, *Law of Scotland Relating to Debt*, 33.
[38] *Thomson* v. *Geekie* (1861) 23 D. 693, 701; *Cunninghame* v. *Boswell* (1868) 6 M. 890.
[39] *Christie* v. *Matheson* (1871) 10 M. 9; *Smellie's Exrx.* v. *Smellie*, 1933 S.C. 725.
[40] See *Williamson* v. *Williamson's Tr.*, 1948 S.L.T. (Notes) 72.
[41] *Gatty* v. *Maclaine*, 1921 S.C. (H.L.) 1.

condition as to appropriation by the debtor, are imputed *primo loco* to interest due on the debt and only the balance is applied in reduction of the principal.[42] Once an extract decree for payment, including a decree upon registration for execution, has been obtained, however, interest runs on the whole amount, principal and interest, contained in the extract.[43]

Deduction of tax

5–24   In the ordinary case interest on a bond for money lent is payable gross, but tax at the standard rate must be deducted from interest which is chargeable to tax under case III of Schedule D if it is paid (a) by a company or local authority otherwise than in a fiduciary or representative capacity; (b) by or on behalf of a partnership of which a company is a member; or (c) to a person whose usual place of abode is outside the United Kingdom unless the payments are made by or to a bank carrying on banking business in the United Kingdom.[44]

Consent to registration for preservation and execution

5–25   See paragraphs 4–60 to 4–73 *supra*.

Stamp duty

5–26   Stamp duty is not payable on a personal bond.[45]

Assignations and discharges

5–27   As to assignations and discharges of personal bonds, see paragraphs 7–05 to 7–19 and 10–13 to 10–21 *infra*.

II. BOND OF ANNUITY

5–28   A bond of annuity is a personal bond whereby the granter is obliged to pay to the grantee, not a capital sum, but a continuing payment at stated terms for a period, definite, as for a stated period of years, or indefinite but bound to occur, as during the lifetime of the granter or grantee. It may be made gratuitously or for consideration.

5–29   In modern practice bonds of annuity are most frequently used (1) to make gratuitously a recurrent periodic payment to the grantee in order to provide income benefit; (2) where it is convenient to purchase an annuity, usually from an assurance company, either by an individual as part of investment policy or by executors or trustees in order to implement directions of the truster without having to prolong

---

[42] *Wilson's Trs.* v. *Watson & Co.* (1900) 2 F. 761.
[43] Debtors (Scotland) Act 1838, s. 5.
[44] Interest on money is excluded from the scope of ss. 52 and 53 of ICTA 1970 (which permit deduction of tax from annual payments) but deduction of tax is mandatory in the three cases (a) to (c) above under s. 54 of the Act, subject to the qualification as to payments by or to banks mentioned in the text.
[45] Finance Act 1971, s. 64(1).

administration; or (3) where the object is to provide income benefit to the grantee combined with savings in income tax.

Duration

5–30   It is essential that the period during which the annuity is to be payable is clearly defined. In particular, care should be taken to provide whether payment is to cease on the death of the granter or the annuitant or on the death of either of them. If no period for termination of the payments is specified in the bond the presumption of law is that the obligation ceases on the death of the annuitant, but if the bond states that the annuity will be payable for a specified period, such as the life of the granter, there is no room for the application of that presumption and the annuity will continue to be payable to the executors of the deceased annuitant so long as the granter survives.[46] In the case of bonds granted without consideration where the parties are individuals it will usually be intended that payment of the annuity should cease on the death of either and provision to that effect should be included in the bond. It is particularly important to provide that payment shall cease on the granter's death in gratuitous bonds since the continuing liability of his executors will not form a deduction from the value of his estate for the purposes of capital transfer tax.[47] The presumption above mentioned that in the absence of any period of duration specified an annuity ceases on the death of the annuitant applies when the annuity is created by *inter vivos* deed; there is no such presumption when the annuity is created by testamentary gift.[48]

Apportionment

5–31   Annuities accrue from day to day unless there is a special stipulation to the contrary.[49] In practice apportionment should be avoided by inserting in the bond of annuity a provision that the last payment actually made before the date of termination of the obligation shall be the final payment due and that apportionment is excluded.[50]

Alimentary annuities

5–32   If an annuity is to be effectually made alimentary, it is necessary that it be protected by a trust.[51] An alimentary annuity so created cannot be assigned or renounced by the annuitant and is not subject to the diligence of his or her creditors save for alimentary debts[52] or to the extent

---

[46] *Reid's Exrx.* v. *Reid*, 1944 S.C. (H.L.) 25.
[47] Finance Act 1975, Sched. 10, para. 1(3). ,
[48] *Fleming* v. *Reuther's Exrs.*, 1921 S.C. 593.
[49] Apportionment Act 1870, s. 2.
[50] See style: para. 5–34.
[51] *White's Trs.* v. *Whyte* (1877) 4 R. 786; *Murray* v. *Macfarlane's Trs.* (1895) 22 R. 927; *Kennedy's Trs.* v. *Warren* (1901) 3 F. 1087; *Dunsmure's Trs.* v. *Dunsmure*, 1920 S.C. 147; *Dempster's Trs.* v. *Dempster*, 1921 S.C. 332; *Branford's Trs.* v. *Powell*, 1924 S.C. 439; *Forbes's Trs.* v. *Tennant*, 1926 S.C. 294.
[52] *Harvey* v. *Calder* (1840) 2 D. 1095; *Lord Ruthven* v. *Pulford*, 1909 S.C. 951.

that the court allows it to be subjected to diligence so far as in excess of a reasonable amount having regard to the annuitant's station in life.[53] An annuity, if it is to be effectively alimentary, cannot be provided by the annuitant himself or out of funds provided by him, since that offends against the rule that a person cannot put his own property *extra commercium* while still retaining benefit from it himself.[54] There is one exception to that rule, namely, that a married woman in an antenuptial marriage contract may contribute funds of her own and create an alimentary liferent or annuity in her own favour.[55] Arrears of alimentary payments, however, are arrestable.[56] In practice bonds of annuity do not usually provide that the annuity is to be alimentary. If in special circumstances it is desired that it should be alimentary (a) the funds which provide it cannot be derived directly or indirectly from the annuitant, (b) the bond should be granted in favour of trustees for the annuitant with an express declaration that the payments are alimentary, and (c) there should be no power given to the annuitant to burden or surrender or dispose of the annuity since such provisions are inconsistent with the alimentary character of the annuity.[57] If an alimentary annuity is directed by testamentary provision the testamentary trustees need not execute a bond of annuity in implement of the direction; they simply make the payments to the legatee as part of the administration of the trust.

Legal qualities of annuities—succession

-33   An annuity payable under a personal bond of annuity, being a tract of future time, is heritable in the succession of the debtor[58] and is a burden on his heritable estate. That rule is elided, however, if a capital sum is made over to provide the annuity, since the character of the fruits of the capital sum will be determined by the nature of the sum itself.[59] In the succession of the creditor, however, annuities, whether heritably secured or not, are moveable except for the purposes of *jus relicti* or *jus relictae* or legitim.[60]

Gratuitous unsecured bond of annuity—Non-alimentary—Fixed period or earlier death of either party—No apportionment

-34   I, A (*designed*) for the love, favour and affection which I bear to B (*designed*) hereby undertake[a] to pay to the said B or his/her

---

[53] *Livingstone* v. *Livingstone* (1886) 14 R. 43; *Cuthbert* v. *Cuthbert's Trs.*, 1908 S.C. 967; *Coles*, 1951 S.C. 608.
[54] *White's Trs.* v. *Whyte, supra*; *Eliott* v. *Purdom* (1895) 22 R. (H.L.) 26; *Lord Ruthven* v. *Drummond*, 1908 S.C. 1154.
[55] *Douglas Gardiner & Mill* v. *Mackintosh's Trs.*, 1916 S.C. 125, 127.
[56] *Muirhead* v. *Miller* (1877) 4 R. 1139.
[57] *Dow* v. *Kilgour's Trs.* (1877) 4 R. 403; *Branford's Trs.* v. *Powell, supra*. For a style, see para. 5–36.
[58] *Reid* v. *McWalter* (1878) 5 R. 630; *Countess de Serra Largo* v. *De Serra Largo's Trs.*, 1933 S.L.T. 391.
[59] *Hill* v. *Hill* (1872) 11 M. 247.
[60] Titles to Land Consolidation (Scotland) Act 1868, ss. 3, 117; Conveyancing (Scotland) Act 1874, s. 30.

assignees[a], an annual sum of £600 for the period of   years or
during my life[b] or the life of the said B,[c] whichever of these three
periods shall be the shortest, by equal quarterly[d] payments of £150
each commencing the first payment on 1st May 1986 for the quarter
preceding[e] and the next payment on 1st August 1986 and so forth
quarterly thereafter until termination upon the expiry of whichever
of the said three periods shall be the shortest; declaring that the
final payment shall be that actually made immediately prior to such
termination and no further payment nor accrued proportion of any
payment shall be due or made[e]: And I consent to registration hereof
for preservation and execution. (*To be attested*)

NOTES
[a] Executors or representatives are omitted since the obligation terminates on the death of either party.
[b] It is usually advisable for the obligation to terminate on the death
of the granter—see para. 5–30.
[c] It is also advisable that the obligation terminates on the death of
the annuitant. If it is desired to continue the benefit to his or her
widow or widower or family a new bond can be granted in the
knowledge of the circumstances of the family at the time.
[d] For annual or half-yearly payments adjust appropriately.
[e] If payments are to be made in advance substitute "succeeding" for
"preceding" and amend the concluding part of the declaration thus:
"and no proportion of the final payment shall be repayable."

*Gratuitous bond of annuity—Non-alimentary—Fixed period—No
apportionment—For minor grandchild*

5–35   I, A (*designed*), bind myself to pay to B (*designed*) and C (*designed*)
and such other persons as may hereafter be appointed or assumed
into the trust hereby created and the survivors and survivor of them
as Trustees for the purposes aftermentioned (the persons for the
time being acting as Trustees hereunder being hereinafter called
"the Trustees") an annual sum of . . . . pounds for
the period of seven years from First September Nineteen hundred
and eighty five or during my lifetime or during the lifetime of my
grandson D (*designed*), whichever of these three periods shall be
the shortest, commencing the first payment on First September
Nineteen hundred and eighty six for the year preceding and continuing thereafter with an annual payment on the First day of
September in each year during the said period of seven years or my
lifetime or the lifetime of the said D, whichever of these three
periods shall be the shortest; declaring that the said annual payments shall cease upon my death or upon the death of the said D
during the said period of seven years, in which event the final payment will be that actually made preceding such death and no further
payment or accrued proportion of any payment shall be due or
made: But the said annual payments shall be made to the Trustees
and applied by them for the following purposes:– (First) For payment of the expenses of administering and winding up the trust
hereby created and (Second) I direct the Trustees to pay or apply
the said annual payment to or for behoof of the said D for the purpose of his education and maintenance in such way and manner as
the Trustees in their sole discretion may think proper: And the
Trustees shall have the fullest powers, privileges and immunities

competent to gratuitous trustees in Scotland and shall not be responsible for errors or omissions but only for wilful default: And I authorise the Trustees to appoint any one of their number or any other person to be factor, accountant or solicitor for the trust hereby created with the usual remuneration for his services. (*To be attested*)

Bond of annuity—Alimentary

-36   An alimentary bond of annuity for an adult may be modelled on the style in paragraph 5–35 with appropriate modifications but in lieu of purpose (Second) a provision on the following lines may be inserted:

(Second) I direct the Trustees to pay or apply the said annual payment to or for behoof of the said D and that as a strictly alimentary provision not assignable nor capable of anticipation by him nor subject to his debts or deeds nor liable to the diligence of his creditors.

Purchased annuities

-37   Annuities purchased from assurance companies are now widely used as a central element in investment and income planning with taxation benefits. The detailed structure of schemes involving the use of purchased annuities varies with circumstances and requires consultation with solicitors and tax advisers in each particular case but typical situations in which such annuities may be useful are: (1) Where an elderly person has capital which he or she may use in the purchase of an annuity with a view to securing a greater net income than can be obtained from investment of the capital. The element of each annuity payment which represents a return of the capital invested in its purchase is not liable to tax as income of the annuitant, and assurance companies have considerable investment expertise and enjoy certain tax reliefs from general annuity business: the combination of these factors may enable a significantly larger net income to be available to the purchaser of an annuity than would result from personal investment of the capital by him. The risk of early death of the annuitant can be restricted in effect if payment of the annuity is guaranteed for a minimum period notwithstanding the earlier death of the annuitant (an annuity certain). (2) A variant of this method where the purchaser has a valuable residence is to adopt a home income plan whereby the assurance company advance capital on a heritable security over the residence and the advance is then invested in the purchase of an annuity. (3) A school fees plan whereby either by way of a composition fee scheme operated by the school or a trust fund scheme for provision of school fees operated by an assurance company a capital sum is invested in annuities to provide school fees, with taxation benefits.

5–38   Where a legacy of non-alimentary annuity is conferred in a will and all the other purposes of the will have been implemented the expense of continuing trust administration may be avoided by the purchase of the annuity from the government or an assurance company. In these circumstances, however, the legatee may claim the capitalised value of the annuity in preference to the purchased annuity.[61]

If the annuity is alimentary the purchase of an annuity by the trustees is technically objectionable since the legatee cannot grant to the trustees an effective discharge of an alimentary provision.[62]

5–39   Each assurance company determines its own style of annuity policy but the normal elements contained in such policies comprise (1) a narrative of delivery to the company as the basis of the contract effected by the policy of a proposal and declaration and payment of the capital sum by the person effecting the policy; (2) an obligation by the company to pay the annuity mentioned in the schedule to the policy on proof of age of the annuitant; and (3) a schedule in which are inserted the details of the contract, name and designation of the person effecting the policy and of the annuitant, date of proposal and declaration, capital sum paid, amount and duration of annuity, terms when payable and place of payment, exclusion of apportionment, statement of age of annuitant and any special conditions. If the annuity is to be alimentary the policy will provide for payment to trustees.

Tax covenants

5–40   Bonds of annuity are commonly used to confer income benefits upon the grantee which, by reason of revenue legislation, are greater than the cost to the granter of providing them. The circumstances in which such bonds are most effective in tax savings are that the annuity payments are provided from profits or gains of the granter which are brought into charge to income tax and upon which he is paying tax at the standard rate or more, whereas the grantee does not have an income, including the annuity payments, which renders him liable to payment of income tax or, being a charity, is exempt from income tax. The granter is entitled to deduct from each payment of the annuity income tax at the standard rate current at the date when the payment is due and the grantee reclaims the tax so deducted. The granter does not require separately to account for the tax deducted: it is already covered by the tax on the profits or gains from which the annuity payment has been made. In the case of bonds in favour of persons other than charities the annuity payment must be due for a period which may exceed six years (seven years is usual); if the grantee is a charity the period must be such that it may exceed three years.[63] In the case of bonds in favour of charities

---

[61] *Dow* v. *Kilgour's Trs.* (1877) 4 R. 403.
[62] *Smith and Campbell* (1873) 11 M. 639; *Cosens* v. *Stevenson* (1873) 11 M. 761; *White's Trs.* v. *Whyte* (1877) 4 R. 786.
[63] ICTA 1970, ss. 52, 434, 528(3), amended as to charities by FA 1980, s. 55.

there is the further benefit that for payments which do not exceed £5000 gross in any year of assessment relief is allowed to the granter from higher rate tax and investment income surcharge.[64]

5-41   In the case of bonds of annuity in favour of persons other than charities the style in paragraph 5–34 *supra* may be used. Charities normally provide brief styles of covenant but care should be taken to provide (if it is not included in the style furnished) that the payments will terminate on the death of the granter within the period covenanted.

5-42   In the ordinary case purchased *life* annuities are treated as containing a capital element and an income element. Only the income element is taxable as income in the hands of the annuitant: income tax is not payable on the capital element.[65]

III. Bond of Cash Credit

5-43   A bond of cash credit is usually granted in favour of a bank or financial house with the object of constituting an obligation, possibly with additional personal security such as guarantees or in conjunction with heritable security, for repayment of sums advanced and/or to be advanced on a current account, fluctuating from time to time, with interest. In modern banking practice bonds of cash credit are used most frequently when a heritable security is taken since the bond provides in probative form a personal obligation which may be referred to in a standard security in Form B of Schedule 2 to the Conveyancing and Feudal Reform (Scotland) Act 1970. The practice of banks varies but if the security is by way of personal guarantees it is generally more convenient not to incorporate the guarantors as co-obligants in the bond of cash credit but to have a separate document of guarantee which may incorporate a limitation of the guarantor's liability to a stated maximum amount and also makes clear that the liability of the guarantor commences only upon a demand for payment made by the bank upon the guarantor.[66] Bonds of cash credit are now less frequently used where security is provided in the form of moveable collateral such as stocks or life assurance policies, since there is no requirement that the documentation be in probative form, as in the case of a heritable security: the obligation of the debtor can be sufficiently constituted by the record of the transactions on current account in the books of the creditor and the documents constituting the security can be widely framed to comprehend the debtor's whole obligations to the creditor whether on current account or otherwise.

---

[64] FA 1980, s. 56, as amended by FA 1983, s. 23.
[65] ICTA 1970, s. 230.
[66] See para. 5–61.

Style—by individual in favour of bank

5-44 I, A (*designed*) bind myself and my executors and representatives whomsoever all jointly and severally to pay to the X Bank (*designed*) (hereinafter called "the Bank") within the Registered Office of the Bank in   all sums which are now and which may at any time hereafter become due to the Bank in any manner of way by me, either solely or jointly with any person or persons or corporation, company, firm or other body, and whether as principal or surety, all which sums shall be so paid by me or my foresaids to the Bank either on demand or in accordance with any separate agreement in writing entered into by me with the Bank providing for payment otherwise than on demand, with interest on such sums severally from the respective times of advance or becoming due until payment at the rate or rates charged and computed as may be provided in any such separate agreement or otherwise in accordance with the ordinary practice of the Bank from time to time (the Bank being entitled, subject and without prejudice to the provisions of any such separate agreement, to fix such rates of interest and alter the same from time to time); Declaring that (FIRST) the said sums shall, without prejudice to the foregoing generality, include all moneys for which I am now or may become liable to the Bank upon any banking account anywhere operated upon by me or with my authority and upon bills, promissory notes, letters of credit, guarantees and other documents of any kind and all discount, commission and banking charges (SECOND) the interest charged and computed as aforesaid shall include interest as well after as before any decree obtained by the Bank for the said sums (THIRD) nothing herein contained shall prejudice or affect any guarantees or any securities over any property of any kind which the Bank may at any time hold for any of the said sums or interest and the Bank shall have full power in their sole discretion to discharge or release any such guarantees or securities in whole or in part or to sell, dispose of or otherwise deal with any such securities or any property comprised therein without applying the same or the proceeds thereof towards payment of the said sums or interest, and (subject only to their obligation to hold just count and reckoning in accordance with law) the actings of the Bank in the exercise of the powers hereby conferred upon them shall in no way prejudice or affect the obligation hereby undertaken (FOURTH) the Bank may at all times in their sole discretion without prejudicing or affecting any securities or other rights available to them in relation to the obligation hereby undertaken (i) terminate, vary or increase any credit given to me or my foresaids (ii) grant to me or my foresaids or to any other person any time or other indulgence (iii) renew any bills or notes or other negotiable securities (iv) compound with me or my foresaids or any other person or guarantor (v) accede to any trust deed and draw dividends or (vi) exercise any right competent to me or my foresaids to redeem any security over my heritable or moveable property ranking prior to or *pari passu* with the security over that property or any part thereof held by the Bank and to charge the cost thereof against me or my foresaids and may do all or any of the foregoing things without notice to me or my foresaids or to such other person or guarantor (FIFTH) my current or any other banking account may be kept at any office or branch of the Bank and may from time to time be transferred to any other office or branch of the Bank (SIXTH) the obligation hereby undertaken shall be a continuing obligation and, notwithstanding any operations upon any of my accounts with the Bank and whether such accounts shall be in debit or credit and whether the sums due hereunder shall be at any time settled or repaid, the said obligation shall, along with any securities held therefor, remain in full force and effect until discharged in writing and (SEVENTH) a Certificate signed by a General Manager, Assistant General Manager, Secretary or Law Secretary or any other signing official authorised by the Bank at any of their offices shall ascertain and constitute conclusively the amounts of principal and interest due to the Bank hereunder by me or my foresaids and no suspension of a charge, or of a threatened charge, hereunder shall pass, nor any sist of execution be granted, except on consignation; And I consent to registration hereof and of any such Certificate as aforesaid for execution. (*To be attested*)

Parties—variations

5–45 (a) **Two or more granters in respect of a joint account.** The bond will be granted by both or all of the debtors, thus:

> We, (*names and designations of both or all granters*) bind ourselves and our respective executors and representatives whomsoever all jointly and severally to pay to the X Bank (*designed*) (hereinafter called "the Bank") within the registered office of the Bank in   all sums which are now and which at any time hereafter may become due to the Bank in any manner of way by us or either/ any of us either solely or jointly with any person or persons or corporation, company, firm or other body, and whether as principal or surety, all which sums (continue as in style in paragraph 5–44, substituting the plural for the singular in subsequent references to the granters).

5–46 (b) **Partnerships**. The bond is usually framed widely to bind the firm and its partners as partners and as trustees for the firm and as individuals in respect of all sums due by the firm or any of the partners or by any firm or other body of which any of the individual granters is or may become a partner, thus:

> We the firm of A B & Co. (*designed*) and we A, B and C (*all designed*) the individual partners of the said firm as such partners and as trustees for the said firm and as individuals bind the said firm of A B & Co. and us the said A, B and C as such partners and trustees and as individuals and our respective executors and representatives whomsoever all jointly and severally to pay to the X Bank (*designed*) (hereinafter called 'the Bank') within the

registered office of the Bank in   all sums which are
now and which may at any time hereafter become due to the
Bank in any manner of way by the said firm or by us the said A,
B and C or any of us as such partners or as individuals either
solely or jointly with any person or persons or corporation, company, firm or other body, and whether as principal or surety or
by any firm of which any of us the said A, B and C is or may
become a partner, all which sums (continue as in style in paragraph 5–44 with appropriate alterations in references to the
granters).

5–47   In terms of section 18 of the Partnership Act 1890 a continuing guar-
anty or cautionary obligation given to a third person in respect of the
transactions of a firm is, in the absence of agreement to the contrary,
revoked as to future transactions by any change in the constitution of
the firm. It is therefore desirable in a bond of cash credit by a partnership to incorporate an agreement to the contrary in order to ensure that
the obligations of all the granters continue in force notwithstanding
changes in the firm by death or retiral of partners or the assumption of
new partners. For that purpose a clause should be inserted on the following lines:

Notwithstanding the death, retirement, substitution or addition of
any partner in the said firm of A B & Co. or any other change in the
partners or in the name or constitution of the said firm of A B &
Co. the obligations hereby undertaken shall subsist and be enforceable and we the said A, B and C and our respective foresaids shall
continue to be liable for all sums due and that may become due to
the Bank hereunder until formal application to be relieved of future
liability is made in writing to and granted by the Bank.

A clause in those terms would probably not be sufficient to impose continuing liability in circumstances such as occurred in *Hay & Co.* v.
Torbet[67] where the obligations of a partnership were transferred to a
limited company.

5–48   (c) **Companies.** In modern practice lenders to an incorporated company
to which the Companies (Floating Charges and Receivers) (Scotland)
Act 1972 applied (now incorporated in Part XVIII of the Companies
Act 1985) tend to constitute the obligation of the debtor company by
way of a floating charge with the benefit of the security which it provides. Where for any reason such a charge is not being created a bond of
cash credit in the form in paragraph 5–44 may be taken, the obligation
being expressed as binding the company and its successors all jointly and
severally. In certain circumstances the creditor may wish the directors of
the company to guarantee the obligations of the company: that may be
done either by joining the individual directors as co-obligants in the
bond but more commonly is effected by way of a separate guarantee.

---

[67] 1908 S.C. 781.

5–49 **(d) Unincorporated bodies.** The legal position of a voluntary association such as a club or society is peculiar in that it is not recognised as an entity endowed with legal personality and has no existence in law distinct from the aggregate of its members. A creditor pursuing such an association for debt requires to call not only the association but also its responsible office bearers[68]; although it is competent to sue an unincorporated association in the sheriff court in its own name[69] the problem of enforcing the decree by diligence presents difficulties. A club or society normally provides in its constitution for the appointment of trustees who hold its funds and property, but frequently they may be unwilling to undertake personal liability as individuals for its obligations. Where a bond of cash credit is being granted by a club or society the usual method adopted is that the bond is granted by the club or society and its trustees but only in that capacity and not as individuals. A bond in that form enables the creditor to sue the club or society and the trustees as such, when the funds and property of the body will be available in or towards payment of the obligation. If the personal obligation of any person or persons as individuals is also required, that may be created by a separate guarantee. A suitable style of bond may be:

WE, the   Club (*address*) (hereinafter called "the Club") and we, A, B and C (*designed*) the present Trustees for the Club BIND the Club and us the said A, B and C as such Trustees but not personally or as individuals and our successors in office whomsoever, all jointly and severally, to pay to the X Bank (*designed*) (hereinafter called "the Bank") on demand within the registered office of the Bank in   all sums which are now and which may at any time hereafter become due to the Bank in any manner of way by the Club or by us the said A, B and C or our foresaids as Trustees foresaid either solely or jointly with any person or persons or corporation, company, firm or other body, and whether as principal or surety with interest on such sums severally from the respective times of advance or becoming due until payment at the rate or rates charged and computed in accordance with the ordinary practice of the Bank from time to time (the Bank being entitled to fix such rates of interest and alter the same from time to time without notice); DECLARING that (FIRST) the said sums shall, without prejudice to the foregoing generality, include all moneys for which the Club or we or our foresaids as Trustees foresaid are or may become liable to the Bank upon any banking account anywhere operated upon by the Club or with the authority of us or our foresaids as Trustees foresaid and upon bills, promissory notes, letters of credit, guarantees and other documents of any kind and all discount, commission and banking charges, (SECOND) the interest charged and computed as aforesaid shall include interest as well after as before any decree obtained by the Bank for the said sums, (THIRD) nothing herein contained shall prejudice or affect any

---

[68] *Bridge* v. *South Portland Street Synagogue*, 1907 S.C. 1351.
[69] Sheriff Courts (Scotland) Act 1907, Sched. 1, r. 14 (as substituted by S.I. 1983 No. 747).

guarantee or any securities over any property of any kind which
the Bank may at any time hold for the said sums and interest and
the Bank shall have full power in its sole discretion to discharge or
release any such guarantees or securities in whole or in part or to
sell, dispose of or otherwise deal with such securities or any property comprised therein without applying the same or the proceeds
thereof towards payment of the said sums or interest, and the actings of the Bank in the exercise of the powers hereby conferred
upon it shall in no way prejudice or affect the obligation hereby
undertaken, (FOURTH) the Bank may at all times in its sole discretion without prejudicing or affecting any securities or other
rights available to it in relation to the obligation hereby undertaken (i) terminate, vary or increase any credit given to the said
Club or to us or our foresaids as Trustees foresaid, (ii) grant to the
said Club or to us or our foresaids as Trustees foresaid or to any
other person any time or other indulgence, (iii) renew any bills or
notes or other negotiable securities, (iv) compound with the said
Club or us or our foresaids as Trustees foresaid or any other person or guarantor, (v) accede to any trust deed and draw dividends,
or (vi) exercise any right competent to the said Club or to us or our
foresaids as Trustees foresaid to redeem any security over our
heritable or moveable property ranking prior to or *pari passu* with
the security over that property or any part thereof held by the
Bank and to charge the cost thereof against the said Club or us or
our foresaids as Trustees foresaid, and may do all or any of the
foregoing things without notice to the said Club or to us or our foresaids as Trustees foresaid or to such other person or guarantor,
(FIFTH) the current or any other banking account of the said Club
or of us or our foresaids as Trustees foresaid may be kept at any
office or branch of the Bank and may from time to time be transferred to any other office or branch of the Bank, (SIXTH) the
obligation hereby undertaken shall be a continuing obligation and,
notwithstanding any operations upon any accounts with the Bank
and whether such accounts shall be in debit or credit and whether
the sums due hereunder shall be at any time settled or repaid, the
said obligation shall, along with any securities held therefor,
remain in full force and effect until discharged in writing,
(SEVENTH) notwithstanding the death, retirement, substitution
or addition of any Trustee of the Club or any other change in the
Trustees or in the name or the constitution of the Club the obligation hereby undertaken shall subsist and be enforceable and we
the said A, B and C and our foresaids as Trustees foresaid shall
continue to be liable as such Trustees for all sums due and that
may become due to the Bank hereunder until formal application is
made to the Bank in writing to be relieved of future liability and
(EIGHTH) a certificate signed by the General Manager, Assistant
General Manager or Secretary or any other signing official authorised by the Bank at any of its offices shall ascertain and constitute
conclusively the amounts of principal and interest due to the Bank
hereunder by the Club or us the said A, B and C or our foresaids
as Trustees foresaid and no suspension of a charge, or of a threatened charge, hereunder shall pass, nor any sist of execution be
granted, except on consignation: And we the granters hereof consent to registration hereof and of any such certificate as aforesaid
for execution. (*To be attested*)

Advances

5–50   The bond is an "all moneys" obligation, comprehending all advances of any kind made and that may be made by the creditor bank to the debtor or for which the debtor may become responsible to the creditor in any capacity. The actual amount due at any time, including interest, may be ascertained and made specific for the purposes of summary diligence by a certificate of any signing official.[70]

Limit of credit

5–51   It is unusual to specify any maximum amount in the bond itself. The creditor may impose a limit upon the debtor's credit but it is plainly undesirable to specify any restriction in the obligation of the debtor to repay all sums actually advanced. The position in relation to guarantors is different: the guarantor may be unwilling to undertake an unrestricted cautionary obligation and a maximum limit of his liability may be included in the document of guarantee.

Interest

5–52   In normal practice a bank adds interest to the principal advanced at half-yearly or other periodic intervals. The effect is to convert the interest to principal, and interest then runs on the increased amount.[71] If the obligation of the debtor under the bond is unsecured, interest can be claimed in sequestration or liquidation of the debtor only up to the date of sequestration or winding-up,[72] but if there is any residue of the estate after discharge of the debts ranked the creditor may require any further interest payable in terms of the bond.[73] If, however, the obligation in the bond is secured, *e.g.* by a floating charge or a heritable security, interest is recoverable from the proceeds of sale of the security subjects, notwithstanding the liquidation or sequestration of the debtor, up to the date of actual payment.[74]

Guarantees

5–53   A bond of cash credit may be supported by personal security by way of a guarantee, normally in the form of a separate document. A suggested style follows.

---

[70] See para. 4–64.
[71] *Reddie* v. *Williamson* (1863) 1 M. 228; *Gilmour* v. *Bank of Scotland* (1880) 7 R. 734; *Commercial Bank of Scotland Ltd.* v. *Pattison's Trs.* (1891) 18 R. 476.
[72] Bankruptcy (Scotland) Act 1913, s. 48; Companies Act 1985, s. 613.
[73] Goudy, *Bankruptcy*, 318.
[74] *National Commercial Bank of Scotland* v. *Liquidators of Telford Grier Mackay & Co. Ltd.*, 1969 S.C. 181; Conveyancing and Feudal Reform (Scotland) Act 1970, ss. 13, 42.

To X Bank (*designed*)

I, B (*designed*) hereby guarantee to pay to you on demand all sums and obligations now due or which may hereafter become due to you from time to time by A (*designed*) (hereinafter referred to as "the Principal") and of all interest due or to become due by the Principal thereon at the usual rate or rates charged by you and also of all banking charges and commissions due or to become due by the Principal to you, and that whether such sums and obligations are or may become due to you by the Principal by way of overdrafts or loans upon one or more current accounts, loan accounts including term loan accounts or other accounts in name of the Principal and/or in any trading name or names of the Principal or by way of guarantees granted by you for behoof of the Principal or due to you by the Principal in any other manner of way whatsoever. And I agree and declare (1) that the claim under this Guarantee shall be sufficiently ascertained by a statement made out from the books of you the said Bank and certified by the Secretary, Law Secretary or other officer thereof, and the balance appearing due thereon shall be exigible from me at any time upon a demand being made therefor (2) that it shall be in the power of you the said Bank at your own discretion and without consulting me to transact or compromise with or give time to the Principal as if the Principal were the only party bound or liable without thereby impairing or affecting my liability hereunder (3) that this Guarantee shall be a continuing Guarantee and shall not be determined by my death or by any change in the name or constitution of your Bank and shall remain in force until recalled by me or my executors or representatives in writing (4) that this Guarantee is granted in addition and without prejudice to any other securities or remedies which you now or may hereafter hold for all or any of the debts or obligations of the Principal, all or any of which securities or remedies you may surrender, abandon or realise without consulting me and without impairing or diminishing my liability hereunder and (5) that until your whole claims against the Principal are satisfied I shall not be entitled to delivery of this Guarantee nor to rank on the estates of the Principal in respect thereof nor to demand an assignation of your claim against the Principal nor to have the benefit of any such other securities or remedies held by you. And as a separate and independent stipulation I agree and declare that any sum or sums ascertained as aforesaid which may not be exigible from me under the foregoing guarantee by reason of any legal limitation, disability or incapacity on or of the Principal shall nevertheless be recoverable from me as if I were sole or principal debtor. But I hereby specially stipulate that my liability under this Guarantee shall not exceed the sum of £   sterling and interest thereon at the rate or rates foresaid from the date to which interest was last charged or debited against the Principal. (*To be attested*)

A guarantee by several guarantors may be in similar style, the obligations being undertaken jointly and severally or *pro rata* with individual limits of liability.

Liabilities of principal debtor and guarantors

5–54 **(a) Guarantee not an indemnity.** Although in practice the creditor bank will normally regard the principal debtor as the primary obligant, the guarantee is not an indemnity since the guarantor undertakes to pay upon demand by the bank. In certain circumstances the bank may not wish to exhaust its legal remedies against the principal debtor before calling upon the guarantor to make payment, *e.g.* where the principal debtor is plainly insolvent and has no assets of significant value so that sequestration proceedings may be unproductive.

5–55 **(b) Death of either party.** The death of the principal debtor closes the current account and restricts the liability of guarantors to the amount then due with interest until payment. The death of a guarantor does not have that effect and his executors remain liable for subsequent advances on the account unless and until they intimate to the bank that they are terminating their liability under the guarantee, which they may do only as regards subsequent transactions.[75]

5–56 **(c) Insolvency.** If the principal debtor becomes insolvent and the bank accedes to a trust deed for his creditors or enters into any voluntary composition arrangement or compromise of his liability the effect in law would be to liberate guarantors,[76] but that result is negatived contractually in the bond and by the power to compromise reserved in the guarantee. No such effect results from the sequestration or liquidation of the debtor.[77] In terms of the guarantee the bank reserves the right to rank in the sequestration of the principal debtor, and may proceed against the guarantor for any balance; the guarantor is not entitled to rank in the sequestration for the balance he has to pay since that would conflict with the rule against double ranking.[78] If, however, a guarantor pays the debt in full, but only in such circumstances, the guarantee preserves his right to rank in the sequestration of the debtor and to obtain an assignation of the bank's claim and of any rights or securities held by the bank. As to bankruptcy of the guarantor and the rights of co-guarantors *inter se*, see paragraphs 6–32 and 6–34 to 6–36 *infra*.

5–57 **(d) Continuing obligation.** In terms of the bond itself and of the guarantee the obligations of the principal debtor and the guarantor are continuing obligations. That provision is designed to exclude the application of the rule in *Clayton's* case[79] whereby payments for credit

---

[75] *British Linen Co.* v. *Monteith* (1858) 20 D. 557.
[76] *Allan, Allan & Milne* v. *Pattison* (1893) 21 R. 195.
[77] Bankruptcy (Scotland) Act 1913, s. 52; Companies Act 1985, s. 613.
[78] *Anderson* v. *Mackinnon* (1876) 3 R. 608; *Mackinnon* v. *Monkhouse* (1881) 9 R. 393.
[79] *Devaynes* v. *Noble* (1816) 1 Mer. 529, 572.

of the account, unless specially ascribed, would have been applied towards the discharge of the earliest advances in respect of which guarantees or any other security had been given and payments debited to the account would have been treated as unsecured advances.

5–58 **(e) Actions of creditor affecting liability of guarantors.** By reason of the equities afforded to cautioners, actions of the creditor which may prejudice cautioners have the effect of releasing the latter from their obligation. These are treated more fully later[80] but they include discharge or release of a co-guarantor or securities, giving time or other indulgence to the principal debtor, renewing bills or negotiable securities or compromising claims. In the bond and the guarantee it is usual to contract out of that result by express agreement.

5–59 **(f) Invalidity of principal obligation.** Since a guarantee is an accessory obligation it will be impliedly discharged if there is no enforceable principal obligation. If the obligation of the principal debtor has not been effectively constituted, *e.g.* by reason of some lack of capacity or power of the debtor to incur the obligation, the guarantors would be freed from their obligation. To avoid that result the guarantee includes a special stipulation that in any such case the guarantee may still be enforced as if the guarantor were the principal debtor.

Prescription

5–60 **(a) Principal debtor.** The obligation of the principal debtor is to make payment of the advances, with interest, either on demand by the creditor bank or in accordance with any separate written agreement providing for payment otherwise. Since the bond of cash credit is probative the short negative prescription of five years does not apply to the debtor's obligation thereunder,[81] save as regards interest which has not been converted into capital.[82] The relevant periods of negative prescription after which the obligations of the principal debtor, if not judicially interrupted or relevantly acknowledged, are extinguished are (i) 20 years from the date when payment is demanded *quoad* the principal, and (ii) five years from the date of demand *quoad* unconverted interest. When the obligation of the principal debtor is extinguished by prescription that of the cautioner as an accessory obligation is extinguished also.

5–61 **(b) Guarantors.** The obligation of a guarantor is expressed as exigible on demand by the creditor. Since the longer period of 20 years does not apply to cautionary obligations even although constituted by a probative writ,[83] the obligation of the guarantor is extinguished on the expiry of

---

[80] See paras. 6–20 to 6–30.
[81] Prescription and Limitation (Scotland) Act 1973, Sched. 1, para. 2(*c*).
[82] *Ibid.*, Sched. 1, paras. 2(*c*) and 1(*a*)(i).
[83] *Ibid.*, Sched. 1, para. 2(*c*).

five years after the date when the creditor requires the guarantor to pay.[84]

Securities

5–62   (a) **Heritable securities.** Formerly there were difficulties in constituting heritable security for the fluctuating sums due from time to time under a bond of cash credit because of the provision of the Bankruptcy Act 1696 (c.5) which invalidated securities for debts contracted after the infeftment of the creditor and the rule of feudal law that a real burden upon land must be of a specific amount. Section 7 of the Debts Securities (Scotland) Act 1856 permitted a bond for cash credit and disposition in security for a stated principal sum plus interest for three years at 5 per cent. Difficult problems were encountered as to the operation of the statutory limit[85] and in practice heritable security for fluctuating sums was normally created in the form of a disposition of the security subjects *ex facie* absolute qualified by an agreement that it was truly in security of advances on an account, with interest, and setting out the detailed terms of the loan arrangements.[86] These forms of security are now largely of historical interest (although older securities by way of *ex facie* absolute disposition qualified by agreement may still regulate some loan arrangements) since the Conveyancing and Feudal Reform (Scotland) Act 1970 permits heritable securities for varying sums advanced and to be advanced to be created only in the form of a standard security. Since that enactment heritable securities for advances on cash credit taken either in the form of a standard security in Form A of Schedule 2 to the 1970 Act incorporating both a personal obligation under a cash credit arrangement and the heritable security for the advances with interest or, much more commonly, by way of a separate bond of cash credit and a standard security in Form B of that Schedule.[87]

5–63   (b) **Moveable securities.** Securities in respect of cash credits over moveable property may take various forms according to the nature of the security property, *e.g.* stock exchange securities, life assurance policies, interests in trust estates, etc.[88] Shares of companies which are not listed on the Stock Exchange are not usually acceptable as securities for advances on cash credit because of restrictions on transfer and limited marketability.

Stamp duty

5–64   Stamp duty is no longer payable upon a bond of cash credit or a standard security.[89]

---

[84] *Royal Bank of Scotland Ltd.* v. *Brown*, 1983 S.L.T. 122.
[85] See Burns, 476–477.
[86] *Ibid.*, 489–491.
[87] 1970 Act, s. 9.
[88] For styles see Chap. 7.
[89] Finance Act 1971, s. 64.

IV. IOU

Form

5–65   In short-term transactions between individuals an acknowledgment of receipt of money lent with an implied obligation to repay may be created in the form of an IOU. The document must be holograph of the granter,[90] must contain the words "I owe you" or the letters "IOU," must state the sum due and must be signed by the granter. It need not be, although it usually is, addressed to a particular person.[91] It should bear a date. It is usually expressed thus:

Glasgow
(Date)

> To Robert Jones
> IOU £100
>   (sgd.) David White.

Effect

5–66   An IOU is merely an acknowledgment of debt with an implied obligation to repay.[92] Although it does not expressly bind the granter to make repayment it is evidence of the debt and is a sufficient warrant to found an action for repayment.[93] It is then for the granter to establish that payment has been made or that the implied obligation to repay has been discharged, so that the IOU is no longer a living document of debt. He may do so by parole evidence.[94]

It is not a promissory note nor a negotiable instrument,[95] but it may be assigned. If, however, the document contains, in addition to the acknowledgment of debt, an express undertaking to repay on demand or at a fixed date, it may be treated as a promissory note.[96] The implied obligation to repay arises only upon demand and so, unless the IOU expressly provides for payment of interest, interest is due only from the date of citation in an action to enforce payment.[97] For a fuller discussion of the nature of an IOU and defences against payment thereunder see Wilson, *Law of Scotland Relating to Debt*, at pages 108, 109.

V. Negotiable Instruments

5–67   Negotiable instruments such as bills of exchange, promissory notes and cheques also create a primary obligation to pay. Summary diligence is

---

[90] *Haldane* v. *Speirs* (1872) 10 M. 537, 541.
[91] *Macpherson* v. *Munro* (1854) 16 D. 612.
[92] *Black* v. *Gibb*, 1940 S.C. 24.
[93] *Neilson's Trs.* v. *Neilson's Trs.* (1883) 11 R. 119; *Black* v. *Gibb, supra* at 28.
[94] *Bishop* v. *Bryce*, 1910 S.C. 426.
[95] *Todd* v. *Wood* (1897) 24 R. 1104.
[96] Bills of Exchange Act 1882, s. 83.
[97] *Winestone* v. *Wolifson*, 1954 S.C. 77.

competent upon bills of exchange and promissory notes,[98] but not upon cheques.[99] The law and practice in relation to such documents is within the field of mercantile law rather than conveyancing.[1]

---

[98] Bills of Exchange (Scotland) Act 1772, s. 42.
[99] *Glickman* v. *Linda*, 1950 S.C. 18.
[1] For details see Walker, *Principles*, II, 441 *et seq.*; Marshall, *Scots Mercantile Law*, Chap. 7.

CHAPTER 6

SECONDARY OR CONTINGENT OBLIGATIONS

I. CAUTIONARY OBLIGATIONS

I. CAUTIONARY OBLIGATIONS

Nature

–01   A cautionary obligation has been defined as "an accessory obligation or engagement, as surety for another, that the principal obligant shall pay the debt or perform the act for which he has engaged, otherwise the cautioner shall pay the debt or fulfil the obligation."[1] It is distinguishable from (1) an independent obligation as where a person undertakes direct liability to a creditor for a debt which had been originally due by another[2] or grants a bond of corroboration,[3] (2) a representation as to credit,[4] (3) delegation as where a cautioner assumes the liability of the principal debtor and releases him from his obligation,[5] (4) indemnity which may be a simple undertaking by one person to another undertaking repayment of loss incurred in a particular transaction as distinct from a trilateral arrangement involving the creditor, the principal debtor and the cautioner,[6] or (5) insurance which is an obligation between the

---

[1] Bell, *Prin.*, s. 245.
[2] *Morrison* v. *Harkness* (1870) 9 M. 35; *Stevenson's Tr.* v. *Campbell & Sons* (1896) 23 R. 711.
[3] *Yuill's Trs.* v. *Maclachlan's Trs.*, 1939 S.C. (H.L.) 40.
[4] *Union Bank of Scotland* v. *Taylor*, 1925 S.C. 835.
[5] *Jackson* v. *MacDiarmid* (1892) 19 R. 528.
[6] *Simpson* v. *Jack*, 1948 S.L.T. (Notes) 45.

insurer and the insured person to indemnify against loss from the occurrence of a particular event.[7]

Use

6-02   Cautionary obligations or guarantees are used in a wide variety of circumstances including bonds of caution in respect of the intromissions of executors-dative or judicial factors, guarantees of financial accommodation by banks or other commercial lenders and guarantees in mercantile transactions.

Form

6-03   In practice a cautionary obligation may be created (1) by a tripartite written agreement amongst the creditor, the principal debtor and the cautioner, or (2) by an obligation constituted in writing or otherwise between the creditor and the principal debtor and a separate obligation, which must be in writing,[8] whereby the cautioner guarantees, either wholly or to a specified extent, the obligation of the principal debtor to the creditor. Under the first method several parties bind themselves jointly and severally as co-obligants in the document which constitutes the obligation although one of them is truly the principal debtor and the others are cautioners. By the second method, the separate bond of caution or guarantee stamps the granter with the character of a cautioner. Both methods are in common use but in mercantile and banking transactions the second is frequently preferred since (i) the separate document accommodates more easily a limitation of the cautioner's maximum liability if that is desired and (ii) the obligation of the cautioner is usually expressed as arising when the creditor demands payment from the cautioner so that the short negative prescription of five years commences to run against the creditor in a question with the cautioner only from the date when the creditor requires payment from the cautioner.[9] It is not clear whether a cautionary obligation requires probative writing but probably not.[10]

Proper and improper caution

6-04   An obligation is one of proper cautionry where the fact that the parties are principal debtor and cautioner appears on the face of the document or documents, but it is improper caution where the parties are bound as co-obligants with nothing in the documentation which discloses or necessarily infers that one of them is the principal debtor and

---

[7] *Laird v. Securities Insurance Co. Ltd.* (1895) 22 R. 452; *Re Law Guarantee Trust and Accident Society Ltd., Liverpool Mortgage Insurance Co.'s Case* [1914] 2 Ch. 617.
[8] Mercantile Law Amendment (Scotland) Act 1856, s. 6.
[9] *Royal Bank of Scotland Ltd.* v. *Brown*, 1983 S.L.T. 122.
[10] *Wylie & Lochhead Ltd.* v. *Hornsby* (1889) 16 R. 907; *Snaddon* v. *London Edinburgh & Glasgow Assurance Co. Ltd.* (1902) 5 F. 182.

the other or others are merely cautioners. Clearly, when the obligation of the cautioner is contained in a separate bond of caution or guarantee, the transaction is one of proper caution. If all the parties are bound as co-obligants in the deed creating the obligation of debt, the transaction may still be one of proper caution if (i) some of the parties are expressly bound only as cautioners or guarantors, (ii) the deed contains a clause of relief whereby one of the granters who is truly the principal debtor binds himself to relieve the others of liability, or (iii) there is a separate bond of relief to the same effect which is intimated to the creditor. Apart from these formal methods of establishing proper cautionry in the case of co-obligants the same legal position may result if the creditor is made aware of the true relationship by clear inference from the terms of the documents[11] or if it is proved that he knew the true relationship of the parties.[12] The importance of the distinction between proper and improper cautionry is that in proper cautionry the creditor has certain duties to the cautioner which, if not observed, may result in release of the latter from his obligation,[13] whereas in improper cautionry the creditor may treat all the parties as co-obligants leaving a cautioner who pays to establish and operate his right of relief against the party who was truly the principal debtor.

Bonds of caution

–05 Documents of guarantee in the traditional form of a bond of caution are still used in respect of the intromissions of persons appointed by the courts to administer the property of others, *e.g.* executors-dative or judicial factors. The cautioner must be subject to the jurisdiction of the Scottish courts and must not be beneficially interested in the property to be administered by the executor and the court must be satisfied that he has sufficient financial resources to guarantee the amount of the estate involved.[14] In practice bonds of caution are generally granted by assurance companies in exchange for payment of a premium.

Bond of caution—Executor dative—Company cautioner

Sheriff Court of

We (*name and registered office (or local office) of assurance company cautioners*) do hereby, as Cautioners and Sureties acted in the Court Books of   Bind and Oblige ourselves and our whole funds and property that the sum of (*gross amount of estate*) contained[a] in the Confirmation-Dative of the deceased (*name and designation*) wherein (*name(s) and designation(s) of Executor(s)*) has/have been decerned and is/are to be confirmed[b] Executor/

---

[11] *Mackenzie* v. *Macartney* (1831) 5 W. & S. 504.
[12] Gloag and Irvine, 674 *et seq.*
[13] See paras. 6–25 *et seq.*
[14] Currie on *Confirmation*, 232–233.

Executors dative *qua*   to the said deceased, shall be made
free and furthcoming to all parties having interest therein, as law
will, *(name(s) of Executor(s))* the said Executor/Executors being
always bound to relieve us as Cautioners in the premises: And both
parties subject themselves, their executors and successors to the
jurisdiction of the Sheriff Principal of   in the premises,
and appoint the Sheriff Clerk's Office in   as a domicile
whereat they may be cited to all diets of Court at the instance of all
and sundry as law will, holding any citation legally affixed and left
for them or their foresaids upon the walls of the said Office as sufficient as if they were personally summoned. (*To be attested*)

NOTES
[a] In small estates substitute "to be contained" for "contained."
[b] In small estates substitute "is/are to be decerned and confirmed"
for "has/have been decerned and is/are to be confirmed."

Mercantile guarantees

6–06   These may be granted for a single transaction or in respect of a continuing trading account. The former may be given by letter; the letter is
more commonly expressed in a document of guarantee. Writing is
essential but for documents *in re mercatoria* attestation or holograph
writing is not required.[15]

Letter of guarantee—Single transactions

6–07   (*Address*)
                                                          (*Date*)
            (*Name and address of Grantee*)

            Dear Sirs,
              In respect that you are selling to (*name and address of person
whose obligation is guaranteed*) approximately   tons of steel
at the price of £   per ton and delivering same to him on or
before (*date of delivery*) to be paid for not later than   , I
guarantee payment of the price thereof up to a maximum sum of
£   which sum is the limit of my liability hereunder.
                                                          (*Signature*)

Continuing guarantee—Trading account of firm

6–08   We, A, B and C (*all designed*), the whole partners of the firm of A
B & Co. (*designed*), hereby as such partners and as trustees for the
said firm and as individuals all jointly and severally, guarantee payment of all sums due and that may hereafter become due to (*name
and designation of grantee*) by the said firm in respect of goods supplied to or to the order of the said firm by the said (*grantee*) but subject to the limit of our liability aftermentioned[a]: This guarantee

---

[15] Mercantile Law Amendment (Scotland) Act 1856, s. 6; *B.O.C.M. Silcock Ltd.* v. *Hunter*, 1976
S.L.T. 217.

shall be a continuing and covering obligation applicable to all goods supplied as aforesaid and the obligation hereby undertaken shall continue in force notwithstanding any change in the partners or in the name or constitution of the said firm of A B & Co.[b]: But we specially stipulate that our liability under this Guarantee shall not exceed the sum of £   . (*To be attested*)[c]

NOTES

[a] If it is desired to obviate release of the guarantors by changes in trading terms or giving time or other indulgences insert provisions on lines of condition (2) of style in para. 6–09.

[b] The object is to elide termination of liability under section 18 of the Partnership Act 1890.

[c] Attestation is not legally necessary in a mercantile guarantee but is usual in a formal guarantee of this kind.

Another form—Letter of Guarantee—Trading Account

6–09

(*Address*)
(*Date*)

To . . . .
. . . .

In consideration of your selling goods, advancing money and giving credit to A.B. & Co. (*designed*), I, C (*designed*) hereby guarantee that due payment will be made to you of all debts and advances which are already owing to you or which may from time to time be owing to you by the said A.B. & Co.: And I expressly agree and declare—

(1) That this Guarantee shall be a continuing and covering obligation and that my liability hereunder shall not be affected in any way or held as discharged unless with your written consent:

(2) That you shall have the full power and liberty (without notice to me and without in any way affecting my liability hereunder) at any time and from time to time to extend or limit the period or otherwise alter the terms of credit to the said A.B. & Co.: to hold or renew any bills, promissory notes or securities which you may at any time receive from them or from others on their behalf and to release or give up the same or any of them: to allow the said A.B. & Co. and the granters of such documents any time or indulgence: and to accede to any trust deed or composition arrangement by the said A.B. & Co. or the granters of such documents in whatever terms the same may be expressed:

(3) That no change in the partners or name or constitution of your firm or in the name or constitution of said A.B. & Co. shall release me from liability hereunder:

And I agree to renounce the benefit of division: Declaring however that my liability under this Guarantee shall be restricted to the sum of £   of the ultimate loss which may be sustained by you in respect of your whole transactions with the said A.B. & Co. after placing to the credit of the sums due to you all dividends recovered

by you from their estate, but that I shall nevertheless be bound to
pay the said sum of £   immediately upon payment thereof
being required by you and notwithstanding that the amount of your
ultimate loss on said transactions may not then have been ascertained.

Yours faithfully,

. . . .

Bank guarantees—current accounts, etc.

6–10   For bonds of cash credit and guarantees see paragraphs 5–44 and 5–53
et seq., *supra*.

Principal debt and guarantee in single document

6–11   In certain circumstances it may be convenient to constitute the principal obligation and also a guarantee in a single bond. If the obligation of
the guarantors is limited or partial that should be specified, and for the
purposes of prescription it is desirable that the obligation of the guarantors should arise only on demand by the creditor.[16]

*Bond—Repayment of loan—Principal and cautioners—Limitation of
liability of cautioners*

I, A (*designed*) grant me to have instantly (*or* "now and formerly"
as the case may be) borrowed and received from B (*designed*) the
sum of £   which sum I the said A as principal and we C
(*designed*) and D (*designed*) as cautioners and sureties[a] and full
debtors for and with the said A bind and oblige ourselves jointly
and severally and our respective executors and representatives
whomsoever all jointly and severally without the necessity of discussing them in their order to repay to the said B his executors or
assignees whomsoever at the term of   19   within
with a fifth part more of liquidate penalty in case of failure and the
interest of said principal sum at the rate of   per cent per
annum from the date hereof to the said term of payment and half
yearly, termly and proportionally thereafter during the not-
payment thereof and that at two terms in the year   and
          by equal proportions beginning the first term's payment at
the said term of   next for the interest due preceding that
date and the next term's payment thereof at   following and
so forth half yearly termly and proportionally thereafter during the
not-payment of the said principal sum with a fifth part more of the
interest due at each term of liquidate penalty in case of failure in the
punctual payment thereof: Providing always that (1) the liability of
me the said C or my foresaids hereunder shall not exceed the sum of
£   with interest thereon at the rate foresaid (2) the liability of

---

[16] See para. 6–03.

me the said D or my foresaids shall not exceed the sum of £ with interest thereon at the rate foresaid (3) the liability of each of us the said C and D or our respective foresaids shall be enforceable only upon demand made in writing by the said B or his foresaids to us or our respective foresaids[b] and (4) neither of us the said C or D or our respective foresaids shall be entitled to rank on the estates of the said A or his foresaids in competition with the said B or his fore-saids[c,d]: And I the said A bind myself and my foresaids to free and relieve the said C and D and their respective foresaids of and from payment of the said sums principal, interest and penalties or any part thereof and all loss, damage or expenses which they may incur in respect of their obligations as cautioners hereunder[e]: And we the said A, C and D consent to registration hereof for preservation and execution. (*To be attested*)

NOTES

[a] The obligation is of proper caution.

[b] The obligation of the cautioners is enforceable only after written demand and negative prescription (five years) commences to run only thereafter.

[c] Only B may rank in the bankruptcy of A. C and D may not rank because of the rule against double ranking in bankruptcy.

[d] If it is desired to obviate release of cautioners by change in terms of contract or indulgences by creditor insert provision on lines of condition (2) of style in para. 6–09.

[e] The obligation of relief, although implied, is expressed to facilitate action and diligence.

Parties—capacity and power

6–12 It is important that in any situation involving a cautionary obligation the creditor is satisfied that both the principal debtor and the cautioner have power to enter into their respective obligations. If the principal debtor enters into an obligation which he cannot lawfully undertake, not only is it unenforceable against him but the cautioner is also free since his obligation is accessory and depends upon the existence of a valid principal obligation. Particular care is required in the case of the following parties:

(a) Pupils or minors. Transactions which involve the participation of persons under full age, whether a pupil and his tutor or a minor with or without consent of his curator and whether in the capacity of principal debtor or cautioner, should be avoided. If a minor is the principal debtor the contract is open to reduction within the *quadriennium utile* on the grounds of minority and enorm lesion, thus releasing the cautioner, and if the minor is cautioner lesion is presumed.[17]

(b) Partnerships. Loans to a firm may be, and cautionary obligations undertaken by a firm normally will be, outwith its ordinary business

---

[17] Bell, *Prin.*, s. 2100.

transactions, so that one of the partners cannot effectively bind the firm.[18] The signatures of all partners are required.

(c) **Companies.** Prior to the enactment of the European Communities Act 1972[19] it was necessary to examine the memorandum and articles of association of a company which proposed to undertake a cautionary obligation in order to ensure that the company and its directors had power to make guarantees; a power to lend did not imply power to guarantee and it was necessary to demonstrate that the guarantee was incidental or conducive to the company's objects.[20] The matter became of peculiar importance in modern company practice involving the grant of a debenture by a holding company incorporating guarantees, sometimes with heritable security, by subsidiary companies, some of which derived no obvious benefit from the debenture moneys. The risk to the creditor of *ultra vires* acts of this kind is now significantly reduced by the provisions of section 9(1) of the 1972 Act but until the extent of the protection given by the subsection is more clearly defined by judicial decision, particularly on the matter of good faith, it is suggested that creditors should be satisfied that there is a clear power in the memorandum and articles of the company guarantor.[20a]

(d) **Agents.** An agent may not have authority to enter into a cautionary obligation or even a representation as to credit which binds his principal.[21]

Several cautioners

6–13   In a transaction where there are to be several cautioners for a single obligation each enters into the transaction on the understanding that the others are also bound and if any of the others are not effectively obligated the other signatory cautioners are not liable.[22]

Relationship and rights of parties

6–14   Because of the equities which the law admits for the benefit of cautioners in a question with the creditor and as amongst the cautioners themselves there are certain precautions which should be taken both as to representations inducing a cautionary obligation and as to the subsequent actings of parties while a cautionary obligation is in force and on its termination. These may conveniently be considered with regard to the relationships between (1) creditor and cautioner, (2) principal debtor and cautioner, and (3) cautioners *inter se*.

---

[18] Partnership Act 1890, s. 7; *Fortune* v. *Young*, 1918 S.C. 1.

[19] s. 9(1).

[20] *Shiell's Trs.* v. *Scottish Property Investment Building Society* (1884) 12 R. (H.L.) 14; *Small* v. *Smith* (1884) 10 App. Cas. 119, H.L.; *Life Association of Scotland* v. *Caledonian Heritable Security Co. Ltd.* (1886) 13 R. 750.

[20a] See *Rolled Steel Products (Holdings) Ltd.* v. *British Steel Corporation*, [1985] 2 W.L.R. 908.

[21] See as to the authority of an agent, *Hamilton* v. *Dixon* (1873) 1 R. 72; *Hockey* v. *Clydesdale Bank Ltd.* (1898) 1 F. 119; *Fortune* v. *Young, supra*.

[22] *Paterson* v. *Bonar* (1844) 6 D. 987; *Scottish Provincial Assurance Co.* v. *Pringle* (1858) 20 D. 465.

Creditor and Cautioner

(a) Representations

6–15   Usually when a guarantee is being sought it is in the interests of both the creditor and the principal debtor to obtain it and in these circumstances there is a risk that a guarantor may be induced to undertake a cautionary obligation by information as to the debtor's creditworthiness or financial position and the availability of other guarantees or securities which may amount to misrepresentation. The danger is alleviated by the provisions of section 6 of the Mercantile Law Amendment (Scotland) Act 1856 which require that representations as to the character, conduct, credit, ability (to pay),[23] trade or dealings of any person made for the purpose of enabling such person to obtain credit must be in writing but that requirement probably would not apply if the cautionary obligation was in the form of a negotiable instrument.[24] The section applies to representations by the agent of a bank.[25] It must be kept in view, however, that "a contract of guarantee, like any other contract, is liable to be avoided if induced by material misrepresentation of an existing fact, even if made innocently,"[26] and there can be circumstances when it is obvious that the intending guarantor is under a serious misapprehension as to the state of indebtedness of the person whose credit he is guaranteeing and the creditor takes no action to correct it, which may have that result.[27] In practice the creditor should not, so far as possible, participate in discussions with the proposed guarantor leading to the grant of a guarantee but should leave that matter to arrangement between the debtor and the intending guarantor, and should in no circumstances make any representations in writing.

(b) Extent of liability of cautioner

6–16   An obligation of guarantee may be made in respect of a particular advance, in which case it terminates when that advance is repaid.[28] It may also be made in respect of a continuing account but subject to a maximum figure of liability. In such a case it is important that the document of guarantee makes it clear that the guarantee does not terminate when the maximum amount is reached but continues thereafter so long as the account runs but subject to restriction of the cautioner's liability to the maximum sum stated.[29] Since a guarantee is construed *contra*

---

[23] *Irving* v. *Burns*, 1915 S.C. 260.
[24] *Walker's Trs.* v. *McKinlay* (1880) 7 R. (H.L.) 85.
[25] *Clydesdale Bank Ltd.* v. *Paton* (1896) 23 R. (H.L.) 22; *Union Bank of Scotland* v. *Taylor*, 1925 S.C. 835.
[26] *Mackenzie* v. *Royal Bank of Canada* [1934] A.C. 468, *per* Lord Atkin at 475.
[27] *Royal Bank of Scotland* v. *Greenshields*, 1914 S.C. 259, *per* Lord President (Strathclyde) at 268.
[28] *Scott* v. *Mitchell* (1866) 4 M. 551.
[29] *Veitch* v. *National Bank of Scotland*, 1907 S.C. 554; *Harmer & Co.* v. *Gibb*, 1911 S.C. 1341; *cf.* *Buchanan* v. *Main* (1900) 3 F. 215.

proferentem[30] the proper drafting method is to stipulate expressly that the guarantee is continuing and covering and to specify separately any limit of the guarantor's liability that has been agreed.[31]

(c) Enforcement

6–17   In improper cautionry the creditor may enforce payment against the guarantor without first exhausting his remedies against the principal debtor (the benefit of discussion) and he also has that right in a case of proper cautionry under statute.[32] Since cautionry is an accessory obligation the guarantor may plead in a question with the creditor any defences available to the principal debtor [33] and if a guarantor pays a claim against which the principal debtor had a valid defence he forfeits his right of relief.[34]

(d) Revocation

6–18   Where no limit of time is stipulated in the document of guarantee the guarantor is entitled to terminate his liability but only as regards any future advances and, subject to giving reasonable notice, he may require the principal debtor to relieve him of liabilities he may already have incurred by procuring and delivering a discharge of the guarantor's obligations by the creditor.[35]

(e) Bankruptcy of principal debtor

6–19   The basic rule is that only the amount due by the debtor to the creditor can be admitted to ranking in the sequestration of the debtor; the guarantor may be ranked in respect of any amount he has paid to the creditor but to that extent he ranks in place of the creditor whose claim is to that extent reduced.[36] If the guarantor is liable for the whole debt he may elect to pay it in full, obtain an assignation of the creditor's claim and rank in place of the creditor.[37] If the guarantee has been of a fixed amount the guarantor may pay that amount and rank for it in place of the creditor; alternatively, if the creditor ranks for the full amount, the guarantor's liability is limited to the amount he has guaranteed under deduction of the dividend received by the creditor.[38] If, however, the guarantee is of the whole debt subject to a limit of the amount for which the guarantor is liable, the creditor is entitled to rank for the whole debt and recover the balance, after crediting the dividend, up to the limit for

---

[30] *Aitken's Trs.* v. *Bank of Scotland*, 1944 S.C. 270.
[31] See styles at paras. 5–53 and 6–08.
[32] Mercantile Law Amendment (Scotland) Act 1856, s. 8.
[33] Bell, *Prin.*, s. 251.
[34] *Maxwell* v. *Earl of Nithsdale* (1632) Mor. 2115.
[35] *Doig* v. *Lawrie* (1903) 5 F. 295.
[36] *Anderson* v. *Mackinnon* (1876) 3 R. 608; *Mackinnon* v. *Monkhouse* (1881) 9 R. 393.
[37] *Harvie's Trs.* v. *Bank of Scotland* (1885) 12 R. 1141.
[38] *Veitch* v. *National Bank of Scotland Ltd.*, 1907 S.C. 554.

which the guarantor is liable.[39] In the event of the guarantor having paid part of the debt before the debtor's sequestration, the creditor must deduct that payment and rank only for the balance, whether or not the guarantor has claimed a ranking for the amount which he paid.[40] It is clearly in the interests of the creditor to have the right to rank for the whole debt and to recover the balance in full from the guarantor, at least up to the limit of the latter's liability: hence the special clauses excluding the guarantor's right to rank in the sequestration of the debtor in competition with the creditor included in the styles in paragraphs 5–53 and 6–11.

(f) Release from cautionary obligations

6–20 Apart from express discharge by the creditor of a guarantor's obligation, a guarantor may be liberated from it in a number of ways, chiefly (i) illegality of the principal obligation, (ii) discharge of the principal obligation, (iii) extinction of the principal obligation by prescription, (iv) the death of the principal debtor or creditor, (v) giving time to the principal debtor, (vi) releasing securities held for the debt, (vii) discharging a co-guarantor, (viii) alteration of the contract between the creditor and the principal debtor, (ix) neglect by the creditor to the prejudice of the guarantor, and (x) prescription of the guarantor's obligation. It is possible to preclude release of the guarantor in certain of the circumstances above mentioned by express provisions in the guarantee which reserve the creditor's right to do any of the acts specified without the guarantor being liberated and it is customary for banks or other professional lenders to frame documents of guarantee appropriately— see style in paragraph 5–53 *supra*.

6–21 **(i) Illegality of principal obligation.** From the fact that cautionry is an accessory obligation, the failure to constitute an enforceable principal obligation nullifies any obligation which a guarantor has purported to undertake. The rule is, "No principal debtor, no cautioner." So if the principal obligation has been entered into by a person who lacks the capacity or power to do so or the bargain involved is for any reason illegal or unenforceable, *e.g.* a postponed heritable security in favour of a building society, any purported guarantee of the obligation is unenforceable. The risk of a defect in the principal obligation may be guarded against in the document of guarantee by providing that in such a case the guarantor in effect assumes the liability in a question with the creditor— see style in paragraph 5–53 *supra*.

6–22 **(ii) Discharge of principal obligation.** It also follows from the accessory nature of the guarantor's obligation that there must be a principal obligation in existence. So an express discharge by the creditor of the

---

[39] *Harvie's Trs.* v. *Bank of Scotland, supra.*
[40] *Mackinnon's Tr.* v. *Bank of Scotland*, 1915 S.C. 411.

obligation of the principal debtor without the consent of the guarantor has the effect of liberating the guarantor from his obligation,[41] except when the principal debtor has been sequestrated.[42] (The exception does not extend to the situation where the debtor has granted a trust deed for creditors although power to accede to a composition arrangement is frequently reserved by the creditor in the documentation.)

6–23   (iii) **Extinction of principal obligation by prescription.** Again for the reason that a cautioner's obligation is accessory, it ceases if the principal obligation is extinguished by prescription. Where the principal obligation is to pay money and is constituted by a probative writ the period of negative prescription is 20 years,[43] but the obligation to pay each instalment of interest prescribes in five years from the date on which it becomes payable.[44] Where the debt is not constituted or evidenced by probative writing the short prescription of five years applies. The *terminus a quo* for any period of prescription is (a) in the case of a single debt, the date upon which it becomes payable[45]; (b) in the case of an obligation, not being part of a banking transaction, to pay money in respect of goods supplied or services rendered in a series of transactions charged on continuing account, the date on which payment for the goods last supplied or the services last rendered became due[46]; (c) in the case of a loan repayable on a stipulated date, that date[47]; (d) in the case of a loan where there is no stipulated date for repayment, *e.g.* a current banking account, the date when a written demand for repayment is made by or on behalf of the creditor to the debtor.[48] In all cases the running of prescription may be interrupted by the making of a relevant claim, *e.g.* raising an action for payment, lodging a claim in the bankruptcy of the debtor or notifying the claim in an arbitration process, or by such performance, *e.g.* making part-payment, or written admission by the debtor, as constitutes a relevant acknowledgement.[49] It follows that, whenever the relevant *terminus a quo* occurs and prescription commences to run upon the principal obligation, the creditor, if he wishes to ensure that the obligation of the guarantor is not lost, must either ensure that prescription of the debtor's obligation is interrupted by making a relevant claim or obtaining a relevant acknowledgment or require payment from the guarantor and enforce it, if need be, by court proceedings.

6–24   (iv) **Death of principal debtor or creditor.** The death of the principal debtor, unless there are special conditions in the contract of guarantee

---

[41] *Fleming* v. *Wilson* (1823) 2 S. 336; *Aitken's Trs.* v. *Bank of Scotland*, 1944 S.C. 270.
[42] Bankruptcy (Scotland) Act 1913, s. 52.
[43] Prescription and Limitation (Scotland) Act 1973, s. 7 and Sched. 1, para. 2(c).
[44] *Ibid.*, Sched. 1, para. 1(a) and exclusion from para. 2(c).
[45] *Ibid.*, ss. 6(3) and 7(1).
[46] *Ibid.*, Sched. 2 para. 1(1) and (4).
[47] *Ibid.*, Sched. 2, para. 2(2)(a).
[48] *Ibid.*, Sched. 2, para. 2(2)(b).
[49] *Ibid.*, ss. 6, 7, 9 and 10.

which provide otherwise, terminates the obligation of a guarantor as regards future transactions: the guarantor remains liable only for obligations previously incurred by the debtor which were covered by the guarantee.[50] The death of the creditor has a similar effect: the guarantor's liability, unless otherwise provided in the contract of guarantee, brings the obligation of the guarantor to an end as regards subsequent transactions. The death of the guarantor does not terminate the obligation of guarantee: his executors remain liable not only for obligations covered by the guarantee incurred before his death but also for such obligations incurred under a continuing guarantee after his death unless and until terminated by his executors intimating withdrawal of the guarantee *quoad* any subsequent liabilities. That liability continues until withdrawal even although the executors of the guarantor were unaware of the guarantee, and the creditor does not have a duty to inform the executors of it.[51] In guarantees of a continuing account in banking transactions it is customary to stipulate expressly that the death of the guarantor will not terminate liability under the guarantee[52] although in practice the creditor bank will frequently close the account when it becomes aware of the death of the guarantor and will advise the guarantor's executors of the liability of the debt as then existing. If the executors of a deceased co-guarantor in a joint and several guarantee give notice of termination of liability for future transactions the account should be closed and fresh guarantees obtained for the new account, since the obligations of the other co-guarantors for future advances are significantly affected by the termination of the liability of the deceased guarantor.

5–25 **(v) Giving time to principal debtor.** Any act by the creditor whereby he disables himself from suing the principal debtor for immediate payment and so prevents the guarantor, who would stand in his place, from doing so is an alteration of the contract which was guaranteed and so liberates the guarantor from his liability. The principle of liberation by giving time does not apply to mere failure to press the debtor for payment or to claim in the debtor's bankruptcy because the guarantor has a remedy available in such circumstances by paying the debt, obtaining an assignation of it and himself exercising the creditor's rights.[53] If, however, the creditor agrees not to sue,[54] or takes a bill payable at some future time for the debt,[55] or agrees to take payment by instalments,[56] the guarantor is released, since he is debarred from suing the debtor and may thereby

---

[50] Gloag, *Contract*, 361; *Reddie v. Williamson* (1863) 1 M. 228; *Woodfield Finance Trust (Glasgow) Ltd. v. Morgan*, 1958 S.L.T. (Sh.Ct.) 14.
[51] *British Linen Co. v. Monteith* (1858) 20 D. 557; *Caledonian Banking Co. v. Kennedy's Trs.* (1870) 8 M. 862.
[52] See style in para. 5–53.
[53] *Hay & Kyd v. Powrie* (1886) 13 R. 777; *Hamilton's Exr. v. Bank of Scotland*, 1913 S.C. 743.
[54] *Hay & Kyd v. Powrie, supra.*
[55] *Johnstone v. Duthie* (1892) 19 R. 624.
[56] *Wilson v. Lloyd* (1873) L.R. 16 Eq. 60.

suffer prejudice. The guarantor does not require to establish that he has actually suffered prejudice,[57] nor does it matter that, before time was given, the guarantor had already sought to repudiate liability on other grounds.[58] The guarantor is not liberated, however, merely because the creditor, after the guarantee has been given, supplies goods allowing an ordinary period of credit or takes a bill of ordinary duration for the price.[59] When a guarantee is taken for a continuing account or series of transactions the creditor may, and should, reserve power to give time without thereby releasing the guarantor.[60]

6–26   **(vi) Giving up securities.** Since a guarantor has the right, on payment of the debt guaranteed, to an assignation of any securities held for it, the voluntary release of a security by the creditor without the consent of the guarantor liberates the guarantor from his obligation,[61] but only to the extent of the value of the security released.[62] If, however, it was agreed that the creditor should seek repayment from the security before requiring payment from the guarantor, then the surrender of the security discharges the obligation of the guarantor completely.[63] The guarantor may also be liberated through failure of the creditor to complete title to a security to the extent that the guarantor loses the benefit of it.[64] In a document of guarantee, at least for a continuing account where other securities have been or may be taken, the creditor may reserve the right to release securities without the guarantor being thereby liberated to any extent.[65]

6–27   **(vii) Discharge of co-guarantor.** Where several guarantors are bound jointly and severally the discharge of any one of them by the creditor without the consent of the others is deemed by statute to discharge all the others, except in the case of discharge of a cautioner who has become bankrupt.[66] This statutory provision does not apply if the cautioners are not bound jointly and severally but each only for a specific amount,[67] nor if the rights of the other co-guarantors are expressly reserved in the discharge,[68] nor if the creditor simply gives time to one co-guarantor[69] or undertakes not to sue him.[70] The right to release co-guarantors without affecting the liability of the others may be reserved to the creditor in the guarantee.[71]

---

[57] *Johnstone* v. *Duthie, supra*; *Polak* v. *Everett* (1876) 1 Q.B.D. 669.
[58] *Johnstone* v. *Duthie, supra.*
[59] *Calder & Co.* v. *Cruikshank's Tr.* (1889) 17 R. 74.
[60] See styles, paras. 5–53 and 6–09.
[61] *Sligo* v. *Menzies* (1840) 2 D. 1478.
[62] *Wright's Trs.* v. *Hamilton* (1835) 13 S. 380.
[63] *Drummond* v. *Rannie* (1836) 14 S. 437.
[64] *Fleming* v. *Thomson* (1826) 2 W. & S. 277.
[65] See style, para. 5–53.
[66] Mercantile Law Amendment (Scotland) Act 1856, s. 9.
[67] *Morgan* v. *Smart* (1872) 10 M. 610; *Union Bank of Scotland* v. *Taylor*, 1925 S.C. 835, 841.
[68] *Thompson* v. *Lack* (1846) 3 C.B. 540; *North* v. *Wakefield* (1849) 13 Q.B. 536.
[69] *Kearsley* v. *Cole* (1846) 16 M. & W. 128, 136.
[70] *Muir* v. *Crawford* (1875) 2 R. (H.L.) 148.
[71] See style, para. 5–53.

-28 **(viii) Alteration of contract.** If the creditor and the principal debtor amend their contract in such a way as to alter the guarantor's liability without his consent he is liberated. Examples of changes which have had that result were increase of the weekly payments by the borrower under a personal credit agreement[72] and the taking of a trust deed from the debtor by creditors in a composition contract which had been guaranteed by a cautioner.[73] Novation of the contract, as when the original debt is discharged and a new debt substituted, releases the guarantor from his obligation.[74]

-29 **(ix) Neglect by creditor to prejudice of guarantor.** Any action or failure to take action by the creditor which may adversely affect the liability of the guarantor has the effect of liberating him. Great delay in enforcing the creditor's rights against the debtor,[75] and taking decree against the debtor for the full amount when payment by instalments had been guaranteed by the cautioner without informing the cautioner,[76] were acts which were held to have released the cautioner. On the other hand the fact that the creditor had reason to suspect forgery by the principal debtor and did not disclose that to a guarantor of the debtor's account with his bankers did not release the guarantor, but it was observed that the position might have been otherwise if the bankers had thereafter given further accommodation so as to increase the debtor's obligations without advising the guarantor of their doubts as to the debtor's honesty.[77] Neglect by the creditor is of particular importance in relation to fidelity guarantees—see paragraph 6–37.

(g) Prescription of guarantor's obligation

-30 A cautionary obligation is extinguished if it has subsisted for a period of five years after the date when it became enforceable unless a relevant claim has been made by the creditor or the obligation has been relevantly acknowledged in terms of the Prescription and Limitation (Scotland) Act 1973.[78] This short prescription applies notwithstanding that the guarantee is constituted or evidenced by a probative writ[79] or that it is contained in a probative writ wherein the debtor and guarantor are bound jointly and severally as co-obligants, *e.g.* as in improper caution, unless the creditor establishes that the particular co-obligant is truly a principal debtor or that, if he is not truly a principal debtor, the original creditor was not aware of that fact at the time when the writ was

---

[72] *N. G. Napier Ltd.* v. *Crosbie*, 1964 S.C. 129.
[73] *Allan, Allan & Milne* v. *Pattison* (1893) 21 R. 195.
[74] *Commercial Bank of Tasmania* v. *Jones* [1893] A.C. 313.
[75] *Macfarlane* v. *Anstruther* (1870) 9 M. 117.
[76] *Murray* v. *Lee* (1882) 9 R. 1040.
[77] *Bank of Scotland* v. *Morrison*, 1911 S.C. 593.
[78] s. 6 and Sched. 1, para. 1(g): it is a contract or promise. As to relevant claim and relevant acknowledgment, see ss. 9, 10.
[79] *Ibid.*, Sched. 1, para. 2(c).

delivered to him.[80] It will be comparatively seldom that the original creditor was unaware of the true relationship of the parties, so that for practical purposes the short prescription will usually apply to all cautionary obligations, however constituted. The date when the obligation of the guarantor becomes enforceable is ascertained upon construction of the relevant document but where the guarantee is contained in a separate writing and is expressed as payable on demand the *terminus a quo* of the period of prescription is the date when the creditor formally requires the guarantor to pay, not the date when the principal debtor was in default.[81] In such a case the creditor should exercise care in communicating with the guarantor and in particular, if he is informing the guarantor that the principal debtor is in default and that the creditor proposes to await the completion of bankruptcy or liquidation proceedings, he should make it plain that the letter is not at that stage a demand or request for payment from the guarantor.

Principal Debtor and Cautioner

(a) Right of relief

6–31   A guarantor is entitled to be relieved by the principal debtor repaying to him any amounts he has been required to pay to the creditor under the guarantee.[82] The obligation of relief may be expressed in proper caution, but the law implies it and an express obligation of relief is mainly of value if security is given. In improper caution it is competent to establish the true relationship of the parties by parole evidence.[83] The guarantor may sue the debtor not only when he has paid under the guarantee but also if the debtor is *vergens ad inopiam*[84] and by virtue of the right of relief he may retain against an arresting creditor funds held by him for the principal debtor.[85] The right of relief is lost, however, if the guarantor pays to the creditor a claim against which the principal debtor had a valid defence.[86]

(b) Right to assignation

6–32   When a guarantor pays the debt in full he is entitled to require from the creditor an assignation of the debt, with the benefit of any diligence done upon it, and of any securities held by the creditor for it.[87] He cannot insist upon assignation, however, if only a partial payment has been made, *e.g.* where the guarantor was bankrupt and a dividend was paid

---

[80] *Ibid.*, Sched. 1, para. 3.
[81] *Royal Bank of Scotland Ltd.* v. *Brown*, 1983 S.L.T. 122.
[82] Bell, *Prin.*, ss. 245, 255; *Doig* v. *Lawrie* (1903) 5 F. 295.
[83] *Hamilton & Co.* v. *Freeth* (1889) 16 R. 1022; *Crosbie* v. *Brown* (1900) 3 F. 83.
[84] *Kinloch* v. *McIntosh* (1822) 1 S. 491.
[85] *McPherson* v. *Wright* (1885) 12 R. 942.
[86] *Maxwell* v. *Earl of Nithsdale* (1632) Mor. 2115.
[87] *Sligo* v. *Menzies* (1840) 2 D. 1478.

to the creditor by his trustee.[88] The creditor may refuse an assignation if he has a legitimate interest to retain the security[89] but not simply because he wishes to retain the security in respect of another debt due to him by the principal debtor for which the security was not previously held.[90]

(c) Ranking in bankruptcy of debtor

–33 The right of a guarantor to rank in the bankruptcy of the debtor on paying the creditor in full has already been considered.[91]

Cautioners Inter Se

(a) Relief

–34 In proper cautionry where several cautioners are bound jointly for payment of debt none can be sued for more than his *pro rata* share (*beneficium divisionis*), unless any of them is insolvent in which event he is ignored in making the division.[92] Where several cautioners are bound jointly and severally the creditor may require payment in full from any one of them, in which event the cautioner who pays is entitled to relief from the others to the extent that the payment made exceeds his share.[93] Even where cautioners are bound for fixed amounts any of them who pays more than his proportionate share may recover the excess from the others so far as within the limit amounts of their respective liabilities.[94]

(b) Communication of securities

–35 In theory all cautioners have a right of recourse against the whole funds of the principal debtor in satisfaction of his obligation of relief and so may claim the benefit of any securities provided by the debtor to any of the cautioners, even although the other cautioners have not stipulated for security.[95] The principle does not apply where each of the cautioners is bound for a specific sum,[96] nor where the security was provided by a third party for the benefit of one of the cautioners,[97] nor where one cautioner had stipulated for security for his exclusive benefit and the other cautioners had known of and had consented to the arrangement.[98]

---

[88] *Ewart* v. *Latta* (1865) 3 M. (H.L.) 36.
[89] *Mitchell* v. *McKinlay* (1842) 4 D. 634; *Guthrie & McConnachy* v. *Smith* (1880) 8 R. 107.
[90] *Fleming* v. *Burgess* (1867) 5 M. 856.
[91] See para. 6–19.
[92] *Buchanan* v. *Main* (1900) 3 F. 215.
[93] *Marshall & Co.* v. *Pennycook*, 1908 S.C. 276.
[94] *Morgan* v. *Smart* (1872) 10 M. 610.
[95] Bell, *Prin.*, s. 270; Bell, *Comm.*, I, 367; *Campbell* v. *Campbell* (1775) Mor. 2132.
[96] *Lawrie* v. *Stewart* (1823) 2 S. 368.
[97] *Coventry* v. *Hutchison* (1830) 8 S. 924; *Scott* v. *Young*, 1909 1 S.L.T. 47.
[98] *Hamilton & Co.* v. *Freeth* (1889) 16 R. 1022.

(c) Communication of benefits

6–36   If one of several cautioners pays the debt and obtains a discount or effects a compromise whereby less than the full amount is accepted he is bound, when exercising his right of relief against the other cautioners, to communicate the benefit of the deduction.[99] So if A and B are cautioners bound jointly and severally for £10,000 and A settles the creditor's claim for £7000, he may claim relief from B only to the extent of £3500.

Fidelity Guarantees

6–37   A guarantor of the intromissions of an agent or factor or of the fidelity of an employee has the benefit of the equities in favour of a cautioner already described and throughout the relationship the creditor has the duty of communicating to the guarantor any matters which may affect his obligation and, in the case of an employee, of exercising proper supervision. Failure in these respects may result in the guarantor being released.

6–38   Where the guarantee is of the intromissions of a factor the guarantor should be informed initially of the scope of the factor's duties and responsibilities and is entitled to assume that there are regular periodic accounts of intromissions properly checked by the creditor and, in the case of intromissions of substantial amount, duly audited. A properly drawn document of guarantee will contain an admission by the guarantor that he has received all necessary information as to the nature and extent of the factor's duties and responsibilities but it is thought that such an admission will not protect the creditor if there has been serious misrepresentation. Likewise the guarantee may absolve the creditor from the duty of examining or checking the factor's accounts or having them audited, but it is doubtful whether such a provision would protect the creditor if there is gross negligence in supervision of accounts or failure to obtain accounts prepared at periodic intervals.

6–39   In the case of a guarantee for the fidelity of an employee the creditor, if he is aware of previous defalcations by the employee, must inform the guarantor of those facts or the guarantor will not be bound.[1] If the guarantee does not stipulate for any particular checks or special precautions the guarantor will not avoid liability on the ground that greater care in supervision would have prevented the occurrence of the acts in respect of which the guarantee was given,[2] although probably a guarantor is entitled to assume that checks usual in the business of the employer, as

---

[99] Bell, *Prin.*, s. 270.
[1] *Smith* v. *Bank of Scotland* (1829) 7 S. 244; *French* v. *Cameron* (1893) 20 R. 966.
[2] *McTaggart* v. *Watson* (1835) 1 S. & McL. 553.

in the case of a bank official, will be duly made.[3] On the other hand if the guarantee stipulates that particular checks are to be carried out and there is failure to do so the guarantor will be released from his obligation.[4] A change in the duties of the employee guaranteed will liberate the guarantor even although the loss did not arise from the change.[5] A guarantee in general terms of the intromissions of an employee, not limited as to time, was held to continue enforceable although the employee's engagement was renewed after the expiry of the period of his employment during which the guarantee was given.[6] It is essential that the employer gives immediate notice to the guarantor when any defalcation by the guaranteed employee occurs; failure to do so timeously may liberate the guarantor.[7] As a matter of practice the granter of a fidelity guarantee for an employee should specify his duties, stipulate for regular checks upon his intromissions and provide for notice of any irregularities being given within a very short period after their discovery.

Stamp Duty

6–40   A guarantee was formerly regarded as liable to stamp duty, not as a bond but as an agreement.[8] Stamp duty upon agreements which did not contain a clause of registration was abolished[9] and so no stamp duty is payable upon a bond of caution or separate guarantee which does not contain a clause of registration. A bond incorporating the principal obligation and a cautionary obligation as in the style in paragraph 6–11 *supra*, which contains a clause of registration, is also exempt from stamp duty.[10]

II. CORROBORATIVE OBLIGATIONS

Nature

6–41   A corroborative obligation, although related to an existing obligation, is not accessory: it is a new and independent obligation[11] and the document which creates it should contain within it all necessary particulars to enable the obligee to sue upon it without production of the deed which constituted the original obligation.[12]

---

[3] *Falconer* v. *Lothian* (1843) 5 D. 866, 870.
[4] *Haworth & Co.* v. *Sickness and Accident Assce. Assn. Ltd.* (1891) 18 R. 563.
[5] *Bonar* v. *McDonald* (1850) 7 Bell's App. 379.
[6] *Nicolsons* v. *Burt* (1882) 10 R. 121.
[7] *Snaddon* v. *London, Edinburgh & Glasgow Assce. Co. Ltd.* (1902) 5 F. 182.
[8] *North of Scotland Bank* v. *Inland Revenue*, 1931 S.C. 149.
[9] Finance Act 1970, ss. 32(*a*), 36(8), Sched. 7, para. 1(2)(*a*), Sched. 8, Pt. IV.
[10] Finance Act 1971, s. 64(1).
[11] *Yuill's Trs.* v. *Maclachlan's Trs.*, 1939 S.C. (H.L.) 40.
[12] *Beg* v. *Brown* (1663) Mor. 16091; *Johnston* v. *Orchardtoun* (1676) Mor. 15798; *Coult* v. *Angus* (1749) Mor. 17040.

Use

6–42   Corroborative deeds are used frequently in heritable conveyancing, normally to correct some defect in an existing title, as in the case of a corroborative disposition where there has been a mistake or omission of a necessary consent in an earlier conveyance.[13] Formerly bonds of corroboration were extensively used in relation to heritable securities[14] but the need for them has now been restricted by statute[15] and in the case of standard securities variations in the personal obligation may now be effected by simpler documents.[16] Bonds of corroboration are still used, although less frequently, in moveable conveyancing, in the circumstances outlined in the following paragraphs.

6–43   A bond of corroboration may be granted by the original obligant for the purpose of (1) varying or enlarging the original obligation, *e.g.* by increasing the rate of interest, (2) curing some defect in the original document of obligation, (3) accumulating interest in arrear by adding it to principal, or (4) avoiding the loss of unpaid interest through negative prescription for which the period is now five years[17] or of principal where the relevant period in the case of an obligation constituted by probative writ is 20 years.[18] When the original obligation has been supported by a guarantee and it is not clear that the guarantee is enforceable only on demand so that there is a risk of the guarantor's obligation being extinguished by the short negative prescription a bond of corroboration may be taken from the guarantor to provide a relevant acknowledgment which will interrupt the running of prescription, although the same result may be achieved by a simpler form of unequivocal acknowledgment of continuing liability.[19] A bond of corroboration may also be granted by a third party when the creditor requires an additional obligant, in which case it is peculiarly important that the amount of principal and interest is clearly stated to enable the creditor to enforce payment by the new obligant and to use summary diligence without reference to the original document of obligation.[20]

Prescription

6–44   The effect of prescription on a corroborative obligation depends upon the character of the right corroborated. If the corroborative deed confers or fortifies a real right of ownership in land or a right in land of a lessee under a recorded lease and the corroborative deed is itself either

---

[13] Burns, 545.
[14] Burns, 545 *et seq.*
[15] Conveyancing (Scotland) Act 1874, s. 47 as amended by Conveyancing (Scotland) Act 1924, s. 15.
[16] Conveyancing and Feudal Reform (Scotland) Act 1970, s. 16; Halliday, 164–166.
[17] Prescription and Limitation (Scotland) Act 1973, s. 6 and Sched. 1, para. 1(*a*)(i).
[18] *Ibid.*, s. 7 and Sched. 1, para. 2(*c*).
[19] *Ibid.*, s. 10(1)(*b*).
[20] *Coult* v. *Angus, supra.*

recorded in the Register of Sasines or is part of a progress of titles upon which registration of a title in the Land Register follows, then negative prescription has no application to the corroborative deed since a real right of ownership in land or of the lessee under a recorded lease is imprescriptible.[21] If the obligation corroborated is within any of the categories affected by the short prescription specified in Schedule 1 to the Prescription and Limitation (Scotland) Act 1973 then it will be extinguished on the expiry of five years from the date when it became enforceable unless kept alive by a relevant claim or relevant acknowledgment or constituted by a probative deed and, even when so constituted, if it relates to an obligation for payment of a principal sum and interest, it may be extinguished after five years *quoad* the obligation to pay interest and after 20 years *quoad* the obligation to pay the principal sum. It should be kept in view that the corroborative obligation is independent and it may be extinguished by the operation of the relevant prescription even although the original obligation remains enforceable.[22] It follows that the creditor in a prescriptible corroborative obligation should review the position at intervals of less than five years and take the steps necessary to obtain a relevant acknowledgment.

Style

5–45 Although a corroborative obligation may be created by a relatively informal document it should (a) contain all the particulars necessary to enable its enforcement without reference to the deed which created the obligation corroborated, and (b) be in probative form to ensure that, at least as regards a principal sum, the longer period of prescription of 20 years will apply. Consideration should also be given (if appropriate) to the inclusion of a provision that the corroborative obligation is only enforceable on demand by the creditor in order to defer the *terminus a quo* of prescription. A bond of corroboration in formal style is given below.

Bond of corroboration—Original and new obligant

We, A and C (*both designed*) CONSIDERING that by bond dated   I the said A bound myself, my executors and representatives whomsoever to make payment to B (*designed*), his executors or assignees, of the principal sum of £1000 and that at the term of Martinmas then next with a fifth part more of liquidate penalty in case of failure and the interest of the said principal sum at the rate of Ten pounds per centum per annum from the date of the said bond to the said term of payment and half yearly, termly and proportionally thereafter during the not payment as the said bond more fully bears; AND NOW 'SEEING that the said principal sum of £1000 Sterling is still unpaid and that on condition of a bond

---

[21] Prescription and Limitation (Scotland) Act 1973, ss. 7(2) and 8(2) and Sched. 3, (*a*) and (*b*).
[22] *Yuill's Trs.* v. *Maclachlan's Trs., supra.*

of corroboration being granted by us, the said A and C, the said B has agreed to allow payment thereof to be deferred until the term aftermentioned; THEREFORE and in corroboration of the original bond above narrated and without prejudice thereto or to any diligence that has followed or may be competent to follow thereon, *sed accumulando jura juribus*, we the said A and C bind ourselves and our respective executors and representatives whomsoever, without the necessity of discussing them in their order, all jointly and severally, to make payment to the said B or his executors or assignees of the said principal sum of £1000 and that* at the term of Martinmas next, within (*specify the place of payment*) with a fifth part more of liquidate penalty in case of failure and the interest of the said principal sum at the rate of Ten pounds per centum per annum from the   day of   to the said term of payment and half yearly, termly and proportionally thereafter during the not payment thereof, and that at two terms etc. (*as in form of Personal Bond*). (*To be attested*)

NOTE
* If it is desired to defer the obligation of C until B requires him to pay, insert after the asterisk the words, "subject always to the proviso after written in the case of the obligation of the said C," and add subsequently: "Provided always that the obligations of the said C or his foresaids hereunder shall become enforceable only upon demand by the said B or his foresaids and not sooner."

III. OBLIGATIONS OF RELIEF

Constitution

6–46   Obligations of relief occur in a variety of circumstances but may be broadly classified as (1) obligations of relief arising by implication of law from the relationship of parties, (2) obligations of relief undertaken conventionally by agreement, and (3) obligations of relief implied by law but fortified by express agreement.

Obligations of relief implied by law

6–47   In certain relationships an obligation of relief is implied by law. Examples are (1) the obligation of a principal to relieve his agent of contractual liabilities undertaken on behalf of the principal within the scope of the agent's authority, (2) the obligation of a principal debtor to relieve a guarantor of payments made under the guarantee, (3) the obligation of each of several co-obligants bound jointly and severally to relieve the others of his proportionate share of liability, (4) the obligation of each partner of a firm to relieve the other partners of his appropriate share of a liability of the firm, and (5) the obligation of each of several joint wrongdoers to contribute his proportion of damages incurred. Such obligations concern conveyancers only as the legal background to particular documents and are not treated in this section.

Obligations of relief imposed conventionally

6–48 Obligations of relief are commonly undertaken by agreement in certain types of transaction. Examples are (1) contracts of sale or lease of heritable property where a liability is payable by one party but in terms of the contract he is relieved of the liability, in whole or in part, by the other, *e.g.* apportionment of local rates, etc., (2) agreements for dissolution of partnership which include an undertaking by the continuing partners to relieve the outgoing partner or partners of liabilities of the firm incurred during the subsistence of the partnership which is now being dissolved, and (3) undertakings by beneficiaries at the close of administration of a trust or executry estate to relieve the trustees or executors of any liabilities of the estate which may subsequently be discovered. The terms of such obligations are treated *infra* under the relevant sections relating to sales and leases of heritable property, partnership and trusts and executries.

Obligations of relief implied by law and fortified by express agreement

6–49 Where an obligation of relief is implied by law it may be fortified, particularly in the case of cautionary obligations, by a separate bond of relief. A right of relief implied by law, except in relation to a cautionary obligation, may be enforced only when the person entitled to relief has actually paid the debt or been distressed for payment: relief cannot be recovered in respect of an anticipated claim.[23] A cautioner, however, may require the principal debtor to relieve him of the contingent obligation for past advances before he has been required to make any payment under the guarantee.[24] In these circumstances the document of guarantee will be in the possession of the creditor who cannot be required to surrender it except upon payment of the debt and it is of value to the cautioner to have an express bond of relief from the debtor upon which to found an action of relief. Other reasons for having an express bond of relief in cautionary obligations are:

(1) If the principal debtor and cautioner are bound jointly and severally in a single document of obligation (improper caution) it is desirable that the cautioner should have written evidence from the principal debtor as to the true relationship. That can be established by inference from the terms of the principal deed[25] or by parole evidence,[26] but a bond of relief containing an express admission of the relationship avoids the need of inference or proof and authorises summary diligence.

(2) If in addition to a guarantee security for the principal obligation has been provided by a third party it may be unclear whether the

---

[23] *Eliott's Trs.* v. *Eliott* (1894) 21 R. 858; *Roughead* v. *White*, 1913 S.C. 162.
[24] *Doig* v. *Lawrie* (1903) 5 F. 295.
[25] *Devlin* v. *McKelvie*, 1915 S.C. 180.
[26] *Thow's Tr.* v. *Young*, 1910 S.C. 588.

security is to be applied in relief of the guarantor or *vice versa*[26]; a bond of relief may assist in clarifying the matter although, unless the third party has consented to or been aware of the bond when the security was given, it may not be conclusive.

(3) If the cautioner is to have security for his contingent obligation over moveable property of the principal debtor the bond of relief may contain an assignation in security in appropriate form. If the security is over heritable property the bond of relief will constitute a probative obligation and a standard security in Form B of Schedule 2 to the Conveyancing and Feudal Reform (Scotland) Act 1970 will create the heritable security.

Style

6–50   Where a single guarantor is involved and there are no special circumstances or complexities a bond of relief in the following style may be used.

Bond of relief—Single cautioner

I, A (*designed*) considering that [B (*designed*) and myself have signed a bond dated   in favour of (*name and address of bank*) in respect of all sums due and to become due by me to the said Bank but that the said B has done so only as cautioner for me and that I am the only true debtor] *or* [B (*designed*) has signed a guarantee dated   in favour of (*name and address of bank*) in respect of all sums due or that may become due by me to the said Bank], hereby undertake to relieve the said B and his executors or representatives of the obligations undertaken by the said B under the said [bond] [guarantee] at any time on demand by the said B or his foresaids, and for that purpose I bind myself and my executors and representatives whomsoever, without the benefit of discussion, to pay to the said B or his foresaids within the head office of the said Bank at any time on demand as aforesaid the whole amount of principal and interest due by me or my foresaids to the said Bank at the time of such demand as the said amount shall be ascertained by a certificate under the hand of an official of the said Bank which I agree to authorise the said Bank to furnish at the request of the said B or his foresaids, but subject to the condition that the said B or his foresaids shall be bound to account to me or my foresaids for the amount so paid under deduction of all sums for which he or they may be liable under the said [bond] [guarantee] and all expenses incurred or that may be incurred in connection therewith, with interest at the rate of   per centum per annum on all sums disbursed by the said B or his foresaids until repaid: And I consent to registration hereof for preservation and execution. (*To be attested*)

---

[26] *Thow's Tr.* v. *Young*, 1910 S.C. 588.

Complex cases—several parties

6–51   In special cases, as where the guarantee is of a loan of minimum duration[27] or other guarantors or third parties who provide security are involved, more elaborate provisions in a bond of relief may be required. It must be kept in mind that (a) the rights and obligations of the guarantor in questions with the creditor will be regulated by the document constituting the guarantee and not by a subsequent bond of relief to which the creditor is not a party, and (b) the rights and obligations *inter se* of any one guarantor under a bond of relief and of other guarantors or persons providing security will not be conclusively determined by the bond of relief unless such other parties have consented to it or have entered into their obligations or provided security with knowledge of its terms.

---

[27] See Burns, 494.

CHAPTER 7

TRANSFER OF INCORPOREAL MOVEABLE RIGHTS
ABSOLUTELY AND IN SECURITY

Introduction

7–01   This chapter deals with the transfer of incorporeal moveable rights, both absolutely and in security. Commercial paper such as bills of exchange, promissory notes and cheques are documents more within the field of mercantile law and are not dealt with in this work, except incidentally. The transfer of corporeal moveables on sale or in security is treated in Chapter 8 *infra*.

I. VOLUNTARY TRANSFER OF INCORPOREAL RIGHTS—GENERAL PRINCIPLES

(1) Assignable and Non-Assignable Rights

7–02   In general incorporeal moveable rights are assignable unless they involve an element of *delectus personae* or are declared non-assignable by statute. The principal non-assignable rights are: (a) Contracts of service, which can be assigned only if the employee consents.[1] (b) The share of a partner in the partnership is usually declared unassignable by a provision in the contract of partnership, but, even if not so prohibited, assignation by a partner of his share does not make the assignee a partner nor entitle him to interfere in the management or administration of the partnership business nor inspect its books: the assignee is entitled only to the assigning partner's share of profits (and must accept the account of profits agreed to by the partners) and on dissolution of the partnership to receive the assigning partner's share of the firm's assets and an account as from the date of dissolution to ascertain that share.[2] (c) Rights which are in the nature of privileges granted to a particular person.[3] (d) Goodwill which is personal to the cedent.[4] (e) Liferents are not assignable in the sense that the assignee becomes the liferenter; the liferent still ceases on the death of the person on whom it was conferred by the deed which created it, but the payments, if not declared alimentary, are assignable. (f) Alimentary rights declared to be so in the deed which creates them and properly protected by a trust,[5] except so far as in excess of reasonable requirements for maintenance[6]; the actual alimentary payments as they are received[7] and any arrears[8] are assignable. (g) Social security benefits.[9] (h) Pensions payable under approved occupational pension schemes.

Building or engineering contracts (*locatio operis faciendi*) may, subject to any express stipulations in the contract itself, be assignable or assignable to some degree largely depending upon whether or not *delectus personae* is involved,[10] but the right of the contractor to payment of amounts due or to become due under the contract may be assigned.

(2) Effect of Assignation—Assignatus Utitur Jure Auctoris

7–03 The effect of an absolute assignation duly intimated is to divest the cedent completely and to put the assignee in his place but in accordance with the maxim *assignatus utitur jure auctoris* the assignee acquires only such right as the cedent himself had. The assignee may enforce the right assigned by any legal process which would have been available to the cedent and grant a valid discharge upon payment or performance. On the other hand any pleas or defences competent against the cedent are available to the debtor in a question with the assignee, even when the

---

[1] *Berlitz School of Languages* v. *Duchêne* (1903) 6 F. 181.
[2] Partnership Act 1890, s. 31.
[3] *Leith Dock Commissioners* v. *Colonial Life Assurance Co.* (1861) 24 D. 64; *Orr Ewing* v. *Earl of Cawdor* (1884) 12 R. (H.L.) 12.
[4] *Rodger* v. *Herbertson*, 1909 S.C. 256.
[5] *White's Trs.* v. *Whyte* (1877) 4 R. 786.
[6] *Cuthbert* v. *Cuthbert's Trs.*, 1908 S.C. 967; *Coles*, 1951 S.C. 608.
[7] *Hewats* v. *Roberton* (1881) 9 R. 175.
[8] *Drew* v. *Drew* (1870) 9 M. 163.
[9] Social Security Act 1975, s. 87; Supplementary Benefits Act 1976, s. 16.
[10] Gloag, *Contract*, 416–419.

assignation has been taken in good faith and for value,[11] rights of compensation pleadable by the debtor against the cedent are available against the assignee if they existed before the assignation was granted[12] but not if created subsequently[13] and if the right assigned is terminable or defeasible on the occurrence of any event the right taken by the assignee likewise ceases if that event happens.[14] If, however, the cedent's right is subject to a latent trust or claim in favour of a third party and the assignee takes for onerous consideration and in good faith without knowledge of the latent trust or claim, the third party cannot plead the principle of *assignatus utitur jure auctoris* so as to prevail against the right taken by the assignee.[15]

7–04   In practice the proposed assignee should examine the documents which created the right that is being assigned to ensure that there are no conditions affecting it which are unacceptable and that there are no circumstances in which the right may terminate or be reduced. Inquiry should be made to confirm that no payments to account of the debt have been made and that there is no counterclaim or right of compensation available to the debtor against the cedent. It is not necessary, however, to inquire as to the existence of latent trusts in favour of third parties unless there is anything in the documents examined or the information furnished which indicates the possible existence of a latent claim so that failure to make further inquiry might preclude good faith.

II. Assignations—Particular Rights

(1) Personal Bonds

Pre-contract investigations

7–05   When a personal bond is being acquired for value it is necessary to ensure (a) that the bond has been validly executed, (b) that there have been no payments to account nor any claim of compensation available to the debtor against the cedent,[16] and (c) that no preferential right to the bond has been acquired by diligence or otherwise by creditors of the cedent.[17] Inquiry should also be made as to the ability of the debtor in the bond to make repayment. If the bond is being purchased from an assignee or the executors of the original creditor the validity of the previous assignation or the inclusion of the bond in the confirmation, as the case may be, should be investigated. In such circumstances the cedent or the executors should also be satisfied that there have been no payments

---

[11] *Buist* v. *Scottish Equitable Life Assurance Society* (1878) 5 R. (H.L.) 64.
[12] *Shiells* v. *Ferguson, Davidson & Co.* (1876) 4 R. 250.
[13] *Macpherson's J.F.* v. *Mackay*, 1915 S.C. 1011.
[14] *Johnstone-Beattie* v. *Dalzell* (1868) 6 M. 333.
[15] *Somervails* v. *Redfearn* (1813) 1 Dow 50.
[16] See paras. 7–03 and 7–04.
[17] See *Globe Insurance Co.* v. *McKenzie* (1850) 7 Bell's App. 296.

to account nor rights of compensation nor release of any cautioners for the sum due under the bond, since the implied warrandice *debitum subesse* may render him liable for the full amount in the bond in a question with the purchaser.[18] Inquiry should be made as to whether the bond has been registered for execution and, if so, the extract decree should also be assigned.[19]

Form of assignation

–06   The Transmission of Moveable Property (Scotland) Act 1862 authorises assignation of a personal bond in the forms prescribed in Schedule A (separate) or Schedule B (endorsed). Although the use of those forms is not obligatory, one or other is normally used in practice.

Original creditor—separate assignation

–07   I, A (*designed*), in consideration of the sum of £   now paid to me by B (*designed*) do hereby assign to the said B and his executors or assignees the Bond granted by C (*designed*) dated   by which he bound himself to pay to me the sum of £   at the term of   with interest at the rate of   per centum per annum, which interest is hereby assigned for the period from and after the term of   . (*To be attested*)

Original creditor—endorsed assignation

–08   I, A (*designed*), in consideration of the sum of £   now paid to me by B (*designed*) do hereby assign to the said B and his executors or assignees the foregoing Bond granted in my favour, with interest from and after the term of   (*To be attested*)

Derivative creditor—separate assignation

–09   I, A (*designed*), in consideration of the sum of £   now paid to me by B (*designed*) do hereby assign to the said B and his executors or assignees the Bond granted by C (*designed*) by which he bound himself to pay to D (*designed*) the sum of £   at the term of   with interest at the rate of   per centum per annum, which interest is hereby assigned for the period from and after the term of   ; To which Bond I acquired right by Assignation by the said D in my favour dated   .[a,b] (*To be attested*)

NOTES
[a] In the deduction of title each writ specified should be described by reference to names and designations of parties and date; the provisions of the Conveyancing (Scotland) Act 1924 dispensing with designations of parties are not applicable in moveable conveyancing.
[b] The omission of a deduction of title, it is thought, does not invalidate the assignation so long as the cedent is entitled to the bond

---

[18] *Houston* v. *Corbet* (1717) Mor. 16619; *Reid* v. *Barclay* (1879) 6 R. 1007.
[19] See para. 4–72.

assigned and the links in his title are delivered to the assignee so that on challenge he may substantiate his title. In any event the linking deeds should always be delivered to the assignee[20] or, if they are common writs such as a confirmation, the assignation should incorporate an obligation to make them forthcoming.

Partial assignation

7–10   If the bond is assigned only partially the assignation should be qualified appropriately, *e.g.* "but only to the extent of £   of principal, with interest on the said sum of £   from and after the term of   ."

Original creditor—separate assignation—decree of registration

7–11   I, A (*designed*), in consideration of the sum of £   now paid to me by B (*designed*) do hereby assign to the said B and his executors or assignees (one) the Bond granted by C (*designed*) in my favour dated   and registered in the Books of Council and Session on   , by which he bound himself to pay to me the sum of £   at the term of   with interest at the rate of   per centum per annum, which interest is hereby assigned for the period from and after the term of   ; and (two) the decree by the Lords of Council and Session at my instance against the said C for the sum contained in the said Bond, which decree was obtained by registration as aforesaid and is dated the said   with the extract thereof and warrant therein contained and all that has followed or is competent to follow thereon. (*To be attested*)

If any other form of diligence has been used the charge or decree should also be assigned.[21]

Warrandice

7–12   The statutory forms do not contain a clause of warrandice, which is normally left to implication of law in the circumstances of the transaction. If a different degree of warrandice is intended, particularly if it is to be qualified in any respect, an express clause should be inserted concluding with the words "and no further or other warrandice is to be implied."[22]

Consent to registration

7–13   A consent to registration for execution is inappropriate; the cedent is not the debtor in the obligation. A consent to registration for preservation is unnecessary; the assignee may register the assignation for that purpose without the need of express consent.[23]

---

[20] The assignation carries all deeds relating exclusively to the debt assigned *Finlaw* v. *Earl of Northesk* (1670) Mor. 6544.

[21] For a style see Burns, 29.

[22] Burns, 28; see *Ferrier* v. *Graham's Trs.* (1828) 6 S. 818.

[23] Transmission of Moveable Property (Scotland) Act 1862, s. 1.

Stamp duty

-14   An assignation of a bond is exempt from stamp duty.[24]

Intimation of assignation

-15   An assignation when delivered is good against the cedent and his executors[25] but intimation of it is necessary to interpel the debtor from paying principal or subsequent interest to the cedent[26] and to divest the cedent and complete the title of the assignee.[27] If the debtor pays to the cedent after intimation he may be liable to pay again to the assignee.[28] It is the date of intimation, not the date of the assignation, which determines the priority of the assignee's right in competition with any other assignation[29] or diligence by the creditors of the cedent. A solicitor may be liable for professional negligence if he fails to intimate an assignation promptly.[30] The debtor's private knowledge of the assignation will interpel him from paying to the cedent[31] but does not affect rights of priority in a competition with other assignees or creditors of the cedent.[32] Intimation is unnecessary where the assignee is the debtor since normally in those circumstances the obligation will be extinguished *confusione*.

Methods of intimation

-16   **(a) Notarial.** Older methods of intimation of an assignation,[33] although still competent, have been superseded in practice by the procedure prescribed by section 2 of the Transmission of Moveable Property (Scotland) Act 1862. The notary accompanied by two witnesses delivers to the debtor a copy of the assignation (or if the deed of assignation contains other provisions a copy of the part which effects the assignation), certified as correct, and a certificate in the form of Schedule C to the Act is executed by the notary and the witnesses. If intimation cannot be made personally to the debtor the copy may be left at his house and the person with whom it is left is named in the certificate.

-17   **(b) Postal.** Section 2 of the 1862 Act also authorises postal intimation. The assignee or his agent transmits a certified copy of the assignation by post to the debtor and obtains a written acknowledgment of receipt from the debtor. Again, if the assignation contains other provisions a copy only of the relevant part effecting the assignation need be sent.

---

[24] Finance Act 1971, s. 64(1).
[25] *Grant* v. *Gray* (1828) 6 S. 489; *Brownlee* v. *Robb*, 1907 S.C. 1302.
[26] *McDowal* v. *Fullertoun* (1714) Mor. 840; *Grigor Allan* v. *Urquhart* (1887) 15 R. 56.
[27] *Lord Rollo* v. *Laird of Niddrie* (1665) 1 Br. Sup. 510.
[28] *Macpherson's J.F.* v. *Mackay*, 1915 S.C. 1011.
[29] *Campbell's Trs.* v. *Whyte* (1884) 11 R. 1078.
[30] *Lillie* v. *Macdonald*, Dec. 13, 1816, F.C.
[31] *Leith* v. *Garden* (1703) Mor. 865.
[32] *Lord Rollo* v. *Laird of Niddrie, supra.*
[33] For details see Craigie, *Moveable Rights*, 242–243.

Persons to whom intimation is given

7–18   Intimation to several debtors, whether bound jointly and severally or not, should be made to all of them.[34] Intimation to one of a body of trustees has been held sufficient,[35] but for safety it is recommended that it be given to all the trustees. Where the debtor is a pupil intimation should be made to the pupil and his tutor, and if a minor to the minor and his curators (if any).[36] Intimation to a company should be made to the company at its registered office, but an assignation of uncalled capital of a company requires to be intimated to all its shareholders.[37] Intimation to a firm should be made to the firm *socio nomine* and to all its partners.[38] Intimation may be made to a person furth of Scotland by post in conformity with the 1862 Act or, if the address of the debtor is unknown, edictally.[39] Intimation of a debt due by a principal debtor and a cautioner may be made to the principal debtor without being made also to the cautioner,[40] but intimation only to the cautioner is not sufficient to prevent *bona fide* payment by the principal debtor to the cedent, which also liberates the cautioner.[41]

Constructive intimation

7–19   Certain conduct on the part of the debtor may be regarded as equivalent to intimation. Examples are: (1) Payment to account of principal, or payment of interest, to the assignee.[42] (2) Action or diligence by the assignee against the debtor founded on the assignation.[43] (3) Written promise by the debtor to pay to the assignee.[44] (4) The debtor being a party,[45] not merely a witness,[46] to the assignation. (5) Production of the assignation in a multiplepoinding to which the debtor is also a party.[47] (6) Intimation in correspondence to the debtor or his agent replied to by either of them.[48] (7) Intimation to a factor for the debtor and entry made in the debtor's books,[49] although as a general rule intimation to the debtor's factor is not sufficient.[50] (8) Attendance and voting at a meeting of partners by an assignee of a share in the firm.[51]

---

[34] Ersk. III, v, 5.
[35] *Jameson* v. *Sharp* (1887) 14 R. 643.
[36] Montgomerie Bell, *Lectures*, 314.
[37] *Ballachulish Slate Quarries* v. *Bruce* (1908) 16 S.L.T. 48.
[38] *Hill* v. *Lindsay* (1846) 8 D. 472.
[39] Montgomerie Bell, *Lectures*, 314–315.
[40] *Mosman* v. *Bells* (1670) 2 Br.Sup. 457.
[41] *Lyon* v. *Law* (1610) Mor. 1786.
[42] *Livingston* v. *Lindsay* (1626) Mor. 860.
[43] *Whyte* v. *Neish* (1622) Mor. 854; *Dougal* v. *Gordon* (1795) Mor. 851.
[44] *Home* v. *Murray* (1674) Mor. 863.
[45] *Turnbull* v. *Stewart* (1751) Mor. 868.
[46] *Murray* v. *Durham* (1622) Mor. 855.
[47] *Dougal* v. *Gordon, supra*
[48] *Wallace* v. *Davies* (1853) 15 D. 688.
[49] *Earl of Aberdeen* v. *Earl of March* (1730) 1 Pat.App. 44.
[50] Montgomerie Bell, *Lectures*, 318.
[51] *Hill* v. *Lindsay, supra*.

(9) Registration of the deed containing the assignation in the Register of Sasines,[52] but not in the Books of Council and Session.[53]

(2) Life Assurance Policies

Value of policy

7–20   The assignee is primarily concerned as to the value of the policy. Relevant particulars, if necessary ascertained by inquiry authorised by the cedent made to the assurance company, include the amount assured, record of bonus additions to date, date of maturity of the policy and surrender value. It should also be verified that the premiums are not in arrear, that the assurance company have no existing claims against the assured which could be set off against the sum due under the policy,[54] and that no notices of previous assignations of or securities over the policy have been received by the company.

Conditions of policy

7–21   It is essential that the age of the assured has been admitted in, or by endorsement on, the policy; if not, the assured should be required to furnish the necessary evidence to the assurance company and have the policy endorsed with an admission of age. Likewise the policy and any endorsements should be examined for conditions which, if breached, would invalidate the policy, *e.g.* the assured going abroad or travelling by aircraft other than as a fare-paying passenger.

Insurable interest

7–22   If the policy has been effected on the life of another the insurer must have had an insurable interest in the life of the assured[55] which must be a pecuniary interest[56] and must have existed when the policy was effected even although it has ceased when the policy matures.[57] A defence by the assurance company on the ground of lack of insurable interest may be waived by the assurance company[58] and Burns[59] suggests that, if there is any doubt as to insurable interest, the company should be asked to admit the interest when the assignation is being negotiated.

---

[52] *Paul* v. *Boyd's Trs.* (1835) 13 S. 818; *Edmond* v. *Magistrates of Aberdeen* (1858) 3 Macq. 116; *Rodger* v. *Crawfords* (1867) 6 M. 24.
[53] *Tod's Trs.* v. *Wilson* (1869) 7 M. 1100.
[54] *Borthwick* v. *Scottish Widows' Fund* (1864) 2 M. 595.
[55] Act 14 Geo. III, c. 48.
[56] *Simcock* v. *Scottish Imperial Insurance Co.* (1902) 10 S.L.T. 286.
[57] *Dalby* v. *India and London Life Assurance Co.* (1854) 15 C.B. 365.
[58] *Hadden* v. *Bryden* (1899) 1 F. 710.
[59] At 683.

Proof of death

7-23   One of the risks of taking an assignation of a life policy is that the life assured may become untraceable and the assignee may not know whether he has died. If the assignee has undertaken liability for payment of the premiums (which is normal in the case of an absolute assignation) he would under the former law have required to continue to pay the premiums unless the assurance company agreed otherwise, since section 11 of the Presumption of Life Limitation (Scotland) Act 1891 provided that the Act did not apply to a claim against an insurer under a life policy.[60] The Presumption of Death (Scotland) Act 1977, however, provides that a decree in an action of declarator of death, which may be raised by any person having an interest, is conclusive for all purposes[61] although, if the decree is subsequently varied (as when the person presumed dead reappears), any capital sum paid by an insurer as a result of the decree may be repayable.[62] However, insurance against that risk will normally have been effected.[63] It may prove possible to avoid the expense of an action if the assurance company agrees to make payment on the production of evidence by persons having knowledge of the assured that he is almost certainly deceased.

Title of cedent

7-24   Apart from the limitations in the power or capacity of particular persons or bodies already considered,[64] the case of assignations by trustees requires special mention. Trustees have power to sell a policy of assurance if a general power of sale is included in the trust deed or, if not so included, by virtue of section 4 of the Trusts (Scotland) Act 1921 provided that a sale is not at variance with the terms or purposes of the trust. If, however, the policy is the subject of special directions in the trust deed, *e.g.* bequeathed to or to be held for the liferent of particular beneficiaries, the statutory power may not be available. If the circumstances are such that the premiums continue to be payable after the trust commences the trustees have a duty to preserve its value for the benefit of the trust estate and they may either sell and assign it if they have power to do so, or surrender it[65] or convert it into a paid-up policy.[66] In the absence of express power to continue to pay the premiums it seems doubtful whether the trustees have any power under statute to do so, and if an individual trustee pays further premiums personally he cannot enforce realisation of the policy to recoup himself and in any event is

---

[60] *Murray* v. *Chalmers*, 1913 1 S.L.T. 223.
[61] s. 3.
[62] s. 5(3)(*b*).
[63] s. 6(1).
[64] See Chap. 2.
[65] *Schumann* v. *Scottish Widows' Fund* (1886) 13 R. 678.
[66] *Re Equitable Life Assurance Society of U.S. and Mitchell* (1911) 27 T.L.R. 213; *Re Fleetwood's Policy* [1926] Ch. 48.

only entitled to be repaid in so far as there has been benefit to the estate.[67]

Policies under Married Women's Policies of Assurance Acts

7-25   Policies of assurance effected under the Married Women's Policies of Assurance (Scotland) Act 1880 or the Married Women's Policies of Assurance (Scotland) (Amendment) Act 1980 constitute trusts within the meaning of the Trusts (Scotland) Act 1921[68] and the trustee has the powers under section 4 of the 1921 Act and, so far as not at variance with the terms or purposes of the trust, the powers in relation to the policy specified in section 2(2) of the 1980 Act. It would not appear, however, that any of the statutory powers would authorise sale and assignation of the policy since the trust has been constituted for the benefit of the spouse or children of the person who effected the policy. It would seem that the trustee or trustees of the policy, if a sale or assignation of it is desired, would require either to seek special power to sell under section 5 of the 1921 Act or to apply for variation of the trust purposes under section 1 of the Trusts (Scotland) Act 1961.[69]

Delivery of policy

7-26   An assignation of a life policy should in all cases be accompanied by delivery of the original policy with any endorsements of it. If for any reason the original policy is not available for delivery and a copy is tendered the assignee incurs the risk that the policy has been used to create an equitable security by deposit in England or any country where security by deposit is permitted by law,[70] although normally that requires notice to the assurance company[71] and will be disclosed on inquiry of the company. A further risk is that the policy has become subject to a lien, e.g. that of a solicitor for his professional account, although the right of lien does not extend to secure cash advances by the solicitor.[72] If the policy to be assigned has been lost the assurance company should be asked to issue a duplicate policy (although not all companies will do so) and to confirm that no changes or assignments of the policy have been intimated, that the policy is valid and in force and that on maturity payment will be made without the need of any consent or indemnity. Subject to the reply received, it may be desirable to obtain from the cedent an indemnity against all claims, liabilities, loss and expenses which may be incurred by the assignee in establishing a claim for payment of the proceeds of the policy.[73]

---

[67] *Brown* v. *Meek's Trs.* (1896) 4 S.L.T. 46.
[68] 1980 Act, s. 2(1).
[69] Now permissible: 1980 Act, s. 4.
[70] *Scottish Provident Institution* v. *Cohen* (1888) 16 R. 112.
[71] *Pearson* v. *Amicable Assurance Office* (1859) 27 Beav. 229. As to constructive notice see *Re Weniger's Policy* [1910] 2 Ch. 291.
[72] *Wylie's Exrx.* v. *McJannet* (1901) 4 F. 195.
[73] See Burns, 686.

Premiums

7–27   In the case of an absolute assignation on sale the usual arrangement will be that the assignee pays the future premiums necessary to keep the policy in force. Premiums on life policies are not subject to apportionment *ex lege*[74] and so any arrangement whereby apportionment of premiums is regulated should be made a matter of express stipulation. If at the time when the bargain is being made the premiums are in arrear or the current premium has not been paid but the days of grace have not expired, the seller should be required to make payment and, in the case where any premium is in arrear, to produce evidence from the assurance company that the policy remains in force. If the company requires any additional payment to procure that result the seller should be responsible for it. If the seller is unable to pay the arrears of premiums or the premium currently due but both parties desire the transaction for purchase of the policy to proceed, it is essential that the policy be kept in force and the purchaser may pay the arrears of premium with any interest required by the assurance company and also the current premium, but only if (a) there is a binding bargain for assignation of the policy, and (b) the purchaser is satisfied that the seller has a valid title to the policy: the total amount so paid by the purchaser will be deducted from the price at settlement.

Death of seller before settlement

7–28   If the transaction for the assignation of the policy is one of sale, the seller should stipulate that in the event of his death before settlement the contract of sale will be terminated in order that his representatives will receive the full amount due under the policy rather than the lower price which would have been payable by the purchaser.

Warrandice

7–29   The warrandice implied by law in a sale of a life policy is fact and deed and *debitum subesse*. In the normal case that is adequate and need not be expressed in the assignation, but, to guard against the possibility of some curable defect in the title to the policy not created by the cedent and to ensure that the cedent will be liable for the expense of remedying it, absolute warrandice may be desirable.[75] If for any reason warrandice is to be restricted to fact and deed only, that should be stated with the addition that no further or other warrandice is granted or is to be implied.[76]

---

[74] Apportionment Act 1870, s. 6.
[75] See Burns, 688.
[76] See *Ferrier* v. *Graham's Trs.* (1828) 6 S. 818.

Form of assignation

7–30   A short form of assignation of a life assurance policy is prescribed by the Policies of Assurance Act 1867. It runs:

I, A (*designed*) in consideration of £   do hereby assign unto B (*designed*), his executors, administrators or assigns the policy of assurance (*identify the policy by reference to the assurance company, number, sum assured and date*). (*To be attested*)

This form may be used in simple cases: a fuller form is given in paragraph 7–31 *infra*.

Assignation of life policy—with profits[a]

7–31   I, A (*designed*), in consideration of the sum of £   paid to me by B (*designed*) hereby assign to the said B absolutely the policy of assurance granted by the X Assurance Company of (*chief office*) in my favour on my own life for the sum of £   with profits payable [on the   day of   (*year*) or][b] on my death [if earlier][b] numbered   and dated   on which there is a premium of £   payable on the   day of   in each year while the policy is in force, the last payment being due on   ; Together with the said sum of £   and all bonus and other additions which have accrued or may accrue thereon and my whole right, title and interest present and future in or to the said policy and the whole bonus and other additions and benefits of any kind which have arisen or may arise in respect of the said policy in any manner of way; With full power to the said B to surrender, convert, assign or otherwise deal with the said policy and any bonus or other additions as fully and freely as I could have done myself;[c,d] And I grant absolute warrandice.[e] (*Stamp clause*)[f]

NOTES
[a] If the policy is without profits the references to bonus additions may be omitted but to cover any possible unanticipated benefits a general reference to any benefits of the policy may be inserted.
[b] Appropriate to endowment policies: for whole life policies may be omitted.
[c] This power may strictly be unnecessary but the expression of it avoids all questions.
[d] If the cedent is not the person assured, insert a deduction of title on the lines of that in para. 7–09.
[e] See para. 7–29.
[f] See para. 7–33.

Assignations of life policy subject to debt

7–32   If the policy assigned is subject to any secured debt due to a third party or a debt due to the assurance company the assignation should contain a provision that it is conditional upon the assignee undertaking liability for payment of the debt. For styles see *Encyclopaedia of Scottish Legal Styles*, Volume 1, Numbers 444, 445.

Stamp duty

7–33   An assignation of a life policy is liable to *ad valorem* stamp duty as a conveyance on sale. The duty is based on the consideration or, if it confers a substantial benefit on the assignee, the surrender value of the policy, and an assignation which is not duly stamped confers no right on the assignee to sue for or give a valid discharge of the sum assured.[77] If a policy is assigned subject to a debt (other than a loan by an assurance company on its own policy) and the assignee accepts liability for payment of the debt, the amount of the debt is added to the consideration for the purpose of determining the amount chargeable to stamp duty.[78] That rule applies even if the debt is irrecoverable.[79]

Notice of assignation

7–34   The Policies of Assurance Act 1867 provides for notice of assignations of life policies and the method of notice prescribed in the Act is normally used in practice. The assurance company must state on the policy its principal place of business at which notices of assignation may be given.[80] In practice a notice of assignation is sent in duplicate to the company and a principal officer of the company stamps an acknowledgment upon the duplicate copy and returns it to the sender.[81] A fee not exceeding 25p is chargeable by the company.[81]

Form of notice

7–35   To X Assurance Co. Ltd.,
               (*Address of principal office*)

               Notice is hereby given that by assignation dated   A (*designed*) assigned absolutely to B (*designed*) the policy of assurance granted by the X Assurance Co. Ltd. in favour of A on his own life for the sum of £   number   dated   with all bonus and other additions accrued or that may accrue thereon and the whole benefits thereof.
               Dated at   the   day of   .

                                                            XY & Co.
                                                Agents for the said B.

(3) Reversionary Interests

Types of reversionary interest

7–36   In this chapter reversionary interests include (1) a prospective interest or *spes successionis* such as a possible future interest either by

---

[77] Stamp Act 1891, s. 118.
[78] *Ibid.*, s. 57.
[79] *Inland Revenue* v. *North British Railway Co.* (1901) 4 F. 27.
[80] s. 4.
[81] s. 6.

testamentary disposition or by way of prior or legal or succession rights in the estate of a person still living, (2) a non-vested or defeasible right in property comprised in a trust estate already operative, and (3) a right in property comprised in a trust estate which is vested and indefeasible but not yet due or payable. Reversionary rights are not commonly assigned as commercial transactions although the purchase of reversionary interests is occasionally made, but they are relatively common by way of gift or for taxation purposes and are frequently assigned in security.

Prospective interest or spes successionis

7–37   An assignation of a *spes successionis* in the estate of a person not yet deceased was held incompetent in the old case of *Bedwells and Yates* v. *Tod*,[82] mainly on the ground that there was no person to whom the assignation could properly be intimated, but that decision seems inconsistent with later cases[83] and the view now generally accepted is that a *spes successionis* is assignable.[84] Clearly an assignation of a *spes successionis* is subject to serious risks which may render it of no or significantly less value. The *spes* will be of no value if the granter of the assignation predeceases the person in whose estate the *spes* subsists. If the *spes* depends wholly upon testamentary provisions by that person in favour of the cedent it may be defeated by voluntary change in testamentary provisions or by the operation of the *conditio si testator* which will revoke an existing will. Even if the cedent is a child of the person in whose estate the *spes* subsists its value, even if the cedent survives, may be diminished *inter alia* by a second marriage which may introduce a claim for *jus relictae* or *jus relicti* and in the case of intestacy prior rights, the birth of other (including illegitimate) children, divorce, the effect of capital transfer tax or decrease in the amount of the estate by reason of *inter vivos* gifts or a decline in value of the property held. The combination of those risks will normally render impracticable an absolute assignation of a *spes* for value, since insurance of the risks will not be obtainable or obtainable only at an unacceptable premium, and there is the further practical danger that intimation of a sale of the *spes* to the person in whose estate it subsists may induce an alteration in testamentary provisions which will adversely affect the interest of the cedent. For all these reasons absolute assignations of a mere *spes* on sale are rare, and absolute assignations of a *spes* are normally gratuitous, made with the object of preventing an accretion of wealth to a cedent who already has substantial assets. Assignations of a *spes* in security of debt are more common, usually as a *tabula in naufragio* when the cedent is unable to offer sufficient securities of a more acceptable kind.

---

[82] Dec. 2, 1819, F.C.
[83] *Trappes* v. *Meredith* (1871) 10 M. 38; *Coats* v. *Bannochie's Trs.*, 1912 S.C. 329.
[84] Walker, *Principles*, III, 580.

Non-vested interest in expectancy—existing trust

7–38   Where the granter of the assignation has a non-vested interest as a
beneficiary under a trust deed which is already operating the major risk
is that he predeceases the occurrence of the event upon which his interest would have vested. That risk can usually be covered by insurance at
a premium depending mainly upon the amount involved and the relative ages and states of health of the cedent and the person upon whose
death the contingent interest of the cedent will vest. The trust deed
should be examined carefully and also the latest trust accounts and the
value and nature of the investments held by the trustees. Matters to be
considered include (1) whether the interest of the cedent is subject to
defeasance otherwise than by failure to survive the vesting date, (2)
whether any of the investments held are speculative or subject to
special hazards,[85] (3) if investments have been recently realised
whether there is unsettled liability for capital gains tax in excess of the
annual relief available to the trustees, (4) the amount and incidence of
capital transfer tax which may become payable upon vesting of the
cedent's interest, (5) if the trust is testamentary and the cedent and
other children of the testator will share the residue whether, if any of
the other residuary legatees has died, his children may be entitled to his
share, even although there is no express destination-over to them, by
reason of the *conditio si institutus* and whether the cedent and any of
the other residuary legatees have made an election in respect of their
legal rights and particularly whether any child of the testator who has
predeceased him has left children who are not yet of an age to make
the election, (6) whether there are discretionary legacies or any other
discretionary provisions whereby the amount of the trust estate or the
interest of the cedent may be diminished,[86] and (7) whether there are
annuities which may continue after the vesting date and may require
the appropriation of capital to provide for them. It is desirable that the
assignation should incorporate all rights and interests, absolute or contingent, competent to the cedent either under the trust deed or by
operation of law in the very widest terms. Possible interests which
should be brought within the scope of the assignation include interests
which may arise by accretion when another joint beneficiary predeceases the vesting date or under the law of intestate succession if there
should be partial intestacy. The principles which affect vesting and
other considerations relative to vesting are beyond the scope of this
work but an outline of the more important of them is given in dealing
with Wills and Succession.

---

[85] The discretion of trustees as to investments is not affected by a third party having acquired a right
to a beneficiary's interest: see *Brower's Exr.* v. *Ramsay's Trs.*, 1912 S.C. 1374.
[86] See *Chambers' Trs.* v. *Smiths* (1878) 5 R. (H.L.) 151; *Train* v. *Clapperton*, 1908 S.C. (H.L.) 26.

Vested interest not yet payable—existing trust

-39   Where the granter of the assignation has a vested interest in a trust estate it is necessary to examine the trust deed and confirm that his interest is not subject to defeasance in any circumstances. The latest trust accounts and the value and nature of the investments held should also be considered. Also relevant are the matters numbered (2), (3), (4), (6) and (7) in paragraph 7–38 *supra*. The possible amount and incidence of capital transfer tax upon the cessation of a liferent on the expiry of which the interest of the cedent will become payable should also be taken into account. Inquiry should be made as to any advances by the trustees to the cedent which will be deductible from his interest and, in the case of a testamentary trust where the cedent is a child or grandchild of the testator and it may be open to claim legitim and possibly advantageous to do so, whether any advances were made by the testator to the cedent which could be brought into account in such a claim on the principle of collation *inter liberos*. Again, as in the case of a non-vested interest, the assignation should be framed so as to comprehend all possible interests which may accrue to the cedent by accretion or under the law of intestate succession in the case of partial intestacy.

The deferment and contingency factors

-40   The price or value of a reversionary interest acquired, whether vested or not, should be calculated after applying to the estimated value a discount for deferment based upon the anticipated period which will elapse before the cedent becomes entitled to the interest acquired. In the case of a non-vested interest the price or value should be further reduced in respect of the risk of defeasance, normally taken as the amount of the premium payable for insurance of the risk.

Styles

Assignation of non-vested interest—Residue

-41   I, A (*designed*), Considering that the late B (*designed*) (hereinafter called "the testator") by his Trust Disposition and Settlement dated   and registered in the Books of Council and Session on   conveyed his means and estate to C, D and E (*designed*) as trustees for the purposes therein mentioned[a] and *inter alia* (*briefly narrate purposes other than those relating to residue*) and in the   and   places directed the trustees to hold the residue of his estate for behoof of his widow F in liferent and such of his children as should survive the failure or termination of the said liferent, equally among them, in fee[b]; Further Considering that the testator was survived by the said F and three children, namely, G, H and myself, all of whom still survive, and that I shall be entitled to not less than one-third of the said residue on the death of the said F if I survive her and may become entitled to a further share in the event of the predecease of the said G or H[c]; And Now Seeing that I have sold my whole rights and interests in the estate of the testator to K (*designed*) for the sum of £   of which sum I acknowledge receipt, Therefore I hereby assign to the said K absolutely the whole right, share and interest of every kind and description whatsoever, heritable and moveable, real and personal, present and future, now belonging or which may hereafter belong to me, in and to the estate of the testator under the said Trust Disposition and Settlement and also under common law or otherwise in any manner of way, together with the whole claims, benefits and advantages of every kind arising or that may arise therefrom; together also with the said Trust Disposition and Settlement and the whole provisions thereof so far as I have or may acquire right thereto and the whole trust estate, both capital and income, to which I am or may become entitled and all powers competent to me thereunder: With full power to the said K and his executors or assignees whomsoever to claim, sue for, receive, discharge, sell, assign or otherwise deal with the said whole right, share and interest or any part thereof, and to do everything in relation to the same that I could have done myself before granting these presents or which I or my executors or representatives might have done if these presents had not been granted[d]: And I grant absolute warrandice: (*Stamp clause*) (*To be attested*)

NOTES
[a] If there has been a change in the personnel of the trustees specify those now acting.
[b] If there is a destination-over to children of a predeceasing child that should be narrated (although the *conditio si institutus* may well apply in the absence of such a destination).
[c] If there is such a destination-over, add "without leaving children who survive the vesting date."
[d] It is assumed that the contingency assurance to cover the risk of the cedent predeceasing the vesting date has been effected by the assignee. If the policy has been effected by the cedent it will also be assigned as in the style in paragraph 7–31.

Assignation of vested interest—Residue

7–42   I, A (*designed*), Considering that the late B (*designed*) (hereinafter called "the testator") by his Trust Disposition and Settlement dated   and registered in the Books of Council and Session on   conveyed his means and estate to C, D and E (*designed*) as trustees for the purposes therein mentioned and *inter alia* (*briefly narrate purposes other than those relating to residue*) and in the   and   places directed the trustees to hold the residue of his estate for behoof of his widow F in liferent and his issue *per capita* in fee; Further Considering that the testator was survived by the said F and three children, namely G, H and myself, all of whom still survive, and that I am entitled to one-third of the said residue payable on the death of the said F and may become entitled to a further share in the event of the said G or H predeceasing the said F[a]; And Now Seeing that I have sold my whole rights and interests in the estate of the testator to K (*designed*) for the sum of £   of which sum I acknowledge receipt, Therefore I hereby assign to the said K absolutely the whole right, share and interest of every kind and description whatsoever, heritable and moveable, real and personal, present and future, now belonging or which may hereafter belong to me, in and to the estate of the testator under the said Trust Disposition and Settement and also under common law or otherwise in any manner of way, together with the whole claims, benefits and advantages of every kind arising or that may arise therefrom; together also with the said Trust Disposition and Settlement and the whole provisions thereof so far as I have or may acquire right thereto and the whole trust estate, both capital and income, to which I am or may become entitled and all powers competent to me thereunder: With full power to the said K and his executors or assignees whomsoever to claim, sue for, receive, discharge, sell, assign or otherwise deal with the said whole right, share and interest or any part thereof, and to do everything in relation to the same that I could have done myself before granting these presents or which I or my executors or representatives might have done if these presents had not been granted: And I grant absolute warrandice: (*Stamp clause*) (*To be attested*)

NOTES
[a] Accretion would operate because of the *per capita* direction—*Barber* v. *Findlater* (1835) 13 S. 422. In the absence of such a direction the share of each child would vest on the death of the testator, without accretion if one should predecease the liferentrix. Nevertheless it is advisable to assign all possible interests: the interest of a predeceasing child might accrue to the others by succession on the death of the predeceaser intestate.

Assignations of other interests in trust estates

7–43   Other interests in trust estates may be assigned, *e.g.* legacies, nonalimentary liferents or legal rights. For styles of such assignations see *Encyclopaedia of Scottish Legal Styles*, Volume 1, Numbers 447, 449 and 452.[87]

Stamp duty

7–44   An assignation for a price or by way of gift is liable to stamp duty as a conveyance on sale. If the consideration or value is such that exemption from stamp duty or duty at less than the full rate may be applicable a stamp clause in appropriate terms should be inserted.

Intimation

7–45   An assignation of an interest in a trust estate should be intimated to all the trustees individually and to the agents who administer the estate on behalf of the trustees. Intimation to one of two trustees was held sufficient in one case[88] but the circumstances were special. The opinion was expressed judicially that intimation to the law agents for the trustees was sufficient,[89] but the safe and proper course is to intimate to all the trustees and the agent administering the trust.

---

[87] These styles are still applicable with appropriate amendments in relation to death duties (now capital transfer tax) and the stamp clause.
[88] *Jameson* v. *Sharp* (1887) 14 R. 643.
[89] *Browne's Trs.* v. *Anderson* (1901) 4 F. 305, *per* Lord Justice-Clerk and Lord Moncrieff at 310, 313.

(4) Special Forms of Assignation

Stocks, shares and other securities

7-46   A simple form of transfer of certain securities is authorised by the Stock Transfer Act 1963.[90] The names of the registered holders as appearing on the certificate(s) for the security, the transferors, should be given; if a single transferor, the address should also be stated. The full names and addresses of the transferee(s) should be inserted. The consideration money, the name of the undertaking, a full description of the security and the number of shares, stock or other security transferred (in words and figures) are stated with a statement that the transferor(s) transfer the security specified to the transferee(s). The transfer is signed by the transferor(s) and the execution need not be attested.[91] The securities which may be so transferred are (1) securities issued by any company within the meaning of the Companies Act 1948 except a company limited by guarantee or an unlimited company, (2) securities issued by any body incorporated in Great Britain under any enactment or by Royal Charter except a building society or an industrial or provident society, (3) Government securities, except stock or bonds in the Post Office register (now National Savings Stock Register) and national savings certificates (both of which have special forms of transfer), (4) securities issued by any local authority, and (5) units of a unit trust scheme.[92] In stock exchange transactions the particulars of the consideration and of the transferee may be supplied by a broker's transfer form.[93] Stamp duty on the price is payable at the full rate for conveyances on sale (currently £1 per cent).[94] Completion of the transferee's title to the securities transferred is effected by registration of the transfer in the register of the company and the issue of a new certificate in name of the transferee.[95] In the case of stock exchange transactions the Talisman system authorised by the Stock Exchange (Completion of Bargains) Act 1976 enables transfers to be made to a stock exchange nominee company and the transfers to be recorded by computerised processing in the registers of the company.

Rights in inventions

7-47   **(a) Trade marks.** A registered trade mark may be assigned either in connection with the goodwill of a business or not.[96] It may be assigned in respect of all or some of the goods in relation to which it was registered[97] but not so that more than one person would have exclusive rights

---

[90] s. 1 and Sched. 1.
[91] Except a transfer executed notarially on behalf of a person who is blind or unable to write, which must be attested (s. 2(4)).
[92] s. 1(4).
[93] s. 1(2) and Sched. 2.
[94] Finance Act 1984, s. 109.
[95] *Tennant's Trs.* v. *Tennant*, 1946 S.C. 420.
[96] Trade Marks Act 1938, s. 22(1).
[97] *Ibid.*, s. 22(2).

to use identical or similar trade marks with the likelihood of deceit or confusion.[98] If there is a possibility of such confusion the proprietor of the trade mark who proposes to assign it may seek a certificate from the Registrar whether the proposed assignation will be valid or not.[99] Associated trade marks may be assigned only as a whole and not separately.[1] The assignation may be made (using the English form) thus:

> This assignment made the   day of   between A (*designed*) (hereinafter called "the vendor") and B Limited (*designed*) (hereinafter called "the purchasers") witnesseth
> Whereas the vendor is the registered proprietor of the trade mark numbered   and dated   in class of goods (advertised in Trade Marks Journal No.   page   ) And whereas the purchasers have requested the vendor to assign to the purchasers the said trade mark which the vendor has agreed to do
> Now this indenture witnesseth that in pursuance of the said agreement and in consideration of the price of £   paid to the vendor by the purchasers the receipt of which is hereby acknowledged the vendor doth assign to the purchasers and their successors and assigns All that the said registered trade mark herein before mentioned and all the rights and privileges appertaining thereto [including the goodwill of the business concerned in the goods in respect of which the said trade mark is registered][a] To hold the said trade mark rights privileges [and goodwill][a] unto the purchasers and their successors and assigns absolutely. (*Stamp clause*) (*To be attested*)

> NOTE
> [a] To be inserted where goodwill of a business is also assigned.

Stamp duty as a conveyance on sale.

The purchasers' title is completed by application to the Registrar to register their title.[2]

7–48 **(b) Patents.** Patents registered under the Patents Acts 1949 and 1977 and any licences or sub-licences may be assigned absolutely or in security[3] by probative or holograph writing.[4] Because of the many complexities of patent law, transactions involving the assignation of patents should be entered into with the advice of a registered patent agent. Assignations are liable to stamp duty as conveyances on sale. The title of the assignee is completed by registration of the assignation in the Register of Patents.[5]

7–49 **(c) Registered designs.** A design registered under the Registered Designs Act 1949 or any licence to use such a design may be assigned[6]

---

[98] *Ibid.*, s. 22(4).
[99] *Ibid.*, s. 22(5).
[1] *Ibid.*, s. 23(1).
[2] *Ibid.*, s. 25.
[3] 1977 Act, s. 31(3), (5). See Patents Rules 1978 (S.I. 1978 No. 216).
[4] *Ibid.*, s. 31(6).
[5] *Ibid.*, s. 32(2)(*b*).
[6] 1949 Act, s. 2(2).

and the title of the assignee is completed by application to the Registrar (the Comptroller-General of Patents, Designs and Trade Marks) in prescribed form[7] and registration of the title of the assignee or notice of his interest.[8] Stamp duty on the assignation is as a conveyance on sale.

7-50   **(d) Copyright.** Copyright in a literary, dramatic, artistic or musical work is assignable but only if assigned in writing.[9] The assignation may be total or partial, and in the latter case may transfer the right to one or more of the classes of acts which the assigner has exclusive right to do and may apply to one or more countries or to part of the period for which the copyright subsists.[10] Licences to use a copyright mark may also be assigned unless there is *delectus personae*.[11] Stamp duty on the assignation is as for a conv⋯ ⌐nce on sale.

7-51   **(e) Public lending rights.** Under the Public Lending Right Act 1979 authors may be entitled to receive payments from a central fund in respect of their books lent to the public by local library authorities in the United Kingdom. Such a public lending right is assignable[12] and an entry may be made of the assignee's title in the register kept by the Registrar of Public Lending Right on application in prescribed form.[13] Stamp duty on the assignation is as a conveyance on sale.

7-52   **(f) Plant breeders' rights.** Provision is made by the Plant Varieties and Seeds Act 1964 for an exclusive right being granted by the Controller of the Plant Varieties Rights Office to sell or produce the reproductive material of the plant variety and to exercise certain other rights specified in Schedule 3 to the Act. The holder of the right may assign it or grant licences under it.[14] Stamp duty on assignations is as for a conveyance on sale. Notice of assignations should be given to the Controller.[15]

III. Assignations of Incorporeal Rights in Security

General

7-53   Incorporeal rights which are assignable may normally be made the subject of security. The documentation may be either expressly as security for a personal obligation or by way of *ex facie* absolute assignation or transfer qualified by a separate document to the effect that the transaction is truly one which creates a security. The forms of assignation or transfer are appropriate to the nature of the right assigned and the

---

[7] Design Rules 1949 to 1978.
[8] 1949 Act, s. 19.
[9] Copyright Act 1956, s. 36(1) and (3).
[10] *Ibid.*, s. 36(2).
[11] See Walker, *Principles*, III, 556.
[12] 1979 Act, s. 1(7)(*b*).
[13] *Ibid.*, s. 4.
[14] 1964 Act, ss. 4(4) and 8.
[15] For details of procedures see Plant Breeders' Rights Regulations 1965 (S.I. 1965 No. 65).

creditor's title should be completed by intimation or notice as in the case of an absolute assignation or transfer. An assignation or transfer in security does not in a question between the debtor and the creditor divest the former of ownership of the security subject, and it is the duty of the creditor, subject to the terms of the relevant documents, to consult the debtor in any dealings with it. Accordingly it is necessary to incorporate in the documents any powers of dealing with the security subject which the creditor considers he may require.

Securities created by an incorporated company over incorporeal moveable property which falls within any of the categories specified in section 410 of the Companies Act 1985 must be completed by registration of particulars of the charge within 21 days after the date of its creation. Registration of fixed and floating charges is considered in a subsequent volume.

(1) Securities over Life Assurance Policies

Preliminary inquiries

7–54   The prospective creditor is concerned as to the value of the policy offered as security, its conditions, the existence of an insurable interest if the policy has been effected on the life of another and the prospective debtor's title to the policy. Investigations on these matters should *mutatis mutandis* be similar to those already outlined in relation to an absolute assignation of a life policy in paragraphs 7–20, 7–21, 7–22 and 7–24 *supra*.

Maintaining the policy in force—future premiums

7–55   Normally the debtor will continue liable for payment of future premiums and observance of the other conditions of the policy. The creditor should take power in the event of failure by the debtor to pay premiums to advance the premiums and recover the amounts paid with interest. In the event of subsequent sequestration of the debtor the creditor can claim in the sequestration the amount of premiums advanced plus interest to the date of sequestration but he is not entitled to claim in respect of the value of future premiums.[16]

Creditor's powers

7–56   An assignation of a life policy in security does not imply a power of sale or surrender. It is essential to incorporate express powers enabling the creditor to deal with the policy by sale or surrender and the conditions upon which such powers can be exercised. Power to receive the

---

[16] *Deering v. Bank of Ireland* (1886) 12 App. Cas. 20.

policy moneys on surrender or upon maturity of the policy and to grant a discharge therefor should also be conferred.

Assignation in security—principles

7–57   The style of the assignation may be either a grant expressly in security or *ex facie* absolute qualified by agreement. Formerly it was the practice to include very detailed powers and rights relating to such matters as the inclusion of substituted policies, the right to receive or surrender bonus additions, to convert or agree to changes in the terms of the policy, to exercise options, etc.[17] It is suggested that these are unnecessary. A general power to do everything in relation to the policy is sufficient since, when the assignation has been intimated to the assurance company, it will not issue a substituted policy or deal with any important matters in respect of it without consulting the creditor and the general power and the strength of a creditor's negotiating position will sufficiently ensure that his wishes in any such matter will prevail.

Bond and assignation of life policy in security

7–58   I, A (*designed*) grant me to have instantly borrowed and received from B (*designed*) the sum of £   which sum (*ordinary form of personal bond as in para.* 5–03 *supra*): And in security of the obligations before and after written I assign to the said B and his foresaids redeemably as aftermentioned but irredeemably in the event of a sale or surrender by virtue hereof a Policy of Assurance granted by the   Assurance Company of (*chief office*) in my favour on my own life for the sum of £   [with profits][a] numbered   and dated   ; Together with all bonus and other additions accrued or that may accrue thereon[b] and all benefits and advantages whatever that may arise therefrom, and my whole right, title and interest therein; With full power to the said B and his foresaids to ask, sue for, uplift and discharge all sums due or that may become due thereunder, and to sell,[c] assign, surrender or take over the said Policy and uplift and recover and grant discharges for the proceeds thereof, and generally to do everything in relation to the said Policy that I could have done if these presents had not been granted, but the rights of the said B or his foresaids under this power shall be exercisable only after the expiry of seven days after written notification by or on behalf of him or them sent by post or delivered to me or my foresaids or my or their agent at my or their last known address of the intention to exercise such rights or any of them: And I bind myself and my foresaids to observe the whole conditions of the said Policy and without prejudice to that generality to pay when due the premiums and any other sums necessary to keep the said Policy in force and to exhibit receipts therefor not less than 14 days before the expiry of the days of grace for payment thereof and in the event of my or their failure to do so I hereby authorise the said B or his foresaids, if they think proper, but without any obligation on him or them to do so, to pay the same

---

[17] See, *e.g.* Burns, 692 *et seq.*

with right to recover any sums so paid with interest at the said rate of   per cent. per annum from the respective dates of payment until repaid: Provided always that all sums or value received and all payments made, with interest thereon, by the said B and his foresaids in the exercise of the foregoing powers shall be credited or debited as the case may be in the final accounting between him or them and me or my foresaids: And I agree that the amount due at any time shall be conclusively ascertained and constituted by a certificate under the hand of the said B or his foresaids or his or their agent without production of vouchers: And I reserve power of redemption at any term of Whitsunday or Martinmas on three months' notice in writing upon payment of all sums due hereunder and expenses[d]: And I have delivered the said Policy to the said B[e]: And I grant absolute warrandice: And I consent to registration for preservation and execution. (*To be attested*)

NOTES

[a] Omit in the case of a without profits policy.

[b] This provision should be included *quantum valeat* even if the policy is initially without profits.

[c] If desired the power of sale may be expressed as exercisable by public or private sale and without advertisement but *quaere* whether such a provision would excuse the creditor from securing the best price reasonably obtainable?

[d] If desired a provision as to persons dealing with the creditor on the lines of that in the style in para. 7–60 may be inserted.

[e] Delivery of the policy should always be required—see para. 7–26.

Assignation of life policy (policies) in security of current banking account[a]

7–59   I, A (*designed*) in security of all sums and obligations I may at present or at any future time be owing or under to (*name and address of bank*) either solely or jointly with any person or persons or corporation, company, firm or other body, and whether as principal or surety, hereby assign to the said (*bank*) and their assignees the following Policy/Policies of Assurance, viz:– (*specify policy or policies by reference to assurance company, life assured, amount, number and date*); Together with all bonus and other additions declared and to be declared in respect of the said Policy/Policies and all benefits and advantages whatever that may arise therefrom and my whole right, title and interest therein; with full power to the said (*bank*) and their foresaids to ask, sue for, uplift and discharge all sums due or that may become due thereunder, and to sell, assign, surrender or take over the said Policy (Policies or any of them) and recover and grant discharges for the proceeds thereof,[b] and generally to do everything in relation to the said Policy/Policies that I could have done if these presents had not been granted; And I bind myself to observe the whole conditions of the said Policy/Policies and to pay the several premiums and any other sums necessary to keep the said Policy/Policies in force, and failing my doing so I authorise the said (*bank*) or their foresaids, if they think proper but without any obligation on them to do so, to pay the same and debit me with the amount; And I agree that a statement of any such payments of premiums and other sums as aforesaid, with periodical interest at the usual rates charged by the said (*bank*), certified by the (*officials* *authorised by the bank to sign such statements*) for the time shall be sufficient without any other voucher to constitute and ascertain the amount thereof.[c] (*To be attested*)

NOTES

[a] This form is shorter than the style in para. 7–58. It omits (1) the obligation to credit recoveries from sale or surrender of the policy/ policies (which would be implied by law), (2) the right of redemption (also implied in a security unless negatived), (3) the statement that the policy has been delivered (the normal bank procedures ensure that it will be), and (4) the consent to registration for execution (which already exists in a separate bond creating a general cash credit obligation).
[b] See note [c] to style in para. 7–58.
[c] If desired a provision as to persons dealing with the creditor on the lines of that in the style in para. 7–60 may be inserted.

Agreement qualifying absolute assignation of life policy[a]

7–60   Agreement between A (*designed*) and B (*designed*)
Whereas by Assignation dated   the said A assigned to the said B a Policy of Assurance granted by the   Assurance Company of (*chief office*) in favour of the said A on his own life for the sum of £   numbered   and dated   And whereas the said Assignation, although *ex facie* absolute, was truly granted in security of sums due by the said A to the said B and it is proper that the terms of the security arrangement should be reduced to writing Therefore the parties hereto agree as follows:–
1. Notwithstanding that the said Assignation is *ex facie* absolute the said B admits and declares that the said Policy is and shall be held by him in security of (*specify the obligation in full including interest—if for a continuing account add* "and shall be a continuing and covering security"—*with consent to registration for execution*) (hereinafter called "the loan obligation").
2. The said A shall observe the whole conditions of the said Policy and pay regularly the annual premiums and any other sums necessary to keep the said Policy in force and shall not do or suffer to be done anything whereby the said Policy may become void or voidable: if the said Policy for any reason shall become void the said A will immediately at his own expense do all things necessary to restore the same or to effect a substituted policy to secure the same amount with the like benefits to the satisfaction of the said B.
3. In the event of the failure by the said A to pay when due any premium or premiums or other sums necessary to keep the said Policy in force the said B shall be entitled but not bound to pay the same and the amount or amounts so paid shall be added to the sum due under the loan obligation with interest at the rate payable thereunder from the date or dates of payment until repaid.
4. Without prejudice to the provisions of Clause 3 hereof, in the event of failure by the said A to perform or implement the whole obligations undertaken by or imposed on him under the loan obligation or these presents the said B shall have full power to sell the said Policy publicly or privately and with or without advertisement[b] or in his option to surrender the said Policy and to receive, uplift

and recover the proceeds thereof and apply the same in reduction of the sums due by the said A to him, and no person acquiring right to the said Policy shall be bound or entitled to inquire whether the conditions attached to the exercise of such power have been observed or to see to the application of such proceeds and any such person shall be fully acquitted and secured by any assignations, receipts or discharges granted to him by the said B.

5. On repayment of all sums due under the loan obligation and these presents the said B will retrocess the said Policy (so far as not previously disposed of hereunder) to the said A or his executors or representatives at his or their expense with warrandice from fact and deed only.

6. The whole expenses and outlays of both parties in connection with the said Assignation and these presents shall be borne by the said A. (*To be attested*)

NOTES

[a] This agreement may be used in conjunction with an assignation as in para. 7–30 or 7–31.

[b] As to power to sell publicly or privately and with or without advertisement, see note [c] to para. 7–58.

Assignation by creditor of bond and assignation of life policy in security

7–61 The creditor may assign a bond and assignation of a life policy in security: the following style in paragraph 7–62 is by the executor of the creditor. If the original security documentation was in the form of an *ex facie* absolute assignation and related agreement and the assignee is aware of that fact both the policy and the agreement require to be assigned and, to avoid any question as to *delectus personae* in the original bargain, the consent of the debtor may be desirable. In such a case it is more convenient to have the original loan documents discharged and the policy retrocessed and new loan documentation prepared between the debtor and the proposed assignee.

Assignation of bond and assignation in security by executor of creditor[a]

7–62 I, C (*designed*), Executor of the deceased B (*designed*) conform to Confirmation by the Sheriff of   dated at   the (*date*) in consideration of the sum of £   paid to me by D (*designed*) hereby assign to the said D and his executors and assignees a Bond and Assignation in Security for the sum of £   granted by A (*designed*) in favour of the said B dated   with interest from   As also the Policy of Assurance granted by the   Assurance Company of (*chief office*) in favour of the said A on his own life for the sum of £   numbered   and dated   together with the said sum thereby assured and all bonus or other additions thereto and all benefits and advantages that may arise therefrom and that in security as stated in the said Bond and Assignation in Security: To which Bond and Assignation in Security I acquired right by the said Confirmation: And I grant warrandice from my own facts and deeds only. (*To be attested*)

NOTE
a Assignation of bond and assignation as in style in para. 7–58.

Assignation by creditor of life policy on sale under powers in security deed

7–63   If a life policy which has been assigned in security by a bond and assignation in security is sold by the creditor it is necessary for the purchaser to be satisfied that the power of sale has become exercisable and has been properly exercised in accordance with the terms of the security deed. The position is similar if the security was created by *ex facie* absolute assignation qualified by agreement and the purchaser is aware that the assignation was truly in security. In the latter case if the purchaser was not aware that the assignation was by way of security and there have been no circumstances to put him on his inquiry on that matter his title to the policy will not be affected by any irregularities in the exercise of the creditor's power of sale: the question of improper exercise of the power will concern the debtor and the creditor. In most cases however the fact that the original assignation was truly in security will be known to the purchaser. The style of assignation in the following paragraph is framed on that basis.

Assignation of life policy by creditor on sale

7–64   I, B (*designed*) Considering that the policy of assurance aftermentioned was assigned to me by [Bond and Assignation in Security granted by A (*designed*) in my favour dated   ] [Assignation by A (*designed*) in my favour which was truly granted in security in terms of Agreement between the said A and me dated   ] and that I am entitled to sell the said policy in accordance with the terms of the said [Bond and Assignation in Security] [Agreement] in respect that (*narrate shortly the circumstances in which the power of sale has become exercisable*) And further considering that I have sold the said policy to C (*designed*) at the price of £   of which I acknowledge receipt Therefore I hereby assign to the said C absolutely the Policy of Assurance granted by the X Assurance Company of (*chief office*) in favour of the said A on his own life for the sum   of   £   with   profits   [payable   on   the   day of   (*year*)] or on his death if earlier numbered   and dated   on which there is a premium of £   payable on the   day of   in each year while the policy is in force, the last payment being due on   ; Together with the said sum of £   and all bonus and other additions which have accrued or may accrue thereon and my whole right, title and interest present and future in and to the said policy and the whole bonus and other additions and benefits of any kind which have arisen or may arise in respect of the said policy in any manner of way: With full power to the said C to surrender, convert, assign or otherwise deal with the said policy and any bonus or other additions as fully and freely as I could have done myself: And I grant warrandice from fact and deed only[a]: (*Stamp clause*) (*To be attested*)

NOTE

[a] The purchaser may wish absolute warrandice, which would impose on the seller a warranty of the validity of the policy. That may, however, not be unfair.

Stamp duty on securities over life policies

7–65   Stamp duty is not payable upon a bond and assignation of a life policy in security (paragraphs 7–58, 7–59), nor an assignation thereof (paragraph 7–62).[18] An *ex facie* absolute assignation and relative agreement (paragraph 7–60) should be submitted for adjudication of stamp duty but will normally be adjudged as not liable to duty being a mortgage.[18] An assignation of a life policy on sale by the creditor (paragraph 7–64) is liable to duty as on a conveyance on sale.

Notice

7–66   Notice of a bond and assignation in security (paragraphs 7–58, 7–59) or of an assignation thereof (paragraph 7–62) should be given to the assurance company in the form in paragraph 7–35 save that it should be stated in describing the deed that the assignation is in security. Notice of an assignation which is *ex facie* absolute can be simply in the form in paragraph 7–35. Notice of an assignation of the policy itself (paragraph 7–64) should also be in the form in paragraph 7–35.

(2) Securities over Reversionary Interests

General

7–67   When a reversionary interest, whether prospective, non-vested or vested is being made the subject of security the considerations already outlined in relation to absolute assignations as to the nature of the interest, insurance of contingencies in the case of non-vested interests, the deferment factor, etc. require to be taken into account—see paragraphs 7–36 to 7–40 *supra*. In addition, since the right is to be transferred only in security, it is essential to incorporate in the documentation a

---

[18] Finance Act 1971, s. 64(1).

statement of the rights of the creditor to enforce the security in the event
of default by the debtor in making repayment of the amount advanced.

*Bond and assignation in security—non-vested reversionary interest—
contingency insurance effected by debtor*

7–68   I, A (*designed*), grant me to have instantly borrowed and received
from B (*designed*) the sum of £   which sum (*ordinary form of
personal bond as in para. 5–03 supra*): And in security of the obligations before and after written I assign to the said B and his foresaids redeemably as aftermentioned but irredeemably in the event
of a sale or realisation by virtue hereof my whole right, share and
interest of every kind and description whatsoever, heritable and
moveable, real and personal, now vested in or belonging to me[a]
and which may hereafter vest in or belong to me as residuary legatee or by accretion or otherwise in the estate of the deceased C
(*designed*) under his Trust Disposition and Settlement dated
              and registered in the Books of Council and Session
on   , the Trustees at present acting thereunder being D, E
and F (*all designed*), and also under common law or otherwise in
any manner of way, together with the whole claims, benefits and
advantages of every kind arising or that may arise therefrom;
together also with the said Trust Disposition and Settlement and
the whole provisions thereof so far as I have or may acquire right
thereto and the whole trust estate, both capital and income, to
which I am or may become entitled and all powers competent to me
thereunder: With full power to the said B and his foresaids to claim,
sue for, receive, discharge, sell [publicly or privately and with or
without advertisement], assign or otherwise deal with the said
whole right, share and interest or any part thereof and to do everything in relation to the same that I or my foresaids could have done
if these presents had not been granted and that without any consent
or concurrence of me or my foresaids: And in further security of the
said obligations I assign to the said B and his foresaids redeemably
as aftermentioned but irredeemably in the event of a sale by virtue
hereof a Policy of Assurance granted by the   Assurance
Company of (*chief office*) on my own life for the sum of
£   payable in the event of my dying during the lifetime of G
(*designed*) which policy is numbered   and dated
              and on which there is an annual premium of £   pay-
able on   in each year, together with all bonus and other
additions accrued or that may accrue thereon[b] and all benefits and
advantages whatever that may arise therefrom, and my whole right,
title and interest therein: With full power to the said B and his foresaids to ask, sue for, uplift and discharge all sums due or that may
become due under the said Policy and to sell,[c] assign or surrender
the said Policy and to grant discharges for the proceeds thereof, and
generally to do everything in relation to the said Policy that I could
have done if these presents had not been granted: And I bind
myself and my foresaids to observe the whole conditions of the said
Policy and without prejudice to that generality to pay when due the
premiums and any other sums necessary to keep the said Policy in
force and to exhibit receipts therefor not less than 14 days before
the expiry of the days of grace for payment thereof and in the event
of my or their failure to do so I hereby authorise the said B or his

foresaids, if they think proper but without any obligation on him or them to do so, to pay the same with right to recover any sums so paid with interest at the said rate of   per cent. per annum from the respective dates of payment until repaid: Provided always that all sums received from the said estate or the said Policy and all payments made with interest thereon by the said B and his foresaids in the exercise of the foregoing powers shall be credited or debited as the case may be in the final accounting between him or them and me or my foresaids: And I agree that the amount due at any time shall be conclusively ascertained and constituted by a certificate under the hand of the said B or his foresaids or his or their agent without production of vouchers: And I reserve power of redemption at any term of Whitsunday or Martinmas on three months' notice in writing upon payment of all sums due hereunder and expenses: And I have delivered the said Policy to the said B: And I grant absolute warrandice: And I consent to registration for preservation and execution. (*To be attested*)

NOTES
[a] Although the interest in residue has not yet vested there may be a vested interest to claim legal rights which has not been discharged.
[b] The assurance is normally effected on a non-participating basis but the reference to bonus additions should be inserted *quantum valeat*.
[c] In the circumstances sale by the creditor of the policy covering the contingency of survivance is improbable but the power should be given.

Contingency insurance—variations

7–69   The style in the foregoing paragraph is applicable where the contingency assurance has been effected by the debtor on an annual premium basis. Alternative arrangements are: (1) The policy is effected by the debtor for a single premium, in which case the obligation of the debtor to pay premiums and the right of the creditor to do so if the debtor fails to make the payments will be omitted. (2) The creditor may effect the policy on an annual premium basis in which case the deed should narrate the obligation of the debtor to pay premiums and the right of the creditor to do so on failure as in the foregoing style should be inserted. (3) The creditor may effect the policy on a single premium basis, the amount of the single premium being included in the sum advanced, and the fact narrated, with a provision that the proceeds of the policy if it becomes payable will be credited against the amount due under the bond.

Bond and assignation in security—vested reversionary interest

7–70   I, A (*designed*), grant me to have instantly borrowed and received from B (*designed*), the sum of £   which sum (*ordinary form of personal bond as in para. 5–03 supra*); And in security of the obligations before and after written I assign to the said B and his foresaids redeemably as aftermentioned but irredeemably in the event of a sale or realisation by virtue hereof my whole right, share and interest of every kind and description whatsoever, heritable and moveable, real and personal, now vested in or belonging to me and which may hereafter vest in or belong to me as residuary legatee or by accretion or otherwise in the estate of the deceased C (*designed*) under his Trust Disposition and Settlement dated   and registered in the Books of Council and Session on   , the Trustees at present acting thereunder being D, E and F (*all designed*), and also under common law or otherwise in any manner of way, together with the whole claims, benefits and advantages of every kind arising or that may arise therefrom; together also with the said Trust Disposition and Settlement and the whole provisions thereof so far as I have or may acquire right thereto and the whole trust estate, both capital and income, to which I am or may become entitled and all powers competent to me thereunder: With full power to the said B and his foresaids to claim, sue for, receive, discharge, sell [publicly or privately and with or without advertisement], assign or otherwise deal with the said whole right, share and interest or any part thereof and to do everything in relation to the same that I or my foresaids could have done if these presents had not been granted and that without any consent or concurrence of me or my foresaids: Provided always that all sums received from the said estate by the said B and his foresaids shall be applied in reduction of the amount due by me or my foresaids hereunder: And I agree that the amount due at any time shall be conclusively ascertained and constituted by a certificate under the hand of the said B or his foresaids or his or their agent without production of vouchers: And I reserve power of redemption at any term of Whitsunday or Martinmas on three months' notice in writing upon payment of all sums due hereunder and expenses: And I grant absolute warrandice: And I consent to registration for preservation and execution. (*To be attested*)

Assignation of vested or non-vested reversionary interest in security of current account—no contingency insurance

7–71   An assignation of a reversionary interest, vested or not, may be taken in favour of a bank or other lending institution. The personal obligation may be created in a separate bond of cash credit or may be constituted simply by the lender's record of transactions on the current account. The security over the reversionary interest may be in addition to other securities held for the debtor's obligation and, even if not vested, may be taken without the lender requiring a contingency insurance, and may be in the following style.

I, A (*designed*), in security of all sums and obligations which I may now or at any future time be owing or under to the (*name and addresss of bank*) either solely or jointly with any person or persons or corporation, company, firm or other body, and whether as principal or surety, hereby assign to the said (*bank*) and their assignees whomsoever my whole right, share and interest of every kind and description whatsoever, heritable and moveable, real and personal, now vested in or belonging to me and which may hereafter vest in or belong to me as residuary legatee or by accretion or otherwise in the estate of the deceased C (*designed*) under his Trust Disposition and Settlement dated   and registered in the Books of Council and Session on   , the Trustees at present acting thereunder being D, E and F (*all designed*), and also under common law or otherwise in any manner of way, together with the whole claims, benefits and advantages of every kind arising or that may arise therefrom; together also with the said Trust Disposition and Settlement and the whole provisions thereof so far as I have or may acquire right thereto and the whole trust estate, both capital and income, to which I am or may become entitled and all powers competent to me thereunder: With full power to my said assignees and their foresaids to claim, sue for, receive, discharge, sell publicly or privately and with or without advertisement, assign or otherwise deal with the said whole right, share and interest or any part thereof and to do everything in relation to the same that I could have done if these presents had not been granted and that without my consent or concurrence: And I grant absolute warrandice: (*To be attested*)

Security over reversionary right constituted by absolute assignation and relative agreement

–72   A security over a reversionary interest in a trust estate may be created by an *ex facie* absolute assignation in the style in paragraph 7–41 (nonvested) or paragraph 7–42 (vested) qualified by a separate agreement to the effect that the assignation is truly in security and containing the terms of the security arrangement. If the interest assigned is not vested there may also be an absolute assignation of the contingency assurance policy in the style in paragraph 7–30 or 7–31, also qualified by the agreement.

Agreement relative to absolute assignation of non-vested residuary right and contingency insurance policy

–73   Agreement between A (*designed*) and B (*designed*) Whereas by Assignation dated   the said A has assigned to the said B his whole right, share and interest in the estate of the deceased C (*designed*) under his Trust Disposition and Settlement dated   and registered in the Books of Council and Session on   or otherwise in the said estate; And Whereas the said A by Assignation dated   assigned to the said B a Policy of Assurance granted by the X Assurance Company of (*chief office*) in his favour on his own life for the sum of   payable in the event of the said A dying during the liftime of D (*designed*) which Policy is numbered   and dated   and on which there is an annual premium of £   payable on   in each year; And Whereas the said Assignations, although *ex facie* absolute, were truly granted in security of sums due by the said A to the said B and it is proper that the terms of the security arrangement should be reduced to writing Therefore the parties hereto agree as follows:–
1. Notwithstanding that the said Assignations are *ex facie* absolute the said B admits and declares that the said right, share and interest of the said A in the estate of the said deceased C and the said Policy

of Assurance are and shall be held by the said B in security of (*specify the obligation in full, including interest—if for a continuing account add* "and shall be a continuing and covering security"— *with consent to registration for execution*) (hereinafter called "the loan obligation").

2. As regards the said right, share and interest of the said A in the estate of the said deceased C the said B shall have the whole powers and rights expressed in the said Assignation thereof all completely within the discretion of the said B as if the said Assignation were absolute and not by way of security subject only to the obligation of accounting aftermentioned.

3. As regards the said Policy of Assurance (*incorporate the rights of B as in paragraphs 2, 3 and 4 of style in paragraph 7–60*).

4. Upon final accounting the said A shall be bound to repay to the said B the amount due under the loan obligation including any arrears of interest and any premiums advanced by the said B with interest thereon as aforesaid, but there shall be credited to the said A any sums received by the said B from the said estate or from the said Policy in the exercise of his rights and powers under this Agreement. On repayment by the said A of all sums due under the loan obligation and these presents the said B will retrocess the said right, share and interest in the said estate and the said Policy (so far as not previously disposed of hereunder) to the said A or his executors or representatives at his or their expense with warrandice from fact and deed only.

5. The whole expenses and outlays of both parties in connection with the said Assignations and this Agreement shall be borne by the said A. (*To be attested*)

Stamp duty

7–74   Stamp duty is not payable upon a bond and assignation of a reversionary interest in security (paragraphs 7–68 and 7–70) nor upon an assignation thereof in security of a current account (paragraph 7–71).[19] An *ex facie* absolute assignation and relative agreement should be submitted for adjudication of stamp duty but should normally be adjudged as not liable to stamp duty as a mortgage.[19]

Intimation and notice

7–75   Intimation of the assignation of a reversionary interest in security by any of the styles in paragraphs 7–68, 7–70, 7–71 or 7–72 should be made to all the trustees of the trust estate and also to the solicitor or other agent of the trustees. Intimation is normally made either postally or by procuring a minute signed by the trustees acknowledging intimation— see paragraphs 7–17 and 7–18 *supra*. Where a policy of assurance is effected, notice of the assignation of the policy in security should be given to the assurance company—see paragraph 7–66.

---

[19] Finance Act 1971, s. 64(1).

(3) Securities over Stocks and Shares

General

7-76 Stocks or shares of public companies or Government stocks may be made the subject of security, usually in relation to current accounts in banking. Shares of private companies are not normally acceptable as security because of the restrictions on transfer which may be contained in the articles of association. The security is constituted by transfer of the stocks or shares to the creditor bank, or its nominee company, duly registered, qualified by a letter by the debtor to the bank confirming that the stocks or shares are held in security of the debtor's obligations to the bank and the terms upon which they are to be held. Sometimes a bank will advance money on the mere deposit of securities without actually having them transferred but that is not a proper security in Scotland.

Back letter—security over stocks and shares

7-77   To   Bank
        (*Address*)

GENTLEMEN,
  With reference to the securities which I have deposited with or transferred to or may deposit with or transfer to you or your nominees from time to time, I hereby authorise you to hold said securities as a general security for all or any advances or obligations which I [or A (*designed*)] or any company or firm of which I am [or the said A is] or may become a partner, however the same may for the time be constituted, may now or at any future time be owing or under to you and interest thereon at the rate charged by you from time to time in accordance with your normal practice, without prejudice to any other securities or remedies which may already or hereafter be held by or available to you. And I hereby authorise you to sell or realise said securities or any of them at any time and in such manner as you may think proper, and to apply the proceeds of such sale or realisation, and also all interest, dividends, bonuses and other rights received or to be received therefrom or accruing thereon in settlement or reduction of said advances and obligations and interest thereon, accounting to me for any surplus, [provided always that your right to sell or realise said securities shall be exercisable only after the expiry of seven days following written notification by you to me of your intention to do so]. Declaring that, notwithstanding any liability on you to account for said securities, you shall not be under any obligation to account for or reconvey the securities bearing the numbers or other identification marks of those deposited or transferred or held as aforesaid.[20]
  And I further agree that I shall not be entitled to rank on the estate of [the said A or] any [other] person, company or firm for whose obligations the said securities are or may be held in respect

---

[20] See *Crerar* v. *Bank of Scotland*, 1922 S.C. (H.L.) 137.

of the said securities or the proceeds thereof until your whole claims against [the said A or] any [other] such person, company or firm are satisfied. And I undertake to put you or your nominees in funds to meet any calls which may be made in respect of any partly paid shares deposited or transferred by me.

Yours faithfully,

. . . .

Obligations of creditor

7–78   When any bonus or rights issues are made in respect of stocks or shares held in security it is the duty of the creditor, subject to any express powers contained in the security documents, to consult the debtor as to the manner in which the issues should be dealt with.[21] A provision in the form in the preceding paragraph will enable the creditor to determine any question on that matter in view of his right to receive the proceeds of bonus or other rights but in practice the debtor is often consulted, particularly in the case of rights issues where payment for the rights is involved. A more difficult problem may arise in exercising voting rights on any contentious issue of importance. As registered proprietor the creditor will be entitled to exercise voting rights in respect of the stock or shares and if the debtor wishes to reserve them the security document should be modified appropriately.

Bearer shares

7–79   American, Canadian or other foreign states frequently issue bearer certificates transferable on delivery. Usually such certificates state the name of the registered holder and contain a statement that they are transferable only by him personally or by attorney, and on the reverse a form of transfer and appointment of an attorney is printed. These documents are not truly negotiable in Scotland since a subsequent holder, until he is registered as proprietor, cannot sue in his own name, and the dividends will continue to be paid to the original holder until a transfer is registered. In practice therefore the safe course is to have the transfer form completed by the debtor as the registered holder and have the shares registered in the name of the creditor or his nominee company.

Stamp duty

7–80   The transfer of the stock or shares, certified as being by way of security for a loan, will be stamped 50p. The back letter is not liable to stamp duty. Where a blank transfer is dated it should be stamped within 30 days.

---

[21] *Waddell* v. *Hutton*, 1911 S.C. 575.

(4) Securities over Special Kinds of Incorporeal Rights

General

-81   Securities may be created over a considerable variety of incorporeal moveable rights, usually of the nature of rights to sums of money. Examples are sums payable from funds in a building society or a trustee savings bank or a joint stock bank, investments in Government stocks registered on the National Savings Stock Register, and bills of exchange. Securities of those kinds are sometimes taken by banks or other financial institutions as security for advances on current account.

Documentation and procedure

-82   The security over such rights is normally effected by (1) delivery to the creditor of any relevant document evidencing the debtor's right, *e.g.* passbook, certificate or the bill of exchange together with the appropriate form of withdrawal or repayment signed by the debtor or endorsement of the bill of exchange, (2) a back letter granted by the debtor to the creditor setting out the terms of the security arrangement, and (3) where desired and necessary intimation to the person or body in whose hands the funds due to the debtor are located (not necessary in the case of a bill of exchange being a negotiable instrument).

Back letter

-83   A specimen style of back letter, varying according to the nature of the right over which the security is constituted, might be as follows:–

To   Bank
(*Address*)

Gentlemen,
    With reference to the [Share Account No.   of the
Building Society in my name] [Special Investment Account
No.   of the   Trustee Savings Bank in my name]
[Certificate No.   for £   (*description of stock*) registered
on the National Savings Stock Register in my name] [sum due to me
or that may become due to me on current account with your Bank]
[sum of £   lodged by your Bank on the Money Market on my
behalf and any sums that may at any time hereafter be lodged by
your Bank on the Money Market on my behalf] [four bills of
exchange for the sums of £   , £   , £   and £
respectively and dated   ,   ,   and   respectively, duly endorsed, drawn by us on   and accepted by
them], I have herewith delivered the relevant [Share Account Pass
Book] [Special Investment Account Pass Book] [Certificate] [bills
of exchange] together with a [withdrawal receipt form duly signed]
[withdrawal receipt form duly signed] [application for encashment
form duly completed and signed] [bills of exchange drawn,
accepted and endorsed in your favour] to hold as a general security
for any advances and obligations which I (*name and address of*

debtor) or any company of which I may be a director or any firm—however the same may from time to time be constituted—of which I am or may at any time be a partner, may now or at any future time be owing or under to you. And I authorise you to [uplift the amount due with accrued interest on the said Share Account] [uplift the amount due with accrued interest on the said Special Investment Account] [uplift the amount payable under the said application for encashment] [uplift all or any amounts lodged on my behalf with the Money Market Department of your Bank] at any time you may think it expedient to do so and to apply the same in settlement or reduction of the said advances or obligations, with interest, accounting to me for any surplus [provided always that your right to uplift the said amount [any of the said amounts] and to apply it as aforesaid shall be exercisable only after the expiry of seven days following written notification by you to me of your intention to do so.] (*Where bills of exchange are held specific authority to encash them is not required but there should be inserted* "And I hereby dispense with the presentation and negotiation of any or all of the said bills of exchange"). And I confirm that the security held in terms of this letter shall be without prejudice to any other securities or remedies which may now or hereafter be held by or available to you. And I agree that I shall not be entitled to rank on the estates of any company or firm for whose advances or obligations the security in terms of this letter is held in respect of any sums [uplifted] [received] in accordance with the powers herein contained nor to have the benefit of any securities now or hereafter held by you from any such company or firm until your whole claims against them are satisfied.

Yours faithfully,

. . . .

Completion of creditor's title

7–84   In order to complete the creditor's title and to afford protection against fraudulent withdrawal or encashment or diligence by other creditors the back letter should, except where the security subject is a negotiable instrument, be intimated to the body liable in payment, but the creditor bank may be content to rely upon the honesty of the debtor and accept the risk of diligence by a third party without formally intimating the security.

Security for bridging loan—irrevocable mandate

7–85   When contracts for the sale of one heritable property and the purchase of another have been entered into, the price of the property purchased may have to be paid before the proceeds of the sale of the property sold are available, and a temporary loan from bankers is required to bridge the gap. In such circumstances the practice of bankers is to take an irrevocable mandate from the borrower, addressed to the solicitors handling the sale transaction, instructing them to pay to the bankers the proceeds of the sale when received under deduction of sums secured on the property sold and the fees and expenses of the solicitors in respect of the sale. The mandate should be adopted as holograph by the borrower and intimated to the solicitors concerned from whom an acknowledgment should be received. If the borrower is a limited company the mandate may require registration in the Register of Charges as a charge on an interest in land.[22] Where the amount of a bridging loan to an individual does not exceed £15,000 the procedure for fixed-sum credit under the Consumer Credit Act 1974 must be followed—see para. 8–26 *infra*.

Securities for special loans under statute

–86   Loans may be made or guaranteed by the Government for particular purposes, *e.g.* loans to small firms under sections 7 and 8 of the Industry Act 1972 as amended, on condition of the borrower providing security over its assets (which may be wholly or partly moveable). The documentation is normally in a form prescribed by order under the statute or adjusted by the relevant Government department.

Securities over book debts and sums due under construction contracts

–87   Securities over book debts are considered in Chapter 8 and securities over sums due under construction contracts in Chapter 12.

---

[22] Companies Act 1985, s. 410(4)(*a*).

CHAPTER 8

VOLUNTARY TRANSFER OF MOVEABLE PROPERTY
ABSOLUTELY OR IN SECURITY

(1) ABSOLUTE TRANSFER

(1) Absolute Transfer

General principles

8–01   At common law a transfer of ownership of corporeal moveable property may be effected by a person having a title or right to the property delivering it to another—*traditionibus non nudis pactis dominia rerum transferuntur*. A contract to transfer corporeal moveables, without delivery of the property, does not transfer a real right of ownership but merely creates a personal obligation.[1] The usual title to transfer corporeal moveable property is ownership but the right to sell such property is conferred upon others in certain circumstances by common law and under statute.[2] Further, the rule that delivery is essential to an effective transfer of a real right of property, particularly on sale, has been radically altered by the Sale of Goods Acts.[3,4]

Delivery

8–02   Delivery may be actual, constructive or symbolical. Actual delivery may be effected by the transfer of physical possession of the property or of the key to the premises where it is stored. Constructive delivery may consist in the transfer of a document of title which places goods under the control of the transferee, as by giving a delivery order addressed to an independent storekeeper who has custody of the goods or endorsing and delivering the storekeeper's warrant for the goods, together with intimation to the storekeeper.[5] Symbolical delivery may be effected by transfer of a document of title, *e.g.* endorsation and delivery of a bill of lading, which is recognised as a symbol of ownership of the goods to which it relates and entitles the endorsee to take delivery of the goods when unloaded.[6]

Registration

8–03   In the case of certain kinds of corporeal moveable property, *e.g.* ships or aircraft, transfer of ownership is effected by statutorily prescribed documents and registration in the appropriate register.[7]

Gift

Inter vivos gifts

8–04   A gift of corporeal moveables *inter vivos* requires both delivery and evidence of *animus donandi* since the presumption of law is against

---

[1] *Clark* v. *West Calder Oil Co.* (1882) 9 R. 1017, 1024.
[2] See para. 8–06 and Walker, *Principles*, III, 430–439.
[3] See para. 8–05.
[4] For a fuller discussion of these principles see Walker, *Principles*, III, 427 *et seq.*; Gloag and Henderson, 568, 569.
[5] *Inglis* v. *Robertson & Baxter* (1898) 25 R. (H.L.) 70.
[6] For a fuller account of actual, constructive and symbolical delivery see Walker, *op. cit.*, III, 429, 430.
[7] See paras. 8–54 *et seq.*

donation.[8] Evidence of intention to make a gift may be established by a document expressing that intention, however informal, or admission on oath by the donor or by parole evidence, but delivery is also essential. In order to be effective delivery should involve the transfer of possession to the donee and dispossession of the donor.[9]

Sale of Goods

Preliminary

8–05   At common law in Scotland a contract for the sale of goods, whether existing specific goods or goods not yet in existence or not yet in a deliverable state, did not transfer ownership of the goods until delivery. The Mercantile Law Amendment (Scotland) Act 1856 and the Sale of Goods Act 1893 altered the Scottish common law and substituted the English rules whereby the property in specific or ascertained goods passes when the parties to the contract of sale intend it to pass or, in the case of future or unascertained goods, when goods of that description in a deliverable state are unconditionally appropriated to the contract. The law of sale of goods has now been consolidated in (1) the Sale of Goods Act 1979 superseding the Act of 1893 and incorporating the relevant provisions of the Misrepresentation Act 1967 (s. 4(2)) and the Supply of Goods (Implied Terms) Act 1973 (ss. 1 to 7), (2) the Consumer Credit Act 1974 (in relation to sales by hire-purchase), and (3) the Unfair Contract Terms Act 1977. As regards sales involving parties outwith the United Kingdom the Uniform Laws on International Sales Act 1967 may also be relevant, but may be excluded by agreement of the parties. In matters not affected by those statutes the common or statute law of Scotland continues to apply, *e.g.* capacity and power to contract, misrepresentation and fraud, bankruptcy, landlord's hypothec and sequestration for rent. An exposition of the current law of sale of goods is outwith the scope of this work but its principles must be kept in view in framing conditions and contracts of sale.[10]

Capacity and power to sell

8–06   As has already been noted[11] the usual title to sell corporeal moveable property is that of ownership on the principle that no person can confer a better title than he has himself—*nemo dat qui non habet*—but under statute and at common law a non-owner may in certain circumstances

---

[8] See Walker, *op. cit.*,III, 440, 441; Gloag and Henderson, 569.

[9] Walker, *op. cit.*, III, 440. Dispossession of the donor may be important in certain circumstances in relation to capital transfer tax. For example, if a parent and child both live in a house owned by the parent and the parent makes a gift to the child, evidenced in writing, of furniture in the house, and both parties continue to live in the house and make use of the furniture, there can be a question whether the gift has been completed by delivery and on the subsequent death of the parent the value of the furniture may be liable to tax at the higher rate applicable to transfers on death.

[10] As to principles of the modern law of sale of goods see Walker, *op. cit.*, III, 433 *et seq.*; Marshall, *Scots Mercantile Law*, Chap. 4.

[11] At para. 8–01.

confer a valid title to corporeal moveables. The principal examples are (1) sales under the Factors Acts or any special common law or statutory power of sale or under an order of court,[12] (2) a sale by a seller having a voidable title which has not been avoided at the time of sale to a buyer in good faith without knowledge of the defect in the seller's title,[13] (3) a sale by a seller who continues in possession of the goods sold to a buyer purchasing in good faith without notice of the previous sale,[14] (4) a sale by a purchaser who, with the consent of the seller, has obtained possession of goods although ownership of the goods has not yet passed to him, to a buyer in good faith without notice of the right of the original seller in respect of the goods,[15] (5) a sale by a mercantile agent who is in possession of goods, with the consent of the owner, made in the ordinary course of business as a mercantile agent to a buyer acting in good faith without notice that the agent was not authorised to sell,[16] (6) a sale by a hirer or purchaser of a motor vehicle under a hire-purchase or conditional sale agreement before the right of property in the vehicle has passed to him made to a private purchaser, either directly or after a sale to a trade or finance purchaser, provided that the private purchaser buys in good faith without notice of the hire-purchase or conditional sale agreement,[17] (7) sales by particular persons in special circumstances under powers at common law or by statute,[18] and (8) sales made with the authority of the courts.

Implied conditions and warranties

8–07   The Sale of Goods Act 1979, substantially restating and consolidating earlier legislation, implies certain conditions and warranties. The distinction made in English law between these two terms is not applicable in Scotland, where a failure to perform a material part of a contract of sale entitles the buyer to reject the goods and treat the contract as repudiated or to retain the goods and claim damages[19] and a breach of warranty is deemed to be a failure to perform a material part of the contract.[20] The principal terms implied by the Act relate to time of payment,[21] title to sell,[22] sales by description[23] or by sample[24] or both[23] and

---

[12] Sale of Goods Act 1979, s. 21(2).
[13] Ibid., s. 23.
[14] Ibid., s. 24.
[15] Ibid., s. 25.
[16] Ibid., s. 25. See Factors (Scotland) Act 1890, ss. 8, 9.
[17] Hire-Purchase Act 1964, s. 27 re-enacted with changes in terminology by the Consumer Credit Act 1974, Sched. 4, para. 22. The 1974 Act provisions are effective as from May 19, 1985—S.I. 1983 No. 1551 (C. 44), art. 4.
[18] For a list of these see Walker, *Principles*, III, 438, 439.
[19] 1979 Act, s. 11(5).
[20] Ibid., s. 61(2).
[21] Ibid., s. 10.
[22] Ibid., s. 12.
[23] Ibid., s. 13.
[24] Ibid., s. 15.

quality and fitness of the goods.[25] The implied terms may be negatived or varied by express agreement, or by the course of dealing between the parties, or by such usage as binds both parties to the contract, but an express condition or warranty does not negative a condition or warranty implied by the Act unless inconsistent with it.[26] In practice conditions of sale or a contract of sale in which any of the implied conditions or warranties are being negatived or varied should contain an express exclusion, total or partial, of any of the statutorily implied terms which it is intended to disapply or alter. It must be kept in view, however, that the Unfair Contract Terms Act 1977 (ss. 20, 21) provides that a purported exclusion or restriction of liability for breach of obligations arising from section 12 of the 1979 Act (implied terms about title) is void, and that a purported exclusion or restriction of liability for breach of obligations arising from section 13 (sales by description), section 14 (implied conditions as to quality or fitness), or section 15 (sales by sample) of the 1979 Act is void against the consumer in a consumer contract and in the case of any other contract may be of no effect if it fails to satisfy the "reasonableness" test defined in section 24 of the 1977 Act. Parties to a contract of sale of goods to consumers should also keep in view the terms of orders made for the protection of consumers under the Fair Trading Act 1973 and the Consumer Safety Act 1978.

Conditions of sale or purchase and contracts of sale—practice

8–08   Contracts of sale or agreements to sell[27] are usually concluded in practice by the adoption by the parties of conditions of sale printed on quotations or purchase orders or, in the case of more important transactions, by the adjustment of a formal contract. The terms of sale vary according to the nature of the goods, whether specific goods in stock, a specified quantity of commodities of a particular description or in accordance with sample, specific articles, machinery designed for a specified purpose, etc.[28]

Specimen conditions of sale—goods manufactured by seller

8–09   The following specimen conditions are designed for use in respect of the sale of articles manufactured by the seller to a trade customer who will dispose of them by retail sale to consumers for use as separate items. For conditions where the goods sold are to be incorporated in works constructed under a building or engineering contract see Chapter 12, *infra*. (The conditions are based on styles published by the Institute of Purchase and Supply whose permission is gratefully acknowledged).

---

[25] *Ibid.*, s. 14.
[26] *Ibid.*, s. 55.
[27] For the distinction between a contract of sale and an agreement to sell, see 1979 Act, s. 2.
[28] For building and engineering contracts which include an element of sale see Chap. 12. For consumer credit and credit sales and conditional sales see paras. 8–11 *et seq.*

Definitions
1. "Seller" shall mean the person, firm or company [who issues the Quotation] [to whom the Purchase Order is issued].

"Buyer" shall mean the person, firm or company [to whom the Quotation is issued] [by whom the Purchase Order is issued].

"Quotation" means the quotation issued by Seller to Purchaser which specifies that these conditions apply to it.

"Purchase Order" means the purchase order issued by Purchaser to Seller which specifies or accepts, expressly or by implication, that these conditions apply to it.

"goods" include all goods [specified in the Quotation so far as included in Buyer's order or orders to purchase] [covered by the Purchase Order].

"packages" include bags, cases, carboys, cylinders, drums, pallets, tank wagons and other containers.

"Contract" means the contract between Seller and Buyer for purchase of the goods consisting of [the Quotation and any relative Purchase Order] [the Purchase Order], these conditions and any other documents (or parts thereof) specified in [the Quotation and any relative Purchase Order] [the Purchase Order]. Should there be any inconsistency between the documents comprising the Contract, they shall have precedence in the order listed in this definition.

Quality
2. In the absence of a specification or sample, all goods supplied shall be within the normal limits of merchantable or industrial quality[a] and are supplied subject to the conditions afterwritten.

NOTE
[a] The term "merchantable quality" is defined in section 14(6) of the Sale of Goods Act 1979, but a fuller definition is under consideration by the Law Commissions following upon a remit of January 1979 by the Lord Chancellor.

Delivery
3. The date of delivery of the goods shall be that specified in the Purchase Order unless otherwise agreed between Seller and Buyer. Seller shall furnish such programme(s) of manufacture and delivery as Buyer may reasonably require and Seller shall give notice to Buyer as soon as practicable if such programme(s) are or are likely to be delayed.

All goods will be delivered at the delivery point specified in the Purchase Order. If goods are incorrectly delivered, Seller will be responsible for any additional expense incurred in delivering them to their correct destination.

Passing of property and risk
4. The property and risk in the goods shall remain in Seller until they are delivered at the point specified in the Purchase Order.[a]

NOTE
[a] As to provisions where the Seller wishes to retain the right of property in the goods until receiving payment (a Romalpa type clause) see paragraphs 8–42 et seq.

Price and terms of payment

5. The price shall be that stated or ascertained in accordance with the [Quotation and any relative Purchase Order] [Purchase Order].[a,b,c] Unless otherwise stated in the [Quotation and relative Purchase Order] [Purchase Order], payment of the price will be made within [28] days of receipt of the goods and agreement of invoice. Value Added Tax, where applicable, shall be shown separately on all invoices as a strictly nett extra charge.

NOTES

[a] See Sale of Goods Act 1979, s. 8.

[b] The quotation should state the period for which the price or prices quoted remain valid.

[c] Where the sale is of goods to be manufactured it may be in the interests of Seller to incorporate a price adjustment formula to take account of increases in the cost of labour and materials. An independent recognised basis should be used, *e.g.* the indices published by the Department of Employment/Trade and Industry in the *Monthly Digest of Statistics*.

Loss or damage in transit

6. Buyer shall advise Seller and the carrier (if any) in writing, otherwise than by a qualified signature on any delivery note, of any loss of or damage to the goods within the following time limits:

(i) Partial loss, damage, defects or non-delivery of any separate part of a consignment shall be advised within 7 days of the date of delivery of the consignment or part consignment.

(ii) Non-delivery of the whole consignment shall be advised within 21 days of notice of dispatch.

Seller shall make good free of charge to Buyer any loss of or damage to the goods where notice is given by Buyer in compliance with this condition, provided that Buyer shall not in any circumstances claim damages in respect of loss of profit.

Acceptance

7. In the case of goods delivered by Seller not conforming with the Contract whether by reason of being of quality or in a quantity measurement not stipulated or being unfit for the purpose for which they are required where such purpose has been made known in writing to Seller, Buyer shall have the right to reject such goods within [days] [a reasonable time][a] of their delivery and to purchase elsewhere as near as practicable to the same Contract specifications and conditions as circumstances permit but without prejudice to any other right which Buyer may have against Seller, and the making of payment shall not prejudice Buyer's right of rejection. Before exercising the said right to purchase elsewhere Buyer shall give Seller reasonable opportunity to replace rejected goods with goods which conform to the Contract.

NOTE

[a] If a particular period is specified the Contract may be vulnerable on the ground that it is an unreasonably short period under the Unfair Contract Terms Act 1977. The "reasonable time" alternative is safer; it has the disadvantage of being imprecise but that would be determined by the usage of trade, and there is some

protection for Seller in respect that Buyer must give an opportunity
of remedying the breach before purchasing elsewhere.

Variations
8. Seller shall not alter any of the goods except as directed in writing
by Buyer; but Buyer shall have the right from time to time during
the execution of the Contract, by notice in writing, to direct Seller
to add to or to omit or otherwise vary the goods, and Seller shall
carry out such variations and be bound by the same conditions, so
far as applicable, as though the said variations were stated in the
Contract.

Where Seller receives any such direction from Buyer which
would occasion an amendment to the Contract price, Seller shall
with all practicable speed advise Buyer in writing to that effect stating the amount of any such amendment.

If in the opinion of Seller any such direction is likely to prevent
Seller from fulfilling any of his obligations under the Contract he
shall so notify Buyer and Buyer shall decide with all practicable
speed whether or not the same shall be carried out and shall confirm his instructions on that matter in writing. Until Buyer so con-
firms his instructions they shall be deemed not to have been given.

Patent rights
9. Seller will indemnify Buyer against any claim for infringement of
Letters Patent, Registered Design, Trade Mark or Copyright by the
use or sale of any article or material supplied by Seller to Buyer and
against all costs and damages which Buyer may incur in any action
for such infringement or for which Buyer may become liable in any
such action. Provided always that this indemnity shall not apply to
any infringement which is due to Seller having followed any instruction furnished or given by Buyer or to the use of such article or
material in a manner or for a purpose or in a foreign country not
specified by or disclosed to Seller, or to any infringement which is
due to the use of such article or material in association or combination with any other article or material not supplied by Seller.
And provided also that this indemnity is conditional on Buyer giving to Seller the earliest possible notice in writing of any claim being
made or action threatened or brought against Buyer and on Buyer
permitting Seller at Seller's own expense to conduct any litigation
that may ensue and all negotiations for a settlement of the claim.
Buyer on his part warrants that any instruction furnished or given
by him shall not be such as will cause Seller to infringe any Letters
Patent, ·Registered Design, Trade Mark or Copyright in the
execution of the Purchase Order.

Force majeure
10. If a delivery by Seller, or the acceptance by Buyer of a delivery, is
delayed or prevented because the manufacture of the goods, their
delivery to Buyer's Works by usual route, or the consumption or
use of the goods by Buyer in the ordinary course of his business has
been or is being prevented or hindered by circumstances beyond
the reasonable control of either party, including any form of
Government intervention, strikes and lockouts relevant to the Contract, delays by Sub-Contractors (but only where such delays were
beyond the control of the Sub-Contractor concerned), such
delivery shall be suspended, and if it cannot be made within a

reasonable time after the due date, the delivery may be cancelled by either party by letter or cable to the other. Where more than one delivery is to be made under the Contract, deliveries not cancelled will be resumed as soon as the circumstances causing the delay cease, but, except where both parties otherwise agree, the period during which deliveries are to be made will not be extended. Buyer shall pay Seller such sum as may be equitable in respect of work performed prior to cancellation.[a]

NOTE

[a] The Buyer should only pay an equitable sum in respect of cancellation charges, taking account of the loss that may be incurred by both parties and the degree to which such losses are insurable. The Seller should be covered by insurance in respect of consequential losses, e.g. loss of profits, loss of other contracts, interruption of business etc. and fire or explosion at Seller's Works. Negotiations should therefore be restricted to costs in respect of materials and labour actually expended up to the date of cancellation.

The Seller is not entitled to impose any additional charges in respect of the storage of goods during a force majeure situation unless there is provision for such extra charges in the terms of the contract.

A delivery extension granted under a force majeure situation also extends the period before which liquidated damages (if any) are payable.

Where a price is established relative to a given quantity, no variation in that price basis should be allowed if the Buyer is forced to take a reduced quantity due to a declaration of force majeure.

Assignment and sub-letting

11. The Contract shall not be assigned by Seller nor sub-let as a whole. Seller shall not sub-let any part of the work without Buyer's written consent, which shall not be unreasonably withheld, but the restriction contained in this clause shall not apply to sub-contracts for materials, for minor details, or for any part of which the makers are named in the Contract. Seller shall be responsible for all work done and goods supplied by all Sub-Contractors.

Copies and sub-orders

12. When Buyer has consented to the placing of sub-contracts copies of each sub-order shall be sent by Seller to Buyer immediately they are issued.

Progress and inspection

13. Buyer's representatives shall have the right to progress and inspect all goods at Seller's works and the works of Sub-Contractors at all reasonable times and to reject goods that do not comply with the terms of the Contract. Seller's sub-contracts shall be made accordingly. Any inspection, checking, approval or acceptance given on behalf of Buyer shall not relieve Seller or his Sub-Contractors from any obligation under the Contract.

Buyer's rights in specifications, plans, process information etc.

14. Any specifications, plans, drawings, process information, patterns or designs supplied by Buyer to Seller in connection with the Contract shall remain the property of Buyer, and any information derived therefrom or otherwise communicated to Seller in connection

with the Contract shall be kept secret and shall not, without the consent in writing of Buyer, be published or disclosed to any third party, or made use of by Seller except for the purpose of implementing the Contract. Any specifications, plans, drawings, process information, patterns or designs supplied by Buyer must be returned to Buyer on fulfilment of the Contract.

Free issue materials
15. Where Buyer for the purposes of the Contract issues materials "free of charge" to Seller such materials shall be and remain the property of Buyer. Seller shall maintain all such materials in good order and condition subject, in the case of tooling, patterns and the like to fair wear and tear. Seller shall use such materials solely in connection with the Contract. Any surplus materials shall be disposed of at Buyer's discretion. Waste of such materials arising from bad workmanship or negligence of Seller shall be made good at Seller's expense.

Hazardous goods
16. Hazardous goods must be marked by Seller with International danger symbol(s) and display the name of the material in English. Transport and other documents must include declaration of the hazard and name of the material in English. Goods must be accompanied by emergency information in English in the form of written instructions, labels or markings. Seller shall observe the requirements of U.K. and International Agreements relating to the packing, labelling and carriage of hazardous goods.

   All information held by, or reasonably available to, Seller regarding any potential hazards known or believed to exist in the transport, handling or use of the goods supplied shall be promptly communicated to Buyer.

Packages
17. Where Buyer has an option to return packages and does so, Buyer will return such packages empty in good order and condition (consigned "carriage paid" unless otherwise agreed) to Seller's supplying Works or depot indicated by Seller, and will advise Seller the date of despatch.

   Packages returned promptly in the manner aforesaid shall be subject to an allowance at Seller's standard rate operating at the time of delivery to Buyer.

   Where goods are delivered by road vehicle, available empty packages may be returned by the same vehicle.

   Where goods are delivered by tank wagons these will be emptied and returned without delay.

Indemnity
18. Seller shall as soon as reasonably practicable in his option either repair or replace any goods which are proved to have been or become defective (expressly excluding defects occasioned by improper storage or usage by Buyer or any third party or by any other cause for which Seller or his Sub-Contractors are not responsible) during the period of 12 months from putting into service or 18 months from delivery,[a] whichever shall be the shorter. Repairs and replacements shall themselves be subject to the foregoing obligations for a period of 12 months from the date of delivery. Seller shall further be liable in damages (if any) directly resulting from

any such defects but any such liability shall be limited to the price of the defective goods and Seller shall not in any event be liable for loss of profit or any consequential loss, however incurred.[b]

The foregoing states the entire liability in contract and in negligence of Seller in respect of goods which are defective, other than liability arising under condition 6 hereof, and all warranties expressed or implied under the Sale of Goods Act 1979 or other statutes or at common law are, so far as it is competent to do so,[c] expressly excluded.

NOTES

[a] Shorter or longer periods may be appropriate in particular cases.

[b] This limitation would in most cases, it is thought, satisfy the "reasonableness" test imposed by the Unfair Contract Terms Act 1977 (s. 17) upon standard form contracts which are not consumer contracts.

[c] See Unfair Contract Terms Act 1977.

Insolvency of seller

19. If Seller [shall pass a resolution for winding up (not being a members' winding up for the purposes of reconstruction or amalgamation), or if the court shall make an order that the Seller shall be wound up, or if a receiver or manager of any property of the Seller shall be appointed][a] [or any firm of which he may be a partner shall become insolvent or notour bankrupt, or if a trust deed is granted by him or such firm for behoof of creditors][b] Buyer may, without prejudice to any of his other rights, terminate the Contract forthwith by written notice to Seller [or to any liquidator or receiver][a] [or trustee in sequestration or under a trust deed][b] without compensation to Seller.[c]

NOTES

[a] Applicable where Seller is company.

[b] Applicable where Seller is individual.

[c] Minor adjustments are required where Seller is a firm.

Quotation or tender conditions

20. The conditions submitted or referred to by Seller when quoting or tendering shall form part of the Contract unless otherwise stipulated by Buyer and confirmed by Seller in writing.[a]

NOTE

[a] See *Roofcare Ltd.* v. *Gillies*, 1984 S.L.T. (Sh.Ct.) 8.

Arbitration

21. All disputes, questions or differences at any time arising under, out of or in connection with the Contract shall be referred to the decision of an arbiter to be agreed between the parties or, failing such agreement, to be appointed at the request of either party by the President of the Law Society of Scotland, and the decision of such arbiter shall be final and binding.

Law of the contract

22. The Contract shall be subject to the law of Scotland.

(2) Transfer on Loan or in Security

Principles

8–10   The rule of the common law which requires transfer of corporeal moveable property in order to create a real right of ownership applies also to transfers in security: a transfer, actual, contructive or symbolical, of the relevant property is essential to the creation of a real right of security over it. That principle is preserved in the Sale of Goods Act 1979[29] which ensures that the rules as to passing of property without delivery do not apply to a transaction in the form of a sale which is intended to operate by way of security.[30] To this principle, however, there are important exceptions. Securities over corporeal moveable property without possession are recognised in particular relationships, such as the rights of hypothec of a superior or landlord.[31] Certain kinds of securities without possession may be created by agreement either at common law, as in the case of bonds of bottomry or respondentia and agreements for retention of title until payment for goods sold, or under statute, such as hire-purchase and conditional sales, agricultural credits and mortgages of ships and aircraft. In this chapter the more important securities created conventionally are considered, namely, agreements in the field of consumer credit, agreements for retention of title and mortgages of ships and aircraft. Securities (or quasi-securities) over corporeal moveables under building or engineering contracts are treated in Chapter 12 *infra* and floating charges, which are initially inchoate securities over heritable and moveable property, are dealt with in a subsequent volume.

Consumer Credit

(i) Hire-Purchase, Credit Sales and Conditional Sales

Preliminary

8–11   The principal transactions which involve transfer of corporeal moveable property in which credit is given to or provided for the purchaser are hire-purchase, credit sales and conditional sales. The statutory definitions of these terms in the Consumer Credit Act 1974[32] (which broadly correspond to their ordinary usage) are: (1) A hire-purchase agreement is an agreement, other than a conditional sale agreement, under which goods are hired in return for periodical payments and the property in the goods will pass upon (i) the exercise of an option to purchase, (ii)

---

[29] s. 62(4), re-enacting the Sale of Goods Act 1893, s. 61(4).
[30] *Jones & Co.'s Tr.* v. *Allan* (1901) 4 F. 374; *Gavin's Tr.* v. *Fraser*, 1920 S.C. 674; *Newbigging* v. *Ritchie's Tr.*, 1930 S.C. 273.
[31] For a fuller account of legal hypothecs see Walker, *Principles*, III, 418–422.
[32] s. 189.

the doing of any other specified act by any party to the agreement, or (iii) the happening of any other specified event. (2) A credit sale agreement means an agreement for the sale of goods, other than a conditional sale agreement, under which the purchase price or part of it is payable by instalments. (3) A conditional sale agreement is an agreement for the sale of goods under which the purchase price or part of it is payable by instalments and the property in the goods is to remain with the seller (although the buyer may have possession) until such conditions as to the payment of instalments or otherwise as may be specified in the agreement are fulfilled.

Common law

-12   The common law with regard to hire-purchase, credit sales and conditional sales continues to apply so far as not modified or extended by legislation, but the statutory changes, enacted mainly with the object of protection of consumers, are substantial. The undernoted texts may be consulted for an account of the substantive law, both common law and statute.[33]

The legislation

-13   Hire-purchase, conditional sale and credit sale agreements under which the hire-purchase or total purchase price does not exceed £15,000 and where the hirer or buyer is not a body corporate are subject to statutory regulations, the principal statutes currently in force being the Hire-Purchase Act 1964, the Hire-Purchase (Scotland) Act 1965, the Advertisements (Hire-Purchase) Act 1967 and the Consumer Credit Act 1974. The Act of 1974 prospectively repeals all the earlier relevant legislation but most of its provisions become operative only when detailed regulations are promulgated. The regulations relating to the form and content of documents apply on and after May 19, 1985,[34] and from that date all the main provisions of the Act will be in force. The law as stated in this chapter is that applicable on and after that date.

Consumer Credit Act 1974

-14   This is a comprehensive statute designed to incorporate within a single code the former piecemeal legislation with regard to loan credit[35] and sale credit.[36] As its name implies the Act regulates transactions with individual[37] consumers, whether of consumer credit or consumer hire

---

[33] Goode, *Introduction to the Consumer Credit Act 1974*; Guest and Lomnicka, *An Introduction to the Law of Credit and Security*; Walker, *Principles*, III, 5.34; Gloag and Henderson, XIX; Halsbury's *Laws of England*, Vol. 22, Hire-Purchase and Consumer Credit.
[34] Consumer Credit Act 1974 (Commencement No. 8) Order 1983 (S.I. 1983 No. 1551 (C. 44)).
[35] Moneylenders Acts 1900 and 1927; Pawnbrokers Acts 1872 and 1960.
[36] Hire-Purchase Act 1964; Hire-Purchase (Scotland) Act 1965.
[37] Defined to include partnerships or other unincorporated bodies not consisting entirely of bodies corporate—s. 189(1).

business, usually entered into by commercial credit companies which are licensed under the Act.[38] The principal provisions of the Act apply to regulated agreements, *i.e.* consumer credit agreements (including hire-purchase, credit sales and conditional sales) where the credit provided does not exceed £15,000[39] and is more than £50 and is not an exempt agreement under section 16 of the Act (which excludes agreements where the creditor is a local authority or building society or other bodies specified by order) and certain agreements specified by order where the number of payments to be made by the debtor is small, the rate of total charge for credit does not exceed a specified rate or the agreement has a connection with a company outside the United Kingdom or the agreement relates to electricity, gas or water metering equipment which is exempted by order[40]). The special protection given by Part III of the Hire-Purchase Act 1964 to a private purchaser of a motor vehicle buying in good faith from a hirer under a hire-purchase agreement or a buyer under a conditional sale agreement, although the property in the vehicle had not at the time of disposal vested in such hirer or buyer, remains, and will as from May 19, 1985, be regulated by that Part of the 1964 Act as restated with changes in terminology in Schedule 4, paragraph 22, to the 1974 Act. It should be noted that certain provisions of the 1974 Act apply also to unregulated consumer credit agreements, such as the right conferred upon the courts to reopen any credit bargain which it finds extortionate.[41]

Other relevant legislation

8-15   In addition to the 1974 Act there are other statutes which may be relevant to hire-purchase, conditional sales or credit sales. The principal Acts are: (1) Emergency Laws (Re-enactments and Repeals) Act 1964 as amended by the 1974 Act[42] (relating to hire-purchase, hiring and credit sales of certain kinds of goods as regards minimum deposits and the maximum period for duration of agreements),[43] (2) Fair Trading Act 1973 as amended by the 1974 Act[44] (relating to antecedent negotiations), (3) Counter-Inflation Act 1973 as amended and Price Commission Act 1977 (relating to control of prices), (4) Unfair Contract Terms Act 1977 (relating to unreasonable exemptions from and exclusion of liability), and (5) Sale of Goods Act 1979 (in relation to implied terms in credit sales and conditional sales).

---

[38] ss. 21–42.
[39] s. 8(2): £5,000 increased to £15,000 as from 20.5.85.
[40] s. 16. Relevant orders as to exempt bodies and agreements: S.I. 1980 No. 52; S.I. 1981 No. 964; S.I. 1982 No. 1029.
[41] ss. 137–140.
[42] Sched. 4, para. 23.
[43] The current order is S.I. 1982 No. 1034.
[44] Sched. 4, para. 37.

Regulated agreements[45]

–16 The 1974 Act makes detailed provisions with regard to regulated agreements. These include provisions with regard to (1) advertising,[46] (2) canvassing off trade premises,[47] (3) quotations,[48] (4) disclosure of specified information,[49] (5) withdrawal from a prospective agreement,[50] (6) the form and contents of agreements and the signing thereof,[51] (7) supplying copies of agreements,[52] (8) cancellation rights of a debtor or hirer,[53] (9) liability of a creditor for breaches of contract or misrepresentation by supplier,[54] (10) notice by creditor before enforcing contract,[55] (11) notice of default and restriction of creditor's remedies on default[56] or death[57] of debtor, (12) rebates on early settlement,[58] (13) termination by debtor,[59] and (14) securities (normally personal guarantees).[60]

–17 Regulated agreements—procedure. Parts IV to VII of the Act contain provisions with regard to the procedure in relation to regulated agreements as to seeking business (including advertising, canvassing off trade premises, quotations and display of information), entering into agreements (including disclosure of information, antecedent negotiations and the debtor's rights of withdrawal from prospective agreements), the rights of parties (including the rights of the debtor to have copies of unexecuted and executed agreements and notice of his rights of cancellation), the rights of cancellation available to the debtor, the rights and duties of parties during the currency of agreements, variation and discharge of agreements, alienation of the goods and rights upon termination or default (including the creditor's rights of repossession) and arrangements upon early settlement. For an account of the law on those matters see the undernoted texts.[61]

---

[45] For definition of regulated agreement see para. 8–14.

[46] ss. 43–47; Consumer Credit (Advertisement) Regulations 1980 (S.I. 1980 Nos. 54, 1360); Consumer Credit (Exempt Advertisements) Orders 1980 (S.I. 1980 Nos. 53, 1359).

[47] ss. 48, 49.

[48] s. 52; Consumer Credit (Quotations) Regulations 1980 (S.I. 1980 Nos. 55, 1361).

[49] s. 55.

[50] ss. 57, 59; Consumer Credit (Agreements to enter Prospective Agreements) (Exemptions) Regulations 1983 (S.I. 1983 No. 1552).

[51] ss. 60–65; Consumer Credit (Agreements) Regulations 1983 (S.I. 1983 No. 1553).

[52] ss. 62, 63; Consumer Credit (Cancellation Notices and Copies of Documents) Regulations 1983 (S.I. 1983 No. 1557).

[53] ss. 64, 67–73; S.I. 1983 No. 1557 *supra*; Consumer Credit (Notice of Cancellation Rights) (Exemptions) Regulations 1983 (S.I. 1983 No. 1558); Consumer Credit (Repayment of Credit on Cancellation) Regulations 1983 (S.I. 1983 No. 1559).

[54] s. 75; See *United Dominions Trust* v. *Taylor*, 1980 S.L.T. (Sh.Ct.) 28; *Porter* v. *General Guarantee Corp.* [1982] R.T.R. 384.

[55] s. 76; Consumer Credit (Enforcement, Default and Termination Notices) Regulations 1983 (S.I. 1983 No. 1561).

[56] ss. 87–93; S.I. 1983 No. 1561 *supra*.

[57] s. 86.

[58] ss. 94, 95; Consumer Credit (Rebate on Early Settlement) Regulations 1983 (S.I. 1983 No. 1562).

[59] ss. 99–103; S.I. 1983 No. 1561 *supra*.

[60] ss. 105–113; Consumer Credit (Guarantees and Indemnities) Regulations 1983 (S.I. 1983 No. 1556).

[61] Walker, *Principles*, III, 5.34; Halsbury's *Laws of England*, Vol. 22, Consumer Credit. These texts state the law as at the time of their publication; for the law after May 19, 1985, it is necessary to refer also to the regulations noted in para. 8–16.

8–18   **Types of regulated agreements.** The Consumer Credit Act 1974 introduced new and complex definitions in order to provide a coherent new code for consumer credit transactions. In the first place the Act makes a distinction between two types of regulated agreement based on the purpose for which the credit is available, *viz.*: (1) A restricted-use credit agreement is a regulated consumer credit agreement (i) to finance a transaction between the debtor and creditor,[62] or (ii) to finance a transaction between the debtor and a person other than the creditor, *e.g.* the supplier of goods,[63] or (iii) to refinance any existing indebtedness of the debtor, whether to the creditor or any other person.[64] (2) An unrestricted-use credit agreement is a regulated consumer credit agreement which is not a restricted-use credit agreement.[64a] In the second place the Act distinguishes between different types of agreement based upon the function of the credit supplied, *viz.*: (1) A debtor-creditor-supplier agreement is a regulated consumer credit agreement which is (i) a restricted-use credit agreement to finance a transaction between the debtor and the creditor,[65] or (ii) a restricted-use credit agreement to finance a transaction between the debtor and a third person (the supplier) made by the creditor under or in contemplation of arrangements between the creditor and the supplier,[66] or (iii) an unrestricted-use credit agreement made by the creditor under pre-existing arrangements between the creditor and a person (the supplier) other than the debtor in the knowledge that the credit is to be used to finance a transaction between the debtor and the supplier.[67] (2) A debtor-creditor agreement is a regulated consumer credit agreement which is not a debtor-creditor-supplier agreement.[68] In addition there may be consumer hire agreements which are regulated agreements between a person and an individual[69] which (i) are not hire-purchase agreements, (ii) are capable of subsisting for more than three months, and (iii) do not require the hirer to make payments exceeding £15,000.[70] The Act also contains provisions with regard to multiple agreements[71] and linked transactions.[72] In relation to corporeal moveable property the kinds of agreement most commonly used are contracts of hire-purchase, conditional sale agreements and lease purchase agreements involving a financial institution, supplier and purchaser with a fixed price and definite amount of credit. The first two (hire-purchase and conditional sale agreements) are

---

[62] s. 11(1)(*a*).
[63] s. 11(1)(*b*).
[64] s. 11(1)(*c*).
[64a] s. 11(2).
[65] s. 12(*a*).
[66] s. 12(*b*).
[67] s. 12(*c*).
[68] s. 13.
[69] As defined in s. 189(1) to include a partnership or other unincorporated body not consisting entirely of bodies corporate.
[70] s. 15: the limit is to be increased from £5000 as from 20.5.85.
[71] s. 18.
[72] s. 19.

debtor-creditor-supplier agreements of the restricted-use credit agreement type and the third (lease purchase agreement) is a consumer hire agreement. All of these, if within the category of a regulated agreement as defined in the 1974 Act, are subject to the statutory provisions.

8–19 Existing form of regulated agreements. The form of document at present in use for hire-purchase or conditional sale agreements normally comprises five main sections, namely: (1) The Heading which forms the first page and describes the type of agreement in prominent lettering. (2) Special provisions such as a direct debiting mandate addressed to the bankers of the customer[73] instructing payment to the creditor of the periodic sums which will become due under the agreement and an insurance protection in respect of those periodic sums—these may be completed or not in the option of the customer. (3) Customer details including name and designation and such personal and business information as the creditor wishes in order to enable him to assess the advisability of the transaction. (4) A Schedule which contains all the information peculiar to the particular transaction, *e.g.* name and address of the customer and his bankers, description of the goods concerned and details of their insurance and a statement of the cash price and periodic payments. It also contains, where appropriate, notice of the customer's right to terminate. At the end of the Schedule boxes are provided for signature by the customer and two witnesses and for execution by the creditor. (5) The standard terms of the agreement including the name and designation of the creditor and incorporating the Schedule as part of the agreement.

8–20 Form of regulated agreements on and after May 19, 1985. For regulated agreements entered into on and after May 19, 1985, a similar layout may be adopted with such alterations as will be required to comply with the provisions of the Act which then come into force.[74] Restricted-use debtor-creditor-supplier agreements for fixed sum credit providing for repayment by specified instalments at stated intervals may be broadly on the following lines:

8–21 *(1) Heading.* The first page of the document will state prominently its character, *e.g.* "[Hire-Purchase Agreement] [Conditional Sale Agreement] regulated by the Consumer Credit Act 1974."

8–22 *(2) Special provisions.* This part may be as in present practice.

8–23 *(3) Customer details.* This also may be in the existing form.

8–24 *(4) Schedule.* (a) The Schedule will contain the name and postal address

---

[73] For convenience "customer" is used throughout as referring to the debtor or purchaser. See S.I. 1983 No. 1553, para. 5.
[74] Consumer Credit (Agreements) Regulations 1983 (S.I. 1983 No. 1553).

of the customer, a description of the goods, the cash price, the amount of any advance payment to be made by the customer and the nature of the payments, the amount of the credit to be provided (the difference between the cash price and any advance payment), the charges for the credit, the total amount payable by the customer, the amounts and dates of the periodic repayments,[75] a prominent statement of the APR (the annual percentage rate of the total charge for credit),[76] and a statement of any security provided by the customer sufficient to identify it.[77]

(b) CANCELLATION RIGHTS. A cancellable agreement is a regulated agreement where antecedent negotiations[78] included oral representations made when in the presence of the customer by an individual acting as or on behalf of the negotiator[78a] unless the unexecuted agreement is signed by the customer at the business premises of the creditor or the negotiator. If the agreement is cancellable a notice of the customer's cancellation right must be included in a box, normally in the Schedule, in the form prescribed.[79] It is advisable that in practice the agreement is signed by the customer on the business premises of the creditor or the supplier who negotiates the sale and a declaration is inserted in the Schedule signed by the customer that he is signing the agreement on such premises.[80]

(c) TERMINATION RIGHTS. It is necessary to include, normally in the Schedule, a statement of the customer's right of termination in the exact form contained in the regulations.[81]

(d) REPOSSESSION RIGHTS. It is also necessary to include, normally in the Schedule, a statement of the creditor's rights to repossess the goods in the exact form contained in the regulations.[82]

(e) GENERAL STATEMENT OF RIGHTS. It is also necessary to insert, again normally in the Schedule, a general reference to the rights of the customer under the 1974 Act in the precise form prescribed by the regulations.[83]

(f) CUSTOMER'S DECLARATION. The Schedule should also include (although not required by the 1974 Act) a declaration by the customer on certain matters, e.g. (1) that the agreement is being signed on the premises of the seller or a dealer supplying the goods,[84] (2) that he has seen a written statement of the cash price of the goods which corresponds exactly with that shown in the Schedule, (3) that he has carefully

---

[75] *Ibid.*, Sched. 6, para. 5.
[76] *Ibid.*, Sched. 7, as to permissible methods of disclosure of APR.
[77] See S.I. 1983 No. 1553, Sched. 1, para. 21, as to further details of security. If the normal practice of the creditor in the type of transaction concerned is not to require security the form may omit the statement of security.
[78] Defined in Consumer Credit Act 1974, s. 56(1).
[78a] 1974 Act, s. 67.
[79] S.I. 1983 No. 1553, Sched. 2, Pt. I, Form No. 2.
[80] See customer's declaration, para. 8–24 (f).
[81] S.I. 1983 No. 1553, Sched, 2, Pt. I, Form No. 5.
[82] *Ibid.*, Sched. 2, Pt. I, Form No. 9.
[83] *Ibid.*, Sched. 2, Pt. I, Form No. 12.
[84] See para. 8–24 (b).

examined the goods, and (4) that he has checked the details in the Schedule and has read the terms of the Schedule and the Agreement which follows.

(g) SIGNATURE OF CUSTOMER AND EXECUTION ON BEHALF OF CREDITOR. The Schedule will end with a signature box in exactly the relevant form prescribed by the regulations (including the date of signature) and should be executed by the customer within that box.[85] The signature of the customer should be attested by two witnesses, who add their addresses. The Schedule should also be executed by or on behalf of the creditor.

8–25 *(5) Agreement.* (a) The Agreement, which may be printed immediately after the Schedule, will be in a standard form applicable to (i) all hire-purchase transactions or (ii) all conditional sale transactions, as the case may be. It will record the agreement of hire-purchase or conditional sale between the parties, the creditor being named and designed and thereafter referred to as "the owner" (hire-purchase) or "the seller" (conditional sale) and the debtor being the person named in the Schedule (which is incorporated by reference as part of the Agreement) and designed as "the hirer" (hire-purchase) or "the purchaser" (conditional sale).[86]

(b) INITIAL AND PERIODIC PAYMENTS. The Agreement will contain the obligation of the hirer or purchaser to pay the initial instalment or deposit and the periodic payments of rent or price, all as specified in the Schedule, with interest at a stated rate upon any arrears of payment.[87]

(c) EXCLUSION OF WARRANTIES AND CONDITIONS. There will be an exclusion of the condition as to merchantable quality of the goods in respect of such defects as are specified in the Agreement or are or ought to have been discovered by the hirer or purchaser on examination before the Agreement was made.[88]

(d) DELIVERY OF GOODS. Since the owner or seller, who is merely financing the transaction, is not normally the manufacturer of the goods nor has had physical control or possession of them, there will be an express exclusion of his liability for delay in delivery and a statement that the goods will be at the risk of the hirer or purchaser from the time of purchase and that the acceptance of delivery by the hirer or purchaser shall be *prima facie* evidence that they have been examined by him and are in good and satisfactory condition.

(e) INSURANCE OF GOODS. The hirer or purchaser will undertake to insure the goods comprehensively forthwith for their full value and also to insure against third-party liability in respect of their use, and to

---

[85] *Ibid.*, reg. 6 and Sched. 5, Pt. I, Form No. 1 (hire-purchase agreements) or Form No. 3 (conditional sale agreements).

[86] *Ibid.*, reg. 5.

[87] *Ibid.*, Sched. 1, para. 22.

[88] Sale of Goods Act 1979, s. 14(2). The implied conditions as to title, conformity of goods with description or sample and quality or fitness for purpose cannot be excluded (Unfair Contract Terms Act 1977, s. 20).

maintain the insurance during the currency of the Agreement, to exhibit receipts for premiums and to indemnify the owner or seller against any liability or loss from failure to insure adequately. When insurance is effected the insurers are to be notified that the goods are the property of the owner or seller and the policy endorsed accordingly. The owner or seller will reserve the right to effect such insurances at the expense of the hirer or purchaser if the latter fails to do so.

(f) TITLE TO GOODS. A statement will be included that the goods will remain the property of the owner or seller until full payment or early settlement and, in the case of a hire-purchase agreement, exercise of the option to purchase, with prohibition of sale, assignment or charge of the goods or creation of any lien thereon or pledging the credit of the owner or seller for repairs to the goods.

(g) OPTION TO PURCHASE (HIRE-PURCHASE). In the case of hire-purchase agreements there will be a provision that the hirer has an option to purchase the goods on full payment of all rental instalments.

(h) EARLY SETTLEMENTS. There will be provision as to the right of the hirer or purchaser to effect early settlement on payment of the balance of the periodic payments subject to a rebate calculated in accordance with the Rule of 78.[89]

(i) DEFAULT AND TERMINATION. Provision will be made as to the rights of parties and procedure on default and repossession or termination which must be in conformity with the relevant provisions of the 1974 Act and relevant regulations.[90]

(j) OTHER CLAUSES. The Agreement will also incorporate other provisions which the creditor may wish to stipulate, *e.g.* proper restrictions as to use and maintenance of the goods, payment of licence duties and registration fees and rates and taxes in respect of the premises where the goods are kept, authority to the creditor to make inquiries to enable him to consider the application for the credit and to communicate information in relation to the transaction to third parties and a statement of the date when the Agreement comes into force (normally the date of its execution by the creditor).

(ii) Moneylending

Consumer Credit Act 1974

8-26   As from May 19, 1985, the Moneylenders Acts 1900 and 1927 are repealed.[91] Loans by moneylenders licensed under the Act to carry on

---

[89] 1974 Act, ss. 94–97: Consumer Credit (Rebate on Early Settlement) Regulations 1983 (S.I. 1983 No. 1562). For explanation of Rule of 78 see Sch. 2 to Regulations.

[90] 1974 Act, ss. 87–103; Consumer Credit (Enforcement, Default and Termination Notices) Regulations 1983 (S.I. 1983 No. 1561).

[91] Consumer Credit Act 1974, s. 192(1) and Sch. 5; Consumer Credit Act 1974 (Commencement No. 8) Order 1983 (S.I. 1983 No. 1551 (C. 44)), Art. 5.

consumer credit business are debtor-creditor agreements and are regulated agreements unless exempt as exceeding £15,000 in amount[92] or as low-cost credit agreements.[93] As from that date moneylending transactions are subject to the provisions of the 1974 Act with regard to advertising[94] and canvassing[95] and loan agreements must conform to the relevant provisions of the Consumer Credit (Agreements) Regulations 1983.[96]

The practice in relation to regulated debtor-creditor agreements including both fixed-sum credit and running-account credit, *e.g.* as provided by a bank, may be outlined as follows:–

(a) *Fixed-sum credit* Where a personal loan of a fixed amount not exceeding £15,000 is given by the bank, then the agreement relating to it must comply in all respects with the provisions of the Consumer Credit (Agreements) Regulations 1983 applicable to regulated agreements.[96] It will normally include a statement of the amount of the loan, the total charge for credit, the total sum repayable, the A.P.R., a description of any security to be provided by the debtor in terms sufficient to identify it, the rights of the debtor to cancel the agreement, the rights of the debtor to terminate the agreement, the circumstances in which the bank may terminate the agreement and apply funds of the debtor in any other account towards payment of sums due under the agreement and, if more than two persons are named in the agreement as debtors, the imposition of joint and several liability. In addition it may be stipulated that the bank may make such enquiries about the debtor's financial affairs as it sees fit. The procedure under sections 62 to 64 of the 1974 Act as to the furnishing of copies of the agreement and giving notice of cancellation rights must be followed.

(b) *Running-account credit* Overdraft facilities provided by a bank on current account in the ordinary course of business without any special written agreement are exempt from the requirements of the 1974 Act.[96a] Where there is a written agreement regulating advances on current account which do not exceed £15,000, however, the Act applies to them, the form and contents of the agreement are broadly similar to those described above in respect of fixed-sum credit and the procedure under sections 62 to 64 of the Act must be followed. It is not permissible to avoid the application of the 1974 Act by stipulating in the agreement a credit limit in excess of £15,000 if the debtor cannot draw at any one time an amount which, so far as it represents credit, exceeds £15,000, or if at the time when the agreement is made it is probable that the debit balance on the account will not at any time exceed £15,000.[96b] The provisions of the

---

[92] Regulations in draft and awaited.
[93] 1974 Act, s. 16(5)(*b*); Consumer Credit (Exempt Agreements) Order 1980, (S.I. 1980 No. 52).
[94] 1974 Act, ss. 43, 44, 46, 47.
[95] *Ibid.*, ss. 48–50, 53, 54.
[96] S.I. 1983 No. 1553.
[96a] s. 74(1)(*b*).
[96b] s. 10(3)(*b*)(i) and (iii).

Act regarding regulated agreements also apply, even when the credit limit exceeds £15,000, if the agreement provides that if the debit balance rises above an amount not exceeding £15,000 the rate of total charge for credit increases or any other condition favouring the bank comes into operation.[96c]

Regulated credit agreements with heritable security are considered in Volume III.

(iii) Pawnbroking

Consumer Credit Act 1974

8–27   As from May 19, 1985, the Pawnbrokers Acts 1872 and 1960 are repealed.[97] The term "pawnbroker" is not used in the Act but the sections relating to pledges[98] do not apply to non-commercial agreements, *i.e.* they do apply to agreements by a pawnbroker in the course of his business.[99] As from the above date pawnbroking transactions may be within the category of regulated agreements (for all purposes of the Act if the loan exceeds £50) and the procedure, forms of pawn receipts and combined agreements and pawn receipts and the rights of parties are regulated by the Act and relative regulations.[1]

(3) PARTICULAR TRANSACTIONS INVOLVING TRANSFER OF MOVEABLE PROPERTY ABSOLUTELY AND/OR IN SECURITY

(i) Sale and Purchase of Business

Types of sale transaction

8–28   The sale of the business of an individual or partnership may be of the whole business including heritable and moveable assets, including goodwill, or a sale of the assets only. Where the seller is an incorporated company the sale of the business is normally effected by a purchase of the shares of the selling company although it may take the form of purchase of its assets only. This chapter relates to sales by individuals or unincorporated bodies such as partnerships[2] and in general it is more convenient for the transaction to take the form of a sale of all the assets, which may include goodwill.

[96c] s. 10(3)(*b*)(ii).
[97] Consumer Credit Act 1974, s. 192(1) and Sched. 5; Consumer Credit Act 1974 (Commencement No. 8) Order 1983 (S.I. 1983 No. 1551), art. 5.
[98] ss. 114–122.
[99] *Ibid.*, s. 189(1).
[1] 1974 Act, ss. 114–122; S.I. 1983 Nos. 1553, 1565–1568.
[2] For sales by incorporated companies, *e.g.* takeovers, reference should be made to standard texts upon company law and precedents.

Specification of assets

8–29   In a sale of assets it is necessary to specify the assets sold with some particularity. The more important items are:

(a) Heritable property. The business premises, whether owned or leased, will be included with the usual conditions appropriate to a sale and purchase of heritage.[3] It may be convenient to have a separate contract of sale of the heritage, expressed as conditional upon the agreement for sale of the moveable assets and possibly incorporated as a schedule to the main agreement for sale.

(b) Corporeal moveable property. Major items of plant, machinery or equipment and motor vehicles should be specified individually; lesser items of furniture and equipment may be included in an appropriately comprehensive description. Stock, if of significant value and variable in amount from time to time, may be purchased at valuation on the basis of wholesale price or value by a valuer mutually appointed: if the value of the stock can be estimated with reasonable accuracy it may be purchased at an agreed figure specified. The books and records of the business should also be delivered, subject to a right of access to them by the sellers for a limited period for the purpose of collecting outstanding accounts or adjustment of pre-sale tax liabilities.

(c) Incorporeal moveable property. The goodwill and firm name and any copyrights, patents, trade marks and trade lists should be mentioned. Existing contracts, if they are to continue to be carried on by the purchaser, should be assigned and the sellers should be taken bound, particularly if there is any possible element of *delectus personae* involved, to grant mandates to the purchasers in respect of them. Large contracts involving sub-contractors, performance bonds, etc., involve a commercial appraisal of potential profit and liabilities and may require consent of other parties. In all cases where further documentation is required the sellers should be taken bound to grant the necessary deeds, *e.g.* assignation of patents or trade marks.

Price—allocation

8–30   The total price should be stated with allocation of it between the more important items. The sellers should consider liability to capital gains tax, possibly as affected by roll-over relief (where the proceeds of sale are to be expended in acquiring new assets within the same classes of assets as those sold[4]) or relief on disposal on retirement where the individual sellers are 60 years of age or over.[5] The purchasers will be concerned as to the amount allocated upon heritable property in relation to liability for *ad valorem* stamp duty on the conveyance, and the sum allocated

---

[3] See Chap. 15 *infra.*
[4] Capital Gains Tax Act 1979, ss. 115–121.
[5] *Ibid.*, s. 124.

upon particular assets as forming the basic acquisition price for capital gains tax on subsequent disposals. Capital allowances should be considered by both parties (balancing adjustments and future allowances).[6] On these matters tax advisers should be consulted and the allocation agreed between the parties but the amounts ascribed to particular assets must be in reasonable relationship to their true values.

Date of sale

8–31   The date of sale should be specified but special consideration as to the date for the purposes of transfer of undertakings is required.[7]

Employees

8–32   The position of employees of the business requires special consideration in view of the Transfer of Undertakings (Protection of Employment) Regulations 1981.[8] The transfer of a business does not operate so as to terminate the contract of employment of any person employed by the transferor immediately before the transfer; the contract continues as if originally made between the employee and the transferee.[9] If before or after the sale of the business an employee is dismissed and the principal reason for dismissal is the transfer of the business or a reason connected with the transfer, the dismissal will be treated as unfair,[10] unless it can be shown that there is an economic, technical or organisational reason entailing changes in the workforce of either sellers or purchasers before or after the transfer.[11] As regards trade unions an existing collective agreement between the transferor and a trade union will in general continue in force as between the transferee and the trade union.[12] If the undertaking purchased continues after the transfer to maintain an identity separate from that of the remainder of the transferee's undertaking an independent trade union recognised by the transferor before the transfer will be deemed to have been recognised by the transferee[13] and a duty is imposed upon both transferor and transferee to consult the recognised trade union long enough before the transfer to permit consultation with the trade union's representatives with regard to any employee who may be affected by the transfer.[14] The transfer of the contract of employment or a collective agreement does not extend to rights under recognised occupational pension schemes.[15] Provisions in

---

[6] Capital Allowances Act 1968; Finance Act 1971, ss. 40–50; Finance Act 1984, ss. 58–62.
[7] See para. 8–32.
[8] S.I. 1981 No. 1794.
[9] *Ibid.*, reg. 5.
[10] *Ibid.*, reg. 8(1).
[11] *Ibid.*, reg. 8(2).
[12] *Ibid.*, reg. 6.
[13] *Ibid.*, reg. 9.
[14] *Ibid.*, reg. 10.
[15] *Ibid.*, reg. 7.

any agreement purporting to contract out of regulations 5, 8 or 10 are void.[16]

8-33 The provisions of the Regulations point to the need for the parties at an early stage in the negotiations for the sale of a business to consider whether any employees will be affected and, if so, to initiate consultations with representatives of the relevant trade union immediately. As yet there has been little judicial interpretation of the Regulations but the following suggestions on relevant matters are offered:

(1) The different terminology "employed immediately before the transfer" and "completion of a relevant transfer" in regulation 5 apparently involves different points of time. The prudent construction in relation to dismissal of employees would seem to be to regard the relevant date as being that when the parties commenced serious negotiations for the transfer as distinct from mere preliminary soundings.[17] It may be advantageous to stipulate in the agreement the time of transfer for purposes of the Regulations which may be stated as the date on which agreement to the sale was reached in principle.

(2) It will be in the interests of both parties to ensure that so far as practicable any of the employees whose employment is not to be continued are dismissed for an economic, technical or organisational reason within regulation 8(2). A dismissal for such a reason avoids only the penalties for unfair dismissal; the employee will still be entitled to redundancy payment under the Employment Protection (Consolidation) Act 1978 as amended by the Employment Act 1980. Where employees are to continue in the employment of the purchasers a letter should be sent to each by the sellers informing him of the sale and that he will automatically become employed by the purchasers and the purchasers should also send to each such employee a letter confirming employment on the same terms and conditions (save as to pension scheme but offering, if contemplated, membership of the purchaser's pension scheme).[18]

(3) The purchasers will require to estimate the potential liabilities in respect of claims for unfair dismissal and redundancy and modify the price offered for the business appropriately.

(4) Appropriate clauses and warranties in relation to continued employment and termination of employment should be included in the agreement for sale.[19]

Restrictive covenants

8-34 The inclusion of restrictive covenants should be considered. These will require to satisfy the test of reasonableness in relation to area and period of restraint.

---

[16] *Ibid.*, reg. 12.
[17] See *Teesside Times Ltd.* v. *Drury* [1980] I.C.R. 338, C.A.
[18] Employment Protection (Consolidation) Act 1978, ss. 94, 82.
[19] See para. 8–35, cl. 9.

Agreement for sale of business by partnership to limited company

8–35

AGREEMENT
between
A, B & Co. (*designed*) and A (*designed*), B
(*designed*) and C (*designed*), the whole
partners thereof, of the first part

and

D & Co. Limited (*designed*), of the second
part.

DEFINITIONS In this Agreement the following words and
expressions shall have the following meanings:–

Word or Expression	Meaning
the Vendors	the parties of the first part
the Purchaser	the party of the second part
the Business and Assets	the property agreed in Clause 1 to be sold
the Date of Sale	5th November 1984
Completion	completion of the sale and purchase in accordance with Clause 7
Completion Date	5th November 1984

PRELIMINARY
(A) The Vendors have for some years past carried on in partnership
together the business of   from premises at 10 Gorbals Street,
Edinburgh.
(B) The Vendors have agreed to sell and the Purchaser has agreed to
purchase the said business and the goodwill and other assets thereof
hereinafter mentioned for the consideration and upon and subject to the
terms hereinafter appearing.

THEREFORE THE PARTIES AGREE as follows:–
    1. THE Vendors shall sell as Beneficial Owners and the Pur-
chaser shall purchase free from any lien, charge or encumbrance save as herein otherwise disclosed as from the close of
business on the Date of Sale the whole stock-in-trade, all work
in progress and the goodwill of the said business together with
the benefit of all pending contracts engagements and orders to
which the Vendors are entitled in connection therewith and
the right (so far as the Vendors can grant the same) to use the
name "A, B & Co." as part of the name of the Purchaser and
to represent the Purchaser as carrying on the said business in
continuation of or in succession to the Vendors and (except as
hereinafter provided) all other property rights and assets
belonging to the Vendors in connection with the said business;
    Provided that there shall be excluded from the sale hereby
agreed upon:–
(i) all book and other debts belonging to the Vendors and all bills
receivable held by the Vendors and all rights in relation thereto and

the benefit of all securities therefor and of all guarantees in respect thereof;

(ii) all pre-paid charges and deposit receipts belonging to the Vendors and all temporary loans made by the Vendors;

(iii) all cash in hand and at bank;

(iv) (*Specify any articles to be excluded from sale*)

2. WITHOUT prejudice to the provisions of Clause 1 the Business and Assets shall include:–

(a) the heritable property specified in Part I of the First Schedule hereto together with all servitudes and rights pertaining thereto and all buildings and structures on such property;

(b) all fixed plant machinery and equipment on the property referred to in (a) above specified in Part II of the First Schedule hereto except property belonging to suppliers of gas, water, electricity, telegraphic or other services;

(c) the motor cars, furniture and equipment belonging to the Vendors in connection with the said business specified in Part II of the First Schedule hereto;

(d) the benefit of the policies specified in Part III of the First Schedule hereto;

(e) the whole stock-in-trade of the said business having the agreed value of £ specified in Part IV of the First Schedule hereto which value forms part of the total consideration specified in Clause 5 hereof. PROVIDED THAT any increase or decrease in the value of the stock-in-trade at Completion above or below the said agreed value, as the amount of such increase or decrease shall be agreed by the parties or failing agreement shall be determined by a valuer mutually chosen, shall be added to or deducted from the said consideration.

3. THE heritable property included in the sale hereunder is sold subject to the servitudes, burdens, conditions and provisions affecting the same specified in Part I of the First Schedule but otherwise free from encumbrances.

4. THE Vendors shall (subject to the provisions of Clause 11 (a) and (b)) pay, satisfy and discharge all the debts, liabilities and obligations whatsoever incurred by the Vendors in connection with the said business down to the Date of Sale including claims of any kind by sellers or purchasers in respect of goods sold and claims in respect of services supplied on or prior to that date and shall at all times keep the Purchaser indemnified from and against all such debts, liabilities and obligations.

5. THE consideration for the sale shall be the sum of £ which shall be paid to the Vendors in cash on Completion, subject to any adjustment thereof in respect of the value of stock-in-trade in accordance with Clause 2(e) hereof.

6. THE consideration shall be allocated as follows:–

(a) to such of the assets in relation to which a specific amount is stated in the First Schedule, there shall be allocated that amount;

(b) subject as aforesaid the allocation shall be made in accordance with the provisions of the Second Schedule in respect of the classes of assets referred to therein and the balance (if any) remaining after such allocation shall be allocated to goodwill.

7. (A) COMPLETION of the sale and purchase hereunder shall take place on the Completion Date.

(B) Upon Completion the Vendors shall:–

(1) execute and deliver to the Purchaser together with the relevant documents of title such conveyances, transfers, assignations and other deeds as the Purchaser may require to vest in the Purchaser the full benefit of the properties, rights and assets hereby agreed to be sold and the full benefit of this Agreement and shall permit the Purchaser to enter into and take possession of the Business and Assets;

(2) make delivery to the Purchaser of all property hereby agreed to be sold which is capable of transfer by delivery;

(3) make delivery to the Purchaser of all subsisting contracts and licences in connection with the said business and all books, records and other documents relating to the said business and such lists of customers and other information or documents in relation to the said business as the Purchaser may reasonably require;

Provided that the Vendors shall be afforded reasonable access to the said books, records and documents if and whenever required for any purpose including purposes incidental to the collection of any book debts owing to the Vendors at the Date of Sale which are not collected by the Purchaser for the account of the Vendor pursuant to Clause 11(b).

(C) Upon Completion the Purchaser shall pay to the Vendors the consideration provided by Clause 5.

(D) Upon Completion all agreements and arrangements between the Vendors or any of them and any company associated with the Vendors or any of them by common ownership in so far as they affect the Business and Assets shall be cancelled by mutual consent of the parties thereto without compensation.

(E) On the Completion Date the partnership carried on by the Vendors under the name "A, B & Co." shall cease trading and by 31st January 1985 the said partnership shall be dissolved and without prejudice to the provisions of Clause 4 hereof and save as otherwise expressly provided herein the Vendors will be responsible for and discharge all debts, liabilities and obligations whatsoever of or relating to the said firm (including all taxation liabilities) and shall at all times keep the Purchaser indemnified from and against all such debts, liabilities and obligations.

8. BY not later than 28th October 1984 the Vendors at their expense will notify (in terms agreed with the Purchaser) all customers and other parties having relations with the business. [An advertisement will be adjusted between the parties and inserted in
       and such other newspapers, if any, as the Purchaser may select.] The expenses of the notices to customers will be borne by both parties equally. [The expenses of advertisements will be borne by the Purchaser.]

9. (A) For the purposes of this Agreement "the Employees" shall mean the employees of the Vendors listed in the Third Schedule hereto.

(B) In accordance with the Transfer of Undertakings (Protection of Employment) Regulations 1981 the employment of the

Employees shall be automatically transferred to the Purchaser with effect from the Date of Sale.

(C) The Vendors hereby agree to indemnify and keep indemnified the Purchaser against any claim by any of the Employees arising solely from an act or omission of the Vendors before the Date of Sale which is deemed to be an act or omission of the Purchaser in accordance with said Regulations.

(D) The Vendors warrant that, save as disclosed to the Purchaser in writing, no claims of any kind have been made by any of the Employees against the Vendors during   years prior to the Date of Sale and that they know of no facts which have occurred within the said years which could give rise to any such claim; and the Vendors have made or will make available to the Purchaser all documents which are or could be relevant to any such claim or potential claim.

(E) The Vendors warrant that at the Date of Sale they employ only the Employees listed in the Third Schedule hereto, having the salaries and length of service therein specified and further warrant that any employees who have been dismissed by them since (*date when agreement in principle to sale was reached*) were dismissed for economic, technical or organisational reasons entailing changes in the Vendors' workforce.

[(F) The Vendors hereby agree to effect a policy of insurance to cover any claims made against them by the Purchaser under subclauses C, D or E of this Clause up to a limit of £   in respect of any one claim and to exhibit the said policy to the Purchaser within 28 days after the Date of Sale, and to maintain the said policy in force for a period of   years after the Date of Sale.]

(G) Subject to the obligations of the Vendors under sub-clauses C, D, E [or F] of this Clause the Purchaser shall be liable to meet claims by any of the Employees for unfair dismissal or redundancy payments.

10. ALL amounts payable or receivable in respect of the said business which are of a periodical nature (including rents, rates, insurance premiums, gas, water, electricity and telephone charges, royalties and other outgoings or receipts relating to the said business, salaries, wages and other emoluments, statutory contributions and income tax deductible under P.A.Y.E. for which an employer is accountable and employer's contributions to retirement benefit schemes in respect of employees of the Vendors transferred to the Purchaser) shall unless otherwise agreed be apportioned between the Vendors and the Purchaser as at the Date of Sale on a day to day basis or, in relation to amounts payable specifically referable to the extent of user of any property or rights, according to the extent of such user.

11. THE Purchaser shall after Completion:–

(a) Carry out and complete for its own account all the current contracts and engagements of the Vendors in connection with the said business (other than any expressly excluded hereunder or pursuant hereto) and shall indemnify and keep indemnified the Vendors in respect thereof but shall not be liable to pay any sums owing to the creditors of the Vendors at the Date of Sale.

(b) Be entitled but not bound to collect and receive for the account of the Vendors and without expense to the Vendors all

book debts owing to the Vendors at the Date of Sale in connection
with the said business and to apply the net proceeds thereof in or
towards payment of sums owing to creditors of the Vendors at the
Date of Sale and subject thereto to pay the net proceeds thereof to
the Vendors or as they may from time to time direct;

Provided that the Purchaser shall not be under any obligation to
take any proceedings or any other action with a view to collecting
such book debts other than the rendering of accounts to the debtors
in accordance with the normal practice of the Purchaser in connection with its own business but shall not (except as mentioned in sub-
paragraph (c) below) waive or release any such debts without the
prior written approval of the Vendors and shall from time to time
furnish to the Vendors particulars of all receipts under this sub-
clause. The Vendors shall be at liberty to collect on their own
behalf any of the said book debts which remain outstanding after
six months from the Completion Date.

(c) Be entitled with a view to preserving the goodwill and conti-
nuity of the said business at its discretion to settle as it thinks fit any
claim by or dispute with any customer or other person falling to be
dealt with under Clause 4 but so that any payment or allowance or
forbearance to the customer or other person in connection with
such settlement shall be for the account of the Vendors and be
deemed a liability of the Vendors for the purposes of Clause 4 only
to the extent of the amount which the Vendors in the circumstances
would themselves pay or allow or forbear from taking action to collect.

12. IN so far as any licences or consents from third parties may be
required for the transfer of any assets to the Purchaser hereunder
the Vendors shall use their best endeavours to procure the same at
their expense (including application to the Courts if any such
licence or consent is unreasonably refused) and until such licences
or consents have been obtained shall hold the assets in question in
trust for the Purchaser as from the Completion Date.

13. THE Vendors jointly and severally undertake with the Purchaser:–

(a) notwithstanding Completion to continue to give to the Purchaser at the Purchaser's expense such information and assistance
as it may reasonably require relating to the said business and the
know-how connected therewith and in particular relating to persons
who have dealt with the said business, its current contracts and
engagements and debtors and creditors;

(b) to pass on promptly to the Purchaser any inquiries relating to
the said business received after Completion;

(c) from time to time after Completion to execute such further
deeds as the Purchaser may reasonably require for the purpose of
vesting in it the full benefit of this Agreement and of the properties,
rights and assets hereby agreed to be sold.

14. THE Vendors HEREBY JOINTLY AND SEVERALLY
REPRESENT AND WARRANT TO AND UNDERTAKE with
the Purchaser as to the matters contained in the Fourth Schedule
hereto; Provided that all such representations and all warranties
relating to facts in existence at the date hereof shall apply subject to
any matters expressly disclosed in writing to the Purchaser prior to
the date hereof and all such undertakings as relate to the future

shall be subject to any exceptions to which the Purchaser may have expressly agreed in writing either before or after the date hereof.

15. THE Purchaser hereby undertakes with the Vendors to give to the Vendors at the Vendors' expense such information and assistance as they may reasonably require relating to the said business and particularly in connection with the assets referred to in Clause 2 and the collection of any sums due or to become due to the Vendors in respect of such assets.

[16. THE Vendors HEREBY JOINTLY AND SEVERALLY FURTHER UNDERTAKE with the Purchaser that neither the Vendors nor any company, firm or person carrying on any business in succession to the Vendors or any of them will:–

(a) at any time after Completion carry on under the name A, B & Co. or any name which is likely to be confused therewith within a radius of   miles from any place where the said business is now carried on any business which is likely to compete with the said business as now carried on;

(b) at any time after Completion canvass or solicit the custom in relation to any business competing or likely to compete with the said business as now carried on of any person who has within the period of twelve months prior to the Completion Date been a customer of or had dealings with the said business;

(c) for a period of   years after Completion be engaged, concerned or interested directly or indirectly and whether as principal, agent, employee, shareholder (except in a public limited company) or otherwise in any business competing with the said business of the Vendors within a radius of   miles from any such place aforesaid;

(d) at any time make use of or disclose or divulge to any third party any technical or commercial information of a secret or confidential nature relating to the said business.]

17. THE Vendors shall forthwith on the execution hereof enter into an agreement in the form contained in the Fifth Schedule hereto for the sale by the Vendors to the Purchaser of the heritable property specified in Part I of the First Schedule hereto, the price therein stipulated forming part of the total consideration payable to the Vendors in Clause 5 hereof.

18. ALL warranties, representations, undertakings and other obligations made or undertaken by the parties hereto under the terms of this Agreement shall (except in so far as the same may be fully performed on Completion) continue in full force and effect notwithstanding Completion hereunder.

19. (A) THE Vendors shall pending Completion supply to the Purchaser such information and certificates as the Purchaser may reasonably require having regard to the warranties and undertakings on the part of the Vendors contained in the Fourth Schedule hereto concerning the Business and Assets.

(B) If it shall be found prior to Completion that there is any breach or non-performance of any of the warranties or undertakings on the part of the Vendors or any of them contained herein and the Purchaser would thereby be materially and adversely affected the Purchaser shall be entitled by notice in writing to the Vendors to rescind this Agreement, but failure to exercise such right shall not in any way prejudice or affect the right of the Purchaser to claim damages in respect of such breach or non-performance.

20. WITHOUT prejudice to any express provision herein contained it is agreed and declared that all the obligations of the Vendors under this Agreement are joint and several obligations.

21. ANY notice requiring to be served on any of the parties hereto may be served in the case of the Vendors on (*Vendors' solicitors*) and in the case of the Purchaser on (*Purchaser's solicitors*) each of whom shall be deemed (unless and until notice has been given revoking such agency and nominating another agent with an address in Scotland for this purpose) to be the agent of such party to give and receive all such notices. Any such notice if sent by recorded delivery post shall conclusively be deemed to have been received when the same would have been received in the ordinary course of post.

(*To be attested*)

THE FIRST SCHEDULE

PART I

Property

Section 1   Clause 2

Short Particulars of Property	Agreed Value
10 Gorbals Street, Edinburgh	£20,000

Section 2   Clause 3

Matters subject to which the property is sold.

The whole servitudes burdens conditions and provisions referred to in the title deeds thereof.

PART II   Clause 2

Section 1 — Plant and Equipment
(*Specify all major items of plant, machinery or equipment*)
Together with all other plant, machinery, equipment, tools and furnishings within the heritable property specified in Part I of this Schedule.

Section 2 — Motor Vehicles
(*Specify all motor vehicles stating registration numbers*)

Section 3 — Furniture and Equipment
The whole furniture and equipment within the
heritable property specified in Part I of this
Schedule, but excluding (*specify any articles to be
retained by Vendors*)

Note   *If a value is to be attributed on allocation of
the price specify above opposite item under heading Agreed Value.*

| PART III | Clause 2 |

Policies of Insurance and Assurance

Motor Vehicles
(*Specify policies and vehicles covered*)

Fire and other risks and other property and assets
(*Specify policies with main particulars thereof*)

PART IV	Clause 2
	Agreed Value
Stock-in-trade	£

THE SECOND SCHEDULE

ALLOCATION OF PURCHASE CONSIDERATION
Clause 6(b)

The amounts to be allocated upon assets other than the property
specified in the First Schedule for which an Agreed Value is therein
specified shall be the amounts at which the same stand in the books
of the Vendors as at the Date of Sale after providing for
depreciation down to such date (in cases where it is the practice of
the Vendors to charge depreciation) in accordance with the practice
adopted by the Vendors in making up their accounts for the year
ended   1984.

THE THIRD SCHEDULE
Clause 9

LIST OF EMPLOYEES OF VENDORS

[*Insert list of employees with particulars of salaries and length of service*]

THE FOURTH SCHEDULE
Clause 14

WARRANTIES AND UNDERTAKINGS
The representations warranties and undertakings herein contained
shall be true and correct at Completion and at the close of business
on the Date of Sale as well as at the date hereof and the expression
"Completion" shall include "the close of business on the Date of
Sale." Each of the representations warranties and undertakings

herein contained is without prejudice to the other representations warranties and undertakings and no paragraph of this schedule shall limit or govern the extent or application of any other paragraph thereof. The Vendors hereby agree with the Purchaser to indemnify and keep indemnified the Purchaser against all loss damages costs actions proceedings claims demands and expenses arising from each and every breach of the representations warranties and undertakings.

1. (a) That the information given by or on behalf of the Vendors to the Purchaser in the course of the negotiations leading to this Agreement was and remains true and that after making all proper inquiries none of the Vendors is aware of any fact or matter concerning the financial position or prospects of the Vendors in relation to the said business which has not been disclosed to the Purchaser and the disclosure of which might reasonably have been expected to affect the willingness of the Purchaser to purchase the said business or the price at or the terms upon which the purchase is made.

(b) That the Vendors have a good marketable title to the property specified in Part I of the First Schedule subject to the servitudes burdens conditions and provisions specified in such Part I and the said property complies (as to buildings and use) with the Town and Country Planning Acts and all bye-laws and regulations affecting the same and all covenants (other than covenants for repair state and condition) restrictions and conditions affecting such property have been and will down to Completion continue to be observed and performed and such property is not affected by any of the following matters:–

  (i)   Any closing order, demolition order or clearance order;
 (ii)   Any enforcement notice which has not been complied with;
(iii)   Any outstanding or anticipated notice, requirement or scheme of any district, regional or other authority or town planning or building regulations or any time limit restricting any relevant planning consent;
 (iv)   Any compensation received or receivable consequent upon a refusal of any planning consent or the imposing of restrictions in relation to any planning consent;
  (v)   Any order or proposal publicly advertised or of which written notice has been received for the compulsory acquisition or requisition of the whole or any part thereof or the modification of any Planning Permission or the discontinuance of any use or the removal of any building;
 (vi)   Any agreement with a Planning Authority regulating the use or development thereof;
(vii)   Any outstanding notice or complaint from any Inspector or Authority;

(c) The Vendors are the beneficial owners of the Business and Assets and have a good and marketable title thereto free from all liens charges bills of sale hire purchase agreements credit sale agreements agreements for payment on hiring or deferred terms in respect thereof and any other encumbrances whatsoever.

(d) That the said business has since the Balance Sheet Date of   1984 been carried on by the Vendors in the normal and usual course of business and so as to maintain the same as a going concern with adequate stock-in-trade and that no unusual or long-term commitments have been entered into in connection with the said business save as already disclosed in writing to the Purchaser or will be entered into prior to Completion without the express written consent of the Purchaser.

(e) That since the said Balance Sheet Date no assets of the Vendors used or enjoyed by the Vendors in connection with the said business have been disposed of or will until Completion be disposed of except in the normal course of carrying on the said business and no security, charge or lien has been or will pending Completion be created or agreed to be created or permitted to arise in respect of any such assets and no hire-purchase commitments have been or will pending Completion be entered into in respect of any such assets.

(f) That save as already disclosed in writing to the Purchaser there are not in existence any Service Agreements with employees engaged in the said business which cannot be terminated by twelve weeks' notice or less without giving rise to any claim for damages or compensation and that save as aforesaid there are not in existence any retirement, death or disability benefit schemes or obligations to or in respect of employees of the Vendors whom the Purchaser is employing pursuant to Clause 9.

(g) The Vendors will use all reasonable endeavours to procure that the employees of the Vendors listed in the Third Schedule to this Agreement remain in that employment until Completion on the same terms as hitherto except as may otherwise be agreed to or requested by the Purchaser.

(h) The Vendors are not under any contractual obligation to increase the rates of remuneration or pay any bonus to any employees engaged in the business at any future date with or without retrospective effect and the Vendors will not prior to Completion without the prior written consent of the Purchaser increase the rate of remuneration or alter the terms of service of any employee.

(i) That the Vendors are not engaged in any litigation in connection with the said business (other than normal debt-collection by the Vendors) and that to the best of the knowledge and belief of the Vendors no such litigation is threatened or expected in connection with the said business.

(j) That the Vendors will at the Purchaser's expense pending Completion maintain in force all such insurances in relation to or in connection with the said business as are normally kept in force by the Vendors and will forthwith cause the interest of the Purchaser to be noted on the relevant policies.

(k) The Balance Sheet and Profit and Loss Accounts of the Vendors for the period ended   1984 and for previous years as disclosed to the Purchaser are in accordance with generally accepted accounting principles, are accurate in all material respects and present or reflect a true and fair view of the Business and there has been no material deterioration in the financial position and prospects of the Vendors since that date.

NOTE
It may also be necessary to include warranties in relation to taxation matters, which should be adjusted with the advice of the tax advisers of the parties.

THE FIFTH SCHEDULE
(*Missives of Sale and Purchase of heritable property 10 Gorbals Street, Edinburgh in normal terms expressed as conditional upon completion of the sale of the business and assets of A, B & Co.*)

(ii) *Sale and Purchase of and Securities over Book Debts*

Preliminary

8–36   Sales of book debts are commonly effected (a) upon the bankruptcy or liquidation of the creditor, or (b) in the ordinary course of business by way of a debt factoring or invoice discounting transaction.

Sales on bankruptcy or liquidation

8–37   Upon sequestration of the creditor book debts due to him may be sold by his trustee in bankruptcy by public auction but only more than 12 months after the date of the deliverance actually awarding sequestration.[20] As to procedure and styles of articles of roup and assignations see the undernoted text.[21] The liquidator of a limited company may sell book debts due to it publicly or privately at any time.[22] A trustee acting under a trust deed for creditors will normally have power to sell book debts publicly or privately at any time.

Factoring or discounting of book debts

8–38   The normal practice of providing immediate finance on the security of book debts is to enter into a factoring and discounting agreement with a company engaged in the business of debt factoring, the usual basis being that the factoring company purchases existing debts due at the amount thereof under deduction of a discount being a stated percentage and future debts as they come into existence at a price similarly discounted. Where the creditor in the debts purchased is a limited company the terms of the agreement will determine whether the arrangement constitutes a charge registrable under section 410 of the Companies Act 1985.[23] For special considerations regarding factoring of book debts in Scotland, see *Tolley's Factoring* by F. R. Salinger, paragraphs 7.33 *et seq.*

---

[20] Bankruptcy (Scotland) Act 1913, s. 133; *Stewart* v. *Crookston—Galbraith* v. *Stewart*, 1910 S.C. 609. The length of time which must elapse before sale is permissible and the need for sale by auction have been criticised—see Scottish Law Commission Report on Bankruptcy (Scot. Law Com. No. 68), para. 10.12.

[21] Burns, 141–144.

[22] Companies Act 1985, ss. 539(2)(a) and 598(2).

[23] See *Ladenburg & Co.* v. *Goodwin, Ferreira & Co. Ltd and Garnett* [1912] 3 K.B. 275; *Saunderson & Co.* v. *Clark* (1913) 29 T.L.R. 579; *Re Law, Car & General Insurance Corp. Ltd.* (1911) 55 Sol.J. 407, affd. [1911] W.N. 101, C.A.; *Re David Allester Ltd.* [1922] 2 Ch. 211; *Re George Inglefield Ltd.* [1933] Ch. 1, C.A.; *Ashby, Warner & Co. Ltd.* v. *Simmons* [1936] 2 All E.R. 697, C.A.; *Re Kent and Sussex Sawmills Ltd.* [1947] Ch. 177; [1946] 2 All E.R. 638.

Protection of factor

8–39   The commercial risks in factoring debts are customarily minimised by provisions in the agreement of purchase. These include (1) the imposition of a limit upon the aggregate indebtedness of any one debtor, (2) the specific exclusion of specified non-approved debts, (3) a right of recourse against the creditor which requires him in certain circumstances to repay on notice the amount paid for a particular debt or debts, and (4) an irrevocable power of attorney by the creditor in favour of the factor to execute deeds in favour of the factor such as an assignation of the debts which may be formally intimated or to take other action for perfection of the factor's title to goods or rights, although the assignation would involve payment of stamp duty.

Insolvency of creditor

8–40   It is not customary for the sale and transfer of the book debts to the factor to be intimated to the debtors, although the factor is entitled to do so, with the result that the factor does not have a completed title to the debts. The factor is exposed to the risk of insolvency of the creditor when a receiver, liquidator or trustee in bankruptcy may have a claim to the debts preferable to that of the factor. To guard against that contingency the agreement normally provides that upon payment of the whole or any part of the purchase price of the debts they will be held by the creditor in trust for the factor. It is thought that this creates a trust valid in Scots law since the agreement constitutes a written declaration of trust intimated to the factor as beneficiary over identified subjects.[24,25]

Agreement for the factoring or discounting of debts

8–41   AGREEMENT[25a]
between
A B Limited (*designed*) (hereinafter called "the Factor" which expression shall include the Factor's assignees except where the context requires otherwise)
and
C D Limited (*designed*) (hereinafter called "the Client")

1. DEFINITIONS:
(1) In this Agreement, except where the context otherwise

---

[24] See *Clark, Taylor & Co. Ltd.* v. *Quality Site Development (Edinburgh) Ltd.*, 1981 S.L.T. 308 at 310, 311.

[25] The dictum in *Export Credits Guarantee Dept.* v. *Turner*, 1981 S.L.T. 286 at 290 that debts cannot become part of trust subjects unless the creditor divests himself of them by assignation intimated to the debtors is thought to be too widely stated. A trust properly created over assigned debts is effective in a question between the truster (or his trustee in bankruptcy or its liquidator) and the beneficiary; the effect of intimation is to make the right real in a question with the debtors or third parties.

[25a] This style is based on a form of agreement provided by Anglo Factoring Services Ltd., 44 Old Steine, Brighton.

requires, the singular shall include the plural and vice versa, the masculine shall include the feminine and neuter and vice versa and the following expressions shall have the meanings assigned to them below:

"Approved receivable"
Any receivable which (i) falls within any permitted limit (and where there are two or more receivables owing by the same Debtor the receivables shall be treated for this purpose in the order in which they become due for payment) and (ii) in relation to which the Client is not in breach of any warranty or undertaking contained in this Agreement and (iii) is not a receivable or within a class of receivables specified in paragraph 1 of the Schedule.

"Associate of the Client"
A director, shareholder or employee of the Client or a person whose relationship to the Client is within the meaning of associate as defined by Section 184 of the Consumer Credit Act 1974.

"Collection date"
(1) As regards a receivable paid in cash, the date of receipt from the Debtor and as regards a receivable paid by cheque or other instrument, the date on which the amount of the same is collected from the drawee or acceptor; or (2) Such other date as may be specified in paragraph 2 of the Schedule.

"Commencement date"
The date specified in paragraph 12 of the Schedule.

"Date of insolvency"
(1) In the case of bankruptcy, sequestration or winding up by the court, the date of the adjudication order, sequestration award or winding up order respectively by the court having jurisdiction.
(2) In the case of a voluntary winding up, the date of the effective resolution for voluntary winding up by members of the Debtor.
(3) In the case of the appointment of a receiver, the date of the appointment.
(4) In the case of any arrangement or trust deed for creditors, the date when the same is made.

"Debtor"
Any person who is or may become indebted in respect of any receivable or prospective receivable.

"Delivery"
(1) In the case of goods, despatch in the United Kingdom to the Debtor or his agent.
(2) In the case of services, completion of their performance.

"Goods"
Any merchandise and, where the context so admits, any services (and "sale of goods" shall include the provision of services).

"Insolvency"
(1) Bankruptcy.
(2) Sequestration.

(3) Winding up by reason of inability to pay debts.

(4) The appointment of a receiver of any part of the property or assets of the Debtor, or the making of an arrangement, formal or informal, with or for the benefit of the general body of the Debtor's creditors, including a trust deed for creditors.

"Legal representative"
The Debtor's executor, administrator, trustee in bankruptcy, liquidator or other person for the time being entrusted by law with the management of the Debtor's assets or affairs.

"Notified receivable"
A receivable notified to the Factor under clause 7(2).

"Permitted limit"
A limit established by the Factor at its sole discretion on application to it by the Client in relation to any Debtor for the purpose of determining the extent to which the aggregate indebtedness of any Debtor at any one time comprises approved receivables.

"Purchase price"
The price payable by the Factor under clause 3 in respect of a receivable.

"Receivable"
The amount (or where the context so requires, a part of the amount) of any indebtedness incurred or to be incurred by the Debtor under a supply contract.

"Recourse"
The right of the Factor to require the Client to repurchase a notified receivable at a price equal to the amount remaining unpaid by the Debtor in respect thereof.

"Supply contract"
A contract for the sale of goods by the Client.

"Unapproved receivable"
A receivable that is not an approved receivable.

(2) Expressions which, in or for the purpose of any proceedings outside Scotland or England, have no precise counterpart in the jurisdiction in which those proceedings take place, shall be construed as if bearing the meaning of the closest equivalent thereto in the jurisdiction concerned.

2. TRANSFER OF RECEIVABLES

(1) The Client agrees to sell and the Factor to purchase all receivables, existing at the commencement date or arising thereafter during the currency of this Agreement, in relation to any Debtor of the class or description specified in paragraph 3 of the Schedule. The ownership of each such receivable shall, as regards receivables existing at the commencement date, vest in the Factor on that date and, as regards future receivables, vest in the Factor automatically upon the same coming into existence.

(2) Upon any receivable vesting in the Factor under sub-clause (1) there shall also automatically vest in the Factor all the Client's rights under or in relation to the relevant supply contract (including the right to rescind or terminate such contract and/or to accept a return of goods comprised therein), all instruments and real and

personal securities taken or held by the Client in connection therewith and all the Client's right and title to the goods comprised in the supply contract.

(3) The Client shall at the request of the Factor and at the Client's expense execute a formal written assignment or assignation to the Factor of the receivables, rights, instruments and securities referred to in sub-clauses (1) and (2) and deliver to the Factor any such instrument or security with any necessary endorsement or other signature. Upon payment by the Factor of the whole or any part of the purchase price of any receivable the Client shall hold such receivable and the rights, instruments and securities relating thereto on trust for the Factor.

3. PURCHASE PRICE

(1) The purchase price of each receivable vesting in the Factor under clause 2(1) shall be the amount (including any tax) payable by the Debtor in respect thereof as notifed by the Client under clause 7(2) less (i) any discount or other deduction allowed or allowable by the Client to the Debtor in relation thereto, and (ii) the administration charges provided by Clause 4.

(2) Except as provided by sub-clauses (3)–(5) the purchase price of a receivable shall be paid by the Factor to or for the account of the Client on the collection date thereof or, as regards an approved receivable, on the date of any earlier insolvency of the Debtor.

(3) At any time after the expiry of 24 hours of receipt by the Factor of notification under clause 7(2) relating to an approved receivable, the Factor shall at the request of the Client prepay in whole or in part such percentage of the purchase price of the receivable as is set out in paragraph 4 of the Schedule subject to deduction of the discounting charge specified in paragraph 5 of the Schedule.

(4) The Factor shall not be obliged to make any such payment or prepayment whilst any winding up petition is pending against the Client or whilst any act of bankruptcy committed by the Client remains an available ground for a bankruptcy petition. At any time when the Factor is entitled to terminate this Agreement under clause 18(2) the Factor may, whether or not exercising its right to terminate, withhold all prepayments and recover any prepayment which shall have been made in respect of any receivable then unpaid.

(5) The Factor shall at any time be entitled to set off against any payment due to the Client any amount payable or prospectively payable by the Client to the Factor, whether under this Agreement or otherwise.

(6) Unless otherwise agreed by the Factor at the request of the Client, the purchase price of all receivables shall be payable in Sterling.

(7) Where a receivable is payable otherwise than in Sterling in the United Kingdom, (i) bank charges for collection and/or conversion into Sterling shall be deducted in arriving at the purchase price and (ii) the purchase price shall be computed by reference to the rate of exchange ruling in London on the collection date or any earlier date of insolvency of the relevant debtor, but for administrative convenience and for the purpose of computing the administration charge in accordance with Clause 4, the Factor may provisionally apply the rate ruling in London on the date of receipt by the Factor of the notification relating to the receivable, making such adjustments as

may thereafter be necessary. Similar provisions shall apply to payment of the repurchase price where the Factor has recourse in relation to a receivable to which this clause applies and such repurchase price shall be computed at the same rate as that applied to the purchase price of the receivable to which it relates.

4. ADMINISTRATION CHARGES

The administration charge to be deducted in computing the purchase price payable by the Factor under clause 3(1) shall be such percentage as is specified in paragraph 6 of the Schedule (or such other percentage as shall have been agreed by the parties in writing) of the gross value of each receivable notified to the Factor, such gross value to be computed before deduction of any discounts or other deductions allowed or allowable by the Client to the Debtor. Any additional administration charge for which provision is made in paragraph 7 of the Schedule shall be payable to the Factor by the Client as therein provided.

5. STATEMENTS OF ACCOUNT

The Factor shall send a statement of account to the Client at least once in every month and such statement shall be deemed to be correct and shall be binding on the Client unless the Client notifies the Factor of an error therein within thirty days of the date of its despatch.

6. WARRANTIES BY CLIENT

The Client warrants:–
(1) that the Client's business is as stated in paragraph 8 of the Schedule;
(2) that the Client has not granted any disposition or any charge or other encumbrance which affects or may affect any of the receivables the subject of this Agreement;
(3) that prior to the making of this Agreement the Client has disclosed to the Factor every fact or matter known to the Client which the Client knew or ought to have known might influence the Factor in its decision whether or not to enter into this Agreement and, if so, the terms of the Agreement, including any term as to recourse, prepayment, establishment of any permitted limit or designation of any receivable or class of receivables as unapproved;
(4) that every Debtor has an established place of business and is not an associate of the Client.

7. UNDERTAKINGS BY CLIENT

The Client undertakes:–
(1) to ensure that the warranties given in clause 6 in relation to the making of this Agreement shall, unless otherwise agreed by the Factor, remain in force in relation to the continuance of the Agreement and throughout the currency thereof, and to perform any outstanding or continuing obligations of the Client to every Debtor under the relevant supply contract or any related contract;
(2) promptly to notify the Factor, in such manner and with such particulars and documents evidencing the receivable as the Factor may from time to time require, of every receivable sold by the Client to the Factor, as soon as the relevant goods have been delivered or, if so required by the Factor, at any other time;
(3) to ensure that except as otherwise approved by the Factor in writing every contract relating to a notified receivable (a) shall be

made in the ordinary course of the Client's business; (b) shall provide for terms of payment not more liberal than those set out in paragraph 9(a) of the Schedule; (c) shall be subject to the law of the country or one of the countries specified in paragraph 9(b) of the Schedule; and (d) shall provide for the relevant invoice to be expressed and payment to be made by the Debtor in the currency specified in paragraph 9(c) of the Schedule;

(4) to ensure that every notified receivable shall be payable by the Debtor as a legally binding obligation without defence, counterclaim or set-off and that neither the Debtor nor his legal representative will dispute liability in respect thereof;

(5) as regards every notified receivable, to give to the Debtor such written notice of transfer of the receivable to the Factor as may be required by paragraph 10 of the Schedule;

(6) to notify the Factor promptly in writing of any disagreement between the Client and any Debtor relating to any receivable and to supply to the Factor a copy of any credit note issued to a Debtor as soon as such credit note is issued;

(7) to deliver direct to the Factor (or, if so required by the Factor, direct to a bank account specified by the Factor) any remittance received by the Client in payment of or on account of any receivable, and pending such delivery to hold such remittance in trust for the Factor and separate from the Client's own moneys;

(8) to co-operate fully with the Factor in the collection of any receivable and the enforcement of payment thereof, whether by proceedings or otherwise, and to indemnify the Factor against all legal and other costs and expenses incurred in connection with such enforcement so far as it relates to an unapproved receivable;

(9) in the case of undisclosed factoring or discounting, to maintain proper credit controls and to act promptly and efficiently in the collection of the receivables;

(10) to comply with any requirement of the Factor that the Factor's prior consent be obtained to the issue of any credit note to any Debtor;

(11) not to rescind, terminate or vary any contract relating to a notified receivable without the prior consent of the Factor;

(12) not to assign, charge or otherwise encumber any receivable the subject of this Agreement, nor enter into any other agreement for the factoring or discounting of any receivables (whether or not the subject of this Agreement) without the prior written consent of the Factor.

8. RECOURSE

As regards (i) each unapproved receivable, (ii) each receivable which comprises solely discount wrongly claimed or deducted by the Debtor and (iii) each receivable which the Debtor is or claims to be unable to pay by reason of legal constraints or acts or orders of government, the Factor shall have recourse to the Client on the expiry of notice to the Client of the length specified in paragraph 11 of the Schedule. The Factor will credit the Client with all sums subsequently recovered by the Factor in respect of such receivable as the result of enforcement of rights, title or securities vested in the Factor under clause 2(2). The said receivable, rights, title and securities shall, unless otherwise determined by the Factor, remain vested in the Factor and will continue to be held in trust by the Client for the Factor until the repurchase price has been fully discharged, whether by payment to the Factor or by set-off of an amount credited to the Client under the provisions of this Agreement.

9. VALUE ADDED TAX

(1) For the purpose of securing recoupment of value added tax invoiced to a Debtor who becomes bankrupt or suffers sequestration or goes into liquidation the Client agrees:–

(i) that where legal ownership of the receivable is still vested in the Client, the Factor shall be at liberty to lodge a proof of debt in the Client's name for the amount of the receivable exclusive of value added tax;

(ii) that where legal ownership of the receivable has passed to the Factor, the Factor shall be at liberty to re-assign the receivable to the Client (for a nil consideration in the case of an approved receivable);

and that in either such case the Client shall use its best endeavours to recover such value added tax and shall promptly remit to the Factor, and meanwhile hold on trust for the Factor, any dividend received or value added tax recovered by the Client.

(2) Sub-clause (1) shall not apply in relation to any receivable in respect of which the Factor has exercised its right of recourse under clause 8.

10. APPROPRIATION AND DIVISION OF RECEIPTS

(1) In any case in which approved and unapproved receivables may be owing by the same Debtor then, subject to the provisions of sub-clause (2), the Factor shall be entitled (notwithstanding any contrary appropriation by the Debtor) to appropriate any payment or other benefit received in discharge of or on account of receivables owing by such Debtor, and any credit or allowance granted by the Client to the Debtor, in discharge of or on account of any approved receivable in priority to any unapproved receivable.

(2) Any divided or other benefit received from the estate of a Debtor following the date of insolvency, shall be divided between the Factor and the Client pro-rata to the aggregate amount of approved and unapproved receivables owing by the Debtor at the date of insolvency.

11. CREDIT BALANCES

The Client hereby irrevocably authorises the Factor to make payment in settlement of any credit balance which may arise on any Debtor's account in the Factor's records, whether such credit balance arises from the issue of a credit note by the Client or otherwise.

12. COLLECTION OF RECEIVABLES

Where notice of transfer of a receivable to the Factor has been given to the Debtor, then until a receivable has become revested in the Client in accordance with clause 8, the Factor shall have the sole right to collect the receivable and to enforce payment thereof in such manner and to such extent as it shall in its absolute discretion decide, and to institute, defend or compromise in the name of the Factor or the Client and on such terms as the Factor thinks fit any proceedings brought by or against the Factor in relation to the receivable.

13. CLIENT'S ACCOUNTS AND RECORDS

The Client shall permit the Factor and its authorised agents at all reasonable times to inspect all or any of the Client's records and documents relating to any transaction giving rise to a receivable or relating to the financial position of the Client. The Client shall furnish to the Factor at the Factor's request a copy of any balance sheet, account or statement produced by the Client showing its financial position or the results of its operations.

14. POWER OF ATTORNEY

The Client hereby irrevocably appoints the Factor and the Directors and Secretary for the time being of the Factor jointly and each of them severally to be the attorneys or the attorney of the Client to execute or sign in the Client's name such deeds and documents, to complete or endorse such cheques and other instruments, to institute or defend such proceedings and to perform such other acts, as the Factor may consider necessary in order to perfect the Factor's title to any receivable or goods or any right, instrument or security taken or arising in connection therewith or to secure performance of any of the Client's obligations under this Agreement.

15. CANCELLATION OF PERMITTED LIMIT

Any permitted limit may be cancelled or varied by the Factor in its absolute discretion by written or oral notice to the Client and such cancellation or variation shall take effect forthwith except in relation to receivables arising from goods sold and delivered before receipt of the said notice by the Client.

16. CHANGE IN CONSTITUTION OF CLIENT

This Agreement shall remain effective notwithstanding any change in the constitution, composition or legal personality of the Client, whether by death, retirement, addition or otherwise.

17. PLURALITY OF CLIENTS

Where two or more persons are named as Client in this Agreement, the undertakings and warranties contained in this Agreement shall be deemed to be given by each of them, their liability hereunder shall be joint and several and the Factor shall be at liberty (i) to release or conclude a compromise with any one or more of them without affecting its rights against the other or others and (ii) to treat a notice or demand by the Factor to any one or more of them or to the Factor by any one or more of them as a notice or demand given to or by the other or others (but the Factor shall not be obliged to treat such notice or demand in the manner aforesaid).

18. COMMENCEMENT AND TERMINATION

(1) This Agreement shall commence on the date specified in paragraph 12 of the Schedule and, subject to the provisions of subclause (2), shall continue for the minimum period specified in paragraph 13 of the Schedule and thereafter until terminated by the expiry of any notice specified in that paragraph.

(2) If at any time the Client shall (i) become insolvent (ii) call any meeting of creditors or, being a body corporate, pass a resolution for winding up otherwise than by reason of insolvency or, being a partnership, be dissolved or (iii) commit any material or persistent breach of this Agreement, or if any person who has given to the Factor a guarantee or indemnity in respect of the Client's liabilities to the Factor shall give notice terminating the guarantee or

indemnity or shall become insolvent, then in any such event the Factor shall be at liberty to terminate this Agreement forthwith by notice.

(3) Upon termination under sub-clause (2), the Client shall become liable forthwith to repurchase at the value notified to the Factor all receivables then outstanding, whether approved or unapproved, but so that none of the said receivables shall revest in the Client until the repurchase price of all such receivables has been paid.

(4) Subject to the provisions of sub-clause (3) and of clause 3(4), such termination shall not affect the rights and obligations of the parties hereto in relation to such receivables which came into existence prior to termination, which shall remain in full force and effect until duly extinguished.

19. EXCLUSION OF OTHER TERMS; PRESERVATION OF FACTOR'S RIGHTS

(1) This Agreement, including the Schedule and any Special Conditions set out in paragraph 14 thereof, contains all the terms agreed between the Factor and the Client to the exclusion of any representations or statements made by or on behalf of the Factor, whether orally or in writing, prior to the making of this Agreement.

(2) The Factor's rights under this Agreement shall not in any way be affected by any delay or failure to exercise any right or option, whether under this Agreement or otherwise, nor by the grant of time or indulgence to the Client or to any Debtor, guarantor or indemnifier.

20. NO ASSIGNATION OR DELEGATION BY CLIENT

The Client shall not be entitled to assign any of its rights or delegate any of its duties under this Agreement without the prior written consent of the Factor.

(To be attested)

THE SCHEDULE

1. Receivables within permitted limit which are not approved- (clause 1(1)):

2. Collection date otherwise than as defined (clause 1(1)):

3. Debtors for inclusion (clause 2(1)):

4. Prepayment percentage (clause 3(3)):

5. Discounting charge (clause 3(3)):

   (a) Rate:

   (b) Method of calculation:

6. Administration charge (clause 4) (exclusive of Value Added- Tax):

7. Additional administration charges (clause 4):

8. Nature of Client's business (clause 6):

9. Client's contract with Debtor (clause 7(3)):

    (a) Terms of Trade:

    (b) Governing Law:

    (c) Currency of invoices:

10. Notices to Debtors (clause 7(5)):

11. Recourse for receivables unapproved (clause 8):

    (a) For breach of warranty or undertaking:

    (b) For any other reason:

12. Date of commencement of Agreement (clause 18):

13. Period of Agreement (clause 18):

14. Special Conditions:

(To be executed)

(4) Special Provisions in Contracts of Sale of Moveable Property

(i) Reservation of Title Clauses

Preliminary

8–42   The seller of specific goods on credit may wish to reserve right to the goods or the proceeds of their resale until he himself has received payment of the price due to him. In effect the seller is seeking to have security over the goods without retaining possession which is inconsistent with the principles of Scots law, save in the field of floating charges by incorporated companies, and it has proved difficult to devise provisions in contracts of sale which are effective for that purpose and are acceptable to both parties.

Sale under suspensive condition

8–43   It is competent for a seller of specific goods to reserve the right of disposal of the goods until certain conditions are fulfilled, in which case, notwithstanding delivery of the goods to the purchaser, the property in the goods does not pass to the purchaser until the conditions are fulfilled.[26] In certain circumstances, dependent upon the wording used, such a provision may be construed as making the transaction one of security excluded from the operation of the Sale of Goods Act.[27] The effect of such a condition, either under the Act[28] or at common law,[29] is that the purchaser cannot give a valid title on resale until the condition has been implemented. For that reason such a condition is normally unacceptable to a purchaser of specific goods which he proposes to resell. Alternatively the property in the goods may pass to the purchaser on delivery subject to the retention of beneficial ownership by the seller until payment of the price,[30] but in that case, where the purchaser is a limited company, the arrangement may constitute a charge which requires registration in order to be valid against its liquidator.[31]

Agency

8–44   If title to the goods is reserved to the seller but the purchaser is authorised to resell, the arrangement is in effect that the purchaser resells as agent for the original seller. That arrangement has the disadvantage that, if it is disclosed to a sub-purchaser, the original seller may become liable as principal to implement the conditions of the sub-sale including the warranties implied by sections 12 to 15 of the 1979 Act.

Trust

8–45   In modern commercial practice attempts have been made to solve the problem by insertion of a clause designed to create a fiduciary relationship between the seller and the purchaser whereby, until the price has been paid, the goods are held by the purchaser in trust for the seller. In England this device succeeded in one case[30] but failed in others,[31] but as yet it has not been effective in Scotland.[32] It is clear that the Scottish courts do not regard with favour a device designed to create what is in effect a security over moveable property without possession which could seriously affect the objectives of the law of bankruptcy and liquidation[33]

---

[26] Sale of Goods Act 1979, s. 19.
[27] *Ibid.*, s. 62(4).
[28] *Ibid.*, s. 21.
[29] *Murdoch & Co. Ltd.* v. *Greig* (1889) 16 R. 396.
[30] *Aluminium Industrie Vaassen* v. *Romalpa Aluminium Ltd.* [1976] 2 All E.R. 552; [1976] 1 W.L.R. 676.
[31] *Re Bond Worth* [1979] 3 All E.R. 919; *Borden (U.K.) Ltd.* v. *Scottish Timber Products Ltd.* [1979] 3 W.L.R. 672, C.A. *Cf. Clough Mill Ltd.* v. *Martin*, [1985] 1 W.L.R. 111.
[32] *Clark Taylor & Co. Ltd.* v. *Quality Site Development (Edinburgh) Ltd.*, 1981 S.L.T. 308; *Emerald Stainless Steel Ltd.* v. *South Side Distribution Ltd.*, 1983 S.L.T. 162; *Deutz Engines Ltd.* v. *Terex Ltd.*, 1984 S.L.T. 273.
[33] *Clark Taylor & Co. Ltd.*, *supra* at 311.

but it may be possible, within the principles of the law of trusts, to achieve the desired result. It is suggested, albeit with some hesitancy in view of the Scottish decisions, that an effective fiduciary relationship may be created by a clause which contains an express condition and declaration that (1) specified existing goods sold are held in trust by the purchaser for the seller until payment in full of the price of the goods when the trust will terminate, and (2) the proceeds of sales by the purchaser of the goods or any part of them will be placed in a separate bank account in name of the purchaser expressed as being in trust for the seller, and, where the purchaser is a limited company, the condition is registered as a charge. The subject of the trust is the goods themselves and should not be expressed as the payments to be received on resale since these will not be in existence when the trust is created[34]; the right to the payments should be left to the principle of tracing the proceeds of trust subjects. There should be no qualification inconsistent with the existence of the trust,[35] but it is thought that the stipulation that the trust will terminate upon full payment of the price is not so inconsistent, since trusts may be created for a specified limited period.[36] The condition that proceeds of sub-sales are to be placed in an earmarked bank account not only assists in tracing proceeds but fortifies the concept of trust.[37] The registration of the condition as a charge where the purchaser is a limited company may be of value lest the arrangement may for any reason be ineffective as a trust but may be sustained as a charge which is effective against a receiver or liquidator.[38] It is considered that a clause in those terms would enable the original seller to trace the proceeds of any part of the goods sold and that the right to trace the goods themselves would probably be exercisable where the goods had been mixed with others (*commixtio*) but not where they had been used in the manufacture of new products (*specificatio*). Such a trust, it is thought, would be valid in a question between the seller and a trustee in bankruptcy, liquidator or receiver on insolvency of the original purchaser, but if the goods have been resold to a subsequent purchaser who has no knowledge of the trust the original seller cannot recover from him.[38a]

(ii) Restrictive Covenants

In sale of business

8-46   In the absence of any contractual restriction the seller of a business with its goodwill is free to establish a competing business, the only

---

[34] *Kerr's Trs.* v. *Inland Revenue*, 1974 S.L.T. 193 at 198, 200; *Export Credits Guarantee Dept.* v. *Turner,* 1979 S.C. 286, 294.
[35] *e.g.* as in *Export Credits Guarantee Dept.*, *supra.*
[36] *e.g.* until the termination of a liferent.
[37] *Jopp* v. *Johnston's Tr.* (1904) 6 F. 1028.
[38] See *Re Bond Worth, supra.*
[38a] *Archivent Sales and Devpt. Ltd.* v. *Strathclyde Regional Council*, 1985 S.L.T. 154.

restraint imposed by law being that he may not canvass the customers of the business he has sold.[39] Accordingly it is the usual practice for purchasers of a business to insert in the contract a provision restricting the activities of the seller in order to protect the goodwill of the business he has bought.[40] Any such provision, to be enforceable, must be reasonable as to the geographical area of the restriction, the period of its endurance and the extent of the restraint imposed, the general principle being that the provision will be enforced by the courts only if it is in terms reasonably designed to protect the goodwill of the business purchased.

8–47 **(i) Geographical area.** The area within which the restriction operates must be no wider than is reasonably necessary to protect the interest of the purchaser and so may vary in accordance with the nature of the business and the area within which it traded. One test of reasonableness was laid down in the leading case of *Nordenfelt* v. *Maxim Nordenfelt Guns and Ammunition Co.*[41] For a useful analysis of other decisions in which the restriction has been held to be reasonable or otherwise see the undernoted text.[42]

8–48 **(ii) Period of endurance.** The reasonableness test is applicable also to the period for which the stipulated restriction is imposed.[43] In the case of a local trade a period of five years may be regarded as maximum and one to two years as more reasonable.[43a]

8–49 **(iii) Extent of restraint.** Again the restriction upon the working or trading activities of the seller must be no greater than is reasonably necessary to protect the purchaser's interests.[44] The restraint should apply only to working or trading in the same line of business as that which has been sold. On the other hand it is permissible, in order to prevent evasion of the bargain, that the seller is restricted, not only personally as an individual but as a director of a company or as partner in a firm which carries on a competing business within the area and during the period of the restriction.

Style

8–50 For a possible style of restrictive covenant see paragraph 8–35, clause 16. That clause is framed in wide terms but the periods and areas to be inserted therein should be the minimum necessary to protect the interests of the purchaser.

---

[39] *Trego* v. *Hunt* [1896] A.C. 7.
[40] See Gloag, Contract, 571, 572; Walker, *Contracts*, (2nd ed.) 12.33.
[41] [1894] A.C. 535.
[42] Walker, *Contracts*, (2nd ed.) 12.28.
[43] For illustrative cases see Walker, *op. cit.*, 12.29.
[43a] *Randev* v. *Pattar*, 1985 S.L.T. 270.
[44] *Mulvein* v. *Murray*, 1908 S.C. 528.

In sale of goods

8–51   It is a familiar practice for manufacturers or wholesalers to bind
retailers to purchase specified products only from them, *e.g.* supplies of
petrol to garages or liquors to licensed premises, thus creating guaranteed outlets. Frequently such solus agreements are combined with the
provision of loan finance or specially favourable terms of purchase of
the products, but the fact that the restriction is imposed as a condition of
a heritably secured loan does not protect it from attack as being
unreasonably wide.[45] Solus agreements are subject to the test of reasonableness. In recent cases relating to garages periods of seven and a half
years,[46] twenty one years,[47] and ten years[48] were held to be too long and
the agreements were unenforceable, but a period of four years and five
months was held to be reasonable.[47] The maximum duration of solus
agreements is now regulated in the case of petrol by orders under the
Monopolies and Mergers Act 1965 and in the case of beer by EEC
Regulations. The maximum period of a solus petrol tie is five years, and
any connected loan or credit arrangement must be terminable by the
borrower after expiry of the period of five years.[49] The maximum period
of an exclusive purchasing agreement for specified beers is ten years but
if for both specified beers and other drinks the maximum period is five
years.[49a] If the seller wishes to impose periods up to the maxima this can
conveniently be done by listing the specified beers and minimum quantities thereof to be purchased in one schedule and the specified beers and
other drinks and minimum quantities thereof to be purchased in another
schedule and providing that the tie shall operate for different periods
within the maximum appropriate to each type of goods specified in the
two schedules. Exclusive purchasing agreements relating to liquors and
other drinks combined with loan agreements and heritable security are
complex documents which vary with the practice of different sellers and
normally include provisions as to protection of the licensed premises of
the buyer, powers to the seller to enter into possession on default, etc.
The particular provisions relating to exclusive supply of liquors may be
in the style in paragraph 8–52 *infra*; a style of solus agreement for petrol
is given in paragraph 8–53 *infra*.

Style—solus agreement—liquors—specimen clauses

8–52   (1) This Agreement shall subsist (a) in respect of the type of
goods specified in column 1 of Schedule A hereto for a period of 10
years and (b) in respect of the type of goods specified in column 1 of
Schedule B hereto for a period of 5 years, in both cases from and
after the execution of this Deed by the Seller.

---

[45] *MacIntyre* v. *Cleveland Petroleum Co. Ltd.*, 1967 S.L.T. 95.
[46] *Regent Oil Co.* v. *J.T. Leavesley (Lichfield)* [1966] 1 W.L.R. 1210.
[47] *Esso Petroleum Co.* v. *Harper's Garage (Stourport) Ltd.* [1968] A.C. 269.
[48] *MacIntyre* v. *Cleveland Petroleum Co. Ltd.*, *supra*.
[49] Solus Petrol Order 1966 (S.I. 1966 No. 894) as amended.
[49a] EEC Regulation 1984/83.

(2) Throughout the respective periods above mentioned the Buyer shall purchase from the Seller or its nominees for consumption on or off the premises at   all beers and other drinks specified in column 1 of Schedules A and B hereto not less in each year than the quantity of each type of beer and other drinks specified in column 2 of the said Schedules. For the purpose of establishing the total amount of such beers and other drinks purchased in each year (i) the period of a year shall be calculated from the anniversary of execution by the Seller of this Deed, (ii) any lesser period will be calculated proportionately and (iii) the quantity purchased shall be ascertained from the records of the Seller and will be conclusively determined by a certificate of the accountants (auditors) of the Seller for the time being and the Buyer shall not either directly or indirectly during the said respective periods buy, receive or sell or dispose of or permit to be bought, sold or disposed of at or from the said premises any of the said goods other than such as shall have been purchased from the Seller or its nominees.

(2) Purchases from the Seller shall be from the Seller's current free trade price list only.

(3) In the event of inability of the Seller to supply any of the said goods the Buyer may, with the written consent of the Seller, which shall not be unreasonably withheld, acquire the same elsewhere but only until the Seller can resume supplies and in any event in no greater quantity than the Seller has been unable to supply on a week to week basis.

(4) In no circumstances shall any such inability to supply render the Seller liable to the Buyer or release the Buyer from liability to perform his (its) obligations hereunder save to the extent above stated.

SCHEDULE A

1	2
Types of beer (*list*)	Minimum quantity to be purchased in each year (*specify*)

SCHEDULE B

Types of beer and other drinks (*list*)	Minimum quantity to be purchased in each year (*specify*)

Style—solus agreement—petrol service station[49b]

8–53   MOTOR FUELS SUPPLY AGREEMENT

SERVICE STATION known as ....
at ....

AN AGREEMENT between (i) .... COMPANY LIMITED
of .... (Supplier) and (ii) . . . .
of .... (Dealer).

[49b] The style of agreement is based on that used by Esso Petroleum Co. Ltd., whose permission is gratefully acknowledged.

WHEREBY IT IS AGREED as follows:

1. (1) The Supplier agrees to sell to the Dealer and the Dealer agrees to buy from the Supplier the Dealer's total requirements of motor fuels for resale at the Service Station for a period of   years from the   19   (or the date of first delivery of Supplier's motor fuels whichever is the earlier).

   (2) The price shall be Supplier's Wholesale Schedule Price to Dealers at the date of delivery and each delivery shall be upon Supplier's standard conditions of sale as indicated to the Dealer from time to time.

   (3) The Dealer agrees to make payment to Supplier for the motor fuels on or before delivery as Supplier may from time to time require and any concession granted by Supplier may be withdrawn at any time. Payment shall be made by direct debit or in such other manner as Supplier may from time to time require.

2. SUPPLIER AGREES

   To allow the Dealer on all motor fuels purchased by the Dealer under this Agreement a rebate of   per litre calculated quarterly in arrear up to the 28th February, 31st May, 31st August and the 30th November in each year, and paid as soon as possible thereafter.

3. THE DEALER AGREES

   (1) To give Supplier at least two clear working days notice of the Dealer's requirements of motor fuels and to take delivery at such times as may reasonably be required by Supplier in the largest possible loads.

   (2) Before completing any sale transfer or lease of the Service Station premises or business or making any other arrangement under which any person commences to carry on business there in succession to the Dealer to notify Supplier in writing and procure that any purchaser transferee or lessee of the Service Station premises or successor in business to the Dealer enters into an agreement with Supplier and the Dealer whereby such purchaser transferee lessee or successor as the case may be is substituted for the Dealer for all future purposes of this Agreement in relation to the interest transferred including this sub-clause.

   (3) Not to apply to or use in connection with any of the motor fuels supplied as aforesaid any trade mark, brand name or denomination other than that under which such motor fuels were supplied to the Dealer by the Supplier.

   (4) To permit the erection and removal of an Identification Sign if required by the Supplier.

4. PROVIDED ALWAYS AND IT IS HEREBY AGREED THAT

   (1) (a) Neither party shall be liable for any failure to fulfil any term of this Agreement if fulfilment is delayed, hindered or prevented in whole or in part by any circumstance whatsoever which is not within its immediate control, including but without limiting the generality of the foregoing:

   (i) strikes, lock-outs, labour disputes of any kind, partial or general stoppages of labour (including working to rule), refusals to perform any kind of work (whether or not any of the foregoing are lawful, or relate to that party's own employees or others);

(ii) war, hostilities, terrorist activity, or any local or national emergency;

(iii) any regulation, order or request of, or restriction imposed by any international, national, provincial, port or other public authority or any person purporting to act for such authority;

(iv) breakdown of or accident to plant, machinery or facilities;

(v) failure of or hindrances to transportation;

(vi) in the case of the Supplier, failure of or shortage in any of Supplier's or its suppliers' existing or contemplated sources of supply of the motor fuels, or of the crude petroleum or other feedstock from which they are derived, or any reduction in Supplier's stocks thereof (for whatever reason) below levels which Supplier in its absolute discretion considers necessary;

(vii) the threat or reasonable apprehension of any of the foregoing events.

(b) If any such circumstance affects Supplier's fulfilment of any term of this Agreement:

(i) Supplier shall be at liberty to withhold, reduce or suspend deliveries hereunder to such extent as Supplier in its absolute discretion may think fit and in particular (without limitation to the generality of the foregoing, and subject to Supplier's operating requirements) to allocate on any fair and reasonable basis according to Supplier's discretion between Supplier's customers (including the Dealer) such motor fuels as may be available to Supplier in the ordinary and usual course of Supplier's business and to effect deliveries thereof at such times and in such manner as Supplier may decide;

(ii) Supplier shall in no case be bound to purchase or otherwise obtain or arrange for deliveries of the motor fuels, crude petroleum or other feedstock from which they are derived to make up inadequate supplies or to replace deliveries so withheld, reduced or suspended;

(iii) The Dealer shall be free to purchase from any other supplier those quantities of motor fuels which Supplier fails to deliver hereunder provided that the Dealer has given in respect of each and every delivery 24 hours' prior notice to Supplier's local Regional Office of his intention to purchase from such supplier. The Dealer shall maintain a record of such purchases which shall be made available to Supplier upon request.

(2) Supplier shall be entitled to determine this Agreement at any time if the Dealer fails to carry out any of the Dealer's obligations herein or enters into any arrangement with creditors or becomes notour bankrupt or has a receiver or liquidator appointed, but without prejudice to any of Supplier's other rights or remedies which may have accrued hereunder.

(3) As from the commencing date of this Agreement any

previous Motor Fuels Supply Agreement between Supplier and the Dealer relating to the Service Station is hereby determined.

(4) In the case of a partnership the obligations of the Dealer shall be binding on all the partners jointly and severally.

5. DEFINITION
   The term "Service Station" shall include any adjoining land which may be used for the retail sale of motor fuels by or for the benefit of the Dealer and/or sharing access to or from the existing premises.

DATED this   day of   19

FOR AND ON BEHALF OF SUPPLIER..............................

Witness...................... Witness ....

Address...................... Address ....

                                    (Sole Proprietor)
                                    (Partners)
BY OR ON BEHALF OF THE DEALER................. (Director)

Witness...................... Witness ....

ADDENDUM for signature by non-occupying proprietor/lease-holder.

In consideration of Supplier agreeing to enter into the above written supply agreement with the Dealer I/we hereby undertake to observe and perform (as appropriate to my interest in the Service Station premises or business) and to procure the observance and performance of all the terms and conditions thereof.

Name ....

Address ....

Signed ....

Witness...................... Witness ....

Address...................... Address ....

(5) TRANSFER OF SPECIAL SUBJECTS ABSOLUTELY OR IN SECURITY

(i) Ships

Sale

8–54   The sale of a ship is usually effected by a memorandum of agreement stating the terms of the contract, price, deposit (if any), time of payment, inspection of the ship afloat and in dry dock, taking over of on-board stores and fuels and other more detailed matters. The memorandum contains also the obligation of the Sellers in exchange for the price to grant and deliver a legal bill of sale of the vessel. The actual transfer of ownership is effected by a bill of sale in the form prescribed by the Commissioners of Customs and Excise with the consent of the Department of Trade and Industry under powers contained in the Merchant

Shipping Act 1894, s. 65, Sched. 1, Pt. I, Form A, as amended by the Merchant Shipping Act 1965, ss. 7(1) and (2),Scheds. 1 and 2. For styles of initial memorandum of agreement and bill of sale see *Encyclopaedia of Forms and Precedents* (Butterworth), Volume 21. The bill of sale must be registered at the port of registry of the ship. The transferee must make a statement of his qualification as a British subject to own a British ship and a declaration that no unqualified person is entitled as owner to any legal or beneficial interest in the ship.[50]

Mortgage

8–55   A registered mortgage over a British ship or any share in it must be in the statutory form prescribed by the Merchant Shipping Act 1894,[51] or as near to that form as circumstances permit. The mortgage must be registered[52] and priority among mortgages is determined by the respective dates of their registration.[53] On default by the mortgagor the mortgagee whose mortgage is first registered may sell the ship; subsequent mortgagees require the consent of every prior mortgagee or an order of the court.[54] Registered mortgages may be transferred in prescribed form[55] and are transmissible on death or bankruptcy of the mortgagee or otherwise by operation of law, subject to compliance with the 1894 Act by the person taking the mortgagee's interest.[56] For styles of mortgages and transfers thereof see the *Encyclopaedia* above mentioned— para. 8–53. A mortgage by a limited company is registrable as a charge in the Register of Charges.[57]

(ii) Aircraft

Sale

8–56   An aircraft registered in the United Kingdom Register of Aircraft kept by the Civil Aviation Authority may be sold by a contract of sale in appropriate terms and the purchaser must inform the Authority of the transfer of ownership within 28 days.[58] Only qualified persons may hold a legal or beneficial interest in an aircraft so registered.[59] The contract for sale is subject to the statutory conditions of the Sale of Goods Act 1979 and the Unfair Contract Terms Act 1977 and, if the sale is on hire-purchase or credit, the provisions as to minimum deposits and maximum periods of repayment under the current consumer credit regulations.

---

[50] Merchant Shipping Act 1894, ss. 25, 26.
[51] s. 31, Sched. 1, Pt. I, Form B.
[52] s. 31.
[53] s. 33.
[54] s. 35.
[55] s. 37, Sched. 1, Pt. I, Form C.
[56] s. 38.
[57] Companies Act 1985, s. 410(4)(*d*).
[58] Air Navigation Order 1980 (S.I. 1980 No. 1965), art. 4(11), (12).
[59] As to qualified persons, *ibid.*, art. 4(3).

Mortgage

8–57   Mortgages of aircraft are regulated by the Mortgaging of Aircraft Order 1972[60] with special provisions as to its application to Scotland.[61] A Register of Aircraft Mortgages is kept by the Civil Aviation Authority and the Order contains provisions regulating the priority of mortgages (including special provisions for entering priority notices in advance of registration of the mortgage itself).[62] The legal effect of a mortgage in Scotland upon default by the mortgagor or owner of the aircraft and the rights of the mortgagee upon such default, together with rules for application of moneys received on sale of the mortgaged aircraft by the mortgagee, are the subject of detailed provisions in Schedule 2 to the Order.

8–58   Styles of aircraft mortgage and the transfer and discharge thereof are prescribed for Scotland in Schedule 2 to the Order and the forms of entries in the Register are prescribed in Schedule 1 to the Order. A mortgage of an aircraft by a limited company is registrable as a charge in the Register of Charges.[63] Special provisions as to mortgaging of aircraft may be made by Order in Council,[64] but until an Order is made under the 1982 Act the provisions of the 1972 Order as amended will continue in force.[65]

(iii) Petroleum

The statutory background

8–59   The Petroleum (Production) Act 1918[66] prohibited the searching or boring for petroleum within the United Kingdom except by persons acting on behalf of the government or holding a licence from the Ministry of Munitions. The Act did not affect the property rights of petroleum *in situ*. The Petroleum (Production) Act 1934[67] went considerably further than the 1918 Act (which it repealed) and vested in the Crown the property in petroleum existing in its natural state in strata in Great Britain together with the exclusive right to search and bore for and get it. For the purpose of this Act "petroleum" was defined as including any mineral oil or relative hydrocarbon and natural gas existing in its natural condition in the strata but excluding coal or bituminous shales or other stratified deposits from which oil can be extracted by destructive distillation. Provision was made for the Secretary of State to grant licences to search for and work petroleum in specified areas in return for a

---

[60] S.I. 1972 No. 1268 as amended by S.I. 1981 No. 611.
[61] *Ibid.*, Sched. 2.
[62] *Ibid.*, art. 14.
[63] Companies Act 1985, s. 410(4)(*d*).
[64] Civil Aviation Act 1982, s. 86.
[65] Interpretation Act 1978, s. 17(2)(*b*).
[66] 8 & 9 Geo. 5, c. 52.
[67] 24 & 25 Geo. 5, c. 36.

consideration by way of royalty or otherwise payable to the Exchequer. Power was conferred upon the person holding a licence to acquire compulsorily rights to enter on land for the purpose of getting, carrying away, storing, treating and converting petroleum.

8–60   In 1958 the Continental Shelf Convention was adopted by the United Nations Conference on the Law of the Sea. For the purpose of the Convention the term "continental shelf" means[68]

"(a) . . . the sea-bed and subsoil of the submarine areas adjacent to the coast but outside the area of the territorial sea to a depth of 200 metres or, beyond that limit, to where the depth of the superjacent waters admits of the exploitation of the natural resources of said areas; (b) . . . the sea-bed and subsoil of similar submarine areas adjacent to the coasts of islands."

The Convention gives coastal states the exclusive right to explore and exploit the natural resources of their respective areas of the continental shelf. The Convention further provides that the boundary of a continental shelf appertaining to a state is to be determined by agreement with the other state or states concerned or, in the absence of agreement, by a median line or other equidistance principle unless special circumstances justify another boundary line.

8–61   After the United Kingdom had acceded to the Continental Shelf Convention there was enacted the Continental Shelf Act 1964[69] which provided for the vesting in the Crown of all rights exercisable by the United Kingdom outside territorial waters with respect to the sea-bed and subsoil and their natural resources excepting coal. Provision was made for the Crown to designate areas within which these rights would be exercisable. In relation to petroleum the relevant provisions of the 1934 Act were made applicable.

8–62   The Mineral Workings (Offshore Installations) Act 1971[70] instituted a register of offshore installations and made provision for the construction and survey of such installations, their management and safety regulations.

8–63   In order to facilitate development of offshore petroleum the Offshore Petroleum Development (Scotland) Act 1975[71] authorised the acquisition, by agreement or compulsorily, of land in Scotland urgently required for sites for construction of platforms, pipe-lines, shore terminals and access, housing or other services or facilities relating to the exploration for or production of offshore petroleum. It also provided for the designation of areas in any part of the sea surrounding Scotland which is within United Kingdom territorial waters by order of the

---

[68] Art. 1.
[69] 1964 c. 29.
[70] 1971 c. 61.
[71] 1975 c. 8.

Secretary of State and for the granting of licences by the Secretary of State for the carrying out of operations within such designated sea areas in relation to exploration for or production of offshore petroleum.

8–64　　As a result of the steep increases in the value of oil the method of securing income for the Exchequer from the production of offshore petroleum by way of royalties yielded a revenue disproportionately small in relation to the value of the product, and the Oil Taxation Act 1975[72] introduced a new system designed to secure a greater share of the profits for the state. For the purposes of the Act "oil" includes petroleum and natural gas won under authority of licences granted under the 1934 or 1964 Acts. The Act introduced a new tax, the petroleum revenue tax, charged on the assessable profit of each participator in such licensed operations, the assessable profit being calculated in accordance with detailed provisions prescribed.

8–65　　The Petroleum and Submarine Pipe-Lines Act 1975[73] established the British National Oil Corporation with extensive powers to search for, get, treat and deal in petroleum and its derivatives and to secure government participation in activities connected with petroleum in the territorial waters adjacent to the United Kingdom and the sea in any area designated under the Continental Shelf Act 1964. The revenues obtained by the Corporation are paid into a National Oil Account established by the Act. The 1975 Act also substantially altered the model clauses in petroleum production licences in both seaward and landward areas. As regards seaward areas the model clauses provided for an initial licence period with an option to the licensee to continue it for any part of the area for a further and much longer period. In practice licences for exploration and production are now granted for an initial period of four years with provision for a first extension of three years and a further extension of 30 years in respect of the part of the licensed area in which the licensee wishes to continue operations.

8–66　　**The licence.** The first step in relation to submarine petroleum is the issuing of a licence by the Secretary of State to a company engaged in the exploration for and production of petroleum. The general form of licence is regulated by Schedule 5 to the Petroleum (Production) Regulations 1976[74] subject to variations in particular cases. The licence confers on the licensee an exclusive right to search for and get petroleum in the sea-bed and subsoil of a specified area or block for an initial period with an option to the licensee before the expiry of that period to continue the licence as to part of the licensed area (the continuing part) and

---

[72] 1975 c. 22.
[73] 1975 c. 74.
[74] S.I. 1976 No. 1129.

to determine it as regards the remainder of the area (the surrendered part). The period of continuation is a maximum of 40 years but is now more commonly 30 years. In consideration of the grant of the licence the licensee is obliged to make payments based upon the assessable profit of the participators in the project computed in accordance with the principles prescribed by the Oil Taxation Act 1975. The licence also provides for approval by the Government of production programmes and control of certain aspects of development wells, observance by the licensee of good oilfield practice and avoidance of harmful methods of working, approval by the Government of operators, compliance with safety, health and welfare instructions and various other practical matters. The licence also contains restrictions upon assignation of rights under the licence, powers of the Minister as to revocation of the licence in certain circumstances and provisions as to arbitration (paragraphs 39, 40 and 41 of Schedule 5 to the Petroleum (Production) Regulations 1976), all of which are of importance to prospective lenders on security.

–67 The operating agreement. The size of the operations and the finance involved usually make the formation of a consortium of companies (which frequently include companies registered abroad, notably in the U.S.A.) necessary or desirable. The participators in the project enter into an *operating agreement* which commonly *inter alia*:

(a) defines the initial percentages according to which the costs are to be shared, and the oil produced is to be owned;

(b) designates an operator who is responsible for the conduct of operations with defined powers and functions;

(c) prescribes rules for the conduct of and voting at meetings of consortium members at which various policy decisions may be taken;

(d) provides for a working programme, budgeting reports, etc.;

(e) provides for independent drilling operations in cases where not all the parties decide to participate in the cost;

(f) sets out the basis of charging expenses and reimbursing the operator;

(g) provides for possible changes in ownership percentages particularly where financial obligations are not met;

(h) provides for the basis on which oil may be uplifted;

(i) confers certain potentially valuable rights of pre-emption of the shares of defaulting consortium members and rights of veto of assignment, etc.

Mortgaging of a participator's share is usually permitted subject to conditions, *e.g.* observance of the terms and conditions of the operating agreement, notice of the transaction to the other participators, any necessary government consents and the consent of the other participators which shall not be unreasonably withheld. North Sea operating agreements now generally are governed by English law.

–68 Illustrative agreement. Where one of the holders of the licence is a

United Kingdom subsidiary of an overseas (particularly U.S.A.) parent company, there is frequently an agreement known as an illustrative agreement in terms of which the parent company provides the benefit of financing expertise and the parent company is entitled to the benefit of the petroleum produced. Commonly both parties are required to grant security for their respective interests.

8–69   **The participation agreement with British National Oil Corporation.** This document is entered into between British National Oil Corporation and the participators and usually confers on the corporation an option to acquire oil at market price. The form of the document varies both in its content and as to whether it is granted before or after arrangements for security have been made. The participation agreement is generally included in the documents specified in a security although the concept of assignment of an option rather than an interest does not always consort easily with the Scottish concept of an assignation in security.

8–70   **The pipe-line or terminal operating agreement.** An agreement of this kind is generally required when more than one consortium and more than one field share the same pipe-line or terminal facilities. Sometimes such agreements are entered into by the operator in each consortium on behalf of the other members of the consortium and the total number of parties may be very large, which can create problems with regard to intimation. The "hardware" involved comprises a field facility, *e.g.* drilling apparatus, production platform, single buoy mooring system, storage tanks and/or pipe-line system and terminal facilities.

8–71   **Contractual documents and documents creating securities.** The licence is silent as to governing law but is generally regarded as being governed by the law applicable to the sector in which the licensed area is situated. Partly for the reasons developed in paragraph 27 of the Regulations, licences in respect of areas within the Scottish sector are construed in accordance with the law of Scotland. Since most of the companies concerned are English the basic contractual documentation regulating the interests and obligations of the parties who are involved in the development of the area is usually framed in English form. The normal security is a debenture in English form constituting an equitable charge which is usually declared to be a fixed charge over the listed agreements referred to above and the field facilities and a floating charge over these and all the remaining assets of the companies concerned including in particular the petroleum produced and the proceeds of sale thereof. Where the lender wishes a security under Scots law the form of document is normally an assignation in security whereby there is assigned to the lender the whole right, title, interest and benefit of the borrower (either in immediate security or in the event of default as defined in a related loan agreement) in the licence, the operating agreement and the other agreements above mentioned. The assignation in Scottish form is normally additional to an English debenture and is thought to be necessary because the English charge would not be recognised as creating a fixed security under Scots law. In addition there is a floating charge, duly registered, over all the assets of the borrower because in Scots law a receiver appointed under an all assets charge will be recognised and it affords the most convenient method of enforcing the security.

CHAPTER 9

DELIVERY OF DEEDS

Mutual and unilateral deeds

9–01 A mutual deed, whether bilateral or multilateral, which creates rights or obligations of parties having different interests, is effective once it has been duly executed by all the parties, without delivery.[1] The principle

---

[1] Ersk., III, ii, 44; Bell, *Prin.*, s. 84.

applies even where the deed has been executed in duplicate and one copy has not yet been delivered to one of the parties.[2] The *ratio* of the principle is that the deed, or both copies of it, will ultimately be in the possession of the party who last executes it; he will be entitled to enforce the deed, since it has been delivered to him executed by all the other parties and his execution makes it a binding agreement, whereas, if delivery of the deed or a copy of it to the other parties were necessary, the situation would be that one party would be bound by it while the others were not. Accordingly, the rule is that the party who holds the fully executed document holds it for all the parties and against all the parties.[3]

–02   On the other hand a unilateral deed, whether onerous or gratuitous, even when duly executed, does not take effect in favour of the grantee until it has been delivered to him; the granter, in addition to executing the deed, must put it beyond his power to alter or cancel it by giving physical possession of it to the grantee or performing some act which in law is equivalent to delivery of the deed.[4]

Acceptance of delivery

–03   Although the ordinary rule is that delivery is made whenever the granter of a unilateral deed has done what he can to complete it, as by putting it in the post addressed to the grantee or his agent or entrusting it to someone to post it,[5] delivery of a deed which imposes obligations on the grantee is completed only when the grantee accepts it.[6]

Revocation before delivery

–04   A unilateral deed may be revoked or altered by the granter at any time before it has been delivered, subject to any contractual obligation such as missives of sale which require him to deliver a deed in implement of the contract. If there are several co-granters any one of them may resile before the deed is delivered to the grantee or his agent[7] and the transmission of the deed amongst them does not bar resiling by any of them.[8] Where a deed has been signed by one of several co-obligants but he dies before the deed has been delivered, his executors are not bound, since the implied mandate by the deceased to deliver the deed has fallen on his death.[9]

---

[2] *Robertson's Trs.* v. *Lindsay* (1873) 1 R. 323.
[3] *Ibid.*, *per* Lord President Inglis at 326.
[4] See paras. 9–11 to 9–15.
[5] *Crawfords* v. *Kerr* (1807) Mor. v. "Moveables," App. No. 2.
[6] *Dowie & Co.* v. *Tennant* (1891) 18 R. 986.
[7] *McGill* v. *Edmonston* (1628) Mor. 16991; *Glendinning* v. *Wyllie* (1634) Mor. 16992.
[8] *McAlister* v. *Swinburne & Co.* (1874) 1 R. 166, 958.
[9] *Life Association of Scotland* v. *Douglas* (1886) 13 R. 910.

Effect of delivery as between parties

9–05   In any question between the granter and the grantee a unilateral deed becomes effective only upon delivery. The deed may stipulate a date (which may be other than the date of delivery) upon which rights conferred by the deed pass to the grantee, but it is only upon delivery that these rights become enforceable at all; thereafter the grantee may enforce them with effect from the date stipulated in the deed. Also, if rights conferred by the deed are such that they will become real rights of property only upon further procedure such as registration in an appropriate register, although the rights are created real only when registration has been effected, the personal right to the property is completed on delivery of the deed. In *Thomas* v. *Lord Advocate*[10] the proprietor of heritable subjects executed a disposition of them in favour of his son. It was delivered to the son's agents on May 6, 1945, but entry was postponed till Whitsunday 1945. The proprietor died on May 12, 1950, and the issue was whether the gift had been made within five years before his death in which event the subjects would have been liable to assessment for estate duty. It was held that upon delivery of the deed on May 6, 1945, the gift of a personal right to the subjects had been completed although the benefit of possession prior to May 15, 1945, formed no part of the gift, with the result that the subjects were not assessable to estate duty. In *Gibson* and *Hunter Home Designs Ltd.*[11] missives for the sale of a house were completed and the price had been fully paid but the feu disposition of the property had not been delivered when the selling company was wound up. It was decided that, until the delivery of the feu disposition, the seller, in a question with the purchaser, was not divested of any part of his real right of property in the subjects.

Proof of delivery

9–06   Whether delivery has been made is a question of fact, to be decided on evidence. The onus of proving delivery rests on the party who founds on the deed,[12] but there are certain presumptions arising from the circumstances in which the deed is found.

Deed in possession of grantee

9–07   There is a strong presumption that a deed in possession of the grantee has been delivered.[13] The presumption may be rebutted by proof that the possession was obtained by fraud,[14] or only for safe custody,[15] or subject to a condition suspensive of delivery,[16] or for a purpose

---

[10] 1953 S.C. 151.
[11] 1976 S.C. 23.
[12] *McAslan* v. *Glen* (1859) 21 D. 511.
[13] Walker and Walker, *Evidence*, 59.
[14] *Mair* v. *Thoms' Trs.* (1850) 12 D. 748.
[15] *McAslan* v. *Glen, supra.*
[16] *Semple* v. *Kyle* (1902) 4 F. 421.

inconsistent with an intention to place the deed outwith the granter's control.[17] If the document is gratuitous the strong presumption against donation requires clear evidence of delivery *animo donandi*.[18] Proof in rebuttal of the presumption may be *prout de jure*,[19] unless it is alleged that the deed was held by the grantee in trust for the granter when the proof of trust is restricted to writ or oath.

Deed in possession of granter

-08   If the deed is still in the possession of the granter the presumption is against delivery, subject to the qualification aftermentioned where the granter may be the natural custodier of the deed.[20] Even where there was clear evidence of the granter's intention to deliver the deed but he died before actually carrying out that intention, it was held that delivery had not been effected.[21]

Deed in possession of agent for either party

-09   Possession of the deed by an agent acting exclusively for either the grantee or the granter raises the same presumptions as possession of the deed by the party himself, *i.e.* if held by the grantee's agent delivery is presumed to have been made[22] and *vice versa* if held by the agent for the granter.[23]

Deed in possession of third party

-10   Where the deed is in the possession of a third party such as an agent who acts for both the granter and the grantee it is a question of circumstances to be determined by evidence whether delivery has taken place or not, but in general delivery will be presumed if the deed is onerous but not if it is gratuitous.[24] These presumptions, however, are comparatively slight and may be rebutted by any reasonable evidence to the contrary.[25] In *Mair* v. *Thoms' Trs.*[26] a bond and disposition in security for £900 was granted and delivered to an agent acting for both the granter and the grantees; £900 had been paid by the lenders to the agent but he

---

[17] Gloag, *Contract*, 71.

[18] *Sharp* v. *Paton* (1883) 10 R. 1000.

[19] *McAslan* v. *Glen, supra.*

[20] See paras. 9–22 to 9–25.

[21] *Stamfield's Creditors* v. *Scot's Creditors* (1696) 4 Br. Supp. 344. *Cf. Life Association of Scotland* v. *Douglas, supra.* Contrast *Crawfords* v. *Kerr, supra,* where the deed had been handed to a servant to put in the post.

[22] Bell, *Prin.*, s. 23.

[23] *Irvine* v. *Irvine* (1738) Mor. 11576; *McManus's Tr.* v. *McManus,* 1978 S.L.T. 255, 257.

[24] Ersk., III, ii, 43; Bell, *Prin.*, s. 23; Gloag, *Contract,* 72.

[25] See for examples *Ramsay* v. *Maule* (1828) 6 S. 343; affd. (1830) 4 W. & S. App. 58, 73; *Stewart* v. *Stewart* (1842) 1 Bell's App. 796.

[26] (1850) 12 D. 748.

paid only £669 to the borrower and it was held that the bond had been delivered only to the extent of £669 and to the extent of the balance of £231 was held by the agent on behalf of the borrower. In *Lombardi's Tr.* v. *Lombardi*[27] a gratuitous disposition of one-half share of a dwelling-house by a husband in favour of his wife was handed by the husband to a solicitor acting for both spouses and it was held that in the circumstances there was an implied instruction to the solicitor to hold it for the benefit of the wife and that delivery had been effected.

Donations

9–11 Because of the strong presumption against donation the mere fact that delivery has been made of corporeal moveable property, where physical transfer gives a complete title, is not sufficient to establish ownership; if it is admitted that the property was acquired by way of gift the donee must prove that there was *animus donandi*[28] and proof of the relevant circumstances *prout de jure* is competent. If, however, the donation was of property, such as heritable property, where the transfer to the donee was by a deed of conveyance and the donee has a completed *ex facie* absolute title, averments by the donor or his representatives that donation was not intended and that the property is truly held on behalf of the donor or for purposes inconsistent with absolute ownership by the donee amount to a declarator of trust and can be proved only by the writ or oath of the donee.[29] In the case of gratuitous deeds it may be of importance to establish the date of delivery, as when the deed is challenged as a fraudulent alienation in bankruptcy. In the old case of *Gordon* v. *Maitland*[30] it was decided that, in the absence of evidence to the contrary, delivery was presumed to have been made on the date of execution of the deed of transfer, but that presumption will readily yield to evidence of facts and circumstances which establish a different date.[31]

Equivalents to Delivery

(a) Registration in the Books of Council and Session

9–12 Registration of a deed in the Books of Council and Session for preservation or for preservation and execution affords a strong presumption that the deed has been delivered.[32] In one case,[33] where a deed conveying heritable property under reservation of a liferent and all moveable

---

[27] 1982 S.L.T. 81.
[28] *Brownlee's Exrx.* v. *Brownlee*, 1908 S.C. 232, 239; *Grant's Trs.* v. *McDonald*, 1939 S.C. 448, 471; Gloag, *Contract*, 70; Walker and Walker, *Evidence*, 55, 56.
[29] *Burnet* v. *Morrow* (1864) 2 M. 929; *Newton* v. *Newton*, 1923 S.C. 15.
[30] (1757) Mor. 11161.
[31] See *McManus's Tr.* v. *McManus, supra*; *Lombardi's Trs.* v. *Lombardi* 1982 S.L.T. 81.
[32] *Tennent* v. *Tennent's Trs.* (1869) 7 M. 936; *Obers* v. *Paton's Trs.* (1897) 24 R. 719.
[33] *Leckie* v. *Leckie* (1776) Mor., App. "Presumption," No. 1.

property of which the granter might be possessed at his death had been recorded for preservation, and the granter subsequently executed another deed disposing of the subjects to other persons, it was decided that the original registered deed had been delivered as regards the heritable property but not as regards the moveable property, but the basis of the distinction does not appear from the report.

(b) Registration in the Register of Sasines or the Land Register of Scotland

9–13   Registration of a conveyance or a heritable security in the Register of Sasines also raises a presumption in favour of delivery, even although the deed remains in the custody of the granter.[34] The grantee has a completed title and the presumption of delivery can only be rebutted in special circumstances such as evidence by writ or oath that the property was held by the grantee in trust.[34] In *Cameron's Trs.* v. *Cameron*[35] money was advanced by a father and secured by a bond and disposition in security in favour of the father as trustee for his daughter and provided that the discharge by the father would be sufficient. The bond was recorded in the Register of Sasines, but was not delivered to the daughter who was unaware of its existence. After the father's death the daughter claimed that the bond was held by the deceased in trust for her. It was decided by a court of seven judges (Lord Kyllachy dissenting) that no effectual trust had been created in favour of the daughter. The *ratio* of the decision was that the object of registration of the bond was to complete title to the security in a question with the borrower but not to operate as effectual delivery in a question with the beneficiaries in the trust, and that as there had been no intimation of the existence of the trust to the beneficiary delivery had not been effected.[36] The decision in *Cameron's Trs.* was distinguished in *Linton* v. *Inland Revenue*[37] where a father purchased a farm and with his consent the disposition was granted in favour of his two pupil daughters and recorded in the Register of Sasines. The father in his capacity as tutor to his daughters claimed repayment of Schedule A income tax, and the court held that there had been a completed donation of the farm to the daughters, an argument for the Inland Revenue that the father as their tutor was a trustee for his daughters being rejected. It would appear that registration of a title in the Land Register would raise the same presumption of delivery of the deed upon which registration was based as in the case of registration of the deed in the Register of Sasines.

---

[34] *Burnet* v. *Morrow, supra.*
[35] 1907 S.C. 407.
[36] This decision was followed in *Drummond* v. *Mathieson*, 1912 1 S.L.T. 455, but doubts were expressed *obiter* as to its soundness by Lord Shaw in *Carmichael* v. *Carmichael's Exrx.*, 1920 S.C. (H.L.) 195 at 205.
[37] 1928 S.C. 209.

(c) Intimated assignation

9–14　　An onerous assignation of a debt intimated to the debtor is equivalent to delivery, even although the deed of assignation has not been delivered to the assignee, on the ground that the assignee would have been entitled to require delivery.[38] Where the assignation is gratuitous the question is more difficult, but probably the answer is the same.[39] In *Jarvie's Tr.* v. *Jarvie's Trs.*[40] Lord President Inglis explained the principle thus: "If you execute an assignation, that is made effectual by intimation without delivery, just as a conveyance of land is effectual without delivery if you take an infeftment in favour of a third party. The infeftment and the intimation complete the right, and afford a complete publication or equivalent to delivery."[41] The Lord President distinguished the legal result of an intimated assignation from that where a title to moveable property (a life policy) is taken in name of a third party; in that case some form of intimation to the party benefited is necessary.[42] And the principle applies only where there is an assignation duly intimated. In a rather special case where a receipt was granted by A in terms whereby he acknowledged that the sum paid was to be placed to the credit of B it was decided that the effect was simply to create an implied obligation upon A to account to B and that A's trustee in sequestration had a preferable right.[43]

(d) Title in name of third party

9–15　　The fact that A in transacting with B has taken the title to moveable or heritable property in the name of C does not of itself constitute a completed gift to C[44]; delivery of the deed or document of title to the donee or actings equivalent to delivery are necessary to establish *animus donandi*.[45] In *Carmichael* v. *Carmichael's Exrx.*[46] a father effected a policy of assurance on the life of his pupil son which provided that during the son's minority the father would be entitled to the surrender value of the policy and that, if the son died before attaining majority, the premiums then paid should be repaid to the father, but if the son attained majority and continued to pay the premiums the sum assured would be payable on his death to the son's executors, administrators or assigns. As an alternative the son was entitled at majority to exercise certain

---

[38] *Dick* v. *Oliphant* (1677) Mor. 6548; *McLurg* v. *Blackwood* (1680) Mor. 845.
[39] Gloag, *Contract*, 74.
[40] (1887) 14 R. 411.
[41] At 416.
[42] See para. 9–16.
[43] *Arnott* v. *Drysdale* (1863) 1 M. 796.
[44] *Hill* v. *Hill* (1755) Mor. 11580 (bond); *Walker's Exr.* v. *Walker* (1878) 5 R. 965 (bond of harbour trustees); *Crosbie's Trs.* v. *Wright* (1880) 7 R. 823; *Jamieson* v. *McLeod* (1880) 7 R. 1131; *Lord Advocate* v. *Galloway* (1884) 11 R. 541 (deposit receipts); *Cameron's Trs.* v. *Cameron*, 1907 S.C. 407 (heritable security).
[45] *Thomson's Exr.* v. *Thomson* (1882) 9 R. 911; *Boucher's Trs.* v. *Boucher's Trs.* (1907) 15 S.L.T. 157.
[46] 1919 S.C. 636; revd. 1920 S.C. (H.L.) 195.

options including the conversion of the policy into a cash payment or a fully-paid policy. The father paid all the premiums during the son's minority. The son died after attaining majority but before the next premium fell due and without having exercised any of the options. He knew of the existence of the policy, but it had not been delivered or intimated to him by his father. It was held that, although the policy had never been delivered to the son either actively or constructively, its terms taken in conjunction with the whole circumstances, showed that the son had acquired a *jus quaesitum tertio* under it and that the proceeds fell to his executrix. An argument that the mere existence of the contract by which the policy was effected conferred a *jus quaesitum tertio* on the son, without more, based on a passage from Stair,[47] was rejected. Lord Dunedin's interpretation of that passage, which involved a departure from its grammatical construction by making irrevocability a condition and not a consequence of the gift, has been criticised,[48] but the decision stands and the requirement of intimation to the *tertius* as a condition of irrevocability is consonant with the principles of donation where the gift is made by direct grant.[49]

The decision in *Carmichael* was considered in *Allan's Trs. v. Lord Advocate*[50] and Lord Reid concluded that, while it may be possible to make a provision in favour of a third party irrevocable by the terms of the contract itself, generally it is not and then other evidence of intention is required.

(e) Trusts—deed of trust not delivered

9–16 The rule that delivery is required before a gratuitous deed is effective applies to a deed of trust; until the deed is delivered it remains within the control of the granter to cancel or alter it.[51] That rule applies where third parties are appointed as trustees, but difficult questions may arise where the deed has been granted in favour of the truster as sole trustee and he retains the deed under his own control. In such circumstances some form of intimation of the existence of the trust to the beneficiaries may be regarded as equivalent to delivery.[52] Intimation to one of several beneficiaries is equivalent to delivery to all of them since a trust cannot be irrevocably established in part.[53] Constructive delivery to the beneficiaries is effected by intimation to a person who was in such relationship with them as to render intimation to him equivalent to intimation to

---

[47] Stair, I, x, 5.

[48] T. B. Smith, *Studies Critical and Comparative*, 183; J. T. Cameron, 1961 J.R. 103; A. Rodger, 1969 J.R. 128; D.N. MacCormick, 1970 J.R. 228; Scottish Law Commission, Memorandum No. 38, *Constitution and Proof of Voluntary Obligations: Stipulations in favour of Third Parties* (1977).

[49] As a practical matter it would be highly inconvenient if the law were otherwise: see W. W. McBryde, "Jus Quaesitum Tertio," 1983 J.R. 137.

[50] 1971 S.C. (H.L.) 45, 54.

[51] *Connell's Trs. v. Connell's Tr.*, 1955 S.L.T. 125.

[52] *Allan's Trs. v. Lord Advocate, supra; Clark's Trs. v. Inland Revenue*, 1972 S.C. 177; *Kerr's Trs. v. Inland Revenue*, 1974 S.L.T. 193.

[53] *Allan's Trs. v. Lord Advocate, supra.*

them,[54] but the intimation must be made simultaneously with or subsequent to the creation of the trust and communications as to intentions
made by the truster before creating the trust do not amount to intimation.[55]

Deeds not requiring Delivery

(a) Testamentary writings

9–17   Testamentary writings are not intended to take effect until the
granter's death and may be revoked by him at any time during his life. If
they are found among the granter's papers after his death and not
revoked they are effective without delivery.[56] Even if a testamentary
writing has been delivered to a beneficiary the granter's right of revocation remains.[57]

(b) Clause dispensing with delivery

9–18   A gratuitous deed, even although it contains a clause dispensing with
delivery, is not an effectual gift *inter vivos* unless it is delivered.[58] If it is
found in the repositories of the granter when he dies and has not been
revoked it is effective as a *mortis causa* bequest, but its effect is testamentary, not as an *inter vivos* gift.[59]

(c) Mutual deeds

9–19   For the reasons already given[60] mutual deeds are effective when fully
executed by all parties, without delivery.

(d) Deeds where the granter reserves an interest

9–20   A deed in which the granter reserves an interest, such as a liferent in
his own favour, is, if onerous, effective without delivery since it is presumed that the granter retains the custody of the deed, not because his
intention is not final, but on account of his own interest.[61] If the deed is
gratuitous, however, and has not been delivered its effect is only testamentary; it may be revoked by the granter but, if not revoked, it will be
effective without delivery.[62]

---

[54] *Clark's Trs.* v. *Inland Revenue, supra.*
[55] *Kerr's Trs.* v. *Inland Revenue, supra.*
[56] Ersk., III, ii, 44; Bell, Prin., s. 24.
[57] *Miller* v. *Dickson* (1826) 4 S. 822; *Clark's Exr.* v. *Clark*, 1943 S.C. 216.
[58] *Leckie* v. *Leckie* (1776) Mor. App. "Presumption," No. 1.
[59] Gloag, *Contract*, 67.
[60] Para. 9–01.
[61] Bell, *Prin.*, s. 24; Montgomerie Bell, *Lectures*, 108, 109.
[62] *Hadden and Lawder* v. *Shorswood* (1668) Mor. 16997; *Stark* v. *Kincaid* (1679) Mor. 17002.

(e) Deeds which the granter is under an antecedent obligation to deliver

9–21   If the granter is under an unconditional antecedent obligation to deliver a deed, it is effective without delivery, since the grantee had power to compel delivery.[63] It may be observed, however, that the right of the grantee in such circumstances is not in all respects equivalent to his right had the deed in fact been delivered. The right of the grantee is in the nature of a *jus crediti*, not a real right in property conveyed by the deed, and in the event of bankruptcy of the granter his trustee will have a preferable claim,[64] unless the deed is granted in implement of a *novum debitum*.[65]

(f) Deeds of which the granter is the natural custodier

9–22   Deeds granted by a father in favour of his wife or children are treated in leading older texts[66] as exceptions from the general principle which requires delivery of the deed to the grantee in order to make it effectual. The primary authority for this exception is Stair who states simply that writs granted by parents in favour of their children are effectual without delivery.[67] It is clear that the rule which dispenses with the need for delivery in such deeds now requires considerable qualification and difficult questions have arisen with regard to the effect of the rule, even when it is applicable, and, in recent texts, whether in modern society the rule has any real content.

9–23   **(i) Qualifications of the rule—the need for other indications of the granter's intention to make a completed donation.** It can be stated with reasonable certainty that where a man executes a deed making provision for his wife or children from his own funds then the fact that he is the natural custodier of the deed does not, of itself, in the absence of other evidence of intention to make a completed gift, import delivery to the grantee: the deed remains, as the money formerly was, under the granter's own control.[68] Evidence is necessary to establish an intention on the part of the granter to make a completed donation, in which case the rule that delivery is not required by reason of the granter being natural custodier will apply to the effect of dispensing with delivery of the deed. Important circumstances leading to that conclusion are intimation of the deed to the grantee or knowledge of its existence,[69] registration of the deed (a transfer of shares) in the books of the company together

---

[63] *Cormack* v. *Anderson* (1829) 7 S. 868; *Montgomerie Bell, Lectures*, 110.

[64] *Bank of Scotland* v. *Liquidators of Hutchison, Main & Co. Ltd.*, 1914 (S.C.) H.L. 1; *Gibson and Hunter Home Designs Ltd.*, 1976 S.C. 23.

[65] *Cormack* v. *Anderson, supra*; *Bank of Scotland* v. *Stewart*, Feb.. 7, 1811, F.C.; *Stiven* v. *Scott* (1871) 9 M. 923, *per* Lord President Inglis at 933.

[66] Bell, *Prin.*, s. 24; Montgomerie Bell, *Lectures*, 109; Craigie, *Moveable Rights*, 101.

[67] I, vii, 14.

[68] *Hill* v. *Hill* (1755) Mor. 11580, cited with approval *Walker's Exr.* v. *Walker* (1878) 5 R. 965, 968 and *Jarvie's Tr.* v. *Jarvie's Trs.* (1887) 14 R. 411, 415. (Where a stranger grants a deed in favour of a child and delivers it to the father of the child the position is different: the presumption is that the father holds the deed as the natural custodier of his child's property (*Hill* v. *Hill, supra*)).

[69] *Smith* v. *Smith's Trs.* (1884) 12 R. 186; *Carmichael* v. *Carmichael's Exrx.*, 1920 S.C. (H.L.) 195.

with a letter by the father to his law agents stating that he had originally made over the shares to his son and retained no interest in them,[70] registration of the deed in the Books of Council and Session[71] or registration of the deed in the Register of Sasines[72] although that may not necessarily be conclusive since the granter's object may have been to complete the title as against the debtor and not to effect delivery in a question between himself and the grantee.[73] The rule has no application where the deed by the granter is conceived in favour of third persons as trustees for his wife or children; in that case the trustees, not the granter, are the proper custodiers of the deed and delivery to the trustees is required.[74] Where the deed is granted in favour of the granter himself as trustee for his wife or children it is probably necessary that intimation of the deed or at least knowledge of its existence by the beneficiaries or some of them or a person acting on their behalf is necessary if the deed is not delivered or registered.[75]

9–24   **(ii) Effect of the rule.** The rule as originally stated by Stair did not make it clear whether its application in appropriate circumstances resulted in a completed gift *inter vivos* of the subject of the deed or merely a donation effective only *mortis causa* revocable by the granter during his lifetime and vulnerable to the diligence of his creditors, *i.e.* was its effect contractual or merely testamentary? In the case cited by Stair[76] and other early decisions[77] the question arose after the death of the granter and established only that the deeds were effective *mortis causa*. McLaren[78] and Gloag[79] take the view that the effect of the rule is testamentary so that the deed is effectual only on the death of the granter, revocable by him during his lifetime and of no effect in a question with his creditors. The correctness of that view has been challenged by later writers[80] and it is inconsistent with the decisions in relatively modern cases where the effect was that of a completed gift *inter vivos*.[81] It has been suggested[82]

---

[70] *Inland Revenue* v. *Wilson*, 1928 S.C. (H.L.) 42.

[71] *Obers* v. *Paton's Trs.* (1897) 24 R. 719; *Tennent* v. *Tennent's Trs.* (1869) 7 M. 936, 948.

[72] *Stewart* v. *Rae* (1883) 10 R. 463; *Linton* v. *Inland Revenue*, 1928 S.C. 209.

[73] *Cameron's Trs.* v. *Cameron*, 1907 S.C. 407 (although the decision has been criticised—Gloag, *Contract*, 74; *Carmichael* v. *Carmichael's Exrx.*, *supra* at 205—and has been examined in some detail in Wilson and Duncan, *Trusts*, 42–45).

[74] *Connell's Trs.* v. *Connell's Tr.*, 1955 S.L.T. 125.

[75] *Allan's Trs.* v. *Lord Advocate*, 1971 S.C. (H.L.) 45; *Clark's Trs.* v. *Inland Revenue*, 1972 S.C. 177; *Kerr's Trs.* v. *Inland Revenue*, 1974 S.L.T. 193 although these decisions are not strictly in point since the beneficiaries, except to some extent in *Clark's Trs.*, were not in a relationship to the granter which would have made him natural custodier of deeds for their benefit.

[76] *Bairns of Wallace of Ellerslie* v. *His Heir* (1624) Mor. 6344.

[77] *Cardross* v. *Mar* (1639) Mor. 11440; *Aikenhead* v. *Aikenhead* (1663) Mor. 16994; *Monro* v. *Monro* (1712) Mor. 5052; *Adair* v. *Adair* (1725) Mor. 17006.

[78] *Wills and Succession*, 419, 420.

[79] *Contract*, 67.

[80] Wilson and Duncan, *Trusts*, 40; Clive, *Husband and Wife*, 302, 303.

[81] *Forrest* v. *Wilson* (1858) 20 D. 1201; *Smith* v. *Smith's Trs.* (1884) 12 R. 186; *Linton* v. *Inland Revenue*, 1928 S.C. 209; *Inland Revenue* v. *Wilson*, 1928 S.C. (H.L.) 42. (The rule of natural custodier was the ground of decision in *Forrest* and *Smith*, but the other two cases involved deeds by a father in favour of a child and retention of the deeds by the father, and in all cases there was an effective gift *inter vivos*).

[82] Clive, *op. cit.*, 303.

that the rule of natural custodier is not of universal application since there are several special destination cases[83] which would have been decided differently if the rule had been regarded as applicable but on the special facts of the cases cited it appears to have been conceded that the destinations had only testamentary effect.[84]

9–25   **(iii) Is the rule still applicable?** It is suggested by Clive[85] that in the changed social situation of today there is now no *rule* that the husband is the natural custodier of his wife's deeds, that in certain circumstances a wife might equally be regarded as the natural custodier of her husband's deeds and that everything depends on the facts of the particular case. That statement may be accepted as broadly correct, but with minor qualifications. The rule was frequently applied in pre-1900 decisions but is scarcely referred to in subsequent cases, the decisions being based on the facts of the particular case. Nevertheless the rule that the husband is natural custodier has not been declared obsolete and it is still true that in most families the husband administers the family investments and keeps the documents of title to them in his own custody.[86] The law now appears to be that the facts indicative of intention are of great importance, but if a man has provided from his own funds property placed by him in the names of his wife or children and has retained custody of the relevant documents of title, the principle embodied in the rule may still apply, not because the husband is to the same extent as formerly deemed in law to be the natural custodier of deeds in favour of his wife, but because the facts in the particular case establish that he was in that position.

9–26   **(iv) Conclusions.** It is submitted that the law as it now stands may be summarised thus: If (i) a man has granted a deed which makes provision for, or has taken the title to property in the names of, his wife or children, (ii) the funds required to implement the provision or to acquire the property will be or have been provided wholly by the husband or father, not under any obligation but gratuitously, and (iii) the deed or documents of title to the property have been retained in custody of the husband or father, then (a) if there are circumstances which indicate an intention on his part to make an immediate gift the deed or documents will be effective as a completed gift *inter vivos* without delivery but (b) if there is insufficient evidence of such an intention but there has been no

---

[83] *Walker's Exr.* v. *Walker* (1878) 5 R. 965; *Perrett's Trs.* v. *Perrett*, 1909 S.C. 522; *Dennis* v. *Aitchison*, 1923 S.C. 819, affd. 1924 S.C. (H.L.) 122.

[84] All those cases involved securities provided from the husband's own resources taken in the names of the spouses with a destination to the survivor. The husband retained possession of the certificates and there were no additional facts indicative of an intention by the husband to make a completed gift *inter vivos*.

[85] *Op. cit.*, 303.

[86] It is a common experience of solicitors, where the estate of a deceased husband is being administered, to find in his repositories certificates for securities in joint names of the spouses or in the name of his wife alone; when the estate is that of a deceased wife the converse of that situation is comparatively rare.

revocation of the gift, expressly or impliedly, by the husband or father during his lifetime and no diligence of creditors affecting the subject of the deed or documents has occurred, the deed or documents, although undelivered will constitute an effective testamentary bequest upon his death.[87]

---

[87] On the subject of delivery of deeds generally, see W. W. McBryde, "Delivery of Deeds," 1981 J.L.S. 132, 181.

CHAPTER 10

TRANSMISSION AND DISCHARGE OF MOVEABLE RIGHTS
AND OBLIGATIONS

I. TRANSMISSION

323

I. TRANSMISSION

Death

10–01   On the death of a person the beneficial right to his corporeal and incorporeal moveable property passes to the persons entitled to succeed to it under the law of intestate succession or in terms of testamentary writings of the deceased or by virtue of destinations in the documents of title to particular items of property.[1] The administrative title to the whole property of the deceased vests in his executor[2] who has the duty of ingathering, administering and disposing of it according to law. The formal title of an executor is Confirmation, either a testament-dative (intestate succession) or a testament-testamentar (testate succession), which is the judicial ratification of the appointment of the executor and constitutes his title to deal with the estate of the deceased. The law of intestate and testate succession, the procedure for appointment of an executor and his rights and duties with regard to the administration of the estate, both moveable and heritable, of the deceased are dealt with in the later volume of this work relating to succession.

Judicial Transmission

(a) Bankruptcy

10–02   Upon sequestration the act and warrant of confirmation in favour of the trustee vests in him for behoof of the creditors absolutely and irredeemably as at the date of the sequestration, "the moveable estate and effects of the bankrupt, wherever situated, so far as attachable for debt, or capable of voluntary alienation by the bankrupt, to the same effect as if actual delivery or possession had been obtained, or intimation made at that date, subject always to such preferable securities as existed at the date of the sequestration and are not null or reducible."[3] The effect of this provision is to complete the title of the trustee to the corporeal moveable property of the bankrupt and to incorporeal rights of the bankrupt the transfer whereof would require assignation and intimation

---

[1] Destinations in title documents are not strictly testamentary writings: *Murray's Exrs.* v. *Geekie*, 1929 S.C. 633.
[2] Succession (Scotland) Act 1964, s. 14.
[3] Bankruptcy (Scotland) Act 1913, s. 97(1).

to the debtor in the obligation. If, however, an incorporeal moveable right requires some form of registration for completion of title the effect of the act and warrant is simply an assignation of the right, and registration by the trustee is apparently necessary to complete his title.[4]

4–03 Exceptions from and limitations of trustee's right
(i) Trust Property. Since it is only the property of the bankrupt in the sense of beneficial ownership which passes to the trustee, property held by the bankrupt on trust, whether on a title expressly fiduciary or *ex facie* absolute but truly in trust, is not transferred to the trustee.[5] Cases of property held in trust must be distinguished from cases where the right of beneficial ownership is in the bankrupt but where he is under a personal obligation with regard to it, such as an agreement to sell; in the latter case the ownership of the property passes to the trustee and the person in right of the obligation may only rank in damages for its breach.[6]

4–04 *(ii) Preferable securities.* In terms of section 97(1) of the 1913 Act the moveable property of the bankrupt vests in his trustee subject to such preferable securities over it as exist at the date of sequestration and are not null or reducible. A security over property the transfer of which requires some form of registration for completion of title, even although the creditor has not registered his title to the security at the date of sequestration, may be preferable to the right of the trustee provided that the creditor effects such registration before the trustee registers his title to the burdened property under his act and warrant.[7]

4–05 *(iii) Tantum et tale.* The general rule is that a trustee in bankruptcy takes property *tantum et tale* as it stood in the person of the bankrupt, with the result that the right of the trustee is limited by equitable considerations pleadable against the bankrupt. So property acquired fraudulently by the bankrupt must be restored by the trustee,[8] but unless there has been fraud the trustee is not bound to implement an agreement which the bankrupt was under an obligation of honour to fulfil.[9] Where the bankrupt as factor or agent has immixed moneys of his principals with his own funds, the amounts belonging to his principals, if identifiable, do not pass to the trustee,[10] but to that rule there is an

---

[4] *Morrison* v. *Harrison* (1876) 3 R. 406. The decision related to registration of shares in a company's register, but the principle applies to other transfers where registration is required for completion of title, *e.g.* transfers of ships or mortgages upon ships (Merchant Shipping Act 1894, ss. 27, 38), or patents (Patents Act 1977, s. 33).

[5] *Dingwall* v. *McCombie* (1822) 1 S. 463; *Gordon* v. *Cheyne* (1824) 2 S. 675; *Heritable Reversionary Co.* v. *Millar* (1892) 19 R. (H.L.) 43.

[6] *Wylie* v. *Duncan* (1803) Mor. 10269; *Bank of Scotland* v. *Liquidators of Hutchison Main & Co. Ltd.*, 1914 S.C. (H.L.) 1.

[7] Goudy, 254.

[8] *Fleeming* v. *Howden* (1868) 6 M. (H.L.) 113; *Molleson* v. *Challis* (1873) 11 M. 510; *Colquhouns' Tr.* v. *Campbell's Trs.* (1902) 4 F. 739. See also *A. W. Gamage Ltd.* v. *Charlesworth's Tr.*, 1910 S.C. 257.

[9] *Clyde Marine Insurance Co.* v. *Renwick & Co.*, 1924 S.C. 113.

[10] *Macadam* v. *Martin's Tr.* (1872) 11 M. 33; *Smith* v. *Liquidator of James Birrell Ltd.*, 1968 S.L.T. 174.

exception in the case of moneys belonging to the wife of the bankrupt which she has lent to her husband or permitted to be immixed with his funds when the wife has only a claim in the sequestration postponed to the claims of other creditors.[11]

10–06 *(iv) Property not attachable for debt or capable of voluntary alienation.* Such property is excluded from vesting in the trustee in terms of section 97(1) of the 1913 Act, *e.g.* tools of trade which are not attachable for debt,[12] or alimentary rights although on application to the court by the trustee these may be restricted to a suitable aliment for the bankrupt.[13]

10–07 *(v) Copyright.* Rights of copyright vest in the trustee subject to payment of royalties or a share of profits to the author which would have been payable by the bankrupt.[14]

10–08 **Completion of trustee's title**
Registrable rights. In the case of rights which require registration of a transfer or document of assignation in order to complete title there may be a race for registration between the trustee and a third party having an absolute transfer or assignation of, or a grant of a security over them.[15] It is the duty of the trustee to complete his title to such rights as speedily as is practicable. Title to a heritable security registrable in the Register of Sasines may be completed by the trustee expeding and recording a notice of title using the act and warrant as a link or, where the bankrupt's title to the security has been registered in the Land Register, by production to the Keeper of the charge certificate and the trustee's act and warrant. The title of the trustee to shares or stock of an incorporated company may be completed by exhibition of the act and warrant to the registrars of the company and he may then be registered as a member,[16] although if the shares or stock are of English companies, or of Scottish companies which do not recognise trusts, the trustee will be registered in his individual name. That may be inadvisable if there is uncalled liability upon the shares in which case the trustee may realise them without becoming a member of the company.[17] The title of the trustee to shares in a ship may be completed by lodging with the appropriate registrar of ships a declaration of transmission identifying the ship and containing the statements required in a declaration of transfer accompanied by production of his act and warrant.[18] The title of the

---

[11] Married Women's Property (Scotland) Act 1881, s. 1(4).
[12] *Pennell* v. *Elgin*, 1926 S.C. 9.
[13] 1913 Act, s. 98(2).
[14] *Ibid.*, s. 102.
[15] See para. 10–02. This is the traditional view of the legal position but there can be an argument that the delivered deed has divested the bankrupt of beneficial ownership so that the right does not fall within the assets taken by the trustee—see I. Doran, "Ownership on Delivery," 1985 S.L.T. 165 and other articles there cited.
[16] Companies Act 1985, s. 183(2).
[17] Gower, *Modern Company Law*, 413.
[18] Merchant Shipping Act 1894, s. 27(1).

trustee to a mortgage over a ship or over a share therein is completed by lodging with the appropriate registrar of ships a declaration by the trustee in the form stipulated accompanied by his act and warrant.[19] The title of the trustee to a patent may be registered under section 33 of the Patents Act 1977 by notice to the Comptroller of the Patent Office accompanied by a certified copy of the act and warrant (Patents Rules 1978 (S.I. 1978 No. 216), para. 46 and Form No. 21/77).

10–09 *Assets to which a transfer of title is normally completed by intimation.* Since the act and warrant in terms of section 97(1) of the 1913 Act completes the title of the trustee to such assets as if intimation thereof had been made at the date of the sequestration it is unnecessary for the trustee to intimate his appointment in order to obtain a completed title. In practice, however, it is advisable for the trustee to intimate his appointment to the debtor in the obligation in order to inform him of the trustee's right and to ensure that communications relating to the asset are addressed to him.

(b) Judicial factory

10–10 Where a judicial factor is appointed by the court there is a clear distinction as regards property between the situation where there is an existing person or ward, as in the case of a factor *loco tutoris* or a *curator bonis* to a minor or *incapax*, and that where there is no existing *dominus* of the property, as in the case of a judicial factor appointed on a trust estate. In the former case the appointment of the factor does not strictly involve a transmission of the property of the ward to the factor whose function is only to administer and manage the property of the ward, whereas in the latter case the trust estate vests in the factor, and there is a judicial transmission of the property.[20]

10–11 **Recognition of factor's rights of administration or completion of factor's title.** The procedures with regard to recognition of the factor's administrative rights and powers (where there is an existing ward) or completion of the factor's title (where there is no existing owner other than the factor) in respect of stocks or shares of Scottish or English companies or Government securities are fully treated in Walker, *Judicial Factors,* pages 85–88.

As regards other incorporeal moveable rights such as shares in or mortgages over ships, or patents, the factor's title (where there is no existing owner) may be completed by the respective procedures already described in relation to a trustee in bankruptcy[21] *mutatis mutandis.* If there is an existing ward the relevant registrar should be consulted as to

---

[19] *Ibid.*, s. 38.
[20] Walker, *Judicial Factors,* 83–85: *Inland Revenue* v. *McMillan's C.B.*, 1956 S.C. 142.
[21] Para. 10–08.

the recognition of the factor's rights of administration of and dealing with the property of the ward.

Transmission by Statute

10–12 Rights of shareholders in companies or bodies engaged in industries which are nationalised may be compulsorily acquired by the Government or a government agency. In general such rights and relevant obligations are transferred simply by express provision of statute, subject to payment of compensation, and deeds of transfer are not required.[22]

II. DISCHARGE AND EXTINCTION

Discharges

10–13 An obligation for payment of money, with or without security, is effectively discharged by payment of the amount due evidenced by a receipt, since any grant of security is ancillary to the personal obligation secured and is extinguished when the obligation is implemented.[23] A formal discharge is required when security has been given and the creditor's title to the security subject has been completed by intimation or registration, so that some form of retrocession or registration is necessary to reinstate the debtor in the right to the security subject or to establish that it is no longer burdened by the security. The present chapter deals only with discharges of personal bonds and of securities over moveable property of the kinds whose constitution has been considered in Chapter 7 *supra*: discharges of heritable securities or of trustees upon trust estates and more complex documents of discharge involved in dissolution of partnership, etc., are more conveniently treated in the chapters relating to the relevant subject-matter.

Construction of Discharges

(a) Specific discharge

10–14   A discharge of specified debts or obligations will discharge those but will not, in the absence of words of general discharge, extinguish by implication any other debts or obligations due by the grantee to the granter, even if of a similar kind or arising from the same transaction.[24] Where words of general discharge are added to a discharge of specified

---

[22] See, for examples, Electricity Act 1947, ss. 14, 20; Iron and Steel Act 1967, s. 9; Aircraft and Shipbuilding Industries Act 1977, s. 19.
[23] *Cameron* v. *Williamson* (1895) 22 R. 293, 298.
[24] *Marquis of Tweeddale* v. *Hume* (1848) 10 D. 1053; *Galashiels Provident Building Society* v. *Newlands* (1893) 20 R. 821.

debts or obligations, the general words will be construed as applicable only to debts or obligations of the same nature as those specified.[25]

(b) General discharge

10–15 A general discharge includes all debts of which at its date the granter could demand payment[26] but the court will endeavour to ascertain what was in contemplation of the parties when the discharge was granted. So it may cover debts not yet due[27] or contingent debts,[28] but on the other hand will not cover claims of an extraordinary kind which were not in the contemplation of the parties.[29] For example, it does not cover (i) a claim by a cautioner for relief against the principal debtor when the cautioner had not been required to make payment at the time when he granted the discharge,[30] (ii) liability not yet incurred under a clause of warrandice, (iii) a claim of which the granter of the discharge was unaware,[31] (iv) claims which the granter cannot be assumed to have contemplated[32] and (v) claims which the granter of the discharge had already assigned although the assignation had not been intimated to the debtor.[33] The granter of a discharge cannot plead ignorance of a right or claim of which, after consultation and legal advice, he should have had knowledge.[34]

Form of Discharge

10–16 The general rule is that a discharge should be made and executed in the same way as the obligation which it discharges was constituted—*unumquodque eodem modo dissolvitur quo colligatur*.[35] Accordingly when an obligation has been constituted in writing[36] or is vouched by a document of debt,[37] its discharge may be proved only by the writ or oath of the creditor.[38] As to exceptions to the rule, see Walker and Walker, *Evidence*, at pages 125–128. When a specific debt has been constituted by probative or holograph writing the rule does not go so far as to require that its discharge likewise must be probative or holograph; a receipt signed by or on behalf of the creditor, although neither attested nor holograph, is sufficient evidence of discharge so long as the validity of

[25] Bell, *Prin.*, s. 583; *Talbot* v. *Gudyet* (1705) Mor. 5027; Menzies, *Lectures*, 314, 315.
[26] Bell, *Prin.*, s. 584.
[27] *Adam* v. *Macdougall* (1831) 9 S. 570.
[28] *British Linen Co.* v. *Esplin* (1849) 11 D. 1104.
[29] Bell, *Prin.*, s. 584.
[30] *McTaggart* v. *Jeffrey* (1830) 4 W. & S. 361.
[31] *Greenock Banking Co.* v. *Smith* (1844) 6 D. 1340: *Purdon* v. *Rowat's Trs.* (1856) 19 D. 206.
[32] *Armour* v. *Glasgow Royal Infirmary*, 1909 S.C. 916; *Dickson's Trs.* v. *Dickson's Trs.*, 1930 S.L.T. 226.
[33] *Lady Logan* v. *Affleck* (1736) Mor. 5041.
[34] *Kippen* v. *Kippen's Trs.* (1874) 1 R. 1171.
[35] Walker and Walker, *Evidence*, 124, 125; *Nicol's Trs.* v. *Sutherland*, 1951 S.C. (H.L.) 21, 26, 29.
[36] *Keanie* v. *Keanie*, 1940 S.C. 549; *Nicol's Trs.* v. *Sutherland, supra.*
[37] Gloag, *Contract*, 715; *Thiem's Trs.* v. *Collie* (1899) 1 F. 764, 774, 778, 780.
[38] *McLaren* v. *Howie* (1869) 8 M. 106, 111.

the signature of the receipt is not open to challenge.[38] In general a discharge, however, should be granted in probative form.

Styles of Discharge

Personal bond—endorsed receipt

10–17   (*Place, date*) Received from the within named B the sum of £   within mentioned and all interest due thereon.

Formal discharge—personal bond—separate

10–18   I, A (*designed*) in consideration of the sum of £   paid to me by B (*designed*) hereby discharge a Bond dated   for the sum of £   granted by the said B in my favour and all interest due thereon: And I warrant this discharge at all hands. (*To be attested*)

Formal discharge—personal bond—endorsed

10–19   I, A within designed in consideration of the sum of £   paid to me by B also within designed hereby discharge the foregoing Bond and all interest due thereon: And I warrant this discharge at all hands. (*To be attested*)

Formal discharge—personal bond—assignee or executor of creditor

10–20   I, C (*designed*) in consideration of the sum of £   paid to me by B (*designed*) hereby discharge a Bond dated   for the sum of £   granted by the said B in favour of A (*designed*): To which Bond I acquired right by (*specify the assignation, confirmation or other link whereby the granter acquired right*): (*Clause of warrandice which in the case of an executor will be from fact and deed only but binding the executry estate absolutely*). (*To be attested*)

Partial repayment—personal bond—endorsed receipt

10–21   (*Place, date*) Received from the within named B the sum of £   to account of the within mentioned sum of £   . Balance of principal remaining due £

Discharge and Retrocession

10–22   Where a personal bond has been granted with security in a form which required intimation to the debtor in the security in order to complete the creditor's title, the security subject must be reassigned or retrocessed upon repayment. The retrocession should follow as nearly as may be the wording of the original assignation, and should be intimated to the debtor in the security. Likewise, where a security has been granted in a form which requires registration to complete the creditor's title, a retransfer or assignation is necessary which may be registered to reinvest the debtor in the security subject, *e.g.* a transfer of stocks or shares of companies, a re-assignment of a share in a ship where there has been an

---

[38] *McLaren* v. *Howie* (1869) 8 M.106, 111.

ex facie absolute assignation or a discharge of a mortgage over a share in a ship.

Discharge and retrocession—bond and assignation in security—life policy

-23   I, A (*designed*) in consideration of the sum of £   paid to me by B (*designed*) hereby discharge a Bond and Assignation in Security dated   for the sum of £   granted by the said B in my favour and all interest due thereon: And I retrocess to the said B the Policy of Assurance granted by the   Assurance Company of (*chief office*) in favour of the said B on his own life for the sum of £   [with profits] numbered   and dated   , together with all bonus and other additions and benefits accrued or that may accrue thereon: And I warrant the foregoing discharge at all hands and the foregoing retrocession from my own facts and deeds only. (*To be attested*)

Discharge and retrocession—bond and assignation in security—life policy—executor of creditor

-24   I, A (*designed*), executor-nominate of the deceased B (*designed*) conform to Confirmation by the Sheriff of   in my favour dated at   on   in consideration of the sum of £   paid to me by C (*designed*) hereby discharge a Bond and Assignation in Security dated   granted by the said C in favour of the said B and all interest due thereon: And I as executor foresaid retrocess to the said C the Policy of Assurance granted by the   Assurance Company of (*chief office*) in favour of the said C on his own life for the sum of £   [with profits] numbered   and dated   together with all bonus and other additions and benefits accrued or that may accrue thereon: To which Bond and Assignation in Security I as executor foresaid acquired right by the said Confirmation: And I warrant the foregoing discharge from my own facts and deeds only and I bind the executry estate under my charge to warrant the said discharge at all hands, and I warrant the foregoing retrocession from my own facts and deeds only. (*To be attested*)

Discharge and retrocession—ex facie absolute assignation qualified by agreement—life policy

-25   I, A (*designed*) Whereas by Assignation dated   B (*designed*) assigned to me a Policy of Assurance granted by the   Assurance Company of (*chief office*) in favour of the said B on his own life for the sum of £   numbered   and dated   . And Whereas the said Assignation, although *ex facie* absolute, was truly granted in security of sums due by the said B to me as confirmed by Agreement between me and the said B dated   And Whereas all sums due to me by the said B have now been repaid and all other obligations incumbent on the said B in terms of the said Agreement have been duly implemented; Therefore I retrocess to the said B the said Policy of Assurance together with all bonus and other additions and benefits accrued or that may accrue thereon: And I warrant the foregoing retrocession from my own facts and deeds only. (*To be attested*)

Notice

10–26   Notice of the retrocessions in any of the forms in paragraphs 10–23, 10–24 or 10–25 should be given by the grantee to the assurance company in the form in paragraph 7–35 with the substitution of "retrocession" for "assignation".

Discharge and retrocession—bond and assignation in security—share of residue of trust estate

10–27   I, A (*designed*) in consideration of the sum of £   paid to me by B (*designed*) hereby discharge a Bond and Assignation in Security dated   for the sum of £   granted by the said B in my favour and all interest due thereon: And I retrocess to the said B his whole right, share and interest in the estate of the deceased C (*designed*) under Trust Disposition and Settlement of the said C dated   and registered in the Books of Council and Session on   all as described and assigned in the said Bond and Assignation in Security: And I warrant the foregoing discharge at all hands and the foregoing retrocession from my own facts and deeds only. (*To be attested*)

Discharge and retrocession—ex facie absolute assignation qualified by agreement—share of residue of trust estate

10–28   The deed should follow the same form *mutatis mutandis* as in paragraph 10–25, substituting a retrocession of the right, share and interest in the trust estate for that of the life policy.

Intimation

10–29   Intimation of the retrocession of a reversionary interest in the trust estate in styles in paragraphs 10–27 or 10–28 should be given by the grantee to the trustees of the estate—for method of intimation see paragraph 7–75.

Extinction of Rights and Obligations otherwise than by Discharge

10–30   Rights and obligations may be extinguished by the operation of rules of law without express discharge. The more important circumstances in which these rules apply are compensation, novation, delegation, *confusio*, prescription and *mora*. These rules are not strictly within the compass of a work on conveyancing and are touched upon only incidentally in circumstances to which they may be applicable. For a concise account of them, reference may be made to Walker, *Principles*, Volume II, Chapter 4.10.

PARTNERSHIP

Nature and Incidents of Partnership

–01   Documents relating to partnerships must be framed with knowledge of the nature of the partnership relation and the rights and duties which the law implies or presumes in the absence of express agreement to a different effect. The Partnership Act 1890, although not a complete code of the law of partnership, lays down in succinct form the main principles of the law: for a further account reference may be made to the undernoted texts.[1]

A. FORMATION OF PARTNERSHIP

Policy

–02   When several persons co-operate in the commencement of a business the first question is the selection of the most suitable legal vehicle for the attainment of the objects contemplated. In most situations the choice lies between a partnership, a limited company or a limited partnership. Any business involving a trade, occupation or profession pursued by several persons with a view to profit may be carried on in partnership,[2] but a partnership may not always be the most appropriate vehicle. In the case of a trading business which requires the provision of premises, equipment or stock, much depends upon the scale of the operation. Where the initial capital required is being provided wholly or substantially by the participators, a partnership may be appropriate so that the commercial viability of the business may be established without the expense and administrative procedures required for a limited company; if the business prospers and a satisfactory track record of success has been created the partnership may be converted into a limited company, when finance from outside sources may be obtained for further expansion and the protection of limited liability may be of value in view of the

---

[1] J.B. Miller, *Partnership*; *Lindley on Partnership* (14th ed.).
[2] Partnership Act 1890, ss. 1, 45.

increased potential liabilities resulting from growth. In the case of professions, where the requirement of initial capital is relatively small and the major potential liability is in respect of professional negligence, which is an insurable risk, a partnership is usual. A limited partnership created under the terms of the Limited Partnership Act 1907 is suitable where the business is to be conducted, and liability for its obligations is to be assumed, by one or more general partners, and one or more limited partners contribute capital and have no liability for the debts or obligations of the firm beyond the amount so contributed.

Taxation

11–03   When a partnership is commenced, and indeed throughout its existence when any significant changes are being made, financial advice should be sought with regard to the tax implications of what is proposed. A firm and its partners and their dependants may be affected by income tax and capital allowances, capital gains tax, capital transfer tax, value added tax and stamp duty. In principle policy decisions are taken for commercial reasons but considerations of potential tax liabilities may influence the method to be adopted or may even raise a question as to the advisability of the proposals.

Partnership agreement

11–04   Partnership is a consensual contract normally constituted in probative writing although it may be created by less formal writing or orally and proved *prout de jure* or inferred from facts and circumstances.[3] Where heritable property is involved the contract should always be in probative form.

Partners

11–05   There must be at least two partners (the term "sole partner" is a misnomer[4]) associated in the conduct of a business with a view to profit.[5] The number of partners may not exceed 20, save in the case of firms of solicitors, accountants or stockbrokers,[6] and the Secretary of State may provide by regulations for partnerships of other descriptions being exempted from the restriction.[7] Barristers or advocates may not practise in partnership for reasons of professional etiquette. Since the relation of partnership is contractual the rules of law as to capacity of the persons

---

[3] Bell, *Prin.*, s. 361; Gloag, *Contract*, 191; Walker and Walker, *Evidence*, s. 147.
[4] *Wallace* v. *Wallace's Trs.* (1906) 8 F.558.
[5] 1890 Act, s. 1(1).
[6] Companies Act 1985, s. 716(1) and (2).
[7] Companies Act 1985, s. 716(3); for details of other kinds of partnership so exempt see Lindley, *op. cit.*, 67, 68.

contracting are applicable,[8] but companies if empowered by their constitution, firms and bodies of trustees may become partners.

Firm name and nature of business

1–06   The name of the firm should be stated in the contract of partnership. If it is a descriptive name registration of the firm name is no longer required since the Registration of Business Names Act 1916 has now been repealed,[9] but the provisions of section 4 of the Business Names Act 1985 with regard to the disclosure of the names of the partners in business letters and other documents issued by the firm must be observed. The nature of the firm's business should also be stated: it may be relevant with regard to the implied agency of a partner in transactions with third parties.

Place of business

1–07   It is customary to state the principal place of business in the contract of partnership usually with the addition of "and/or such other place or places as the partners shall from time to time agree" or similar wording.

Endurance

1–08   The period of endurance of a partnership may be specified, usually with a provision that it will continue thereafter subject to the right of any partner to terminate the partnership by written notice of stated length on or after the expiry of the specified period. Alternatively, the period may be left flexible with provision that it will terminate on written notice of specified length. Even if the partnership is created only for a specific period without any provision as to continuance thereafter, it will be deemed to continue after the expiry of that period and the rights and duties of the partners remain the same so far as consistent with the incidents of a partnership at will.[10] The drafting of the clause specifying the period of the partnership requires care. In particular (1) a provision that the contract will endure for a stated period and will continue *thereafter* until terminated by notice will not entitle a partner to give notice to terminate as at the expiry of the stated period,[11] (2) phrases which provide for termination by mutual consent, *e.g.* "the partnership will continue for 3 years and thereafter until terminated by mutual consent," bind the parties to continue in partnership until *all* the partners agree to dissolution or until one of them dies.[12] When the stated period of endurance of the partnership expires and there is no contractual provision for

---

[8] Enemy aliens and pupils cannot become partners; as to minors, insane persons, bankrupts, married women, corporations and firms see J.B. Miller, *Partnership*, Chap. II.
[9] Companies Act 1981, s. 119(5) and Sched. 4.
[10] 1890 Act, s. 27(1).
[11] *Marshall* v. *Brinsmead* (1912) 106 L.T. 460.
[12] *Moss* v. *Elphick* [1910] 1 K.B. 846.

its continuance thereafter it is always desirable, if the partners wish to continue, to have a written extension of the contract for a further period. If the partnership is allowed to continue as a partnership at will it must be kept in view that not all of the terms of the original contract will be consistent with a partnership at will.[13]

Capital

11–09 The initial capital of the partnership and the respective shares of each partner therein should be stated: if no such statement is made the presumption is that the capital is shared equally by the partners.[14] (i) Where a new business is being commenced and the capital is provided by the partners in cash the total capital and the respective amounts contributed by each partner should be stated. (ii) If a new partnership is created by the assumption of a new partner or partners the capital of the former partnership and the shares of the "old" partners therein may be adopted, without revaluation, as the contributions of the "old" partners to the capital of the new firm and the share of capital of a new partner will be the amount of any cash contribution made by him. If the assets of the former partnership are to be revalued, however, the incidence of capital gains tax, subject to roll-over relief, has to be considered. A decision on election for continuance under section 154(2) of the Income and Corporation Taxes Act 1970 and its effect on the tax liabilities of the old and new partners and upon capital allowances and losses also requires consideration and consultation with financial advisers.[15] (iii) If the contribution to capital by any of the partners consists of heritable property it is advisable that it should be conveyed to the partners as trustees for the firm. Since a partnership, although it has a separate legal personality distinct from the partners as individuals, cannot sustain the feudal relationship, the title to heritage is taken in the names of the partners as trustees; upon subsequent changes in ownership, as by the retirement or assumption of partners, the title to the property devolves in accordance with the law of trusts under section 20(2) of the 1890 Act but rights of beneficial ownership will be regulated by the partnership agreement as altered by the subsequent documents effecting the changes. Alternatively the partner may retain ownership of the property in which case there should be a lease of it to the partnership and the contribution of the partner concerned to the capital of the firm is restricted appropriately. (iv) In a trading partnership which is formed to exploit patents or inventions belonging to one of the partners the contract should specify whether these are to be property of the partnership or are to remain in the ownership of the particular partner with right to

---

[13] As to the kind of provisions which may and may not be so consistent see J.B. Miller, *Partnership*, 437, 438.
[14] Partnership Act 1890, s. 24(1).
[15] Lindley, *op. cit.*, 881, 882, 892 *et seq.*

the firm to use them, so that in the event of dissolution it will be clear to whom they belong.

–10 Drawings from capital. If the initial capital of a firm is little more than adequate to provide the fixed and working capital necessary for the conduct of its business, it will seldom be in the interests of the partnership to permit a major drawing from capital by any of the partners, save in special circumstances, and there may in future be a requirement for the contribution of further capital. It will usually be suitable to provide for the contribution of additional capital or withdrawal of capital as may be agreed by the partners from time to time on the broad principle that the capital shall be maintained at such amount as will be sufficient for the conduct of the business.

–11 Interest on capital. Provision should be made for interest on the share at credit of the capital account of each partner at a rate to be determined by the partners from time to time. The 1890 Act provides that a partner is not entitled, before the ascertainment of profits, to interest on the capital subscribed by him.[16] That provision leaves uncertain (i) whether the interest is not payable before or does not commence to run until the ascertainment of profits and (ii) the date as at which the profits are ascertained, *e.g.*, at the conclusion of the financial year or upon completion of the audited accounts. In a firm where interest is to be payable on capital, provision should be made for the interest being calculated on the amount at credit of the capital account of each partner at periods to be agreed by the partners from time to time. For example, where the sums at credit of the capital accounts of the different partners fluctuate significantly during each year the arrangement agreed by the partners might be that interest would be based on the sum at credit of each partner's capital account at the end of each calendar month for the month succeeding and that the total of the monthly sums of interest should be calculated and credited to each partner at the close of the firm's financial year. The rate so determined may be approximately that available from Government securities, so that there is little incentive for a partner to seek to withdraw capital for personal investment. Interest on a partner's share of capital in the firm is treated as earned income for income tax purposes, although this is of less importance than formerly since the abolition of earned income relief and investment income surcharge. Interest on capital will be payable before divisible profits are ascertained: interest on special advances by any partner should be at a rate to be agreed when the advances are made and should be payable before interest on capital.[17] It is not usual or necessary to provide for the making of special advances in the contract of partnership; it can be regulated by *ad hoc* agreement if the need arises.

---

[16] s. 24(4).
[17] If no rate of interest on advances is stipulated, 5 per cent will be payable: 1890 Act, s. 24(3).

Shares of profit

11–12   Subject to agreement express or implied the profits of the partnership business are shared equally among the partners who are liable to contribute equally to any losses.[18] In a properly drawn contract of partnership the respective shares of profit and liability for loss should be specified in order to avoid questions as to unequal sharing which may be implied from actings or other circumstances.[19] If any partners are remunerated wholly or partly by way of salary, it should be debited as a first charge on profits and the remainder of profits divided in the stipulated proportions. It is sometimes provided that the remuneration may be varied by agreement among the partners but that is unnecessary; it will always be open to make such variation by subsequent agreement. In certain cases the share of profits of a partner may be made subject to a guaranteed minimum figure. In such a case it should be made clear whether a deficiency in one year may be set off against a surplus in another year.

Liability for loss

11–13   It should be kept in view that, although the capital contributions of the partners are in different proportions from those in which they share profits, any losses which have to be met from capital will be contributed in proportion to the respective shares of profit and not in proportion to the respective amounts of capital.[20] The application of this rule may raise difficult questions where there are salaried partners and the contract should make express provision on the matter.

Drawings to account of profits

11–14   The rights of partners to make drawings in anticipation of profits should be regulated by the contract of partnership. The provision may take the form of specifying the amounts of and the periods at which drawings may be made or may be flexible by stipulating that the amount of drawings will be determined by agreement of the partners from time to time so that a decision can be made in consideration of the financial position of the business and the needs of the particular partner. Specific provision may be included for repayment of overdrawings at the end of the financial year of the business.

Provision of capital from profits

11–15   Where a partner is unable to contribute his share of capital initially, provision may be made for a proportion of his share of profits, or an amount of his profits in excess of a stated annual figure, being left in the business towards making up his contribution to capital. In such

---

[18] 1890 Act, s. 24(1).
[19] See J.B. Miller, *op. cit.*, 400–404: Lindley, *op. cit.*, 469 *et seq.*
[20] For illustrations of the application of this rule see Lindley, *op. cit.* 651, 652 and authorities cited.

circumstances consideration should be given as to the liability of the partner concerned to contribute to losses which may require to be met from capital.

Books and accounts

-16 The contract should provide for the keeping of books and accounts of the business of the partnership, to be balanced at a fixed date in each year and audited by professional accountants. The audited accounts will be signed and docquetted by the partners within a stated period after completion. If the accuracy of the accounts is challenged by any partner he should be required within that period to submit stated objections in writing; if these cannot be agreed amongst the partners there should be provision for determination of the question by arbitration. If a partner neither signs nor objects in writing within the stated period, he will be held to have accepted the accounts. A qualification may be inserted to the effect that the accounts and balance sheet may be opened upon the ground of palpable or manifest error such as a patent *error calculi*.[21] A provision as to the accounts and balance sheet being conclusive, however stringently framed, will not be binding if there has been dishonesty or fraudulent concealment of material facts.[22] It is not usual, and seldom desirable, for assets to be re-valued on the occasion of each annual balance and normally it is stipulated that no value is placed upon goodwill; the revaluation of assets or goodwill may be provided for upon dissolution but not in the annual accounts.

Custody of books

-17 The contract may provide expressly that the books of the partnership shall be kept at the premises, or one of several premises, where the business of the partnership is carried on, but that is not usually necessary.[23] In the absence of specific provision any partner is entitled to access to the books of the business and the firm's place of business, or its principal place of business, is obviously most convenient for that purpose. If any one or more of the partners are to have custody of the firm's books upon dissolution, appropriate provision should be made in the contract.[24]

Banking arrangements

-18 The contract may provide that the firm's bank account may be kept with a named bank or such other bank as the partners may from time to time agree. The arrangements as to signature of cheques drawn on the firm's account may vary but the normal provision is that cheques may be signed by any partner but only in relation to the proper business of the

---

[21] *Law* v. *Liddell's Trs.* (1862) 24 D. 577, 584, 585; *Ex p. Barber* (1870) L.R. 5 Ch. App. 687.
[22] *Blisset* v. *Daniel* (1853) 10 Hare 493.
[23] 1890 Act, s. 24(9).
[24] *Blair* v. *Hunters* (1888) 15 R. 1094.

firm. Cheques to account of shares of profit or for withdrawal of capital may require signature by more than one partner or by a specified partner. It is advisable for the banking arrangements to be set out in the contract: if that is not done an agreement on the matter would, unless specially provided otherwise, be determined by a majority of the partners.[25]

Powers and duties of partners

11–19   **(a) Time and attention to business.** Where all partners are engaged exclusively in the work of the firm the contract should stipulate that all the partners should devote their whole time and attention to its business. If any of the partners is not to be so obliged an appropriate provision would be that he should devote such time to the affairs of the business as may be necessary to discharge such duties as are allotted to him or alternatively, depending on circumstances, only such time and attention as he shall consider proper. It will seldom be practicable to specify his obligations with more precision in the original contract: the time devoted to the business of the partnership may change in relation to the requirements of the firm or of the other business activities in which he may be engaged and his contribution to the firm can be assessed and, in the case of a relatively short period of endurance of the partnership, reflected in his share of profits on a subsequent renewal of the partnership.

11–20   **(b) Personal appointments.** It may frequently happen that individual partners, particularly when they are professionally qualified, hold or may be offered personal appointments which are outwith the ordinary business of the partnership. In order to promote and preserve harmonious relationship amongst partners it is suggested that, save in exceptional circumstances, (i) the remuneration received in respect of such offices should form part of the income of the firm rather than be retained by the individual partner and (ii) acceptance of any new appointment should require the approval of all, or a majority of, the partners.

11–21   **(c) Prohibited acts.** It is advisable to prohibit expressly in the contract of partnership acts which may be harmful or costly to the partnership or damaging to its reputation. The acts specified will vary to some extent with the nature of the business. The list in clause 10 of the style in paragraph 11–43 *infra* is not exhaustive but indicates some of the more important acts which may be prohibited except with the written consent of the other partners. There may also be certain acts which are prohibited in the circumstances of a particular firm, *e.g.*, engaging in any other business or occupation (full-time partner) or engaging or

---

[25] 1890 Act, s. 24(8).

dismissing employees, or selling or disposing of property of the firm except in the ordinary course of business.

–22 **(d) Decision-making powers.** In terms of the 1890 Act any difference arising as to ordinary matters connected with the business of the partnership may be decided by a majority of the partners,[26] but (i) a change in the nature of the partnership business requires the consent of all partners,[26] (ii) no person may be introduced as a partner without the consent of all existing partners,[27] and (iii) a partner may not be expelled by a majority of partners unless power to do so has been conferred by express agreement of the partners.[28] These statutory rules may be varied by agreement.[29,30] Express variation is required where (i) a partner or partners wish to reserve the right to introduce a person, *e.g.* a relative, into the partnership, (ii) it is desired that voting shall not be on the basis of a simple majority, each partner having one vote, but weighted in relation to the respective shares of profit of the partners, or (iii) more detailed provisions are desired as to the circumstances in which and the conditions on which a partner may be expelled.[31] In certain partnerships the right to determine the policy of the firm, either on particular matters or generally, may be reserved to a senior partner or partners.

Pensions and life assurance

–23 In order to discharge or limit the obligations, contractual or moral, of the partners in the event of sickness, death or retirement of a partner a pension and life assurance scheme may be adopted by the partnership. An approved scheme is tax efficient since the premiums, subject to a restriction in any one year to $17\frac{1}{2}$ per cent of net relevant earnings, are deductible from partnership profits for income tax purposes.[32] It will seldom be practicable to have a pension and life assurance scheme approved before the contract of partnership is signed so that the contract will include only an obligation to participate in a scheme approved by the partners.

Incapacity of partner

–24 It is advisable to include in the contract specific provisions for dissolution of the partnership in the event of permanent incapacity of a partner, since a partner cannot be expelled unless a power to do so has been conferred by express agreement amongst the partners.[33] The

---

[26] s. 24(8).
[27] s. 24(7).
[28] s. 25.
[29] s. 24 (chapeau).
[30] For the interpretation of the statutory rules see J.B. Miller *op. cit.* 182–188.
[31] See para. 11–25.
[32] Income and Corporation Taxes Act 1970, s. 227 as amended by Finance Act 1980, s. 31.
[33] 1890 Act, s. 25.

relevant clause should include (a) a definition of permanent incapacity, (b) the right of the other partners to dissolve the partnership upon specified notice, (c) the devolution of the share and interest of the incapacitated partner in the firm upon the other partners and the payment or other consideration to be made to the incapacitated partner or his dependants, and (d) continuance of the partnership by the other partners.

Expulsion of partner

11–25   The contract should confer, on the occurrence of certain specified events affecting any partner, a right to the other partners to expel the partner concerned. It is suggested that in all partnerships the occurrence of any of the following events should, either automatically or on the expiry of a short period of written notice by the other partners, result in the partner concerned ceasing to be a partner: (i) notour bankruptcy or the granting of a trust deed for his creditors or entering into a composition or other arrangement for the benefit of his creditors generally, (ii) continued absence from business for a stated period, or (iii) becoming lunatic or insane. Other events which may entitle the other partners to expel the defaulting partner after a longer period of written notice should be considered, such as (i) in the case of a professional partnership, committing an act of professional misconduct, (ii) doing any of the acts prohibited by the contract (expressed as any of such acts or any of a serious nature or particular acts specified), (iii) gross neglect of the business of the partnership, (iv) acting so as to bring the name of the partnership into disrepute, or (v) acting contrary to good faith among the partners. It may be arguable whether the actings of the partner are within any of the above categories; that will be a question to be determined under the arbitration clause aftermentioned.

Retirement of partner

11–26   It is suggested that in most partnerships, and in particular in professional partnerships, the contract should provide for automatic retirement of a partner at the end of the firm's accounting year during which he has attained a stated age. It is also suggested that such a provision should be absolute. If any qualification is inserted, *e.g.* unless otherwise agreed, there could be awkward and embarrassing decisions if there was a division of opinion amongst the partners: in the absence of any qualification it would always be open to the partners, if all desired that the partner due to retire should continue, to agree to that course when the occasion arose, although in large professional partnerships the effect of creating a precedent would require to be carefully considered. Apart from compulsory retirement power may be conferred on a partner to retire voluntarily on attaining a specified age, and such a power is necessary if he is to be entitled to do so during the period stipulated for endurance of the partnership. In the event of retirement, whether compulsory or voluntary, it is necessary to define the terms on which, as between himself and the other partners, he does so.

Death of partner

–27   Subject to any agreement amongst the partners the death of any partner dissolves the partnership.[34] It will normally be desired that on the death of a partner the remaining partners will be entitled to acquire his share and interest in the business on terms defined in the contract.

Entitlement of outgoing partner

–28   Where the share of an outgoing partner is acquired in terms of the contract by the continuing partners in any of the situations envisaged in paragraphs 11–24 to 11–27 *supra*, the basis upon which payment is to be made to the outgoing partner or his representatives should be prescribed in the contract. The sum to be paid in respect of the share of the outgoing partner may be ascertained in different ways but most commonly it will be determined (a) by reference to profits, (b) on the basis of book value of assets, or (c) on the basis of revaluation of assets.

–29   **(a) Profits basis.** Determination of the sum to be paid by reference to profits of the business may be suitable where the principal asset of the business is goodwill, since that basis does not reflect the value as such of the business premises, stock and other assets. It is most appropriate in professional or other partnerships where the value of physical assets is relatively small. The sum may be a capital figure based upon a specified percentage of the profits of the firm as shown in the last completed accounting year immediately preceding the date of dissolution, or of the average of the profits in the last two or three years preceding that date, or a greater number of years' purchase of a lesser percentage of such profits. Alternatively the payment may take the form of a stated percentage of the profits of the firm for a specified period after dissolution, although this latter basis is less tax efficient for the outgoing partner since the payments will be assessable to income tax upon the recipient and has the further disadvantage of imposing difficulties upon the remaining partners in assuming new partners or otherwise altering the organisation of the partnership.

–30   **(b) Book value of assets.** In some circumstances the payment to the outgoing partner or his representatives may be stated as his share of capital, either (i) as shown in the balance sheet of the firm at the end of the last accounting period, without revaluation, with the addition of a further sum in respect of his share of profits for the period subsequent to the date of that balance sheet, or (ii) as shown in a balance sheet of the firm

---

[34] 1890 Act, s. 33.

prepared as at the date of dissolution. It should be made clear that, even if such balance sheet has not been adjusted and audited at the date of dissolution, it will nevertheless form the basis of the payment when finalised and accepted by the partners.

It should be stipulated that the balance sheet will be prepared on the same principles as applied in accordance with the accounting practice of the firm, so that, if no value has been placed on goodwill in former balance sheets, it will be entered at a nil value in the relevant balance sheet.

11–31   **(c) Revaluation of assets.** Where the partnership has fixed and/or current assets of substantial value the most equitable basis for determining the value of the share of an outgoing partner will be to provide for the preparation of accounts and a balance sheet as at the date of dissolution, with a right to the outgoing partner or his representatives to require that the assets be revalued as at that date by a valuer or valuers to be nominated by the arbiter appointed in terms of the arbitration clause.[35] The sum payable to the outgoing partner or his representatives will be the amount of his capital ascertained after the revaluation including any undrawn profits.

Certain matters require special consideration, *viz.*

11–32   *(i) Goodwill.* Even although the contract provides for revaluation of assets on dissolution it may nevertheless be advisable to exclude revaluation of goodwill. It is often difficult to assess with accuracy the value of goodwill on a dissolution since it may be affected by the cessation of the outgoing partner's connection with the firm and the circumstances in which it occurs. It is suggested that, if in previous accounts it has not been the practice of the firm to attribute any value to goodwill, the right to require any value to be placed on it on dissolution should be negatived. Even where a value has been placed on goodwill in former accounts there is much to be said for repeating the value shown in them adjusted only upon the same principles as have been applied in the previous accounting practice of the firm, without any special reappraisal of its value.

11–33   *(ii) Bankruptcy of partner.* It may be desirable to exclude revaluation of assets when the cause of dissolution is the bankruptcy of a partner. A revaluation normally produces a greater figure than book value, so that the effect would be to benefit the creditors of the bankrupt partner at the expense of the other partners in circumstances where the immediate prospects of the business might be adversely affected by his bankruptcy.

11–34   *(iii) Income tax.* The liability of the firm to income tax will not be

---

[35] Revaluation of assets would be implied by law in the absence of a provision to the contrary: *Cruikshank* v. *Sutherland* (1922) 92 L.J.(Ch.) 136; *Noble* v. *Noble*, 1965 S.L.T. 415; *Shaw* v. *Shaw*, 1968 S.L.T.(Notes) 94; *Clark* v. *Watson*, 1982 S.L.T. 450; *cf. Thom's Exrx.* v. *Russel & Aitken*, 1983 S.L.T. 335.

adjusted until some time after the date of dissolution. The contract should provide that the balance sheet prepared as at the date of dissolution should take into account the liabilities of the partners as such for income tax up to the date of dissolution. In practice an estimated figure will be inserted in the balance sheet, to be adjusted when the actual liabilities are agreed with the Inland Revenue.

1–35 **Terms of payment of outgoing partner's shares.** The continuing partners will normally be allowed a stated period such as two, three, four or five years to make the payment to the outgoing partner or his representatives by annual instalments with interest on the outstanding balance at a stipulated rate from the date of dissolution until payment, with power to anticipate the payments with consequent adjustment of interest. The payments of capital are not assessable to income tax nor allowable as a charge for income tax on the assessments of the continuing partners.

1–36 **Annuity to outgoing partner or his dependants.** In circumstances where no pension or superannuation scheme has been adopted, or where the provisions for the outgoing partner are inadequate, the contract may provide for an annuity to the outgoing partner or the widow or children of a deceasing partner of a stipulated annual amount for life or a stated period. The widow or children may enforce such a provision on the principle of *jus quaesitum tertio*. Income tax at standard rate is deductible from the payments and constitutes a charge on the profits of the continuing partners.[36]

1–37 **Restrictive covenant in partnership agreement.** In certain cases it may be desired to include in the contract of partnership a restrictive covenant designed to restrain an outgoing partner from competing with the business carried on by the continuing partners.[37] Any such restriction, to be enforceable, must be reasonable as to period and area. If the outgoing partner has received payment for his share in the former firm including goodwill the legal test of reasonableness applied by the courts would probably be that appropriate to a seller-purchaser relationship; if otherwise, the courts would probably decide upon a fair construction of the partnership agreement as a whole.[38] For a specimen clause see paragraph 11–44 (note (a) to clause 12).

1–38 **Tax election.** When a change in the partnership occurs, as by the death, bankruptcy, expulsion or retirement of an existing partner, the partnership will be deemed to have been discontinued for tax purposes[39] but, where at least one of the partners is a member of both the old and new firms, all the partners of the old and new firms and in the case of a deceased partner his personal representatives may elect to have

---

[36] Income and Corporation Taxes Act 1970, s. 52.
[37] For an account of the legal background see J.B. Miller, *op. cit.*, 120–123.
[38] J.B. Miller, *op. cit.*, 121.
[39] Income and Corporation Taxes Act, s. 154(1).

assessments made on a continuing basis by giving notice within two years of the date of change to the Inspector of Taxes.[40] The notice of election will also be treated as notice for the purposes of stock relief.[41] The decision as to making such an election will vary with circumstances and should always be taken with financial advice, but generally it will be advantageous to elect for the continuing basis if the profits of the business have been and are expected to continue on an upward trend. Since all partners and the representatives of a deceased partner must sign the notice of election it is desirable to insert a provision in the contract obliging the outgoing partner or his representatives to join in giving such a notice if so requested by the continuing partners on the basis that the outgoing partner or his representatives will be indemnified against any increase in income tax payable by him or them in excess of that which would have been payable by him or them if the notice had not been given. For a specimen clause see paragraph 11–43, clause 16.

Dissolution arrangements

11–39   When a partnership is dissolved and it is not proposed to continue the business the rule for distribution of its assets in section 44 of the 1890 Act will normally be appropriate and need be varied in the contract only for some special reason, e.g. a provision that one of the partners will be entitled to purchase a particular asset at valuation by an independent valuer. It is always desirable, however, to specify the person or persons who will be responsible for supervising the process of winding up the affairs of the firm. He may be a specified partner or partners, or a person to be nominated by the partners upon dissolution, but the more usual practice is to name in the original contract of partnership a neutral person having appropriate qualifications. The auditors of the firm are frequently nominated.

Arbitration

11–40   It will seldom be desirable for disputes between partners to be the subject of litigation in open court and so an arbitration clause should be included in the contract and resort to the courts under section 3 of the Administration of Justice (Scotland) Act 1972 should be expressly excluded. The matters to be determined by arbitration should be expressed comprehensively to cover all questions as to the construction of the contract or arising therefrom, whether between the partners or their representatives and whether arising during the continuance of the partnership or after its dissolution, the only excluded matters being those on which a decision is otherwise specifically provided for in the contract.

---

[40] *Ibid.*, s. 154(2) as amended by Finance Act 1971, s. 17.
[41] Finance Act 1976, Sched. 5, para. 21(3).

Consent to Registration

11–41 In formal contracts of partnership a consent to registration of the deed itself and of any decrees arbitral following upon it for execution should be inserted.

Styles—short form—two partners—new business

11–42 PARTNERSHIP AGREEMENT
between
A (*designed*) and B (*designed*)
The parties have agreed to carry on business as partners under the firm name of A, B & Co. at   on the following conditions:–

1. The partnership shall endure for   years from   .
2. The capital shall be £   contributed equally by the partners.
3. Profits shall be shared and losses borne by the partners equally.
4. A profit and loss account and balance sheet shall be prepared at   in each year and audited by   or other accountants mutually agreed. The accounts shall be signed by the partners within one month after completion of the audit and if not so signed shall be conclusive unless objected to in writing within that period.
5. In the event of the death or bankruptcy of either partner (the outgoing partner) the other partner shall be entitled in his option to acquire the share and interest of the outgoing partner in the firm at a price to be fixed as follows:
   (i) If said event occurs before   (*end of first year*) the price shall be the amount contributed to the partnership by the outgoing partner, under deduction of all sums drawn out by that partner, with interest at 10% per annum on the balance outstanding from time to time until the date of death or bankruptcy.
   (ii) If said event occurs on or after   (*end of first year*) the price shall be the figure at which the share and interest of the outgoing partner stood in a balance sheet of the firm prepared on the normal date of balancing accounts last preceding said event, without any revaluation of assets, under deduction of all sums subsequently drawn out by the outgoing partner, with interest at 10% per annum on the balance outstanding from time to time between the date of such balance sheet and the date of death or bankruptcy.
6. Payment of the price ascertained under clause 5 shall be made by   equal (half yearly) (quarterly) instalments commencing (six months) (three months) after the date of such death or bankruptcy with interest at 10% per annum on the balance of the price outstanding from time to time until paid. The remaining partner shall produce to the representatives of the outgoing partner evidence of discharge or payment of all liabilities of the firm which existed at the date of death or bankruptcy within (three) (six) months thereafter.
7. In the ascertainment of the foregoing price or in the balance sheet on which it is based no amount shall be included for goodwill.
8. If the remaining partner does not exercise the option of acquiring the share and interest of the outgoing partner under clause 5 the affairs of the firm shall be wound up under the control of the remaining partner and the assets shall be distributed in accordance with section 44 of the Partnership Act 1890.

9. The remaining partner, if he acquires the share and interest of the outgoing partner under clause 5, shall be entitled to possession and ownership of the whole books and records of the firm. If clause 8 operates the remaining partner shall have possession of the books and records of the firm, subject to reasonable access by the outgoing partner or his representatives, and may deliver them for the purposes of the winding up or dispose of them one year after its completion.

10. All disputes and differences which may arise between the partners or between either of them and the representatives of a deceased partner or the creditors of an insolvent or bankrupt partner as to the meaning, intent or construction of this agreement or the implement thereof or any other matter in relation to the partnership or its dissolution and winding up, whether arising during the existence of the partnership or after its termination, shall be referred to an arbiter mutually chosen or, failing agreement, to be appointed on the application of any party by   and the decision of such arbiter shall be final and binding on all concerned. The application of section 3 of the Administration of Justice (Scotland) Act 1972 is expressly excluded. (*To be attested*)

Stamp duty nil.

Standard style—full form—three partners

11–43
CONTRACT OF PARTNERSHIP
among
A (*designed*) (hereinafter called "Mr A")
B (*designed*) (hereinafter called "Mr B")
and
C (*designed*) (hereinafter called "Mr C")
WHEREAS the parties hereto have agreed to carry on business together in partnership as   , THEREFORE the parties AGREE:

Firm Name and Place of Business
1. The parties shall carry on the business of   in partnership under the firm name of A, B & Co. at   and/or elsewhere as may be agreed.

Endurance
2. The partnership shall [commence] [be held to have commenced] on   and, subject to the provisions hereof, shall continue until   and from year to year thereafter until dissolved by written notice given by any partner to the other partners not less than   months prior to   (*end of initial period of endurance*) or any subsequent anniversary thereof.

Capital
3. The capital of the partnership shall be such sums contributed by the partners in such proportions as may be agreed by the partners from time to time and the respective contributions of the partners to capital shall be credited in the books and accounts of the partnership. Each partner shall maintain at credit of his capital account at least such sum

as the partners shall mutually agree so that the total at credit of the capital accounts of the partners shall be adequate for the efficient conduct of the business. Interest shall be payable on the sum standing to the credit of the capital accounts of each partner at the end of each (*calendar month or longer period*) at the rate of per cent per annum or such other rate as shall be mutually agreed from time to time but shall be calculated and become payable only upon completion of the annual accounts of the partnership. Interest on capital shall be credited to the capital accounts of the partners before the profit for the year is ascertained.

Profits and Losses

4. The partners shall be entitled to the profits of the partnership and shall bear any losses (*equally or in stated proportions*) which may be varied as the partners may mutually agree in writing from time to time. The partners shall be entitled to draw in anticipation of profits such amounts and at such times as the partners may mutually agree [in writing].

Books and Accounts

5. Proper books shall be kept in which all financial transactions of the partnership shall be entered and the books shall be brought to a balance on the day of in each year. A Balance Sheet as at that date, with Profit and Loss Account for the period to that date, shall be prepared and audited by Chartered Accountants, or such other Accountants as the partners may from time to time agree. Copies of the audited Balance Sheet and Account shall be furnished to each partner as soon as practicable and the principal copy thereof shall be submitted for signature by each of the partners and, when so signed, shall be conclusive. If the Balance Sheet and Account are not signed by any partner within a period of months after being submitted to him they shall be deemed to have been approved by such partner unless written objections to them have been stated by him within the said period. Failing agreement among the partners such objections shall be disposed of by an independent accountant to be mutually agreed by the partners or, in the absence of such agreement, to be nominated by the Arbiter aftermentioned; the accountant shall have power to employ any professional services which he may deem necessary for determination of the dispute. The decision of such independent accountant shall be conclusive

and he shall have power to sign the Balance Sheet and Account with any amendments he shall consider proper. The Balance Sheet and Account may be challenged within three months after signature by the partners or independent accountant or Arbiter, as the case may be, on the ground of any palpable error or omission but subject to the rectification thereof shall remain final and binding on all concerned. In any Balance Sheet no sum shall be placed on the value of goodwill.

Use of Firm Name and Bank Accounts
6. Each of the partners shall be entitled to sign the firm name but only in connection with the business of the partnership. All correspondence, documents and writings in any way relating to the business of the partnership shall so far as possible be given or taken in name of the partnership. The partnership will maintain a bank account or accounts in the name of the firm into which all sums received from the business shall be paid or credited. Cheques drawn on the bank account may be signed by any partner in the firm name but no cheques shall be drawn except in settlement of the debts or obligations of the partnership or payments to partners authorised hereunder or specially authorised by all the partners.

Time and Attention
7. Each partner shall devote his whole time and attention to the business of the partnership and shall not without the consent of the partners engage in any other business or apply for, or allow himself to be nominated for or elected to any position which would prevent him from devoting his whole time and attention to the business of the partnership.

Pensions and Insurances
8. [A pension and life assurance scheme shall be established for the benefit of the partners and their dependants in terms to be agreed by the partners] [Each partner shall effect and maintain at his own expense policies of life assurance and pension, family income benefit and permanent sickness benefit in terms to be approved by the partnership, and shall if required satisfy the auditors of the partnership accounts that his obligations under this Clause have been fulfilled].

Decisions
9. Where any decision is required to be taken or any act authorised by or in relation to the partnership such decision shall be taken or such act shall be authorised, in default of unanimous agreement of the partners, [by a simple majority of votes of the partners] [by a majority of the partners and in ascertaining

such majority the partners' votes shall carry weight in proportion to the size of the respective shares for the time being of the partners in the profits of the partnership]. In the event of equality of votes Mr. A. shall have a casting vote.

Prohibited Acts 10. No partner shall, without the express consent of the other partners, do any of the following acts:

(a) draw, accept or endorse any bill of exchange or promissory note, or contract any debt, on account of the partnership, or in any manner pledge its credit or employ its funds, except in the normal course of its business;

(b) lend money to, or give credit to or have dealings on behalf of the partnership with any person, firm or company whom the other partners have forbidden him to lend to or give credit to or have dealings with respectively;

(c) release, compromise or compound any debt owing to, or any claim of, the partnership;

(d) take any steps by way of management, control or conduct of the partnership business which are not in accordance with policy laid down by the partnership;

(e) on behalf of the partnership, guarantee payment of or discharge any sum or claim, other than by way of undertaking given in the normal course of business of the partnership;

(f) whether on behalf of the partnership or as an individual, become cautioner for or grant any guarantee or security for any person, firm or company;

(g) as an individual, enter into any speculative transactions other than by way of investment of his own free capital exclusive of any capital belonging to him in the business of the partnership;

(h) knowingly do or permit anything to be done whereby the partnership property may be subjected to diligence of any kind; or

(i) assign or charge his share and interest in the partnership or any part thereof.

If any partner shall act in any way contrary to the provisions of this Clause he shall indemnify the partnership for any loss resulting therefrom.

Expulsion 11. If any partner shall

(a) become notour bankrupt or enter into

any composition or arrangement for the
benefit of his creditors generally,

(b) do any act prohibited by Clause 10
hereof,

(c) grossly neglect the business of the partnership,

(d) act in such a way as to bring his name or
the reputation of the partnership into disrepute,

(e) [commit any act of serious professional
misconduct], or

(f) act in any respect contrary to the provisions of this Contract or to good faith
between partners

then, in any of these events, the other
partners may expel the partner concerned
with effect from such date as shall be specified in a written notice given by or on behalf
of such other partners to the partner concerned who shall be deemed to have ceased to
be a partner on such date.

Retirement

12. (1) A partner shall retire from the partnership at the end of the accounting year of
the partnership in which he attains the age of

(2) Any partner may retire from the partnership on giving not less than six months'
notice in writing to the other partners.

(3) If a partner (i) becomes of unsound
mind, as evidenced by a medical certificate,
(ii) becomes in the reasonable opinion of his
partners incapable of contributing effectively
to the business of the partnership or of
managing his financial affairs or (iii) is absent
from business without the consent of his
partners for a continuous period of
consecutive months or an aggregate of
days in any period of   consecutive
years, he shall be deemed to have retired
from the partnership on the expiry of a period
of   months' written notice given to him
by the other partners.

Continuance of
Partnership

13. In the event of the death of any partner,
or the expulsion or retirement of any partner
by the operation of Clause 11 or Clause 12
hereof, this Contract shall not *ipso facto* be
terminated but shall, unless otherwise
agreed, continue as regards the other
partners. The share of profits or losses of the
outgoing partner after such event shall be
divided among the remaining partners in proportion to their existing shares as provided by
Clause 4 hereof.

Payments on
Death, Expulsion
or Retirement

14. In the event of the death of any partner, or the expulsion or retirement of any partner by the operation of Clause 11 or Clause 12 hereof,

(a) the whole assets (including the firm name, goodwill, work in progress, furniture, fittings and equipment, cash balances and books and records) of the partnership shall become the exclusive property of the remaining partners who shall settle the whole debts and obligations of the partnership as at the date of such death, expulsion or retirement. Any outgoing partner in whom any heritable property which is an asset of the partnership is vested, or the Trustee of any such partner, shall, whenever called upon to do so, execute a deed conveying such property to the remaining partners or their nominees at the expense of the remaining partners;

(b) a Balance Sheet shall be prepared in terms of Clause 5 hereof (in which no value shall be placed upon the goodwill of the partnership) as at the date of the death, expulsion or retirement of the outgoing partner. The outgoing partner or his Trustee (except in the case of expulsion by the operation of Clause 11 hereof) shall be entitled to require that any asset or group of assets (other than goodwill) of the partnership be valued for the purpose of any such Balance Sheet by a valuer mutually chosen or, failing agreement, to be nominated by the Arbiter aftermentioned. Such Balance Sheet shall take into account all liabilities of the partners as such for income tax to the date of death, expulsion or retirement and make due provision therefor. The sum at credit of the outgoing partner shall be ascertained from such Balance Sheet and paid by the remaining partners to the outgoing partner or his Trustee by equal half-yearly instalments, commencing six months after the date of death, expulsion or retirement, as the case may be, with interest (except in the event of expulsion by the operation of Clause 11 hereof) also payable half-yearly on the same dates at the rate of   per cent per annum on the amount from time to time outstanding, with power to the remaining partners to accelerate payment of all or any of said instalments with corresponding reduction of interest;

(c) if the capital account of the outgoing partner ascertained as in sub-clause (b) of this Clause is at debit the amount due shall be paid forthwith by the outgoing partner or his Trustee to the remaining partners.

Dissolution by Notice 15. If the partnership is dissolved by notice given under Clause 2 hereof and the partners to whom such notice is given intimate to the partner who has given such notice within three months of the date of receipt thereof that they intend to continue the partnership business, the provisions of Clause 14 hereof shall apply as if the partner who has given such notice had retired in terms of Clause 12(2) hereof.

Tax Election 16. An outgoing partner or his Trustee shall, if so requested by the remaining partners, join with them in giving to H.M. Inspector of Taxes any election notice required in respect of income tax under sub-section (2) of section 154 of the Income and Corporation Taxes Act 1970 or any statutory replacement or amendment thereof, and in any such case the remaining partners shall indemnify the outgoing partner or his Trustee against any additional aggregate liability for income tax (including higher rate tax) which may be payable by him as a result of giving such notice.

Dissolution and Winding up 17. Upon final dissolution of the partnership, if the partners do not otherwise agree, the whole assets of the partnership, including the firm name and goodwill (if any), shall be realised to the best effect and after settlement of all obligations of the partnership the net proceeds shall be divided under the supervision of the Auditors of the partnership for the time being.

Interpretation 18. In this Contract
(a) words importing the singular shall include the plural, and *vice versa*;
(b) words importing the male gender shall include the female gender;
(c) the word "Trustee" shall include any testamentary trustee, executor-nominate, executor-dative, trustee in bankruptcy, trustee under a trust deed for behoof of creditors and any judicial factor or *curator bonis*.

Arbitration 19. If during the continuance of the partnership or after its termination any dispute, question or difference shall arise between the partners or the Trustee of any partner or any of them, the decision of which is not otherwise hereinbefore specially provided for, as to the meaning, intent or construction of these presents or the accounts or transactions of the partnership, the expulsion or retirement of any partner, the dissolution or winding up of the partnership, or any valuation herein provided for or the rights or liabilities of any partner or the Trustee of any partner hereunder, or otherwise in relation to the partnership, the same shall be referred to an Arbiter to be mutually chosen by the parties to any such dispute, question or difference or, failing agreement, to be appointed on the application of any such party by [the President of the Law Society of Scotland] [the Sheriff Principal of   ]; [such Arbiter shall have power to assess and award damages] and the decree or decrees arbitral of such Arbiter, interim or final, shall be conclusive and binding on all concerned and the application of section 3 of the Administration of Justice (Scotland) Act 1972 is expressly excluded.

Registration 20. The parties consent to registration hereof and of any decree arbitral to follow hereon for preservation and execution.

(*To be attested*)
Stamp Duty 50p.

Notes on standard full form

1–44 General note. The standard form of contract of partnership is substantially based upon the style of Partnership Agreement prepared by the Styles Committee of the Law Society of Scotland 1980 (J.L.S., W153).

CLAUSE 1

It may be desired to include a reminder of the requirements of the Business Names Act 1985 as to business names and disclosure of the names of partners.

"There shall be displayed prominently at all premises at which the business of the firm is carried on a notice containing the names and addresses of all partners of the firm for the time being and the names of all partners shall be written or printed on all communications of the firm as required by section 4 of the Business Names Act 1985."

CLAUSE 2

(a) It is sometimes provided that notice must be given by a majority of the partners. In general, however, it is preferable to terminate the partnership on notice by any partner as it is undesirable to continue the business in association with a reluctant partner.

(b) The stipulation that notice may be given for termination only upon

the date of the annual balance of accounts is convenient, but termination on prescribed notice at any time after expiry of the original period of endurance may be permitted although it may involve preparation of accounts for a part year.
(c) See paragraph 11–08.

Clause 3

(a) Alternatively the sums to be contributed to capital may be specified.
"The initial capital of the partnership shall be £   contributed [*equally or in stated amounts by each partner*]; any additional capital required for the proper conduct of the business shall be provided by the partners in such proportions as may be mutually agreed from time to time."
(b) The provision as to maintenance of each partner's minimum amount of capital may be strengthened by an express obligation to make up any deficiency immediately upon being required to do so by the other partners.
(c) As to contributions to capital in the form of property see paragraph 11–09 (iii) and (iv).
(d) If no interest is payable on capital, that should be stated.
(e) As to policy considerations in relation to interest and periods of calculation see paragraph 11–11.

Clause 4

(a) If any partner is to receive a salary either instead of or in addition to a share of profits, special provision is required:
"Mr C shall receive a salary of £   per annum payable monthly in arrear [but shall not otherwise be entitled to participate in the profits of the partnership] [in addition to his share of profit aftermentioned]. His salary shall be debited in the accounts of the firm before the profit for the year is ascertained."
(b) In certain businesses, *e.g.* a farm, one of the partners may be resident on the premises and may act as manager of the business.
"Mr A shall be [The partners may appoint one of their number to be] managing partner. He shall be entitled to free occupation, board and service in the [farmhouse of   ] [property at   ] for himself and his family and to receive a salary of £   per annum payable monthly in arrear in addition to his share of profit aftermentioned. The cost of said board and service and said salary shall be debited in the accounts of the firm before profit for the year is ascertained."
(c) Salaried partners who do not otherwise participate in profit should be indemnified against loss.
"Mr C shall have no liability for any losses incurred by the partnership and shall be entitled to be indemnified by the other partners against any such liability."
(d) If motor cars are required for use by partners in the conduct of the business special provision may be made in the contract.
"In respect that each of the partners requires a motor car for the conduct of his part of the business of the partnership there shall be purchased or provided for each partner at the expense

of the firm a motor vehicle of a type and cost to be determined by the partners. The whole cost of running the said vehicles, including licensing, insurance, repair, maintenance and running costs, shall be a charge on the profit of the partnership and the intervals at which the said vehicles are replaced shall be decided by the partners."

(e) Any other expenses or outlays which may usually be incurred according to the nature of the business may be specified as in note (d) above as charges on the profit of the business, *e.g.* travelling and board expenses, attendance authorised by the partners at business or professional conferences, etc.

CLAUSE 5

(a) The clause is comprehensive with provision for determination of objections by an independent accountant. A simpler version may provide for determination by the auditors.

(b) The entry of goodwill at nil value is optional. See paragraph 11–16.

(c) In a partnership of solicitors the keeping of accounts is governed by professional requirements.

"Books shall be kept in accordance with Rule 8 of the Solicitors (Scotland) Account Rules 1981 as amended from time to time and the Solicitors (Scotland) Accountant's Certificate Rules 1981 as amended from time to time."

CLAUSE 6

(a) As to power of a partner to bind the firm see Partnership Act 1890, ss. 5, 6.

(b) It may be desired to prohibit expressly the power of a partner to grant obligations binding the firm otherwise than in the ordinary course of its business or to use the credit of the firm for private purposes.

"No partner shall be entitled to grant obligations under the firm name, save in the ordinary course of the business of the partnership, except with the consent in writing of the other partners nor to implicate the firm in liability for his debts or obligations as an individual."

See 1890 Act s. 7.

(c) The name and branch or branches of the firm's bankers may be specified in the contract.

"The partnership will maintain a bank account or accounts in the name of the firm which shall be kept with the   Branch of the   Bank or such other branch or Bank as the partners may agree."

CLAUSE 7

If any of the partners is not required to devote his whole time and attention to the business of the partnership the clause will be restricted in its application to the full time partners and provision on the following lines inserted in respect of the part time partner.

"Mr A shall devote such time and attention to the business of the partnership [as may be necessary to discharge such duties as are allotted to him] [as he may consider necessary]."

CLAUSE 8

A pension scheme has taxation benefits—see paragraph 11–23. As to income tax and capital transfer tax implications, see Lindley, *Partnership* (14th ed. 887–890 and 917–919).

CLAUSE 9

(a) See paragraph 11–22. If the decision on any matter is to require unanimous approval of all partners, or all partners other than the one concerned, the clause should be modified appropriately.
  "The provisions of this Clause shall not apply to (i) any fundamental change in the nature of the business or (ii) the introduction of a new partner, either of which shall require the unanimous consent of all partners, or (iii) the expulsion of a partner, which shall require the unanimous consent of all the other partners."

(b) If any partner has a reserved right to introduce a new partner head (ii) in (a) above should be deleted.
  "Mr. A shall be entitled at any time to appoint his *(relative, preferably a named relative or person)* to become a partner in the firm on such terms as may be agreed or, failing agreement, as may be determined by the Arbiter aftermentioned. The introduction of any other person as a partner shall require the unanimous consent of all partners."

CLAUSE 10

As to other acts which may be prohibited in particular cases see paragraph 11–21.

CLAUSE 11

(a) Sub-head (e) of the clause is appropriate where any partner is professionally qualified.

(b) Any question as to whether a right to expel has arisen in terms of the clause will be decided by the arbiter.

CLAUSE 12

(a) In the event of retirement a restrictive covenant may be added. See paragraph 11–37.
  "Any partner retiring or being deemed to have retired under this Clause agrees with the other partners and each of them that he (the retiring partner) will not during the period of   years immediately following such retirement act for or solicit either by himself or as a partner, director or employee of any other person, firm or company any [customer] [client] of the partnership [other than his relatives or a family business owned or controlled by his relatives] and that he will not

practise as a   either by himself or as the partner,
director or employee of any person, firm or company which
shall include or refer to the name of 'A, B & Co.' or any part
of such name or which shall include or refer to the name or
names of any firms whose [businesses] [practices] have been
incorporated in the partnership of the existing business of A,
B & Co. other than his own name, and further that he will not
within the said period of   years and within a radius of
          miles from   practise as a   either by
himself or as a partner, director or employee of any person,
firm or company."

(b) This clause poses difficult problems of drafting and may vary in different partnerships. Although a partner may not be certifiable as of
unsound mind under (3)(i), he may have suffered mental or physical deterioration which makes his continued participation in the
partnership undesirable. If a decision on that matter were left to the
opinion of his partners, without qualification, the provision could
be used unfairly to procure the retirement of a partner of whom the
other partners for any reason wished to be rid in circumstances
where none of the grounds of expulsion under Clause 11 was applicable. The qualification "reasonable" in (3)(ii) may involve arbitration on challenge, but is weighted to some extent in favour of the
other partners since, if the arbiter considers that there is any proper
reason for the opinion of the other partners, their opinion will prevail.

(c) The periods to be inserted in (3)(iii) are for consideration and
agreement.

CLAUSE 13

This clause negatives dissolution which would otherwise be implied
by law on a change in the personnel of the partners.

CLAUSE 14

(a) The payment provided for in the clause is based upon the outgoing
partner's share as shown in a balance sheet at date of outgoing with
a right to have assets (excluding goodwill) revalued (except in the
case of expulsion).

(b) If the sum payable to the outgoing partner is calculated on a profits
basis (see paragraph 11–29) it should be considered whether the
payment should be a capital sum payable by instalments with interest, which may have capital gains tax implications, or income
payments for a stated period in the nature of pension payments,
which will be paid under deduction of income tax.

(c) As to policy in relation to payments under this clause see paragraphs 11–28 to 11–36.

CLAUSE 15

(a) The provision in this Clause can result in problems of tactics if the
partners are in disagreement as to continuing the business together
but none wishes to be bought out. In such circumstances no partner
desires to give the others the opportunity of doing so by giving

notice, and an impasse is created which can only be resolved by negotiation.

(b) One option to avoid that situation is to provide that on notice given by any partner the right to acquire the share of that partner is conferred upon a named senior partner or partners. That may be appropriate when the goodwill of the business substantially belongs to the named partner or partners, but it would enable them to give notice and in effect expel the other partner or partners even although none of the grounds of expulsion in Clause 11 existed.

(c) Another option is to provide that on notice being given dissolution and winding up under Clause 17 would ensue, a result which would follow if Clause 15 were simply omitted.

(d) Since notice can be given only when the initial period of the partnership under Clause 2 has expired, the selection of a short initial period and a provision on the lines of option (b) above may be advisable. Once the success of the association has been established a renewal of the partnership with a provision on the lines of (a) or (c) may be inserted.

(e) If a choice has to be made between the provisions of this Clause (option (a)) and a provision on the lines of option (c), the former is marginally preferable, since in the circumstances indicated in (a) above the giving of notice is discouraged and allows time to negotiate arrangements for dissolution by agreement, whereas under option (c) the threat of notice by a dissident partner, with consequent winding up and possible competition among partners in bidding to acquire the assets of the business, may create an atmosphere which is not conducive to dissolution by agreement (which usually is more advantageous to all parties than winding up).

CLAUSE 16

See paragraph 11–38.

CLAUSE 17

The supervision of the winding up may in appropriate circumstances be entrusted to a named partner or partners. It will usually be preferable, however, to have this function exercised by independent professionally qualified accountants, such as the auditors.

CLAUSE 19

(a) This clause is comprehensive of all questions which may arise from the contract, whether during its existence or after its termination, and between any of the parties who may be concerned.

(b) It may not always be desirable to confer power on the arbiter to award damages: *in dubio* it is preferable to omit it.

CLAUSE 20

The inclusion of this clause will render the deed liable to stamp duty of 50p. If the clause is omitted no stamp duty is payable.

Medical Partnerships

–45 Partnerships of medical practitioners operating within the National Health Service are subject to special conditions and reference should be made to the memorandum *Medical Partnerships under the National Health Service (Scotland)* (1982 edition) published by the Scottish General Medical Services Committee and the Scottish Council of the British Medical Association.[42] For further guidance see the undernoted texts.[43] The principal statutory provisions are contained in the National Health Service (Scotland) Acts 1972 and 1978. Proposed partnership agreements may be submitted for opinion as to their suitability to the Advisory Group on Partnerships of the Scottish General Medical Services Committee.[44] Some of the more important matters are outlined in the following paragraphs.

Goodwill

–46 A medical practitioner whose name has been entered in any list of medical practioners undertaking to provide general services under the National Health Service may not lawfully sell the goodwill or any part of the goodwill of his practice,[45] and any person who sells or buys such goodwill is guilty of an offence.[46] In order to obviate concealed sales of goodwill: (1) The sale or let of premises previously used by the practitioner for the purposes of the practice for a consideration substantially in excess of their value without goodwill is deemed to be a sale of the goodwill: (2) There is also a deemed sale of goodwill where (i) any valuable consideration other than the performance of services is given by a partner or proposed partner as consideration for his being taken into partnership, or (ii) any valuable consideration is given to a partner on his retirement or to his personal representatives on his death in excess of sums due to him in respect of past services or his share in the assets of the partnership, or (iii) services are performed by a partner for substantially less than they are worth, or (iv) a practitioner performs services as an assistant for substantially less than they are worth and subsequently succeeds to the practice or a share in it, or (v) a practitioner or his personal representatives agree for valuable consideration to do or refrain from doing any act for the purpose of facilitating the succession of another to the practice or any part thereof, or (vi) a practitioner gives valuable consideration to another practitioner or his representatives and succeeds to the practice or part thereof.

---

[42] Copies obtainable from British Medical Association (Scottish office), 7 Drumsheugh Gardens, Edinburgh.

[43] Noel Leigh Taylor, *Doctors and the Law*; J. Leigh Taylor, *Medical Malpractice*; S.A.A. McLean, *Legal Issues in Medicine*; *National Health Service Superannuation for Scotland*, published by Scottish Home and Health Department.

[44] 7 Drumsheugh Gardens, Edinburgh.

[45] 1978 Act, s. 35(1).

[46] *Ibid.*, Sched. 9 para. 1.

Sharing of profit

11–47   The area health board must be satisfied that the income of any partner
cannot at any time fall below one-third of the net income of the partner
with the largest share. (To avoid concealed sale of goodwill—see head
(iii) of preceding paragraph.) It is recommended that the partnership
agreement should provide for subsequent increases to junior partners at
stated intervals.

Special earnings, allowances or awards

11–48   The partnership agreement should state whether special earnings,
allowances or awards, e.g. seniority payments, vocational training
allowances, postgraduate training allowances, academic prizes or
travelling scholarship awards, are to be retained by the individual
partner or are to form part of the general income of the partnership.

Incapacity

11–49   In view of the essentially personal services performed, provisions for
short term and long term incapacity, holidays and study leave and in the
case of females maternity leave require special consideration and should
always be included.

Superannuation

11–50   Contributions of the individual partners to the National Health Service (Scotland) Superannuation Scheme may be assessed on different
bases, but generally are related to shares of profits (as varied from time
to time) or shares of profits plus any other superannuable remuneration
received from a health board.[47] The partnership agreement should
specify the basis to be adopted.

Capital

11–51   In view of the prohibition upon sale of goodwill it is desirable to
specify with some particularity the principal assets of the practice to be
valued on termination of the partnership.

Restrictive covenants

11–52   Restrictive covenants on the outgoing of a partner must satisfy the
condition of reasonableness imposed by law but in the case of a medical
partnership regard must be had to the special feature that each of the
partners is under a separate contract with a health board and the restriction must not be so stringent as to found an argument that it forms an
element in the prohibited sale of goodwill.

---

[47] See National Health Service (Superannuation) (Scotland) Regulations 1980, reg. 68(2)(*b*).

Style of medical partnership (National Health Service)[48]

1–53

CONTRACT OF PARTNERSHIP
among
Dr. A (*designed*)
Dr. B (*designed*)
and
Dr. C (*designed*)

WHEREAS the parties hereto have agreed to carry on the profession of General Medical Practitioners THEREFORE the parties AGREE:

Firm Name and Place of Practice

1. The practice shall be carried on in   and district under the firm name of

Endurance

2. [As clause 2 of Standard Style]

Capital

3. The capital of the partnership shall comprise:

(a) [the surgery premises at   and/or any other premises agreed by the partners] [the tenants' interest in leased surgery premises at   and/or any other premises leased to the partnership] [the rights of occupancy of all the partners in any Health Centre made available by the National Health Service, declaring that on the retirement or death of any partner his rights of occupancy therein, if made available by the relevant Health Board, shall be available to the remaining partners],

(b) the whole furniture, fittings, appliances, drugs, bottles, utensils and other contents of the surgery premises,

(c) the sum from time to time standing to the credit of the partnership Bank Account,

(d) such further sums as may from time to time be required for the conduct of the partnership practice to be contributed by the partners in the proportions in which at the time they share in the profits of the partnership, and

(e) such other assets as are purchased from time to time out of partnership funds.

3A. (a) Each partner shall himself provide and maintain a dwellinghouse suitable and convenient for his work in the practice and pay the whole expenses thereof. If any such dwellinghouse is used for the work of the practice, the partnership shall pay to such partner (in full of rent, rates,

---

[48] The style is based on a style provided by Mr J. Cameron Henderson of Bird Semple & Crawford Herron, Glasgow.

taxes, heating, cleaning, lighting and attendance) such sum as may be allowed for income tax purposes for such use and as the partners may from time to time agree.

(b) Each partner shall provide and pay the initial and running costs of all motor cars required by him for his work in the practice.

(c) The whole expenses of all surgery premises and the cost of all surgical instruments required by the partners shall be borne by the partnership.

Profits and Losses 4. (a) Seniority payments, post graduate training allowances and vocational training allowances shall be retained by the partner to whom they are awarded and shall not form part of the income of the partnership.

(b) For the purpose of superannuation each partner's remuneration shall be deemed to be the same proportion of the total remuneration of the partners (being remuneration earned in respect of providing General Medical Services under the provisions of the National Health Service (Scotland) Act 1978) as the proportion of his share in net profits, and written notice shall be given to the appropriate Health Board(s). In calculating the division of net profits of the partnership as provided in sub- clause (c) of this Clause each partner shall be deemed to have received to account of his share of such profits the amounts of any deductions made in respect of his superannuation contributions under the National Health Service (Scotland) Superannuation Regulations.

(c) The partners shall be entitled to the net profits of the partnership, and subject to Clause 8 hereof shall bear any losses (*equally or in stated proportions keeping in view the limits of differentials—see paragraph 11–47*) which may be varied as the partners may mutually agree in writing from time to time. The partners shall be entitled to draw in anticipation of profits such amounts as the partners may mutually agree [in writing].

Books and Accounts 5. Proper books shall be kept by each partner and entries shall be made immediately therein of all attendances upon patients, receipts, payments and all such other matters as are usually entered in the books of a medical practice. The books of the partnership shall be brought to a balance on [*continue as in clause 5 of Standard Style*].

Bank Account

6. All sums (save as provided in Clause 4(a) or 7(b) hereof) received by all partners on behalf of the partnership shall be paid into a Bank Account kept in name of the partnership. Cheques on the Bank Account shall be signed by any partner in the firm name but no cheques shall be drawn except for payment of debts of the partnership, or payments authorised in terms of Clause 4(c) hereof to account of shares of profits of partners, and no accounts shall be paid until they have been approved by all partners.

Time and Attention

7. (a) Each partner shall employ himself diligently in the practice and no partner shall engage in any other undertaking or business requiring his personal attention. In the event of any partner holding or obtaining any appointment or making any profit by consultation the salary or fees therefrom shall be earnings of the partnership. No partner shall accept or resign from any personal appointment, office or contract without the consent of the other partners. In the event that payment for any such appointment is taxed on the basis of Schedule E the partners agree to refer to the Auditors of the partnership accounts any adjustment of taxation which the Auditors may consider to be equitable, whether during the endurance of the partnership or on its termination, between the partners.

(b) In the event that any of the partners, with the consent of the other partners, undertakes duties for any deputising service in his free time, he shall be entitled to retain any fees earned.

Negligence and Insurance

8. Each partner shall be liable personally to pay, and so indemnify the partnership against, any damages or compensation recovered against him or the partnership by reason of any negligence or misconduct on his part. Each partner shall maintain himself in membership of a Medical Defence Union.

Employees and Assistants

9. Such employees (other than household domestics) or qualified assistants as may from time to time be required for the work of the practice shall be engaged and, except in the case of flagrant misconduct, be dismissed only with the consent of all partners, provided that servants employed at the residence of any one partner may be engaged and dismissed by

that partner alone. Any qualified assistant so employed shall serve all partners.

Holidays, Study Leave and Maternity Leave

10. (a) Each partner shall be entitled to at least weeks' absence for holiday in each year of the partnership, Dr. to have the first choice in fixing the time for holidays. During the absence on holiday of one partner, the remaining partners shall undertake his duties, unless the partners agree that a locum is required when the cost of providing the locum shall be borne by the partnership. A partner shall also be entitled to such periods of absence for study to be taken at such times as the partners mutually agree.

(b) [In the event that Dr. shall require maternity leave she shall be entitled to be absent from the practice for a period to be agreed but not exceeding thirteen weeks, without loss of remuneration, and on the basis that the partnership will provide at its expense a locum for the period of absence. Should the absence extend on medical grounds beyond thirteen weeks, the cost of a locum will be borne by Dr. herself.]

National Service

[11. If at any time during the partnership any partner shall be called up for national service any pay received by such partner shall be paid to the partnership and included in its profits, but this provision shall not apply to any allowances, gratuity or prize money. During the absence on national service of any partner the other partners shall be entitled in their sole discretion to engage a competent registered medical practitioner as a locum at the expense of the partnership. A partner absent on national service shall be entitled to receive his share of net profits as herein provided and notice to dissolve the partnership shall not be given solely on the ground of such absence. The foregoing provision shall apply also to short periods of call up for annual training, and the period or periods of such training, unless of a duration of more than four weeks in any one year, shall not affect the right of a partner to his full annual holiday.]

Prohibited Acts

12. No partner shall, without the express consent in writing of the other partners, do any of the following acts:

(a) on behalf of the partnership or as an individual, become a cautioner or grant any guarantee or security;

(b) as an individual, enter into any

speculative transaction other than by way of investment of his own free capital;

(c) use the name of the partnership or deal with the property thereof for purposes other than those of the partnership;

(d) commit any breach of the provisions herein contained and on his part to be observed or performed;

(e) commit any act of serious professional misconduct; or

(f) do or suffer to be done anything whereby the interests of the partnership may be in danger of being seriously injured.

If any partner shall act in any way contrary to the provisions of this Clause he shall indemnify the partnership for any loss resulting therefrom.

Incapacity 13. (a) In the event of any partner being absent from the practice beyond the periods allowed in Clause 10 [or Clause 11] hereof save with the consent of the other partners or become from any cause incapacitated from performing his fair share of the work of the practice he shall (and in the case of incapacity after an absence of ninety days), if required in writing by the other partners to do so, provide at his own expense a competent qualified medical practitioner as substitute, but nothing herein contained shall imply a right to any partner to absent himself from his duties in the practice.

(b) In the event of any partner becoming by reason of illness or accident incapable of performing general medical services in private practice or under the National Health Service Scheme, he shall be entitled at any time to retire from the partnership with immediate effect on giving written notice to the other partners of such retirement, stating the reason for it. In such event the provisions of Clause 16 hereof shall apply.

Dissolution 14. (a) In the event of the death, notour bankruptcy or insanity of a partner, or if the name of a partner be removed for any cause from the Medical Register or the Medical List of any Health Board, the partnership shall be dissolved.

(b) The partnership may be dissolved by notice in accordance with Clause 13(b) hereof.

(c) In the event of (i) the incapacity of any partner continuing for more than six consecutive calendar months or for more than two hundred days in all in any period of twenty four consecutive calendar months or (ii) any partner committing a breach of any of the provisions of Clause 12 hereof, the other partners may, in their option, dissolve the partnership by notice in writing at such date as may be specified in the notice. For the purpose of this Clause "incapacity" shall, in the event of dispute, be determined by the decision of a consulting specialist mutually agreed by the partners or, in default of agreement, nominated by the Arbiter aftermentioned on the application of any of the partners.

Accounts and Payments on Dissolution

15. If the partnership shall be dissolved a Profit and Loss Account and Balance Sheet shall be prepared up to the date of dissolution in accordance with the terms of this Contract and the balance due to or by each partner in respect of undrawn or overdrawn profits shall be paid to or repaid by him within one month after final adjustment of the Account and Balance Sheet, due allowance being made for all obligations of the partnership, including outstanding liability for income tax on the profits of the partnership. The said Balance Sheet shall state the value of the capital (including cash and other assets but excluding goodwill) and the share of each partner therein, and the value of the share of any outgoing, defaulting, incapacitated or deceased partner shall be paid to him or his Trustee, as the case may be, by the surviving or continuing partners [by four equal quarterly instalments, payable without interest three, six, nine and twelve months after the date of adjustment of the accounts] [*or on other terms to be agreed*], provided that if, after the date of dissolution, all parties intend to continue in practice, settlement may be effected *pro tanto* by the division of the assets among them at the values shown in said Balance Sheet.

Appointments

16. In the event of the retirement of a partner from practice in the area of the partnership practice or in the event of the death of a partner, he or his Trustee, as the case may be, shall use his best endeavours to secure for the surviving or continuing partners or their nominees all public and other medical and surgical appointments held by the outgoing or deceased partner at the time of his retirement or death, and he shall do all acts and things necessary to transfer or have transferred all persons on the list of the outgoing or

deceased partner under the National Health Service (Scotland) Act 1978 or any act amending the same to the lists of the surviving or continuing partners or to the lists of their nominees.

Arrangements on Dissolution

17. (i) If the partnership shall be dissolved, all partners shall be entitled to continue to practise on their own account within the area of the partnership practice, but Dr. A shall have the exclusive right of occupancy of any lock-up surgery then used by the partnership.

(ii) If the partnership shall be dissolved, and one or two partners only intend to continue in practice in the area of practice these two or one or other of them as they may then agree shall have an option for a period of one month of purchasing with vacant possession (i) any lock-up surgery belonging to the firm and (ii) any dwellinghouse owned and occupied by the outgoing or deceased partner within the area of practice, if it be then the intention of such outgoing partner or representatives of a deceased partner to sell such dwellinghouse. The remaining partners shall pay for said surgery and/or dwellinghouse such sum(s) (in which no allowance shall be made for goodwill) as shall be fixed, failing agreement, by a valuer nominated by the Arbiter aftermentioned as representing the fair market value(s) thereof with vacant possession, which value(s) shall be ascertained and agreed before the option is exercised.

(iii) If the partnership shall be dissolved, any rights of occupancy (by lease or otherwise) of any surgery premises, shall, if any partners intend to continue to practise in the area of the practice, be available for the exclusive use of the continuing partner(s) subject to them or him freeing and relieving the outgoing partner(s) or the representatives of a deceased partner of all future liabilities related thereto.

Change of Circumstances

18. If, as a result of the publication or coming into effect of any Act amending or repealing the National Health Service (Scotland) Act 1978, or any Regulations made under that Act or such amending or repealing Act, it shall appear to any partner that the continuation of the partnership in terms of these presents would be impossible or impracticable or a hardship to him, he shall be entitled, failing

agreement between the parties, to require that there shall be referred to the Arbiter aftermentioned the questions (a) whether the partnership shall continue, and (b) if so, on what terms, and (c) if not, on what terms it shall be dissolved, and the Arbiter has hereby power conferred upon him to answer said questions, to declare that the partnership should be dissolved, or the terms and conditions, if any, on which it should be varied, if and to such extent as he may deem just and equitable; and in making his award the Arbiter shall have due regard to the rights and liabilities of the parties immediately prior to the coming into effect of the said amending or repealing Act or the said Regulations as the case may be.

19. [As in Clause 16 of Standard Style]
20. [As in Clause 18 of Standard Style]
21. [As in Clause 19 of Standard Style]

(*To be attested*)   Stamp Duty nil.

B. Assumption of New Partner

Assumption in terms of right reserved in original contract

11–54   In certain contracts of partnership a right may be reserved to a partner or partners to introduce a son or daughter into the partnership. The right may be expressed without specifying the terms as to contribution to capital or share of profits. That leaves it within the power of the partners to make the terms of admission unattractive. Alternatively the contract may provide for the new partner to acquire a proportion of the capital and share of profits of the partner who is entitled to introduce him.[49] Save in the case where the capital and share of profits are to be found wholly from the share of the introducing partner having the right of introduction it is probably preferable to stipulate the right but leave the conditions to be agreed among the partners. When the relationship of the partners is harmonious, the right will be respected and fair terms can be agreed in the knowledge of the circumstances of the partnership at the time.

Voluntary assumption of new partner

11–55   It may be advisable to make the initial endurance of the partnership relatively short, *e.g.* one year during which the quality of the new partner's contribution to the business may be assessed. To provide against the possibility of that being unsatisfactory clause 15 of the standard style may be altered thus: "15. In the event of the partnership

---

[49] For a style and notes see Burns, 118 *et seq.*

being dissolved by notice given under clause 2 hereof and (*the old partners*) intimating to (*the assumed partner*) within three months of the date of receipt thereof that they intend to continue the business of the partnership, the provisions of clause 14 hereof shall apply as if (*the assumed partner*) had retired in terms of clause 12(2) hereof as at the date of termination specified in said notice."

Terms and conditions of new partnership

-56   The new contract of partnership may be on the same lines as the standard style with appropriate alteration of the preamble. Alternatively a Supplementary Minute of Partnership (which effectively creates the new partnership) may be executed which adopts the continuing provisions of the former Contract of Partnership that are to be applicable to the new firm. Whatever its form the deed should specify (1) the period of endurance of the new partnership, (2) the contributions to capital of the old partners (normally the sums at credit of their capital accounts in the balance sheet of the former firm as at the date of its dissolution, without revaluation of assets) and the contribution to capital (if any) of the new partner (3) the shares of profits and losses of the partners and (4) whether the new partner is to be responsible, along with the old partners, for the liabilities of the former partnership (normally he will undertake that responsibility save in special circumstances).

Style

-57   SUPPLEMENTARY MINUTE OF PARTNERSHIP
among
A (*designed*) (hereinafter called "Mr. A")
B (*designed*) (hereinafter called "Mr. B")
C (*designed*) (hereinafter called "Mr. C")
and
D (*designed*) (hereinafter called "Mr. D")

WHEREAS Mr. A, Mr. B and Mr. C have carried on the business of A, B & Co. in partnership in terms of Contract of Partnership dated   and it has been agreed to assume Mr D as a partner THEREFORE the parties AGREE:

1. The firm name shall be A, B & Co. and the business shall be carried on at   and/or elsewhere as may be agreed.

2. The partnership shall [commence] [be held to have commenced] on   and, subject to the provisions hereof, shall continue until the   day of   and from year to year thereafter until dissolved by written notice given by any partner to the other partners at least [six] [three] months prior to (*original date of termination specified above*) or prior to (*anniversary of original date of termination*) in any year thereafter.

3. The initial capital of Mr. A, Mr. B and Mr. C shall be the sums at credit of their respective capital accounts as shown in the Balance

Sheet of the former partnership of A, B & Co. prepared as at (*date of dissolution of former partnership*). The initial capital of Mr. D shall be £   . (*Continue as in Standard Style to end of Clause*).

4. The partners shall be entitled to the profits of the partnership and shall bear any losses in the proportions of (*state proportions for each partner*) which may be varied as the partners may mutually agree in writing from time to time. The partners shall be entitled to draw in anticipation of profits such amounts and at such times as the partners may mutually agree [in writing].

5. The provisions of clauses 5 to 14 inclusive of the said Contract of Partnership of the former firm of A, B & Co. shall apply to the partnership hereby created to the same effect as if these clauses were incorporated herein.

6. (*Insert clause on the lines of Clause 15 of Standard Style or clause in paragraph 11–55 as may be preferred*).

7. Clause 16 of the said Contract of Partnership of the former firm of A, B & Co. shall apply to the partnership hereby created. Further, in respect of the termination of the said former firm and the commencement of the partnership hereby created Mr. D shall, if so requested by the other partners, join with them in giving the like notice and in that event shall have the like indemnity by the other partners *mutatis mutandis* as are contained in the said clause 16.

8. The provisions of clauses 17, 18 and 19 of the said Contract of Partnership of the former firm of A, B & Co. shall apply to the partnership hereby created to the same effect as if these clauses were incorporated herein.

9. The parties consent to registration hereof and of any decree arbitral to follow hereon for preservation and execution.

(To be attested)

Stamp 50p.

NOTE

The clauses in the Contract of Partnership of the former firm referred to are as in the Standard Style.

Taxation

11–58   As regards income tax and capital allowances an election for continuance is competent—see clause 7 in paragraph 11–57 *supra* and Lindley on *Partnership* (14th ed.) ps. 873 *et seq*. As regards capital gains tax, particularly where there is a capital contribution by the incoming partner or where assets of the former firm are revalued, see Lindley, *op. cit.*, ps. 895 *et seq*.

As regards capital transfer tax when there is a connected relationship between one of the partners of the former firm and the assumed partner see Lindley, *op. cit.* ps. 913, 914.

Stamp duty

-59 Stamp duty will be 50p if clause 9 is included: if not, no stamp duty is payable. In the circumstances where A is providing the capital of D (his son) clause 3 should make no reference to the balance sheet of the former firm but should simply state the initial capital of A as £   (being his capital as in that balance sheet reduced by the amount transferred to D), the capital of B and C as £   and £   (the sum at credit of their respective capital accounts in the former firm) and the capital of D as £   (the sum transferred to him by A).

C. DISSOLUTION

Documentation

-60 Upon dissolution of a partnership the primary objective of any documentation is to ensure that the terms of dissolution are properly recorded. Subject to that, however, there are important considerations affecting stamp duty and income tax which may determine the most suitable form of any documents required.

Dissolution on Retirement or Death of Partner where other Partners are Continuing—Stamp Duty and Taxation

-61 **(a) Stamp duty.** If the contract of partnership has made provision for the ascertainment of the value of the share and interest of the outgoing or deceased partner and payment therefor by instalments (*e.g.* clause 14 of Standard Style), no further agreement on dissolution is required. Receipts for the stipulated payments, the last of which bears to be in full and final settlement of the interest of the outgoing partner or his representatives in the firm, will not normally involve liability for stamp duty.[49a] On the other hand if the contract has made no such provision, or if the provisions in the contract are being altered by agreement at the time of dissolution, a Minute of Dissolution may be required to record the arrangement or the altered arrangement, although that document may attract *ad valorem* stamp duty if the value of the share of an outgoing or deceased partner is being transferred to continuing partners, and it will usually be advisable to incorporate in such a deed arrangements on ancillary matters such as a restrictive covenant (where the outgoing partner is living) and tax election.

-62 **(b) Capital Gains Tax.** Where a partner retires and his share and interest is acquired by the continuing partners there is a disposal of his share and a charge to capital gains tax will be incurred subject to (i) relief under section 126 of the Capital Gains Tax Act 1979, which is available in the case of a family partnership where the disposal is not made as part of a

---

[49a] See para. 11–65.

bargain at arm's length, or (ii) relief under section 124 of the Capital Gains Tax Act 1979 where the retiring partner has attained the age of 60. No capital gains tax liability arises on dissolution by the death of a partner nor where the bargain is not one of purchase of the outgoing partner's share so long as it is expressed as an annuity given independently of the disposal of the partner's share and not as a consideration for that disposal.

11–63   (c) Income Tax. Where payment is made in respect of a purchase of the share of a retiring or deceased partner by the continuing partners, it is of a capital nature and income tax will be payable only on the interest on any instalments of the payment. Where an annuity is paid to the retiring partner or the representatives or dependants of a deceased partner, not expressed as consideration for his share in the business, the payments of the annuity are income payments, taxable by deduction under section 52 of the Income and Corporation Taxes Act 1970 and constituting a charge on the income of the continuing business. The payments will be treated as income in the hands of the recipient, taxed by deduction but liable to be brought into account for higher rate tax.

11–64   (d) Capital transfer tax. Where a partner dies and the contract of partnership has provided for the acquisition of his share by the surviving partners without any payment for goodwill that arrangement will normally be treated as full consideration in money's worth for the right to acquire the share of the deceased partner and the amount to be included in the estate of the deceased partner for the purpose of the charge to capital transfer tax will be the sum payable by the surviving partners, ignoring any value for goodwill.[50] In the absence of any such provision the value of the share in the business will be assessed on normal principles of valuation, i.e. its value in the open market either on a going-concern basis (which will take into account the value of the share of goodwill) or on a break-up basis, subject to any reliefs available, e.g. business property relief[51] and/or agricultural property relief.[52]

Receipts

11–65   Where a retiring partner withdraws what is due to him as agreed with the other partners who continue the business and a receipt for the sum received is thereafter granted by the retiring partner, then, so long as there is no writing which effects an assignation of his interest to the continuing partners, it is considered that no liability to stamp duty will be incurred.[53] Likewise, where the contract of partnership has provided for

---

[50] Capital Transfer Act 1984, s. 163; *Att. Gen.* v. *Boden* [1912] 1 K.B. 539, but see *Perpetual Executors & Trustees Association of Australia* v. *Commissioners of Taxes for Australia* [1954] A.C. 114 (P.C.). See also *Ventisei* v. *Ventisei's Exrs.*, 1966 S.C. 21.
[51] Capital Transfer Tax Act 1984, ss. 103 to 114.
[52] *Ibid.*, ss. 115 to 130.
[53] *Garnett* v. *I.R.C.* (1899) 81 L.T. 633, 637; *cf. Fleetwood-Hesketh* v. *I.R.C.* [1936] 1 K.B. 351.

payment by instalments in respect of the share and interest of the retiring partner, simple receipts for each instalment do not involve liability to stamp duty.

Receipt by retiring partner—single payment

–66 (*Place, date*) Received by me A (*designed*) from the firm of A, B & Co. (*designed*) the sum of £   in full settlement of my whole share and interest in the said firm.

Receipt by retiring partner—last instalment of payment under contract of partnership

–67 (*Place, date*) Received by me A (*designed*) from the firm of A, B & Co. (*designed*) the sum of £   which, together with instalments each of £   previously paid to me, with interest thereon also paid to me, are in full and final settlement of my whole share and interest in the said firm.

Minutes of Dissolution

–68 Where a formal agreement recording the terms of dissolution is required[54] the style of deed will vary with circumstances. The three styles printed below are applicable where (i) a partner is retiring and his share in the business is being transferred to the continuing partners in exchange for a consideration in cash, (ii) a partner is retiring and is receiving an annuity or pension, and (iii) the business is being wound up and its assets distributed among the partners.

Minute of dissolution—retiring partner—transfer of interest to continuing partners for cash payment

–69 MINUTE OF DISSOLUTION
of
A, B & Co. (*designed*)
among
A (*designed*) (hereinafter called "Mr. A")
B (*designed*) (hereinafter called "Mr. B")
and
C (*designed*) (hereinafter called "Mr. C")

WHEREAS the parties hereto have carried on business in partnership as   under the firm name of A, B & Co. [in terms of Contract of Partnership among them dated   ]; AND WHEREAS Mr. A is retiring from the partnership as at   (*date*) THEREFORE the parties AGREE:

1. The partnership shall terminate [be deemed to have terminated] on   .

2. The parties shall sign a notice in terms adjusted between them which shall be inserted in the Edinburgh Gazette. Copies of said

---

[54] See para. 11–61.

notice shall be sent to persons who have dealt with the firm during the last   years.

3. The whole assets of every kind of the said firm shall be retained by Mr. B and Mr. C to be owned by them in such proportions as they may mutually agree and Mr. A hereby assigns to Mr. B and Mr. C his whole share and interest therein and in the business carried on by the said A, B & Co. and binds himself and his executors and representatives to execute and deliver to Mr. B and Mr. C all further conveyances, deeds and writings necessary or convenient for that purpose. Mr. B and Mr. C shall be entitled to continue business under the firm name of A, B & Co. but Mr. A shall not be entitled to use the said firm name or any name of which B or C shall form part.

4. [*Restrictive covenant, if desired*]

5. Mr. B and Mr. C shall pay to Mr. A [on   (*date of dissolution*)] [on the execution of this deed, (*if later*)] the sum of £ which Mr. A accepts in full settlement of his whole share and interest in the said firm and the assets thereof. [From that sum there shall be deducted any amount overdrawn by Mr. A as shown in a Balance Sheet of the said firm as at   (*date of dissolution*)].

6. Mr. B and Mr. C jointly and severally undertake liability for the whole debts and liabilities of the said firm and shall be entitled to use the name of Mr. A in recovering debts or claims due to the said firm, Mr. B and Mr. C being bound to relieve Mr. A of all expenses that may be incurred in relation to debts, liabilities or claims due by or to the said firm.[55] Mr. B and Mr. C shall exhibit to Mr. A or his representatives within   months of the date or last date of execution hereof receipts or discharges of all debts and liabilities of the said firm existing at   (*date of dissolution*).

7. [Tax election binding on Mr. A—see clause 16 of Standard Style of Contract of Partnership—para. 11–43].

8. All stamp duties in connection with the dissolution, fees for Gazette notice and the cost of other advertisements and circulars in relation to the dissolution shall be borne by Mr. B and Mr. C. (*Stamp clause if appropriate*).

(*To be attested*)

Stamp duty as conveyance on sale.

Documentation—Retiring Partner receiving an Annuity

11–70   The form of documentation depends upon the nature of the bargain and in particular whether the annual payments are to be of a capital or income character, and tax advisers should be consulted as to the precise terms of the agreement necessary to achieve the desired result. Factors which indicate that the annual payments are of a capital nature are (i) that the agreement was one of sale and purchase of the retiring

---

[55] It will usually be necessary to qualify this undertaking by excepting the liability to income tax on Mr. A's share of profits in respect of the period prior to dissolution—see *Stevens* v. *Britten* [1954] 1 W.L.R. 1340.

partner's share in the business and its assets even although the price was
measured by the profits of the business in future years[56] or past years,[57]
(ii) that there was no express stipulation for deduction of tax,[58] and (iii)
that a single sum was payable even though expressed in the form of
annual payments over a stated period.[58] On the other hand if it is
intended that the annual payments should be of the nature of income,
then (i) the agreement to make the payments should be divorced from
any provisions for the acquisition of the retiring partner's share by the
continuing partners and (ii) the annual payment should expressly be
stated to be subject to deduction of tax.[59]

Annuity as consideration for share—payments of capital

1–71   1, 2, 3 and 4. [*As in style in para. 11–69*]
5. Mr. B and Mr. C shall pay to Mr. A [the sum of £   payable by
equal instalments of £   on the   day of   in
each of the   years (*state the calendar years*)] [per cent of
the profits (before tax) of the continuing firm of A, B & Co. in each
of the   years ending on   (*date of annual accounts
and calendar years*) payable three months after said dates in each
year] without deduction of income tax and without interest, which
payments Mr. A accepts in full settlement of his whole share and
interest in the firm of A, B & Co. and the assets thereof.
6, 7 and 8. [As in style in para. 11–69].

(*To be attested*)

Stamp duty as conveyance on sale based on value of annuity.

Income annuity

1–72   1, 2, 3 and 4 [As in style in para. 11–69]
5. Mr. B and Mr. C shall pay to Mr. A [on   (*date of dissolution*)] [on the execution of this deed, (*if later*)] the sum of £   [60]
which Mr. A accepts in full settlement of his whole share and interest in the said firm and the assets thereof.
6. Mr. B and Mr. C will pay to Mr. A by way of acknowledgment of
his past services to the said firm [an annual sum of £   (during his
lifetime) (during the period of   years) payable on the
day of   in each year] [per cent of the profits (before
tax) of the said firm of A, B & Co. in each of the   years ending
on   (*date of annual accounts and calendar years*) payable
three months after said dates in each year] under deduction of
income tax at standard rate current at the date of each payment.

---

[56] *I.R.C.* v. *Ledgard* [1937] 2 All E.R. 492.
[57] *Inland Revenue* v. *Hunter*, 1955 S.C. 248.
[58] *Inland Revenue* v. *Hogarth*, 1941 S.C. 1.
[59] Annual payments to a retiring partner, even for a relatively short period, are not treated as income
of the continuing partners: Income and Corporation Taxes Act 1970, s. 457.
[60] This amount depends on the bargain. If Mr. A is to receive the full amount at credit of his capital
account (and the annuity is additional) that amount will be inserted. If Mr. A is accepting a lesser payment and the annuity is truly part consideration the lesser sum (so long as it is not manifestly illusory)
will be inserted.

7, 8 and 9. [As in clauses 6, 7 and 8 of style in para. 11–69]

(*To be attested*)

Stamp duty as conveyance on sale on amount in clause 5.

Alternatively, an agreement on the foregoing lines but with the omission of clause 6 may be executed and thereafter a bond of annuity granted by the continuing partners in favour of Mr. A. This may be preferable where the relationship of the parties is such that Mr. A can rely upon the continuing partners honouring the arrangement to grant the bond of annuity subsequently.

Minute of Dissolution—Distribution of Assets

11–73

MINUTE OF DISSOLUTION
of
A, B & Co. (*designed*)
between
A (*designed*) (hereinafter called "Mr. A")
and
B (*designed*) (hereinafter called "Mr. B")

WHEREAS the parties hereto have carried on business in partnership as   under the firm name of A, B & Co. [in terms of Contract of Partnership between them dated   ] and they have agreed to dissolve the said partnership as at   ; AND WHEREAS final accounts of the partnership as at the date of dissolution have been prepared and examined and the parties are satisfied that a fair basis of settlement of their interests in the said firm is that hereinafter contained THEREFORE the parties AGREE:

1. Mr. A shall receive (*specify the assets and cash (if any) to be taken by Mr. A*).

2. Mr. B shall receive all the other assets of the said firm including goodwill but he shall not be entitled to use the firm name or any name of which A is part. Mr. B will indemnify Mr. A against all debts and liabilities of the business of A, B & Co.[61] and shall, if required by Mr. A, exhibit evidence of settlement thereof within months of the date of dissolution above mentioned.

3. Mr. A and Mr. B will execute and deliver all documents necessary or convenient to transfer assets of the said firm to the party entitled thereto in accordance with this agreement.

4. Subject to the implement of the terms of this agreement the parties discharge each other of all claims and matters relating to the said partnership and business.

5. [*As in clause 2 of style in para. 11–69*].

6. [*Provision as to expenses*].

---

[61] Qualify if necessary as regards liability to income tax on Mr. A's share of profits prior to dissolution—para. 11–69, note 55.

7. The parties consent to registration hereof for preservation and execution.

(*To be attested*)

Stamp 50p.

Heritable Property of Partnership

1–74 Heritable property owned by a partnership will have been, and property leased to it may have been, taken in the names of individual partners as trustees for the firm.[62] Upon a dissolution of the firm by retiral of a partner who is one of the named trustees it is advisable to procure the signature of the retiring partner to a deed which transfers the title to trustees for the continuing firm so that it is unnecessary to obtain his signature to any future dealing with the property during his lifetime and incidentally is a precaution against the trust lapsing through the deaths of all the original trustees. The form of deed appropriate depends upon the terms of the title. If the original title was taken in the usual form, *e.g.* "to A, B and C, the partners of the firm of A, B & Co. and the survivors and survivor of them as trustees for the said firm of A, B & Co. and the partners thereof present and future" it is thought that the reference to future partners necessarily implies that the objects of the trust as originally constituted include the partners of any new firm which continues to carry on the business of A, B & Co. In these circumstances it may be argued that a deed of assumption of the new partners as trustees and a minute of resignation by the retiring partner (with consequent economy in stamp duty) are sufficient, since there has been no change in the objects of the trust as originally created, only a change in the personnel of the trustees. If, however, the original title of the trustees was taken in more limited terms without reference to future partners a disposition of the property or an assignation of the lease, as the case may be, in favour of the new trustees is appropriate, which is *prima facie* liable to stamp duty as a conveyance on sale,[63] since there would be a transfer of property to a new trust for different beneficiaries.

1–75 Where heritable property is let to the firm by a lease which continues after the date of dissolution, or where heritable property owned by the firm is subject to a security, it is important that on dissolution by the retiral or death of a partner the obligations of the outgoing or deceased partner under the lease or the security should be discharged by the landlord or creditor. The obligation of relief by the continuing partners in the document of dissolution may be insufficient protection if the firm and its partners subsequently become insolvent.

---

[62] See para. 11–09(iii).

[63] If the Minute of Dissolution is liable to *ad valorem* stamp duty as a conveyance the disposition or assignation should be submitted for adjudication with the minute, when duplication of stamp duty may be avoided.

D. Limited Partnerships

Statutory creation

11–76   The Limited Partnerships Act 1907 authorised the formation of limited partnerships, consisting of one or more general partners and one or more limited partners. The liability of a limited partner for the debts and obligations of the firm is restricted to the amount of his contribution to the capital of the firm and he may not take part in the management of the partnership business[64]; he is in effect a sleeping partner with limited liability. The general partners conduct the business of the partnership and, like members of an ordinary partnership, are liable for all its debts and obligations.[65] For a full account of the nature of a limited partnership, the rights and obligations of the partners *inter se* and in relation to third parties dealing with the firm and its dissolution and winding up, reference may be made to the undernoted texts.[66] A limited partnership must be registered as such.[67]

Use

11–77   Limited partnerships are not in common use save for special reasons, since private limited companies providing limited liability for all participators are usually preferred. A limited partnership has certain advantages, *e.g.* its profits are liable to income tax and not corporation tax and its accounts need not be disclosed to the public. It has proved useful as a method of evading the statutory protections given to agricultural tenants by the Agricultural Holdings Acts, the method being to create a limited partnership in which the landlord is the limited partner, the general partner is the person who actually carries on the business but the lease is granted in favour of the partnership. The contract of partnership confers power on the limited partner to dissolve the partnership, thereby terminating the lease and so circumventing the security of tenure which the partnership tenant would otherwise have.[68]

Contract of partnership

11–78   The contract of partnership may be framed along the lines of an ordinary partnership subject to the compliance of its provisions with the 1907 Act. It should specify the full names and designations of the partners, the firm name, the nature of the business, the principal place of business, the period of endurance, a statement that the partnership is

---

[64] Limited Partnerships Act 1907, s. 6(1).

[65] *Ibid.*, s. 4(2).

[66] J.B. Miller, *Partnership*, 583 *et seq.*; *Lindley on Partnership* (14th ed.), 823 *et seq.* See also Limited Partnerships Rules 1907 as amended by Limited Partnerships (Amendment) Rules 1972 (S.I. 1972 No. 1040) and 1974 (S.I. 1974 No. 560).

[67] 1907 Act, s. 5.

[68] Gill, *Law of Agricultural Holdings in Scotland*, 3. See *Inland Revenue* v. *Graham's Trs.*, 1971 S.C.(H.L.) 1.

limited and the description of each partner as a limited or general partner as the case may be and the capital contributed by each limited partner and each general partner. Provision should be made for the sharing of profits or losses, but the liability of a limited partner for losses should be restricted to the amount of his capital contribution. The usual provision as to books and accounts will be included. Prohibited acts should include in the case of a limited partner withdrawal of any part of his capital[69] and contribution to and participation in any way in the management of the business and he will have no power to bind the firm.[70] A limited partner will have power to assign his share with the consent of the general partners when the assignee will become a limited partner in his place,[71] but any such change must be advertised in the Edinburgh Gazette.[72] The provisions in respect of a limited partner upon dissolution should be stated, the statutory background being that subject to any agreement expressed or implied between the partners a limited partner may not dissolve the partnership by notice[73] nor is the partnership determined by his death or bankruptcy.[74]

Registration

1–79   A Scottish limited partnership must be registered in the Register of Companies, Edinburgh.[75] Registration is effected by delivery or transmission by post to the Registrar of Companies of a statement signed by all the partners, both limited and general, containing particulars of (1) the firm name, (2) the general nature of the business, (3) the principal place of business, (4) the full names of all partners, (5) the period for which the partnership is to endure and the date of its commencement, (6) a statement that the partnership is limited and the description of every limited partner as such, (7) the sum contributed by each limited partner and whether paid in cash or how otherwise paid, and (8) the capital duty payable.[76,77]

---

[69] 1907 Act s. 4(3).

[70] *Ibid.*, s. 6(1).

[71] *Ibid.*, s. 6(5)(b).

[72] *Ibid.*, s. 10.

[73] *Ibid.*, s. 6(5)(e).

[74] *Ibid.*, s. 6(2). As to possible problems see Lindley, *op. cit.*, 851.

[75] *Ibid.*, s. 5.

[76] *Ibid.*, s. 8

[77] Capital duty is payable at £1 per cent on the total amount of the capital contributions of the limited partners; Finance Act 1973, ss. 47, 48 and Sched. 19.

CHAPTER 12

BUILDING, ENGINEERING AND OTHER CONSTRUCTION CONTRACTS

Introductory

12–01 Contracts for the construction of buildings or engineering works are normally entered into on the basis of model conditions of contract published by professional institutions.[1] The contract documents usually comprise a tender submitted by the contractor for performance of work specified in drawings and/or bills of quantities and/or specifications issued by the employer and a formal agreement between the employer and the contractor to carry out the work for the price tendered or for work as measured at stipulated rates upon model conditions appropriate to the nature of the contract. In addition there may be a performance bond whereby a bank or other body guarantees payment of a stated sum if the contractor defaults in implementing his part of the contract. The standard work on the law relating to such contracts is Hudson's *Building and Engineering Contracts*[2] and useful commentaries on the model forms are undernoted.[3] More specialised types of contract such as shipbuilding contracts are usually adjusted in relation to the particular vessel but many relatively standard clauses are customarily incorporated although their precise terms are negotiable between the contracting parties. Export contracts are frequently guaranteed by the Export Credits Guarantee Department by a specific guarantee in a form adjusted by the department.

12–02 An exhaustive examination of the various model conditions and standard clauses is outwith the scope of a general work on conveyancing; the present chapter is restricted to a commentary on some of the more common conditions from the Scottish legal and conveyancing aspects. Styles of particular clauses may be found in the standard contracts or conditions already mentioned or in Butterworth, *Encyclopaedia of Forms and Precedents*, Volume 3.

PRELIMINARY CONSIDERATIONS

Planning and building—statutory regulations

12–03 Before building or engineering operations which constitute a development within the meaning of the Town and Country Planning (Scotland) Act 1972[4] commence planning permission must be obtained from the

---

[1] *e.g.* Standard Form of Building Contract published by Scottish Building Contract Committee, Conditions of Contract published by the Institution of Civil Engineers (ICE Conditions), the Institution of Mechanical Engineers (I Mech E Conditions) or the Institution of Electrical Engineers (IEE Conditions). Works for Government departments usually incorporate General Conditions of Government Contracts for Building and Engineering Works - see *J.B. MacKenzie (Ed.) Ltd.* v. *Lord Advocate*, 1972 S.C. 231.

[2] (10th ed., 1970) with 1979 Supplement.

[3] Sir D. Walker-Smith and H.A. Close, *The Standard Form of Building Contracts*; D. Keating *RIBA Contracts*, W.J. Creswell *Building and Engineering Contracts*, (Building Contracts); M.W. Abrahamson *Engineering Law and ICE Contracts*, (Civil Engineering Contracts); I.N. Duncan Wallace *Building and Civil Engineering Contracts*, (both Building and ICE Contracts); K.F.A. Johnston *Electrical and Mechanical Engineering Contracts*, (I Mech. E and IEE Contracts).

[4] s. 19. As to operations which are within the definition of "development" see E. Young, *The Law of Planning in Scotland*, 64 *et seq.*

appropriate planning authority,[5] and there are special provisions with regard to particular classes of buildings.[6] It is also necessary to obtain a building warrant under the Building (Scotland) Acts 1959 and 1970 from the authority responsible for building control in the area[7] whose function is to ensure that the proposed structure complies with the current Building Standards (Scotland) Regulations. The obtaining of such permissions and warrants is the responsibility of the employer and his professional advisers. As to procedure in making application for planning permission or a building warrant see the statutory provisions and regulations undernoted.[8]

Title conditions and other restrictions

12–04   Since it is the duty of the employer to give the contractor possession of the site or premises where the work is to be performed,[9] it is necessary to ensure that there are no conditions of title, servitude rights, rights of way or other rights which would prohibit or restrict completion of the contract works.[10] Special attention should be given to the existence of public services such as electricity, gas or telephone cables or pipes or sewers in or over the site which may be affected by the proposed works and, where necessary, the employer should arrange for their protection or rerouting.

DOCUMENTS

Kinds of documents

2–05   All or some of the documents involved in the negotiations and final contract are (1) the general conditions of contract, (2) the specification, (3) the bills of quantities, (4) the drawings, (5) the schedule of rates, (6) the tender, (7) the formal contract, and (8) the performance bond.

General conditions of contract

2–06   Usually one of the standard forms of conditions already referred to in paragraph 12–01 *supra* appropriate to the nature of the works to be carried out is adopted. Some of the conditions which have important legal implications are considered later in this chapter.

---

[5] As to regional, district and general planning authorities see Local Government (Scotland) Act 1973, s. 172 and Sched. 22.

[6] *e.g.* listed buildings—1972 Act. ss. 53, 162, and Town and Country Planning (Listed Buildings and Buildings in Conservation Areas) (Scotland) Regulations 1975 (S.I. 1975 No. 2069) as amended by S.I. 1977 No. 255.

[7] Normally the district or islands council—Local Government (Scotland) Act 1973, s. 134.

[8] Town and Country Planning (Scotland) Act 1972 s. 24; Town and Country Planning (General Development) (Scotland) Order 1981 (S.I. 1981 No. 830) as amended; Building (Scotland) Act 1959 s. 24; Building (Procedure) (Scotland) Regulations 1971, (S.I. 1971 No. 746 (s. 104)).

[9] See *MacKay & Son* v. *Leven Police Commissioners* (1893) 20 R.1093.

[10] *e.g.* a servitude of access as in *Armia Ltd.* v. *Daejan Developments Ltd.*, 1979 S.C.(H.L.) 56.

Specification and bill of quantities

12–07   The employer and his technical advisers prepare a specification which indicates the design of the works and may be subdivided into different items of work and may specify also the method of performance. The contractor is invited to price the various items. In larger contracts a bill of quantities is prepared by a quantity surveyor indicating in more detail the preliminary site work and the work of construction and the contractor prices each of the items in the bill of quantities. The contents of the bill of quantities vary according to the nature of the work: in building contracts there are separate bills for each trade involved and in civil engineering contracts separate bills for each stage of the preparatory work on site and the actual construction works. Standard methods of measurement are specified.

Drawings

12–08   The employer's architect or engineer prepares drawings which should contain sufficient detail to enable the contractor to carry out the work and (where there are no bills of quantities) to assess the price. More detailed working drawings may be provided later but if these disclose items which could not have been inferred as necessary from the drawings provided at the stage of tender the contractor may have a claim for additional payment.

Schedule of rates

12–09   Where the full extent of the work required to complete the contract cannot be ascertained with precision when the contract is being entered into a schedule of rates may be incorporated showing the prices to be charged for particular types of item, often with provision for escalation of the quoted prices which may arise from increases in the cost of materials and labour between the date of the contract and the time when the work is performed.[11]

Tender

12–10   In some cases, particularly civil engineering contracts, standard forms of tender are issued by the employer but in other cases the contractor submits a tender of a less formal type, but in all cases tenders are made on the basis of the general conditions, drawings, specifications, bills of quantities and schedule of rates issued by the employer and specify a date for completion of the works.

Prices should be quoted for each separate item in the specification or bill of quantities in order to facilitate comparison of the tenders received.

---

[11] See para. 12–22.

Formal contract

2–11 The formal agreement to contract may be in a standard form prescribed by the employer[12] or it may be left to the acceptance of the tender subject to all the conditions thereof. An agreement usually specifies the parties, contains a general description of the works, states the contract price (if a lump sum) or refers to a schedule of rates in appropriate cases, and incorporates the general conditions (either by way of an appendix or by reference to standard conditions) and the tender, drawings, specification, priced bill of quantities and, where applicable, schedule of rates as parts of the contract. Important contracts should be formally executed.

Performance bond

2–12 Where completion of the contract is to be guaranteed by a third party (normally a bank or financial house) a performance bond will be executed by the guarantor.[13]

Construction of documents

2–13 In the construction of the documents constituting the contract the ordinary rule applies that the intention of parties is to be ascertained by considering the documents as a whole.[14] Where a special *ad hoc* provision is stipulated which is inconsistent with general standard conditions the former will normally prevail.[15] In some forms of general conditions express provision is made regulating the order of preference in construction between general conditions and particular conditions in bills of quantities or other documents incorporated in the whole contract.

FORMATION OF CONTRACT

Invitation to tender

2–14 An invitation to tender is simply an indication of willingness to treat and acceptance of a tender is necessary before a binding contract is completed.[16] It is unnecessary to state that the lowest or any offer may not be accepted. However, if it is stated that the lowest tender will be accepted that amounts to an offer and the lowest tenderer may claim that there is a concluded contract.[17] An invitation to tender may be

---

[12] The Scottish Building Contract Committee and the ICE Conditions prescribe a form of contract.
[13] See para. 12–50.
[14] See para. 4–26.
[15] *The Brabant* [1967] 1 Q.B. 588.
[16] *Spencer* v. *Harding* (1870) L.R. 5 C.P. 561.
[17] *Paton* v. *Macpherson* (1889) 17 R. 52.

revoked and a tender may be withdrawn at any time prior to acceptance.[18]

Tenders are usually stated to be open for acceptance only for a specified period, but even without such a stipulation a tender lapses if not accepted within a reasonable period.[19]

Acceptance of tender

12–15   Acceptance, without qualification, of a tender sent by post constitutes a concluded contract[20] as from the date when the acceptance is posted.[21] Qualifications in the tender or acceptance require confirmation by the other party before a binding contract exists.[22]

Collusive tendering

12–16   Agreements to refrain from tendering or to tender at an artificially high price are not illegal at common law but are void and unenforceable under the Restrictive Trade Practices Act 1956[23] unless registered and, if part of a course of conduct, may be struck at as restricting or preventing competition under the Competition Act 1980.[24]

Misrepresentation

12–17   If a contractor is induced to enter into a contract by fraudulent misrepresentation of fact he may resile from the contract or claim damages or both.[25] If the misrepresentation is innocent arising from a mistake made honestly and not negligently the contract thus induced is reducible so long as *restitutio in integrum* is possible,[26] but damages are not recoverable.[27] If a contractor continues with the work after discovering an innocent misrepresentation he loses his right to rescind[28] and may only claim the price fixed by the contract.[29]

EEC conditions

12–18   In the case of certain types of contract, *e.g.* public works contracts of substantial value,[30] directives issued by the Council of Ministers of the European Communities should be observed with regard to procedure for advertising and awarding contracts.[31] Also for certain export

---

[18] *J.M. Smith Ltd.* v. *Colquhoun's Tr.* (1901) 3 F. 981; Bell, Prin., s. 73.
[19] *Murray* v. *Rennie* (1897) 24 R. 965; *Lawrence* v. *Knight* 1972 S.C. 26.
[20] *Tancred, Arrol & Co.* v. *Steel Company of Scotland Ltd.* (1890) 17 R.(H.L.) 31.
[21] *Dunlop* v. *Higgins* (1848) 6 Bell's App. 195.
[22] *Wylie & Lochhead* v. *McElroy & Sons* (1873) 1 R. 41.
[23] ss. 1, 6 and 9.
[24] s. 2.
[25] *Moss & Co. Ltd.* v. *Swansea Corp.* (1910) 74 J.P. 351. *Cf. Smith & Houston Ltd.* v. *Metal Industries (Salvage) Ltd.*, 1953 S.L.T.(Notes) 73.
[26] *Boyd & Forrest* v. *Glasgow & South Western Rly. Co.*, 1914 S.C. 472, revd. 1915 S.C.(H.L.) 20.
[27] *Brownlie* v. *Miller* (1880) 7 R.(H.L.) 66; *Dunnett* v. *Mitchell* (1887) 15 R. 131.
[28] *Ormes* v. *Beadel* (1860) 2 De G. F. & J. 333.
[29] *Boyd & Forrest* v. *Glasgow & South Western Rly. Co.*, *supra.*
[30] At least £415,000.
[31] See Halsbury's *Laws of England* (4th ed.) Vol. 4, paras. 1149 *et seq.*

contracts, particularly in relation to plant and machinery and its erection abroad, model conditions have been published by the Economic Commission for Europe which, although not compulsory, are being widely adopted.[32]

Local authority contracts

2–19 A local authority must make standing orders with respect to the making of contracts for the execution of works.[33] A contractor is not bound to inquire whether the standing orders have been complied with, and non-compliance with the orders does not invalidate a contract.[34]

PARTICULAR PROVISIONS

(a) Price

Ascertainment

2–20 The price will normally be determined by the contract, and may be in the form of a total sum based on specifications or priced bills of quantities, but where the extent of the work cannot be ascertained initially the ultimate price will be determined in accordance with a schedule of rates. Most building and engineering contracts provide for remeasurement of the work: where the price has been based on drawings or specifications, without bills of quantities, remeasurement affects only extra payment for variations authorised by the employer's architect or engineer in the course of construction but, where there have been bills of quantities, the contractor is normally entitled to require remeasurement and adjustment of the price based on the new measurements of the work contracted for and any variations.

Variations

2–21 In building contracts variations which may result in adjustment of the price are usually carefully defined[35] but normally include alterations or omissions of any work, alterations of the kind or standard of materials, alterations or omissions in access to the site or limitations upon working space or time or the execution of the works in any specific order. In civil engineering contracts adverse physical conditions or the existence of artificial obstructions together with variations ordered by the employer's engineer in the quality, form, position, dimension, level or line or the sequence, method or timing may justify variations in the price.[36] Provision should be made for the instructions of the architect or orders of

---

[32] See K.F.A. Johnston, *Electrical and Mechanical Engineering Contracts*.
[33] Local Government (Scotland) Act 1973, s. 81(2).
[34] *Ibid.*, s. 81(4).
[35] See Scottish Building Contract, cl. 13.
[36] See ICE Conditions, cll. 12, 51.

the engineer being in writing and acknowledged or confirmed by the contractor. In shipbuilding contracts modifications and extras are similarly provided for, the employer notifying the shipbuilder of any alterations or additions required and the shipbuilder formulating proposals for incorporating them in the vessel. Claims for adjustment of the price are conditional upon those procedures being observed.

Fluctuations

12–22   In contracts where the work of construction will extend over a relatively long period a clause should be inserted in the contract providing for appropriate increases in the cost of materials and labour. The former are normally based upon the increase between the cost of materials at the date of contracting and their cost at the date of procurement for the purposes of the contract as shown in appropriate published indices. Variations in labour costs are assessed similarly, usually on the basis of the fluctuations shown in the index figures published by H.M. Stationery Office for the various trades involved. In certain cases it may be appropriate also to provide for increases in the contractor's establishment charges (often taken as a percentage of labour costs) and possibly a percentage of the whole increases in respect of profit to the contractor.

Instalments of price

12–23   It is a common feature of construction contracts that provision is included for payments to account of the price being made as the work progresses. These may be made either on completion of specified stages of the work (in building or shipbuilding contracts) or at stated intervals, often monthly, on submission of statements of the estimated contract value of the work done and materials delivered to the site (in engineering contracts). Certificates of the employer's architect or engineer or other representative authorising interim payments are required before the payments are made.

Retention

12–24   In building and civil engineering contracts it is customary to retain from each instalment payment a stipulated percentage of the payment to be released at a later date. It is usual for the retention money to be released in two instalments, one upon practical or substantial completion and the other on expiry of the maintenance or defects liability period after completion. The standard conditions or model forms of contract contain detailed rules as to the ascertainment of retention money and its release.[37] The retention money is held by the employer in trust for the contractor and is normally placed in a separate bank account, but any interest accrued during the period of retention belongs

---

[37] See ICE Conditions, cl. 60, and Scottish Building Contract cl. 30.

to the employer.[38] In shipbuilding contracts the stage payments are usually so adjusted that up to 10 per cent of the price is paid only after sea trials and acceptance of the vessel: it is not customary to retain part of the price during any subsequent guarantee period.

Value added tax

12–25 The contract price excludes value added tax but the contractor is entitled to payment with each instalment of the price of the amount of tax on materials and services provided by him in respect of which the tax is payable and to receive the amount thereof in addition to the instalment payment.[39]

Export contracts

12–26 (i) **Export credits guarantee.** In the case of contracts of substantial amounts where the employer is a foreign person or company or body it is customary for the contractor to obtain a specific guarantee from the Export Credits Guarantee Department in exchange for a premium. The guarantee is in a form adjusted by the department but in general insures the contractor against non-payment by the employer to the extent of a stated percentage (often 90 per cent) of the contract price subject to a maximum liability specified. The causes of loss covered are stated in the guarantee but generally include failure of the employer to make payment under the contract for reasons including political events, economic difficulties or the operation of law outwith the United Kingdom or the occurrence outwith the United Kingdom of war, revolution or natural catastrophe.

(ii) **Method of payment.** The contract may provide for the employer giving irrevocable letters of credit to bankers in the United Kingdom for the estimated amount of each stage payment authorising payment to the bankers of the contractor upon presentation of the appropriate certificates that the payment is due. In order to minimise postal delays provision may be made for the certificates to be telexed between the parties and their bankers.

(iii) **Rate of exchange differentials.** If payment is not to be made in sterling the contract should provide for increase or decrease in each payment in accordance with fluctuations in the rate of exchange between sterling and the selected currency from the rate of exchange ruling at the date of the contract. If supplies of machinery or special prefabricated parts are to be obtained from foreign sub-contractors or suppliers there should be similar provisions to take account of rate of exchange differentials between the respective currencies of the United Kingdom and the countries of the sub-contractors or suppliers.

---

[38] See Scottish Building Contract, cl. 30.5.
[39] See Scottish Building Contract Supplemental Conditions (VAT Agreement); ICE Conditions cl. 70.

(b) Performance by Contractor

Time for completion

12–27   The contract will normally stipulate a date for completion of the works. Where time is not of the essence of the contract[39a] failure to complete timeously entitles the employer to damages[39b] but not usually to rescind the contract. If, however, the contractor can show that the work has been delayed by reason of extra work ordered by the employer or his architect or engineer or by reason of any act of the the employer and the works have been completed within a reasonable time the employer cannot claim damages.[39c] Where time has been stipulated to be of the essence of the contract, or has been made so by the employer giving notice requiring completion within a specified reasonable time, failure to complete timeously may entitle the employer to treat the failure as repudiation of the contract.[40]

Extension of time

12–28   Modern construction contracts require the contractor to make a written application for extensions of time stating the reasons and the expected period of delay, and the architect or engineer may give an extension in writing of the period for completion.[41] A similar procedure is usually incorporated by express provision in shipbuilding contracts.

Liquidate damages for delay

12–29   It is usual to provide in construction contracts for payment of liquidate damages in the event of failure by the contractor to complete the works (or specified sections of the works) within the time for completion stipulated in the contract as extended by any duly authorised grants of extension.[42] Care must be taken to ensure that the liquidate damages stipulated are a genuine pre-estimate of the loss and not a penalty, and it may be prudent to state that expressly[43] although such a statement is not conclusive of the character of the payments.[44] For a review of the factors relevant to the determination of whether or not a stipulated payment is liquidate damages or a penalty see the undernoted text.[45] In construction contracts the damages are usually stated as a specified sum per day, week or month of the delay beyond the date for completion, which

---

[39a] It is not of the essence of the contract in most model conditions: Scottish Building Contract, Abstract of Conditions App. II; ICE Conditions, cl. 43 and App.

[39b] *Port Glasgow Magistrates* v. *Scottish Construction Co. Ltd.*, 1961 S.L.T. 319.

[39c] *Holme* v. *Guppy* (1838) 3 M. & W. 387; *T. & R. Duncanson* v. *Scottish County Investment Co. Ltd.* 1915 S.C. 1106; *Charles Rickards Ltd.* v. *Oppenheim* [1950] 1 K.B. 616.

[40] *Charles Rickards Ltd.* v. *Oppenheim, supra.*

[41] Scottish Building Contract, cl. 26; ICE Conditions, cl. 44.

[42] See Scottish Building Contract, cl. 24.2; ICE Conditions, cl. 47.

[43] See ICE Conditions, cl. 47(1)(a) and (3).

[44] *Dunlop Pneumatic Tyre Co. Ltd.* v. *New Garage and Motor Co. Ltd.* [1915] A.C. 79 at 86.

[45] Walker, *Contracts*, (2nd ed.) 355 *et seq.*

prima facie favours the interpretation of liquidate damages; on the other hand a provision that the contractor should forfeit the retention money would be a penalty since the amount of the retention money varies according to the amount of work carried out and is unrelated to the loss caused to the employer by the delay in completion.[46]

The fact that it may be difficult to estimate with precision the actual amount of the damages that may result from delay favours the construction that the stipulated amount is of the character of liquidate damages.[47] The value of a provision for liquidate damages is that it avoids the need to assess and prove the actual loss, and in contracts where the amount of the potential loss from delay may be very substantial and incapable of pre-estimate the clause may be useful as a means of limiting the contractor's liability.[48] If the provision is construed as a penalty it is not enforceable[49] and the actual loss sustained by the employer may be recovered as damages.[50] It is usually provided in construction contracts that the stipulated liquidate damages may be recovered by way of deduction from any sum otherwise payable by the employer to the contractor.[51] It should be noted that provisions for liquidate damages for delay do not exclude the right to recover damages at common law where there has been breach of contract which occasions the delay.[51a]

Force majeure clauses

2–30   In model contracts or standard conditions provisions are included permitting extensions of time for completion of the works by reason of the occurrence of events outwith the control of the contractor. The events which will justify an extension of time may be specified particularly[52] or in general terms[53] and the contractor is required to notify the architect or engineer within a stipulated period after the occurrence of the relevant event claiming an extension of time in order that a certificate of extension may be granted. In contracts which are not in model form nor regulated by standard conditions it is essential in the interests of the contractor that a clause be incorporated which will excuse non-timeous performance where delay is caused by circumstances outwith his control. In framing such a clause the draftsman must ensure (i) that general descriptive phases such as "act of God" or "force majeure" cover all the contingencies envisaged, and (ii) that the operation of the *ejusdem generis* rule of construction will not result in an unintended limitation of the

---

[46] *Public Works Commissioner* v. *Hills* [1906] A.C. 368, P.C.
[47] *Clydebank Engineering Co. Ltd.* v. *Castaneda* (1904) 7 F.(H.L.) 77.
[48] *Cellulose Acetate Silk Co. Ltd.* v. *Widnes Foundry (1925) Ltd.* [1933] A.C. 20.
[49] *Robertson* v. *Driver's Trs.* (1881) 8 R. 555, 562.
[50] *Dingwall* v. *Burnett* 1912 S.C. 1097.
[51] See ICE Conditions, cl. 47(4).
[51a] *Chanthall Investments Ltd.* v. *F.G. Minter Ltd.* 1976 S.C. 73.
[52] See Scottish Building Contract, cl. 25.
[53] ICE Conditions, cl. 44.

scope of general words added to a particular list of events.[54] "Act of God" includes an extraordinarily high tide,[55] an unprecedented rainfall,[56] an extraordinary frost[57] or snowfall,[58] or a fire caused by lightning[59] but does not include a fog,[60] an ordinary snowfall[61] or a fire not caused by lightning.[62] "Force majeure" is wider in meaning than "act of God"[63] and includes a strike or breakdown of machinery,[64] difficulties caused by war[65] or refusal of an export licence.[66] A clause which simply specified "usual force majeure clauses to apply" was held void for uncertainty.[67] A reasonably comprehensive clause might be:

> "Provided always that no liability shall arise for delay in completion (delivery) occasioned by strikes, riots, civil commotion, lockouts, go-slow, work to rule or trade disputes affecting employees of the contractor or any of his sub-contractors or manufacturers or suppliers of machinery or other components or materials or sub-contractor's equipment, hostilities (whether war has been declared or not), fire, accident, storm or tempest, any Government intervention, any delay in approval of drawings by the employer or by any other cause (whether of a character similar to the foregoing or not) not being within the control of the contractor."

Sub-contracts

12–31   In many construction contracts particular parts of the work are performed by specialist sub-contractors. In general, contracts should be so framed that any sub-contractors are selected by the main contractor who remains fully responsible to the employer for implementation of the whole contract. In such cases the employer may sue only the main contractor since he has no direct contractual relationship with the sub-contractor and it is for the main contractor to require performance of the sub-contract. From this relationship difficult drafting and procedural problems arise of which the following are the most important. (1) The sub-contract should mirror the provisions of the main contract as regards the sub-contracted work and a copy of the main contract should be furnished to the sub-contractor so that he is aware of the full circumstances. (2) Any subsequent variation in the conditions of the main

---

[54] See *The Admiralty* v. *Burns*, 1910 S.C. 531.
[55] *Nichols* v. *Marsland* (1876) 2 Ex.D. 1, C.A.
[56] *Thomas* v. *Birmingham Canal Co.* (1879) 49 L.J.Q.B. 851. An unusually heavy rainfall such as the contractor should have been prepared for is not enough (*Dixon* v. *Metropolitan Board of Works* (1881) 7 Q.B.D. 418).
[57] *Blyth* v. *Birmingham Waterworks Co.* (1856) 11 Exch. 781.
[58] *Briddon* v. *Great Northern Rly. Co.* (1858) 28 L.J. Ex. 51.
[59] *Keighley's Case* (1609) 10 Co. Rep. 139a at 140.
[60] *Liver Alkali Co.* v. *Johnson* (1874) L.R. 9 Exch. 338.
[61] *Fenwick* v. *Schmalz* (1868) L.R. 3 C.P. 313 at 316.
[62] *Forward* v. *Pittard* (1785) 1 Term Rep. 27 at 33.
[63] *Lebeaupin* v. *Crispin* [1902] 2 K.B. 714 at 718–721.
[64] *Matsoukis* v. *Priestman & Co.* [1915] 1 K.B. 681, but *quaere* as to a lockout?
[65] *Tennants (Lancashire) Ltd.* v. *C.S. Wilson & Co. Ltd.* [1917] A.C. 495, H.L.; *Peter Dixon & Sons Ltd.* v. *Henderson Craig & Co.* [1919] 2 K.B. 778, C.A.
[66] *Walton (Grain and Shipping) Ltd.* v. *British Italian Trading Co. Ltd.* [1959] 1 Lloyd's Rep. 223.
[67] *British Electrical and Associated Industries (Cardiff) Ltd.* v. *Patley Pressings Ltd.* [1953] 1 W.L.R. 280.

contract which may affect a sub-contract should be made only after consultation between the main contractor and the sub-contractor to ensure that the latter cannot avoid liability under the sub-contract by reason of alterations to which he was not a party. (3) The provisions as to liquidated damages in the main contract may require modification in the sub-contract; where the amount of the sub-contracted work is relatively small a sub-contractor may be unwilling to accept responsibility for substantial liability under the main contract resulting from delay or defects in performance of the sub-contracted work. (4) The sub-contractor must intimate promptly to the main contractor any claims for extensions of time for completing the work of the sub-contract so that the main contractor may apply timeously for an extension. (5) Throughout the progress of the contract the main contractor must provide any drawings or specifications required for the work of the sub-contract; a *force majeure* clause excusing delay through lateness of a sub-contractor will not avail the main contractor if the sub-contractor's delay was due to non-timeous furnishing of necessary information by the main contractor.

Nominated sub-contractors

2–32   In a considerable number of contracts increase in specialisation results in the employer stipulating that particular parts of the works will be carried out by sub-contractors nominated by the employer or his architect or engineer or that particular supplies be obtained from specified suppliers. Elaborate provisions in respect of nominated sub-contractors or suppliers are contained in most model contracts or standard conditions,[68] but in general the drafting objective is to secure that the nominated sub-contractors or suppliers are in contractual relationship with the main contractor and not directly with the employer. Usually the main contractor is entitled to offer reasonable objection to the employment of a nominated sub-contractor. The amount payable to a nominated sub-contractor or supplier is generally included as a prime cost item in the main contract and the proportion of a stage payment due to the sub-contractor or supplier must be paid punctually by the main contractor to the sub-contractor or supplier, often with a provision that, if not so paid, the amount may be deducted by the employer from the next stage payment and paid by the employer direct to the sub-contractor or supplier save when the main contractor is bankrupt.

(c) Materials and Plant

Vesting of materials and plant

2–33   In the normal situation where the employer has ownership or a long lease of the land on which the construction work is being carried out the

---

[68] See Scottish Building Contract, Pt. 2, cll. 35 and 36; ICE Conditions, cll. 58,59 A, B and C.

materials as they are incorporated in the structure become the property of the employer on the principle of *inaedificatum solo, solo cedit*. The ownership of materials brought on to the site or stored off-site for the purposes of the works should be regulated by the contract: certainly it should stipulate that such materials if paid for by the employer should be his property.[69] The contractor's plant is in a different position: even if temporarily attached to the structure or the site it remains the property of the contractor. Shipbuilding contracts present special features in respect that (1) the ship is being built on land belonging to the ship-builder and in any event is not being attached to the land and (2) materials brought into a shipyard, unless specially adapted for a particular vessel, may be used in any of several vessels. For that reason it is customary to regulate the passing of property in a ship in the contract itself and the contractual provisions vary according to the bargain between the parties; in some cases the property in the materials passes as they are incorporated in the ship whereas in other cases the property passes only on acceptance of the completed ship. In law a shipbuilding contract is a sale of goods rather than a *locatio operis faciendi* and the rule is that the property in the ship passes when the parties intend it to pass. So materials even when marked for construction of a particular ship will not normally pass to the employer until incorporated in the ship[70] and very clear language in the contract is necessary to achieve a different result.[71]

(d) Determination on Breach of Contract

12–34 (i) **Common law.** It should be kept in view that, apart from contractual provisions, a breach of a condition which goes to the root of the contract may entitle the innocent party to treat such breach as implied repudiation of the contract. If he does so the contract is terminated in the sense that there is no contract which remains to be performed but the rights of parties are nevertheless assessed in terms of the contract.[72] Moreover in the case of a fundamental breach of contract the party in breach may lose the protection of an exclusion clause designed to limit his liability, even where the clause in terms would cover the situation.[73]

12–35 (ii) **Express powers to terminate.** Frequently construction contracts confer on the employer power to terminate the contract in the event of specified defaults by the contractor. A clause of this kind should also state the rights and duties of the employer and contractor if the

---

[69] *e.g.* Scottish Building Contract, cl. 16.

[70] *Seath & Co.* v. *Moore* (1888) 13 R. (H.L.) 57; *Reid* v. *Macbeth & Gray* (1904) 6 F.(H.L.) 25.

[71] *Re Blyth Shipbuilding and Dry Docks Co. Ltd.* [1926] Ch. 494; *cf. Re Walker, ex p. Barter* (1884) 26 Ch. D. 510.

[72] *Heyman* v. *Darwins Ltd.* [1942] A.C. 356.

[73] *Harbutt's Plasticine Ltd.* v. *Wayne Tank & Pump Co. Ltd.* [1970] 1 Q.B. 447, C.A. This decision is difficult to reconcile with earlier authorities such as *Suisse Atlantique Société* v. *N.V. Rotterdamsche Kolen Centrale* [1967] 1 A.C. 361.

employer exercises his right to terminate.[74] The events which justify the exercise of the power to terminate vary with the nature of the contract but usually include abandonment of the work, failure to proceed with the work after the expiry of written notice by the architect or engineer, failure or refusal to remedy defective work after the like notice or assignation or sub-letting of the contract or part of it without the approval of the employer or his architect or engineer.[75] The rights of the employer on such termination should include the right to have the work completed by another and to recover the excess cost from the contractor,[76] the vesting of the property in materials on site in the employer,[77] the retention by the employer of sums due to the contractor as set off against the employer's loss,[78] the right either (i) to use the contractor's plant for completion of the works or (ii) to require the contractor to remove it from the site and, if not so removed within a reasonable time, to sell it and credit the proceeds to the contractor in the final accounting[79] and the right to require the contractor to assign to the employer any sub- contracts and the benefit of any agreement for supply of goods or materials required for the execution of the contract.[80] In general the rights given to the employer should be such as to enable him to have the work completed by another contractor as expeditiously as possible and to charge the defaulting contractor with the extra cost under deduction of any sums due to him for work which he has performed but for which payment has not been made at the date when the contract is terminated. It is thought that in no circumstances should a contractor accept liability for consequential loss or damage which in certain cases could be substantial depending upon circumstances not known or not fully known to the contractor when the contract was made. If the cause of termination is the insolvency of the contractor a provision that the materials and plant of the contractor will thereupon vest in the employer is invalid in a question with the trustee in bankruptcy or liquidator of the contractor as being an attempt to control the use, after bankruptcy, of property vested in the bankrupt at the date of sequestration.[81] If such a provision is to be effective against a trustee or liquidator it should be expressed as a forfeiture of the materials and plant upon failure by the contractor to implement the contract, not upon insolvency of the contractor,[82] and the scheme of drafting should be to provide that materials and plant of the contractor are deemed when on the site to be property of the

---

[74] See for example Scottish Building Contract, cl. 27; ICE Conditions, cl. 63.
[75] For a list of events decided by the courts to authorise determination of a contract by the employer see Halsbury's *Laws of England* (4th ed.), Vol. 4, para. 1239.
[76] *e.g. Walker* v. *London and North Western Rly. Co.* (1876) 1 C.P.D. 518.
[77] See *Roach* v. *Great Western Rly. Co.* (1841) 1 Q.B. 51.
[78] *e.g.* Scottish Building Contract, cl. 27.4.
[79] See Scottish Building Contract, cl. 27.4; ICE conditions, cl. 63(i).
[80] See ICE Conditions, cl. 63(2).
[81] *Re Walker, ex p. Barter* (1884) 26 Ch. D. 510, C.A.
[82] See *Re Keen and Keen ex p. Collins* [1902] 1 K.B. 555; *Hart* v. *Porthgain Harbour Co. Ltd.* [1903] 1 Ch. 690.

employer and will re-vest in the contractor upon completion of the works.[83]

12–36   Sometimes express conditions are included in the contract to provide for its determination by the contractor in stated circumstances. The events specified may comprise failure by the employer to settle stage payments after certification of the relevant part of the works, or suspension of the work for a specified continuous period by reason of *force majeure*, or default by the employer in providing necessary drawings or instructions or materials which the employer had undertaken to supply or procure, or bankruptcy of the employer.[84] Upon such determination the employer remains liable for the cost of work completed and any direct loss to the contractor (including direct loss under sub-contracts or contracts already entered into by the contractor for supply of materials) and the contractor is entitled to remove his plant from the site.[85] Shipbuilding contracts normally include provisions for determination of the contract either by the employer or the shipbuilder in specified circumstances. The employer may determine the contract upon failure by the shipbuilder to implement the contract in any fundamental respect, other than delay in completion, after the expiry of notice in writing by the employer requiring him to do so or by failure to complete the vessel within a stated period after the contractual date for delivery. The shipbuilder may determine the contract upon failure of the employer to settle a valid claim for a stage payment or award by the arbiter. Either party may be entitled to determine the contract by reason of *force majeure* which continues for a specified continuous period. Notice of determination after a stated period must be given; the other party, if the right to terminate is challenged, may require the decision of the arbiter and the contract continues in operation until the arbiter issues his decision. The respective rights of the employer and the shipbuilder upon termination of the contract by either party are usually expressed in detail but the terms differ in particular contracts and depend to some extent on the negotiating strength of the parties. Where the right of termination is exercised by the employer he will usually be entitled to arrange for the completion of the vessel by another contractor and to take over the benefit of existing contracts for supplies of materials upon payment to the shipbuilder for the value of the work done on the vessel, the shipbuilder being liable in payment of damages for direct loss, often quantified at a particular amount of agreed liquidate damages. Alternatively the employer may be entitled to abandon the uncompleted vessel to the shipbuilder upon payment by the latter of a more substantial sum of liquidate damages. Where the right of termination is exercised by the shipbuilder on account of default by the employer the shipbuilder

---

[83] See ICE Conditions, cll. 53, 54.
[84] *e.g.* Scottish Building Contract, cl. 28.1.
[85] See Scottish Building Contract, cl. 28.2.

usually has the option of (i) selling the uncompleted vessel or the materials incorporated in it after dismantling or (ii) completing and selling the vessel, with provision for a final accounting between the parties debiting against the employer all sums due but unpaid under the contract at the date of termination, all costs incurred by the shipbuilder on the vessel including dismantling or completion as the case may be and the expenses of selling and a stated percentage of profit applied to the total of these amounts, and crediting the instalments paid by the employer and the sums received on sale. If determination occurs by reason of *force majeure* the same provisions as to dismantling or completing the vessel, sale and accounting usually apply, save that when the right to terminate in such circumstances is exercised by the shipbuilder the element of profit may be modified or excluded.

(e) Assignation

(i) By employer

2–37   An employer may assign the benefits and obligations of a construction contract as between him and the assignee but the assignation does not relieve the cedent from his obligations to the contractor.[86] If the assignee agrees to pay the contractor, however, and the contractor continues with the work, he may sue the assignee for payment in respect of work done after the assignee has undertaken the obligation to pay.[87]

(ii) By contractor

2–38   A contractor may assign his rights under the contract, primarily rights to receive payment of sums due and to become due under the contract and right to the retention money when payable,[88] but he cannot assign his obligations of performance except with the consent of the employer[89] and in most standard conditions assignation by the contractor without consent of the employer is prohibited.[90] Partial assignation by way of sub-contracting may be permissible so long as there is no element of *delectus personae* involved[91] and provided the contract contains no provision which prohibits it without the consent of the employer or his architect or engineer,[92] but the main contractor remains responsible for the proper execution of the sub-contracted part of the work.

---

[86] *Bailey* v. *Thurston & Co. Ltd.* [1903] 1 K.B. 137, C.A.
[87] *Oldfield* v. *Lowe* (1829) 9 B. & C. 73. See *I.R.C.* v. *Rennell* [1964] A.C. 173 at 194 and *Jones* v. *Padavatton* [1969] 1 W.L.R. 328 at 333.
[88] *Re Tout and Finch Ltd.* [1954] 1 W.L.R. 178.
[89] *Tolhurst* v. *Associated Portland Cement Manufacturers (1900) Ltd.* [1902] 2 K.B. 660 (assignment upheld but on ground that the benefit and not the burden of the contract was assigned).
[90] See ICE Conditions, cl. 3.
[91] See Gloag, *Contract*, 421.
[92] See ICE Conditions, cl. 4.

(iii) Bankruptcy or liquidation of employer

12–39   If the employer becomes bankrupt or is liquidated the contractor is not obliged to continue the work: the rights of the employer pass to the trustee or liquidator and only if he elects to adopt the contract with acceptance of the liabilities of the employer to make the contractual payments need the contractor resume performance.

(iv) Bankruptcy or liquidation of contractor

12–40   If the contractor becomes bankrupt his rights under the contract vest in his trustee[93] so far as assignable,[94] who may adopt it, or disclaim it leaving the employer to claim damages.[95] If the contractor being a company is wound up the contract does not vest in the liquidator but he has similar rights to adopt or disclaim it.[96] The employer's claim for damages may be set off against moneys due to the contractor at the date of bankruptcy or liquidation even if the latter have been certified by the architect or engineer as payable.[97] As to the effect of bankruptcy or liquidation of the contractor upon contractual provisions regarding the vesting of materials and plant in the employer see paragraph 12–34 *supra*. Where the contractor becomes bankrupt and has failed to pay sums due to a sub-contractor the main contract may expressly authorise payment by the employer directly to the sub-contractor[98] provided that the authorisation is not expressed as operating on the insolvency of the contractor.[99]

(f) Completion

Completion and acceptance

12–41   Most formal contracts include express provisions for a final architect's certificate (building contracts)[1] or engineer's completion certificate (engineering contracts).[2] In shipbuilding contracts an acceptance certificate is normally granted by the employer or his authorised representative after completion of satisfactory sea trials. The issue of such certificates precludes objections to defects, whether patent or not,[3]

---

[93] Bankruptcy (Scotland) Act 1913, s. 97(1).
[94] See Gloag, *Contract*, 425–427; *Anderson* v. *Hamilton & Co.* (1875) 2 R. 355 at 363.
[95] *Kirkland* v. *Cadell* (1838) 16 S. 860 at 881.
[96] *Asphaltic Limestone Concrete Co.* v. *Glasgow Corporation*, 1907 S.C. 463; *Crown Estate Commissioners* v. *Liquidators of Highland Engineering Ltd.* 1975 S.L.T. 58.
[97] On the ordinary principles of retention of liquid debts against illiquid sums in bankruptcy. See special conditions of contract in ICE Conditions, cl. 63(4); Scottish Building Contract, cl. 27.4.
[98] See Scottish Building Contract, cl. 27.4.2.2.
[99] When it will be invalid as designed to defeat the law of bankruptcy—see *Re Walker, ex p. Barter*, *supra*. It may be valid if the right to pay is expressed as exercisable on the occurrence of some other event, *e.g.* if the contractor delays to pay the sub-contractor timeously, *Re Tout and Finch Ltd.* [1954] 1 W.L.R. 178; *British Eagle Ltd.* v. *Air France Ltd.* [1975] 1 W.L.R. 758.
[1] See Scottish Building Contract, cl. 30.
[2] See ICE Conditions, cl. 48.
[3] *Ayr Road Trs.* v. *Adams* (1883) 11 R. 326.

subject to the qualification that the contractor will remain liable for rectification of defects within any stipulated maintenance period.[4] Where there has been no such final or acceptance certificate the contractor may still be liable for work which is incomplete or badly done[5] and the making of stage payments or entering into possession of the building does not infer waiver of objections by the employer or his acquiescence in non-compliance with the conditions of the contract.[6]

Defects liability or maintenance period

2–42 Final certificates or formal acceptances are normally granted subject to an obligation upon the contractor to remedy defects within a stipulated defects liability or maintenance period, after which, or by instalments during which, the retention moneys are released. It is important in the interests of the contractor that his liability during such period is restricted to completing any unfinished work and repairing defects which are due to his fault and that it does not extend to rectification of all defects even although not attributable to his work.[7] The actual phraseology, too, is important. An obligation to rectify defects would extend only to putting right any actual defect and would not usually include an obligation to remedy damage due to some external cause during the defects liability period. An obligation to repair would probably impose a similar liability, but an exclusion of fair wear and tear should be expressed.[8] An obligation to maintain and uphold may be rather more onerous; although, in a relatively short period of maintenance, replacement should not be necessary, the obligation might extend to alterations or improvements necessary for proper use of the building or works.[9]

(g) Arbitration Clause

(i) Arbiter

2–43 Frequently the architect or the engineer is appointed as arbiter.[10] Although he also has the function of certifying the work as it progresses he is not thereby disqualified from exercising the office of arbiter[11] unless he has expressed views on the issue in evidence in a court action[12] or in correspondence.[13] Alternatively the arbiter may be an

---

[4] See para. 12–42.
[5] *Munro* v. *Butt* (1858) 8 E. & B. 738; *Sumpter* v. *Hedges* [1898] 1 Q.B. 673.
[6] *Whitaker* v. *Dunn* (1887) 3 T.L.R. 602.
[7] See ICE Conditions, cl. 49.
[8] See ICE Conditions, cl. 49(2).
[9] *Sevenoaks etc. Rly.* v. *London, Chatham & Dover Rly.* (1879) 11 Ch. D. 625.
[10] See ICE Conditions, cl. 66.
[11] *Scott* v. *Carluke Parochial Board* (1879) 6 R. 616; *Mackay* v. *Barry Parochial Board* (1883) 10 R. 1046; *Halliday* v. *Duke of Hamilton's Trs.* (1903) 5 F.800; *Scott* v. *Gerrard*, 1916 S.C. 793; *Crawford* v. *Northern Lighthouses Commissioners*, 1925 S.C.(H.L.) 22.
[12] *Dickson* v. *Grant* (1870) 8 M. 566.
[13] *Maclauchlan & Brown* v. *Morrison* (1900) 8 S.L.T. 279.

independent person appointed by agreement of parties or, failing agreement, by the holder of a public or professional office.[14]

(ii) Scope of reference

12-44   The reference to arbitration should cover any dispute or difference between the employer and the contractor in connection with or arising out of the contract whether during the progress of the works or after their completion or abandonment, including any instruction, direction, certificate or valuation by the architect or engineer. It may also cover disputes or differences between the contractor and any sub-contractor. In order to avoid delay it may be provided that the work shall proceed notwithstanding the reference to arbitration. In general an arbiter is not usually empowered to award damages.

(iii) Expert or arbiter

12-45   It is important in drafting the contract to distinguish matters which are to be decided by the architect or engineer or some independent person appropriately qualified acting as an expert and matters where the person who makes the decision is acting as an arbiter. Decisions by a person acting as an expert are made by him using his skill, experience and knowledge, he does not require to hear parties or take evidence and his decision is not subject to appeal. On the other hand an arbiter must observe the ordinary principles of hearing both parties, etc., and his decision on any question of law may be appealed to the Court of Session under section 3(1) of the Administration of Justice (Scotland) Act 1972 unless that right of appeal is expressly excluded by the contract. In shipbuilding contracts it is usual to refer technical matters in connection with the vessel and its equipment to a technical body acting as experts and matters relating to the construction of the contract or the rights, duties or liabilities of the parties thereunder to an arbiter.

(h) Guarantees and Performance Bonds

12-46   Construction contracts frequently require the contractor to provide security, either in the form of a guarantee or a performance bond for due completion of the work undertaken. Government departments and local authorities generally require such security for larger contracts. In turn bankers who enter into such obligations of guarantee or performance often require the contractor to provide security, either personal or by way of assignation of rights to payment under the contract, against any liability which may arise under the guarantee or bond given to the employer. There may also be guarantees required from sub-contractors in respect of their undertakings and bid-bonds guaranteeing that if a contractor's tender is accepted he will execute a binding contract.

---

[14] See Scottish Building Contract, cl. 41.

Writing

-47   A guarantee or performance bond in a building or engineering contract must, as a cautionary obligation, be in writing[15] and in practice is executed in probative form.

Actings to the prejudice of the guarantor

-48   Subject to any express provisions to the contrary contained in the document of guarantee actings of the employer which in any way are inconsistent with the interests of the guarantor or alter the contract performance of which has been guaranteed or could prejudice the rights of the guarantor to contribution or indemnity will release the guarantor from his obligations under the guarantee.[16] In construction contracts actings which may, subject to any conditions in the guarantee which permit them, have the result of releasing the guarantor include the following: (1) Altering the work contracted to be performed (although variations will not have that effect if the contract provided for them[17] or the guarantee permits them[18]). (2) Extending time for completion of the work[19] or failing to inform the guarantor that the work had fallen seriously behind the stipulated time for performance[20] (although again allowance of additional time may be permitted by the contract or the terms of the guarantee[18]). (3) Anticipating payment of instalments to the contractor.[21] (4) Releasing the contractor or a co-guarantor.[22]

Termination of guarantor's liability

-49   The liability of the guarantor will terminate either on completion of the work as evidenced by any final certificate stipulated in the contract or only at the end of the defects liability or maintenance period. It may also be extinguished by the short negative prescription upon the expiry of five years after the obligation of the guarantor became enforceable.[23]

Style—performance bond

-50   In modern practice guarantees for performance of work by contractors usually take the form of a performance bond by bankers, the liability of the bankers being limited to a specified sum.

BY THIS BOND We X Construction Company Limited (*designed*) (hereinafter called "the Contractor") and Y Bank (*designed*)

---

[15] Mercantile Law Amendment (Scotland) Act 1856, s. 6.
[16] As to the general principles of release of guarantors by actings, see para. 6–14 *et seq.*
[17] *United States* v. *Walsh* (1902) 115 Fed. Rep. 697.
[18] See para. 12–50.
[19] *Rouse* v. *Bradford Banking Co.* [1894] A.C. 586.
[20] *Clydebank and District Water Trs.* v. *Fidelity and Deposit Co. of Maryland*, 1916 S.C.(H.L.) 69.
[21] *Warre* v. *Calvert* (1837) 7 A. & E. 143; *General Steam Navigation Co.* v. *Rolt* (1858) 6 C.B.(N.S.) 550, 584.
[22] *Commercial Bank of Tasmania* v. *Jones* [1893] A.C. 313.
[23] Prescription and Limitation (Scotland) Act 1973, s. 6 and Sched. 1, paras. 1(*g*) and 2(*c*).

(hereinafter called "the Surety") are held and firmly bound unto C D & Company Limited (*designed*) (hereinafter called "the Employer") in the sum of £   for the payment of which sum the Contractor and the Surety bind themselves, their successors and assigns jointly and severally by these presents subject to the conditions contained in the Schedule hereto. (*To be attested*).

SCHEDULE

WHEREAS the Contractor by an Agreement made between the Employer of the one part and the Contractor of the other part has entered into a Contract dated   (hereinafter called "the Contract") for the construction and completion of the Works and maintenance of the Permanent Works as therein mentioned in conformity with the provisions of the Contract.

NOW THE CONDITIONS of the foregoing Bond are such that if:–

(a) the Contractor shall subject to Condition (c) hereof duly perform and observe all the terms provisions conditions and stipulations of the Contract in the Contractor's part to be performed and observed according to the true purport intent and meaning thereof or if

(b) on default by the Contractor the Surety shall satisfy and discharge the damages sustained by the Employer thereby up to the amount of the above-written Bond or if

(c) the Engineer named in Clause 1 of the said Contract shall pursuant to the provisions of Clause   thereof issue a Maintenance Certificate then upon the date stated therein (hereinafter called "the Relevant Date")

this obligation shall be null and void but otherwise shall remain in full force and effect but no alteration in the terms of the said Contract made by agreement between the Employer and the Contractor or in the extent or nature of the Works to be constructed completed and maintained thereunder and no allowance of time by the Employer or the Engineer under the Contract nor any forbearance or forgiveness in or in respect of any matter or thing concerning the Contract on the part of the Employer or the said Engineer shall in any way release the Surety from any liability under the said Bond.

PROVIDED ALWAYS that if any dispute or difference shall arise between the Employer and the Contractor concerning the Relevant Date or otherwise as to the withholding of the Maintenance Certificate then for the purposes of the said Bond only and without prejudice to the resolution or determination pursuant to the provisions of the Contract of any dispute or difference whatsoever between the Employer and Contractor the Relevant Date shall be such as may be:

(a) agreed in writing between the Employer and the Contractor or

(b) if either the Employer or the Contractor shall be aggrieved at the date stated in the said Maintenance Certificate or otherwise as to the issue or withholding of the said Maintenance Certificate the party so aggrieved shall forthwith by notice in writing to the other refer any such dispute or difference to the arbitration of a person to

be agreed upon between the parties or (if the parties fail to appoint an arbiter within one month of the service of the notice as aforesaid) a person to be appointed on the application of either party by the President for the time being of the Institution of Civil Engineers and such arbiter shall forthwith and with all due expedition enter upon the reference and make an award thereon which award shall be final and conclusive to determine the Relevant Date for the purpose of this Bond. If the arbiter declines the appointment or after appointment is removed by order of a competent court or is incapable of acting or dies and the parties do not within one calendar month of the vacancy arising fill the vacancy then the President for the time being of the Institution of Civil Engineers may on the application of either party appoint an arbiter to fill the vacancy. In any case where the President for the time being of the Institution of Civil Engineers is not able to exercise the aforesaid functions conferred upon him the said functions may be exercised on his behalf by a Vice-President for the time being of the said Institution. The application of section 3 of the Administration of Justice (Scotland) Act 1972 to such arbitration is expressly excluded. (*To be executed by all the parties*).
Stamp duty nil.

Indemnity to guarantor

2–51   Normally the guarantor bank obtains an indemnity from the contractor against any liability which the bank may incur under the performance bond.

To Y Bank (*designed*)   (Date)

Gentlemen

In consideration of your having at our request joined in the Bond of which the attached is a copy and which has been executed by us as relative hereto we, X Construction Company Limited (*designed*)

(a) agree to keep you indemnified against all actions, proceedings, liability, claims, damages, costs and expenses in relation to or arising out of the said Bond and to pay to you on demand all payments, losses, costs and expenses suffered or incurred by you in consequence thereof or arising therefrom; and

(b) irrevocably authorise you to debit to our Account or an Account in our names all such payments, losses, costs and expenses or the Sterling equivalent thereof; and

(c) irrevocably authorise you to make any payments and comply with any demands which may be claimed from or made upon you under the said Bond whether such demand is made before or after any expiry date expressed therein, and that without any reference to or further authority from us, and agree that any payment which you shall make in accordance or purporting to be in accordance with the said Bond shall be binding upon us and shall be accepted by us as conclusive evidence that you were liable to make such payment or comply with such demand and further that you may at any time determine the said Bond.

(*To be signed by Director or Secretary*)

Securities in relation to Construction Contracts

Security over employer's interests

12–52   Major works of construction are frequently financed by borrowings by the employer to provide payment of the cost of the works. The employer may provide security for the loan over the works themselves if these are heritable, as in the case of buildings or fixed engineering works constructed or installed on land belonging to the employer, by way of a heritable security in the form of a standard security. If, however, the thing constructed is moveable, as in the case of a ship, the position of security over it presents a more difficult problem on account of the rule that a security over moveable property requires delivery and, where the subject of the contract is being constructed on the premises of the contractor, delivery during the course of construction is impracticable. In shipbuilding contracts the security documentation usually comprises (1) a bond by the employer in favour of the lender for repayment of the sum advanced and an assignation in security of the whole rights and interests of the employer under the contract with the shipbuilder including the employer's rights under any performance bond obtained from the shipbuilder and under any insurances effected over the ship under construction, (2) intimation of the assignation to the shipbuilder, (3) an irrevocable order by the employer addressed to the shipbuilder to hold the vessel and all materials appropriated to its construction to the order of the lender, and (4) intimation of the order to the shipbuilder. The value of the security is enhanced if the contract provides for vesting the property in the vessel in the employer as it is being constructed.

Bond and assignation in security—shipbuilding contract

12–53   We A Limited (*designed*) (hereinafter called "the Owner") considering that X Bank (*designed*) (hereinafter called "the Bank") have agreed to grant banking facilities and accommodation to the Owner for the purpose *inter alia* of providing part of the cost of construction of a   vessel to be named   (hereinafter referred to as "the Vessel") being carried out by B Limited (*designed*) (hereinafter called "the Builder") for the account of the Owner under the Contract hereinafter assigned do hereby bind and oblige ourselves and our assignees and successors whomsoever to pay to the Bank within their head office at   all sums which are now or shall hereafter become due to the Bank in any manner of way (and whether or not advanced in respect of the said Contract) by us either solely or jointly with any other person or persons or corporation, company, firm or other body, and whether as principal or surety, all which sums shall be so paid by us or our foresaids to the Bank either on demand or in accordance with any separate Agreement in writing entered into by us with the Bank providing for payment otherwise than on demand (*continue as in normal form of personal bond by company omitting any inappropriate provisions*): And in security of the personal obligations hereinbefore and hereinafter written we the Owner with the consent and

concurrence of the Builder as is testified by the execution of these presents by them do hereby Assign to and in favour of the Bank and their assignees (One) our whole rights, interests and benefits (but not our obligations) under the Contract entered into between the Owner and Builder for the construction of the Vessel dated (which Contract a copy of which forms Part I of the Schedule annexed and executed as relative hereto is hereinafter referred to as "the Contract") including particularly but without prejudice to the foregoing generality all our rights to call for performance of the prestations of the Contract incumbent on the Builder and all our rights to take possession of the Vessel whether completed or incomplete and to finish and complete the same and (Two) all our rights, title and interest in and to the performance bond dated   issued by the Y Bank (*designed*) referred to in clause   of the Contract (a copy of which performance bond forms Part II of the said Schedule) and all benefits thereof including without prejudice to that generality all moneys payable by the said Y Bank thereunder (and we undertake to give written notice of such assignation to the said Y Bank[24]): And we the Owner hereby assign to and in favour of the Bank our whole rights, interests and benefits under all policies of insurance that have been or may hereafter during the existence of this security be effected by us and/or the Builder in respect of the Vessel, its engines, boilers and machinery and all materials appropriated to it including all claims of whatsoever nature and returns or rebates of premiums; and we undertake to deliver to the Bank a letter or letters of undertaking satisfactory to the Bank from the brokers through whom such policies have been effected for the protection of the Bank as assignees of our interests under such policies: And in default in payment of any sums that may be due under these presents or upon failure to implement the obligations and prestations incumbent on us under these presents or any of them the Bank shall be entitled without any notice to us and whenever they see fit but shall not be obliged to enter into possession of the whole subjects hereby assigned in security or any part thereof and also in their sole discretion and at such time or times as they may see fit to sell the said subjects or any part thereof and that on such terms with or without advertisement in whole or in such lots and at such price or prices as they may think proper and otherwise deal with the said subjects in such way as they may think best and in the same manner as if they were absolute owners of the same and to apply the proceeds thereof so realised in or towards payment of any sums owing to the Bank hereunder or otherwise due by us or our foresaids to the Bank, and the surplus (if any) shall be paid to us: And we consent to registration hereof for preservation and execution. (*To be executed by Owner and Builder and to be attested*).
Stamp duty nil.

SCHEDULE

Part I (*Copy Contract*)

Part II (*Copy Performance Bond*)

---

[24] Alternatively the assignation may be intimated by X Bank to Y Bank.

Intimation to builder of above bond and assignation in security

12–54   To B Limited
                        (*address*)

Notice is hereby given that by Bond and Assignation in Security
dated   (a copy of which accompanies this Notice) Á
Limited (*designed*) ("the Owner") assigned to us X Bank
(*designed*) (First) the whole rights, interests and benefits of the
Owner (but not their obligations) under a Contract ("the Contract") entered into between the Owner and yourselves dated
              for the construction of a vessel to be named
("the Vessel") including particularly but without prejudice to the
foregoing generality all the rights of the Owner to call for performance of the prestations of the Contract incumbent on you and all
the rights of the Owner to take possession of the Vessel whether
completed or incomplete and to finish and complete the same and
(Second) all rights interests and benefits of the Owner under all
policies of insurance that have been or may after the date of the
said Bond and Assignation in Security during the existence of the
security thereby created be effected by the Owner and/or you in
respect of the Vessel, its engines, boilers and machinery and all
materials appropriated to it including all claims of whatsoever
nature and returns and rebates of premiums.

Without prejudice to the assignation hereby intimated to you we
have agreed that until we give you notice to the contrary the Owner
may continue to superintend the construction of the Vessel and
may require alterations, additions, extra work and materials in
accordance with the terms of the Contract.

You are requested to execute the acknowledgment endorsed on the
duplicate of this Notice and to return it to us forthwith.

Dated at   on the   day of

For and on behalf of X Bank
. . . . (signature)

[Docquet on duplicate copy:

Received a Notice of which this is a duplicate.
Dated at   on the   day of

For and on behalf of B Limited
. . . . (signature)]

Delivery order to builder

12–55   To B Limited
                        (*address*)

With reference to the Contract entered into between us and you
dated   ("the Contract") for the construction of the vessel
to be named   ("the Vessel") we hereby irrevocably

authorise you to hold the Vessel and all its engines, boilers and machinery and all materials from time to time appropriated to it or them whether in your building yard, workshops, dock or elsewhere to the order and at the disposal of X Bank (*designed*), subject only to your lien as Builder under the Contract.

For and on behalf of A Limited
. . . . Director
. . . . Secretary (Seal)

Intimation of delivery order to builder

2–56   To B Limited
          (*address*)

Dear Sirs

The enclosed Delivery Order addressed to you by A Limited (*designed*) dated   regarding the Vessel to be named   to be constructed by you is hereby intimated to you. You are requested to execute the acknowledgment endorsed on the duplicate of this intimation and to return it to us forthwith.

Yours faithfully

. . . .
For and on behalf of X Bank

Acknowledgment by builders to bank of intimation of delivery order (to be endorsed on the duplicate of the intimation in paragraph 12–56)

2–57   To X Bank
          (*address*)

We hereby acknowledge the foregoing intimation of the Delivery Order addressed by A Limited to us dated   and we confirm that in terms of the said Delivery Order we now hold to your order and at your disposal subject only to our lien as Builder under the Contract entered into between the said A Limited and us dated   relating to the construction of the vessel to be named   ("the Vessel") the Vessel as it is constructed and all its engines, boilers and machinery and all materials from time to time appropriated to it or them whether in our building yard, workshops, dock and elsewhere. In particular without prejudice to the generality of the foregoing we undertake that until the Vessel is delivered to the said A Limited we shall not:

(i) remove or permit or suffer the removal of the Vessel out of Scotland except for the purposes of sea trials nor take the Vessel during the course of sea trials to any place outwith the jurisdiction of a court of the United Kingdom.

(ii) permit or suffer any engines, boilers, machinery or materials which are part of the vessel or which are appropriated thereto to be removed outside Scotland except for the purpose of construction or adjustments thereto, or

  (iii) work on the Vessel other than at our yard, workshops or dock
    at .

For B Limited

. . . . Director

. . . . Secretary (Seal)

Security over contractor's interests

12–58 A contractor usually endeavours to adjust the terms of the contract so
that the expenditure involved in carrying out the work substantially is
financed from instalment payments by the employer, but this is not
always practicable and funds from other sources may be required, frequently by way of borrowing on current account with the contractor's
bankers.

 Bank borrowings may be obtainable under existing loan arrangements such as a bond of cash credit possibly supported by a floating
charge or heritable security, but additionally the bankers may require a
fixed security over the payments due and to become due to the contractor in terms of the construction contract. In such circumstances an assignation of moneys payable to the contractor may be taken. The style of
assignation in the following paragraph is based on the assumption that a
general all moneys bond of cash credit already exists and the object is to
add a fixed security over the payments made or to be made to the contractor under the construction contract.

Assignation in security over contract payments

12–59 We A B Limited (*designed*) in security of all sums and obligations
we may at present or at any future time be owing or under to Z
Bank (*designed*) (hereinafter called "the Bank") either solely or
jointly with any person or persons or corporation, company, firm or
other body and whether as principal or surety do hereby assign to
the Bank and their assignees all sums of money at present due to us
and all sums of money which may hereafter become due to us by X
(*designed*) under a contract between the said X and us dated
    for the construction of   at   or under any
alterations of or additions to the said contract and all extra work of
any kind that may be undertaken by us to the order of the said X in
connection with the said work of construction whether by variation
of the terms of the said contract or independently of it, together
with our whole right, title and interest in and to the said sums of
money hereby assigned and all vouchers and documents of every
kind already granted and which may be granted by the said X or his
(their) architects or engineers or other representatives in connection therewith; surrogating the Bank and their foresaids in our full
right and place in the premises with power to the Bank and their
foresaids to call, sue for, uplift and discharge in whole or in part the
said sums of money hereby assigned, and generally to do everything
in the premises which we could have done before the granting
hereof: And we bind ourselves when required by the Bank or their
foresaids to make forthcoming all documentary and other evidence
requisite in support of the foregoing assignation: (*To be attested*).

Stamp duty nil.

(Intimation of the above Assignation to X in usual form).

Construction contract securities—complex cases

2–60 In large contracts the financial and security arrangements may be much more complex. For example, the potential liability in excess of a stated amount of one bank under a performance bond may be underwritten by another, with a subordinate assignation of security rights. The foregoing styles will generally be susceptible of adaptation to suit more involved arrangements.

CHAPTER 13

AGENCY AND CONTRACTS OF SERVICE

I. AGENCY, FACTORIES AND COMMISSIONS AND POWERS OF ATTORNEY

II. CONTRACTS OF SERVICE

I. Agency, Factories and Commissions and Powers of Attorney

Classes of agents

3–01   Agents may be classified as general or special agents. The former have authority to act for their principals in all matters, or all matters of a particular kind, or all matters within the ordinary course of the business or profession of the agent; the latter have authority to act only in respect of a particular transaction.[1] Another classification may be between non-commercial and commercial agents according to the character of the authority conferred upon the agent as relating to an individual's private affairs or to the conduct of transactions on behalf of a business.

Creation of agency

3–02   Agency may be created expressly as by the grant of a factory and commission or power of attorney, but formal writing is not required and express agency may be established by informal writings or even orally.[2] Agency may also be implied from the actings of parties, or by the operation of law.[3]

Construction of documents creating express agency

3–03   A factory and commission, power of attorney or mandate is strictly construed.[4] The safe practice therefore is to express specifically all powers that may be required since nothing more will be implied. Special powers must be conferred on the factor or attorney to enable him to (i) sell or dispose of heritable property or valuable moveable property,[5] (ii) purchase or feu land or purchase valuable moveable property,[6]

---

[1] *Morrison* v. *Statter* (1885) 12 R. 1152.
[2] *Ross* v. *Cowie's Exrx.* (1888) 16 R. 224.
[3] See Walker, *Principles*, II, 213. In general implied agency is not the concern of conveyancers.
[4] *Goodall* v. *Bilsland*, 1909 S.C. 1152; *Park* v. *Mood*, 1919 1 S.L.T. 170.
[5] Montgomerie Bell, *Lectures*, 448; *Thomas* v. *Walker's Trs.* (1829) 7 S. 828.
[6] Montgomerie Bell, *Lectures*, 448; *Stewart* v. *Johnston* (1857) 19 D. 1071.

(iii) serve an heir,[7] (iv) compromise claims[8] or arbitrate,[9] (v) grant leases,[10] (vi) borrow money on behalf of his principal or grant security over his principal's estate,[11] or (vii) grant a servitude or other permanent right over his principal's heritable property.[12] On the general principle *delegatus non potest delegare* a factor or attorney may not delegate the power conferred upon him to another[13]; he should be authorised to engage the professional services of stockbrokers, solicitors, counsel, accountants or others in the management of the affairs entrusted to him and, if it is intended that he may delegate his powers generally to a sub-agent, power to do so should be given expressly.

Particular matters

13–04   Apart from the powers above mentioned which must be conferred by the deed of appointment if they are to be exercisable by the factor or attorney, there are many special powers which should be considered in circumstances where they may be required. Preliminary inquiry should be made as to the necessity for inclusion of powers to deal with particular matters affecting the granter's affairs and should be expressed in ample terms. Examples are:

(a) **Interests in estates.** If the granter has an interest in an executry or trust estate, power should be given to examine and approve of accounts, to give consents or authorities to trustees or executors (which may be required in circumstances where acts are proposed which the trustees or executors are not technically empowered to do) and to grant discharges and indemnities.

(b) **Investments in companies.** Power to sell securities of companies should normally be included without restriction. Power to purchase such securities may be unrestricted or may be limited if the granter so wishes, but generally it is advisable to confer full powers, including power to accept provisional allocations of shares and to take up or sell rights issued by companies, the only limitation being that stocks or shares purchased should not involve liability beyond the amount invested or be in the form of bearer shares. Full powers should be given to exercise voting rights and to grant proxies.

(c) **Borrowing and securities.** If power to borrow is conferred authority should be included to bind the principal personally or jointly and severally with others and to grant security over the principal's estate with

---

[7] Titles to Land Consolidation (Scotland) Act 1868, s. 29, so far as service procedures still competent under Succession (Scotland) Act 1964, s. 37(i)(*d*), and Law Reform (Miscellaneous Provisions) (Scotland) Act 1980, s. 6.

[8] *Bridges* v. *Willison's Trs.* (1831) 10 S. 43.

[9] *Livingston* v. *Johnson (1830)* 8 S. 594.

[10] Rankine on *Leases*, 46; Paton and Cameron, *Landlord and Tenant*, 57; *Danish Dairy Co. Ltd.* v. *Gillespie* 1922 S.C. 656.

[11] *Sinclair, Moorhead & Co.* v. *Wallace & Co.* (1880) 7 R. 874; Montgomerie Bell, *op, cit.*, 448. Con-*tra* where borrowing necessary to preserve estate: *Thomson* v. *Fullarton* (1842) 5 D. 379.

[12] *Macgregor* v. *Balfour* (1899) 2 F. 345.

[13] *Dempster* v. *Potts* (1836) 14 S. 521.

authority to the creditor to realise the security. If there are existing heritable or other securities in which the principal is creditor, or if power is given to invest in such securities, power should be conferred on the factor or attorney to rearrange the securities both as to capital and interest, to enforce them and grant discharges, to grant assignations, deeds of restriction or postponement, to exercise powers of sale or foreclosure or to accept a substituted security. If there are securities in which the principal is debtor or the factor or attorney has power to grant such securities, power should be conferred to negotiate variations of interest, to arrange assignations or to procure discharges by making repayment and re-borrowing on new security deeds.

(d) Deeds. A general power to grant deeds necessary for the exercise of powers conferred on the factor or attorney should be included and deeds which impose a continuing obligation such as repayment of borrowings with interest or a contingent obligation of warrandice or indemnity should be specially mentioned.

Parties

3–05   **(a) Companies.** Contracts for which writing is required may be made on behalf of a company in writing signed by any person acting under its authority, express or implied.[14] A company may by writing under its common seal empower any person, either generally or in respect of any specified matter, to execute deeds on its behalf in any place outwith the United Kingdom.[15]

3–06   **(b) Trustees.** Trustees have a statutory power, exercisable when not at variance with the terms or purposes of the trust, to appoint factors and law agents.[16] Moreover at common law trustees have an implied power to employ agents, so long as the authority given to the agent does not involve delegation of functions which the trustees should exercise personally.[17] Trust deeds frequently confer express power to appoint agents and pay them suitable remuneration. In general trustees may delegate power to perform executory acts which are within the professional competence of the agent, but decisions on matters of policy or the exercise of discretionary powers must be taken by the trustees personally.

3–07   **(c) Several granters.** Where there are two or more granters it is important to provide that (a) power is conferred by the granters severally to do everything authorised which each of the granters could do severally, (b) in cases where it is intended that the factor or attorney should account to each of the granters separately his obligation of accounting should be so expressed, (c) recall or termination of the appointment by any one of

---

[14] Companies Act 1985, s. 36(1)(*b*).
[15] *Ibid.*, s. 38.
[16] Trusts (Scotland) Act 1921, s. 4(1)(*f*).
[17] *Hay* v. *Binny* (1861) 23 D. 594. See Wilson and Duncan, *Trusts*, 306–310.

the granters should not terminate the authority granted by the others, and (d) the responsibility of each of the granters is limited to his respective several interest. See paragraph 13–15 *infra*.

Joint attorneys

13–08 If two attorneys are appointed it should be stated clearly (a) whether both must concur in any act or whether either of them has power to act independently, (b) whether either is a *sine quo non*, and (c) whether the powers will terminate on the death or resignation of either or will continue to be exercisable by the other. It will usually be convenient to appoint the attorneys jointly and severally, the power if not recalled to continue in force so long as one survives and retains office and each having full power to act by himself alone. Provisions on these lines facilitate the exercise of the power when for any reason one of the attorneys is temporarily unavailable and avoid the need for further documentation if either dies or ceases to act. See paragraph 13–16 *infra*.

Remuneration of agent

13–09 An agent has no right to receive remuneration from his principal unless there is a contract, express or implied, to that effect.[18] A provision should normally be inserted in a factory and commission or power of attorney authorising the factor or attorney to receive remuneration on an appropriate basis of professional charges and empowering him to remunerate any agents whom he may employ.

Actings of attorney

13–10 In important matters which may significantly affect the value of the principal's property or impose liability upon the principal it is good sense for the attorney, even although the proposed action is clearly within the powers conferred upon him, to consult his principal, if available and able to take decisions. Deeds and documents should run expressly in the name of the principal, preferably with any responsibility of the attorney being clearly negatived. Bank accounts should be operated specifically on behalf of the principal[19] and sums of more than, say, £100 should not be kept in hand or in a current account which does not accrue interest. Litigation by a factor or attorney on behalf of his principal raises peculiar difficulties: it seems impracticable to avoid the attorney being personally liable for the judicial expenses of the other party if the principal's assets are insufficient.

---

[18] *Orbiston* v. *Hamilton* (1736) Mor. 4063; *Rondel* v. *Worsley* [1969] 1 A.C. 191.
[19] In which case the attorney will not be liable for debit balances: *Royal Bank of Scotland* v. *Skinner*, 1931 S.L.T. 382.

Termination of office

3–11 The office of a factor or attorney may be terminated (1) on the expiry of the period for which it was created,[20] (2) on complete performance of the relevant transaction,[21] (3) on the death,[22] bankruptcy or winding-up of the principal,[23] (4) by recall of his authority by the principal,[24] or (5) on discontinuance of the business of the principal in respect of which the authority was given.[25] Supervening insanity of the principal, if permanent, terminates the authority of the factor or attorney but *quaere* whether temporary insanity would have that effect,[26] but usually in such circumstances the court will appoint a *curator bonis* who will supersede the factor or attorney in the management of the property of the principal.[27] The resignation, incapacity or death of the factor or attorney will terminate the appointment. In questions with third parties notice must be given of termination of the authority of the factor or attorney in order to put them *in mala fide* if they continue to transact with him.[28] As regards knowledge of termination of his authority by the factor or attorney himself, it should be provided in the deed by which he is appointed that actings under it will be valid and bind his principal until the factor or attorney has received notice of the termination.[29]

Power of attorney by individual—general—wide powers

13–12 I A, (*designed*), whereas I [intend to go abroad][a] [am unable by reason of ill health to attend personally to my affairs][b] and desire to appoint a proper person to manage my affairs do hereby appoint B, (*designed*) to be my Attorney with full power to do everything regarding my estate and affairs which I could have done myself without limitation by reason of anything herein contained; and in particular, but without prejudice to the foregoing generality, I confer upon my Attorney the following powers, all to be exercised or not and, if exercised, then at such time or times and in such manner and generally on such terms and conditions all as he in his sole discretion shall think fit, namely:

(1) To demand, sue for and recover all debts, claims and sums of money due or that may become due to me or exigible by me on any account or in any way, to give time for payment of any debt or claim and to grant receipts or discharges therefor.[c]

(2) To open accounts with any banker or banking company or any building society in the United Kingdom in my name or in his name

---

[20] *Brenan* v. *Campbell's Trs.* (1898) 25 R. 423.
[21] *Black* v. *Cullen* (1853) 15 D. 646; *Gillow* v. *Lord Aberdare* (1892) 9 T.L.R. 12, C.A.
[22] *Life Association of Scotland* v. *Douglas* (1886) 13 R. 910.
[23] *Salton* v. *New Beeston Cycle Co.* (1900) 1 Ch. 43; *Friend* v. *Young* (1897) 2 Ch. 421.
[24] *Walker* v. *Somerville* (1837) 16 S. 217.
[25] *Patmore & Co.* v. *Cannon & Co. Ltd.* (1892) 19 R. 1004; *S.S. State of California Co.* v. *Moore* (1895) 22 R. 562.
[26] *Wink* v. *Mortimer* (1849) 11 D. 995.
[27] *Dick* (1901) 9 S.L.T. 177.
[28] *Pollok* v. *Paterson* Dec. 10, 1811, F.C.; *Campbell* v. *Anderson* (1829) 3 W. & S. 384.
[29] See para. 13–12, cl. 17.

as my Attorney and to operate thereon, or to operate on any such account already opened in my name or to which I am a party, and for that purpose to lodge or deposit moneys and to draw, sign, endorse or negotiate all cheques, coupons, bills of exchange, promissory notes, deposit receipts, interest or dividend warrants, money orders or postal orders and generally all cash and other documents of whatever description which may require to be signed or endorsed by me.[d]

(3) To sell or concur with others in selling by public auction or by private sale any property, heritable or moveable, real or personal, of any kind or description and wherever situated which may belong to me or in which I may be or become interested and whether the title thereto may be in my name or in the names of myself and others or in the name of any person as nominee or trustee for me, and that at such prices and upon such terms as he may think proper.

(4) To purchase or concur with others in purchasing heritable property or real estate in any part of the United Kingdom or to invest in the purchase of government stocks or funds of the United Kingdom, any country of the British Commonwealth or any foreign country or in stocks, securities or funds of any municipal corporation or public trust in the United Kingdom, or in the stocks, shares, debentures or other securities of public or private companies registered in the United Kingdom or elsewhere or in shares, bonds or other securities of unit or other trusts, provided that the certificates for such investments are registered and not to bearer and that the liability incurred is limited to the amount invested, and generally to act in relation to any such purchases or investments made in virtue of the powers hereby conferred upon him.[e]

(5) To accept on my behalf any stocks, shares or securities allotted or provisionally allotted to me, to undertake liability for and make any payments that may be due in respect thereof and to procure the registration thereof in my name or in his name as my Attorney, or to renounce or sell any rights to such stocks, shares or securities; and to attend, act and vote for me at all meetings of and with regard to all matters affecting any company, corporation, trust or other undertaking in which I may be or become interested as a holder of stocks, shares, debentures or other securities or as a creditor or otherwise, or at any class meeting of such holders or creditors, and to grant proxies for others to act on my behalf at any of such meetings, and generally to act for me in the premises as fully and freely as I could have done myself, including without prejudice to the foregoing generality power to agree to liquidation, amalgamation, reconstruction or transfer of any such company, corporation, trust or undertaking.

(6) To grant or accept feus or leases, to excamb land, to consolidate interests of superiority and property, to improve or reconstruct or concur with others in improving or reconstructing heritable or real property, to accept renunciations of leases, input and output tenants, pay and receive rents, feuduties, ground annuals and ground rents, to redeem or accept redemption of feuduties or ground annuals, to alter or vary rents, and all on such terms and conditions as my Attorney may think proper, and generally to do all acts or things which he may consider necessary or desirable in relation to

the management of heritable or real property in which I may be interested.

(7) To lend money upon the security of any moveable or personal property, or upon the security of any heritable property or real estate in the United Kingdom, on such terms and conditions as my Attorney shall think proper, and to rearrange or vary all loans or securities, whether made by myself or by him on my behalf, from time to time or to require repayment thereof or enforce the security therefor and generally to do all such acts or things in relation thereto as my Attorney may deem fit.

(8) To borrow money on my behalf binding me and my executors and representatives jointly and severally for repayment thereof and that on such terms and conditions as my Attorney may think fit, and to grant security therefor over any part of my property, heritable or moveable, real or personal, and to rearrange or vary the terms of any borrowings whether made by myself or by him on my behalf, or the securities therefor, including without prejudice to that generality to make repayment thereof or arrange for loans or advances in substitution therefor and generally to do all such acts or things in relation thereto as my Attorney may deem fit.

(9) To grant, execute and deliver or to accept any deeds or documents necessary or appropriate to the exercise of any of the powers hereby conferred upon my Attorney, including without prejudice to that generality feu grants, dispositions, deeds of conditions relating to land or buildings, deeds of excambion, leases, standard securities, mortgages, assignations, variations, discharges, deeds of restriction or disburdenment, transfers of stocks, shares or other securities, renunciations, acceptances, applications for registration and receipts.

(10) To make on my behalf all returns required for government or local taxation or rating, to adjust valuations and assessments, to claim all repayments, rebates or allowances to which I may be entitled and to make any relevant appeals, and that as regards all periods past, current or future.

(11) To appear and claim for me in the bankruptcy or liquidation of any person or company indebted to me and to concur in any arrangement in connection therewith.

(12) To examine, prepare and adjust all accounts between me and any other person or persons and to claim or pay any sums which he may be satisfied are payable to or by me, and to compound, compromise, submit to arbitration and settle claims of any kind due to or payable by me.

(13) To raise or defend all actions or judicial or other proceedings in which I am or may be interested so far as he may consider necessary or expedient and to refer to arbitration any questions or disputes in which I am or may become involved, to appeal against, enforce or implement any judgment, order or award and to appear or instruct appearance on my behalf before any tribunal, commission or other official inquiry.

(14) To employ bankers, brokers, solicitors, counsel, accountants, managers, factors or agents of any kind for the management of any

of my affairs and to pay them appropriate remuneration for their services.

(15) To appoint an attorney or attorneys under my Attorney for all or any of the purposes herein contained and to remunerate him or them for their services and to revoke such appointment or appointments at any time.

(16) I provide and declare that all acts and deeds done or granted by my Attorney in virtue of the powers hereby conferred shall be as valid and binding as if done or granted by myself; and persons paying money or transferring property to my Attorney shall not be concerned with or be bound to see to the application thereof; and I bind myself to ratify, approve of and confirm all that my Attorney or any attorney under him or any agent appointed by either of them shall do or cause to be done in virtue of the powers herein contained.

(17) And I further provide and declare that this Power of Attorney shall remain in force until recalled by me in writing; but until my Attorney shall have received notice of such recall or of other termination hereof my Attorney shall be entitled to continue to act hereunder; and all powers herein conferred shall be operative and may be acted and relied upon by third parties upon production of a copy hereof certified as required by the Powers of Attorney Act 1971 or an extract hereof from the Books of Council and Session until they shall have had notice of such recall or other termination however occasioned.

(18) And my Attorney shall be bound as by acceptance hereof he binds himself to account to me for his intromissions in virtue hereof and to make payment to me of whatever balance may be due to me after deduction of remuneration for his services, including remuneration on the appropriate scale for any professional services rendered by him, and all charges and expenses upon being relieved of all obligations and liabilities undertaken or incurred on my behalf; but declaring that my Attorney shall incur no responsibility whatever in respect of the actings, intromissions or management of any bankers, brokers or other agents employed by him or of any substitute Attorney whom he may appoint.

(*To be attested*)   Stamp duty nil.

NOTES
[a] If the granter proposes to return from time to time and wishes the power to remain in force notwithstanding temporary returns add "and may be absent for a considerable period and from time to time."
[b] It is not necessary to state any reason for granting. If the statement of a reason may be restrictive it can be omitted.
[c] As to possible interest in trust estates or in succession see more detailed clauses in paras. 13–13 and 13–14.
[d] If the granter already has any banking accounts abroad this clause may be extended to authorise continued operation of such accounts by the attorney but it is normally undesirable to authorise the attorney to open new banking accounts except in the United Kingdom. Express power to overdraw bank accounts may be included if desired.

e Foreign investments are authorised except in municipal corporations or public trusts which are restricted to the United Kingdom but may be extended to foreign countries if desired. Investment in bearer securities is not authorised: if the granter already holds these it may be desirable to authorise the Attorney to retain or sell them. The restriction of liability to the amount invested would not prohibit the acceptance of rights issues with liability for payment by further instalments: that is specifically authorised in clause (5).

Special powers

13–13 **Interests in trust estates.** If the principal has an interest in any trust estate fuller powers to deal therewith may be inserted.

"In respect that I am or may be a beneficiary under (*specify the trust so as to identify it*) I empower my Attorney to require, sue for and receive transfer or payment of all property and moneys due and to become due to me from the same, to examine, approve or disapprove and adjust all accounts of or relating thereto, to give and undertake on my behalf to the trustees of the said trust such consents, authorities and instructions as my Attorney may think fit and to grant receipts and discharges for property and moneys transferred to me and to discharge the said trustees of their actings, transactions, intromissions and management, with obligations of indemnity, warrandice and relief restricted to the amount or value of any property or moneys received by me or on my behalf from the trust estate."

13–14 **Interests in executry estates.** Where the principal has an interest in executry estate being or about to be administered by an executor-nominate or executor-dative who is not the principal the general power to recover moneys due to the principal and to grant receipts or discharges (clause (1) of style in paragraph 13–12) will normally suffice. Any right to claim legal rights is personal to the principal[30] and cannot be delegated to his attorney. If the principal has been or is to be the executor, fuller powers on the following lines may be inserted.

(*a*) *Executor-nominate not yet confirmed.* "In respect that X (*designed*) died at   on   and that I am the executor nominated by (him)(her) in (his) (her) will dated   and that I am about to enter on the possession and management of the estate of the said deceased and that it is necessary that I should obtain, record and exhibit an inventory of the said estate but by reason of my absence abroad it would be inconvenient for me to do so personally, I authorise and empower my Attorney to give up an inventory of the said estate, make oath thereto, record the same in the books of the appropriate court and crave confirmation thereof in my favour as executor foresaid; and also" (*continue as in common clauses infra*).

(*b*) *Executor-nominate already confirmed.* "In respect that I have been appointed and confirmed as executor-nominate of the

---

[30] *Lawson* v. *Young* (1854) 16 D. 1098.

deceased X (*designed*) conform to confirmation by the Sheriff of
at   dated   and that I am (about to enter
on) (have yet to complete) the administration and management of
the estate of the said X, but by reason of my absence abroad it
would be inconvenient for me to do so personally I authorise and
empower my Attorney" (*continue as in common clauses infra*).

(*c*) *Executor-dative not yet appointed.* "In respect that I am a
and one of the next-of-kin of the deceased X (*designed*)
and that I am about to apply to be decerned and confirmed as (his)
(her) executor-dative but that by reason of my absence abroad it
would be inconvenient for me to do so personally I authorise and
empower my Attorney for me and in my name to present a writ in
the appropriate court and obtain decernitur in my favour as
executor foresaid, and thereafter to give up an inventory of the
estate of the said X, make oath thereto, record the same in the
books of the said court and to crave confirmation thereof in my
favour as executor foresaid; and also" (*continue as in common
clauses infra*).

(*d*) *Executor-dative already appointed but confirmation not yet
obtained.* "In respect that I have been decerned executor-dative of
the deceased X (*designed*) conform to decree by the Sheriff of
dated   and that I am about to enter" (*continue as
in (a) above*).

(*e*) *Executor-dative appointed and confirmation obtained.* "In
respect that I have been appointed and confirmed as executor-
dative of the deceased X (*designed*) conform to confirmation by the
Sheriff of   at   dated   and that" (*continue
as in (b) above*).

Common clauses. "to take all other steps necessary to complete
my title to the estate, heritable or moveable, real or personal, of
the said X in any country [and to obtain and pay premiums in
respect of any bonds of caution or indemnities for the purpose of
obtaining administrative title to the estate of the said X or any part
thereof in Scotland or elsewhere;][a] to adjust and pay all
government taxation payable in respect of the said estate and all
debts and liabilities due by the said X or his estate."

NOTE
[a] Executor-dative only.

13–15   Several granters. The style in paragraph 13–12 may be adapted with
alterations as follows:

Appointment. "Severally and respectively appoint B (*designed*)
to be the Attorney for each of us to do everything regarding our
respective estates which we respectively could have done if present
without limitation by reason of anything herein contained; and in
particular, without prejudice to the foregoing generality, we
severally and respectively confer upon our Attorney the following
powers," *etc.*

Special clause (before clause (18)). "And we specially provide and declare that (i) this deed shall be construed and acted upon in all respects as if we had granted separate powers of attorney in favour of the said B in the same terms as those present *mutatis mutandis* (ii) our Attorney shall have no power to bind any (either) of us in obligations or liabilities incurred with reference to the estate of the other (others) (iii) we undertake no liability to our Attorney except with reference to our respective estates only and (iv) this Power of Attorney, although recalled or otherwise terminated as regards one of us, shall not thereby be recalled or terminated as regards the other (others)."

Accounting clause (in lieu of clause (18)). "And our Attorney shall be bound as by acceptance hereof he binds himself to account to each of us separately for his intromissions with our respective interests and estates in virtue hereof and to make payment to each of us respectively of whatever balance may be due to each of us respectively after deduction of remuneration for his services, including remuneration on the appropriate scale for any professional services rendered by him, and all charges and expenses upon being relieved by each of us respectively of all obligations and liabilities undertaken or incurred on behalf of such one of us; and the decision of our Attorney as to the apportionment as between our respective estates of all sums received or expended, including his remuneration and expenses, shall be conclusive and binding upon each of us respectively: and we declare that our Attorney shall incur no responsibility whatever in respect of the actings, intromissions or management of any bankers, brokers or other agents employed by him or of any substitute Attorney whom he may appoint."

13–16 Joint attorneys. The appointment may run:

"I hereby appoint B (*designed*) and C (*designed*) and each of them by himself alone and the survivor to be my Attorneys (each of them separately and the survivor being hereinafter referred to under the expression "my Attorneys" and all powers hereby conferred on my Attorneys being exercisable by either of them alone while both hold office or after the resignation or death of the other)."

13–17 Powers for specific purposes. A factory and commission or power of attorney may be granted for specific purposes. Styles of deeds for the purpose of the management and sale of heritable property, power to sell a particular heritable property or a *pro indiviso* share therein and power to borrow money and grant security in special terms are contained in Burns, *Conveyancing Practice* (4th ed. pages 61–63), and are still appropriate.

Proof of instruments creating powers of attorney

13–18 The contents of a power of attorney or factory and commission may be proved by means of a copy authenticated on each page and at the end by the granter or by a solicitor or stockbroker in the way prescribed by section 3 of the Powers of Attorney Act 1971. When a copy has been made and so authenticated the contents of the original deed may also be proved by a copy of the copy similarly authenticated.

Certificate at the end of each page

I certify this page to be a true and complete copy of the corresponding page of the original instrument.

> (*Signature of granter, solicitor or stockbroker*)

Certificate at the end of complete copy

I certify the foregoing reproduction to be a true and complete copy of the original instrument.

> (*Signature of granter adding "granter of the said instrument" or of solicitor or stockbroker adding profession and address*)

A copy of an authenticated copy may be similarly authenticated substituting references to the authenticated copy for references to the original instrument.

Powers of attorney for use abroad for commercial purposes

13–19   Powers of Attorney are frequently granted authorising acts to be carried out abroad by an agent on behalf of a commercial concern. These vary from comprehensive powers to manage a branch business or factory abroad to specific powers to complete a particular transaction or carry out a particular act. Styles are given in paragraphs 13–20 and 13–21 of special powers to enter into a contract and to effect stoppage *in transitu*. For other illustrations of general and special powers for use abroad reference may be made to Butterworth, *Encyclopaedia of Forms and Precedents*, Volume 1, "Agency". In order that the deed may be acceptable abroad it is necessary that the authenticity of the signature(s) and the validity of execution of the deed are certified by a notary public and that the status of the notary public and his entitlement to grant the certificate are certified by a holder of responsible public office, *e.g.* the provost or a magistrate.[31] In the case of a power of attorney for use abroad it is recommended that the principal deed, rather than an authenticated copy, be used. For some foreign countries the requirements may be different and it may be desirable to enquire of the nearest relevant consulate.

Power of attorney to negotiate contract abroad

13–20   To all to whom these presents shall come, we, X and Company Limited, (*designed*) send greeting: whereas we have resolved to appoint B, (*status and designation*) to act as our Attorney for the purpose of negotiating with (*name and designation of foreign*

---

[31] For forms of certificate see para. 13–20.

contracting party) a contract for the building, supply and delivery and guarantee of marine vessels in accordance with terms, conditions and specifications to be arranged and completed by the said B: therefore we do hereby nominate and appoint the said B to act as our Attorney for the purposes of negotiating on our behalf and entering into the said contract with the appropriate (ministers or) officials of the said   and to that end to adjust, sign, execute and deliver on our behalf all documents necessary or incidental to the purposes aforesaid: And we agree that this Power of Attorney shall subsist until notice of its recall has been received by you.

(*To be attested*)   Stamp duty nil.

Certificate of notary public annexed

I, (*name and address of notary public*), Notary Public by Royal Authority duly admitted and sworn, do hereby certify and make known to all to whom these presents shall come and may concern that the Power of Attorney hereunto prefixed was of the day and date thereof duly executed and sealed, and as and for their own act and deed in due form of law delivered by X and Company Limited of (*address*) aforesaid, the granters thereof, and it was subscribed for and on behalf of the said Company by AB, one of their Directors, and CD, the Secretary of the said Company, and that the signatures "AB" and "CD" appended to the said Power of Attorney are of the respective proper handwritings of the said AB and CD. And I further certify that, under the Articles of Association of the said X and Company Limited, the said Power of Attorney has been duly executed by the said X and Company Limited. In faith and testimony whereof, I have hereunto set my hand and affixed my Notarial Seal, this   day of   in the year of our Lord One thousand nine hundred and   (Signature of notary public) Glasgow (date). (Seal of notary public).

It is hereby certified that   who has issued the foregoing Certificate is a Notary Public and that in the said capacity he is entitled to issue Certificates of that nature.

(*Provost*) (*Magistrate*)

Power of attorney to effect stoppage in transitu[32]

13–21   We, A and Company Limited (*designed*) whereas on or about (*date of despatch of goods*) we consigned the goods specified in the schedule hereto to Z Limited of (*address*) and in the events which have happened we are entitled to stop the said goods in transit and wish to do so. Therefore we hereby appoint A (*designed*) as our Attorney for us and in our name to ask, demand, sue for and recover possession from any person who may have possession of the same such of the said goods and also any other goods consigned by us to the said Z Limited whether specified in the said schedule or not as have not at the time of such demand or taking possession been delivered to the said Z Limited: and we authorise our Attorney (1) to notify any person who may have possession or custody of such goods as aforesaid of our intention to stop them in

---

[32] Style based on style in Butterworth's *Encyclopaedia of Forms and Precedents*, Vol. 1, 282.

transit in order to prevent them reaching the said Z Limited and to prohibit any person from doing any act whereby the said goods may reach the possession of the said Z Limited; (2) on non-delivery of any of such goods upon demand to prosecute any action or legal procedure to compel delivery thereof; and (3) to sell any of such goods as may lawfully be sold and account to us for the proceeds of such sale: And we agree to ratify all things that our said Attorney may do or cause to be done in the execution of the power herein conferred upon him: (And we declare that this deed shall be irrevocable for a period of   months from the date hereof).

(*To be attested*)   Stamp duty nil.

     Schedule
     (*List of goods*)
         (*To be executed*)
   (*Certificates as in style in para. 13–20 to be appended*)

II. CONTRACTS OF SERVICE

Introduction

13–22   Legislation has now in many respects impinged upon freedom of contract between employer and employee, and contracts of service or employment must be framed to comply with any statutory provisions applicable. Some of the more important matters which are subject to statutory control are: (1) the employment of women, children and young persons[33]; (2) discrimination against employment on grounds of race[34] or sex[35] and as to differentials in the terms and conditions of employment of men and women[36]; (3) the control of the hours and conditions of work in certain employments[37]; (4) minimum wages, holidays and holiday remuneration in particular trades established on the recommendations of wages councils[38]; and (5) permitted deductions from wages.[39] For a fuller account of the legislation see the undernoted texts.[40]

Capacity of parties

13–23   The ordinary rules as to capacity to contract apply to contracts of employment. A minor who contracts without his curator's consent may reduce the contract on the ground of enorm lesion.[41]

---

[33] Factories Act 1961; Mines and Quarries Act 1954; Children and Young Persons (Scotland) Act 1937.
[34] Race Relations Act 1976.
[35] Sex Discrimination Act 1975.
[36] Equal Pay Act 1970.
[37] *e.g.* Shops Act 1950 (shops); Films Act 1960 (cinemas); Baking Industry (Hours of Work) Act 1954 (bakeries); Agricultural Wages (Scotland) Act 1949 (agriculture); Transport Act 1968 (road transport); Merchant Shipping Act 1970 (shipping); Banking and Financial Dealings Act 1971 (banks).
[38] Wages Councils Act 1979.
[39] Truck Acts 1831 to 1940; Payment of Wages Act 1960.
[40] Walker, *Principles*, II, 237 *et seq.*; Halsbury's *Laws of England*, Vol. 16, "Employment."
[41] *Faulds* v. *British Steel Corporation*, 1977 S.L.T. (Notes) 18.

Formation and terms of contract

3-24   A contract of employment for a period of more than one year must be constituted by writing of both parties which is probative, holograph or adopted as holograph.[42] An improbative contract may be validated *rei interventu*.[43] Alteration of a written contract for more than a year can be proved only by writ or oath.[44] These rules apply to a contract of apprenticeship.[45] In practice a contract of employment should specify the period of endurance and provide that it shall continue on the expiry of that period until terminated by notice given by either party.[46]

The terms of the contract are negotiable and vary with circumstances. The styles in paragraphs 13–27 and 13–28 *infra* are typical of many normal contracts but special benefits may be incorporated, *e.g.* (a) membership of medical care schemes (b) payment of school fees for family where service abroad is required (c) interest free or low interest loans (d) financial assistance regarding house purchase where the employee is required to move his operating base or (e) profit sharing or share option schemes. Where any such special benefits are conferred it is essential that the taxation implications are carefully considered.

Written Particulars of Terms of Employment

3-25   The Employment Protection (Consolidation) Act 1978, Part I, requires an employer within 13 weeks after the beginning of the employment to give to the employee a written statement of the principal terms of his employment. The statement must identify the parties, specify the date when the employment began and, if it is for a fixed term, when it expires, and state whether any employment with a previous employer counts as part of the employee's continuous period of employment and, if so, specify the date when the continuous period of employment began. It must also contain particulars of the terms of employment as at a specified date not more than one week before the statement is given. The particulars to be given are: (1) the scale of remuneration or the method of calculating remuneration, (2) the intervals at which it is paid, (3) any terms or conditions relating to hours of work, (4) any terms or conditions relating to holiday entitlement, including public holidays, incapacity for work due to sickness or injury, including any provision for sick pay, and pensions and pension schemes, (5) the length of notice which the employee is obliged to give and entitled to receive to determine the contract of employment, and (6) the title of the employee's

---

[42] *Stewart* v. *McCall* (1869) 7 M. 544; *Nisbet* v. *Percy*, 1951 S.C. 350; *Murray* v. *Roussel Laboratories Ltd.*, 1960 S.L.T. (Notes) 31; *Cook* v. *Grubb*, 1963 S.C. 1.

[43] *Cook* v. *Grubb*, *supra*, at p. 16.

[44] *Dumbarton Glass Co.* v. *Coatsworth* (1847) 9 D. 732; *Ayr District Board of Control* v. *Lord Advocate*, 1926 S.L.T. 223.

[45] *Grant* v. *Ramage & Ferguson* (1897) 25 R. 35.

[46] See para. 13–27, cl. 1.

job.[47] As regards pension schemes it is unnecessary to provide particulars of these if the employee's rights depend on the terms of a pension scheme established under statutory authority where the body administering the scheme is required to give new employees information as to their pension rights; there may be an occupational pension scheme which contracts out of the earnings-related part of the State pension scheme and the particulars must state whether or not a contracting-out certificate is in force. The statement of particulars must also include a note of any disciplinary rules applicable to the employee (usually by way of reference to a document accessible to the employee which specifies the rules) and must specify a person to whom the employee may apply in relation to any disciplinary decision regarding him or any grievance and the steps in procedure consequent upon any such application.[48] If there are no particulars to be specified on any of those matters that fact should be stated.[49] Subsequent changes in the terms or conditions specified in the statement must be notified in writing by the employer to the employee not later than one month after each change.[50]

Exclusion from requirement of written particulars when there is a written contract of employment

13–26   When the parties have entered into a formal written contract of service, a copy of which has been furnished or made available to the employee, it is unnecessary to give a separate written statement of the particulars in paragraph 13–25 *supra*, provided that the contract contains express terms affording the particulars that would have been required in such a statement and a note must be given to or be accessible to the employee with regard to disciplinary rules and contracting-out of the State pension scheme.[51] In practice it is desirable to avoid the administrative work of issuing a separate statement when a formal contract has been made and so it is essential to ensure that any such contract covers all the matters which the written particulars would have specified.[52] The styles which follow in paragraphs 13–27 and 13–28 contain the particulars which the Act requires to be stated and a separate statement is not necessary.

Contract of service—staff employee

13–27   AGREEMENT
                                    between
          A B & Company Limited (*designed*)
          (hereinafter called "the Company") of the one part
          and

---

[47] Employment Protection (Consolidation) Act 1978, s. 1(1) to (3).
[48] *Ibid.*, s. 1(4).
[49] *Ibid.*, s. 2(1).
[50] *Ibid.*, s. 4.
[51] *Ibid.*, s. 5.
[52] *i.e.* those contained in ss. 1(3) and 2 of the Act.

part.   (hereinafter called "the Employee") of the other

Whereas the Employee is in the employment of the Company as (*title of job*) of the Company

Now it is hereby agreed as follows:–

1. This Agreement shall operate from the   day of for the term of   years and shall continue thereafter unless and until terminated by either party giving to the other at least thirteen weeks notice in writing.

2. The Employee shall unless prevented by ill-health devote the whole of his time and attention during usual working hours to the duties assigned to him hereunder or pursuant hereto and shall well and faithfully serve the Company and use his utmost endeavours to promote the interest of the Company. The Employee shall not without the consent of the Company accept any other appointment and shall not either alone or jointly with or as manager servant or agent for any other person directly or indirectly engage or be concerned in any business of any kind whatsoever other than the business of the Company provided always that this clause shall not prevent the Employee being from time to time interested as a holder of securities of a company whose shares are quoted on the Stock Exchange or of a company whose shares are not so quoted but which does not carry on any business of a similar nature to any of the businesses carried on by the Company or by any company which is associated with the Company in any of the relationships specified in section 736 of the Companies Act 1985.

3. The Employee shall obey and conform to all lawful orders regulations and instructions from time to time made or given to him.

4. The Employee shall not at any time either during the period of his employment hereunder or after the termination thereof without the express written consent of the Company first obtained divulge reveal or publish to any person firm or company (other than any officer or employee of the Company whose province it is to know) any of the trade secrets operations processes formulae or methods of the Company or of any of the associated companies of the Company which may have come or may come to his knowledge whether during his employment hereunder or otherwise or any other information whatsoever concerning the business or businesses of the Company or any of such associated companies or the source from which they obtain their materials and will keep with inviolable secrecy all matters entrusted to him, and all notes memoranda records formulae and writings made by him relative to the business of the Company or of such associated companies or to his employment hereunder shall be and remain the property of the Company and shall be handed over by him to the Company or as it may direct from time to time on demand or upon leaving the service of the Company.

5. As remuneration for his services hereunder the Company shall pay to the Employee a salary of £   per annum paid four weekly in arrear. This salary will be reviewed periodically.

6. The Employee shall make such journeys on the business of the

Company as may be required of him by the Company and the Company shall reimburse to him all travelling, hotel and other out-of-pocket expenses properly incurred by him in the execution of his duties hereunder. In addition the Company shall grant to the Employee the use of a motor car of the type considered by the Company to be in keeping with the status of the Employee and the Company shall maintain the said motor car and pay all expenses connected therewith including licences, repair costs and those fuel costs directly attributable to the Employee's work with the Company.

7. In addition to the usual public holidays the Employee shall be entitled to such reasonable holiday in each year not in any event being less than four weeks at full salary and to be taken at such time or times as the Managing Director of the Company may approve.

8. All inventions devices processes and designs relating to the business of the Company and all improvements thereon or on any existing inventions devices processes and designs which may be discovered or invented by the Employee during the continuance of his employment hereunder shall become the sole and absolute property of the Company without payment by the Company of any sum other than such (if any) as the Board of Directors of the Company in its absolute discretion may determine *ex gratia* to pay. All such inventions devices processes and designs and all such improvements shall be immediately disclosed to the Company and the Employee at the request and cost of the Company shall join with the Company in applying for letters patent or other protection for all or any of the said inventions devices processes designs or improvements and shall at the request and cost of the Company execute and do all instruments and things requisite to vest in the Company alone or if the Company so requires in any nominee or nominees of the Company all or any such inventions devices processes designs and improvements and any letters patent or other protection that may be obtained in respect of any of them.

9. Notwithstanding anything in this Agreement contained:–
(a) If the Employee shall neglect or fail or refuse to carry out the duties required of him hereunder or shall become bankrupt or insolvent or shall be guilty of any default or misconduct whereby the interests of the Company shall or may be seriously injured it shall be lawful for the Company summarily to determine the Employee's employment hereunder without notice or payment in lieu thereof.
(b) If during the period of this Agreement the Employee shall become unable to fulfil his duties owing to incapacity due to ill-health and such incapacity shall extend for a continuous period of six months, the Company may at the expiry of said period or at any time thereafter, by notice in writing, terminate the employment of the Employee hereunder.

10. If before the expiration of this Agreement the Employee's employment hereunder shall be determined by reason of the liquidation of the Company for the purpose of amalgamation or reconstruction and the Employee shall be offered employment during the remainder of the term of this Agreement with any concern or undertaking resulting from such reconstruction or amalgamation on

terms not less favourable in all respects than the terms of this Agreement the Employee shall have no claim against the Company in respect of the determination of his employment by the Company hereunder.

11. The Employee shall not within a period of two years after the determination of this Agreement canvass, solicit for orders or entice away any person firm or corporation who shall at any time during the continuance of the Employee's employment by the Company whether hereunder or otherwise have had business dealings with the Company.

12. In the event of any dispute or difference arising between the parties hereto as to the meaning or construction of this Agreement or as to the rights duties or obligations of either party hereunder, whether during its currency or after its termination, the same shall be referred to a single Arbiter to be agreed by the parties or, failing agreement, to be appointed by the President of the Law Society of Scotland and the decision of such Arbiter shall be conclusive and binding. (The application of section 3 of the Administration of Justice (Scotland) Act 1972 is expressly excluded).

13. During the last month of this Agreement, both parties shall agree whether the Agreement together with any modifications thereto shall be extended for a further period of   or other number of years. If for any reason either party does not wish to enter into a new Agreement, then the present Agreement will continue thereafter as set out in Clause 1 hereof.

14. Any notice required to be given hereunder must be served by being sent by registered post to the Company at   or (as the case may be) to the Employee at his address hereinbefore mentioned or last known place of abode and any such notice shall be deemed to have been served at the expiration of twenty-four hours after it is posted.

15. In this Agreement the expression "associated company" shall include C Public Limited Company and any company in which C Public Limited Company or the Company has a holding in the issued ordinary share capital and participates in the management of that company.

16. The Employee is a member of The   Staff Pension Scheme and shall be entitled to the benefits provided under the said Scheme and any amendments thereof.

17. The Schedule annexed and executed as relative hereto containing further particulars of employment of the employee required by the Employment Protection (Consolidation) Act 1978 forms part of this Agreement.

(To be attested)

SCHEDULE

1. The usual working hours will be from   a.m. to   p.m. on Monday to Friday of each week (and from   a.m. to   p.m. on each Saturday) during which the employee shall be allowed an interval for lunch at such times as shall be fixed by the Company.

2. The disciplinary rules applicable to the employee are (set out in [*state document containing the Company's disciplinary rules*] which is available in the   department) (*Alternatively state rules in the Schedule itself*).

3. If the employee is dissatisfied with any disciplinary decision relating to him or seeks redress of any grievance relating to his employment he should apply to   for an interview. Further steps consequent on such application are (contained in [*document containing Company's disciplinary rules*]) (set out below).

4. A contracting-out certificate is (not) in force relating to the employment of the employee.

(*To be executed*)

Contract of service—executive director

13–28   AGREEMENT
                              between
A B & Company Limited (*designed*) (hereinafter called "the Company")
                              and
C D (*designed*)(hereinafter called "the Executive")

1. The Company shall employ the Executive and the Executive shall serve the Company such service being based on   as an Executive Director or in such other comparable capacity as the Board of Directors of the Company ("the Board") may from time to time determine. This Agreement shall commence on and shall continue subject as hereinafter mentioned until and thereafter unless and until terminated by either party giving to the other not less than six months previous notice in writing so as to expire on   (*termination date*) or at any time thereafter.

2. During the continuance of his employment hereunder the Executive shall serve the Company to the best of his ability and use his best endeavours to promote the interests and welfare and maintain the goodwill of the Company and of its holding and subsidiary companies and the subsidiary companies of its holding companies if any (as defined by Section 736 of the Companies Act 1985) for the time being (hereinafter together with the Company called "the Group") and shall devote the whole of his working time and attention to the duties of his office.

3. The Executive shall perform such duties and exercise such powers authorities and discretions as the Board shall from time to time delegate to him on such terms and conditions and subject to such restrictions as the Board may from time to time impose.

4. (A) During each of the following periods:–
    (a) the period ending on   (*termination date*);
    (b) the unexpired portion of any period of notice given under Clause 1 hereof whether given
         (i) by the Company or (ii) by the Executive;
    (c) the continuance of this Agreement
    the Executive shall not in any capacity whatsoever or in any manner be engaged or concerned or interested in any business which is detrimental to or in competition with any business

for the time being carried on by the Company or by any company in the Group.

(B) During the continuance of this Agreement the Executive shall not without the previous consent in writing of the Board be directly or indirectly engaged or concerned in the conduct of any other trade or business save as a holder of shares or securities of a company any of whose shares or securities are dealt in on a recognised stock exchange provided that such holdings shall not exceed five per cent of the issued share capital of the company concerned.

5. As remuneration for his services the Company shall pay to the Executive a minimum salary at the rate of £   per annum payable by equal monthly payments in arrear on the last day of each month. Such remuneration shall include any sums receivable as Director's fees from any member of the Group.

6. The Executive shall make such journeys whether in the United Kingdom or otherwise as may be required of him and shall be entitled to be repaid all travelling hotel and other expenses properly incurred by him in or about the performance of his duties hereunder.

7. The Executive shall be entitled to four weeks holiday (exclusive of public holidays) in each calendar year at full salary to be taken at such time or times as the Board may approve. Upon the determination of the Executive's employment hereunder (otherwise than in pursuance of sub-clause (b) or (c) of Clause 12) his entitlement to holiday will be calculated on the basis of 2 days' holiday for each completed calendar month of service in the then current calendar year and payment in lieu will be made for any holidays not taken at the date of such determination.

8. The Company shall provide and maintain a motor car of a type to be decided upon by the Board and shall bear the cost of insuring testing taxing and running the same (including petrol and oil) for the use of the Executive for the performance of his duties Provided always that the Executive shall be responsible for paying for petrol consumed on any occasion when the said motor car is used by him for his private purposes.

9. The Executive subject to the Rules for the time being applicable thereto shall be entitled to become and remain during the continuance of his engagement a member of   Staff Pension and Life Assurance Scheme (*or other scheme if any*) for the time being in force applicable generally to full time officers or employees of the Company or any category thereof including the Executive.

10. A) The Executive shall not at any time either during his employment hereunder or during the period of two years after the determination thereof either on his own account or for any other person firm or company solicit or interfere with or endeavour to entice away from the Company or from any company in the Group any person firm or company who at any time during or at the date of the termination of his employment shall be a customer or in the habit of dealing with the Company or such other company nor induce or seek to

induce any employee of the Company or such other company to leave its service.

B) The Executive shall not divulge or communicate to any person (other than those whose province it is to know the same or with proper authority) any of the trade secrets or other confidential information of or relating to the Company or any company in the Group or of or relating to any customers of the Company or any company in the Group of which he is now possessed or of which he shall become possessed while in the service of the Company. This restriction shall continue to apply after the termination of his employment without limit in point of time.

11. In the event of the Executive leaving the service of the Company or of his employment with the Company being terminated for any reason other than under sub-clause (a) of Clause 12 he shall not for a period of (one) (two) years thereafter be or become in any capacity whatsoever engaged or concerned or interested in any business which is or is to his knowledge about to be engaged within a radius of   miles from   in competition with any business carried on by the Company or by any member of the Group in the course of which or in connection with which the Executive shall have been employed during his appointment provided that this restriction shall not prevent the Executive from holding (by way of investment only) shares or securities of a company any of whose shares or securities are dealt in on a recognised stock exchange provided that such holdings shall not exceed five per cent of the issued share capital of the company concerned.

12. This Agreement shall be subject to termination by the Company by summary notice in writing:–
(a) given at any time while the Executive is incapacitated by reason of ill health or accident from performing his duties hereunder if he shall have been so incapacitated for an aggregate period of 183 days or more in the preceding twelve months; or
(b) if the Executive shall have committed any serious breach or repeated or continued (after warning in writing) any material breach of his obligations hereunder or shall have been guilty of conduct tending to bring himself or the Company or any company in the Group into disrepute; or
(c) if the Executive shall become bankrupt or make any composition or deed of arrangement with his creditors
and the Company shall not be liable in damages to the Executive by reason of any such termination.

13. If before the expiration of the Executive's engagement hereunder (i) his tenure of office shall be determined by the winding-up of the Company for the purpose of reconstruction or amalgamation or (ii) any company in the Group shall request him to enter its service and to terminate his engagement with the Company and the Company shall procure the reconstructed or amalgamated company to employ him or any other company in the Group shall agree to employ him (as the case may be) in service based on   on terms as to remuneration and otherwise not less favourable to him than are provided by this Agreement and for the residue of the

period of this Agreement or for such other period as may be mutually agreed then the Executive shall have no claim against the Company for damages.

14. Notices may be given by either party by recorded delivery letter or by cable or telex message addressed to the other party at (in the case of the Company) its registered office for the time being and (in the case of the Executive) his last known address and any such notice given by recorded delivery letter shall be deemed to have been given at the time at which the letter would be delivered in the ordinary course of post.

15. (*Arbitration clause as in clause 12 of style in para. 13–27*)

The information contained herein and in the following Schedule constitutes a written statement of the terms of employment of the Executive in compliance with the provisions of the Employment Protection (Consolidation) Act 1978.

(To be attested)

SCHEDULE

1. Date of commencement of Period of Employment 19

2. Rate of Remuneration and the intervals at which it is paid are contained in Clause 5.

3. The normal hours of work are currently from 9–00 a.m. to 5–30 p.m. (Monday to Friday) but the Executive is expected and may be required to work reasonable overtime, when necessary, for the performance of his duties without additional remuneration.

4. The terms and conditions relating to holidays and holiday pay are contained in Clause 7 and those relating to sickness are contained in Clause 12(a).

5. The terms and conditions relating to pensions and pension schemes are contained in Clause 9.

6. Particulars as to the length of notice to terminate are contained in Clauses 1 and 12.

7. There are no disciplinary rules applicable to the Executive except as provided in this Agreement and if the Executive is dissatisfied with any disciplinary decision relating to him he should apply orally or in writing to the Chairman of the Company.

8. Any application for the purpose of seeking redress of any grievance relating to the Executive's employment should be made either orally or in writing to the Chairman of the Company.

(To be executed)

Contracts of employment—weekly paid employees

3–29 Weekly paid workers who are not members of staff may be engaged without formal contracts of service for periods which may be less than a year initially. To comply with the statutory requirements a written statement of the terms and conditions of employment must be given by the employer to the employee within 13 weeks after the commencement of his employment. The style which follows in paragraph 13–30 is for general use: where employment in the trade or industry concerned is subject to an order under section 14 of the Wages Councils Act 1979 or where a collective agreement applies briefer forms of statement containing a reference to the order or the collective agreement may be used.[53]

Written statement under section 1 of Employment Protection (Consolidation) Act 1978

13–30
(*Name and address of employer*)
To (*name and address of employee*)   Date

This statement contains particulars, as at the above date, of the terms and conditions of your employment as required to be given to you under section 1 of the Employment Protection (Consolidation) Act 1978.

1. Your employment commenced on   . No employment with a previous employer counts as part of your period of continuous employment (It forms part of a continuous period of employment with   which began on   ).

2. The title of your job is   .

3. Your remuneration is £   per (week) (month) payable at (weekly) (monthly) intervals on the   day of each (week) (month).

4. Your normal hours of work are from   to   daily from Monday to Friday (or otherwise as the case may be). (*Specify any overtime arrangements*).

5. You are entitled to   working days holidays for each calendar year worked or a proportion thereof for part years worked. Holidays will be taken at times convenient to us. In addition you will be entitled to public holidays observed in our trade.

6. You will receive normal remuneration during absence through sickness or accident up to a maximum of   days in any period of twelve months. A medical certificate must be supplied by you for any absence of   or more consecutive working days. You will be required to give credit to us for any national insurance sickness benefits payable to you in respect of any period of absence during which you are remunerated by us.

7. (A contributory pension scheme known as   is provided which you will require to join) (A non-contributory pension scheme known as   is provided under which you are entitled to benefit). Full particulars of the scheme are furnished in a booklet given to you. A contracting-out certificate under the Social Security Pensions Act 1975 is (is not) in force in respect of your employment. (*Adapt as appropriate*)

8. The disciplinary rules which will apply to you and the procedures to be followed if you are dissatisfied with any disciplinary decision

---

[53] For examples see Butterworth, *Encyclopaedia of Forms and Precedents*, Additional Forms 95 2 and 3.

or have any grievance relating to your employment are set out in (*state document containing such rules which is available to employees*) which is available in the   department.

9. (a) The length of notice which you are required to give to terminate your employment is   .
(b) The length of notice which you are entitled to receive from us to terminate your employment is one week while you have been employed continuously for two years and thereafter increasing by one week for each year of continuous employment until you have completed twelve years of such employment after which you will be entitled to receive twelve weeks notice[a]. (*Additional conditions may be specified but are not required under the 1978 Act*).

Please acknowledge receipt hereof (and of the pension booklet) by signing the receipt attached to the duplicate copy hereof and returning it to us.

(*Signature of employer*)

NOTE
[a] These are the minimum periods prescribed by the Employment Protection (Consolidation) Act 1978, s. 49.

Form of receipt

To   (*employer*)   (Date)
From   (*employee*)

I acknowledge receipt of the statement of which the foregoing is a duplicate (and of the pension booklet therein mentioned).

(*Signature of employee*)

Changes in Terms and Conditions of Employment

3–31 When any change is made in the original terms or conditions of employment a further statement must be given by the employer to the employee stating the change. The statement must be given not more than one month after the change.[54] The statement, it is suggested, should be sent in duplicate with an acknowledgement of receipt upon the duplicate to be signed and returned by the employee as in the case of the original statement—see paragraph 13–30 *supra*.

Written statement of changes under section 4 of Employment Protection (Consolidation) Act 1978

3–32 To (*name and address of employee*)
This statement is given pursuant to section 4 of the Employment Protection (Consolidation) Act 1978. The following changes, as provisionally notified to you, have been made in the terms of your employment and are effective as from   (*State the changes*)
Please acknowledge (as in form in paragraph 13–30)
(Receipt on duplicate as in form in paragraph 13–30).

---

[54] Employment Protection (Consolidation) Act 1978, s. 4.

Indentures of Apprenticeship—Training Contracts

13–33   The Employment Protection (Consolidation) Act 1978 applies to contracts of apprenticeship or training. The traditional forms of indentures of apprenticeship or training contracts did not contain all the particulars now required by the Act. Accordingly either (a) the indenture or contract should be amplified to include all the particulars specified in subsection (3) of section 1 of the Act and a note should be given specifying matters in subsection (4) of that section, or (b) the existing forms should continue to be used and a written statement of the particulars required by the Act should be given. The styles in paragraphs 13–34 and 13–35 do not include all the particulars required by the Act and a written statement of particulars must also be given.

Since such contracts are entered into for a fixed period, usually without obligation upon either party to continue an employer-employee relationship thereafter, it is advisable to provide in the contract for renunciation of the rights of the apprentice or trainee at the expiry of the fixed period to claim redundancy payment or to complain of unfair dismissal.[55]

Indenture of apprenticeship—trade

13–34   INDENTURE
                                              between
              A B Limited (*designed*) (hereinafter called "the Company")
                                                and
              C D (*designed*) with the consent of E D (*designed*) as curator
                                        of the said C D.

1. The said C D with the consent of the said E D as his curator binds himself to serve as apprentice to the Company for the period of   years from and after the   day of   , which is the commencement of this indenture notwithstanding the date hereof.

2. The said C D and E D jointly and severally undertake that during the said period the said C D (1) will on every business day within normal working hours faithfully, honestly and diligently serve the Company in their trade of   and all branches thereof and will obey and perform all lawful orders and instructions given to him on behalf of the Company and observe any regulations made by the Company from time to time for the conduct of its works or business (2) will not without the consent of the Company absent himself from the service of the Company (3) will not reveal or disclose any of the affairs or secrets of the Company's business and (4) will not do or knowingly suffer to be done any injury or damage to the property of the Company or of its customers or persons dealing with it; and the said C D and E D jointly and severally agree to make payment of any loss or damage which the Company may

---

[55] 1978 Act s. 142(1) and (2) as amended by Employment Act 1980 s. 8(2).

sustain through the negligence or misconduct of the said C D or by his breach in any respect of his obligations hereunder.

3. The Company undertakes during the said period to teach or cause the said C D to be taught the said trade of   so far as practised by them and so far as the said C D is capable of learning the same.

4. The company shall pay to the said C D wages on the following scale:–
(*Specify wages for each year or period of the apprenticeship*)

5. The Company shall be entitled to suspend or dismiss the said C D on account of incompetence or wilful disobedience, insolence, neglect of duty, idleness, dishonesty or other misconduct.

6. The parties accept that this indenture is a fixed term contract and the said C D with consent of the said E D, in terms of Section 142 of the Employment Protection (Consolidation) Act 1978 as amended by Section 8(2) of the Employment Act 1980, waives any right to complain of unfair dismissal or claim redundancy payment if the said C D is not re-engaged by the Company on the expiry of the period of this indenture.
(*To be attested*)   Stamp duty nil

NOTE
Written statement to be given as required by section 1 of the 1978 Act.

Post-diploma training contract—solicitor

3–35   POST-DIPLOMA TRAINING CONTRACT
between
AB, CD and EF, all Solicitors
in B & Company (*address*)
(hereinafter referred to as "the Employer")
and
GH (*designed*) (hereinafter referred to as "the Trainee")

Whereas the Trainee (One) holds *inter alia* the Diploma in Legal Practice granted by the University of   dated   ; and (Two) has in terms of the Admission as Solicitor (Scotland) Regulations 1981 obtained the written consent of the Council of the Law Society of Scotland (hereinafter referred to as "the Council") to enter into a post-Diploma training contract conform to an Entrance Certificate by the Council dated   .

Therefore the parties agree as follows:

1. This training contract will endure for the period of two years from   which is hereby declared to be the commencement date of said contract, notwithstanding the date or dates hereof.

2. The Employer undertakes:–
(first) to provide training in the work of a solicitor within the scope of their practice, in such areas of work as may be agreed between

the parties hereto, and in so far as the Trainee is capable of learning the same;

(second) to have regard (a) in fixing the rate of remuneration payable to the Trainee to the relevant scale of remuneration recommended by the Council from time to time during the term of this training contract; and (b) in general, to the Guidelines for the Training of Solicitors issued from time to time by the Council;

(third) if requested by the Trainee, and if satisfied on the completion of one year from the date of commencement of this training contract that the Trainee has during that year adequately fulfilled the obligations herein imposed, to certify to the Council that the Trainee is a fit and proper person to be admitted as a solicitor;

(fourth) on the completion of the period of service hereunder to the reasonable satisfaction of the Employer to discharge this training contract.

3. The Trainee undertakes:–

(first) to serve the Employer in their profession as solicitors honestly, faithfully and diligently;

(second) to perform such tasks or to work in such departments of the Employer's business as the Employer may reasonably require;

(third) to treat as strictly confidential the secrets and affairs of the Employer, their staff and clients;

(fourth) not to engage in any other gainful employment during office hours or otherwise absent himself from his Employer's business without the prior consent of his Employer and the Council.

4. The Trainee accepts that this training contract is a fixed term contract, and in terms of Section 142 of the Employment Protection (Consolidation) Act 1978, as amended by Section 8 (2) of the Employment Act 1980, waives any right to complain of unfair dismissal or claim redundancy payment if he is not re-engaged by the Employer on the expiry of this contract.

5. The Employer and the Trainee agree:

(first) that if any dispute shall arise between them in any matter whatsoever in connection with this training contract the same shall be referred for decision to the President of the said Society for the time being or to any person nominated by him and the decision of the President or such other person shall be binding and final;

(second) that in relation to any such reference to the President of the said Society or his nominee, the provisions of Section 3 of the Administration of Justice (Scotland) Act 1972 shall be excluded; and

(third) that this training contract is made under and is subject to the terms of the said Admission as Solicitor (Scotland) Regulations 1981.

(*To be attested*)   Stamp duty nil

NOTES

1. The above contract can only be entered into if the trainee holds an Entrance Certificate issued by the Council of the Law Society of Scotland (Admission of Solicitors (Scotland) Regulations 1981, reg. 8(1)).

2. The contract must be registered with the Council within three months of its commencement and thereafter in the Books of Council and Session (said Regulations, reg. 15(2)).

Discharge of indenture of apprenticeship—trade (as in para. 13–34)
(endorsed)

3–36 We A B Limited, designed in the foregoing indenture, certify that C D also therein designed has served as our apprentice to our satisfaction for the period therein specified.
Stamp duty nil.   (*To be attested*)

Discharge of post-diploma training contract—solicitor (as in para. 13–35)
(separate)

3–37 We A B, C D and E F, all Solicitors in B & Company (*address*) the Employer under a Post-Diploma Training Contract dated
and entered into with G H (*designed*) (hereinafter referred to as "the Trainee") hereby discharge the Trainee of the said Post-Diploma Training Contract and the whole purport and effect thereof and certify that in our opinion he continues to be a fit and proper person to be a Solicitor in Scotland.
Stamp duty nil.   (*To be attested*)

ARBITRATION

A. Submissions

B. Procedure

C. Final Award

Introduction

14–01   A reference to arbitration may be (1) made by the parties voluntarily
when a dispute arises, (2) provided for antecedently in a contract, or (3)
required by statute.[1] If the parties have agreed to arbitrate and the issue
falls within the scope of the arbitration agreement or clause, the jurisdiction of the courts is ousted,[2] subject to the qualification that, in the
absence of express agreement to the contrary, the arbiter may on the
application of a party, and shall if the Court of Session on such an application so directs, at any stage in the arbitration state a case for the
opinion of that court on any question of law arising in the arbitration.[3] It
is for consideration by the parties, when the terms of the reference or of
the arbitration clause in a contract are being adjusted, to agree whether
they wish to incur the expense of a reference to the court of a question
of law: if they do not so wish the application of section 3 of the 1972 Act
should be expressly excluded. Arbitration clauses with exclusion of section 3 are appropriate where (a) the agreement is in respect of a relationship where publication of a dispute would be undesirable (b) the
financial resources of the parties are significantly disparate or (c) the
issues which may arise or have arisen are more appropriate for decision
by a technically or professionally qualified person or involve the exercise
of discretion in a special field.

Capacity of parties

14–02   In general, parties who have power to contract may enter into a submission to an arbiter. The following special cases may be noted:
Trustees have implied power to submit to arbitration all claims connected with the trust estate so long as that is not at variance with the
terms or purposes of the trust.[4] The same power is possessed by persons
within the definition of "trustee" under the 1921 Act, *i.e.* trustees *ex
officio*, executors, nominate or dative, tutors, curators and judicial factors.[5]
Minors. A minor who has no curator has power to submit to arbitration
but it is inadvisable for the other party to do so since the award may be
reduced within the *quadriennium utile*. If the minor has a curator he
may enter into a submission with his curator's consent; the award may
still be reducible, but enorm lesion may be more difficult to establish.
Partnerships. All partners must be parties since a submission is not an

---

[1] *e.g.* Agricultural Holdings (Scotland) Act 1949, s. 74.
[2] *North British Railway Co.* v. *Newburgh and North Fife Railway Co.*, 1911 S.C. 710; *Sanderson &
Son* v. *Armour & Co.*, 1922 S.C. (H.L.) 117, 126; *Crawford Brothers* v. *Commissioners of Northern
Lighthouses*, 1925 S.C. (H.L.) 22; *Farrans* v. *Roxburgh County Council*, 1969 S.L.T. 35.
[3] Administration of Justice (Scotland) Act 1972, s. 3(1). It is too late to raise a question of law under
the section once the arbiter has issued his final award: *Fairlie Yacht Slip Ltd.* v. *Lumsden*, 1977 S.L.T.
(Notes) 41.
[4] Trusts (Scotland) Act 1921, s. 4.
[5] *Ibid.*, s. 2 as amended by Succession (Scotland) Act 1964, s. 20.

act in the usual course of the firm's business where any one partner may bind the firm.[6]

Counsel have implied power to refer a litigation to arbitration without the express authority of their clients.[7]

Solicitors do not have such a power[8] and may be personally liable if their client repudiates their authority to bind him.[9]

Trustees in sequestration may, with the consent of the commissioners, refer to arbitration any questions which may arise in the course of the sequestration regarding the estate or any demand or claim made thereon.[10]

Liquidators. Liquidators in a winding up by the court in Scotland, subject to general rules, have the same powers as a trustee in sequestration,[11] and may refer questions arising in the winding up but it would seem with the sanction of the court or the committee of inspection.[12] In the case of a voluntary winding up it appears that the liquidator may enter into a submission without any consent,[13] save where the winding up is subject to the supervision of the court when the consent of the court seems advisable.[14]

Appointment of arbiter

4–03   An agreement to refer to arbitration is not invalid because the reference is to a person not named, or to a person to be appointed by another person, or to a person described as the holder for the time being of any office or appointment.[15] If the agreement is to refer to a single arbiter to be agreed by the parties and one party refuses to concur in the nomination of such an arbiter, or if the agreement is to refer to two arbiters and one party refuses to name an arbiter, then, in the absence of any effective provision to deal with such circumstance, a sheriff having jurisdiction or the Court of Session will appoint an arbiter on the application of any party to the agreement.[16] Unless the agreement otherwise provides two arbiters who fail to agree may nominate an oversman or the court will do so if the arbiters cannot agree upon the selection of an oversman.[17] The Arbitration (Scotland) Act 1894 does not provide for the situation where an arbiter has been named by the parties but has

---

[6] *Lumsden* v. *Gordon* (1728) Mor. 14567.

[7] *Gilfillan* v. *Monkhouse* (1833) 11 S. 548; *Mackenzie* v. *Girvan* (1843) 2 Bell's App. 43, 53.

[8] *Black* v. *Laidlaw* (1844) 6 D. 1254.

[9] *Livingston* v. *Johnson* (1830) 8 S. 594.

[10] Bankruptcy (Scotland) Act 1913, s. 172.

[11] Companies Act 1985, s. 539(5).

[12] A trustee in sequestration may refer with the consent of the commissioners: the consent of the court or the committee of inspection would appear appropriate in the case of the liquidator and that is consistent with the consent required for compromising claims or questions under s. 539(1)(*f*) of the 1985 Act.

[13] 1985 Act, s 598(2).

[14] *Ibid.*, s. 610(2).

[15] Arbitration (Scotland) Act 1894, s. 1.

[16] *Ibid.*, ss. 2 and 3.

[17] *Ibid.*, s. 4.

failed,[18] and so, where a named person is appointed, it is desirable to have a fallback provision that, whom failing, an arbiter be appointed by agreement or by the holder of a named office. A reference to arbitration in the customary manner of a particular trade is effective,[19] or even a reference to arbitration where there are relevant averments of a custom in the trade concerned.[20] A mere reference to arbitration may enable one of the parties to compel arbitration but is insufficient to require the court to nominate an arbiter.[21] A firm may be appointed as arbiter and may act by one of its partners.[22]

Disqualification of arbiter

14-04 An agreement to refer to an arbiter who is one of the parties,[23] or an architect or engineer employed by one of the parties,[24] is valid, provided that he has not committed himself to a particular view in correspondence or court proceedings or otherwise indicated that he has made up his mind.[25] Although one of two arbiters appointed respectively by the parties acts as agent for the party appointing him the award is not thereby invalidated.[26] Where an arbiter has made an award which is subsequently reduced on the ground that it was *ultra vires* or did not exhaust the reference, it is unclear whether he is *functus officio* and disqualified from again taking up the reference.[27] If after an oversman has issued an award it is found that one of the two arbiters was disqualified the award is thereby vitiated.[28] A judge of the Court of Session may be an arbiter in a commercial case.[29]

Oversman

14-05 The oversman may be appointed by the parties in the submission or, if there is no such appointment, by the arbiters unless their power to do so is excluded in the submission.[30] If the submission is in formal writing the appointment by the arbiters of an oversman should also be in writing.[31] If the arbiters do not appoint an oversman the court may do so.[30] The oversman should be appointed before the procedure in the arbitration is

---

[18] *British Westinghouse Electric and Manufacturing Co. Ltd.* v. *Provost of Aberdeen* (1906) 14 S.L.T. 391.
[19] *Douglas & Co.* v. *Stiven* (1900) 2 F. 575.
[20] *United Creameries Co. Ltd.* v. *Boyd*, 1912 S.C. 617.
[21] *McMillan & Son Ltd.* v. *Rowan & Co.* (1903) 5 F. 317.
[22] *Wm. Dixon Ltd.* v. *Jones, Heard & Ingram* (1884) 11 R. 739.
[23] *Buchan* v. *Melville* (1902) 4 F. 620; *Fleming's Trs.* v. *Henderson*, 1962 S.L.T. 401 (partner of firm party).
[24] *Halliday* v. *Duke of Hamilton's Trs.* (1903) 5 F. 800; *Crawford Brothers* v. *Commissioners of Northern Lighthouses*, 1925 S.C. (H.L.) 22.
[25] *McDougall* v. *Laird & Sons* (1894) 22 R. 71; *McLauchlan & Brown* v. *Morrison* (1900) 8 S.L.T. 279; *Aviemore Station Hotel Co. Ltd.* v. *James Scott & Son* (1904) 12 S.L.T. 494, 495.
[26] *Scorrier Steamship Coasters* v. *Milne*, 1928 S.N. 109.
[27] *Miller & Son* v. *Oliver & Boyd* (1906) 8 F. 390.
[28] *Sellar* v. *Highland Railway Co.*, 1919 S.C. (H.L.) 19.
[29] Law Reform (Miscellaneous Provisions) (Scotland) Act 1980, s. 17.
[30] Arbitration (Scotland) Act 1894, s. 4.
[31] *Davidson* v. *Logan*, 1908 S.C. 350 *per* Lord Ordinary at 363.

commenced so that he may be present at debate and proof before the arbiters, and in arbitrations under the Lands Clauses Acts it is necessary that he is appointed before the arbiters enter upon the matters referred to them.[32] In submissions under the Agricultural Holdings Acts involving straightforward valuations minor irregularities in the appointment and procedure of the oversman will not invalidate the award[33] and references *in re mercatoria* may be conducted without formalities and the awards are nevertheless binding.[34] Burns[35] suggests that (1) if the submission appoints an oversman who fails, the arbiters cannot appoint, (2) if the arbiters appoint an oversman who declines, their power of appointment is not exhausted, and (3) if the oversman accepts but dies, before or after devolution, the power of appointment is exhausted. For a style which caters for events (1) or (3) see paragraph 14–36 *infra*.

Subject-matter

4–06   Submissions to arbitration may be general, embracing all disputes between the parties or all disputes arising from a particular contract, or special, restricted to an issue or issues which are specified in the reference. The former occur frequently in contracts which contain an arbitration clause: the latter in submissions entered into after the dispute has arisen. There may also be mixed general-special submissions where there is a general reference together with a particular specified issue. Since the jurisdiction of the arbiter is derived solely from the contract of submission he cannot decide any question which is not within the scope of the reference.[36] It is important in framing the submission to include all matters which the parties wish to refer and nothing which they do not. In that connection the following matters should be kept in view, *viz.*– (1) Where both special and general matters are to be referred the preferable method is to state the general matters first "including" the special matters; if the special matters precede the general matters the scope of the latter may be restricted by the operation of the *ejusdem generis* rule. (2) If the arbiter is to have power to award damages, that should be expressly conferred, since it will not be implied.[37] (3) If the reference is to "all disputes between the parties" that will not include disputes between the representatives of a deceased party or the trustee in bankruptcy of a party who has been sequestrated: if it is intended that the representatives or trustee should be bound to arbitrate then that should be specified in the submission or arbitration clause. (4) If the reference is contained in an arbitration clause in a contract it should be

---

[32] Lands Clauses Consolidation (Scotland) Act 1845, s. 26.
[33] *Gibson* v. *Fotheringham*, 1914 S.C. 987; *Methven* v. *Burn*, 1923 S.L.T. (Sh. Ct.) 25; *Cameron* v. *Nicol*, 1930 S.C. 1.
[34] *McLaren* v. *Aikman*, 1939 S.C. 222.
[35] At 71.
[36] *Carruthers* v. *Hall* (1830) 9 S. 66; *Calder* v. *Mackay* (1860) 22 D. 741.
[37] *Mackay & Son* v. *Leven Police Commissioners* (1893) 20 R. 1093.

to all disputes in relation to the contract whether arising before or after its termination. A reference of all disputes or differences as to the true intent and meaning of a partnership contract and the carrying into effect of the contract will not empower the arbiter to decide questions with regard to dissolution of the firm.[37a] (5) A mere reference of questions as to the true intent and meaning of a contract will not entitle the arbiter to do more than resolve ambiguities in the contract as distinct from questions arising from its implementation. The scope of a reference may be enlarged by subsequent conduct of the parties.[38]

Form of submission

14–07   Formal contracts of submission should be made in probative or holograph writing; if the subject matter is heritable property they must be, although an informal reference may be validated by homologation or *rei interventus*.[39] References *in re mercatoria* and agricultural references need not be in probative form.[40] In special submissions it is useful to specify each of the questions put in a numbered paragraph: that assists the arbiter in giving precise answers to each and in ensuring that the reference is exhausted. As to appointment of the arbiter or arbiters and oversman see paragraphs 14–03 and 14–05 and as to exclusion of the right to refer questions of law to the Court of Session see paragraph 14–01. It is convenient to include power to the arbiter to appoint a clerk or technical assessor in circumstances where such appointments may be appropriate—see paragraph 14–08. As to the expression of mixed general-special submissions see paragraph 14–35. If the submission includes a valuation consideration should be given to the matter of whether the arbiter should be empowered to decern for the amount.

Procedure

14–08   **Initial steps.** Except in very informal references the first step is for the arbiter or arbiters to accept office by a formal minute, either separate or endorsed on the submission. If the reference is to two arbiters, the oversman should be appointed at this stage, and he also should sign an acceptance of office. If a clerk to the reference is to be appointed that should also be done. It will be the duty of the clerk to communicate the orders of the arbiter to the parties. If the services of a technical assessor are likely to be required, he also should be appointed at the commencement of the proceedings: if the submission does not authorise such an appointment the arbiter should ask permission from the parties to make

---

[37a] See *Roxburgh* v. *Dinardo* 1981 S.L.T. 291.
[38] *North British Railway Co.* v. *Barr* (1855) 18 D. 102; *Orrell* v. *Orrell* (1859) 21 D. 554; *Miller & Son* v. *Oliver & Boyd* (1906) 8 F. 390 at 401.
[39] *Telfer* v. *Hamilton* (1735) Mor. 5657; *Brown and Colvill* v. *Gardner* (1739) Mor. 5659.
[40] *McLaren* v. *Aikman*, 1939 S.C. 222 at 229.

it on the basis that the expenses of the assessor will form part of the
expenses of the arbitration proceedings.

4–09   **Regulation of procedure.** The arbiter is master of the procedure and
may decide all incidental questions which may arise in the course of the
proceedings.[41] It is essential, however, that in the course of the proceedings the arbiter observes the principles of natural justice. In particular
the arbiter should be careful to avoid inspection of the locus in the presence of only one of the parties or his representative and privy communications with one of the parties which are not disclosed to the other. In
general the procedure adopted by the arbiter should follow the lines of
judicial procedure in court actions although there is no strict rule that he
should do so. In arbitrations under the Agricultural Holdings (Scotland)
Act 1949 the code of procedure in the Sixth Schedule to the Act should
be followed.

4–10   **Claim and answers.** The first order is usually for lodgment of a statement of claims within a specified period and answers thereto within a
further period. The order may be more than a bare order to lodge
claims. If the reference relates to the true intent and meaning of a contract or other deed which has accompanied the submission the arbiter
may identify the principal legal issues upon which he wishes the parties
to advance their respective contentions[42]; if the claim arises from actings
of parties the order may indicate the matters of fact upon which the arbiter would wish to have detailed averments. Such indications in the order
may assist in focusing the main issues at an early stage but should be
stated to be without prejudice to the freedom of the parties to include in
the statement of claim, answers and any counterclaim any averments or
representations which they think relevant to the subject-matter of the
reference. The claim and answers should contain condescendence upon
any relevant facts, give adequate notice of legal arguments and state the
basis of any valuation or sum claimed or counterclaimed. In some cases
it may be desirable to allow a further period for adjustment of the claim
and answers. In complex cases a closed record may be helpful, although
that is only a matter of convenience[43]: usually the claimant will be
responsible for preparing it.

4–11   **Hearings.** It may be useful after the submission has been received and
before the order for claims and answers has been made to have a preliminary hearing as to the procedure in the arbitration, *e.g.* the time to
be allowed for preparation of the claim and answers, whether an inspection of the locus is desired and at what stage that may most conveniently

---

[41] *Holmes Oil Co. Ltd.* v. *Pumpherston Oil Co. Ltd.* (1890) 17 R. 624 at 656; affd. (1891) 18 R.
(H.L.) 52.
[42] An early indication of legal issues may assist in avoiding a familiar dilemma, the failure of parties
to deal at debate with a relevant line of authority which the arbiter is left to apply without benefit of
argument by the legal advisers of the parties.
[43] *Christison's Tr.* v. *Callender-Brodie* (1906) 8 F.928 *per* Lord President Dunedin at 931.

be made, etc. Once the claim and answers have been received and adjusted a hearing upon legal arguments or upon the basis of any valuation may be ordered. Where the reference is simply to a man of skill to make a valuation a hearing may be unnecessary,[44] but in almost all cases, and certainly if any of the parties wish it, a hearing should be allowed. If the matters in issue are entirely legal or relate only to the proper basis of a valuation, a hearing on these matters may be sufficient to enable the arbiter to make a final award. If there are questions of mixed law and fact it is usually convenient to have a debate on the legal questions after which the arbiter may either issue an interim interlocutor on the questions of law (which may be useful in directing the matters upon which proof will be competent and relevant) or he may reserve his decision until after the evidence on the facts has been heard (corresponding to a proof before answer situation in court proceedings).

14–12   **Proof.** Where the reference is simply to a man of skill to determine a particular question the arbiter may decide without hearing evidence[45] and indeed in such circumstances evidence is unnecessary and incompetent,[46] and if the arbiter construes a contract in such a way that evidence offered is irrelevant a proof is not required.[47] In general, however, the arbiter should not refuse a proof if there are conflicting averments upon facts which may be relevant. The arbiter does not have power to enforce the attendance of witnesses nor the production of documents but the court on an application by one of the parties may authorise citation of a witness or the taking of his evidence on commission.[48] An oversman may, and in good practice should, be present at the proof; it is unnecessary to obtain the consent of parties to his being present although if he is to participate in the proceedings at the proof it is advisable that he be authorised to do so either in the submission or by a subsequent minute of the parties. Where inspection of a locus is involved the parties should be informed and invited to attend or be represented. If one party elects not to attend or be represented the safe course is for the arbiter to make the inspection unaccompanied by either party and to raise at a subsequent stage of the proof, when both parties or their representatives are available, any questions in relation to the locus upon which he wishes information or explanation.

14–13   **Devolution to oversman.** If the arbiters fail to agree either on procedure[49] or the merits[50] the reference may devolve on the oversman appointed originally, or by a minute signed by the arbiters in the

---

[44] *McNair's Trs.* v. *Roxburgh* (1855) 17 D. 445.
[45] *Paterson* v. *Corporation of Glasgow* (1901) 3 F. (H.L.) 34; *North British Railway Co.* v. *Wilson*, 1911 S.C. 730.
[46] *Logan* v. *Leadbetter* (1887) 15 R. 115.
[47] *Holmes Oil Co. Ltd.* v. *Pumpherston Oil Co. Ltd.* (1891) 18 R. (H.L.) 52.
[48] *John Nimmo & Son Ltd.* (1905) 8 F. 173; *Galloway Water Power Co.* v. *Carmichael*, 1937 S.C. 135.
[49] e.g. *Gibson* v. *Fotheringham* 1914 S.C. 987.
[50] e.g. *McNair's Trs.* v. *Roxburgh* (1855) 17 D. 445; *Crawford* v. *Paterson* (1858) 20 D. 488.

exercise of authority conferred on them by the submission,[51] or by the parties themselves. The devolution may be partial,[49] matters on which the arbiters agree being determined by their decree-arbitral and devolved matters only being decided by an award by the oversman. Where there is partial devolution care should be taken to ensure that the award of the arbiters should deal exclusively with the matters reserved to them and that the award of the oversman should deal only with the matters devolved, and that the two awards taken together should dispose fully of all the matters referred in the submission. Devolution does not imply prorogation of any time limit within which the award is to be made.[52] The nomination of an oversman made at the commencement of the reference does not effect devolution,[53] nor does the fact that the oversman has heard the evidence led before the arbiters.[54] Since the right to devolve arises only when the arbiters have differed in opinion the minute of devolution should state that fact. If one of the arbiters dies, devolution thereafter is incompetent and the submission is no longer effective.

4–14   **Interim decrees.** Power to pronounce interim decrees should be given in the submission; it is doubtful whether in the absence of such a power the arbiter can make an interim or partial award. The power to make interim awards may be useful in bringing the matters to an agreed conclusion more quickly. For example if there are several interconnected matters in the reference, the decision of the arbiter upon one of them with a note of the principles upon which it proceeded may sufficiently indicate to the parties the principles which will be applied to determination of the other matters which may facilitate an agreed settlement of these.

4–15   **Proposed findings.** Frequently an arbiter issues proposed findings and allows the parties to make representations thereon within a stated time, and perhaps orders a further hearing on the representations. In references of any complexity proposed findings are valuable. If the arbiter has erred in law the error may be rectified while the arbitration is still uncompleted[55] by either party applying for a stated case to the Court of Session (where that course is not excluded) or by the arbiter appreciating the error and voluntarily amending the findings in his final award; or he may amend his view similarly if he has misunderstood the evidence on a matter of fact. Moreover if the arbiter in the course of considering proposed findings has doubts upon any matter of law or fact, the issue

---

[51] *McNair's Trs.* v. *Roxburgh, supra.*
[52] *Thomson* v. *Norton* Jan. 28, 1818, F.C.
[53] *Brysson* v. *Mitchell* (1823) 2 S. 382.
[54] See *Crawford* v. *Paterson, supra.*
[55] A reference to the court on a question of law cannot competently be made after the arbitration proceedings have terminated *Johnson* v. *Gill*, 1978 S.C. 74, a decision relating to an agricultural holding, but section 3(1) of the Administration of Justice (Scotland) Act 1972 authorises an application for a stated case "at any stage in the arbitration," which would appear to impose a similar time limitation.

can be focused in the proposed findings so that it may be resolved on representations or after a further hearing.

Final award

14–16   **(1) Simple references.** Where the reference is simply to determine a valuation the award may be a single sentence stating the amount. It is unnecessary to explain the method by which it is calculated.

14–17   **(2) Fuller references.** In the case of fuller references where the arbiter's decision involves construction of deeds or questions of right or title, questions of law or findings in fact and the liabilities of parties which result, whether the reference be under a special or general or mixed special / general submission or under an arbitration clause in a contract, a more detailed award is desirable. The award should contain a brief narrative of the document of reference, acceptance of office by the arbiter or arbiters, the appointment of an oversman (if any) and his acceptance of office, the hearings and proof (if any) and, if there has been devolution on the oversman, the fact that the arbiters have differed and that the reference, or some of the questions if the devolution has been partial, have devolved on the oversman. The operative provisions of the award should deal precisely with all the questions referred,[56] but nothing more. If the submission has stated specific numbered questions, the award should follow the same pattern. The phraseology used in the questions submitted should so far as practicable be adopted in the findings in the award.[57] If nothing is awarded under any particular head of the claim, that should be stated.

14–18   **(3) Expenses.** The award should deal with the expenses of parties and also the expense of the clerk and any legal or other professional services provided for the assistance of the arbiter authorised by the submission or otherwise by the parties. Even if the submission does not confer power to award expenses the arbiter has an inherent power to deal with them, but in that situation it is not a ground for reduction of the award that he does not do so,[58] but *quaere* if the arbiter is asked to determine the question of expenses in the submission. The remuneration of the arbiter himself should *not* be dealt with in the award. At common law an arbiter was not entitled to expenses unless the right to them was conferred in the submission since he was presumed to act gratuitously, but it is now recognised that a professional person acting as an arbiter is entitled to remuneration for his services[59] at an appropriate rate.[60] The amount of his expenses, however, should not be included in the award

---

[56] *Miller & Son* v. *Oliver & Boyd* (1903) 6 F. 77. *Cf. Alston & Orr* v. *Allan* 1910 S.C. 304. See generally *Pollich* v. *Heatley*, 1910 S.C. 469, *per* Lord President Dunedin at 481, 482.

[57] As to objections based on changes in phraseology see *Davidson* v. *Logan*, 1908 S.C. 350, 365, 366.

[58] *Pollich* v. *Heatley*, *supra* at 481, 482.

[59] *Macintyre Brothers* v. *Smith*, 1913 S.C. 129.

[60] See *Wilkie* v. *Scottish Aviation Ltd.*, 1956 S.C. 198.

unless expressly authorised by the parties in the submission or by subsequent agreement, since the amount of the arbiter's remuneration is not within his power to decide and, if disputed, will be determined by the courts. In practice the arbiter usually awards the expenses of parties as taxed by the auditor of the Court of Session or of the sheriff court. In the case of arbitrations under the Agricultural Holdings Acts taxation is by the auditor of the sheriff court.[61] In arbitrations under the Lands Clauses Consolidation (Scotland) Act 1845 the acquiring body in all cases pays the expenses of the arbiter and oversman[62] which include both out-of-pocket expenses and reasonable remuneration.[63]

4–19 (4) **Note to award.** Where the arbitration relates to a simple valuation or an assessment of the adequacy of workmanship or materials which has been submitted to the judgment of the arbiter as a man of skill, it is unnecessary to add a note to the decision: the parties have agreed to rely upon the knowledge and experience of the arbiter and he need not set out the way in which he has reached his findings. It is suggested that in most other cases, and in particular where questions of law or disputed facts are involved, the arbiter should append to the award a note of the reasons for his decision, preferably in the form of distinct statements of the basis of his findings in fact and law where both of those elements are involved. Burns expresses the view[64] that there is no reason why such details should be given since they may simply furnish matter for objection to the decree, but it is more satisfactory to the parties to be apprised of the arbiter's reasons and, even if they should furnish grounds for objection, it is more important that justice be done to the parties than that the arbiter should shield himself from the consequence of error by a judicious silence.

4–20 (5) **Execution.** If the submission has been in probative form so also should be the decree-arbitral.[65] In a case where there was a tested reference *in re mercatoria*, however, an informal award was substained.[66] And in general the rule which requires observance of the statutory solemnities in decrees-arbitral is subject to exception in agricultural references and references *in re mercatoria*.[65] The award should not be signed by the arbiters *and* the oversman.[67]

4–21 (6) **Delivery of award.** The award is not final until it has been put beyond the control of the arbiter by delivery or registration, even although it is in the form of a final decree-arbitral.[68] Even although it has been handed to the clerk, so long as he has not been authorised to

---

[61] Agricultural Holdings (Scotland) Act 1949, Sched. 6, para. 16.
[62] s. 32.
[63] *Murray* v. *North British Railway Co.* (1900) 2 F. 460.
[64] at 74. The court may take the arbiter's note into account in an action for reduction—*Farrans Ltd.* v. *Roxburgh County Council*, 1970 S.L.T. 334.
[65] *McLaren* v. *Aikman*, 1939 S.C. 222 at 227.
[66] *Hope* v. *Crookston Brothers* (1890) 17 R. 868.
[67] *Cameron* v. *Nicol*, 1930 S.C. 1.
[68] *Robertson* v. *Ramsay* (1783) Hailes 912.

issue it, the arbiter may recall and alter it,[69] but if the clerk has been directed to transmit it to the parties that constitutes delivery and the award cannot be recalled or altered.[70] A delivered improbative award may be recalled and replaced by a properly executed award.[71] After delivery the award cannot be amended by the arbiter except as regards a clerical error.[72]

14–22   **(7) Registration.** If the submission contained a clause of consent to registration for execution, the submission and the decree-arbitral may be so registered and it is unnecessary for the decree to contain any such consent. If the submission does not contain any such consent, a consent to registration for execution in the decree is ineffectual since it is the consent of the parties that is required, but in practice it is regularly inserted. Both the submission, if not already registered, and the decree should be lodged for registration[73] and thereafter summary diligence may proceed upon the warrant endorsed on the decree.

Endurance of contract of submission

14–23   The contract of submission may fix a period for decision by the arbiter: if the arbiter fails to pronounce the final decree-arbitral within that period then, unless the parties agree to extend the period, the reference falls. In older practice it was customary to regard a year and a day as an appropriate period for disposal of a reference and there are old authorities, where there was an intention expressed to limit the period but the actual dates were left blank in the submission, to the effect of construing such provisions as being equivalent to a year and a day.[74] In modern practice the imposition of a time limit is unusual and, where it is included, the period is normally stated with precision. There is no jurisdiction in Scottish courts, such as has been conferred by statute upon English courts,[75] to extend the period stipulated in the contract of submission, and, even where a power of extension is conferred on the courts in the contract of submission, it may be exercised only within the period originally stipulated while the arbitration is still "live" and even then the court has a discretion whether or not to grant it.[76] If the contract of submission is silent as to endurance and imposes no time limit, the reference would appear to fall upon the expiry of the period of the long negative prescription (20 years).[77] The parties may agree to extend

---

[69] *Macnair* v. *Gray* (1831) 5 W. & S. 305.
[70] *McQuaker* v. *Phoenix Assurance Co.* (1859) 21 D. 794.
[71] *Bannatyne* v. *Gibson & Clark* (1862) 1 M. 90.
[72] Bell, *Arbitration* , 256, 257.
[73] See *Gracie* v. *Gracie* (1908) 16 S.L.T. 653.
[74] See Burns, 75.
[75] Arbitration Act 1950, s 13(2).
[76] *Paul* v. *Henderson* (1867) 5 M. 613; *Blyth & Blyth's Trs.* v. *Kaye*, 1976 S.L.T. 67.
[77] In *Fleming* v. *Wilson* (1827) 5 S. 906 a submission without limit of time was held not to expire within a year and a day. The categories to which the short negative prescription applies under the Prescription and Limitation (Scotland) Act 1973 do not include any which is appropriate to a reference to arbitration.

a time limit specified in the contract of submission: if that is done before the time limit originally stipulated has expired the arbitration may continue, but if after the expiry of the original time limit it is in effect a new submission.[78] If there has been no agreed prorogation of the time limit actings of parties such as appearing and pleading without taking exception may infer an extension without written agreement.[79] Power may be conferred on the arbiter in the contract of submission to prorogate any time limit which it may contain, but the power must be exercised as an official act of the arbiter in writing[80] before the time limit has expired.[81]

14–24　**Statutory time limits.** The Agricultural Holdings (Scotland) Act 1949[82] requires an arbiter to issue his award within three months of his appointment and it is misconduct by the arbiter to issue an award after the time limit has expired.[83] The time limit may be prorogated by agreement of parties or by the Secretary of State.[82] The Lands Clauses Consolidation (Scotland) Act 1845[84] allows the arbiters and umpire three months to make an award but the parties may agree to extend it.[85]

14–25　**Earlier termination in certain events.** *(a) Death of party or arbiter.* A submission falls on the death of either party.[86] The death of one of a body of trustees who are parties does not have that result if there are remaining or new assumed trustees, since it is the trust and not the individual trustees who are the true party to the reference.[87] The rule that the submission falls on the death of either party does not apply (a) where it is executorial of another contract, as where a contract of sale provided for reference to arbitration to fix the price, on the view that the principal contract remains binding upon the executors of the deceased party,[88] or (b) where the reference is merely to adjust accounts between the parties where there is no pending dispute,[89] nor does it apply to a judicial reference.[90] A submission also falls on the death of the arbiter or one of the arbiters or of an oversman on whom the reference has devolved[91]: it is for consideration whether a contract of submission to two arbiters should provide that on the death of either the reference should devolve on the oversman.[92] If there has been a general reference

---

[78] *Hill* v. *Dundee and Perth and Aberdeen Railway Junction Co.* (1852) 14 D. 1034. See note to style in para. 14–53.
[79] *Paul* v. *Henderson, supra.*
[80] *Gordon* v. *Monteith*, Dec. 10, 1812, F.C.
[81] *Lang* v. *Brown* (1855) 2 Macq. 93.
[82] Sched. 6 para. 8, as amended by Agricultural Holdings (Amendment) (Scotland) Act 1983, s. 5(2)(e).
[83] *Halliday* v. *Semple*, 1960 S.L.T. (Sh. Ct.) 11.
[84] s. 35.
[85] *Caledonian Rly. Co.* v. *Lockhart* (1860) 3 Macq. 808.
[86] Ersk., IV, iii, 29; *Robertson* v. *Cheyne* (1847) 9 D. 599.
[87] *Alexander's Trs.* v. *Dymock's Trs.* (1883) 10 R. 1189.
[88] *Earl of Selkirk* v. *Nasmith* (1778) Mor. 627; cited with approval in *Alexander's Trs.* v. *Dymock's Trs., supra.*
[89] *Alexander's Trs.* v. *Dymock's Trs., supra*, 1194, 1196.
[90] *Watmore* v. *Burns* (1839) 1 D. 743.
[91] Ersk., IV, iii, 34.
[92] See para. 14–36.

to arbitration the death of the arbiter before the arbitration commences does not extinguish the original obligation to refer unless the reference was to a man of skill to make a valuation by the exercise of his own skill and by personal inspection.[93] The bankruptcy of a party does not terminate a submission: the trustee should be informed and may participate (although he may decide not to do so in order to avoid personal liability for expenses) but even if he does not appear the arbitration may proceed and an award may be made.[94]

14–26　　*(b) Impossibility of performance.* If an arbitration cannot be carried out in the manner contemplated by the parties, as where dung and way-going crop were to be valued by personal inspection by the arbiter but had been used and consumed, arbitration is impracticable.[95]

14–27　　*(c) Rescission, frustration or repudiation of principal contract containing arbitration clause.* Where one party contends that a contract containing an arbitration clause has been rescinded or frustrated or repudiated but that is not admitted by the other party, the arbitration clause remains applicable and indeed the question of whether or not rescission, frustration or repudiation has taken place may, depending upon the scope of the clause, be a matter to be determined by arbitration.[96] Where rescission, frustration or repudiation is admitted by both parties to have occurred, there are authorities to the effect that the contract with all its clauses has gone, including the arbitration clause.[97] That proposition may now be regarded as too widely stated as a result of the decision in *Heyman* v. *Darwins Ltd.*[98] In the judgements of the House of Lords in that case it was pointed out that repudiation, not being of the contract but of an obligation undertaken by one of the parties, did not imply repudiation of a clause providing generally for reference to arbitration and the clause survived for the purpose of measuring the claims arising from the breach.

Prorogation

14–28　　The parties may prorogate the period of endurance of the submission. If arbiters or oversman are to be entitled to prorogate, power to do so must be expressly given by the parties, and the oversman may exercise any such power given to the arbiters after the reference has devolved upon him.[99]

---

[93] *Graham* v. *Mill* (1904) 6 F. 886, 892.

[94] *Grant* v. *Girdwood*, June 23, 1820, F.C.

[95] *Graham* v. *Mill, supra.*

[96] *Sanderson & Son* v. *Armour & Co.*, 1922 S.C.(H.L.) 117.

[97] *Hegarty and Kelly* v. *Cosmopolitan Insurance Corpn.*, 1913 S.C. 377; *Johannesburgh Municipal Council* v. *D. Stewart & Co.*, 1909 S.C.(H.L.) 53 as explained in *Sanderson & Son* v. *Armour & Co.*, *supra*; *Hirji Mulji* v. *Cheong Yue Steamship Co. Ltd.* [1926] A.C. 497, 505.

[98] [1942] A.C. 356.

[99] *Glover* v. *Glover and Keir* (1805) 4 Pat. App. 655.

Relationship of courts and arbitration

4–29 **(a) Before arbitration has commenced.** If an alleged reference is contained in an arbitration clause included in a principal contract questions as to (1) the existence or validity of the principal contract,[1] (2) whether there is a question to be referred,[2] and (3) whether the issue is within the scope of the arbitration clause[3] are matters for the courts to decide. If arbitration is directed by reason of a provision of statute then, if the statute expressly requires arbitration, the jurisdiction of the courts is excluded,[4] but not if the provision is merely enabling,[5] and the courts may determine whether the question at issue is within the categories which are required by the statute to be decided by arbitration[6] and whether the necessary conditions for the existence of a claim to arbitration under the statute exist.[7] Normally all such questions come before the courts by the defender pleading the arbitration clause: if that plea is sustained the question is referred to arbitration and the jurisdiction of the courts on the merits of the matter referred is excluded.[8]

4–30 **(b) After arbitration proceedings have commenced.** When arbitration has begun the courts are reluctant to intervene but may interdict the proceedings if the arbiter clearly has no jurisdiction to act[9] or if there is no question to try.[10] Normally, however, the courts will assume that the arbiter will not act outwith his powers nor decide questions that are *ultra fines compromissi* and, if he does so, an appeal to the courts for reduction of the award will then be competent.[11] If the arbiter entertains doubts as to whether any question referred to him is within the scope of the contract of submission or the arbitration clause, as the case may be, it is his duty to explicate his jurisdiction[12] but the courts may ultimately decide if reduction of the award is sought.[13]

4–31 **(c) Enforcement of award.** The arbiter's award is *res judicata* on all issues referred to him,[14] but he has no power to enforce it: that may be done by an action by one of the parties for decree conform.[15] The court may refuse to grant a decree enforcing the award if it has ceased to be binding on the defending party or is in restraint of trade.[16] If the

---

[1] *Ransohoff & Wissler* v. *Burrell* (1897) 25 R. 284; *Hoth* v. *Cowan*, 1926 S.C. 58, 64, 65.

[2] *Mackay* v. *Leven Police Commissioners* (1893) 20 R. 1093; *Woods* v. *Co-operative Insurance Society*, 1924 S.C. 692. See *Allied Airways (Gandar Dower) Ltd.* v. *Secretary of State*, 1950 S.C. 249.

[3] *Crawford Brothers* v. *Northern Lighthouse Commissioners*, 1925 S.C. (H.L.) 22.

[4] *Brodie* v. *Ker*, 1952 S.C. 216.

[5] *Lanarkshire County Council* v. *East Kilbride Town Council*, 1967 S.C. 235.

[6] *Houison-Craufurd's Trs.* v. *Davies*, 1951 S.C. 1.

[7] *Donaldson's Hospital* v. *Esslemont*, 1925 S.C. 199.

[8] *Sanderson & Son* v. *Armour & Co.*, *supra*.

[9] *Sinclair* v. *Clyne's Tr.* (1887) 15 R. 185.

[10] *Parochial Board of Greenock* v. *Coghill & Son* (1878) 5 R. 732.

[11] *Bennets* v. *Bennet* (1903) 5 F. 376; *Moore* v. *McCosh* (1903) 5 F. 946.

[12] *Bell* v. *Graham*, 1908 S.C. 1060.

[13] *Adams* v. *Great North of Scotland Railway Co.* (1890) 18 R. (H.L.) 1.

[14] *Fraser* v. *Lord Lovat* (1850) 7 Bell's App. 171.

[15] Bell, *Arbitration*, 357; *McCosh* v. *Moore* (1905) 8 F. 31.

[16] *Bellshill and Mossend Co-operative Society Ltd.* v. *Dalziel Co-operative Society Ltd.*, 1958 S.C. 400; affd. 1960 S.C. (H.L.) 64.

contract of submission contains a consent to registration of the award for execution summary diligence may be competent.[17]

14-32   **(d) Reduction of award.** The award of an arbiter may be challenged by appeal to the courts, not upon any decision in fact or law which was submitted to him, but on certain grounds under statute or at common law. The Articles of Regulation 1695[18] provided that no award of arbiters pronounced on a subscribed submission was reducible except on the grounds of corruption, bribery or falsehood of the arbiters. There are a number of older reported cases in which attempts were made to extend the meaning of corruption to constructive corruption such as irregularities in procedure,[19] but it is now clear that "corruption" is used in its natural sense.[20] It has been held that unsuccessful applications by the arbiter to each of the parties for a loan did not constitute corruption.[21] It is not corruption for arbiters who are professionally qualified to stipulate for a fee for their services.[22] Acceptance of gifts or hospitality might amount to bribery. There is little authority on the term falsehood in this connection but a forged award would be reducible on that ground.[23]

14-33   At common law the award in an arbitration may be reduced (1) if there has been a breach of natural justice in the course of the proceedings[24] such as hearing only one party,[25] failing to hear parties,[26] refusing to hear proof[27] or refusing to receive a claim from one party,[28] (2) if the award goes beyond the terms of reference,[29] or does not exhaust the reference by deciding upon all the questions submitted,[30] (3) if the arbiter has been misled by improper, fraudulent or even unfair conduct by either of the parties,[31] (4) if the arbiter has taken the opinion of the court on a question of law and then failed to apply it,[32] (5) if the arbiter has a personal interest such as would warrant declinature on the part of

---

[17] See para. 14–22.

[18] s. 25 (issued by Commissioners under authority of Act 1693 c. 34).

[19] *Mitchell* v. *Cable* (1848) 10 D. 1297; *Miller* v. *Millar* (1855) 17 D. 689.

[20] *Adams* v. *Great North of Scotland Railway Co.* (1890) 18 R. (H.L) 1; *Robson* v. *Menzies* 1913 S.C.(J) 90, 94–95. Improper procedure may be a ground for reduction at common law but was wrongly categorised as corruption under the Articles.

[21] *Morisons* v. *Thomson's Trs.* (1880) 8 R. 147—but this is not recommended practice for arbiters!

[22] *Fraser* v. *Wright* (1838) 16 S. 1049.

[23] See *Hardie* v. *Hardie* (1724) Mor. 664.

[24] *Holmes Oil Co. Ltd.* v. *Pumpherston Oil Co. Ltd.* (1891) 18 R. (H.L.) 52 per Lord Watson at 55.

[25] *Sharpe* v. *Bickerdyke* (1815) 3 Dow App. 102; but such conduct is not necessarily fatal if the question on which the party was not heard was answered in his favour: *Black* v. *John Williams & Co. (Wishaw) Ltd.*, 1924 S.C. (H.L.) 22.

[26] *Field & Allan* v. *Lownie*, 1909 2 S.L.T. 317.

[27] *Mitchell* v. *Cable, supra*; *Brown & Son* v. *Associated Fireclay Companies*, 1937 S.C. (H.L.) 42 although refusal to hear evidence was not fatal when the arbiter considered that evidence would be irrelevant.

[28] *Drummond* v. *Martin* (1906) 14 S.L.T. 365.

[29] *Carruthers* v. *Hall* (1830) 9 S. 66; *Miller & Son* v. *Oliver & Boyd* (1903) 6 F. 77; *McIntyre* v. *Forbes*, 1939 S.L.T. 62.

[30] *Pollich* v. *Heatley*, 1910 S.C. 469; *Donald* v. *Shiell's Exrx.*, 1937 S.C. 52; *Dunlop* v. *Mundell*, 1943 S.L.T. 286.

[31] *Logan* v. *Lang* (1798) Mor. App. Arbitration No. 6; *Calder* v. *Gordon* (1837) 15 S. 463.

[32] *Mitchell-Gill* v. *Buchan*, 1921 S.C. 390.

a judge and that interest was not known to the party challenging the award at the time of the agreement to refer or, if subsequently disclosed, either party has not waived the right to object on that ground, or (6) if the award has not been executed in proper form.[33] For a review of the grounds upon which reduction may be sought see the recent case undernoted.[33a] It is competent to reduce an award partially if it is possible to sever the valid and invalid parts[34]; if severance is not possible the whole of a partially invalid award will be reduced.[35]

Practice

4–34   In the conduct of the proceedings an arbiter should be vigilant to avoid any acts which may afford grounds for allegations of partiality, even in minor matters. Each party should be asked to send to the other party copies of correspondence directed to the arbiter and, if that has not been done, the arbiter himself should transmit copies to the other party, correspondence issued by the arbiter should be addressed or copied to both parties, telephone calls with either party should if possible be avoided or made in like terms to both parties, site inspections should be made only in the presence of representatives of both parties or of neither party if either or both have declined to attend after intimation, and invitations to hospitality offered by either party should be declined unless both parties or their representatives are also included in and accept the invitation. If at the commencement or in the course of the proceedings the arbiter finds that he has some possibly disqualifying interest he should communicate the fact to both parties and proceed further only if both parties waive objection. In general he should be reluctant to refuse claims, representations or hearings, even if tendered or requested unduly late, unless plainly irrelevant. Even if no time limit has been imposed upon the endurance of the submission the arbiter, as master of the proceedings, should endeavour to ensure that an award is not delayed: it is a complaint frequently made, although often unjustified, that proceedings in arbitrations are unduly prolonged.

A. SUBMISSIONS

Special / general submission to single arbiter—construction contract

4–35   We AB (*designed*) and CD & Co. Limited (*designed*) Whereas differences have arisen between us with regard to a contract entered into by us dated   for the construction of (*describe briefly*)

---

[33] See para. 14–20.
[33a] *Johnson* v. *Lamb*, 1981 S.L.T. 300.
[34] *Cox Brothers* v. *Binning & Son* (1867) 6 M. 161.
[35] *Miller & Son* v. *Oliver & Boyd, supra.*

we hereby submit all claims, disputes and differences arising out of the said contract to the decision of EF (*designed*) as sole arbiter, including but not limited to the following matters (*specify briefly in numbered heads*): We agree that the arbiter shall be entitled to hear such evidence as he shall consider proper either personally or by commission and to call for production of all certificates, records of site meetings and any other documents which he may consider relevant to the matters hereby referred to him, to inspect the works carried out in pursuance of the said contract and all materials and components relative thereto whether on site or elsewhere and generally to make all such inquiries in relation to the matters hereby referred to him as he in his sole discretion may think proper; to employ such professional, technical or skilled assistance as he in his sole discretion shall think fit but he shall not be bound to do so and shall be entitled to decide in whole or in part by his personal skill and knowledge, to order so far as he thinks fit the execution and performance of works, acts or things and to supervise the execution and completion thereof; to order payment and assess damages and to decern; with power to the arbiter to decern against either party in whole or in part for the expenses of this submission including without prejudice to that generality the expense of these presents and of the decree or decrees arbitral, interim, partial or final and the registration thereof, the expense of all such assistance as is above mentioned and for the remuneration of any clerk to the submission whom he may appoint; And we bind ourselves and our respective executors, assignees, successors and representatives to implement whatever the arbiter shall determine by decree or decrees arbitral, interim, partial or final[a]: (And it is hereby declared that if I the said AB should die during the dependence of this submission the same shall continue in operation and with all that shall then have followed or may thereafter follow thereon shall be binding upon me the said AB and my foresaids and my estate:)[b,c] And we agree that in case no final decree-arbitral shall follow hereon all probation which may be taken hereunder shall be received as legal probation *quantum et quale* in any subsequent submission or process of law between us and our respective foresaids: (The application of section 3 of the Administration of Justice (Scotland) Act 1972 is expressly excluded:) And we consent to registration hereof and any decree or decrees arbitral to follow hereon for preservation and execution.

(*To be attested*)   Stamp 50p

NOTES

[a] The clause which ends at this point will not of itself bind the executors or representatives to continue the arbitration if it is still depending when the death occurs, but will impose liability to implement an award already pronounced before the death (*Robertson* v. *Cheyne* (1847) 9 D. 599).

[b] This clause is intended to preserve the submission even if the death of AB occurs during its dependence. (See *Robertson* v. *Cheyne, supra, per* Lord MacKenzie at 603.)

[c] As to bankruptcy of AB see para. 14–25. The winding-up of CD & Co. Ltd. would produce a similar result.

General submission to two arbiters and oversman—differences between proprietors of adjoining estates

4–36   We AB (*designed*) and CD (*designed*) Whereas the estate of X belonging to me the said AB and the estate of Y belonging to me the said CD adjoin and differences have arisen between us as to the rights of each of us to certain servitudes, common ground, water rights and others for the settlement and determination whereof we hereby submit all claims, disputes and differences relating to the said estates at present existing between us to the amicable and final decision of EF (*designed*) and GH (*designed*) arbiters mutually chosen and in case of difference between them (or failing either of them by death or otherwise) then on JK (*designed*) as oversman (or sole arbiter as the case may be) and failing him as oversman before delivery of a final decree-arbitral whether by death or otherwise and whether before or after devolution then of any other oversman to be chosen by the arbiters which failing to be appointed by the Sheriff Principal of   . This submission while not limited thereto includes the following matters (*specify*)   . And we agree that the arbiters and oversman (or sole arbiter as the case may be) shall be entitled to hear such evidence as they or he shall consider proper either personally or by commission and to require production of all title deeds, correspondence and any other documents which they or he shall consider relevant, to inspect the said estates and any parts thereof and generally to make all such inquiries as they or he shall consider proper; to employ such professional or skilled assistance as they or he shall in their or his discretion think fit but they or he shall not be bound to do so and may decide in whole or in part by their or his personal skill and knowledge; to order so far as they or he may think fit the erection of fences and performance of works of any kind on the said estates which they or he may consider necessary or desirable in relation to the matters hereby referred to them and him; to order the execution and adjust the terms of any such deeds as may in his judgment be necessary or desirable to give effect to his decision; to order payment and assess damages and decern. And we consent to the oversman being present and consulting, advising and participating with the arbiters in all or any of their deliberations and examinations and at any hearing or proof at all stages and taking part in the decision of matters of procedure or otherwise incidental to any proceedings under this submission where the arbiters differ even before devolution and if devolution should take place then to his deciding after or without hearing the opinions of the arbiters and with or without further inquiry or hearings and that whether he was present at the proof or hearings or any other stages or not, all as he in his uncontrolled discretion shall think fit: with power to the arbiters and oversman (or sole arbiter as the case may be) to decern against either party (continue as in 14–35 adapted to apply to two arbiters and oversman). (*To be attested*)   Stamp 50p.

Special submission—ownership of piece of ground—with statement of facts and contentions of parties

14–37   We A & Co. Limited (*designed*) (hereinafter called "A") and B plc (*designed*) (hereinafter called "B") Whereas a dispute as narrated in the Statement of Facts and Contentions annexed hereto has arisen between us as to the ownership of a piece of ground (*described*)

(hereinafter and in the said Statement called "the disputed area")
Therefore we submit to the amicable and final decision of CD
(*designed*) as sole arbiter mutually chosen to investigate all matters
relating to the said dispute and to decide the following questions:–
(1) Is A or B entitled to ownership of the disputed area?
(2) Whether any amending or corrective deeds, plans or other
documents are necessary or desirable to clarify the title of the
party whom the arbiter determines is the owner of the disputed area and whether the same should be recorded?
And we empower the arbiter as he in his sole discretion may think
proper to hear such evidence as to possession of the disputed area
or otherwise as he may think fit and to require production of all title
deeds and other documents which he may consider relevant, to
inspect the disputed area and adjoining lands and generally to make
such enquiries as he may think proper; as also to employ the services of surveyors or other skilled persons although he shall not be
bound to do so but may decide by his own personal skill and knowledge; as also to adjust any such deeds as are referred to in question
2 above; and to decern; with power to the arbiter to decern against
either party in whole or in part for the expenses of this submission
including without prejudice to that generality the expense of these
presents and of the decree or decrees arbitral, interim, partial or
final and the registration thereof, the expense of such assistance as
is above mentioned (and for the remuneration of any clerk to the
submission whom he may appoint): And we bind ourselves and our
respective successors to implement to each other whatever the arbiter shall determine by decree or decrees arbitral, interim, partial or
final: (The application of section 3 of the Administration of Justice
(Scotland) Act 1972 is expressly excluded;) And we consent to
registration hereof and of any decree or decrees arbitral to follow
hereon for preservation and execution.
(*To be attested*)   Stamp 50p.

Annexation—Statement of Facts and Contentions
    (*The Statement will detail the deeds or other documents upon
which the parties found their respective claims to ownership and
averments as to possession and any other facts which the parties wish
to bring to the notice of the arbiter, together with the arguments
based thereon. This form of presentation obviates the need for claims
and answers.*)

*Special submission—informal reference—joint letter—construction of
partnership contract—deceased partner*

14–38   To (*name and address of arbiter*)   (*Date*)
We (First) A (*designed*), Executor-nominate of the deceased B
(*designed*) conform to Confirmation by the Sheriff of
at   dated   and (Second) C (*designed*) in
respect that (1) the said B and C carried on business in partnership
under the firm name of B & C at   under a Contract of
Partnership between them dated   (hereinafter called "the
Contract") (2) the said B died on   and (3) differences have
arisen between me the said A as Executor foresaid and me the said
C as to the proper meaning and effect of certain provisions of the
Contract relating to the payments to be made to me the said A as
Executor foresaid by me the said C, hereby agree to submit to your

amicable and final decision as Arbiter to determine the following questions:–

1. In respect that in terms of Clause 6 of the Contract the payments to be made by the said C to the Executor of the said B are based upon the average turnover of the firm of B & C in the last two complete years prior to the death of the said B "provided that these were reasonably normal years," were the last two such complete years ended on 31st December 1981 and 31st December 1982 reasonably normal years?
2. If the answer to question 1 is in the negative, what would be a reasonable figure of average turnover to be used as a basis in accordance with the said Clause 6?
3. What sums are actually payable to the said A as Executor foresaid by the said C in terms of the said Clause 6 and at what dates?
4. Whether the sums actually payable referred to in question 3 should bear interest and, if so, from what dates and at what rate?

We further agree that (1) you shall be entitled to hear proof and to call for production of any correspondence and to consider such evidence written or oral as you consider relevant to determine the above questions (2) you shall have power to decern against either of us for the expenses in whole or in part incurred by the other of us in respect of this submission (3) the application of section 3 of the Administration of Justice (Scotland) Act 1972 is expressly excluded and (4) any award of the arbiter, interim or final, shall be binding upon us.–

We are,

Yours faithfully

(*Signatures of A and C*)   Stamp duty nil

General submission—sole arbiter—to settle partnership accounts

4–39   We A (*designed*) and B (*designed*) Whereas since   (*date*) we have carried on business in partnership as   under the firm name of A B & Co. without any written contract of partnership but on the basis, which we hereby confirm, that we should contribute equally to capital and share equally the profits or losses of the said business; and whereas the said partnership was dissolved by mutual agreement on   (*date*) and certain disputes and differences have arisen as to our respective rights and obligations and as to the adjustment of final accounts of the said partnership; Therefore we hereby submit to the amicable and final decision of C, chartered accountant, (*address*) as sole arbiter mutually chosen to determine all questions, disputes and differences between us in relation to the said partnership and the dissolution thereof, to decide our respective rights, duties and obligations in connection therewith and to settle and adjust a final accounting between us in respect thereof; And we empower the arbiter to investigate all matters in relation to the affairs of the partnership, to call for and examine all documents and other writings which he may consider relevant, to examine the books and accounts of the said partnership, to obtain such valuations as he may think fit and to take account thereof in adjusting the accounts of the partnership and generally, without limitation by reason of the foregoing, to do everything which in his opinion is necessary in order to decide all claims, accounts and matters between us relating to the said business and partnership, and to decern for whatever sums he may find due by either of us to the other; as also to determine whatever discharges fall to be granted by either or both of us, and to adjust the terms thereof; And we bind ourselves (*continue as in 14–35 adapted as appropriate*).

(*To be attested*) Stamp 50p.

B. PROCEDURE

Minute of acceptance of office—sole arbiter

14–40 I, A (*designed*), arbiter nominated in (Deed of Submission between B (*designed*) and C (*designed*) dated) (the foregoing Deed of Submission) hereby accept office as arbiter thereunder: (And I appoint D (*designed*) to be clerk (and legal assessor) to the reference). (*To be attested*) Stamp duty nil.

Minute of acceptance of office—arbiters and oversman

14–41 We A (*designed*) and B (*designed*), arbiters nominated in (Deed of Submission between C (*designed*) and D (*designed*) dated) (the foregoing Deed of Submission) hereby accept office as arbiters thereunder: And we appoint E (*designed*) to be oversman: And we appoint F (*designed*) to be clerk (and legal assessor) to the reference. (*To be attested*) Stamp duty nil.

Minute of acceptance of office by oversman (endorsed on above)

14–42 I, E, designed in the foregoing Minute, hereby accept office as oversman. (*To be attested*)

First order—one party making claim

14–43 (*Place and date*) The arbiter appoints C (*the Claimant or the First Party adopting the terminology in the Submission*) to lodge his claim within days and allows D (*the Respondent or the Second Party*) to answer same within a further days thereafter; allows both parties to adjust the claim and answers within a further days thereafter; and appoints each party to produce with the claim and answers all written evidence founded upon.

(*Signature of arbiter*)

First order—claims by both parties

14–44 (*Place and date*) The arbiter appoints the parties to lodge their respective claims within days, and allows them a further days thereafter to answer the claim of the other party and to adjust their respective claims and answers; and appoints each party to produce with their respective claims and answers all written evidence founded upon.

(*Signature of arbiter*)

Extension of time for adjustment of claims and answers

4–45   (*Place and date*) The arbiter allows the parties a further period of days to revise and adjust their respective claims and answers.
(*Signature of arbiter*)

Closing record

4–46   It is not always necessary for the arbiter to pronounce an interlocutor formally closing the record, at least in cases where the issues are brought out clearly in the claims and answers. It sometimes happens that at debate arguments are advanced of which the claims or answers have given no proper notice, in which event the arbiter may allow amendment without a formal award of expenses against the party making the amendment, although if a further hearing is required by reason of the amendments he will take that into account in considering the award of expenses at the end of the proceedings. In general in such matters the arbiter should follow the principles which apply in an action in court but need not apply them rigidly. In more complex cases a closed record should be made since it assists in clarifying the issues at debate or proof.

Debate—no formal closing of record

4–47   (*Place and date*) The arbiter appoints parties to be heard before him on the claim (claims) and answers Nos.   and   of process at   on   at   (a.m.) (p.m.).
(*Signature of arbiter*)

Closing record and debate

4–48   (*Place and date*) The arbiter closes the record on the adjusted claim (claims) and answers Nos.   and   of process, and appoints the parties to be heard thereon before him at   on   at   (a.m.) (p.m.).
(*Signature of arbiter*)

Closing record and proof

4–49   (*Place and date*) The arbiter closes the record on the adjusted claim (claims) and answers Nos.   and   of process: (allows the claimant a proof of his averments and the respondent a conjunct probation) (allows the parties a proof of their respective averments and the respondent a conjunct probation)[36]: appoints the proof to commence at   on   at   (a.m.) (p.m.).
(*Signature of arbiter*)

NOTES
(1) It is unusual in practice for the order to state which party will lead in the proof. It may be self-evident or, if not, will usually be agreed

---

[36] See *Magistrates of Edinburgh* v. *Warrender* (1862) 1 M. 13, 14.

between the parties. If parties disagree the arbiter will be better informed to decide the more convenient course after hearing parties before proof commences.

(2) It is usually unnecessary to include a request by the arbiter to the sheriff or the Court of Session to grant warrant for citing witnesses and havers unless either party has indicated beforehand that such a warrant will be required. If that should be required add: "The arbiter respectfully recommends to the Sheriff of   (the Lords of Council and Session) to grant warrant for citing witnesses or havers on the application of either party."

(3) If documents require to be recovered (and the parties do not agree to accept copies as accurate) the arbiter may require to include "the arbiter approves of the specification No.   of process; appoints the clerk to the reference to be the commissioner; respectfully recommends the Sheriff of   (the Lords of Council and Session) to grant diligence and commission conform hereto."

Proof

14–50   The conduct of the proof is determined by the arbiter. In many cases the parties are on friendly terms and arbitration has been invoked to settle an honest difference of opinion as to particular facts and the inference to be drawn from them. In such cases the arbiter (preferably with consent of parties) may dispense with some of the strict procedures of a formal proof in court, *e.g.* the witnesses may not be put on oath. In other cases, however, and particularly when the testimony of witnesses is vital to the outcome, the proof should be formal and on the same lines as in a litigation in court. In all cases the proper procedure of examination, cross-examination and re-examination of witnesses should be adopted, and submissions of each party upon the evidence should be heard. The arbiter may take advantage of the greater latitude that is permissible in arbitration proceedings to put to the parties any inferences from the evidence which he may provisionally have taken and invite comment upon them from the parties (if not already dealt with in their submissions) so that when arriving at his conclusions from the evidence he will have had the benefit of the views of parties. It is now unusual and is unnecessary for the arbiter to pronounce a formal interlocutor making avizandum.

Proposed findings

14–51   (*Place and date*) The arbiter, having heard parties and considered the evidence, the productions and the whole process, issues the subjoined Proposed Findings: Allows the parties to lodge representations thereon within   days from the date hereof.
(*Signature of arbiter*)
Proposed Findings subjoined.
(*Signature of arbiter*)

Prorogation by arbiter[37]

4–52 (*Place and date*) The arbiter (of consent of parties) prorogates the submission to the   day of   .
(*Signature of arbiter*)

Prorogation by parties

4–53 We, A (*designed*) and B (*designed*), the parties to Submission dated   , hereby prorogate the same to the   day of   .

(*To be attested*)

NOTE
If prorogation has not been made before any stipulated date for completion of the arbitration has expired, technically any extension of that period is a new submission. In such circumstances the agreement may be:

We, A (*designed*) and B (*designed*) the parties to Submission dated   which has now expired without being exhausted, hereby renew the said Submission and extend the period thereof to the   day of   ; and of new we submit the whole matters referred in the said Submission to the amicable and final decision of C therein designed as sole arbiter with the whole powers and with the whole clauses contained in the said Submission, other than that which imposed the time limit for decision, to the same effect as if they were incorporated herein:
(*To be attested*)

Devolution on oversman

4–54 We, A (*designed*) and B (*designed*), arbiters appointed by Submission between D (*designed*) and E (*designed*) dated   , having differed in opinion (as regards questions 3 and 4 contained therein), hereby devolve the Submission (but only as regards the said questions 3 and 4) and the (whole matters therein contained) (and the matters therein contained so far as relating to the said questions 3 and 4) upon C (*designed*) the oversman.
(*To be attested*)

NOTE
This should be followed by a formal acceptance of the devolution by the oversman.

C. Final Award

Decree-arbitral (relative to Submission in para. 14–35)

4–55 I, EF (*designed*), arbiter appointed in Submission by AB (*designed*) and CD & Co. Limited (*designed*) dated   , having accepted

---

[37] See para. 14–23.

office as such arbiter, received claims and answers of the parties, (heard the parties by their solicitors (counsel) in debate), allowed proof and heard the same and heard parties by their solicitors (counsel) thereon, (having issued proposed findings and considered representations by the parties thereon), and having fully considered the whole process and evidence and being well and ripely advised on the whole matter, hereby pronounce my final decision and decree-arbitral as follows:– (1) I find that the work of construction of the   referred to in the said Submission has not been satisfactorily completed as regards the items specified in column 1 of the Schedule annexed and signed by me as relative hereto on account of the defects in workmanship and/or materials specified in column 2 of the said Schedule and that the remedial work required specified in column 3 of the said Schedule in respect of each of the respective items shall be carried out by and at the expense of the said CD & Co. Limited as soon as reasonably practicable under my supervision and to my satisfaction. (2) In respect that the whole work of construction of the said   should have been completed in terms of the contract referred to in the Submission (as extended by certificates of the engineer employed by the said AB) by   (*date*) and that by reason of the defects specified in the said Schedule the said   was not available for use on the lastmentioned date, I find that the said CD & Co. Limited are liable to the said AB in the sum of £   per week from the said lastmentioned date until the said remedial work has been completed to my satisfaction, with interest upon the said sum from   (*date when work of contract should have been completed*) at the rate of   % per annum until paid. (3) I find the said CD & Co. Limited liable to pay to the said AB the expenses (including the expense of employment of counsel) incurred by him in respect of the reference as the same shall be taxed by the auditor of the (Sheriff Court at   ) (Court of Session). (4) I find the said CD & Co Limited liable to GH, my clerk and legal assessor, for his remuneration (taxed as aforesaid) (amounting to £   ). And I decern and ordain the said CD & Co. Limited to carry out the remedial work above mentioned, to make payment to the said AB of the sum specified in Clause (2) hereof with interest as therein stated, and to make payment to the said AB and the said GH of the expenses and remuneration above specified with interest thereon from the date hereof at the rate of   % per annum until paid. (And I direct the said GH to register the said Submission and these presents in the Books of Council and Session for preservation and execution on payment of his remuneration).

(*To be attested*)

SCHEDULE

1. Defective Items	2. Nature of Defects	3. Remedial Work Required

(*to be signed by arbiter*)

A note to the findings is superfluous in this case: the Schedule sufficiently explains them.

Decree-arbitral (relative to Submission in para. 14–36)—No devolution

4–56   We EF (*designed*) and GH (*designed*), arbiters appointed in Submission by AB (*designed*) and CD (*designed*) dated   , having accepted office as such arbiters, received claims and answers for the parties, (heard the parties by their solicitors (counsel) on debate,) inspected the locus in presence of parties or their representatives, allowed proof and heard the same and heard parties by their solicitors (counsel) thereon, (having issued proposed findings and considered representations thereon) and having fully considered the whole process and evidence and being well and ripely advised on the whole matter, hereby pronounce our final decision and decree-arbitral as follows:
(1) We find that the boundary between the estates of X and Y in the area where its situation was in dispute is the line lettered A B C D on the plan annexed and signed by us as relative hereto. (2) We ordain the parties at their mutual expense to erect a stob and wire fence along said boundary between the points A and B and the points C and D, such fence to be mutual, and we confirm that the said boundary between the points B and C is the centre line of the stream known as   . (3) We find that the said CD and his successors in the ownership of the estate of Y have a heritable and irredeemable right of servitude to draw water from the loch of   situated on the estate of X for the ordinary agricultural purposes of the estate of Y and for the supply of water to the farmhouse and steading known as   on the estate of Y but for no other purpose and also a heritable and irredeemable servitude right of access for that purpose to said loch as nearly as may be along the line lettered E to F on said plan. (4) We ordain (a) the said AB and CD to execute an agreement under section 19 of the Land Registration (Scotland) Act 1979 in implement of the finding in paragraph (1) hereof and to record the same in the Division of the General Register of Sasines for the County of   within 60 days of the date hereof and (b) the said AB to grant and deliver to the said CD and his successors a deed of servitude in implement of the finding in paragraph (3) hereof within the said period of 60 days and (c) the said CD to record the said deed of servitude in the said Divison of the General Register of Sasines within 30 days after its delivery to him. (5) We find the said AB and CD jointly and severally liable for (a) the remuneration of MN (*designed*) our clerk and legal assessor, modified to the sum of £   and (b) the expenses of preparing and executing the said agreement and deed of servitude and of the registration of the said agreement, the said CD being solely liable for the expense of registration of the said deed of servitude; and save as herein expressly provided we find no expenses due to or by either party: And we ordain and decern the said AB and CD to implement to each other the whole findings and decisions herein contained. (*Direction as to registration for preservation and execution as in para. 14–55, if desired*).
(*To be attested*)

PLAN *identified as that referred to in decree-arbitral*
(*to be signed by arbiters*).

Again a note to the findings is probably unnecessary but may be appended if the arbiters consider any explanations are required.

Decree-arbitral (relative to submission in para. 14–36) by oversman—total devolution

14–57   I, JK (*designed*), oversman appointed in Submission by AB (*designed*) and CD (*designed*) dated   . Considering that EF (*designed*) and GH (*designed*), the arbiters appointed by the said Submission, having differed in opinion regarding the matters thereby referred to them, devolved the same upon me as oversman, and that I accepted office as oversman; Further considering that the arbiters had ordered and received claims and answers for the parties (*narrate other steps in procedure as in para. 14–56*) and that I have now considered the evidence, representations and the whole process and have heard parties by their solicitors (counsel) and being well and ripely advised on the whole matter, hereby pronounce (*continue as in para. 14–56*)

(*To be attested*)

Decree-arbitral—partial devolution

14–58   The arbiters should issue a decree-arbitral upon the matters which they reserved for their own decision, indicating that the other matters had been devolved on the oversman. The oversman should issue a separate decree-arbitral narrating the matters devolved and pronouncing a decree-arbitral on those matters only. The forms of decree-arbitral in paragraphs 14–56 and 14–57, appropriately adapted, may be used.

Decree-arbitral (relative to submission in para. 14–37)

14–59   I, CD (*designed*), arbiter appointed in Submission by A & Co. Limited (*designed*) (hereinafter called "A") and B plc (*designed*) (hereinafter called "B") dated   , having accepted office as such arbiter, considered the Statement of Facts and Contentions annexed to the said Submission and the whole title deeds and productions, heard the parties by their solicitors (counsel) in debate, inspected the disputed area and adjoining lands in presence of the parties or their representatives, allowed proof and heard the same and heard parties by their solicitors (counsel) thereon, (having issued proposed findings and considered representations thereon) and having considered the whole process and evidence and being well and ripely advised on the whole matter, hereby pronounce my final decision and decree-arbitral as follows:–

(1) A is entitled to ownership of the disputed area.
(2) An agreement between the parties under section 19 of the Land Registration (Scotland) Act 1979 in implement of the decision in (1) above showing the disputed area belonging to A is desirable and should be executed by the parties and recorded in the Division of the General Register of Sasines for the County of   .
And I decern and ordain accordingly: I find A and B liable equally for the expense of preparing, executing and registering the said agreement: Further I find B liable to A in two-thirds of the expenses incurred by A in the reference as the same are taxed by the auditor of the (Sheriff Court at   ) (Court of Session). And I find A liable for one-sixth and B liable for five sixths of the

remuneration of M, my clerk and legal assessor, modified to the sum of £ : (*Direction for registration for preservation and execution as in para. 14–55, if desired*).

(*To be attested*)

NOTE Facts The title to the disputed area proponed by A was a Disposition by X Estates Limited in favour of A recorded on 27th January 1971 with entry as at Martinmas 1968. The subjects thereby conveyed were described by reference to a plan attached to the Disposition and by description of boundaries. The plan gave no measurements but the delineation of the boundaries thereon clearly excluded the whole or at least a substantial part of the disputed area, but the subjects conveyed were stated to be bounded by other lands belonging to two third parties Y and Z (who had also derived their titles by separate Dispositions from X Estates Limited) and the titles of those third parties plainly excluded the disputed area. The title to the disputed area proponed by B was a Disposition by X Estates Limited in favour of B recorded on 15th March 1976 which described the subjects conveyed as the whole of a larger area of land which originally belonged to X Estates Limited under exception of the subjects conveyed to A, Y and Z. It was admitted that since before 1970 A had used the whole of the disputed area for the deposit of industrial waste from its factory and that there had been no physical or judicial interruption of that possession until the Submission to me in 1983.

Law There was a conflict in the description by reference to the plan and that by reference to boundaries in the Disposition of 1971. The plan contained no measurements so that no help is to be obtained from measurements to resolve the conflict. In these circumstances it appears to me that the description by boundaries in the Disposition of 1971, interpreted by reference to the description of the boundaries of the lands conveyed to Y and Z, and supported and explained by the possession of the disputed area by A for more than the period of positive prescription peaceably and without judicial interruption, is to be preferred to the description in the same Disposition by reference to the plan. The title of B depends upon the construction of the title deeds of A, Y and Z. For these reasons I consider that A has a valid title to the disputed area.

(*Signature of Arbiter*)

Decree-arbitral (relative to submission in para. 14–38)

14–60 I, (*name and address of arbiter*), arbiter appointed by Joint Letter by A (*designed*) as Executor-nominate of the deceased B (*designed*) and C (*designed*) dated   . Considering that I accepted office as arbiter and have received claims and answers of the parties, heard parties by their solicitors in debate, allowed proof and heard the same and heard parties by their solicitors thereon (and issued proposed findings and considered representations thereon), and having considered the Contract of Partnership referred to in the Joint Letter (hereinafter called "the Contract"), the productions lodged by parties, the evidence given and the whole process and being well and ripely advised on the whole matters referred to me, hereby pronounce my final decision and decree-arbitral as follows:–

1. I find that the two complete years ended on 31st December

1981 and 31st December 1982 referred to in Question 1 of the Joint Letter were reasonably normal years.
2. The answer to Question 2 of said Joint Letter is superseded.
3. The sums payable to the said A as Executor foresaid by the said C in terms of Clause 6 of the Contract are as stated in column 1 of the Schedule annexed and signed by me as relative hereto payable on the dates specified in column 2 of the said Schedule.
4. The sums payable in terms of paragraph 3 above shall bear interest from the respective dates when each sum is payable until paid at the rate of 12% per annum.

And I find that, of consent of parties, no expenses are due to or by either party. (*To be attested*)

NOTE Question 1 The deceased B and C had carried on a professional business in partnership since 1st January, 1978. The annual turnover of the business was £26,050 in 1978, £31,326 in 1979, £30,520 in 1980, £32,156 in 1981 and £37,316 for the period from 1st January 1983 to 24th December, 1983, the date of death of B. It was submitted on behalf of B's Executor that these figures, and particularly the significant increase in 1983, showed that the results of the business in the years 1981 and 1982 were unduly low and failed to reflect the greater value of the business at the date of B's death. The evidence as to the nature of the firm's business demonstrated that its turnover was significantly affected by the periodic occurrence of large individual items and that several of these had happened in 1983 with a resultant increase in turnover. On the whole it appeared to me that the pattern of a general increase in turnover, with fluctuations occasioned by non-recurring items of profitable business, was not unusual in the circumstances of a growing professional business in a period of modest inflation and that the results of the years 1981 and 1982 were not abnormal.

Question 3 Clause 6 of the Contract provided for payment by the surviving partner to the representatives of a deceased partner of ten per cent of the average turnover of the business in its last two completed financial years prior to the death (if these were reasonably normal years) for the one half share in the five years immediately following the death. That provision was ambiguous in respect that it was not clear whether the ten per cent was of the whole of the average turnover or the deceased's one half of it. To assist in resolving that ambiguity I admitted evidence of the circumstances in which the Contract was prepared and first and second drafts were produced. The five words which I have underlined above did not appear in either draft and were plainly a late addition inserted in the principal Contract itself. I also heard oral evidence from C and from the solicitor who framed the Contract. Having considered all the evidence, which confirmed that the five words referred to were a late addition to the Contract, it seemed to me that these words, deliberately added by the parties, must be accorded some significance. Without them it would have been clear that the sum payable would have been ten per cent of the average turnover for five years; the addition of these words could only have been intended to restrict that to one-half of that amount. The sums payable in terms of the Contract by quarterly instalments over a period of five years from 24th December 1983 as contained in column 1 of the Schedule to the decree-arbitral are calculated on that basis.

Question 4 Since some of the instalments are now overdue I consider that interest should be paid on these at 12% per annum, the rate at present awarded on sums contained in decrees of court, from the dates when the instalments were due until paid.

(Signature of Arbiter)

SCHEDULE

Amount of Sum   *Date Due*

(Signature of Arbiter)

Decree-arbitral (relative to submission in para. 14–39)

14–61 I, C *(designed)*, arbiter appointed in Submission by A *(designed)* and B *(designed)* dated   having accepted office as arbiter, received claims and answers for the parties, allowed and heard proof for both parties and heard them by their solicitors (counsel) thereon and being now well and ripely advised on the whole matters referred to me, hereby pronounce my final decision and decree-arbitral as follows: I find that the said B is liable in payment to the said A of the sum of £   , with interest thereon at the rate of   per cent per annum from   until paid, being in full and final settlement and in mutual discharge of all claims and liabilities between the parties in relation to the partnership of A B & Co referred to in said Submission; and I direct that upon payment of the said sum and interest the parties shall execute in duplicate a deed of mutual discharge in terms of the draft No.   of process which draft has been signed by me for the purpose of identification; And I decern and ordain the said B to pay to the said A the said sum of £   , with interest as aforesaid, in exchange for such deed of mutual discharge, one executed duplicate copy whereof shall be retained by each party; and I find the said A and B liable jointly and severally for the remuneration of D *(designed)*, my clerk and legal assessor, (as the same shall be taxed by the auditor of the Sheriff Court of   at   ) (modified to the sum of £   ); and quoad ultra I find no expenses due to or by either party: *(Direction as to registration for preservation and execution as in para. 14–55, if desired)*.

(To be attested)

A note is unnecessary if the reference has involved only the adjustment of accounts in accordance with professional book-keeping and accounting practice. If any questions of fact or law have been determined a note of the arbiter's reasons for his findings is helpful.

Stamp duty

14–62 Stamp duty on a submission is required only where a clause of consent to registration is included. No stamp duty is payable upon an award or decree-arbitral (Finance Act 1949, ss. 35, 52(10) and Sched. 8).

INDEX

Note
Figures in ordinary type refer to text.
Figures in bold refer to styles and figures in parentheses refer to the relevant clause of the style.

477